SECOND EDITION MAKING AMER

About the Authors

John T. Rourke, Ph.D., is a professor of political science at The University of Connecticut. He is the author of *International Politics on the World Stage,* Fifth edition (Dushkin Publishing Group/Brown & Benchmark Publishers 1995), and *Presidential Wars and American Democracy: Rally 'Round the Chief* (Paragon House, 1993); coauthor of *Direct Democracy and International Politics: Deciding International Issues through Referendums* (Lynne Rienner, 1992); the editor of *Taking Sides: Clashing Views on Controversial Issues in World Politics,* Seventh edition (Dushkin Publishing Group/Brown & Benchmark Publishers 1996); and the author of *Making Foreign Policy: United States, Soviet Union, China* (Brooks/Cole, 1990), *Congress and the Presidency in U.S. Foreign Policymaking* (Westview, 1985), and numerous articles and papers. He enjoys teaching introductory classes, and he does so each semester at the university's Storrs and Hartford campuses. Rourke believes that politics affect us all, and we can affect politics. Rourke practices what he propounds; he is involved in the university's internship program, advises one of its political clubs, has served as a staff member of Connecticut's legislature, and has been involved in political campaigns on the local, state, and national levels.

Ralph G. Carter, Ph.D., is an associate professor and former chair of the political science department at Texas Christian University. He is the author of articles in *American Politics Quarterly, Presidential Studies Quarterly,* and of numerous chapters in edited volumes. He has served on the Executive Committee, Governing Council, and Program Committee of the International Studies Association; as president of ISA'S Foreign Policy Analysis Section; as editor of *Foreign Policy Analysis Notes,* and as co–program chair for a conference on the future of U.S. foreign policy at the University of Maryland. He has also served on the Program Committee of the American Political Science Association, representing the Domestic Sources of Foreign Policy Section. From 1974–1978 he was a University Fellow at The Ohio State University. From 1978–1982, he taught both undergraduates and graduate students at Wichita State University. At TCU, he teaches undergraduate courses in Mideast, Russian, and U.S. foreign policy; foreign policy analysis; and introductory courses in both international politics and political science. Carter has been the recipient of numerous teaching awards and recognitions at each of his universities.

Mark A. Boyer, Ph.D., is an associate professor of political science at The University of Connecticut. He is author of *International Cooperation and Public Goods: Opportunities for the Western Alliance* (John Hopkins University Press, 1993), as well as articles in the *Journal of Conflict Resolution, Defence Economics,* the *Review of International Political Economy, Pacific Focus* and a number of chapters in edited volumes. He is a 1992–1993 Pew Faculty Fellow in International Affairs and a 1986–1988 SSRC-MacArthur Fellow in International Peace and Security. He directs the Connecticut Project in International Negotiation (CPIN), which conducts computer-assisted foreign policy simulations for high school students throughout the northeastern United States and was initially funded by grants from the United States Institute for Peace and the National Science Foundation. In all of his courses, he employs a wide mix of teaching approaches, ranging from case teaching to various types of simulations, and is a strong proponent of active forms of learning.

JOHN T. ROURKE
University of Connecticut

RALPH G. CARTER
Texas Christian University

MARK A. BOYER
University of Connecticut

MAKING AMERICAN FOREIGN POLICY

SECOND EDITION

Brown & Benchmark
PUBLISHERS

Madison, WI Dubuque Guilford, CT Chicago Toronto London
Mexico City Caracas Buenos Aires Madrid Bogotá Sydney

Book Team

Acquisitions Editor *Scott Spoolman*
Editor *John S. L. Holland*
Copy Editor *Dorothy Fink*
Production Manager *Brenda S. Filley*
Managing Art Editor *Pamela Carley*
Designers *Harry Rinehart, Charles Vitelli*
Assistant Art Editor *Joseph A. Offredi*
Typesetting Supervisor *Libra Ann Cusack*
Typesetter *Juliana Arbo*
Proofreaders *Jan Jamilkowski, Diane Barker*
Graphics *Charles Vitelli, Shawn Callahan, Lara M. Johnson*
Associate Marketing Manager *Kirk Moen*

President and Chief Executive Officer *Bob McLaughlin*
Vice President of Production and Business Development *Vickie Putman*
Director of Marketing *John Finn*

 **A Times Mirror Company**

Cover © *Daniel J. Cox–Liaison International*
Cover design *Harry Rinehart*
Research *Pamela Carley*

Printed in the United States of America
by Times Mirror Higher Education Group, Inc.
2460 Kerper Boulevard, Dubuque, IA 52001

10 9 8 7 6 5 4 3 2 1

This book is dedicated

from Ralph to Nita Carter, my wife, best friend, and most constructive critic

from Mark to Craig, Dana, and Marissa Boyer, who make life more fun and interesting

from John to the first woman U.S. president

Preface

The purpose of *Making American Foreign Policy*, Second edition, is to illustrate to students how the United States makes its foreign and national policies in the post–cold war world. The ending of the bipolar superpower confrontation between the United States and the Soviet Union, growing global interdependence, and other factors have produced important changes in the way that U.S. foreign policy is made, with shifts in the relative importance of both the various actors and the issues involved. Texts that do not include these changes—such as the growing importance of congressional and public inputs to foreign policy making in an era when there no longer is a consensus on what the U.S. world role should be—no longer accurately reflect the realities of the American foreign policy making process.

The aim of this text is to provide an accurate and up-to-date analysis of the foreign policy making process that will be an effective tool from which professors can teach and students can learn. To meet this goal, there are several standards that have guided our efforts.

Theoretical Sophistication   One criterion that we emphasize is theoretical sophistication. With regard to this standard, we have done two things. First, we have met the sophistication standard by making a real effort to cite, apply, and discuss a strong representation of the most current research available on the U.S. foreign policy process. A quick perusal of the extensive bibliography will indicate that the sources are the most current of any text available in the field. The bibliography also provides students with an array of sources that they can use for further study.

A second way we endeavor to help students think in sophisticated theoretical terms is by analyzing the foreign policy making process with four theoretical models: the presidential, political, administrative, and subgovernment models. Not only do we introduce and explain these models in a separate chapter; we explicitly incorporate them in each subsequent chapter of the book. Thus, policy making models are not just brought up and then forgotten. In *Making American Foreign Policy* the models are an integral part of the book and are used repeatedly and explicitly in a way that students can readily understand.

User Friendly   A second criterion of an effective text is that it must help students to learn. We have borne in mind that we are writing to undergraduates, not colleagues. We have written in a clear, understandable, and lively fashion and have avoided using jargon wherever possible. Furthermore, we have enlivened the presentation by providing information in a variety of visual formats: figures, tables, boxed inserts, editorial cartoons, maps, and photographs. Important concepts are boldfaced, and a glossary is provided. Each chapter has a brief table of contents on its first page; each chapter ends with a numbered summary. There are also numerous headings, italicized words, and other "signposts" to help students understand both the organization and the important points of the narrative. Finally, an appendix illustrates the steps involved in producing a good college research paper. This specific, "how to" approach should be a valuable aid to the student and also should make the instructor's task easier when research papers are a part of the course.

Relevant and Up-to-Date   A third criterion of an effective text is that it engage the reader's interest. We have used several strategies to draw the students into the subject of the text. One approach is to explain to the students why they should care about foreign policy and who makes it. This subject is the focus of a great deal of the first chapter. Keeping the interest of students is also aided by richly illustrating theoretical points and by being up-to-date. We have taken care to use illustrations, with a particular emphasis on the Clinton administration, to support the theoretical points being made.

Dynamic   We believe that a fourth standard of a good text, at least in political science, is that it encourages students not only to think, but to act. We want to empower students to take part in the foreign policy process. We do this in two ways. First, we use the concept of democracy as a theme throughout the book. Our purpose is to foster student thinking about how democratic foreign policy making *is* and how democratic it *ought* to be. Second, we include an appendix illustrating some very specific ways that students can become involved in the foreign policy making process. In this way, we not only encourage students to get involved, but we try to show them how.

Organization   A brief look at the book's contents shows that it features comprehensive coverage of the American foreign policy making process. Chapter 1 establishes the theme of how democratic the foreign policy process is and ought to be. Throughout the text, "is" and "ought to be" are standards about which the reader is challenged to think and to make judgments. This first chapter also conveys to readers how they are affected by foreign policy and why *who* decides *what* American foreign policy will be makes a substantive difference. The setting in which foreign policy is made is explicitly addressed as well. Chapters 2 and 3 analyze the international setting by examining the past and present place of the United States in the international system and how that system constrains U.S. policy. Chapter 4 addresses the domestic setting by taking up American political culture and its impact on policy. Chapter 5 focuses on the human setting, with an emphasis on the nature of humans and how their interactions affect policy making.

In chapter 6, the presidential, political, administrative, and subgovernment models of foreign policy making are introduced, described, and illustrated. Thereafter, these models are used in each subsequent chapter to explain the roles of the various actors in the policy process and the policy making associated with the implementation of policy. Chapters 7, 8, and 9 discuss the presidency, Congress, and the interaction between these two branches in making foreign policy. Chapter 10 covers the bureaucracy, chapter 11 examines interest groups, chapter 12 discusses the media, and chapter 13 explores public opinion and elections. Next, there are two appendixes, which discuss how to write a research paper and how to get personally involved in the foreign policy making process.

Those instructors who used the first edition will notice that there have been some changes in the organization of the text. Our colleagues who reviewed the first edition or who wrote to us spontaneously made several good suggestions that we have adopted. One request was to add more about administrative institutions to the chapter on the bureaucracy. We have done this while still maintaining our emphasis on the dynamic rather than the structure of the foreign policy apparatus. Second, we have responded to those who wished us to enhance and separate our discussions of interest groups and the media. In the first edition these two actors were covered in one chapter; in this edition each has its own chapter and receives greater attention. Third, a number of reviewers praised the last three chapters on the instruments of foreign policy (diplomacy, economics, and violence) in the first edition but commented that they made the book too long to cover adequately in one semester. We found this to be true ourselves, and have dropped those last three chapters. We did, however, move some of the material into the remaining chapters. In particular, those of you who emphasize economics will find a more extensive discussion of the place of the United States in the world economy, which is now included in chapter 3 on the current international system.

Making American Foreign Policy, Second edition, is also accompanied by an instructor's resource guide. It contains chapter abstracts, suggestions for further reading for each chapter, a test bank, and simulation exercises that the instructor can use to involve the students more fully.

In summary, we have been guided by our experiences in teaching American foreign policy making courses and the comments of those who have used this text. Our hope is that we have produced a text that walks a fine line—one which is sufficiently substantive, analytical, and theoretical to satisfy our scholarly expectations, while being interesting enough not to lose the undergraduate reader. We trust that we have found that middle ground, but we welcome your continued comments, criticisms, and suggestions.

TO THE STUDENT

We hope you already realize that American foreign policy affects you directly. The choices made by U.S. foreign policy makers affect your life in a variety of ways: The value of the money in your pocket, the number and nature of jobs awaiting you following graduation, your safety and security both here and abroad, the quality of the physical environment in which you live, and other aspects of your existence are determined, in part, by U.S. foreign relations. Ultimately, American foreign policy makers could make decisions causing you to go off to war, risking death or injury in pursuit of goals thought by them to be important.

Because you are so affected, it is important that you understand the process by which these decisions are made. *Who* makes policy partly determines *what* policy is adopted. Moreover, we live in a democracy. There is no reason that you, as a citizen, should not participate in foreign policy making just as you participate in domestic policy making. Perhaps the most direct way to affect foreign policy is to occupy specific foreign policy making roles in our government. Obviously, the foreign policy officials of tomorrow are the students of today. You, or some of your peers, could be important government officials 20 or 30 years from now.

We have tried to write this text using a straightforward, understandable style. When you are reading it, pay attention to the outline that precedes each chapter. It tells you what is about to be covered. Furthermore, each chapter ends with a numbered summary. While this summary can help you review the scope of the chapter, remember that it is no substitute for carefully studying the chapter.

There are also many visual items here: figures, tables, maps, boxed inserts, and photographs. Pay close attention to them. They have been carefully chosen to help graphically represent many of the ideas presented in the text. However, no one book can include everything you need to know to understand the various topics we treat in the following pages. To help you identify other relevant works, we have used an "in-text" reference system that gives you citations as you read. Thus (Powell, 1993:37) refers to page 37 of the article published by Colin Powell in 1993, which is listed alphabetically in the references at the end of the book.

We have other features that we think you will find useful. For example, important political science terms or concepts are highlighted in boldface. The explanations for such highlighted items can be found in the glossary at the end of the text. Also, we have included two appendixes at the end of the text as well. These are just for your use. One walks you through the steps involved in writing a traditional college research paper. Even if you think you know how to do this, take a look at our suggestions. You may be surprised at what useful tips you can pick up. The other appendix talks in some specificity about how you can affect foreign policy making *right now.* It gives you ideas about how to get involved in the process. More specifically, this appendix provides the names and phone numbers of some groups you might want to contact.

Since we care what you think, we would value your feedback about this book. Have we reached you? Does our approach work, or could it be significantly improved? You are encouraged to share your comments, criticisms, or suggestions by writing to us in care of Brown & Benchmark Publishers, Sluice Dock, Guilford, Connecticut, 06437. This book, just like the broader world in which we live, can be improved, but only if you care enough to think and act.

John T. Rourke
Ralph G. Carter
Mark A. Boyer

ACKNOWLEDGMENTS

In particular, each of the authors is much indebted to his colleagues for their suggestions and support in the writing of this text. Collectively, we would like to thank these reviewers for their insightful criticisms and valuable advice:

Linda Shull Adams	Baylor University
Richard S. Flickinger	Wittenberg University
Martha Gibson	University of Connecticut
Heidi H. Hobbs	Illinois State University
Roy Licklider	Rutgers University
James M. Lindsay	University of Iowa
David S. McLellan	Miami University
Donald A. Sylvan	Ohio State University
Louis M. Terrell	San Diego State University

Our publisher has been steadfast in this endeavor, for which we are immensely grateful. We also thank the important people around us.

J.T.R.
R.G.C.
M.A.B.

CONTENTS IN BRIEF

CONTENTS

Chapter One
DEMOCRACY AND DECIDING FOREIGN POLICY, 1

Chapter Four
POLITICAL CULTURE: THE DOMESTIC SETTING, 89

Chapter Five
THE HUMAN
SETTING, 127

Chapter Ten
THE BUREAUCRACY, 273

Chapter Eleven
INTEREST
GROUPS, 321

Chapter Twelve
THE MEDIA, 349

Chapter Thirteen
PUBLIC OPINION, 372

Countries of the World

Scale: 1 to 125,000,000

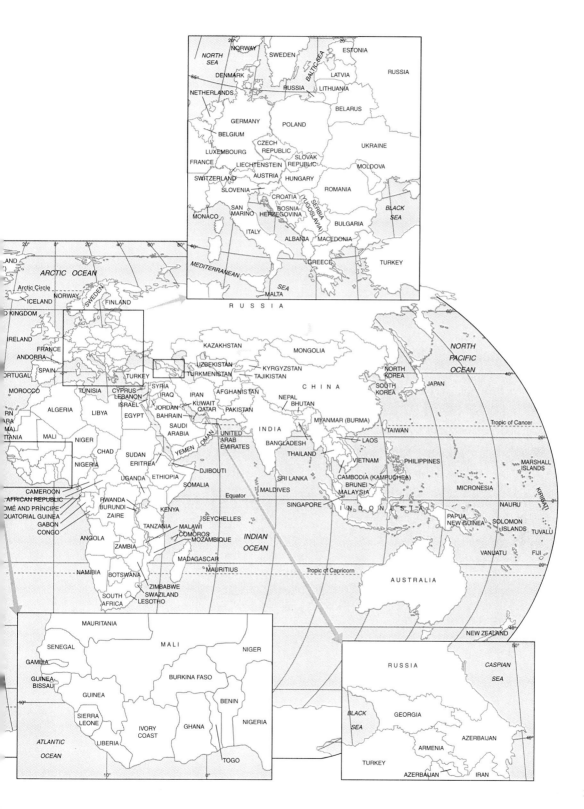

Chapter One

DEMOCRACY AND DECIDING FOREIGN POLICY

Democracy! Now *there* is an idea all Americans can support. The history and rhetoric of the United States abound with declarations of devotion to democracy. The colonists revolted amid democratic demands for "no taxation without representation." They declared independence to pursue their "unalienable rights": "life, liberty, and the pursuit of happiness." Some Americans even trumpet their willingness to make the supreme sacrifice for democracy. "Give me liberty or give me death," Patrick Henry proclaimed. "Live free or die," New Hampshire's license plate asserts defiantly. Ask almost any American to describe the U.S. system of government and he or she will probably begin, "Well, it's a democracy. . . ."

1

MAKING FOREIGN POLICY: WHAT IS, WHY CARE, WHAT OUGHT TO BE

Americans are so used to democracy that they hardly ever think about what it means or how it should work. Virtually everyone supports the concept of democracy. How democracy should work in practice is a different story, however, and there is a significant debate over how applied democracy does and should work. These issues are central to this book. The first concern here is the question of what the policy process *is*. Who makes policy and when? The second issue here is: Why care? What difference does it make to you who makes foreign policy? These two issues lead to a third: What the policy process *ought to be*. How should policy be made in a democracy? Once you have decided this, you can contemplate a fourth issue: How well do the "is" and the "ought to be" coincide? Are you satisfied with the policy process; if not, what should be done to change it?

Making Foreign Policy: What Is?

It is infinitely easier to ask the question, *"What is* the policy process?" than to agree on an answer. Consider the conflicting views of President Harry S. Truman. Feeling feisty one day, as he often did, the president remarked that he had foreign and defense policy making authority that would make "Caesar, Genghis Khan or Napoleon bite his nails with envy" (Rossiter, 1960:30). On another day, Truman had a very different view. He had just met in the Oval Office with president-elect General Dwight D. Eisenhower. "It is going to be tough for Ike," Truman sighed after the general departed. "He'll sit here and he'll say, 'Do this! Do that!' *And nothing will happen.* Poor Ike—it won't be like the Army" (Neustadt, 1960:9).

The exquisite complexity of the foreign policy process is that both of Truman's views were accurate. Sometimes presidents have near-imperial authority. At other times it must seem as if nobody is listening.

The same inconsistency in power that characterizes the presidency is true for the other policy making actors as well. It will be evident as you move through this text that there is considerable variation in the relative foreign policy making strengths of the president, Congress, the bureaucracy, interest groups, the public, and other actors. Compounding that debate is the fact that the political system is in flux because of both international and domestic political changes. Many analysts agree with the recent observation that the "old foreign policy" process, which was "relatively homogeneous, pragmatic, and mostly bipartisan," has been replaced with a "more open and ideological foreign policy making process [that] now encompasses the public, political parties, elections, media, experts, interest groups, Congress *and* the executive branch" (Mann, 1990:14–16).

There are many reasons why bipartisan cooperation has declined. In part the decline is symptomatic of a sharp drop on the domestic front of faith in government. The Watergate scandal that led to the resignation in 1974 of President Richard M. Nixon especially damaged the presidency. That troubled time has been followed by subsequent disclosures of malpractice and even criminality in the government in a number of other scandals. Added to this, a number of domestic factors have increased conflict in the American political system as individuals and interest groups struggle over economic and social issues. Internationally, the Vietnam War and the end of the cold war have destroyed the American anticommunist consensus as the focus of foreign policy, and this has created conflict over what new basic direction U.S. foreign policy should take. Moreover, U.S. economic interdependence with the rest of the world and other factors have increased the links between foreign policy and domestic policy issues. Individuals and interest groups (and their representatives in Congress) are increasingly apt to feel affected by and, thus, to try to influence foreign policy because of its domestic links. This means that U.S. diplomats must engage in a **two-level game** (Boyer, 1995; Mo, 1994; Putnam, 1988). The idea of a two-level game is that, in order to be successful, diplomats have to negotiate with other countries at the international level and with interest groups, Congress, and other policy actors at the domestic level.

All of these stresses have created a diffusion—some people fear a breakdown—of political authority in the United States. People are less willing to trust and frequently less willing to follow political leaders. Polls show, for instance, that whereas approximately 60 percent of Americans in 1964 said that they could trust the U.S. government to do what is right most of the time, by 1993 only slightly more than 10 percent of Americans polled agreed with that statement.[1]

By the same token, Congress is less willing to follow the president (Ripley & Lindsay, 1993). During the cold war era of the 1950s and 1960s, for instance, Congress changed presidential defense spending requests by an annual average of less than 1 percent; during the less threatening 1970s and 1980s, Congress changed the chief executive's defense budget proposals by an average of more than 5 percent (Carter, 1992). More frequently than earlier, opposition in Congress to presidential preferences is based on partisan views. This leaves some observers concerned that the entire foreign policy process is becoming too much a matter of partisan division—an effort to gain partisan advantage—rather than one based on U.S. national interests. Others see the rise in congressional activity as a return to normal patterns. "The postwar [World War II] bipartisan consensus and general congressional acquiescence to the president in foreign policy has historically been the exception rather than the rule in American politics," one scholar writes. This is not necessarily worrisome, she continues, because "conflict between the branches is not inherently bad. Indeed, our system of governing institutions was designed to encourage a degree of conflict to check and balance the powers of each branch against the others" (Gibson, 1994:471).

The willingness of Congress to grant primacy to the president in foreign policy making declined even further with the presidency of Bill Clinton. Congress has been emboldened in part by Clinton's reputation for a lack of foreign policy interest and expertise. One 1995 survey found that only 44 percent of Americans approved of "the way President Clinton is handling foreign affairs."[2] Many scholars agreed. "There has not been a president in my lifetime that is less interested in foreign policy," commented presidential historian Stephen Ambrose. "It seems almost painful to [Clinton]."[3] That attitude is also reflected in Congress. "I have always respected the foreign policy prerogatives of the commander-in-chief," Senator (and former admiral) John McCain (R-AZ) commented in 1995. "But," the senator continued, "I must say . . . [that] my fidelity to that principle has been tested by the frustration I have experienced as I have seen threats left unanswered and opportunities left unexploited by a foreign policy that has—as far as I can determine—no conceptual framework to guide it," and which is marked by "feckless inconsistency."[4] Even some of the president's key congressional allies, such as House Intelligence Committee member Dan Glickman (D-KS), joined the criticism. "You just can't be a leader at home," Glickman said of Clinton, "you have to be a leader abroad as well."[5]

Congressional activity in the foreign policy realm increased even more once the Republicans took control of both houses of Congress in January 1995 and set their sights on ousting Clinton from the White House in 1996. When, for example, Clinton visited Moscow in May 1995 to celebrate the fiftieth anniversary of V-E Day, Senate majority leader and presidential hopeful Robert Dole (R-KS) described the president's efforts as a "failure" and a "fraud" for failing to address strongly enough such issues as Russia's brutal suppression of the revolt in Chechnya and Moscow's proposed sale of nuclear reactor technology and material to Iran. "Clearly," Dole continued, "Congress will be reassessing relations with Russia in the wake of the summit's failure." Dole's criticism brought an angry reply from the administration. "You know," Secretary of State Warren M. Christopher retorted icily, "in my generation there was an old-fashioned custom that Americans did not criticize the president when he was abroad. The thought was in those halcyon days that there would be time enough when the president returned home to assess his performance."[6] It is debatable whether Christopher was correct that the restraint of an earlier era constituted halcyon days, but it is certain that he was right about the increased willingness of many in Congress to differ publicly with the president wherever he might be.

Whatever the public and Congress may feel, presidents are loathe to surrender their foreign policy leadership. In fact, one scholar notes, there is a countervailing and "growing trend toward executive initiative in foreign policy" (Mann, 1990:17). Perhaps because of their diminished ability to count on bipartisan foreign policy support, combined with the mounting frustrations of trying to manage seemingly intractable domestic ills, presidents have become more insistent of their presumed foreign policy prerogatives. They are most assertive during crises, especially when the use of military force is contemplated or occurs. But as we shall see, increased presidential claims of executive prerogative are also evident in other policy areas. The National Security Revitalization Act, sponsored by House Republicans in an effort to change the rules of U.S. participation in UN peacekeeping and to make other alterations in U.S. security policy, was attacked in a joint statement by Secretary of State Christopher and Secretary of Defense William J. Perry. "What is at stake," they said, "is fundamental: the authority of our president to protect the national security. . . . In its present form, the bill unwisely and unconstitutionally deprives the president of the flexibility he needs to make the right choices for our nation's security."[7] Thus, the two senior Cabinet officers went beyond arguing that the National Security Revitalization Act was just bad policy. They characterized the bill as an unconstitutional and dangerous attempt to intrude on the president's proclaimed prerogative to make foreign policy.

Explaining these countervailing trends of both diffusion and centralization of authority and other dynamic aspects that shape U.S. foreign policy will consume a great deal of this book. For now, though, the central point is that there is no single foreign policy process. Instead there are multiple policy processes.

We will, in chapter 6, divide these processes into four models of foreign policy making: the political, the presidential, the administrative, and the subgovernment. You will see in that chapter and elsewhere a point that is particularly relevant to the next section on what the policy process ought to be: Only the political model resembles what you might consider a broadly democratic process. The other three models substantially insulate policy decisions from public input. In the political model, issues are widely debated, and there are a number of foreign policy actors who play a strong role in the process. The president and his executive branch appointees are the dominant decision makers in policy decided according to the presidential model. Congress, the public, and other actors play a much weaker role. Policy decisions according to the administrative model are mostly a function of the career professionals who staff the civilian and military bureaucracies. The subgovernment model describes how policy decisions are made on policy issues that are of little interest to the general political system but are important matters to particular elements of Congress, the bureaucracy, and a limited number of interest groups.

Within which of the models an issue falls depends on numerous variables such as what the issue is and how skillful the president and other officials are. This text will enable you to begin to understand such variables and thus to be better able to see why things happen. It will also help you evaluate whether the various models are satisfactory ways of making policy according to a number of standards, including democracy. With this knowledge about how the process works, you can act to influence policy substance, and to change the process if you wish to and if you try to hard enough.

Making Foreign Policy: Why Care?

At this point, you might reasonably ask, "Who cares who makes foreign policy?" "Sure," you might say, "it is important to think about policy substance, that is, to care *what* U.S. foreign policy is about. But foreign policy process? *How* it is made? That seems pretty arcane and irrelevant."

This would be an understandable first reaction, but the point we are going to make here is that you should care about the **foreign policy process**. In the paragraphs that follow, you will see four reasons to care. First, process affects substance. Who decides influences what gets decided. Second, what policy is decided upon affects you. Third, what the country's elected and appointed leaders want and what you and the majority of other people want are not always the

Foreign policy is not a matter of metaphysics; it happens to people. Army Sergeant Michael D'Adams and his children, Caroline and David, are among those who have to bear the brunt of the decision in Washington to deploy U.S. troops to Bosnia. This picture, taken 10 days before Christmas 1995 at the NATO Air Base in Wiesbaden-Erbenheim, Germany, shows the children and their dad hugging good-bye. The sergeant and 85 other soldiers of the 3rd Corps Support Command were being deployed to Bosnia.

same. Fourth, you can change what policy is and how it is made. In order to do that, though, you have to understand how things work to know if they should change, what you would do to improve things, and how to go about making changes.

Policy Process Affects Policy Substance

How policy is made may not initially seem as provocative as policy substance, but it is no less important. One reason that the policy process is important is because it frequently has a significant impact on the substance of policy. Who decides plays a major role in determining what gets decided.

Foreign aid provides an example. If you are opposed to the current or an expanded level of foreign aid, you would want to increase Congress's role in the policy process. Senator Jesse Helms (R-NC), chairman of the Foreign Relations Committee, argues that "the foreign aid program has spent an estimated $2 trillion [since World War II] of the taxpayers' money, much of it going down foreign rat-holes."[8]

Most legislators are less scathingly critical of foreign aid, but whatever their personal views on aid, they are apt to be more sensitive to the views of the voters about such spending. One public opinion survey taken in 1995 found that 75 percent of all respondents said that the United States spends "too much" on foreign aid, 73 percent thought aid was "wasteful," and 64 percent wanted to cut aid appropriations. If, on the other hand, you favor a robust, well-funded foreign aid program, then you would probably want to see Congress acquiesce to presidential leadership. The president and appointed executive branch officials are more likely than are members of Congress to stress the role of aid as part of maintaining global stability and furthering other broad U.S. goals. J. Brian Atwood, the head of the U.S. Agency for International Development (AID) in the Clinton administration, argues that "when societies fail there are wars and new flows of refugees, and then the world has to spend a lot of money to resolve these problems." Therefore, Atwood reasons, "a little more [foreign aid] investment earlier on might help prevent such crises.[9] Moreover, administration officials are apt to argue that some cuts in foreign aid will imperil the United States. A Republican threat to end financial aid to Russia met with a warning by National Security Adviser Anthony Lake that such a move "could have profoundly negative consequences for our national security" and "do terrible damage to ourselves as well as to the Russians."[10]

There is an even broader possible impact of process on policy. The German philosopher Immanuel Kant suggested in *Perpetual Peace* (1795) that universal democracy would eliminate war because average citizens would not willingly take on the dangers and deprivations of conflict. The spread of democracy in the past few years has sparked renewed interest in Kant's idea. Scholars still debate about why and how often democracies fight. There is, however, a general finding that democracies are very unlikely to wage war against each other (Fearon, 1994; Hagan, 1994; James & Hristoulas, 1994; Raymond, 1994; Dixon, 1993; Lake, 1992; Starr, 1992; Nincic, 1992a). The compatibility of democracies in the international system is further confirmed by a recent study that democracies have higher levels of trade with one another than they have with nondemocracies (Dixon & Moon, 1993). The implication of these findings, combined with the growth in the percentage of countries worldwide that are democracies, is, two other scholars have concluded, that "the process of global democratization may carry long-term prospects of international stability that arise, not out of the missile launchers, but out of popular control of governments and of norms of peaceful resolution of political conflicts associated with democratic political systems" (Maoz & Russett, 1993:636).

Given this relationship between democracy and peace, it is possible to speculate that *degrees of democracy* also affect bellicosity in some circumstances. Specifically, it may be that decisions made in a broad democratic context (wide debate among many influential actors in a society) are less likely to be for war than are decisions made in a much narrower democratic manner, within the confines of the Oval Office or some other executive suite.

It is only fair to note that there is a counterargument: that democracy is bad for foreign policy and international relations. Specifically, some analysts maintain that a highly active role of Congress, the public, interest groups, and other actors in the foreign policy process may lead to compromises in policy that dilute its effectiveness under the old saying that a camel is a racehorse designed by a committee. Critics of democratic foreign policy contend that too much democracy may cause inconsistent policy as first one side, then the other, prevails and changes U.S. policy. This, critics say, creates an impression of incoherence that creates anxieties among allies and impressions of U.S. weakness among potential adversaries. Former British ambassador to the United States Sir Nicholas Henderson once commented that the American system of checks and balances created a process where "the lack of any clearly defined authority on foreign policy" can lead to "the kind of hugger-mugger operations, false disclosures, public recriminations, and congressional hearings" associated with the Irangate scandal, which involved unwise and sometimes illegal arms shipments to Iran and the Contra rebels in Nicaragua. This, Sir Nicholas concluded, contributes to a "continuing unpredictability and weakness in safeguarding the [U.S.] national interest" (Rose, 1988:217). This series of charges and countercharges between advocates of greater or more restrained democracy in the foreign policy process will be expanded upon shortly.

Policy Affects You

A second reason to care about the foreign policy process is that foreign policy affects you continually and often intimately. One way is in the taxes you pay. National defense spending equaled $2,646 for each American household in 1995. Paying for defense also entails budget decisions. During the presidency of Ronald Reagan, for example, defense spending soared while federal funding for colleges and student aid lagged. While the trade-offs between defense and education spending are not direct, it is also true that spending nearly $1 billion per plane for B-2 bombers decreases the funds available for scholarships and student loans.

In the aftermath of the cold war, the budget competition between defense and domestic spending eased somewhat. Clinton vowed during the 1992 presidential campaign to cut $60 billion from the $1.4 trillion that President George H. W. Bush estimated was needed for defense spending during fiscal years (FYs) 1994–1997. The defense budget projections that the Clinton administration made in 1993 more than doubled the projected cuts over four years to $123 billion. Further reductions are unlikely, however. Clinton commented in his 1995 State of the Union address that "we must not cut defense further."[11] Furthermore, the Republican-controlled Congress wants to increase military spending by $20 billion beyond what Clinton has projected

One reason to pay attention to foreign policy is the impact it could have on you. At its extreme, that impact is symbolized in this photograph of two young women at the Vietnam War Memorial in Washington, D.C. They are reacting to one of the letters of anguish that are sometimes left at the memorial by relatives of those who died in Vietnam or by one of the servicemen or -women who survived but cannot forget. The vast majority of the approximately 50,000 Americans who were killed in Vietnam were between 18 and 22 years old.

through the year 2002 and increased Clinton's defense request for FY1996 by $7 billion. Therefore, the trend of recent years will reverse itself defense spending will probably stabilize or increase as a percentage of the federal budget.

It would be an error, however, not to recognize that reductions in national defense spending can also affect you adversely. The post–cold war cuts have cost many workers their jobs. Civilian defense industries have declined, and several rounds of closing or consolidating military bases have eliminated other civilian jobs. The 1995 round alone closed 30 military installations and reduced numerous others in 39 states. Fort Chafee (Arkansas), McClellan Air Force Base and the Naval Shipyard (California), Lowry Air Force Base (Colorado), the Philadelphia Naval Shipyard (Pennsylvania), and other well-known bases will all soon be gone. By 1997 Connecticut is projected to have lost 2.8 percent of the workforce that it had in 1992 because of defense spending cuts. Among other heavily impacted states, Arizona, California, Maine, Maryland, Massachusetts, Mississippi, Missouri, New Hampshire, Vermont, Virginia, and Washington will each lose at least 1.4 percent of its jobs. You may have been one of the laid-off workers; if one of your parents was laid off, it may have changed your college plans; if you had hoped to find a job in a defense-related corporation after graduation, you might want to rethink your goals.

National security policy can also take college-age men and women away from their classes, jobs, and homes unexpectedly. When there is a military draft, the word

Political leaders and the general public often do not agree on what U.S. foreign policy should be. One reason is the demographic differences that exist between those who frequent the Oval Office and the average American. During this meeting in the White House, President Clinton, Vice President Al Gore, and six top advisers were deciding on U.S. policy toward Bosnia. The names of these policy makers are less important than their demographic similarities: They are all white, male, middle-aged, and of European heritage. The majority are lawyers who attended Ivy League universities. When President Clinton came into office, he promised to promote diversity so that decision makers would better reflect the American public. Diversity is not evident in this picture. The question is: If you are not a white, middle-aged male of European heritage, how well do these advisers represent your views?

"unwillingly" can also be added. Eighty-four percent of all Americans killed in Vietnam were between the ages of 18 and 22. It is also increasingly true that combat service includes and imperils women. Two of this book's authors are at the University of Connecticut. So was first-year student Cindy Beaudoin when the Persian Gulf crisis erupted. Cindy was also in the Army National Guard. Along with her unit, Specialist Beaudoin was called to duty and sent to the desert front. She died there in action. In just the 1990s, U.S. combat forces have been deployed to, and sometimes died in, actual or potential combat zones in Bosnia, Haiti, Macedonia, the Persian Gulf, and Somalia. General John Shalikashvili, chairman of the Joint Chiefs of Staff, recently told a contingent of U.S. troops, "Like it or not, most of you will find yourselves in a place you never heard of, doing things you never wanted to do."[12] That is not literally true of all young Americans, but if you have not had to go to war, you may have just been lucky—so far.

Less tragically, your economic circumstances are affected by decisions about trade policy with Japan and many other countries. As you read this, you may be wearing a shirt made in India, sneakers manufactured in China, and a belt produced in Brazil. A lot of vegetables you eat come from Mexico. German, Japanese, and

Korean cars are a common sight on our roads, and they are propelled in part by Saudi, Nigerian, and Venezuelan petroleum. Almost everything you watch or listen to comes from somewhere else. There is much talk of "Buy American" and trade retaliation these days, but increasing tariffs or quotas on such items would frequently increase their cost or limit your choice. You also have to be careful of what initially seems obvious. Some of Ford Motor's cars are built in Mexico; Honda Accords roll off an assembly line in Marysville, Ohio.

You are also affected by the general flow of trade and investment dollars. The United States is the world's largest exporter, and the U.S. Department of Labor estimates that each $1 million in exports creates an average of 19.7 jobs. By this calculation, the flow of goods and services outward employs more than 10 million Americans, about 8 percent of the workforce. The flow of investment dollars into the United States also brings economic benefits. Foreign investors begin new companies in the United States or rejuvenate existing companies that were failing under their previous owners. Foreign investors also buy U.S. Treasury bonds and other debt instruments, thereby helping to finance the U.S. national debt and deficit spending. Without the foreign bondholders, interest rates and inflation would soar for Americans. The inflow of foreign money even helps keep college tuition down. The fifth largest source of U.S. earnings from the export of services is the $6.1 billion that foreign students spend for tuition, room, and board at American colleges. Since foreign students often have to pay more and are less likely to receive scholarship help, their payments ease the financial burden of institutions of higher education. There are also downsides to the international flow of commerce and finance. For example, your job or the job of someone in your family may be threatened by imports or by the decision of an American company to move its operations abroad.

The availability and cost of products you use and your family's economic circumstances are not the only ramifications of economic relations. Policy decisions may bring about types of benefits or costs to you. President Clinton imposed a U.S. trade ban on Iran in April 1994 to retaliate for that country's alleged support of terrorism and its drive to develop nuclear weapons. Few countries joined the U.S. initiative so the embargo's impact on Iran was probably marginal. What is more certain is that those Americans who were involved in creating the $326 million worth of U.S. exports to Iran in 1994 suffered. About half of the U.S. exports to Iran were for oil drilling and associated equipment; perhaps 3,000 American jobs in the oil services industry were lost due to the embargo. American rice farmers lost $75 million in sales to Iran, and other grain and corn farmers also were injured.

The changes in the exchange rate of the U.S. dollar versus other currencies also affect Americans. During early 1995, for example, the dollar dropped 20 percent against the Japanese yen. Just one ramification is that it will cost more for U.S. operations in Japan. Among other such costs, the U.S. embassy in Tokyo had to raise the annual salaries of administrative assistants from $40,000 to $54,000 to offset the devalued dollar. The Mexican peso moved in the opposite direction against the dollar, plummeting in December 1994. That made U.S. goods more expensive in Mexico and Mexican goods less expensive in the United States; such changes brought on a significant trade deficit with Mexico for 1995.

International economics has also become entwined with international environmental policy in ways that affect you. Many scientists believe that there is an environmental threat called global warming that is caused by the blanket effect of carbon dioxide (CO_2) emissions into the atmosphere. The fear is that increases in average temperature associated with global warming could dramatically change the world's and your environment by causing sea levels to rise, the intensity of storms to increase, and fertile areas to become arid. President Bush declared that reducing CO_2 emissions would harm U.S. business and in 1992 refused to sign a United Nations–sponsored treaty committing countries to reducing CO_2 emissions. In 1993 President Clinton reversed U.S. policy and signed the treaty. The list of ways that international relations and foreign policy affect you intimately could continue, but that should not be necessary to make the point that you are not exempt from foreign policy decisions.

The Gap between the Opinions of Leaders and the Public

A third reason to care about the foreign policy process is that there is a considerable gap on some foreign policy issues between social-economic-political leaders and the public. During the country's first 150 years, white Anglo-Saxon Protestant (WASP) males dominated American politics. Policy usually reflected their values and perceptions. More recently, there has been a greater diversity of gender, ethnicity, and race among policy makers and others who influence policy. Still, it would be incorrect to assume that the values and perceptions of those who have political power are the same as the values and perceptions of the average American. White males still predominate.

The education, professions, and economic status of those in power are also usually atypical. One press report calculated that 80 percent of all of Clinton's initial key appointees lived in the Boston–New York or San Diego–San Francisco megalopolises. Forty-four percent of those appointed officials attended Harvard, Yale, or Princeton at some point; two-thirds are lawyers (Dye, 1993).[13] Of the top four foreign policy makers who took office in January 1993, President Clinton is an Oxford- and Yale-educated attorney; Secretary of State Warren M. Christopher was a partner in one of the country's largest and most prestigious law firms; Secretary of Defense Les Aspin went to Yale, Oxford, and the Massachusetts Institute of Technology; and national security adviser Anthony Lake went to Harvard and Cambridge and has a Ph.D. in political science from Princeton. These white, highly educated, middle-aged men are hardly average Americans in cultural background or outlook.

The impact of the cultural differences between the elite (political, business, and other types of leaders) and the mass (most Americans) is perhaps best illustrated by the quadrennial poll done by the Chicago Council on Foreign Affairs and reported in the journal *Foreign Policy*. Table 1.1 on page 14 shows some of the questions asked by the survey and the response of leaders and the public.

While you are thinking about this table, remember two points. First, the opinions of leaders and the public do not always diverge. There are issues on which there was only a small gap between the views of the leaders and of the public (Rielly, 1995). Both groups agreed strongly (by at least 2 to 1 margins) that the United States has a vital interest in Canada, China, Germany, Great Britain, Japan, Mexico, Russia, and Saudi Arabia and that preventing the spread of nuclear weapons and securing adequate energy supplies are very important U.S. policy goals. There are many other issues in which a majority of both leaders and the public agree, but where there is a significant gap is in the levels of support. Both leaders and the public would use U.S. troops if Russia invaded Western Europe, but the leaders (91 percent) were much

(Continued on page 12)

Diplomats and Soldiers: Women and Foreign Policy

Throughout history, women have been little represented in American foreign policy. This is true for both the making and the implementation of policy. At the policy-making level, no woman has ever served as president, vice president, secretary of state, secretary of defense, director of central intelligence, chairman of the Joint Chiefs of Staff, or as the president's national security adviser. Women are also vastly underrepresented in the various layers of these offices and bureaucracies (McGlen & Sarkees, 1993).

Despite his pledge to ensure diversity among policy makers, President Clinton followed the tradition of selecting males for the highest national security and foreign policy posts. The ranking woman that he appointed was Madeleine Albright, the U.S. ambassador to the United Nations. She has defied the stereotype held by some that women may not be tough enough to confront Saddam Hussein and other menacing leaders on the world stage.

After the president and secretary of state, Albright is perhaps the most visible U.S. diplomat. "I meet more foreigners per square inch than anybody else in America," she says of herself.[1] Albright has been a university professor and has directed the Women in Foreign Service Program at Georgetown University, an effort to increase the number of women in the diplomatic service. She has also served as a chief legislative assistant to Senator (and later secretary of state) Edmund S. Muskie (D-ME) and as a staff member of the National Security Council (NSC) in the Carter administration. Albright speaks Czech, French, Russian, and Polish.

At the UN the ambassador has earned a reputation for being blunt beyond the niceties of normal diplomacy. "Madeleine is a person of passionate temper," one diplomat commented with mixed feelings. One widely quoted example of what one newspaper styled Albright's "relentless, combative personal approach" was when she publicly warned Haiti's military junta,

"You can depart voluntarily and soon or you can depart involuntarily and soon."[2]

Albright has been particularly hard on Iraq, once telling the Iraqi minister that a speech he had just given "was one of the most ridiculous delivered at the UN by Iraq."[3] Indeed the Iraqis are so beset by Ambassador Albright that the Iraqi (controlled) press published a scathing poem, the first stanza of which read:

> Albright, Albright,
> Alright, alright.
> You are the worst
> in the night.
> Why do you throw-over
> the peace leaves
> and maintain the papers of fight?
> Why do you hate the day and love the night?
> Don't put out the light.[4]

She has not let the political thrust or dubious literary merit of such attacks deter her. When the Iraqi press characterized her as a snake, the next day she wore a serpent-shaped brooch to a meeting of the Security Council. When an anonymous and chauvinist critic sent her a broom; she displayed it in her office.

Whether they are diplomats or warriors, the percentages of women implementing foreign policy is also limited. Male attitudes toward women have frequently meant that they have been excluded from many roles or, even if given jobs, have been treated with sexist disregard. Nine female agents filed suit against the CIA in 1995 alleging that sexual discrimination had derailed their careers. One of the agents told reporters what happened when she was dispatched to one CIA post. Instead of using her to collect intelligence, her male supervisor assigned her to a desk job and to escort duty for wives of visiting members of Congress. "I've dealt with some real lowlifes," the female agent told reporters, "but my supervisor was . . . [an exceptional] sleazebag . . . ; he

more likely than the public (52 percent) to take that position. Eighty-six percent of the leaders said that the United States has a vital interest in Israel; only 64 percent of the public thought so. Second, it is not important for now to decide whether the

(Continued on next page)

stared at my legs and gave me bad assignments." The CIA has not admitted that the women's charges were valid, but the agency did offer a settlement that included $940,000 in back pay and career-enhancing assignments. The women turned it down, and the case continued. The new CIA director, John Deutch, has also promised that improving the lot of women in the agency "will be a big deal for me," and, in an initial step, he appointed former assistant secretary of the navy Nora Slatkin to the third-ranking post in the CIA. The women in the agency have understandably adopted a wait-and-see attitude. As one explained, "We've heard it from the last two directors, and nothing really changes."[5]

The issue of the roles that women should play in the military provides another example of the limits placed on women. Women make up 11 percent of the military and have moved into more extensive combat positions. The country's four national military academies all admit women, and they perform well. One mark of that occurred in 1995, when cadet Rebecca E. Marier led her 987 contemporaries in West Point's academic, military, and physical programs and graduated first in her class. But other roles, such as ground combat, remain off limits to women. Opponents of women serving in combat worry that women are not physically or psychologically fit for combat. Former Marine Corps commandant general Robert Barrow testified before Congress that "if you want to make a combat unit ineffective, assign women to it. It would destroy the Marine Corps—as simple as that—something no enemy has been able to do in over 200 years."[6] Other opponents maintain that such issues as personal hygiene preclude women from ground combat roles. "Combat means living in a ditch," Speaker of the House Newt Gingrich told an audience, and "females have biological problems staying in a ditch for 30 days because they get infections." The Speaker also suggested that males were more combative, using the logic that "males are biologically driven to go out and hunt giraffes." That line of reasoning did not impress Representative Patricia Schroeder (D-CO), among others. "I have been working in a male culture for a very long time," she observed, "and I haven't met the first one [male] who wants to go out and hunt a giraffe."[7]

It should be noted that the issue of women in combat is not simply a matter of men opposing and women favoring the change. Some women believe that women should not be exposed to enemy fire; some men believe that they should be. "We do not wish to carry a rifle, lug a pack and live the way grunts [infantry soldiers] do," said Marine sergeant Jean Amico.[8] And Air Force reserve sergeant Sarah White, who served on a presidential panel studying the issues, asked, "Where are we headed as a nation when policy is willing to permit the inevitable deaths, degradation, maiming, dismemberment, [and] disablement [of women and their] being burned alive in crashes?" Another panel member, Marine brigadier general Thomas Draude, whose daughter is a Navy pilot, disagreed. "I'm asked would you let your daughter fly in combat with the possibility of her becoming a POW?" Draude noted, "And my answer is yes, because I believe we should send in the best."[9]

The public is also split on the issue of women in combat. One survey found 47 percent in favor, 41 percent opposed, and 12 percent unsure about women serving in combat. Women were only slightly more likely than men to take the affirmative position.[10] Another poll found that if the draft were reinstituted, 65 percent of respondents thought that both men and women should be included. When questions about specific combat jobs were asked, however, support weakened. Of those asked, 54 percent said, for example, that women should not be allowed to serve as infantry soldiers.[11]

The question to ponder and perhaps debate in class is whether U.S. foreign policy can be truly American foreign policy when women are often absent or nearly so from the ranks of those who make and implement decisions.

leaders or the public are correct about the national interest (Neuchterlein, 1993). The point here is that they sometimes disagree, and that raises significant issues about the democratic process (Farkas, 1995).

TABLE 1.1

Policy View	Leaders (Percent)	Public (Percent)	Gap (Percent)
The United States has a vital interest in Egypt	78	45	33
The United States has a vital interest in France	59	39	20
The United States has a vital interest in Ukraine	66	35	31
U.S. troops should be used if North Korea invades South Korea	82	39	43
U.S. troops should be used if the Cuban people try to overthrow Fidel Castro	18	94	76
Controlling and reducing illegal immigration should be a very important U.S. foreign policy goal	28	72	44
Reducing the trade deficit should be a very important U.S. foreign policy goal	59	49	10
Strengthening the UN should be a very important U.S. foreign policy goal	51	33	18
Defending the security of its allies should be a very important U.S. foreign policy goal	60	41	19
Economic competition with Japan will be a critical threat to U.S. interests during the next 10 years	21	62	41
Terrorism will be a critical threat to U.S. interests during the next 10 years	33	69	38
Protecting the jobs of American workers should be a very important U.S. foreign policy goal	57	89	32

Data source: Rielly (1995).

One reason to care about who makes foreign policy is that leaders and the public sometimes disagree on policy. This table shows the percentage of leaders and the public that support a series of policy statements and the gap (difference) between those two percentages.

The Ability to Change Policy

A fourth reason why it is important to understand how policy works is that you can make changes. Policy is not immutable, but it is not easy to persuade or compel those in power to alter the country's direction. For this reason, knowing what policy is and how it was derived increases your ability to change both process and substance if you wish. Note that your ability to have an impact has two related aspects: substance and process.

American citizens now have a greater ability to affect *foreign policy substance* than at any time since the period immediately following World War II. This is because the cold war has ended, and the anticommunist consensus that dominated U.S. foreign policy for decades has vanished. As a result, there is a great debate in Washington, D.C., and throughout the rest of the country as to what the role of the United States should be in the world. That debate will be covered more extensively in later chapters, but for now we can focus on some of the differences between the Republicans who control Congress and the Democrats who control the White House. It is important to see that many of the issues now being debated involve more than their immediate focal point. The larger question behind many issues is the degree of future U.S. involvement in world affairs. The Clinton administration has assailed many of the Republicans' proposed policies as being isolationist. According to the president, efforts to cut the foreign aid budget, for instance, are not just a matter of budget allocations. Rather, Clinton told an audience, "under the cover of budget cutting, back-door isolationists . . . want to cut the legs off our [American] leadership. We did not win the cold war to walk away and blow the peace on foolish, penny-wise, pound-foolish budgeting."[14]

The Clinton administration mounted the same attack on a Republican proposal to abolish several foreign policy agencies and place their functions in the State Department. Republican senator Jesse Helms argued that the foreign policy apparatus is "a mess" and that the consolidation would "be good for the country and be good for the taxpayers, particularly." Speaking on C-Span, Brian Atwood, head of one of the targeted units (the Agency for International Development), labeled Helms's proposal "mischievous" and charged that "it's designed more to pursue an isolationist foreign policy than it is to do something constructive."[15]

The important point here is that whether such issues should be construed in their narrow sense or as debates on U.S. involvement in the world, you can play a role in deciding them. With a presidential election looming in 1996, and with legislative elections every two years, which party's standard bearers control the executive and legislative branches will have a marked impact on foreign policy. Moreover, you can have an impact between elections by becoming active in the ways discussed in Appendix 2, Democracy, Foreign Policy, and You: Making a Difference.

Table 1.2 outlines some of the differences between legislative Republicans and the Clinton administration. A few disclaimers are important. First, not all Republicans and not all Democrats are of one view. Second, the issues and positions are laid out starkly for the sake of clarity. There are, however, many nuances in the issues and the positions of members of both parties. Nevertheless, there are differences, and the table uses the House Republican's Contract with America and other legislative positions to establish contrasts with the foreign policy stand of the Clinton administration.

It is also possible in a democracy to change the *foreign policy process*. A good place to begin thinking about whether you want to change the process is the old saying, "If it ain't broke, don't fix it." That bit of folk wisdom is improved by the corollary, "You can't know why it's broke, or sometimes even if it is broke—much less fix it—unless you understand how it works in the first place." The message is that you must be an educated citizen to be a constructive and effective player in reform. Much of this text is devoted to helping you understand how it works, and the following section provides commentary on the standard of democracy against which you can judge the workings of the process.

Making Foreign Policy: What Ought to Be

Now we can turn to the question of *what ought to be* the policy process. The fundamental dispute is the degree to which foreign policy making should be democratic. To address this question, let us begin with an overview of the debate, followed by a discussion of the origins of U.S. constitutional democracy.

TABLE 1.2 Policy Difference: Congressional Republicans and White House Democrats

Issue	Congressional Republicans	Clinton Administration
Foreign aid funding, general	Reduce	Maintain
Aid to Russia if it sells nuclear technology to Iran	Reduce	Probably continue
Level of U.S. contribution to UN peacekeeping operations	Reduce	Maintain
Funding for international organizations involved in abortions overseas	Ban	Allow
Forbid U.S. soldiers to serve under non-American commanders in UN operations	Favor	Oppose
Move U.S. embassy to Israel from Tel Aviv to Jerusalem by 1997	Move immediately	Settle by diplomacy between Israelis and Arabs
Abolish the Agency for International Development, the U.S. Information Agency, and the Arms Control and Disarmament Agency and merge functions into the State Department	Yes	No
Toughen U.S. economic embargo of Cuba and reverse Clinton's decision to return Cuban boat people to Cuba	Yes	No
Admit Poland and some other East European countries to NATO	Require	Leave open to negotiation
Appoint a special envoy to Tibet	Require	Retain as a matter of presidential discretion
Violate UN embargo on arms shipments to Bosnia	Yes	No

Source: Authors.

Caring about who makes foreign policy is worthwhile because, as this table shows, the two major political parties differ on many foreign policy issues. As a voter, you can help determine which party controls Congress and the White House and, therefore, which set of policy preferences prevails in Washington.

Democracy and Foreign Policy: Introducing the Debate

Democracy has persisted for over two centuries in the United States. So has the debate over degrees of democracy, especially in the realm of foreign policy making. American democracy is admittedly messy, and the issue is whether the political free-for-all that frequently characterizes domestic policy making is also suitable for charting the U.S. course in world affairs.

Sorting out the multifaceted debate over how foreign policy ought to be made is difficult. One of the frustrations involved with writing a textbook is that everything cannot be said at once. There are numerous issues about the workings of a democracy that relate to all the policy making models. *Bureaucracies* are one focus of concern. Some people argue that government now addresses such a wide and complex range of issues that we have slipped into a government by **technocrats** (bureaucrats who are technical experts on one or another issue). At later points in this book, especially in chapter 10, we will discuss the pluses and minuses of technocracy. On the up side, career professionals bring years of experience and technical expertise in their respective fields to foreign policy making. On the down side, there are serious issues about democracy raised by the influence in the foreign policy process of permanent, unelected, often only marginally accountable bureaucrats, who, it is said, are often more interested in their agency's interests than in the nation's interests.

Interest groups are another focus of concerns about democracy. Some people argue that interest groups contribute to democracy by serving to aggregate and channel the policy demands of individuals, groups, and organizations, thus keeping government responsive. Other observers worry that some groups are powerful, while others are weak. This may make for policy by the powerful rather than for policy by the majority, as self-centered interest groups press the government to adopt policies that are in the groups', not the country's, interests.

The concerns about bureaucracies, interest groups, and other policy making actors will be addressed at a later point in this text. In this chapter our discussion of democracy will concentrate on the *role of the president compared to that of Congress and the people*. This wide-angled focus is appropriate as a starting place because the most important policy decisions, such as questions of war or peace, capture wide public interest and the attention of the president and other important political leaders. Arguably, a key test of democracy is how we make these paramount decisions. Are they, and should they be, made by the presidential model or the political model? The origins of our constitutional system are a reasonable place to begin to explore the debate over democracy and foreign policy.

Democracy: Early Foundations, Early Doubts

It is intriguing to wonder what James Madison would have thought of this debate over democratic policy making. Madison, of course, helped write the U.S. Constitution in 1787. He was keenly aware of King George III, and this example of monarchical abuse of power made Madison wary of too much control winding up in the hands of any one branch of government. "If men were angels, no government would be necessary," Madison explained in *Federalist* No. 51. And "if angels were to govern men, . . . controls on government would [not] be necessary." Alas, Madison concluded that neither citizens nor politicians were angels. Therefore, although government was necessary, it was vital to "oblige" the government "to control itself." But how? "Ambition must be made to counteract ambition" was Madison's answer.

The Constitution divided the government into distinct and separate branches to diffuse and balance power. Madison also sought to prevent any branch from amassing too much power at the expense of the others by giving to each "the necessary and constitutional means and personal motives to resist encroachment of the others."

Still, while Madison wanted a restrained presidency, he did not want a weak one. There was no chief executive under the first U.S. constitution, the Articles of Confederation. That arrangement had worked poorly, and the delegates in Philadelphia

The Constitution and Foreign Policy

Congress: Article I, Section 8, establishes most of Congress's powers with respect to foreign policy. It states that "The Congress shall have the Power . . . To regulate Commerce with foreign Nations . . . To establish an uniform Rule of Naturalization . . . To define and punish . . . Offenses against the Law of Nations . . . To declare War . . . To raise and support Armies . . . To provide and maintain a Navy . . . To make Rules for the Government and Regulation of the land and naval Forces; [and] . . . To provide for calling forth the militia [of the states] to . . . repel Invasions. . . ." Less directly, there are two general clauses that affect foreign policy. They are Congress's authority "To make all Laws which shall be necessary and proper for carrying into Execution the foregoing powers [in Article I], and all other Powers vested by this Constitution in the Government of the United States. . . ." and the injunction that "No money shall be drawn from the Treasury, but in Consequence of Appropriations made by Law. . . ." Furthermore, the Senate has two specific powers under Article II that affect foreign policy: to ratify treaties by a two-thirds vote and to confirm presidential appointment by majority vote.

President: Article II, Section 2, establishes the president's role in foreign policy. Under it, "The President shall be Commander in Chief of the Army and Navy of the United States, and of the Militia of the several States, when called into the actual service of the United States; . . . He shall have the Power . . . to make treaties; . . . [and to] appoint Ambassadors . . . [and most] other officers of the United States. . . . He shall receive Ambassadors and other public Ministers." There are two, even less specific phrases in Article II that also come into play. One, in Section 1, holds that "The executive Power shall be vested in a President of the United States of America." The other, in Section 3, mandates to the president that "he shall take Care the Laws be faithfully executed."

Courts: Article III stipulates that "The judicial Powers shall extend to all Cases . . . arising under this Constitution, the Laws of the United States, and Treaties made . . . ; to all Cases affecting Ambassadors; . . . to all Cases of admiralty and maritime Jurisdiction." In the 1803 case of *Marbury v. Madison,* the Supreme Court found that this language meant the courts had the power of "judicial review," that is, they could declare unconstitutional laws passed by Congress or actions taken by the executive.

wanted to establish and empower a chief magistrate. They also saw a special role for the president in foreign affairs. The delegates therefore gave the president important powers in that area. Madison and most of his colleagues were also leery of unrestrained democracy. Pure democracies, Madison wrote in *Federalist* No. 10, "have ever been spectacles of turbulence and contention; . . . as short in their lives as they have been violent in their deaths." For this reason, he explained, the new government was created as a republic—a representative form of government—that filters public sentiment through elected and appointed officials.

These complex motives, plus the need for compromise among the delegates on many issues, spawned constitutional language that is important, yet unsatisfactory. The phrases found in the box above entitled "The Constitution and Foreign Policy" are important because they address basic foreign policy powers. They are unsatisfactory as guides to where power rests because they are imprecise and, therefore, the root of a 200-year-old struggle over conflicting interpretations. This constitutional imprecision means that trying to decide how foreign policy ought to be made by merely debating what the Philadelphia delegates meant or what the Constitution literally says has limited utility. The fact is that scholars often cannot agree about what the Framers intended, and it is extremely unlikely that many original-intent issues will ever be settled. Thus, while it is wise to be informed by the language of the Constitution, it is only one of the factors you should consider when deciding what ought to be.

DEMOCRACY AND FOREIGN POLICY: CONTINUING THE DEBATE

Controversy over the proper role of various actors in the foreign policy making process has, if anything, become more unsettled during the more than 200 years since the Constitutional Convention completed its work in Philadelphia. One answer to the question of who should decide is "we the people." The "we" here does not necessarily imply that most foreign policy should be decided by an ongoing series of national referendums in which citizens vote on whether or not to send aid to the former Soviet republics, to commit U.S. troops to Bosnia, or to ratify trade agreements. Such referendums are not unheard of in other countries, but, whatever their wisdom, such a process is not currently possible in the United States. Therefore, what "we" does imply here is widespread debate over foreign policy issues and influential input by a wide range of national political actors, including public opinion, interest groups, political parties, Congress, the president, and the bureaucracy. One job that you, the reader, have is to decide what you think about the advisability and the efficacy of broad democratic participation in the foreign policy process.

It is not an easy decision. Congress, as we shall see in chapters 8 and 9, has been inconsistent in asserting its authority in the face of unilateral presidential actions and claims of prerogative. Even scholars who spend considerable time studying our government are divided or uncertain. Most often scholars have advocated a strong activist presidency. One scholar wrote during the supposedly too-passive Eisenhower presidency that the president should not be "a Gulliver immobilized by ten thousand cords [but] a kind of magnificent lion who can roam widely and do great deeds" (Rossiter, 1960). In the same vein, a political scientist who analyzed textbooks from the 1950s and 1960s entitled his study, "Superman: Our Textbook President," thereby encapsulating nicely the presidential model that scholars saw and preferred during this period (Cronin, 1970).

The abuse of power by Lyndon B. Johnson and Richard M. Nixon changed the weight of academic analysis. Both presidents assumed many of the airs of royalty. Nixon was especially outrageous. When he traveled, especially abroad, the president was often accompanied by as many as 200 people, including valet, dog handler, butler, wine steward, waiters, cooks, chauffeurs, and barbers and hairdressers. More perniciously, both Johnson and Nixon were insecure personalities who used their offices to attack political opponents. Again, Nixon was worse than Johnson. Nixon and his Oval Office advisers approved domestic espionage operations against political opponents, countenanced burglaries, and took myriad other actions that led even conservatives such as Senator Barry Goldwater (R-AZ) to fret publicly about the growing "Gestapo frame of mind" in the White House (Sherrill, 1979:7). The Watergate scandal was the culmination of this trend and led to Nixon's resignation in disgrace. Scholars, such as Arthur M. Schlesinger Jr. in *The Imperial Presidency* (1973:124), reacted with warnings about the dangers of concentrated presidential power. Schlesinger noted that he, among many others, had earlier "labored to give the expansive theory of the presidency historical sanction." In retrospect, he admitted, it was "wrong" to propound "an uncritical cult of the activist presidency."

Since the Vietnam/Watergate period, academic attitudes about concentrated presidential power have been more mixed. Neither Presidents Gerald R. Ford or Jimmy Carter were especially effective in office, and their weak presidencies caused some pro-presidential power sentiment. Academia's generally low opinion of Ronald Reagan influenced the debate in the opposite direction. Then dismay over secret and illegal Reagan White House operations during the Iran-Contra affair set off renewed academic criticism. Two typical studies concluded that the events demonstrate that the "constitutionalism built around a legislative role in foreign affairs . . . is disappearing" (Elkin, 1991:12) and that the Iran-Contra affair constituted a "fundamental assault on constitutionalism" (Koh, 1990:5).

President Bush's almost unilateral decision to commit the United States to war in the Persian Gulf and subsequent presidential actions engendered yet further criticism of presidential prerogative (Fisher, 1995c; Rourke, 1993). One legal scholar decried the "law's near irrelevance to the events leading up to the war" and argued that the country should begin "shoring up the . . . legal order" (Glennon, 1991b:96, 101). Similarly, another analyst was moved to comment that legitimate power cannot exist that is "not checked, not balanced, not even in the president, not even in foreign affairs" (Henkin, 1990:36).

The presidency of Bill Clinton and the assertiveness of the Republicans in Congress have somewhat muddled the debate over the balance of executive-legislative power. A widespread conception of Clinton as a relatively weak president and the press attention paid to the Republican congressional leadership, especially Speaker Newt Gingrich (R-GA), pressured the president to declare himself during a news conference to be still "relevant." This defensiveness should not disguise the fact that Clinton has continued to insist adamantly that he should dominate foreign policy making. Reflecting that view, Secretary of State Christopher has argued that the Republicans' foreign policy initiatives in Congress are an "extraordinary assault on the president's constitutional authority to manage foreign policy."[16]

This concern with congressional foreign policy is not limited to executive officials. Independent analysts support broad presidential power and worry that disputes between the president and Congress endanger U.S. foreign policy coherence (Turner, 1991; Wiarda, 1990). Scholars of this persuasion feel that there has been a decrease in both the country's foreign policy consensus and presidential authority in foreign affairs in the last 20 years. Two studies that propound this view reflect it succinctly in their titles: *Our Own Worst Enemy: The Unmaking of American Foreign Policy* (Destler, Gelb, & Lake, 1984) and "Making Democracy Safe for the World" (Lowi, 1989). *Our Own Worst Enemy*, for example, bemoans the fact that "the making of American foreign policy has been growing more political," and it worries that "the mass public . . . has become more activist and difficult to lead" (pp. 18, 24). It is worth noting that Anthony Lake, one of the authors of the first study, became President Clinton's national security adviser. Concern about the dangers of democracy are especially strong when national security is at stake. In this realm, one text suggests, "the conduct of foreign policy . . . requires a concentration of executive power" (Spanier & Uslaner, 1994:17).

Given the divisions among scholars, it will be a challenging task for you to decide which approach to making foreign policy you favor. To help you in your deliberations, we will introduce alternatives and continue to outline the arguments for and against broad democratic participation in foreign policy making.

Democracy and Foreign Policy: Two Alternatives

There are two basic alternatives to making foreign policy in a democratic society. One alternative is broad participation in foreign policy making; the other alternative is limited participation in foreign policy. Before addressing these, it is appropriate to note two things. The first is that it is probable that there is no single correct way to make policy. Not every decision should be or can be subject to a vigorous and wide-spread debate throughout the political system. The simple avalanche of decisions that have to be made, their technical detail, and their frequently minor nature dictate, for example, that the more specific an issue is, the more likely it is to be decided by career professionals in the executive branch. Second, it is also the case that there is occasionally a matter so pressing that the president has a duty, not just the authority, to take immediate action. A direct attack on the United States would be one instance that would fit this situational imperative. These two thoughts about what is possible and necessary at the extreme ends of the continuum between routine policy making and crisis decisions do not, however, obviate the fundamental question: In most cir-cumstances, how much democratic participation should there be in the foreign policy making process?

Limited Participation in Foreign Policy Making

The first alternative, limited participation in foreign policy making, involves a process in which relatively few individuals or organizations have an important voice. Depending on the issue and the situation, policy makers may be located in the White House, the bureaucracy, and among a limited range of interest groups. This alternative reflects the presidential, administrative, and subgovernment models of policy making.

General Arguments for Limited Participation   Advocates of the limited for-eign policy participation alternative believe that foreign policy making is best entrusted to a relatively narrow range of political leaders and executive branch experts centered around the president. Those who take this position argue that the world is too com-plex, too fast moving, and too dangerous to be left to slow, contentious democracy. Proponents of this view suggest that the way to achieve foreign policy success lies in leaving foreign policy decisions largely in the hands of the president and immediate White House advisers. These top officials can presumably draw on information and expertise within the executive branch and act with decisiveness and consistency.

Supporters of limited participation in foreign policy making also disparage the quality of the possible input from other actors, such as Congress and public opinion. Those who would limit the role of Congress, for example, worry that Henry A. Kissin-ger was correct when he described its members as "runaway legislative rabble" (Schulz-inger, 1989:130). The public is viewed with a similarly jaundiced eye. Putting it bluntly, Secretary of State Dean Acheson once commented, if public opinion decided foreign policy, "you'd go wrong every time" (Barnet, 1990:15).

It is important to think about whether you agree with the point of view about democracy expressed by Kissinger, Acheson, and some other experienced and eminent foreign policy experts. Democracy at its best is the process of arriving at decisions by taking ideas from many sources, having open discussions, and reaching a consensus or a compromise. Less ideally, democracy can also be marked by individuals and groups greedily pursuing self-serving ends, by raucous conflict, by policy victories being determined by who is more powerful rather than who is right, and by policies shifting as the balance of political power ebbs and flows.

It is because democracy in practice is frequently undisciplined and occasionally venal that many critics are suspicious of too much democracy. These doubters about the democratic process believe that extended foreign policy participation creates uncertainty and inconsistency, which injure U.S. policy. During the crisis with Iraq, for example, President Bush worried that democratic participation by Congress in the decision of whether or not to go to war would be a "kind of hand-wringing operation that would send bad signals to Saddam."[17]

Such views hold that even if there are flaws in centralized decision making, it is better than the alternative of extended participation and input from the public and other sources. Such qualms are as old as the republic and are especially strong where the democratic process intersects the making of foreign policy. A classic statement was provided by French historian and diplomat Alexis de Tocqueville, who traveled to the United States in the early 1800s to visit the new experiment in democracy. Tocqueville declared himself devoted to democracy in his study, *Democracy in America* (1835). Nevertheless, he was filled with angst about what he saw as its popular passions and other troubling tendencies. Democracies, the French analyst asserted, were prone to making policy based on "impulse rather than prudence," a flaw that left them "decidedly inferior" to authoritarian governments in the conduct of foreign policy. Tocqueville's critical theme persists. Amid the assault on presidential power during the 1970s, for example, Secretary of Defense James Schlesinger urged a restoration of presidential prerogative by quoting the French historian and adding, "Let us be sure it [Tocqueville's warning] is not an epitaph" (Rourke, 1983:286). Proponents of executive authority take particular pains to demean the ability of Congress to help decide foreign policy. With "535 members of the House and Senate, each representing a different local constituency," writes former Kennedy White House presidential assistant Theodore Sorensen (1995:518), Congress "cannot match the presidency in exercising foreign policy initiative, description, direction and implementation. We cannot have [what has been described as] '535 ants sitting on a log floating down a turbulent river, each one thinking he's steering.'"

Executive Branch Proponents of Limited Participation As one might expect, presidents and other executive branch officials are among the strongest and most consistent advocates of broad presidential power. They argue that it is both constitutional and necessary. Moreover, Oval Office occupants are increasingly apt to assert unilateral power and to criticize others, especially in Congress, who attempt to intervene in foreign policy making. Presidents have long groused about interference, but they usually grumbled in private. The powerful Franklin D. Roosevelt once fulminated to his staff that senators were "a bunch of incompetent obstructionists," and that "the only way to do anything in the American government [is] to bypass the Senate" (Bohlen, 1973:210). The president even admitted that "I never let my right hand know what my left hand is doing" and conceded that he was "willing to mislead [the country] and tell untruths if that will help win the war" (Clifford, 1993:633). Congress

There is an ongoing and important debate about how much unilateral authority a president should have in making foreign policy, especially in decisions that concern the use of the military. In late 1994 President Clinton decided to remove the military junta in Haiti, by force if necessary. The protesters shown here, who agreed with a majority of Americans, demonstrated against sending U.S. troops to Haiti. The Senate voted 100 to 0 to demand that Clinton get the approval of Congress before sending troops. The president, ignoring both public opinion and the Senate, unilaterally sent the troops. He claimed that he had the right to do so in his role as commander in chief. Is this an acceptable way to determine policy in a democracy?

rankled President John F. Kennedy so much that he once complained even to Soviet leader Nikita S. Khrushchev about the "time-consuming process" involved in consulting Congress. "Well, why don't you switch to our system?" the Soviet totalitarian leader suggested helpfully (Beschloss, 1992:86).

More recently presidents have been ever more willing to assert publicly that they should decide policy and that Congress interferes in that process. Presidential authority temporarily declined in the aftermath of the political upheaval that accompanied the anguish over Presidents Johnson and Nixon stubbornly pressing the war in Vietnam and the abuses of power (symbolized by the Watergate affair) of the Nixon administration. It was not long, however, before Nixon's successors began to chafe under the restraints of such legislation as the War Powers Resolution (1973) and at the general aggravation of dealing with an activist Congress. Gerald Ford warned in his 1976 State of the Union message that "the framers of our Constitution knew from hard experience [that] the foreign relations of the United States can be conducted effectively only if there is a strong central direction." That responsibility, the president told the assembled Congress, "clearly rests with the President." Jimmy Carter sounded the same note, declaring his determination to "preserve presidential capacity to act in the national interest at the time of rapidly changing circumstances."[18]

Ronald Reagan so vigorously attacked the limits on the presidential prerogatives imposed by Congress during the political climate of the 1970s that one national columnist soon warned that "life is being breathed once again into the Imperial Presidency [idea] that . . . no matter how the President decides a foreign policy question . . . Congress and everyone else must accept it or his authority is undermined."[19] George Bush's attitude fitted this mold of the assertive, perhaps imperial, presidency. "Over the last 20 years," he observed disapprovingly, "we have witnessed a departure from the way we have conducted foreign policy for nearly two centuries. Congress has asserted an increasingly influential micro-management of foreign policy" (Fisher, 1990:243).

President Clinton has followed in the mold of his predecessors and repeatedly asserted that he has and should have broad authority to make foreign policy decisions without the legal concurrence of Congress. Chapter 7 will deal extensively with the president's authority as commander in chief, and for our purposes here it will suffice to examine the president's attitude toward Haiti.

Throughout the U.S.–UN confrontation during 1993 and 1994 with the Haitian military junta that had earlier overthrown the rightfully elected President Jean-Bertrand Aristide, Clinton and his supporters claimed that he had the unilateral constitutional authority to take military action if he deemed it appropriate. A series of resolutions introduced in Congress in 1993 to denounce, perhaps even legally bar, a U.S. military intervention prompted concerted counterattacks. Clinton announced that he would oppose any congressional curbs on his foreign policy powers and asserted that he alone "must make the ultimate decision on when to use force."[20] Even former White House Republicans, who were normally critical of Clinton, closed ranks on the question of executive authority. For one, Brent Scowcroft, the national security adviser to Presidents Ford and Bush, editorialized that "trying to legislate foreign policy is simply a bad idea." "Maneuvering in the complex environment of Somalia," he wrote, "or of Haiti or former Yugoslavia, requires the agility of a [presidential] ballet dancer, not the Mack truck of legislation."[21]

The crisis in Haiti moved toward an explosion point in the summer and fall of 1994 in the face of the continued defiant survival of the junta, despite the UN economic embargo, and the tidal wave of Haitian boat people who were reaching Florida's beaches, were being picked up at sea and being interned at the U.S. naval base at Guantanamo, Cuba, or who were perishing at sea. Clinton was politically caught between two contradictory criticisms. On the one hand, many people belabored the president for talking tough but doing nothing. On the other hand, public opinion polls showed that as much as 73 percent of Americans opposed military action against Haiti. Even after Clinton appeared on television two days before the actual invasion was scheduled to commence and argued that taking action was in the national interest, he was unable to persuade a majority of Americans to favor military action.[22]

Eventually Clinton decided to remove the junta by force if necessary and set an invasion date. Congress objected to the president's unilateral decision making and pressed him to ask for legislative authorization to act. The Senate, for example, voted 100 to 0 in favor of a resolution that emphasized the president's obligation to ask Congress before going to war. "I would like to take this opportunity to send a succinct message to President Clinton concerning the projected invasion of Haiti: Don't do it," William V. Roth Jr. (R-DE) proclaimed in the Senate. "I see the congressional requirement for a congressional vote as the mechanism chosen by the Founding Fathers to determine public support before going to war," Representative David E. Skaggs (D-CO) said during debate in his chamber.[23]

Such sentiments did not sway the White House. Instead, according to one news source, Clinton, with "a sweeping assertion of presidential authority," moved "inexorably toward military intervention in Haiti and essentially dared a skeptical Congress to try to stop him."[24] The administration dismissed the legal necessity of seeking congressional authority on the grounds that the president had the authority to act both because he was commander in chief and because the UN had authorized the operation. Clinton took the position that "I would welcome the support of Congress and I hope that I will have that. [But] like my predecessors in both parties, I have not agreed that I [am] constitutionally mandated to get it."[25] Secretary of State Christopher added in another forum that it was "more important to establish and maintain the principle of presidential authority and power" than to mollify Congress.[26]

Any chance that the Congress might act was thwarted when the administration enlisted the Democratic Speaker of the House and the Senate majority leader to block various attempts to bring the issue to a vote in Congress. In fact, some observers charged that the White House had decided on an early date for the invasion to short-circuit a vote in Congress that would be an embarrassingly narrow victory or that might even be negative. "What's most outrageous," Representative Robert G. Torricelli (D-NJ) charged angrily, is that "the administration may be advancing an invasion to bring democracy to Haiti in order to avoid a vote in the U.S. Congress."[27]

Assertions of presidential prerogative have not been limited to crises and the use of military force (Barilleaux, 1988). Although Congress has the clear constitutional authority to appropriate all funds spent by the United States, President Reagan did not think that in foreign affairs he should be limited by such legal niceties. According to his national security adviser, Admiral John Poindexter, the president expressed his wish "to take action unilaterally to provide assistance" to the Contra rebels in Nicaragua if Congress refused to appropriate funds for that effort. Poindexter has recalled that Reagan was "ready to confront Congress on the constitutional question of who controls foreign policy" (Scott, 1994:30). Reagan's wish became his staff's command, and money was illegally diverted to the Contras by national security assistant Lieutenant Colonel Oliver W. North and others. Such acts reflected what Poindexter's predecessor, Colonel Robert C. McFarlane, remembers as an arrogant indifference to the constitutional standing of Congress. In retrospect, McFarlane told the press recently, he believes that "Ronald Reagan should have come forward and had a public argument over what the Constitution intended about the conduct of foreign policy."[28] That did not happen, McFarlane writes ruefully in his ironically entitled memoir, *Special Trust,* because Reagan "lacked the moral conviction and intellectual courage to stand up in our defense and in [the] defense of his policy" (Brinkley, 1994:9).

Presidents also often try to exclude others from the realm of general diplomacy. At one point when Bush tried to withhold some U.S. aid to Israel to pressure its government to follow American wishes on a diplomatic stance, Congress and some interest groups wanted the aid to go forward. What is interesting here is how the president reacted to this democratic policy dispute. Bush alternated between picturing himself as a forlorn figure trying to hold back a tide of congressional irresponsibility and as a warrior aggressively asserting his right to unchallenged foreign policy authority. Speaking to reporters, Bush first cast himself as Peter beside the dike, as "one lonely little guy down here" beset by "something like a thousand lobbyists on the

Hill working the other side of the question." Then he moved to the offensive. "The Constitution charges the president with the conduct of the nation's foreign policy," Bush proclaimed. "There is an attempt by some in Congress to prevent the President from taking steps central to the nation's security. But too much is at stake for domestic politics to take precedence over peace."[29]

President Clinton makes similar claims to foreign policy dominance. When the Republicans swept to a majority in Congress in the 1994 elections, foreign leaders understandably wondered what impact the GOP ascendancy would have on U.S. foreign policy. Clinton was quick to try to reassure them that the Republican landslide victory meant little or nothing to the world. On a foreign trip less than two weeks after the election, the president told a press conference in Manila that a Republican majority in Congress would not have "any impact on our foreign policy" because "the power vested by the Constitution in the president to represent the United States in foreign affairs . . . is quite clear."[30] The White House has also responded to increased congressional activism by trying to paint critics of Clinton's foreign policy as merely motivated by political self-interest. "I can't think of another time when there has been such controversy [over the conduct of foreign policy] between the executive and legislative branches," observed Press Secretary Michael McCurry.[31] The reason for this, he continued, implying selfish bipartisanship on the part of critics, is that "we are seeing foreign policy being used as a device by the president's opponents to define themselves politically." What McCurry did not seem to think was worth considering was that the critics might be motivated by sincere disagreement with Clinton's policy direction and by the right and value of dissenting in a democracy.

As in the realm of national security, former Republican executive officials have supported Clinton's claims to broad foreign policy authority. Former secretary of state in the Bush administration James A. Baker III told a congressional committee that the Clinton administration had experienced "major problems . . . in formulating and implementing its foreign policy." Yet, despite this criticism, Baker warned that "it would be wrong for Congress to meddle too greatly in Clinton's policy." The United States can only lead globally, Baker contended, if Americans "understand that the president has primary responsibility for the conduct of the nation's foreign policy. Attempts at congressional micromanagement were a bad idea when the Democrats were in control [of Congress], and they remain a bad idea today."[32] In sum, then, it may be said that presidents, many other executive officials, and outside analysts who support strong presidential authority in foreign policy making are trying to expand the limits of what the president is solely responsible for and can do unilaterally. The advocates of presidential power also wish to limit the role of Congress in determining the country's foreign policy.

Extended Participation in Foreign Policy Making

The second alternative is extended foreign policy participation. This means a more diverse policy making process that involves a wide range of actors, each with political clout, vigorously debating policy options. Advocates of extended participation make several general arguments.

First, those who support extended participation dismiss the idea that presidents are always coolly rational decision makers—the "Mr. Spock-as-president" image (Barilleaux, 1988:11). To the contrary, the argument goes, presidents are subject to egotism, anxiety, indecisiveness, anger, and all the other frailties of human beings. Second, presidents are not omniscient. Instead they are frequently uninformed or misinformed. Even if accurate information is available, presidents are often unable to assimilate and evaluate the deluge of information that they face. Whatever the cause, presidents, secretaries of states, and other ranking officials may not be as rational or as fully in charge as we imagine. President Nixon and crises he faced in the Middle East provide some examples. During a 1970 civil war in Jordan, Syrian tanks entered the fighting on the rebel side, thereby threatening to set off a general war in the region that might, in turn, lead to a superpower confrontation with the USSR. At the height of the crisis, a group headed by national security adviser Henry Kissinger debated options, including direct U.S. intervention in Jordan. Nixon did not participate nor was he even in the White House. He was, inexplicably, next door at the Executive Office Building, where Kissinger found him concentrating on strikes in the basement bowling alley rather than in the Middle East. Three years later during the 1973 Yom Kippur War between Israel and several Arab neighbors, Washington faced a Soviet threat to intervene on behalf of the Arab countries. The threat was so ominous that the White House ordered an increase in the U.S. DEFCON (defense condition) level, including nuclear readiness, as a counterthreat to the Soviets. It appears from the records of several participants in the decision making group that, again, Nixon did not participate nor approve of the warning to the Soviets. In fact, he was upstairs asleep and did not learn of his country's action until the next morning (Haney, 1992).

Second, advocates of extended participation dispute the idea that there is a wealth of secret information that only top-level decision makers should be privy to and that gives them greater wisdom. Arthur Schlesinger, an aide to President Kennedy, has recommended that the public and Congress stop being cowed by the supposed secret, better information provided by cables from abroad. According to Schlesinger:

> As one who has had the opportunity to read such cables at various times in my life, I can testify that 95 percent of the information essential for intelligent judgment is available to any careful reader of the *New York Times.* Indeed, the American government would have had a much wiser Vietnam policy had it relied more on the *Times;* the estimate of the situation supplied by newspapers was consistently more accurate than that supplied by the succession of ambassadors and generals in their coded dispatches. (Sherill, 1979:64)

Third, those who advocate extended participation in foreign policy making contend that there is greater wisdom in Congress, the people, and other democratic institutions than skeptics are willing to concede. In fact, proponents of this view suggest that there is a certain safety in numbers. Supporters of this approach argue that the odds of policy success will be increased by an open, even conflictive, system in which numerous independent, strong voices are heard (Moens, 1991). In essence, the "extended" element of the concept implies numerous actors in the foreign policy process and "participation" anticipates broad debate within the polity and the various branches of government, with each actor exercising its responsibility and not trying to circumvent constitutional or statutory law.

Typifying this broad participation argument, one scholar, after reviewing the cold war era, has concluded that "policies that have failed have tended to be those adopted by presidents without meaningful debate," whereas successful policies have been those that, in addition to the executive branch, were also "adopted by Congress and the people after meaningful debate" (Ambrose, 1992:136). Even broader studies of U.S. decisions to go to war and other policies make a similar case that greater congressional and popular participation in the foreign policy process is both desirable and possible (Ely, 1993; Weissman, 1995; Mayer, 1992; Barnet, 1990).

The case of Vietnam serves as a poignant illustration. "We were wrong, terribly wrong," former secretary of defense (1961–1968) Robert S. McNamara has written in his memoir of the Vietnam War. "I am writing this book," he says, "to put before the American people why their government and its leaders behaved as they did and what we may learn from that experience." McNamara indicates that there were many short-comings inside the executive councils. Sheer ignorance was one of them. "I had never visited Indochina, nor did I understand or appreciate its history, language, culture, or values," McNamara concedes. "The same must be said," he adds, "about the president and the other high executive officials who sent Americans to that region."[33]

Much more will be said in later pages about the saga of the U.S. involvement in Vietnam, but a full history is not necessary to make the point here that maybe, just maybe, the tragic U.S. involvement in Vietnam might have been avoided if, at various crucial junctures, Presidents Kennedy and Johnson and their executive branch advisers had not proceeded unilaterally, sometimes secretly, and occasionally with deception.

Ask yourself, for instance, what might have been if President Johnson had fully informed the American public about what was occurring in Vietnam and had not rushed the Tonkin Gulf Resolution, authorizing action, through Congress in 1964? American warships, including the USS *Maddox* and the USS *C. Turner Joy*, were in 1964 involved in operations in the Gulf of Tonkin that included measures to discover the radar and other electronic capabilities of North Vietnam and China and to support South Vietnamese seaborne raids on North Vietnam's coast. On the night of July 30–31, a squadron of South Vietnamese patrol boats shelled several North Vietnamese islands. Then, on the evening of August 2, North Vietnamese patrol boats and the *Maddox* clashed. More South Vietnamese raids took place later that night on North Vietnam's mainland. This was followed during the night of August 3–4 by both the *Maddox* and the *Turner Joy* reporting having come under attack. The White House ordered extensive air strikes to be launched against North Vietnam's naval facilities and asked Congress for emergency authorization, the Tonkin Gulf Resolution, to act. Johnson portrayed the North Vietnamese attacks as unprovoked and dastardly. Amid a crisis atmosphere, the Senate quickly passed the resolution with but two dissenting votes. The House of Representatives considered the resolution for a mere 40 minutes before passing it 416 to 0. The president and Congress had taken a major and speedy step down the path that eventually claimed approximately 50,000 American lives.

The president had not, however, told the whole truth. He did not, for example, disclose the association of the U.S. warships with the South Vietnamese raids on the North. Nor did the president tell the public or members of Congress that naval officials near the scene of the second night's (August 3–4) incidents involving the U.S. ships had cabled that the reported contacts with North Vietnamese patrol craft were doubtful because of the bad weather. Johnson himself later admitted that he was unsure of whether the attacks had taken place. Perhaps nothing occurred at all. More than 30 years later, in late 1995, McNamara traveled to Vietnam. There he met General Vo Nguyen Giap, commander of North Vietnam's military forces during the war. What had occurred in the Tonkin Gulf during those nights in August 1964, McNamara asked Giap. Nothing, the general replied.

Be that as it may, if the president had made an open and full report of what was known and what was not, and if he had not tried to stampede Congress and the public into action, the U.S. reaction might have been very different. Senate Foreign Relations Committee chairman J. William Fulbright (D-AK), who agreed to lead the fight for the resolution, has recalled that the president and his advisers were not very candid about what had or had not just happened or about what was on their minds for the future. Fulbright was reluctant to say that the president of the United States had lied to him, but he added, "Not being a professional psychiatrist, all I can say is that I was deceived. The greatest mistake I made in my life was to accept Lyndon's account of what happened" (Miller, 1980:383).

"Why did President Johnson refuse to take the American people into his confidence?" McNamara asks in his memoir. Johnson's "innate secretiveness" is one answer he considers. More important, according to McNamara, was Johnson's "obsession with securing Congress's approval and financing of his Great Society agenda; he wanted nothing to divert attention and resources from his cherished domestic reforms." Johnson had an "equally strong fear of hard line pressure (from conservatives in both parties) for greater— and far riskier—military action that might trigger responses, especially nuclear, by China and/or the Soviet Union." The upshot, McNamara concludes, is that instead of publicly facing the policy uncertainty in Vietnam, "the president coped . . . by obscuring it—an unwise and ultimately self-defeating course."[34]

Fourth, it is important to note that advocates of extended participation do not claim that it will mean flawless foreign policy. Constitutional scholar Alexander Bickel readily concedes, "There is no assurance of wisdom in Congress," nor, he adds correctly, is there "such assurance in the presidency." In sum, Bickel argues, "Singly, either the President or Congress can fall into bad errors. . . . So they can together, too; but that is somewhat less likely, and in any event, together they are all we've got" (Culver, 1990:241).

Similarly, proponents of extended participation reject Dean Acheson's contention that you would be wrong every time if you followed public opinion. It was certainly hyperbole when President Truman commented at a lecture at Columbia University in 1959 that whenever you have an efficient government you have a dictatorship. Yet proponents of open foreign policy making would say that it is equally an overstatement to maintain that if you have a democracy, you have an inefficient government buffeted by ignorant, apathetic, and unstable public preferences. Chapter 13 will review the quality of public opinion, but we can note here that many scholars are not as skeptical as was Acheson.

Fifth, advocates of extended participation make the point that policy success is not the only standard by which to judge policy making. They argue that democracy, the Constitution, and the law are, in and of themselves, important to uphold.

One scholar, after reviewing what he calls the "myth that presidents can under the law decide by themselves to take military action," concludes that debating the wisdom of the chief executive versus that of Congress "is the wrong question." The point, he suggests, is that "we happen to have a Constitution that clearly states where the war-deciding power is located." That is in Congress. Moreover, "it is now cliché to say that we are supposed to be a government of laws, not men" and we should either follow the law or change it by amending the Constitution (Draper, 1995:38).

Representative Lee H. Hamilton (D-IN) made much the same point when trying to educate Oliver North about why the lieutenant colonel's disdain for Congress did not justify his breaking the law by illegally diverting funds to the Contra rebels and then lying about it under oath before Congress. "A democratic government as I understand it," Hamilton explained, "is not a solution, but a way of seeking solutions. It is not a government devoted to a particular policy objective, but a form of government which specifies the means and methods of achieving objectives." The danger, he warned North and the country, is that "if we [subvert] that process to bring about a desired end—we have weakened our country, not strengthened it" (Berman, 1990:125).

SUMMARY

1. Virtually all Americans support democracy rhetorically, but they do not think much about how policy making in their democracy actually works, how it should work, or what difference it makes how foreign policy is made.

2. One reason to care how foreign policy is made is that the process often affects the choice that is finally selected. There is, for example, sometimes a gap between what leaders and average citizens favor. Furthermore, foreign policy intimately affects us all.

3. Foreign policy making is complex, with multiple processes.

4. There is a long-standing and important debate over how democratic the foreign policy process should be. Skeptics do not believe that the public is informed, intelligent, or unemotional enough to play an important role in foreign policy making. The president and much of the executive branch favor enhanced presidential power. Congress, scholars, the media, and the public are both divided and shifting in their views of the proper level of presidential unilateral authority and democratic restraints.

5. Decision making in the White House frequently does not live up to the informed, rational image of the president and his advisers that many Americans have. Factors such as presidential idiosyncrasies often affect decision making substantially and negatively.

6. There are some scholars who believe that enhancing the democratic input into foreign policy through extended participation and multiple advocacy would improve policy.

Chapter Two
THE HISTORICAL INTERNATIONAL SETTING

In the last chapter we saw that the president does not always dominate U.S. foreign policy making. Sometimes, as Truman once grumbled, a president commands "do this, do that," and nothing happens. Americans sometimes share a similar sense of frustration about the inability of the United States always to have its way. After all, the United States has the world's biggest economy, the globe's most powerful military, and an enviable democratic stability. For nearly a half century the country was one of just two superpowers; now it alone can claim that title. To many Americans, it seems as if their country should be able to emulate the proverbial 1,000-pound gorilla. "Where can such a super simian sit?" the query goes. "Anywhere it wants," is the punch line. Alas, it is not true, at least not for the United States.

LIMITED POSSIBILITIES: INTERNATIONAL AND DOMESTIC

Whatever Americans might occasionally wish, political reality limits what even a superpower can or will do. The United States and its foreign policy makers frequently are not free to choose any course. Instead, there are a variety of historical and contemporary forces that either constrain the country from some action or push it toward a particular policy. Some of these forces are external to the United States; others are internal. Understanding what these impediments and imperatives are and how they influence U.S. foreign policy requires a grasp of the international, domestic, and human contexts in which decisions are made. It is also important to look at these forces from the perspective of the history of American foreign policy so that we can recognize how past experiences affect the decisions being made today. To do this, the following four chapters will use what is called a *levels-of-analysis approach* to examine the history and contemporary settings of U.S. foreign policy.

The first level of analysis is the international system, a global concept that we will explain presently. We will identify how the international system limits the freedom of American action in the world. The second level focuses on American political culture and the ways that it constrains the choices available to U.S. officials. The third level involves seeing how human beings—as individuals and interacting in groups—affect the foreign policy process.

Chapters 2, 3, 4, and 5 focus on these three levels. Chapters 2 and 3 examine the international system (how the world is politically structured and how it operates) and how the system influences U.S. foreign policy. American political culture—who we are, how we feel—is also critical, so chapter 4 moves to a different level of analysis and explores the ramifications of American political culture on the country's foreign policy. Chapter 5 takes up the third level of analysis: how individual characteristics and decisional-group dynamics influence policy.

Just to give you a flavor of how these international and domestic constraints work, let us think about the 1990–1991 Persian Gulf crisis and war. The distribution of economic resources and needs in the international system pressed the United States to intervene. Oil is produced in the Middle East and consumed in the industrial countries. When petroleum-producing Iraq seized another major oil source (Kuwait) in August 1990 and threatened others (Saudi Arabia and the oil emirates), could the United States have done nothing? Probably not. There were, of course, several reasons to take action against Iraqi aggression. But even if none of these had existed, it is arguable that the system-level economic realities virtually compelled the United States, as the world's industrial and political leader, to react to aggression in the globe's most important petroleum-producing region. So doing something was not exactly a free choice.

The international system also helped determine what weapons were used in the ensuing war that began in January 1991. The United States and its allies fought a conventional war in the region, but they were not required to do so. George Bush had nuclear weapons at his disposal; Saddam Hussein did not. Theoretically, Bush could have "nuked" Iraq early in the crisis, forcing the Iraqis to withdraw from Kuwait or face total annihilation. There were even a few Americans who advocated that course. But it was never seriously considered. Why? One reason was that using nuclear weapons would have made the United States a pariah among nations. "You lose the moral high ground if you use one of those stupid things," one U.S. military official explained during the crisis.[1]

Thus concern for potential world opinion—and its impact on the future of U.S. political and economic relations in the international system—constrained the United States. There were also domestic impediments. Moral values are part of political culture, and most Americans would have been horrified by a thermonuclear attack on populous Baghdad. There were other international and domestic factors that constrained U.S. choices, including the difficulty in choosing an appropriate target for such a strike. The lesson here is that the United States *could have* used nuclear weapons but *did not*. The reasons it did not are partly related to the nature of the international system and to the characteristics of American political culture.

UNDERSTANDING INTERNATIONAL SYSTEMS

There is an old adage that says "when America sneezes, the world catches a cold." This implies that American decisions—good and bad—have a great effect on world affairs. It says little, however, about the reverse effect: the degree to which the international system colors the American decision making process and constrains foreign policy success. The primary goal of this chapter is to examine the impact of the international system. Before we can do that, though, it is important to understand the concept of an international system. This can be done by thinking about the general nature of a system and the characteristics of the international system.

The Nature of International Systems

Countries operate in a global social-economic-political-geographic environment called the **international system**. On a more intimate level, each of us also exists within a domestic political system—in a family or other social system that influences our behavior. We individuals are likely to stand impatiently in line for a movie ticket rather than rush to the front. We go to work when it would sometimes be more fun to be picnicking. If stopped by a police officer and given a speeding ticket, we are apt to be polite—even though we are angry and upset. One thing to see here is that our behavior is shaped and limited in these situations by the social, economic, and political realities that exist in our domestic political and personal social systems. Second, our responses in most situations are reasonably predictable. The domestic system creates a degree of consistency in our actions and a similarity between how we and others act. Decisions and actions are not foreordained, but norms—what is expected—usually are good indicators of what will happen. In a sense, countries have similar sorts of system restraints on them. They do things or do not do things partly because of the realities of the international system. For instance, American decision makers had a much freer hand in formulating responses to Iraq's invasion of Kuwait in 1990 than would have been the case during the cold war era. American decision makers had more choices available for action in the Persian Gulf because the Soviets were no longer a major player in the region. This does not mean that countries do not have options or that they always act as expected. Human affairs are never completely predictable. But if you understand the nature of the international system, then you can begin to foresee how it will affect the policies of countries such as the United States (O. Holsti, 1991; Pelz, 1991;).

Characteristics of the International System

Once you grasp the fundamental concept that a country operates within a constraining international system, the next step is to discover the specific impact of the system. Various scholars have argued that different types of systems operate in different ways. Because this is true, it is important to identify and remember the specific characteristics of the international system that help shape how countries act in international affairs. These seven characteristics include organizational structure, types of actors, number of poles (power centers), distribution of power assets, norms of behavior, geographic characteristics, and scope and level of interaction.

These characteristics combine to form the international system that American policy makers must confront in their efforts to pursue their foreign policy goals. The system is not a constant for policy makers; it changes over time. Sometimes change is evolutionary—such as the evolution from a multipolar world system at the turn of the twentieth century to the bipolar system that emerged after World War II. Occasionally change is revolutionary, as were the events of 1989–1991. During that period, Eastern Europe broke away from Soviet domination, Germany reunited, then the Soviet Union imploded amid economic collapse and political unrest. On December 25, 1991, the Soviet Union ceased to exist. With its demise the last chapters of the cold war and the bipolar system also entered the history books. The Soviet Union destroyed first the influence and then the very existence of one of the two existing poles, the USSR.

Organizational Structure

The international system is anarchic. The concept of anarchy means that no ultimate authority exists within the international system. There are factors such as norms and power relationships that exist and constrain the behavior of countries and other international actors. Importantly though, there is no vertical authority structure overseeing the actions of countries in the way that the U.S. federal government oversees the actions of the 50 states, thousands of local governments, and 250 million citizens. Instead, nation-states are sovereign actors in the international system. **Sovereignty** means that nation-states legally answer to no higher authority than themselves. Thus the system is organized horizontally rather than vertically, as in a domestic political system.

International relations scholars generally agree that the anarchic nature of the international system is one of the most important characteristics influencing the ways that countries interact with one another. Countries for the most part must rely on themselves. As a result national interest—that is, self-interest—is a primary standard by which a nation-state decides its conduct.

Identifying anarchy as the central characteristic of the international system does not imply that the system is without structure. There is structure, and the characteristics of that structure play an important role in determining how the system works. Nor does the concept of anarchy imply that states are free to do anything they wish in the international arena. Instead countries must, if they are wise, be concerned about how their actions will affect the system and how other actors in the system will respond.

Types of Actors

The types of actors that exist at a given time constitute a second system characteristic. Most prominently, the list of system-level actors includes (national or nation–) *states* (countries). Also important are *international organizations,* such as the United Nations or the European Union, and *transnational actors,* such as multinational corporations (Exxon or Nestlé) or international nongovernmental organizations (Amnesty International or Greenpeace).

Number of System Poles

A third characteristic of system structure is the number of system poles. The number of poles is determined by the number of powerful or dominant actors in the system. Political scientists often distinguish among unipolar, bipolar, tripolar, and multipolar (four or more poles) systems. "Balance of power" is a related and commonly used term. When applied to multipolar systems as an adjective (as in a balance-of-power system), however, the term usually implies a system in which countries fluidly shift alliances to balance the power of a country or an alliance that threatens to achieve hegemony (to dominate the system).

Poles are sometimes established along ideological lines, as they were in the bipolar system that pitted the United States and its allies against the Soviet Union and its allies. Poles may also be defined more purely along competitive economic or military lines when nation-states strive with one another for power and influence within the system. This is what is occurring in the current, evolving multipolar system. Note that the number of poles existing within the system at a particular time partially determines the types of interactions that take place among the major and minor powers of the system. Saddam Hussein might not have decided to invade Kuwait in 1990 if the second pole in the system—the Soviet Union—had not been eliminated as a force that constrained the behavior of those countries allied with it.

Distribution of Power Assets

A fourth characteristic is the distribution of power assets within the system. Power assets determine a country's strength and include military strength, industrial capacity, natural resources, organization, and the level of technological development. From a system perspective, states with more power assets have greater freedom of action within the system than those with fewer assets. Certain power assets, however, are not usable in all situations, and even powerful nations will be subject to limits to maneuverability at times. American frustration during the Iranian hostage crisis (1979–1981), when U.S. military superiority was irrelevant to whether the captives would be released, demonstrates the situational limits on power, even for a superpower.

Norms of Behavior

A fifth system characteristic is determined by international norms of behavior. Norms are standards of behavior that are followed in part because of voluntary compliance by actors who agree with them and recognize the value of an orderly system. Standards are also sometimes enforced by the threat or application of diplomatic,

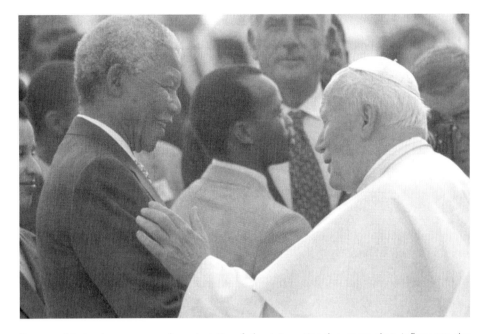

Norms of behavior are one characteristic of the international system that influences the foreign policy of the United States and other countries. During the 1970s and 1980s, global attitudes, including those in the United States, became increasingly intolerant of the racist apartheid system in South Africa. Even though the administration of Ronald Reagan opposed taking strong measures against South Africa, Congress insisted that the United States comply with international norms and join other countries in placing stringent sanctions on South Africa. These eventually helped force the white government to end official segregation and to hold elections in which people of all races and ethnic groups could participate. The results of those elections in 1993 are symbolized in this picture, in which Nelson Mandela, a former political prisoner who became South Africa's first black president, greets Pope John Paul II upon his arrival in Johannesburg in September 1995.

economic, or military sanctions. Moreover, norms often become law in the form of either common law or statutory law. At the international system level, for instance, international law provides a code of conduct for international relations that places boundaries on the actions of states, even if it is not always obeyed. Human rights such as political participation and the fulfillment of basic human needs also sometimes condition the actions of states. As noted, the use of nuclear weapons against a non-nuclear opponent would violate the norms of the system and has been avoided despite the amoral case that could be made for the efficiency of such a strategy.

Geographic Characteristics

Geographic characteristics such as location, size, and topography are a sixth factor that affects national policy. For 150 years geographic isolation allowed the United States usually to shun the conflicts of the European-dominated multipolar system. More recently, the United States has sought to decrease its geographic distance from important regions of the world by establishing alliances with nations around the world and by stationing American military forces overseas for rapid deployment during a crisis (Dalby, 1990). During the political-military crisis with Haiti in 1994, President Clinton was able credibly to threaten the quick use of American military force because of the short distance that Haiti is from the United States. Military force is more constrained across longer distances.

Scope and Level of Interaction

The final international system characteristic is the scope and level of interaction among the actors. Scope of interaction includes the number and variety of related issues on which actors interact. Level refers to the frequency and intensity of those interactions. Both the scope and level of international interactions have increased dramatically in this century as countries have become increasingly *interdependent* on one another. The United States and other countries with large industrial economies, for example, have myriad and frequent contacts as trading partners. These partners are vital as sources of needed commodities and as markets for U.S. exports. And our ability to watch at home the events of the Persian Gulf War as they unfolded is testimony to the speed and frequency of international communication and interaction today.

THE U.S. GLOBAL ROLE: THE GROWTH OF A SUPERPOWER

Americans have interacted with the outside world since the republic began. President George Washington warned about the dangers of forming "permanent alliances" or involving the new country in the power politics of Europe, as such things detracted from the central American interest of commerce and trade. President Thomas Jefferson pointed to the pitfalls of "entangling alliances." Moreover, Americans were long able to follow this advice. The wealth of natural resources available to Americans—especially as they moved westward—and the country's geographic isolation from powerful international system actors allowed U.S. policy makers to be very selective about participation in world affairs. While the great European powers were forced to look outside their borders for new economic resources and markets, the United States built its strength by capitalizing on its expansive and expanding territory and by exploiting the increasingly dominant U.S. position in the Western Hemisphere.

Over time, however, both the United States and the international system changed in ways that promoted expanded U.S. international activity. One change was in U.S. power. It grew: slowly at first, then explosively. As American power expanded, so did the country's ability and confidence to involve itself in international affairs. The international system evolved also. In spite of American isolationist predilections, changes in world technological and economic realities made both U.S. military security and economic prosperity ever more dependent on global conditions. As a result, Americans' traditional isolationist tendencies have wrestled with the pragmatic need for international involvement in order to promote and protect American interests and with the emotional urge to use U.S. power to recreate much of the world in the American image. This isolationist-internationalist tension has been a hallmark of the U.S. role in the international system and continues in the contemporary American system.

The following several sections examine the historic system conditions that have promoted U.S. internationalism. Contemporary conditions will be examined in chapter 3, and chapter 4 will describe the political culture factors that have variously worked to turn the focus of American activity alternatively outward and inward.

For the system perspective, U.S. foreign policy motives can be grouped into four main topics. First, American international activity expanded as U.S. power assets grew and as its relative power as a system actor increased. Second, the United States soon sought to dominate its immediate international environment. By the early 1800s, Americans began to define the Western Hemisphere as the U.S. sphere of influence. Third, international trade thrust American interests outward from the earliest days of the republic. Long before Americans thought of their country as a world actor, the American flag flying from U.S. merchant vessels was a familiar sight in ports around the world. By the late 1800s and early 1900s, the U.S. Navy was never far behind the merchant fleet. Fourth, a combination of the system influences and the political culture factors to be discussed in chapter 4 has made the United States a most un-revolutionary country. Especially in this century, the country became a defender of the status quo both because it equated change with a loss of U.S. power and prestige and because new ideas and new people seemed to threaten Euro-American concepts of world order.

U.S. Power and International Activity Expand

Until recently, American history was marked both by a slow growth of national power and by restrained international activity. Throughout most of the republic's first 200 years, the growth of its power preceded the expansion of internationalism, but the two factors were linked reciprocally.

Power and International Activity to 1900

When the United States achieved independence, it entered a **multipolar**, Euro-centric world. This means that the international system was dominated by four or more powerful countries, in this case located primarily in Europe. Great Britain and France were the two strongest poles. Russia, Prussia, the Austrian Empire, and the Ottoman Empire (centered in Turkey) were also great powers. China still dominated its region. Compared to the great European powers, the United States was weak, its future uncertain. The new country needed time to consolidate itself and increase its strength. It was, therefore, the pragmatic assessment of American weakness that was the primary factor that prompted George Washington and Thomas Jefferson to counsel their country to avoid the perils of international entanglements. John Adams explained in the language and spelling of the time in his diary as early as 1775 that:

> We ought to lay it down as a first principle and a Maxim never to be forgotten, to maintain an entire Neutrality in all future European Wars. . . . [If we are not neutral] foreign Powers would find means to corrupt our People [and] to influence our Councils, and in fine We should be little better than Puppetts danced on the Wires of the Cabinetts of Europe. We should be the Sport of European Intrigues and Politicks. (Paterson, 1989:30)

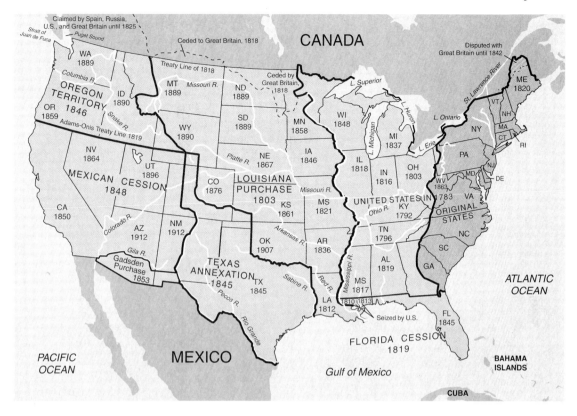

Contrary to the popular idea that early American history was marked by profound isolationism, the United States interacted regularly with other countries. Territorial expansion was a hallmark of the first 125 years of U.S. history, and much of the newly acquired territory was gained from France, Great Britain, Mexico, Russia, and Spain through clashes, negotiations, or purchases. Americans not only acquired all the territory in the so-called continental United States, pictured here, under the self-proclaimed doctrine of Manifest Destiny, but they also acquired Alaska, Hawaii, Puerto Rico, Guam, the Philippines, and other territories through various interactions with other countries. By the year 1900 the United States was one of the world's largest and potentially most powerful countries, and it began to move more frequently and assuredly, if not consistently, into a truly internationalist role in world politics.

Although weak, the newly independent Americans still were able to manipulate the operation of the multipolar international system to their advantage. One scholar theorizes that in the "classical multipolar balance-of-power system" that existed throughout most of the 1700s and 1800s, one rule of conduct for weak states is that "In peacetime, small powers try to play . . . great powers against other great powers in order to maintain independence or gain concessions." Alternatively, "in time of tension or war," small powers that are not directly involved "try to extract concessions for maintaining benevolent neutrality" (Pelz, 1991:53).

Most of the early American leaders understood and followed these principles of system conduct to one degree or another. John Adams and others argued, for instance, that the United States should build up good commercial relations with both Great Britain and France so that neither superpower would be willing to see the United States attacked and subdued by the other. The Americans were also able to take advantage of balance-of-power politics and the Napoleonic war raging in Europe to accomplish such specific goals as acquiring the Louisiana Territory from France in 1803. The transfer of this territory from Spain to France alarmed Americans and there was talk of seizing New Orleans. The reasons behind France's decision to sell the territory to President Jefferson were complex, but in part they stemmed from Napoleon's disinclination to risk conflict with the United States or to prompt an Anglo-American alliance against him.

None of these strictures against foreign entanglement were meant to prevent the United States from having regular political and commercial contacts with many countries. In fact, Washington, Jefferson, and other early leaders viewed such contacts as a source of strength. Nor did they advocate shunning political contacts. They were too realistic for that, understanding as they did that trade and the flag travel together. Moreover, the young republic soon found itself engaged in armed clashes with other countries. Most of these were related to establishing the United States as a fully sovereign country, to protecting U.S. international commerce, and to expanding U.S. territory. The United States also soon sought agreements with other countries. Treaties with Spain (1795) and Great Britain (1783), for example, settled territorial disputes. Frontier tension, the freedom of the seas, and Great Britain's condescending attitude toward its former colony were among the causes of the War of 1812. There were other tensions and even war scares, but Americans eventually secured what they believed to be manifestly their territory through treaties with Spain, France, and Great Britain. The U.S. annexation of Texas did spark war with Mexico (1846–1848), and victory brought more territory under the American flag. Nonetheless, early international interaction was generally related to specific American concerns and did not involve long-term alliances or regularized overseas involvement. None of this constituted classic internationalism as we think of it today and as it will be discussed in chapter 4.

While the country expanded westward, it was also growing economically powerful and immigration was feeding a rapid population growth. Many people did not recognize it at the time, but by the late 1800s the United States had become one of the world's most powerful countries. In 1900, for example, Americans produced more steel than the British and French together, and there were almost as many Americans as there were British and French citizens combined. One estimate of *potential power* based on population and economic strength at the turn of the century calculated that the United States was the world's most powerful country: twice as strong as Great Britain and five times more powerful than France. Only Germany was close, but even Kaiser Wilhelm II commanded only two-thirds of the power potentially available to President William McKinley (Beckman, 1984).

Nevertheless, the United States remained relatively isolationist and its military forces were weak at the turn of the century. *Projectable power,* which includes the ability of a country to deploy its military forces, yields very different results from potential power. The United States' projectable power was only about a third of German or British strength and half of Russian strength. This gap between U.S. potential and projectable power, however, had already begun to narrow. By the late 1800s, the United States was beginning to be more of an international player because of its appetite for foreign resources to fuel economic expansion, its need to gain new markets for products, and its confidence in its burgeoning power. As we will see in a later section of this chapter, the United States began to build a modern navy and to acquire colonies as the century drew to a close. The 1896 Republican national platform called for a "firm, vigorous, and dignified" foreign policy promoted by "naval power commensurate with [America's] position and responsibility." Just two years later, Spain became the first traditional European power to feel the force of stirring American power. The defeat of Spain in 1898, the U.S. acquisition of colonies and dependencies as a result of the Spanish-American War of 1898, and the coming to the White House in 1901 of the assertive Theodore Roosevelt signaled a new foreign policy for a new century.

Power and International Activity, 1900–1945

The first 45 years of the 1900s are a tale of America's emergence as a full-scale internationalist superpower. It was, however, a slow and uncertain metamorphosis to global power. Symbolically, the emerging U.S. presence as a major international player was confirmed by Roosevelt's role as the mediator of the Russo-Japanese War in 1905 and by his 1907 decision to send 16 battleships, the so-called Great White Fleet, to show the flag on a globe-circling voyage.

The first four decades of the twentieth century saw swings in the strength of American attitudes about **internationalism** and **isolationism**. For most of these years, Americans still shied away from the balance-of-power, multipolar world of Europe. Americans viewed European problems as distant, largely irrelevant events from which the United States should stand aloof. World War I, German attacks on U.S. shipping and lives, and the desire of Woodrow Wilson to make the United States a leader in world affairs seemed for a time to turn the country toward internationalism. But the Senate rejected U.S. membership in the League of Nations. Then, with the war won, Americans once again became self-absorbed—first in the ecstasy of the Roaring Twenties, then in the agony of the Great Depression that beset the 1930s.

While Americans faced inward, the international system continued to change and remained unstable. Some political scientists believe that international systems are especially conflict-prone during times of polar shift, when old powers are declining and new powers are rising (Schampel, 1993; Geller, 1992). There are other scholars who see the existence of regular cycles of conflict marked by the fall of old and the rise of new dominant (hegemonic) powers (Goldstein, 1991; Beck, 1991). Arguably, this type of system shift was occurring and created instability throughout the first half of the twentieth century. The dissipated hegemonic power of Great Britain left the multipolar world without a stabilizing hegemon. Other traditional powers (Austria-Hungary, the Ottoman Empire, China) collapsed, while other countries (Germany, Japan, the United States, Russia) each struggled to increase their power, even to become a hegemon. World War I did not fully settle the matter, the old multipolar system limped on, and war was resumed after only two short decades.

The multipolar system finally collapsed in the ashes of World War II. Concurrently, isolationist strength in the United States was eclipsed by participation in the war. Franklin Delano Roosevelt, who had favored joining the League of Nations after World War I, worked hard to shift the United States from a general policy of isolationism to greater internationalism. He brought the country to Great Britain's aid before the war, but isolationism remained so strong that FDR was not able to join

The United States became a powerful global actor in the twentieth century. During World War I, which had its origins in Sarajevo, Bosnia, U.S. power and global interests resulted in Americans entering a war in Europe for the first time. The traumas of that war, including the American soldier seen dying here in France during a mustard gas attack in 1918, caused a U.S. retreat from the global stage during the 1920s and 1930s. World War II once again found Americans at war in Europe and, indeed, around the world. Since then the United States has remained a global power and internationalism has dominated U.S. foreign policy attitudes. Now, however, in the post–cold war era, many Americans are once again questioning U.S. international involvement. The December 1995 deployment of U.S. troops to Bosnia is one focus of this debate.

the war voluntarily as a British ally. Whatever Americans wanted, however, the world and its war came to them on December 7, 1941, at Pearl Harbor. The four years of conflict that followed ended the existing multipolar system and marked the coming of America's age as not only an international power but as a superpower hegemon.

Power and International Activity, 1945–1975

With victory in sight by 1944, President Roosevelt shifted his immediate goals and shepherded the country toward membership in the United Nations and other international organizations. "We have learned that we cannot live alone, at peace," FDR observed in his fourth inaugural address in January 1945. "Our own well-being is dependent on the well-being of other nations, far away. We have learned that we must [not] live . . . as ostriches . . . [but as] citizens of the world, members of the human community."

Roosevelt died soon thereafter, but a number of changes in the international system worked to continue U.S. global involvement (Ambrose, 1991). *Geography* is one system determinant we mentioned earlier. As military technology became vastly more destructive and could be delivered more quickly and at remarkably greater ranges, the oceans flanking the United States offered less protection. The system-level *pattern of interaction* also changed. One example is foreign commerce, which increased rapidly. This made trade and other aspects of international financial relations increasingly important to the economic health of the United States and most other countries. As a result, markets and supply sources had to be secured and trade and monetary stability had to be ensured.

Shifts in the international power structure prompted other important system changes. These left the United States in the enviable, yet burdensome, position of being the world's greatest military and economic power. One notable difference was the *distribution of power resources*. The war destroyed the economies of most of the prewar powers. By contrast, U.S. industrial capacity and infrastructure survived and prospered. Americans produced in 1947 about half the world's steel and commercial energy, and the U.S. gross national product accounted for about half of the entire world's GNP. The distribution of military resources also changed. Most dramatically, the United States possessed, and the Soviet Union soon acquired, atomic weapons. While Soviet economic and military power did not nearly equal U.S. assets, the Soviet Union was geographically close to Western Europe, possessed an imposing army, and had a large population. Also, a significant amount of Soviet industrial and energy production capacity had survived the war or had been rebuilt.

American and Soviet strength stood in contrast to that of most of the other *actors,* who were either defeated or who were so economically exhausted by the cost of victory that they ceased to play a major world role. The result was a change in the system's *number of poles*. The postwar power structure was basically **bipolar** (two powers), in contrast to the prewar multipolar (four or more powers) structure. Some political scientists maintain that bipolar systems are characterized by unrelenting hostility between the two countries competing for global hegemony. True to that theory, the power dynamics of the bipolar system, coupled with ideological differences, seemingly forced the two superpowers into unremitting, cold war competition. They were like two scorpions in a bottle.

Americans reacted to the new system realities with a mix of fear and brashness. On the one hand, bipolar competition put the United States on the defensive as it sought to defend the status quo: the U.S.–created, postwar political and economic system. To Americans, it seemed that the Soviet Union posed a mortal threat and that the United States either had to accept leadership or see the collapse of the "free world." On the other hand, the U.S. status as the world's military and economic colossus created foreign policy assertiveness. "Americans in 1945 were flushed with a sense of power," one diplomatic history explains. The United States began a "zealous pursuit of its goals," with such assertiveness that it sometimes acted with "a diplomatic style befitting the bully on a street corner" (Paterson, Clifford, & Hagen, 1991b:463).

This aggressive anxiety extended American internationalism beyond the end of World War II and helped shape the international system. The bipolar world redefined the concept of American interests. Europe was thrust forward as the central arena of conflict with the Soviet Union. Nowhere would superpower competition be more acute than over divided Germany. The British, French, Soviets, and Americans occupied Berlin after the war. Soon the city became a flash point for superpower conflict in a series of recurring crises, including the Berlin Blockade of 1948–1949 and events surrounding the 1961 construction of the Berlin Wall. Americans believed that conflict in Europe was a result of broken Soviet promises regarding the nature of postwar Europe. To Americans, the Soviets supplied ample evidence of evil intent by refusing to allow Western-style democratic elections after the war in Poland, by dominating

Eastern Europe, and by repressing the people of that region. The United States responded to the perceived threat economically and militarily. The European Recovery Program (the **Marshall Plan**) pumped billions of dollars into Western Europe to restore economic and political stability and to avert leftist political takeovers. Militarily, the United States sponsored formation of the North Atlantic Treaty Organization (NATO) in 1949 and allowed West Germany to rearm in 1954.

The United States also assumed some of the traditional regional responsibilities of the European powers. The 1947 **Truman Doctrine**, announcing U.S. support of Greece and Turkey against Soviet pressure, ushered in the policy of containment of communism. The U.S. position was spurred by Great Britain's financial inability to continue Western guardianship of the Eastern Mediterranean. This region was strategically vital because of the Suez Canal, which connects the Mediterranean Sea to the Indian Ocean through Egypt, and because of the Bosporus and Dardanelles straits in Turkey, which provide choke points that could have been used to deny free passage to the Soviet navy from the Black Sea into the Mediterranean.

The geographic expansion of American power and perceived interests of the United States did not stop in Europe or even at the far shores of the Mediterranean. Soon the U.S. presence girdled the globe. Containment was the primary rationale, but not the only reason. Economic interests, the smug self-assurance that other people would be better off if they adopted American-style political and economic systems, and the sheer assertiveness of superpower status also internationalized American foreign policy.

Americans Define and Dominate a Sphere of Influence

The Western Hemisphere was the earliest and has been the most consistent region of U.S. international activity. Competition among the European powers for international power, territory, and economic opportunities led to development of areas over which they exercised special influence. These are termed **spheres of influence**. During the first great imperial period, Great Britain, France, Spain, Portugal, the Netherlands, and a few other countries divided North and South America into spheres of influence. Various conflicts, such as the French and Indian War (1756–1763), were fought over these spheres. Then beginning with the United States and followed in the early 1800s by many Spanish and Portuguese colonies to the south, revolutionaries established new countries throughout the Western Hemisphere. Once American independence was achieved, the United States also moved to assert its influence in the Western Hemisphere.

The **Monroe Doctrine** of 1823 declared the New World off limits to further colonization by Old World powers and proclaimed American determination to stay out of Europe's affairs. President James Monroe's démarche (a strong policy statement in diplomacy) was based on an idealist mixture of Americans' isolationist sense of moral superiority to Europe and a realpolitik desire to keep European powers at bay and to establish and fortify America's claim to influence in the Western Hemisphere. In reality, though, as one diplomatic historian put it, "the Monroe Doctrine was a bluff" (Jones, 1988:114). It worked and kept European powers from resubjugating newly independent countries or transferring continuing colonies to other European countries. But because the United States was weak, the early success of the Monroe Doctrine was actually based on the multipolar rivalries in Europe, which made them unwilling to risk conflict with one another or with the United States.

In time, American strength grew. After the Civil War, U.S. power helped prevent France from sustaining the reign of Maximilian, an Austrian archduke installed as the emperor of Mexico (1864–1867) by Napoleon III. Still, the U.S. interpretation of the Monroe Doctrine remained generally defensive. That definition changed by the end of the century amid burgeoning American power.

The defeat of Spain in 1898 brought Cuba and Puerto Rico in the Caribbean, as well as the Philippines and Guam in the Pacific, under either direct or indirect U.S. control. The Virgin Islands were purchased from Denmark in 1916. The country of Panama was virtually created by Theodore Roosevelt in 1903. The Americans then dug a canal across it and insisted on a long-term lease. The 1904 **Roosevelt Corollary** to the Monroe Doctrine asserted the U.S. right to intervene in the affairs of other Western Hemisphere nations to stop actions unacceptable to the United States. The American-claimed right to define such wrongdoing was a reflection of the political culture trait of American exceptionalism, or the tendency to view the United States as a unique and morally superior nation. To Americans the corollary justified repeated interventions, and at times occupying forces, in Cuba (1898–1922), the Dominican Republic (1916–1924), Haiti (1915–1934), Honduras (1924–1925), Mexico (1914–1917), and Nicaragua (1912–1933), and the permanent stationing of troops in the Panama Canal Zone. Protecting U.S. economic interest through "dollar diplomacy" and "exporting democracy" to Latin America were vigorously pursued (Lowenthal, 1991).

Still, Americans have always found it troubling to ignore their ideals by using power nakedly. Therefore, the United States

The Nicaraguan revolutionaries who overthrew the Somoza dictatorship in 1979 called themselves Sandinistas in honor of César Augusto Sandino (1895–1934). This man was hailed in his country as a hero but was called a "cold-blooded bandit outside the civilized pale" by President Herbert Hoover. Sandino, who blasted the Monroe Doctrine as meaning "America for the Yankees," was accused of administering "machete justice" to members of the Guardia Nacional. He explained that "liberty is not conquered with flowers."

tried to soften its image of self-interested U.S. domination of its sphere of influence. The most significant step was Franklin Roosevelt's 1933 use of the homey phrase "good neighbor" to denote his policy toward Latin America. The **Good Neighbor Policy** marked an end to prolonged, direct U.S. interventions, but the United States actively continued to foster pro-American regimes throughout Latin America.

The cold war and the containment doctrine gave new impetus to and justification for U.S. domination—albeit usually indirect—of its sphere of influence. The

45

Organization of American States (OAS) was established in 1948 during the early cold war period as an anticommunist alliance. Washington also supported Rafael Trujillo in the Dominican Republic, the Somoza family in Nicaragua, and other odious, right-wing dictatorships as supposed bulwarks against communist movements. Leftist Latin American regimes were attacked. The U.S. Central Intelligence Agency (CIA) was heavily involved in the 1954 overthrow of Guatemala's president Jacobo Arbenz Guzmán. His transgression was to call for land reform. This upset the American-owned United Fruit Company, which warned the State Department that such heresy threatened a communist takeover of all of Latin America.

The situation created in Cuba when rebels led by Fidel Castro toppled right-wing dictator Fulgencio Batista in 1959 was even more alarming to many Americans. Castro survived, however, where other leftist Latin American leaders had not and would not. The attempt of President John F. Kennedy's administration to overthrow Castro in 1961 failed dismally at the Bay of Pigs. Cuba again became a point of superpower conflict in 1962 when the Soviets deployed intermediate-range, nuclear-warhead missiles on the island. This crisis resulted in the U.S. pledge to the Soviets that if they forswore nuclear weapons in Cuba, the United States would never again invade the island. The Western Hemisphere was thus resecured for American interests. In exchange, Castro was secure as the leader of Cuba.

This crisis and the fact that poverty in Latin America could, as it had elsewhere, foster leftist sentiments led Kennedy to shift the emphasis of U.S. hemispheric policy and to try to resurrect the spirit of the Good Neighbor policy. He announced the Alliance for Progress to focus American economic assistance and technical expertise on Latin America in 1961 as a method of nation-building and of "winning hearts and minds" (the so-called WHAM effort) over to the American model of democracy and development. Relations with Latin America slowly improved, but U.S. intolerance of leftist governments continued. As late as 1973 the CIA was involved—albeit indirectly by some accounts—in the overthrow and death of Chile's president Salvador Allende and in the coming to power of rightist dictator General Augusto Pinochet. Moreover, as we will see in the next chapter, Americans' belief in the Monroe Doctrine continued to influence U.S. policy into the administrations of Ronald Reagan and George Bush. This was especially true when it was coupled with an anticommunist impulse, as in El Salvador, Nicaragua, and Grenada. It was also the case, as in Panama, whenever a Latin American government pressed the United States too hard.

The U.S. Expansion in the World Economy

The somewhat ambivalent American quest for political-military power, influence, and prestige was not the only reason why the United States became a player in international affairs. The twin needs for sources of imported raw materials to supply manufacturing and for foreign markets that would help expand the economy also led the United States to look beyond its borders from the beginning of the republic.

Trade, Investment, and Imperialism

Promotion and protection of trade have been an ongoing centerpiece of U.S. international activity. Some of the country's earliest international activity centered on *promoting trade*. The 1794 Jay Treaty both secured favorable status for U.S. trade with

Great Britain and "postponed war with Britain for eighteen years and enabled adolescent America to establish its footing" (Bailey, 1974:79).

Promoting international trade also increased U.S. contacts with other parts of the world, including the Far East. The Treaty of Wanghia with China (1844) guaranteed the United States both most-favored-nation trade status and **extraterritoriality** (the provision that Americans who were accused of crimes in China would be tried before American, not Chinese, courts). Commodore Matthew Perry commanded a squadron of ships that anchored threateningly in Tokyo Bay in 1853; the following year he negotiated a treaty with Japanese officials of the Tokugawa shogunate that allowed the United States to use two Japanese ports. By 1858 U.S. relations with Japan had also been formally initiated, and another treaty granting Americans favorable trade status and extraterritoriality was signed. Still other international activity focused on the need to acquire and secure speedier sea travel to California. In 1850 the United States agreed with Great Britain to cooperate in the building of any future canal across Central America. Five years later an American-owned railroad was built across the Isthmus of Panama (Carruth, 1991).

Protecting trade and a related insistence on freedom of the seas have also been a regular part of U.S. international activity and have led to many military confrontations and clashes. The first was a short, undeclared naval war (1797) with France over commerce and national pride. These themes figured in the U.S. decisions (1805, 1807) to send ships into the Mediterranean to fight the Barbary pirates, who were demanding tribute and seizing American merchant ships. The impressment of American seamen and other issues of commerce were also among the causes of the War of 1812 with the British. As President James Madison told Congress in 1812, war was justified because "British cruisers have been in the continued practice of violating the American flag on the great highway [the oceans] of nations. . . . Such is the spectacle of injuries and indignities which have been heaped on our country." Some 105 years later, President Woodrow Wilson asked for a declaration of war against Germany on much the same grounds. He described German submarines as "outlaws" preying on U.S. shipping in violation of "our right to use the seas . . . [without] unlawful interference." Wilson declared that "we will not choose the path of submission and suffer the most sacred rights of our Nation and our people to be ignored or violated. The wrongs against which we now array ourselves . . . cut to the very roots of human life."

Business expansion, in league with the burgeoning American power discussed earlier, also moved beyond normal promotion and protection of trade and laid the groundwork for **imperialist internationalism**. American business leaders, once their domestic markets were saturated, looked abroad for new ones. Quaker Oats products were sold worldwide. Swift and Armour shipped meats to Europe. Standard Oil exported to Germany, Great Britain, Cuba, and Mexico. International Harvester exported reapers to Russia. As early as 1879, Singer sold more sewing machines abroad than at home.

Overseas investments needed protection, and that, Commodore Alfred Mahan argued in his influential *The Influence of Seapower upon History* (1890), required a modern navy. In turn, a modern navy required secure foreign bases to refuel and resupply the ships. Colonies represented the most secure form of foreign bases. Thus, according to one study, the "loop was closed: great navies required colonies; colonies begat great navies" (Paterson, 1989:367). The United States began building a modern navy; by 1893 it was the seventh-largest in the world, and by 1921 it was the second-largest.

By the late 1800s, the United States began acting like other imperial powers, seeking colonies or areas that could be dominated indirectly. A number of Pacific territories, including Hawaii (1898) and Samoa (1899), were acquired. Victory over Spain brought other territories, including the Philippines. There, it took 70,000 U.S. troops to "restore order" once the Filipinos realized the United States was unwilling to grant them immediate independence. American interests and diplomacy even extended to China. The McKinley administration announced the **Open Door policy** (1899), which demanded that the other imperial powers already in China share that country's resources and markets with the United States. As is frequently the case with American policy, the U.S. move was presented as an effort to save China, while, in reality, it was an effort to save a share of the Chinese market for U.S. exploitation. The Chinese were not fooled by this latest barbarian maneuver; they tried to drive all the foreign devils out in the Boxer Rebellion (1899–1900). The United States responded by sending 5,000 troops to China to protect U.S. interests and to join with European and Japanese troops to keep China safe for foreign domination.

The rise of Japan in the Pacific created new economic and national security worries. During the 1920s, the United States redeployed the main part of its naval fleet to the Pacific in response to Japanese activities in the region. This action provided impetus for the Washington (1922) and London (1930) naval treaties. These pacts sought unsuccessfully to control the naval arms race among France, Great Britain, Italy, Japan, and the United States. Japan's invasion of northern China sparked the 1931–1932 Manchurian Crisis and reinforced American concerns over Japanese intentions. Secretary of State Henry Stimson reiterated the Open Door policy and issued a veiled warning about Japanese expansionism. The coming of World War II in the Pacific is too lengthy a topic to detail here, but suffice it to say that Japanese economic and military expansion, especially its brutal war against China, clashed with both U.S. interests and its sense of morality. This led to economic sanctions against Japan, to increased Japanese efforts to offset the loss of U.S. supplies, and to an increasing sense in both Tokyo and Washington that war was inevitable.

American economic interests also contributed to U.S. political or military intervention in the affairs of other countries. Involvement in Cuba in the 1920s and 1930s, for example, aimed to protect American investment in sugar production. In the 1950s, commercial interests played a large role in the CIA's intervention in Iran (oil) and in Guatemala (United Fruit Company). The International Telephone and Telegraph Company and the CIA promoted the overthrow of President Allende in Chile in 1973. In general, the activities of American multinational corporations produced a tendency for the American government to intervene to serve the economic interests of its citizens.

The United States as International Economic Leader

As the twentieth century progressed, the United States moved to a position of international economic prominence, then dominance. Americans used their leadership position to promote, with a great degree of success, a system-level regime of liberalized trade, investment, and monetary relations.

After World War I, Great Britain declined as the guarantor of low tariffs and other liberal trading practices. Without the once-economically powerful British to set the example for other economies by keeping its markets open to others' goods, there was little incentive for the other powers to practice free trade. The world economy quickly slipped into a mercantilist pattern of trade protectionism, limited currency convertibility, and other such beggar-thy-neighbor policies in the late 1920s and 1930s. In the United States protectionism coupled with isolationism also won out over free trade policies and internationalism. This trend culminated in 1931 when Congress enacted the **Smoot-Hawley Tariff** in an effort to protect American industry in the developing recession and to restrain increasing U.S. involvement in the world economy. Imposing a duty of over 50 percent on imported goods, Smoot-Hawley was the highest tariff on record and a major barrier to foreign access to American markets. Other countries passed similar barriers, and the world economy deteriorated into increased competition for market access and eventually into open conflict.

Liberal economic policy after World War II was designed to prevent a recurrence of the global economic collapse of the 1930s and the war of the 1940s. Policy makers believed that the commercial interests of the United States and the other great powers had caused both the Great Depression and the global conflict. Their logic was simple. "If our businesses are losing markets because of foreign competition," they thought, "we will decide to impose tariffs on imported goods so that our businesses keep their domestic markets. By erecting barriers to the free flow of goods into our economy, we then prompt others to erect barriers to our goods." One result was suffocated business, leading to do-

This haunting photo of a woman in economic desperation during the Great Depression symbolizes one reason why U.S. policy makers took an internationalist economic path beginning in the 1940s. At that time the United States became a principal advocate of liberal international economic policy, including free trade, and other economic interchanges. The General Agreement on Tariffs and Trade and the International Monetary Fund were established to promote these goals. Policy makers believed that high tariffs and other restrictions on international economic interchange had caused the Great Depression. The ensuing worldwide economic hardship created desperation among people that became fertile ground for the rise of fascism and the onset of World War II.

mestic poverty, leading to the rise of demagogic dictators. It is also possible to argue that the retaliatory tariffs pressured the Axis powers (Germany, Japan, and Italy) to expand through conquest in order to thrive economically. Thus, the competition and conflict that ensued in World War II were partly the result of earlier, short-sighted economic policies.

The United States began retreating from protectionism by 1934 with the passage of the Reciprocal Trade Agreements Act, although narrow nationalistic policies remained the dominant feature of international economics until after World War II. But pressure for change was mounting. The deterioration of the international trading system and World War II had the effect of galvanizing international support for the creation of an international economic system centered on free trade. Later, after the allied relationship between the United States and the Soviet Union soured, U.S. policy makers were convinced that reestablishing strong and prosperous Western economies was vital to the containment of Soviet influence.

American policy makers were at the center of this free trade thinking, and they were the leaders in establishing a new international economic system beginning with the 1944 Bretton Woods (New Hampshire) Conference, attended by 44 countries. The ensuing **Bretton Woods international economic system** was designed to remedy the sources of the Great Depression and to provide greater opportunities for the capitalist nations to prosper in the postwar world. Under Bretton Woods, the International Monetary Fund (IMF) and the World Bank were created to provide financial support for postwar recovery and economic development. In 1947 the United States and the other industrialized countries signed the **General Agreement on Tariffs and Trade (GATT)**, creating an organization of the same name as the principal institution working to ensure market access and to liberalize trade policies throughout the world. The rationale for this major change in the international economic system, as Roosevelt's secretary of state Cordell Hull wrote in his memoirs, was that "unhampered trade dovetail[s] with peace; high tariffs, trade barriers, and unfair economic competition, with war" (Cooper, 1987:299). This sentiment toward free trade carried over into the Truman administration and manifested itself in the American postwar trade policy.

All three of these institutions (IMF, World Bank, and GATT) depended for their success on the economic and political strength of the United States. Creating a financial system based on the dollar, as the IMF did, meant that the United States filled the void created earlier in the century by Great Britain's economic decline. Fortunately for the stability of the postwar international system, most American policy makers were willing, and the American economy was able, to assume world economic leadership.

Also, regarding the U.S. role in the international economic system, several subsidiary points are important. One is that the U.S.–led global economic recovery extended little, sometimes hardly at all, to the less developed countries (LDCs) of the world. Instead, the United States and other industrial countries have been accused of using **neoimperialist** policies to create a continuing economic and political **dependencia** system. Under this system, critics allege, the rich got richer and the poor stayed poor and remained dependent on the wealthier countries. Second, free trade did not extend to the industrialized communist countries. To the contrary, containment spurred coordination of export control policies among the Western nations after the war under the auspices of the Coordinating Committee (CoCom), particularly as such policies related to exports of high technology with military applications. This action, in combination with the reluctance of the Eastern Bloc to participate in the capitalist world economy, kept the communist countries relatively isolated economically. Third, the system became much freer, especially in terms of lower tariffs, but totally free trade was never even a near reality. Quotas and other forms of nontariff barriers to trade have continued as more subtle forms of protectionism. Fourth, the United States soon both lost its undisputed economic leadership position and began to waiver in its support of liberal international economic policies. Rising international competition, increased dependence on oil and other imports, domestic budget deficits, and a variety of other factors were seriously beginning to undermine the U.S. economy by the late 1960s. The international worth of U.S. currency became suspect, forcing the United States in 1971 to take the dollar off the fixed gold standard, by which the dollar's value was set at (and redeemable for) 1 ounce of gold = $35. The dollar was no longer a symbol of economic stability. Neither was the U.S. economy. Its continuing travails have caused new, much stronger protectionist pressures in the 1990s.

The United States: A Most Unrevolutionary Country

Americans like to remember that the country was born in revolution and to see themselves as a progressive people open to change. Internationally, at least, this self-image does not fit reality. The United States has a history of *defending the status quo*. Especially since World War II, Americans have felt threatened by changes in the international system for two reasons. One is that the rise of communism and the independence of many new LDCs produced and strengthened ideologies and points of view that were very different from the Euro-American sense of justice and proper conduct. Second, with the United States being by far the most powerful country just after World War II, change necessarily meant an ebbing of relative U.S. power. As the world recovered from war, the American grip on hegemony slipped.

Containing Communism

As discussed, World War II marked the beginning of enduring internationalism in American foreign policy. Prior to the conflict, U.S. international activity had been limited, short-term, and episodic. But a number of factors changed all that after 1945. We have already seen that the United States was the only free-world nation after the war able to institute a stable international political and economic order, and that this accelerated interdependence expanded American interests globally. The nature of the bipolar world also played a role, for it seemed to American and other Western policy makers that the Soviet Union and Soviet-inspired aggression and social turmoil constituted the principal threats to world peace. This perception urged Americans to seek to contain Soviet and communist aggression throughout the world. Containment, in turn, inspired the United States to establish a global military presence and a series of alliances, to intervene militarily on several occasions to counter the communist threat, and to build a massive and expensive arsenal of nuclear and conventional weapons to balance Soviet military might (Melanson, 1991).

As all this suggests, the American role in the world quickly changed from being one of a number of great powers in a multipolar world to being the chief defender of democracy and capitalism in a bipolar world. The Soviet Union, arguably, had much to gain by challenging Western, particularly American, policies and ideas. Also, the communist ideology of the USSR made it seem to be more than a country that was merely seeking to assert itself as a great power. The Soviet Union's communism and the U.S. reaction, based on American political culture, are crucial to under-standing the cold war. Simply put, communism offended many of the American values that will be discussed in chapter 4. Moscow and the then-expanding number of communist countries seemed bent on a radical transformation of the international system in a way designed to destroy U.S. strength and the American way of life. One indication of this ideological hostility is that it dated to the early days of the Bolshevik

The domino theory was a by-product of the containment doctrine. Americans believed that any gain by the communists might set off a global chain reaction, with countries succumbing sequentially until the United States, the last domino, would fall.

revolution in Russia. President Wilson refused to recognize Lenin's government in 1917, and he also sent 15,000 troops to northern Russia and to Siberia to aid French and British efforts in unseating the Bolsheviks (Leffler, 1994).

The effort to defeat communism if possible and contain it when necessary was renewed with vigor after 1945. The image of the Soviet threat was best captured in an article written by State Department official George Kennan (1947) under the pseudonym "X." Entitled "The Sources of Soviet Conduct," it characterized Soviet power as "inexorably" expansionist and warned that it would stop only "when it meets some unanswerable force." Therefore, Kennan urged the West to confront the Soviets "at every point where they show signs of encroaching upon the interests of a peaceful and stable world." Kennan was more concerned with Soviet power than with communist ideology, however, and he later claimed he meant political and economic, not military, confrontation. Nevertheless, his article articulated a growing mood in the United States and helped spawn the **containment doctrine**. This political dogma held that communism, especially backed by Soviet power, presented a deadly threat to the United States and the rest of the free world; that any communist advance was unacceptable; and, therefore, that the West, led by the United States, had to counter every communist thrust no matter where it occurred in the world.

A soon-propounded corollary, dubbed the **domino theory**, helped further explain why even communist advances in remote, small, poor countries were dangerous. The domino theory suggested that, like a row of on-end dominoes successively toppling by striking one another, one communist takeover would lead to another, then another, until the last free world domino, the United States, was imperiled. This imagery explains how years later President Lyndon B. Johnson could, on the one hand, characterize South Vietnam as a "raggedy-ass fourth-rate country," yet, on the other hand, send a half-million Americans to fight there because he believed that if "we don't stop the Reds in South Vietnam, tomorrow they will be in Hawaii, and next they will be in San Francisco" (Paterson, Clifford, & Hagan, 1991b:554).

Containment was the key to U.S. policy for the next several decades. The 1947 Truman Doctrine justified containment around the globe in stark ideological terms; those who believed in freedom, liberty, and democracy had the obligation to defend those threatened with their loss. Congress appropriated money for the Marshall Plan because a weak Western Europe might become a communist Western Europe. In 1950 Washington drafted and adopted the most official containment document: National Security Council Paper Number 68 (NSC-68). This paper concluded that the USSR "seeks to impose its absolute authority over the rest of the world" and urged both a massive U.S. military buildup and the extension of U.S. military protection to the free world in order "to deter, if possible, Soviet expansion, and to defeat, if necessary, aggressive Soviet or Soviet-directed actions of a limited or total character" (Smoke,

1987:60). It went so far as to suggest that during an emergency the United States might need to devote as much as 50 percent of its GNP to national security. The extent of alarm is evident by comparing this figure to the 39 percent of GNP that went to defense spending at the height of World War II (1944). Such an astronomical percentage was never approached: the highest postwar figure (14 percent) came in 1953 near the end of the Korean war. After 1959 defense spending never again reached 10 percent of GNP, even though American forces were larger than they had ever been in peacetime. Still, the trillions of dollars spent by the United States and the Soviet Union are a dubious monument to the hostility that gripped the two superpowers.

Thus, regardless of what Kennan may or may not have meant, the cold war was fully and officially joined and militarized by the late 1940s. Much has been written about the alliances that the United States encouraged and often joined and about the myriad confrontations and clashes with Soviet and other communist countries and movements in the decades that followed. Reflecting on these studies, we can make a few brief points here. One is that the United States did undertake a massive military buildup. Existing biases in the American political culture against defense expenditures and a large standing military faded. Within five years the defense budget tripled and U.S. troop strength increased over 50 percent.

Second, the United States established a series of bilateral and multilateral alliances that committed the country to possible military action around the globe. The North Atlantic Treaty Organization (NATO, 1949) was the most important. Other alliances included the Organization of American States (OAS, 1948), the Australia-New Zealand-United States Tripartite Treaty (ANZUS, 1951), the Southeast Asian Treaty Organization (SEATO, 1954), the Middle East Defense Organization (1955), as well as bilateral treaties with Japan, Formosa, Pakistan, and others.

Third, the United States used its military strength regularly to contain communism and to promote or preserve U.S. interests. There were major wars and high casualties in Korea (1950–1953: 34,000 U.S. battle deaths) and in South Vietnam and bordering areas (1964–1973: 47,000 U.S. battle deaths). In the three decades after World War II, there were also numerous other sizable interventions, including those in Lebanon (1958) and the Dominican Republic (1965); a truly nerve-jarring confrontation with the Soviets (Cuban missile crisis, 1962); and, in total, some 226 threatened or active uses of U.S. military force (Blechman & Kaplan, 1979).

The LDCs as a Cold War Battlefield

One of the most remarkable changes that occurred in the international system after World War II was the end of colonialism and the resulting independence of dozens of new countries. Most of these were in Africa and Asia. Despite the U.S. history as a colony freed by revolution, the American government reacted cautiously to the independence movements and to many of the new countries. This hesitancy had several causes. One is that the anticolonial movements attacked the European colonial powers such as Great Britain and France that were also U.S. NATO allies. Second, many of the new countries did not share Western values, and some leaders were even willing to try socialism and to take aid from the Soviet Union to build up their countries. Many new countries also did not want to be involved in the cold war and declared themselves part of the Nonaligned Movement (NAM). The NAM was formalized in 1961, when the leaders of 25 countries met in Belgrade, Yugoslavia, to discuss mutual economic concerns and to seek ways to end the cold war or at least to stay out of the middle of East-West tensions. Eventually, the NAM grew to 102 members. Whatever the leaders and people of these countries wanted, however, Americans were apt to believe that there could be no neutral position between American good and Soviet evil. This attitude was especially intense amid the virulent bipolar competition that dominated the 1950s and 1960s. Therefore, new countries that did not align themselves with the West were suspected of having pro-Soviet sympathies. Neutralism, nationalism, and socioeconomic experimentation in Africa, Asia, and elsewhere were too often confused with anti-Americanism. Policy makers in Washington either ignored or were suspicious of most new countries or worked to bring down governments that were viewed as too leftist.

One striking example of all this occurred in Vietnam. There, Ho Chi Minh, who was a nationalist long before he was a communist, struggled to free his country from French colonial domination. Ho defeated the French in 1954, and the resulting peace accord created Ho's communist North Vietnam and the U.S.–supported, rightist South Vietnam. After a respite, the movement to unite Vietnam resumed. This time, because of U.S. aid to the South's government and because the rebels were communists, John Kennedy and Lyndon Johnson increasingly committed U.S. forces to the fight in the early 1960s. The effort reaped only death, domestic discord, and eventual defeat. In the end, America retreated.

The End of Consensus

Vietnam marked the outer limit of the expansion of U.S. international influence. The agony of the war also prompted a national questioning of American commitments around the world. The decision in 1969 to withdraw from Vietnam and the gradual U.S. retreat (1969–1975) marked more than just another veering toward isolationism in U.S. history. President Nixon attempted to keep the United States engaged in the world through the enunciation of the **Nixon Doctrine** in July 1969. Stating that American policy in the world would increasingly rely on the support of regional allies as surrogate powers for direct American involvement, the Nixon Doctrine was perceived as a way to retrench explicit and tangible American commitments while still preserving American influence in critical regions of the world.

Even so, American policy makers soon realized that the cold war consensus that had guided U.S. policy since the end of World War II had been shattered. This consensus, which will be discussed extensively in chapter 4, was based on a commitment to contain communism and on an associated determination that the United States should play an active, global role in the international system. Defeat in Vietnam brought the containment doctrine and U.S. internationalism into question. More important, there was no new consensus on the direction of future U.S. foreign policy. The lack of public agreement on what U.S. foreign policy should emphasize left elected policy makers without clear public guidance. Thus the ship of state sailed without clear direction into the uncharted waters of the future.

As you will see in the next chapter, the most recent captain of the ship, President Bill Clinton, wanted primarily to keep the ship of state anchored in home waters so that he could attend to domestic needs. Such was not the fate of this modern mariner, however, and he soon found his captaincy awash in storms that swirled up from the

Balkans on the Adriatic Sea, Somalia on the Gulf of Aden and the Indian Ocean, and Haiti in the Caribbean Sea. The truth is, "we're living in a new and different world and we've got to try to chart a course that is the right course for the United States," Captain Clinton told his passengers, many of whom were not pleased with the course he had set.[2] Indeed Clinton and other top American policy makers might well have been thinking of the poem "Long Trip" by Langston Hughes, which uses the metaphor of land and sea. Mr. Clinton's advisers have depicted themselves as "pioneers, groping their way toward new principles in a post–Cold War world," a report entitled "Unruly Global Village" in the *New York Times* commented.[3] "It is uncharted ground, and they admit[ted] they are having trouble." As the poet Hughes tells us,

> The sea is a wilderness of waves,
> A desert of water.
> We dip and dive,
> Rise and roll, Hide and are hidden
> On the Sea.
>   Day, night,
>   Night, day,
> The sea is a desert of waves,
> A wilderness of water.

SUMMARY

1. American foreign policy makers are not free to make any and every decision that they so desire. The international system—in conjunction with the domestic political culture discussed in chapter 4—limits the maneuverability of policy makers and constrains the numbers and types of choices available in response to foreign policy problems.

2. Additionally, American foreign policy operates in an environment where it has direct effects on other actors and the policies of those other actors have effects on the United States.

3. Historically, the United States has demonstrated an ambivalence toward international involvement that has forced policy to swing back and forth between isolationism and internationalism.

4. Early isolationism, however, did not preclude international involvement. Eventually, international interaction resulted in the development of an American sphere of influence in the Western Hemisphere that was broadened to a global scale after World War II.

5. American economic and commercial interests have also driven the United States to become involved in the outside world. Not only has this meant selling American goods in foreign markets, but it has also meant direct military intervention at times to support American economic concerns.

6. The development of the Soviet Union as the primary adversary and the growth of American power and influence in the world caused the United States to become the defender of the status quo in the post–World War II period. The period was also marked by the most fervent American commitment to internationalism of any time since the birth of the republic.

Chapter Three

THE CURRENT INTERNATIONAL SETTING

Even amid the expected political disputes during the 1992 presidential primary campaign, there was one point of consensus: All the contestants agreed that the cold war was history. They could not, however, come together on the question: Who won? The United States did, asserted President George Bush. "The biggest thing that has happened in the world in my life, in our lives, is this: By the grace of God, America won the cold war," Bush proclaimed to Americans during his 1992 State of the Union address.[1] That is only half right, retorted Democrat Paul Tsongas, "The cold war is over, and Japan won."[2]

The correct answer, of course, is that the world won. Yet despite the fact that neither Bush nor Tsongas had it right, their differing estimates about who won do provide insight into the contemporary status and role of the United States in the international system and American political culture attitudes about the U.S. position and actions in the world.

To review quickly, chapter 2 illustrated how the historic international system setting influenced U.S. foreign policy through the end of the Vietnam War. System-level analysis, as detailed in that chapter, discussed system characteristics and examined how these complex socio-political-economic realities constrain U.S. foreign policy. It is important to have these system characteristics clearly in mind because we will continue our study of them in this chapter and demonstrate how the international system has affected U.S. foreign policy in the contemporary, post-Vietnam period.

THE U.S. GLOBAL ROLE: HEGEMON OR HAS-BEEN?

The international system is in the midst of a rapid and portentous transformation. Much of this has occurred since the Vietnam War era, and it has affected the status and activity of the United States in the international system. As in chapter 2, we will examine the U.S. status and role by considering the following characteristics: power and international activity, definition and domination of a sphere of influence, involvement in the world economy, and attitude toward the status quo and world change.

U.S. Power and International Activity

The transformation of the international system from a bipolar to a multipolar configuration has altered the U.S. world role from the superpower leader of one of two hostile alliances to a key player in a more complex and shifting balance-of-power scenario. The Soviet Union's collapse, on the one hand, left the United States as the world's unquestioned military superpower. On the other hand, the increased economic strength and diplomatic independence of other countries, many of which were U.S. cold war allies, created a multipolar system at least in the economic arena. The U.S. status in the international economic system is relatively less powerful than in international political-military affairs, where it still dominates. In short, the United States is no longer the undisputed world economic leader, and some analysts even claim that the country is in general decline.

Warming Relations with Adversaries

One change in the U.S. global role resulted from an American reevaluation of U.S. commitments in the wake of the loss in Vietnam. Trying to contain communism everywhere was no longer an acceptable option for most Americans. This reevaluation was then accelerated by the decline, then the end, of bipolar conflict. This change pressed American decision makers to reformulate the U.S. role in a world without a primary adversary. Indeed, the fact that the bipolar world had begun to fragment by the early 1970s was one reason that the long Vietnam War was finally settled. The disputes between China and the Soviet Union were so serious that they had nearly gone to war in 1969. The United States still dominated the Western alliance, but its allies in Western Europe and Japan had grown stronger economically and had become more independent politically. One sign of ebbing Western cohesion was the strong criticism by some allies of the U.S. war in Vietnam. As a result of the erosion of the bipolar system, the leaders of the United States, the Soviet Union, and China sought new, more pragmatic relationships with one another. On the U.S. side, President Richard M. Nixon's geostrategic view anticipated that a tripolar (United States–Soviet Union–China) system might be forming. A cardinal rule in a tripolar world is to avoid being on the short side of a two-against-one confrontation, and so Nixon moved to improve relations with both Beijing and Moscow.

Relations with China   One reason that Nixon (1980:126) sought better relations with China was his estimate that it "could become the most powerful nation on earth during the twenty-first century." Second, while he moved to establish détente, or warmer relations, with the Soviet Union, Nixon simultaneously sought to constrain the USSR from imprudent action by creating the possibility of a *de facto* U.S. alliance with China. Threatening the Soviets with a Sino-American combination was later labeled "playing the China card."

As a first step, Nixon ignored his own history as an anticommunist ideologue and traveled to China in 1972 to meet Chairman Mao Zedong. Informal diplomatic relations were established and their importance accentuated by the dispatch of rising Republican star George Bush to head (1974–1975) the U.S. liaison office in Beijing. The trend toward normalizing relations with China was finalized when President Jimmy Carter extended formal diplomatic recognition to China in 1979. His successor, Ronald Reagan, also sublimated ideology to the realities of power politics and treated China cordially. In 1984 he followed Nixon's footsteps to Beijing and told China's communist leaders, "America's door is open to you; and when you walk through, we'll welcome you as our neighbors and our friends."[3]

Still, current relations with China are not trouble free. One sore point is the reaction of many Americans to the massacre of students and other activists in Beijing's Tiananmen Square during the May and June 1989 protest demonstrations and to continued domestic oppression by China's communist government. In the aftermath of the 1989 events, Congress required the president annually to link China's improvement in Beijing's human rights record to China's continued enjoyment of **most-favored-nation (MFN)** trade status, which allows its imports into the United States at the lowest existing U.S. tariff rate. Whatever China's record, the Bush administration continued China's MFN status because it viewed relations with China from a *system-level* perspective. President Bush's secretary of state, James A. Baker III, pointed this out, noting that China has "almost one-fourth of all the people in the world . . . nuclear weapons . . . great influence in the region [and] . . . immense economic potential."[4]

While campaigning for the presidency, Bill Clinton argued emphatically that China's human rights abuses should not be tolerated. He called President Bush's policy toward China "unconscionable" and declared that, as president, "I would deny most-favored-nation status to China, impose trade sanctions and encourage the younger generation's democratic aspirations."[5] Once he became president, Clinton soon learned to appreciate the view of Bush and others that China is a major power that has to be dealt with carefully.[6] Even though the perception of China as a counterweight to the USSR in the international system has been obviated by the latter's demise, the prevailing realpolitik view is that in the new, multipolar system, China may play an important role in providing a balance-of-power hedge again the rise of Japan as a regional political power and as a world economic power. As a result, the Clinton administration has focused much of its China policy on bringing the giant Asian nation into the mainstream of world affairs.

Clinton's most important move was his decision to continue to renew China's MFN status and, in 1994, to "delink" the MFN issue from China's human rights policy. In terms that echoed the arguments of the Bush administration, Clinton justified his change of policy on the grounds that "China has an atomic arsenal and a vote and a veto in the UN Security Council. It is a major factor in Asian and global security."[7] In addition to China's strategic position, another system-level reality that pressed the Clinton White House to downplay China's internal policies was the growing economic interdependence of countries and the importance of China as an export market for U.S. products and investment capital. The risk of economic retaliation if Washington revoked China's MFN status created strong pressures on Clinton from within the United States. Secretary of Agriculture Mike Espy depicted China as "one of our most important agriculture markets," and American businesses also lined up strongly against sanctions on China.[8] Some 300 companies and business groups wrote Clinton a joint letter warning that sanctions against China would damage the U.S. economy. Thus, Clinton's decision was in part, as the *New York Times* wrote cogently, evidence of "the underlying shift evident in all the industrial democracies today: economic con-

Relations between China and the United States have improved greatly since the depths of the cold war, but sharp differences over trade, human rights, and other issues remain. Hillary Rodham Clinton traveled to China in 1995 to speak at the UN's conference on women in Beijing. She did so, however, only after China agreed to release Harry Wu, a Chinese American and a civil rights activist, who had been jailed by Chinese authorities. Then, while speaking to a parallel conference of nongovernmental organizations (NGOs) concerned with women's issues, in Huairou, Clinton launched a veiled attack on the Chinese government for its indefensible effort to block many women from getting to the conference. Beijing was not pleased, and the official newspaper, the *People's Daily*, covered her visit in just one sentence.

cerns have taken center stage in foreign affairs decision-making. This is the age of the Finance Minister. . . .The game of nations is now geo-Monopoly, and it is first and foremost about profits, not principles."[9]

The delinking of trade and human rights did not, however, wipe away sore spots in Sino-American relations. In fact, other aspects of trade continue to rankle. Beijing's lax record of closing down Chinese companies that were producing pirated versions of American music compact discs, software, videocassettes, and other copyrighted properties led Washington in 1995 to threaten sanctions. China backed down, but it remains to be seen how effective Beijing's policing of its domestic manufacturers will be. The large and growing U.S. trade deficit with China looms as an even more troublesome issue. The 1995 deficit of $33.9 billion is second only to the U.S. deficit with Japan ($62.4 billion) and is causing increased pressure by Washington on Beijing to open its markets. China is resisting, claiming, as Foreign Ministry spokesman Chen Jian put it, that "China has made the maximum concessions that a developing country can bear at its current state of development" without risking having its industries overwhelmed by competition from developed countries like the United States.[10] Washington rejects that argument and has been blocking China's desire to sign the General Agreement on Tariffs and Trade (GATT) and join the World Trade Organization (WTO).

Despite these issues, the Clinton administration's effort to maintain reasonable relations with China and to bring it into the mainstream of global affairs has paid some dividends. China's sale of missile and nuclear technology to Iran and some other countries remains an issue. China did agree formally in late 1994 not to sell missiles with ranges of over 185 miles or with payloads in excess of 1,000 pounds. China also apparently played a constructive role in helping defuse the crisis that threatened to explode in 1994 over the demands by the United States and others that North Korea dismantle its nuclear weapons program. And China contributed to the extension in 1995 of the Nuclear Nonproliferation Treaty (NPT) by agreeing to an unlimited extension of the NPT; by not siding with the demand of some important less developed countries that the NPT be renewed only for a short time unless the nuclear powers agreed to dismantle all their nuclear weapons, it again contributed to the extension of the NPT. Also during 1995, other potential discord was smoothed over. China released naturalized American dissident Harry Wu and Hillary Rodham Clinton traveled to China in September to address the UN forum on women's rights. In October, the improved, but not warm, relations between Beijing and Washington were illustrated with protocol symbolism when President Clinton agreed to meet with President Jiang Zemin during his trip to the United States. Clinton would meet with Jiang only in New York at the United Nations, however, and denied to China the mark of warm relations that a meeting at the White House and a state dinner would have signaled.

Relations with the Soviet Union   As the Vietnam War concluded, President Nixon maneuvered in the fragmenting bipolar system to establish improved relations, called **détente**, with the Soviet Union. One Nixon tactic was to assure the Soviets that the United States presented no immediate political or military threat. Among other things, National Security Adviser Henry A. Kissinger told Soviet ambassador Anatoly F. Dobrynin in 1969 that "President Nixon takes into account the Soviet Union's special interests in East Europe and does not intend to do anything that would be assessed in Moscow as a 'challenge' to its position in the region." As for any rhetoric that might emanate from Washington about freeing Eastern Europe from Soviet communism's grip, Dobrynin was told "this is only tribute to some layers of the U.S. population which play a role in American elections."[11]

Nixon and his two successors also sought to better relations through arms control. Nixon and Soviet leader Leonid Brezhnev signed the SALT I (Strategic Arms Limitation Talks) Treaty in 1972, which put numerical ceilings on their respective strategic nuclear weapons systems. Presidents Ford and Brezhnev signed the Vladivostok Accord in 1974, refining that upper ceiling; and Presidents Carter and Brezhnev signed the SALT II Treaty in 1979 to further limit nuclear weapons system expansion.

Then relations with the Soviet Union once again turned sour when in late December 1979 Soviet military forces intervened in Afghanistan to protect the communist regime there from anticommunist guerrillas. The SALT II Treaty was one casualty. Carter recognized that the Senate would not ratify SALT II after the Soviet invasion, and he withdrew the treaty from consideration (Caldwell, 1990). Carter even became something of a born-again anticommunist, telling listeners that the invasion of Afghanistan had "made a more dramatic change in my opinion of what the Soviets' ultimate goals are than anything they've done . . . [since] I've been in office" (Jones, 1988:681). Carter reacted further by imposing economic sanctions on the USSR and by dramatically increasing defense spending. He also enunciated the **Carter Doctrine**, explicitly putting the Soviets on notice that the Persian Gulf was a strategic American interest that the United States would protect militarily if required. The president's new outlook mirrored American public opinion. Growing public worry over Soviet defense spending and adventurism in less developed countries, anger over the seizure of U.S. hostages by Iran, and concern over a U.S. economy plagued by both high unemployment and soaring inflation added to the nagging American sense of post-Vietnam impotence. President Carter told Americans in 1979 that there was an "erosion of our confidence in the future [that] is threatening to destroy the social and the political fabric of America" (Paterson & Merrill, 1995:710). Many citizens agreed and decided that Carter was part of the problem. Ronald Reagan seemed to offer a solution.

Presidential candidate Reagan promised to rectify what he claimed was a Soviet military advantage. The new president's resolve was strengthened by his ideologically based worldview that, one aide commented, was reminiscent of "a kind of 1952 world" demarcated in "black and white terms."[12] Reagan spoke loudly, condemning the USSR as "the focus of evil in the modern world," which would stoop "to commit any crime, to lie, to cheat" to accomplish its goals (Paterson, Clifford, & Hagan, 1995:508). Reagan also called on Congress to fund many new swords to brandish at the Soviets and other antagonists. Reagan accelerated defense spending rapidly, he revived some of the weapons systems shelved by Carter, and he added many new weapons programs, such as the Strategic Defense Initiative (SDI), more commonly known as Star Wars (Carter, 1991). Many critics derided SDI and Reagan's other initiatives. Retired, longtime (1962–1986) Soviet ambassador to Washington Anatoly Dobrynin argues in his 1995 memoirs, however, that Reagan's military policies forced the Kremlin's leaders "to reconsider their positions" and seek greater accommodation with the United States.[13]

The president also pledged the United States to supply anticommunist forces in less developed countries, a stance dubbed the **Reagan Doctrine**. At its root, this interventionist doctrine held, as Reagan said in his 1985 State of the Union address, that the American "mission is to nourish and defend freedom and democracy [to] stand by our democratic allies [and to] not break faith with those who are risking their lives—on every continent, from Afghanistan to Nicaragua—to defy Soviet-supported aggression and secure rights which have been ours from birth." The bottom line, Reagan told Americans, is that "support for freedom fighters is self-defense."

In practice, Reagan was careful not to risk military confrontation with the Soviets (or the Chinese) by firing more than rhetorical salvos. He was much more willing to bring pressure to bear on weaker leftist regimes (Hantz, 1995). Most notably, Reagan tried to topple the Sandinista regime in Nicaragua in a variety of covert and overt ways. He also supplied billions of dollars and American military advisers to support the government of El Salvador in its efforts to fend off a leftist insurgency. Moreover, the president sometimes wielded sticks as well as supplying them. Reagan ordered naval confrontations with and air strikes against Libya (1981, 1986), U.S. forces into Lebanon (1982), and the military invasion of Grenada (1983). Although the Libyan and the Lebanon cases were not related directly to Soviet-inspired encroachments, these instances bore witness to the willingness of the Reagan administration to use military force readily as an instrument of U.S. foreign policy.

The realities of the international system, however, inexorably cooled President Reagan's ideological fervor and even his rhetoric. The bipolar world was crumbling, and even Reagan had to respond realistically. Domestic pressure and the willingness of other countries to sell grain to the USSR persuaded him to end the economic sanctions that President Carter had imposed on the Soviets. Despite the facts that he had opposed the SALT II Treaty and that it did not exist legally, domestic and international pressures persuaded Reagan to comply with SALT II's limits until 1986. By then new, and eventually successful, arms reduction talks with the Soviets were under way.

President Reagan's moderation was further encouraged by the accession to power in March 1985 of a new Soviet leader. Whether motivated by a desire for peace and reform or by an effort to refurbish a crumbling Soviet infrastructure, Mikhail S. Gorbachev shifted Soviet policy and sought accommodation with Soviet opponents. The story of Gorbachev's efforts, the collapse of the Soviet sphere of influence in Eastern Europe, and the fragmentation and final fall of the USSR itself are epic. Suffice it to say that all these changes accelerated international system change to warp speed.

Reagan held his first summit meetings with a Soviet leader when he met Gorbachev in Geneva, Switzerland, in late 1985. "I'll bet the hard-liners in both our countries are bleeding," Reagan whispered without a hint of irony to Gorbachev as they shook hands (Kaiser, 1991:119). During successive summit meetings, the two leaders pledged cooperation, agreed to eliminate medium-range missiles through the Intermediate-range Nuclear Forces (INF) Treaty of 1987, and began the Strategic Arms Reduction Talks (START) negotiations. Much of the world was surprised, and so was Reagan. June 1988 found the old cold warrior and another veteran politician, Mikhail Gorbachev, jointly appearing in Moscow and kissing babies in Red Square. "I never expected to be here," Reagan gushed.[14] The president, along with the world, was being swept forward by the powerful current of international system change.

Just three and a half years later, the torrent of transformation swept away one of the two superpowers. At 7:32 P.M. one frigid Moscow night, the Soviet hammer-and-sickle flag was lowered for the last time from atop the Kremlin and was replaced by Russia's red, white, and blue flag. The death of the officially atheistic USSR came on Christmas night 1991.

Appearing that evening on national television with an erect, even soldierly air, his countenance occasionally showing a small smile of satisfaction, President Bush told Americans that they and their political culture stood triumphant. The cold war "is now over," he said." The Soviet Union . . . is no more." The president went on to characterize the USSR's demise as "a victory for democracy and freedom . . . a victory for the moral force of our values. Every American can take pride in this victory," Bush said. "And on this special day of peace on earth, good will toward men, may God continue to bless the United States of America."

Relations with the Soviet Union, just as those with China, improved slowly, if unsteadily, beginning in the 1970s with President Nixon's policy of détente. In the aftermath of the collapse of the Soviet Union, U.S. relations with the USSR's main successor state, Russia, have further evolved to the point where Moscow and Washington have become mutually supportive on many issues. As a symbol of the change in relations, you can see in this photograph a scene that would have been unimaginable just a few years earlier. The ship is a former Soviet, now Russian, guided missile destroyer, the *Bezudershyn,* passing the Statue of Liberty as it enters New York harbor for a visit in May 1993. The visit of the *Bezudershyn* was the first visit of a Soviet/Russian ship to New York since the Russian Revolution in 1917.

Americans, it seemed, were on top of the world. Within the previous year they had routed Iraq's military and had witnessed the Soviet Union strike its colors. Whether the USSR had been toppled by firm U.S. policy or had fallen victim to its own internal problems hardly mattered. American self-confidence soared. The Russian bear had seemingly been defanged and impoverished and transformed into a sometime supplicant for aid just like one of the real bears in a U.S. national park. Presidents Bush and Clinton both proffered substantial foreign aid to Russia and some of the other former Soviet republics on the grounds that, as Clinton put it, improved U.S. "security and prosperity . . . lie with Russian reform."[15] Congress, it may be noted, has been generally less sympathetic than are presidents to foreign aid to Russia or most other countries, and the Republican Congress elected in 1994 is even less supportive of foreign aid than its Democratic-dominated predecessors. The result is that the flow of aid has been restricted and, given legislative attitudes, the continuation of U.S. economic assistance remains in doubt.

On the military side of the relationship, the change in U.S. relations with Moscow is most starkly seen in the invitation in 1994 by the former adversarial alliance, NATO, to Russia and other one-time parts of the defunct Warsaw Pact to join with NATO in a Partnership for Peace. President Boris Yeltsin has agreed that Russia will join, but he continues to seek special status in this cooperative military venture. Russia has argued that it needs a "special relationship" with NATO that differs from that of its former allies because of its size and power in Europe and the world. One simply amazing symbol of this new cooperation has occurred in Bosnia, where Russian troops are associated with the NATO force there and are serving under an American commander.

While tentative cooperation was emerging in the military realm, President Clinton was nonetheless careful to avoid casting U.S.–Russian relations in overly optimistic terms. In particular, the Russian conflict with rebels in Chechnya and Russian plans to sell nuclear reactors to Iran were points of conflict at the May 1995 meeting to celebrate the fiftieth anniversary of the ending of World War II in Europe.

Cooling Relations with Allies

An irony associated with the end of the cold war is that while U.S. relations with former adversaries have improved gradually, U.S. relations with Japan and Western Europe have waned. To a degree, the bipolar confrontation held the allies together and made them willing to suppress economic and political disputes in the interest of national security and unity. Now, without a looming Soviet threat, the glue of fear that held the alliance system together has weakened. At the same time, Japan, the countries of Western Europe, and that region's collective economic organization, the 15-member European Union (EU) have prospered economically. This new economic strength, coupled with the end of the cold war, has enhanced demands by Japan and Western Europe for a greater say in world affairs. Added to all this is the worry in Europe and Asia that the United States is becoming more isolationist and cannot be counted on to lead and, in particular, to continue to provide the backbone of security relationships. This concern has strengthened the voices of those in Japan and Europe who argue that there is little reason to follow a United States that is unwilling to lead by actions instead of rhetoric. "That [security] linkage has become less convincing to Japanese politicians and the public, and that has a lot to do with the new assertiveness," commented Eisukke Sakakibara, of Japan's Finance Ministry.[16]

The strains between the United States and its erstwhile allies can be grouped into two broad and interrelated categories: The first is political leadership. The second is trade and other international economic relations.

Political Leadership   One source of tension among the industrialized powers is the U.S. desire to exercise continued dominant leadership in the international system. Germany, Japan, and other countries that have become powers in their own right are less inclined than they once were to follow the foreign policy lead of the Americans. This change of attitude by former cold war allies is heightened by the fact that Washington also wants them to share more of the burden of maintaining stability. When, for example, Iraq threatened the status quo in the Persian Gulf, the United States moved militarily with only cursory consultation with its allies during the early portions of the crisis. The allies were expected to line up dutifully and to send troops. Japan, for one, did not because, in part, its constitution (largely imposed by occupying U.S. forces after World War II) forbids the overseas deployment of military forces. That and other instances where Japan has not lived up to U.S. expectations of support sparked official criticism. "Your checkbook diplomacy . . . is clearly too narrow," Secretary of State Baker scolded his hosts during a visit to Japan.[17] Many Japanese responded to such exhortations with puzzled resentment about seeming U.S. hypocrisy. "First Americans taught us that pacifism was a good thing, and then they called us cowards when we did not send troops [to fight Iraq]," a Japanese official grumbled.[18]

The role of U.S. leadership in European affairs has also been unsettled during the transition from a bipolar to a multipolar world. "There is definitely a sense in Europe that a vacuum has developed between Europe and the United States," one ranking U.S. official conceded recently. With "no widespread security threat," he continued, "there is a fear that the essential glue that held the relationship together seems to be coming apart."[19] The course of events in Bosnia illustrates the degree to which most of the countries of Western Europe still desire, albeit reluctantly, the United States to exercise political leadership. Bosnia is, arguably, first and foremost a European concern. Yet the EU and NATO was unable to establish a firm and workable approach to securing peace in Bosnia without U.S. leadership. "Given the instability in Eastern Europe," Germany's defense minister Volker Ruehe commented at one point, "we need the strategic backing of America."[20]

The importance of U.S. leadership also became apparent once President Clinton decided to exercise it. After a series of distressing events during the summer of 1995, including Bosnian Serbs taking 377 UN peacekeepers hostage and shooting down a patrolling U.S. warplane, Clinton began to see that, as one foreign diplomat put it, "Nothing can happen without the Americans; everything can happen with them."[21] Assistant Secretary of State Richard Holbrooke led a high-pressure diplomatic effort that soon convinced the presidents of Bosnia, Croatia, and Serbia (representing the Bosnian Serbs) to agree to face-to-face peace talks. Another indication of the crucial nature of American leadership was the fact that the peace conference convened in Dayton, Ohio. There the U.S. pressure on the Balkan leaders to reach a settlement was intense. Holbrooke, who has a volcanic temper, "frequently used words that are not quotable," reported one diplomat. "I don't think there is anyone Holbrooke didn't yell at at least once."[22] The pressure worked. After 3 weeks the Broats, Muslims, and Serbs all begrudgingly accepted a peace plan. It kept the facade of a single government in place for Bosnia-Herzegovina but, in reality, divided the country's territory into two semiautonomous sections: one for Muslims and Croats, the other for Bosnian Serbs.

The need for American leadership was not over. The United States had to commit 20,000 troops as part of the NATO-led international force (IFOR) of 60,000 soldiers that was needed to patrol the 4 kilometer-wide demilitarized zone that divides the two sections of Bosnia. General John Shalikashvili, chairman of the Joint Chiefs of Staff, was almost certainly correct when he told a Senate committee that "we have seen that [without] America's leadership role, things still don't get put together right." Inasmuch as NATO "has been built around the core of American leadership," the general reasoned, "we, as leader . . . cannot step away" when needed without imperiling the alliance.[23]

Among the many things that remain unclear is how the events in Bosnia will affect U.S.–European political relations in the long run. On the one hand, the American willingness to lead has reinvigorated NATO. One indication of this came when France reversed a policy almost 30 years old and agreed in December 1995 to rejoin NATO military committees and councils. On the other hand, though, it remains true that the Europeans simultaneously resent being told what to do by Washington and, given the nearly 3 years it took Clinton to act, doubt the strength of the U.S. commitment in Europe. Europeans are well aware that Senator John Glenn (D-OH) was not far from wrong when he told Secretary of State Christopher, "With all due respect, I don't think the average American person really feels [an] affinity for NATO now that the cold war is over."[24]

Economic Rivalry   The end of the cold war has also created a climate in which the economic rivalries among Japan, Europe, and the United States have become sharper. The industrial powers no longer need to moderate their economic differences in order to maintain unity in the face of a political-military threat.

The result of these changes has been friction among all the major countries as they grope for a new set of relationship norms. Relations between the United States and Japan have been the focus of the most notable discord. Japan–U.S. economic and political relations will receive considerable attention later in this chapter, but it is important to note that they are the source of tension and uncertainty on both sides of the Pacific. The United States has a long-standing and huge trade deficit ($66 billion in 1994) with Japan. Whatever the rights and wrongs of the views of the two sides, Americans are prone to blame Japan, and President Clinton has increasingly mirrored that sentiment. "America's trade deficit with Japan is not very popular with the American people or the American government," he told Japan's prime minister in 1994 at a joint news conference in Washington, D.C. That is because, Clinton explained, Japan "remains less open to imports than any other country."[25] Clinton's disposition to toughen the U.S. stand against Japan was amplified by Mickey Kantor, the U.S. special trade representative (USTR). Kantor is blunt, some say aggressive. The chief Japanese trade negotiator, Ryutaro Hashimoto, has described Kantor as "scarier than my wife when I come home drunk."[26] Intimidating trade negotiators, it should be noted, is not confined to one side of the Pacific. Hashimoto, who is widely assumed to be maneuvering to become prime minister, is called "the prince" because, according to one Japanese official, "he tends to act like a big shot, that is his style." Nevertheless, the official added, "fundamentally everyone has to say that he is right on this [trade dispute], and the United States cannot take unilateral action when it doesn't like the results of our trade relations."[27]

As you will see in Box 3.1 on pages 68–69, trade friction with Japan has continued to be a central point of policy concern for the Clinton administration. With Washington increasing pressure on the Japanese to make concessions and with Tokyo increasingly resisting the pressure, trans-Pacific economic relations in 1995 were at a 50-year low point.

Moreover, it would be fatuous to imagine that the economic tensions between these two economic superpowers could be isolated and not affect political relations. "We have no intention of undermining the [U.S.] security relationship with Japan or using our military presence there as a tool of trade," commented Jeffrey E. Garten, undersecretary of commerce for international trade. "But," Garten asked rhetorically, "do economic tensions slowly undercut the trust that has to underlie security ties?"

The undersecretary answered his own question: "Yes. Over a long time, absent an identifiable enemy, there is no precedent in history for strong security ties in the face of a highly unbalanced economic and commercial relationship."[28]

While the bulk of U.S. media attention has been on U.S.–Japan discord, U.S. economic relations with Europe also have numerous sore spots. The EU is an economic Goliath with an economy approximately equal to that of the United States, and there have been serious U.S.–EU disputes over such issues as the level of aid to the former Soviet republics, economic sanctions against Iran and Japan, and the protection of agriculture from foreign competition. Recurrent trade friction was finally overcome enough to allow for the completion of the latest revision of the GATT. A multilateral agreement was signed in late 1994 that created the World Trade Organization (WTO) in 1995 and furthered free trade under the GATT. This progress did not dispel the economic maneuvering between the two transatlantic economic superpowers.

Europe, for example, refused to follow the U.S. lead in 1995 and also impose sanctions on Iranian oil imports in retaliation for Iran's alleged nuclear weapons program. "We do not believe in unilateral embargoes," declared France's foreign minister, Alain Juppé. "The right thing to do is to conduct a political dialogue with Iran," advised Günter Rexrodt, Germany's economic minister.[29] Iran's biggest single customer, Japan, also rejected the U.S. initiative. The EU also was highly critical of the U.S. treaty in May 1995 that would impose a 100 percent punitive tariff on Japanese luxury auto imports as part of the Washington-Tokyo trade dispute. Sir Leon Brittain, the EU's chief trade official, said that the U.S. efforts to get Japan to accept quotas of U.S. products "would violate international trade rules." Not only that, but Sir Leon threatened that if the United States did force Japan to comply, the EU "would give very serious consideration to taking action against such an agreement" by filing a complaint with the WTO.[30] At least part of the EU's concern was that if the United States were successful with Japan, sanction-wielding American negotiators might next turn their sights on Europe. In any case, the EU's position brought on a retort by Undersecretary Garten that "the Europeans are acting with great hypocrisy." Garten claimed that the Europeans were just as anxious as the Americans to pry open Japan's markets but that while the Europeans would "scream that we are acting unilaterally," they would also "rush in within minutes to get the benefits of the openings that we achieve."[31]

It is worth adding that many other U.S. trade partners and allies refused to support the U.S. move against Japan out of fear that they would be next on the U.S. sanction list while simultaneously agreeing with the United States that Japan's markets needed to be more accessible. "We are quite sympathetic with America's goals" conceded Sarasin Viraphol, director general for American affairs in the Foreign Ministry of Thailand. "But," he added, "if [the United States] is successful [in] using this weapon on Japan, soon it will use it on all of us." The Thais and others in Asia were also worried that if the dispute were resolved and the U.S. and Japan achieved too great a level of accord, the two economic behemoths might join together to exploit the smaller Pacific Rim countries. "When elephants fight, the grass gets trampled," Sarasin explained, using an old Thai saying, "but when they make love, it's even worse."[32]

U.S. Power: Declining or Returning to Normalcy?

Despite the fact that the United States stands alone as the world's only military-economic-political superpower, there are some analysts who believe that the United States is in decline. They note that U.S. economic preeminence is challenged by the economies of the EU, Japan, and, increasingly, China. They also argue that the United States has squandered and continues to waste too many of its economic resources on

U.S.–Japan Relations: Political Alliance and Economic Conflict?

The "most important bilateral relationship in the world, bar none" (Vogel, 1992:35) . . . this is what former U.S. senator and ambassador to Japan Mike Mansfield once called the U.S.–Japan relationship. Most of us would probably have little difficulty in understanding why he made such a statement, given how often we have heard or read about one aspect or another of this relationship in the news over the past few years. There is much less consensus, however, over how to define the character of the relationship today. Is Japan an American ally and friend, or is Japan an American competitor and maybe even an adversary? The truth of the matter probably falls somewhere in between.

In the early days of the cold war, it was much easier to figure out the U.S.–Japan relationship. The United States helped rebuild Japan after World War II and essentially wrote its constitution and helped create the representative government that Japan has today. They shared a common enemy during the cold war and continue to have formal military security treaty obligations with each other.

Today, however, it is a bit more difficult to identify what commonalities hold the two countries together. The Soviet Union is gone, and Russia (or any other country for that matter) does not present the same type of threat to Japan or to the United States at the moment. And increasingly, the items that gain the headlines are ones of conflict over such exemplary issues as automobile export and import markets in both countries, what were supposed to be cooperative military projects, and, more generally, over whether or not Japan will assume a role in the world commensurate with its economic power.

In the first and most recent case of bilateral difficulty—over automobiles—the conflict came to a head in June 1995, when the office of the U.S. Special

Trade Representative (USTR) moved to impose a 100 percent tariff on the import of Japanese luxury cars to the United States if Japan would not agree to open its markets by June 30. In essence, the Clinton administration took an aggressive trade stance against the Japanese, which USTR Mickey Kantor stated would "break the back" of the collusive relationships that prevent foreign access to the Japanese auto market. Vice President Al Gore added further rhetoric to this tough stand by stating, "We're not going to blink."[1]

In the end, however, it seemed that much of the administration's tough stand was bluster, with little substance to back it up. The main outcome of the agreements reached at the eleventh hour were pledges by private sector firms in Japan to increase imports of foreign-made cars and auto parts. There was no guarantee from the government in Tokyo that these pledges would be met or even how these pledges might be measured. By way of rationalizing the outcome, one senior Clinton administration official said, "We all looked over the precipice and discovered we couldn't see the bottom. The sanctions were a big risk. So we took what we had in hand."[2] One Senate staff member was a bit less positive about the outcome of the talks, and also about the future of U.S. trade relations, when he said that "we've only gone after the manifestation of the problem itself. We're in a cycle of crisis-relief-crisis-relief with the Japanese."[3] In other words, the tension that exists between the two economic giants is far from resolved and will be a continued sticking point for future relations.

Trade conflict has also permeated military issues between the two countries. In November 1988, the Reagan administration signed an agreement with the Japanese government to coproduce the FSX multipurpose jet fighter. Mitsubishi Heavy Industries and overseas adventurism. The cost, critics say, is too little investment in the U.S. infrastructure (such as communication, educational, industrial, and transportation capabilities), thereby sapping American strength. By the critics' standards, statistics such as those shown in Figure 3.1 bear witness to the relative decline of U.S. economic fortunes.

Other analysts disagree. They argue that U.S. defense and other international expenditures are appropriate and that, in any case, the data in Figure 3.1 shows

General Dynamics were identified as the two companies to build the plane. The agreement allowed the Japanese to build a fighter similar to the American F-16, provided General Dynamics with 40 percent of the development work, and included complete Japanese government funding and access by the United States to any technological modifications made by the Japanese to the basic F-16 design.[4]

But because of Congressional pressure and bureaucratic maneuvering by Commerce Department and USTR officials within the successor Bush administration, President Bush reopened negotiations after taking office. Most Congressional opponents to the original agreement wanted the Japanese to buy American F-16s "off the shelf" as at least one way of addressing the huge trade imbalance between the two countries. As Senator Lloyd Bentsen (D-TX) put it, "Japan seems bent on subordinating everything to running a $50 billion to $60 billion a year trade surplus, even to the point of excluding superior imports." Representative Mel Levine (D-CA) echoed those sentiments when stating that "if fighter aircraft is not a clear-cut area in which the U.S. has a comparative trading advantage, then I do not know what is!" Independent trade analyst Clyde Prestowitz summed up the concerns by asking, "Should the United States be helping to create a powerful competitor in its best export industry?"[5]

In the end, the agreement was renegotiated and placed into effect with strong limitations on the amount of U.S. technology to which Japanese firms would have access. On the down side, American firms were prevented from gaining access to technologies, such as those used in the manufacture of composite (plasticlike) aircraft body materials, where the United States lagged behind the Japanese. In a symbolic ending to the renegotiated coproduction ar-rangements that were set up in the Japanese city of Nagoya, the General Dynamics engineers working on the project sit in different buildings from the Japanese engineers to prevent access to sensitive national technologies, and the two teams get together only when collaboration is absolutely essential for the project to move forward.

Lastly, even at the level of global strategy, where the U.S.–Japan relationship has always been the closest, signs of tension are seen. The United States has pushed Japan hard to assume a military role in the world that goes beyond what some have termed "checkbook diplomacy," or funding military operations that benefit Japan but declining to commit and risk Japanese troops or hardware in such situations. These accusations came to a head during the Persian Gulf War in 1990–1991 and have not gone away. Since then, the Japanese government has passed a "PKO" (peacekeeping operation) bill in 1993 that for the first time allows Japanese military participation in United Nations peacekeeping efforts. While some see this as only a nominal commitment to international political-military efforts, it nonetheless is a first move by the Japanese government to assume a role in world political-military issues appropriate to its economic size. One should also remember that U.S. accusations of a meager Japanese military effort are also a bit hypocritical given that the United States helped draft the constitution that explicitly limits Japanese military efforts other than for territorial defense.

As all these examples suggest, U.S.–Japan relations are more unsteady today than they have been at any time since World War II. At the root of these tensions are economic issues that have become more prominent between the allies after the cold war. With this in mind, we are faced with the following question, Can economic competitors remain friends?

FIGURE 3.1   Shares of World GNP Held by the United States, the
European Union, and Japan, 1960 and 1993

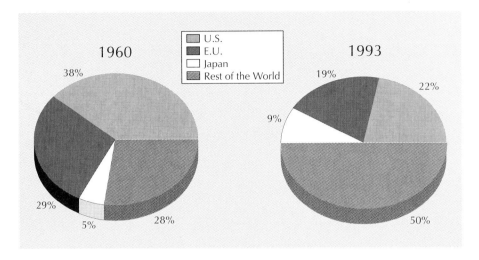

Note: The figures used to derive the charts above were created from a number of sources. In all cases, every effort was made to obtain accurate figures for world GNP. Unfortunately, any figure for GNP is by nature an estimate and should be understood as such.

The United States has experienced relative decline as the world's dominant economic power. The U.S. share of the world's GNP declined from 38% in 1960 to 22% in 1993. Yet, the United States remains the world's largest and most powerful economy.

nothing more than that the U.S. global economic position has returned to normal after an unusually high, early post–World War II level that could not be sustained under any circumstances after World War II.

A 1987 book, *The Rise and Fall of the Great Powers,* by Paul Kennedy is closely associated with the "declinism" theory. Based on his study of the rise and decline of great powers since the year 1500, Kennedy argued that what brought great powers down is **imperial overstretch** caused by trying to exercise too much international control and by too much military spending in the attempt. Such was the experience of the earlier hegemons, including Great Britain, according to Kennedy. And such, he implies, will be the U.S. fate if it does not rein in its international commitments to match its finite economic resources. Other analysts of the declinist school argue that the increase in post–cold war instability will actually accelerate America's decline (Friedberg, 1994). There are even some predictions that the United States may decline to the status of a third-rate, underdeveloped power over the next few decades (Luttwak, 1994).

Yet other analysts reject the declinist argument. They dispute Kennedy's conclusion that U.S. preeminence is vanishing. One counterargument charges that the declinists misconstrue the data. While, according to one scholar, "there is no question that the United States is less powerful at the end than it was in the middle of the twentieth century . . . American preponderance was bound to erode as other nations regained their economic health." Furthermore, he contends, "there is no reason why the world's wealthiest country cannot pay for its international commitments *and* its domestic investments" (Nye, 1990:187).

Another argument against the declinist notion states that only the United States was and still is able to maintain peace and stability in the years ahead and thus *must* continue to play a large role militarily and politically in the world (Neumann, 1993). Such analysts suggest that even if the cold war period did require vast defense spending, the process can be reversed and the United States can be reinvigorated in the new era by the development of a military division of labor with its alliance partners in various regions of the world to optimize political military strength (Bracken & Johnson, 1993; Doran, 1993).

U.S. Power: First Among Equals

The warnings of the declinists and others should be considered carefully, and U.S. economic practices and international activities need to be rethought. It is also almost certainly true that the United States will not be able to dominate world affairs as it did in the cold war era. None of this, however, means that the United States will decline precipitously as a powerful actor in the international system. Indeed, three points can be made to the contrary.

First, the United States has influenced and will continue to influence strongly the structure and operation of the international system in the years ahead. The central role that the United States played in forming the international system and creating international organizations after World War II has secured the country its place in world decisions for some time to come. The United States was, for example, a principal participant in the creation of such international institutions as the UN, GATT, the International Monetary Fund (IMF), and the World Bank. As a founder of these organizations and their rules, the United States was careful to assure itself of a strong role in their future operations. Put simply, the post-1945 international system was molded by Americans, so it will continue to serve their interests and to preserve U.S. power.

Second, U.S. global influences will be preserved also by the assimilation of American international values into the thinking and action of other countries, especially traditional American allies. Some authors assert that the most permanent legacy of U.S. preeminence is the inculcation of a common set of liberal economic and democratic values among the Western nations (Ikenberry & Kupchan, 1990). Moreover, the newly emerging democracies of Eastern Europe and the former Soviet Union are trying to emulate the West, thereby further spreading American influence. From this perspective, for example, "Atlanticism [cooperation based on a common set of ideals held by the advanced capitalist democracies in the United States and Europe] is an organizing principle that helps us see a pattern in a set of shared expectations among [these] countries," and that "the norms and principles of Atlanticism seem secure," even in a rapidly changing international security environment (Wolfe, 1991:138, 162).

Even more expansively, there are scholars who believe that much of the world has adopted many of the Western cultural values promoted by the United States. Russia, the other former Soviet republics, Eastern Europe, and other countries are experiencing the painful transformation from communism to capitalism. Also, democratic government is more widespread than at any time in history. "The triumph of the West, of the Western *idea*," (Fukuyama, 1989:3) believes, "is evident . . . in the total exhaustion of viable systematic alternatives to Western liberalism." Not only that,

Fukuyama sweepingly speculates, but "we may be witnessing . . . the end of history as such: that is, the end point of mankind's ideological evolution and the universalization of Western liberal democracy as the final form of human government." Note that Fukuyama only suggests "we may be witnessing," and many analysts are even more cautious than that; but he does have a point about the spread of international norms based more on the Euro-American tradition than on any other sociopolitical model.

Third, the United States has, and will continue to possess, world-class military and economic power. It is true and to be expected that Japan and the countries of Europe (individually and collectively in the EU) will play a more independent diplomatic role. Germany and Japan, for example, are seeking seats on the UN Security Council. Both countries have adopted legal changes that, for the first time since World War II, allow them to deploy their military forces away from their home countries. Japan has sent noncombat units to aid the UN effort in Cambodia, and Germany has sent support ships to the Adriatic Sea to aid the UN effort in the Balkans. None of this necessarily presages a return to a level of German or Japanese armament that could pose a military threat to the United States. Among other reasons, there is strong domestic opposition in both Germany and Japan to even slight modification of their constitutionally restricted roles, much less any significant remilitarization of their societies. The Japanese and German people have painful memories of their failed attempts at global power in the 1930s and 1940s and the destruction that ensued.

Indeed, there is considerable evidence that despite periodic grumbling, Japan, Germany, and others still expect and want the United States to lead. One Japanese diplomat commented in a private conversation in late 1991, for instance, "Japan makes a good 'number two,' but does not want to bear the burden of becoming a good number one."[33] Thus, in the words of one specialist, "that the Pax Americana is on the wane does not automatically imply that a Pax Nipponica is on the rise (Taira, 1991:59). Attesting to the U.S. role from another point of view, Mahbub ul Haq, of the UN Development Program (UNDP), greeted the news that President Clinton would not attend the UNDP-sponsored summit meeting on world poverty to be held in Denmark in 1995 with the dismayed protest that "this summit without Clinton will be like staging 'Hamlet' without the Prince of Denmark."[34] And from Europe, Dutch minister of cooperation Jan Pronk worried that with respect to global development, "We cannot do it without the United States."[35]

Fourth, some analysts believe that the weight of the various components of international power is changing and that the United States is not necessarily disadvantaged. This view holds that there is an increased importance of "soft" power resources (such as cultural and ideological leadership) that give "co-optive" power (the ability to shape what others *want*) and a decreased importance of "hard" power resources (such as military and economic strength) that give "command" power (the ability to change what others *do*). Moreover, "some of [the changes] may favor the United States" because of its "universalistic popular culture" and other soft power elements that will enhance U.S. co-optive power (Nye, 1990:177–82).

So the epitaph of American vitality is far from written in stone. American policy makers certainly face difficult choices and must surmount serious challenges to U.S. power in the years ahead. Nevertheless, the United States will continue to play a leading, but not unipolar, role in world affairs, even given the fact that by some measures the country is experiencing a relative decline in its power.

The U.S. Sphere of Influence: President Monroe Lives!

If Americans are anxious about their global status, they remain assured about their hemisphere. In fact, the U.S. hold on its sphere of influence in Central America and the Caribbean has tightened somewhat through a mixed carrot-and-stick approach.

Carrots When Possible

One U.S. approach to Latin America is to extend economic carrots and expressions of goodwill in the lineage of Franklin Roosevelt's Good Neighbor policy. This positive approach is not totally altruistic. Instead, aiding the hemisphere's poorer countries helps expand American investment opportunities in the region. Aid also promotes the political stability of Latin American countries. President Carter, for example, eliminated a remnant of earlier U.S. imperialism in Central America by renegotiating the Panama Canal treaties to return control of the canal gradually to Panama. The Caribbean also became the focus of U.S. activity in the 1980s. Economically, Reagan pushed for closer U.S.–Caribbean trade ties with his Caribbean Basin Initiative (Fascell, 1991). Beyond the obvious trade advantages for both sides, Reagan hoped that enhanced prosperity in the region would lessen the attractiveness of communism there. The Bush and Clinton administrations have also followed this economic path. Bush began trilateral negotiations between Canada, Mexico, and the United States to establish a free trade area under the North American Free Trade Agreement (NAFTA). The treaty was signed in 1992, subsequently ratified by the legislatures of all three countries, and went into effect in January 1994.

During the presidential campaign, Clinton had expressed reservations about certain aspects of the Mexico–U.S. accord. After the election, however, Clinton moved strongly to negotiate side agreements with Canada and Mexico aimed at reducing U.S. domestic opposition to NAFTA and to mount a major lobbying campaign that overcame significant early opposition to NAFTA in Congress. Since the creation of NAFTA, the Clinton administration has been at the center of several other efforts to expand U.S. free trade ties with the rest of the Western Hemisphere. On one front, negotiators for the three NAFTA members began negotiations in June 1995 with Chile that, if successful, will add a fourth member to the pact. On a second and even more significant front, President Clinton hosted the leaders of all the hemisphere's countries except Cuba at the Summit of the Americas held in Miami in December 1994. The conferees agreed to strive toward the establishment of the Free Trade Area of the Americas by the year 2005. "When our work is done," Clinton told the conference, "the free trade area of the Americas will stretch from Alaska [forming] the world's largest market."[36]

Recent presidents also have had to address the huge international debt under which many of the Latin American countries are staggering. This debt retards economic growth, reduces social services, and promotes political instability when the countries try to meet payment schedules; the debt harms U.S. banks and other lenders when payments fall behind or are in default. The debt also limits U.S. exports to its southern neighbors. The Reagan administration fashioned the (then-secretary of the treasury James) Baker Plan in 1985, and the Bush administration followed with the (U.S. secretary of the treasury Nicholas) Brady Plan in 1989. Both plans were designed to enhance international debt management aimed at shoring up Latin American economies and at providing greater governmental protection for American lenders to the region. The Brady plan represented a break with past U.S. policy in that it explicitly acknowledged that some of the debt of less developed countries will never be repaid and that both debtor and creditor countries would be injured by an attempt to collect it all. Mexico was the initial country with which specific details were worked out, marking the first time the United States, commercial lenders, and Latin American governments came together to renegotiate debt repayment with U.S. guarantees to the banks. These plans eased the strain but did not fully solve the problem. Many have questioned the Brady Plan's applicability and feasibility beyond this initial agreement.

The most recent evidence of the U.S. effort to assist its southern neighbors during times of economic crisis occurred in late 1994 and into 1995 when the value of the Mexican peso (relative to the U.S. dollar) collapsed. That threatened Mexico's economic and political stability; there was concern that financial panic also might cause Americans numerous difficulties including massive losses from investments in Mexico and a tidal wave of illegal immigrants crossing the border in search of work. Clinton initially offered to lend Mexico $40 billion to stabilize its currency, but Congressional opposition forced the administration to scale back that amount by half. Other financial commitments from Canada and European and global financial organizations such as the International Monetary Fund (IMF) offered another $20 billion, thereby reaching the $40 billion that Clinton had proposed originally. "In the end there is no choice," one administration official explained. "Mexico has become an integral part of the North American market. . . . The two economies are intertwined in trade, in commerce and in the movement of people. And in the end, there is a bigger need to have a stable country on our border."[37]

Sticks When Necessary

There have also been times when Franklin Roosevelt's good neighbor approach of supplying carrots and kind words has been abandoned in favor of Theodore Roosevelt's big stick strategy. For example, even as Carter moved to return sovereignty over the canal to Panama, his subordinates warned that the gesture depended on good behavior by the Panamanians. When asked what would happen if the Panamanians closed the canal, national security adviser Zbigniew Brzezinski growled that, "In that case . . . we will move in and close down the Panamanian government for repairs" (Strong, 1991:280).

Reagan took such belligerency out of the realm of rhetoric and into the arena of action. His administration provided military and economic assistance to the right-wing regimes in Guatemala and El Salvador while overlooking their human rights violations. Because the United States made a commitment to the Soviet Union as part of resolving the 1962 Cuban missile crisis not to topple Fidel Castro's communist regime in Cuba through military means, the Reagan cold warriors could do little about that government besides isolate it and bombard it with propaganda from Radio Martí in Florida. Nicaragua was a different story. That country's president, Daniel Ortega, and his Sandinista government were condemned as communist, and the United States launched a considerable effort to overthrow them. Money and other forms of U.S. assistance—some legal, some not—flowed to the Contra rebels in Nicaragua. Human rights violations were selectively overlooked. The administration condemned the abuses of the Sandinistas; it ignored those of the Contras.

Where financial assistance to anticommunist governments and insurgency did not suffice, the administration considered direct military intervention. The Reagan White House was alarmed by growing Cuban influence and the Cuban-assisted construction of a major airfield in the Caribbean country of Grenada. When, in 1983, the left-wing Grenadan government of Prime Minister Maurice Bishop was overthrown by an even more leftist coup, a U.S. invasion soon followed. Reagan (1990:455) regretted that 19 soldiers had died and 116 had been wounded, but he asserted that "the price would have been much higher if the Soviet Union had been allowed to perpetuate this penetration of our hemisphere." The U.S. action also served as a warning to the Sandinistas in Nicaragua that American military intervention was a possibility. In any case, the president happily recorded, "The Marxists and their Cuban puppeteers [in Grenada] were defeated," and, he exultantly confided to his diary, "Success seems to shine on us and I thank the Lord for it. He has really held me in the hollow of His hand." An interesting historical footnote is that the Grenada's seeming strategic significance faded rapidly. Washington decided in May 1994 to close the U.S. embassy in Grenada and place relations in a consolidated embassy elsewhere in the Caribbean. In a far cry from Reagan's earlier depiction of the critical importance of the tiny island country, a State Department official described it just a decade later as "not really an active post in terms of any of the normal criteria: political and economic reporting, narcotics, or consular affairs."[38]

The waning of the cold war and the advent of the more pragmatic Bush administration led the United States to step back from the ideological focus and to compromise with Congress over the Contra aid issue and the various plans for achieving regional peace (Pastor, 1992). It has even forced the Clinton administration to work toward the elimination of U.S. economic sanctions against Cuba, once a primary symbol of U.S. cold war policy in the Western Hemisphere. Thus far the Cuban government has refused to accept the primary condition for the removal of the sanctions: opening up its political system. The President of Cuba's National Assembly, Ricardo Alarcon, expressed his government's view of the Clinton proposal by stating that Cuba could not agree to any conditions if they were imposed by "the very same nation that refused to accept our independence. Cuba is simply not a U.S. colony."[39]

The cold war troubles in Nicaragua were eventually settled when the United States, the Soviet Union, and the government and rebels in Nicaragua agreed to abide by an internationally supervised election. To nearly everyone's surprise, the opposition coalition headed by Violeta Barrios de Chamorro upset President Ortega in 1990, and the Sandinistas turned over the presidency to her. The equally exhausted sides in El Salvador reached accord in 1992. For the first time in many years, no cold war fighting beset Latin America. If anything, the end of the cold war and the withdrawal of Soviet aid for leftist governments and rebels in the hemisphere solidified U.S. influence. As one newspaper article put it, there was a reemergence of "good neighbors" in the hemisphere based on U.S. preeminence.[40]

Just in case the countries in the Western Hemisphere did not live up to the American image of how a good neighbor should act, there was still the traditional approach to rectifying the lapse. This was dramatically demonstrated when 24,000 U.S. troops invaded Panama on December 20, 1989, and ousted and imprisoned General Manuel Noriega. Most Americans believed that the invasion was justified by Panamanian provocations and by the Monroe Doctrine. An editorial in the *Los Angeles Times* by conservative columnist (and perennial presidential hopeful) Patrick J.

Buchanan entitled "The Monroe Doctrine: Use It or Lose It" reflected the bravado mood of many Americans.[41] Their self-adulation was not widely shared by the international community. To the contrary, both the UN General Assembly and the Organization of American States passed resolutions condemning the intervention.

Continuing the American penchant for military intervention, the Clinton administration eventually resorted to military pressure to reinstate the democratically elected President of Haiti, Jean-Bertrand Aristide, late in November 1994. In contrast to past interventions in the region, most OAS members and the UN Security Council supported this U.S. action. In a televised warning that Teddy Roosevelt would have admired, a stern Clinton told Haiti's military leaders, "The message of the United States to the Haitian dictators is clear. Your time is up—leave now or we'll force you from power."[42] Ultimately, the military junta reluctantly stepped aside even as planes carried U.S. paratroopers toward Haiti. As a result, U.S. forces entered the country peacefully to restore order and democracy. Subsequently, and possibly foreshadowing future similar ventures, U.S. forces handed over military control of Haiti to a UN force in March 1995. One adviser to President Aristide, however, remains circumspect about the prospects for domestic peace when stating that "things aren't going as planned. There is a lot of insecurity, and criminals are claiming the night for themselves."[43] In the longer term, many analysts believe, Haitian domestic stability will only develop with American economic help both in terms of foreign aid and private investment. As one analyst, explained, "any fair economic assessment of Haiti would recognize there's no quick solution."[44]

The United States in the World Economy

The years since Vietnam have been a roller-coaster ride for the U.S. economy. The inescapable reality of the rapidly increasing economic interdependence of countries has inexorably intertwined U.S. economic health and economic decisions with the international system. After the war in Vietnam, the U.S. inflation rate spiraled, partly because of the budget deficits that the war had helped build up. Then a 1973 Arab oil embargo, imposed on the West in retaliation for its support of Israel in the October 1973 Yom Kippur War with Syria and Egypt, made the situation dramatically worse. Global oil prices skyrocketed, quadrupling in 1973–1974 and increasing by a total of 1,500 percent by 1980 after the Iranian revolution and the oil supply disruptions it caused. The results were global recessions during the years 1973–1975 and again in the early 1980s. Oil price increases also caused the accumulation of vast wealth by some members of the Organization of Petroleum Exporting Countries (OPEC). Events and forces such as these pushed foreign economic policy into the arena of "high politics" once occupied only by military security issues (Livingston, 1994).

A time of double trouble, of both a stagnant economy and high inflation—ingloriously dubbed stagflation—plagued the country in the late 1970s and helped drive Jimmy Carter from office. Particularly in such areas as manufacturing and electronics, U.S. corporations began to lose their domestic and foreign markets to companies in Japan and in the newly industrializing countries such as South Korea. As a result, the U.S. trade deficit spiraled and set off escalating calls for trade protectionism. These concerns were seen dramatically once again in the 1992 presidential debates between Bill Clinton and George Bush, as many in the United States began to question an American foreign policy that put foreign concerns ahead of those closer to home—

such as urban blight, unemployment, and crime—with more noticeable local economic impact (Petras & Morley, 1994).

The U.S. Economic Position Weakens in the 1980s

The Reagan administration reacted by rhetorically supporting the principle of free trade while, in practice, significantly increasing the protection of domestic economic interests (Nivola, 1990). In 1981 only 20 percent of U.S. manufactured goods (by dollar value) were protected from foreign competition. By 1989 this share had risen to 35 percent, mostly by imposing **nontariff barriers (NTBs),** such as pressuring other countries to observe what are euphemistically termed voluntary export quotas. The 1980s also saw a number of interactions between the international system and U.S. fiscal policy that spelled trouble for the U.S. economy. Military budgets increased dramatically—despite much rhetoric to the contrary—with relatively little restraint on domestic spending. Reagan also kept taxes down. In short, the United States bought more guns and almost as much butter, did not bring enough money to the store to pay for them, and therefore had to borrow heavily to meet the bill. Massive budget deficits financed by soaring borrowing from domestic and foreign creditors followed. Figure 3.2 displays the upward trend of the federal budget deficit from 1965 to 1991 as both a percentage of gross domestic product (GDP—the sum of all goods and services produced within a country) and total government spending.

This unsound budget policy had a number of effects. First, the huge amount that the federal government had to borrow kept interest rates high in the United States. The high rates attracted capital from abroad, and that kept interest rates in other countries up because there was a greater demand for capital than there was a supply of money. High interest rates also acted to depress the U.S. and world economies and also created resentment among U.S. political allies and economic competitors. Furthermore, the soaring portion of the U.S. budget devoted to paying interest on the national debt further broadened the deficit, thereby causing even more borrowing to pay interest on past borrowing. Because U.S. capital supplies could not meet these borrowing demands, foreign creditors increasingly bought Treasury notes and other U.S. debt instruments, and a significant part of the interest went overseas. This and the spiraling trade deficit turned the U.S. **balance of payments** sharply into the red. By the mid-1980s the United States became the world's most indebted country, owing foreigners a net $645 billion in 1989. In the early 1980s, the United States had been the largest creditor nation.

Second, investment opportunities in the United States and the fact that the U.S. economy was the first to pull out of the recession of the early 1980s forced the value of the dollar higher on international financial markets. President Reagan often equated a strong dollar with a strong America. Yet a strong dollar also made U.S. goods more expensive on world markets and foreign goods less expensive in American markets. This contributed significantly to the increasing trade deficit and declining U.S. competitiveness.

Third, U.S. fiscal and economic problems eroded the U.S. claim to leadership, and during the early 1980s there was increased discord with major U.S. allies. There were differences over trade with the Soviets, with the United States favoring restraint and the Western Europeans disagreeing. The economically empowered U.S. allies demanded more of a share in setting macroeconomic policy; an annual economic summit

FIGURE 3.2

Federal Budget Deficit as Percentage of
Government Spending and GDP

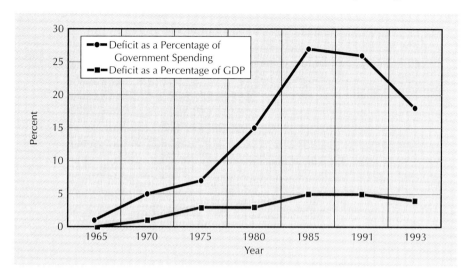

Data source: International Monetary Fund; *World Factbook* (1994).

Increasing budget deficits have weakened the U.S. international economic position by requiring heavy borrowing from abroad to finance the deficit. The figure shows that the deficit has increased as a percentage of government spending and of the U.S. GDP.

of the **Group of Seven** (G-7: Canada, France, Germany, Great Britain, Italy, Japan, and the United States) was instituted in 1975; but the United States continued to insist on leading, and the other industrial powers chafed under what they saw as U.S. unilateralism. By the mid-1980s, the United States began to understand the need to coordinate and consult more closely with its allies on economic policy issues (Boyer, 1993). The G-7's so-called Plaza Agreement (named after the Plaza Hotel in New York City, where the conference was held) of 1985 brought about coordinated intervention in the international currency market and helped change the Reagan administration's policy. Within two years, the value of the U.S. dollar had dropped 42 percent against the Japanese yen and 38 percent against the German mark, and the U.S. trade deficit began to ease as U.S. exports became less expensive in other countries and their products became more expensive in the United States.

Economic Challenges in the 1990s

Even though the Bush and Clinton administrations have continued to support the theory of economic cooperation and have moved reluctantly toward greater economic cooperation with traditional U.S. allies, relations with them over trade issues remain a source of considerable strain. The 1990s are a time of increasing regionalization of the world economy. So far, the regional blocs such as the EU, NAFTA, or the even more loosely organized Asian Pacific Economic Cooperation (APEC) forum have not erected protectionist barriers against one another. But there is concern that regions might do so, thereby touching off a global trade war and restricting inter-regional trade. The difficulty that the world's countries had concluding the current Uruguay round of the GATT negotiations, in part over EU–U.S. differences about agricultural subsidies, made many fear that trade problems would be the set of issues that would permanently drive a wedge between the longtime allies and economic partners.

These fears were proven premature. Albeit several years behind schedule, the world's major trading countries agreed on the new revisions to the GATT and established a new coordinating body, the World Trade Organization. Part of the motive to settle was the recognition by the major economic powers that they benefit from a relatively unrestricted trading system. Part of the motive was fear that without the GATT, protectionist regionalism might take hold, leaving them isolated. The Clinton administration's attention to APEC, for example, was, according to one U.S. official, aimed at letting the Europeans "know that while we all want GATT, there are other options we have with Asia."[45] In contrast to such possible combative regionalism, the restraints on trade restrictions that the GATT provides "make the world safe for regionalism," according to one economist.[46]

Under the new agreement the WTO has the power to monitor free trade and assess penalties on countries violating the agreement, thus giving more power to an international trade organization than ever before. The agreement also requires all signatories to reduce existing tariff levels by an average of one-third and for the first time since 1948 includes agricultural tariffs. It also forces the abandonment of quotas as a way around older GATT rules regarding tariffs, thus requiring Japan to remove its ban on rice imports and the United States to end its quotas on peanuts and textiles, among other products. In another area, to move the GATT into the twenty-first century, the accord requires that all signatories protect intellectual property rights such as patents, copyrights, and computer software. This last item was a particularly sticky negotiating point but one that the United States had been insistent on throughout the negotiations.

Although there was some domestic opposition to the new organization and agreement, it passed through Congress much more easily than did NAFTA a year earlier. The House passed the GATT bill by 288 to 146; the Senate did so by a vote of 76 to 24. The lopsided votes reflected the reality, as Senate minority leader Bob Dole put it, that although the accord was "far from perfect . . . let's face it . . . we're the big beneficiaries, the United States of America, any way you cut it."[47]

Whether that attitude persists remains to be seen. The first major test of the WTO's role of arbitrating trade disputes may well involve the two heavyweights of the economic world: Japan and the United States. As noted, Japan has threatened to challenge the legality of the Clinton administration's auto-import sanctions before the WTO. Hoping to avoid that, Renato Ruggiero, director general of the WTO, termed the contest "a delicate matter with nationalist implications" for both countries and has called on them to settle the issues diplomatically rather than through "a legalistic ruling" by the WTO. At least part of Ruggiero's motivation, one diplomat observed, is his fear that "the WTO will get trampled." What worries the world community most is a nasty nationalist reaction by the United States if it were to lose in the WTO. The irony, Ruggiero noted, is that the potential case would put the United States in a position of "almost defending itself from the system you [Americans] have created. Now there is a feeling that these institutions [like the WTO] take something out of your influence and power."[48] Japan and the United States reached an agreement that avoided sanctions and quotas, and the threatened suits and countersuits were never filed. Still, the WTO will be the scene of future contests.

Holbert, United Feature Syndicate

The U.S. dollar was once considered the most powerful currency in the world. That is no longer true. Between 1985 and 1995, for example, the dollar declined in its exchange rate value versus Japan's yen from $1 = ¥250 to, at its nadir, $1 = ¥85. The fall of the dollar is not all bad. The weaker dollar has, for instance, helped boost U.S. exports. Still, the dollar has probably fallen too far, and, while it has recovered a bit it is unlikely in the foreseeable future to be able to return to the exalted status it once had.

In another economic area, multilateral efforts to harmonize international monetary policy in order to stabilize international currency exchange rates have been considerably less successful in the 1990s than they were in the 1980s. In contrast to the success of the Plaza Accord in achieving the desired movement of exchange rates, the G-7, amid mutual recriminations, has struggled to keep the U.S. dollar from continuing its long decline in value particularly compared to the Japanese yen and the German mark. While the falling dollar generally means that American exports become more attractive to international consumers, it also can mean, over the medium to long term, significant rates of inflation at home. Part of the problem with maintaining the dollar's value has been the linkage of the U.S. and Mexican economies through NAFTA. This linkage became especially acute because the Clinton administration put together a bailout package for Mexico when its latest economic crisis hit in spring 1995. The Europeans did not block the U.S. move to have the IMF put up part of the rescue funds for Mexico, but they did express their displeasure by pointedly abstaining from the vote on the IMF's board of directors.

Soon thereafter, when the G-7 finance ministers met, the atmosphere was captured by one newspaper headline that read, "7 Rich Nations Meet for Talks in Bitter Mood." "In recent years, there has been something of a nonaggression pact in operation," an analyst explained. "No one wanted to bash, because no one wanted to be bashed. Now there is just too much pent-up frustration."[49] The annual meeting of the leaders of the G-7 in Halifax, Nova Scotia, in Canada did little to restore cooperation among the most powerful economies. As U.S. secretary of the treasury Robert

E. Rubin noted ruefully, "coordination proved to be like many other things in economics: something that sounds nice and simple and is anything but simple. It ran into the complexities of economic life."[50]

The 1990s, then, have witnessed both positive and negative developments regarding the future of international economic cooperation. Somewhat surprisingly, the Clinton administration has generally pursued foreign economic policies—for example, approval of NAFTA, creation of the WTO, and laissez-faire monetary policies—that fit more closely with those of Republican predecessors than with Democratic ones.

Defending U.S. Economic Interests: The Persian Gulf

One hallmark of U.S. activity in the international system has been the country's willingness to fight, if necessary, to defend its international economic interests. The unofficial naval war with France in the 1790s, the War of 1812 with Great Britain, and World War I with Germany are just three examples involving freedom of the seas and trade. As chapter 2 discussed, there has also been an imperialist element in U.S. foreign policy, especially during the last 100 years. This has included U.S. domination of areas that are important for resource supply, export absorption, and investment opportunities (Livingston, 1994).

The willingness to defend trade, resources, and other key economic elements in the international system remains a principle of U.S. foreign policy, as was demonstrated by U.S. actions in the Persian Gulf region. When President George Bush hurled a half-million U.S. troops against Saddam Hussein's Iraqi legions in 1991, he was only the latest in a long line of presidents to pledge, threaten, or actually decide to intervene militarily in the petroleum-producing region. The United States has long opposed any consolidation of regional power there, especially if backed by what once was the USSR, because that would threaten energy supplies and low prices. Protecting the region's regimes has, in turn, usually made them compliant with U.S.–led Western demands for steady supplies at low prices. Secret documents declassified in 1992 indicate that as early as 1947 President Harry S. Truman sent a message to the king of Saudi Arabia pledging U.S. "support [of the] territorial integrity and political independence of Saudi Arabia."[51] The late 1950s and early 1960s brought worries that pan-Arab nationalism, led by Egypt's Gamal Abdel Nasser, might threaten the West's interests in the area. This fear, coupled with the potential of outside intervention in Lebanon counter to American interest, prompted President Dwight D. Eisenhower to send U.S. troops to Lebanon in 1958 to fend off a threatened coup against the pro-Western government there. In 1963 President John F. Kennedy sent a U.S. fighter squadron to Saudi Arabia after an attempt by Nasser's supporters to overthrow the Saudi royal régime.

An even clearer and more public assertion of U.S. interests and determination came in 1980. Anxiety about the region after the overthrow of Iran's shah and the Soviet invasion of Afghanistan, both in 1979, prompted President Jimmy Carter to declare, during his 1980 State of the Union address, that any attempt by an outside force to gain control of the Persian Gulf region would be regarded as "an assault on the vital interests of the United States, and such an assault will be repelled by use of any means necessary, including military force."[52]

The Carter Doctrine was first put into action by Ronald Reagan. The long (1980–1988) Iran-Iraq War seemed by 1986 to be going in Iran's favor, and—worse—it spilled into the Gulf, threatening Kuwait and the flow of oil to the West. The U.S.

administration responded by putting U.S. flags on Kuwaiti tankers (thereby making them technically U.S. vessels) and sending the U.S. Navy into the Persian Gulf to protect the reflagged ships. Several limited, although deadly, clashes ensued.

The strength of the U.S. commitment to the defense of its economic interests in the region received its greatest test in August 1990, when Iraq invaded Kuwait. Making good on over three decades of American assurances, President Bush acted to protect Saudi Arabia and, later, to drive Iraqi forces from Kuwait. President Clinton has also demonstrated the U.S. commitment to preventing any other power from dominating the gulf region. He responded in June 1993 to an alleged plot to assassinate former president Bush during a visit to Kuwait by launching airstrikes against Iraq. "Don't tread on us," Clinton warned Baghdad.[53] Then in October 1994, when Iraq moved military units to its border with Kuwait, Clinton ordered a rapid buildup of U.S. forces in the region and warned Iraq to pull its soldiers back from the frontier.

The U.S. response to the Gulf crisis clearly shows several things about how the international system affects U.S. foreign policy. First, petroleum is an essential resource. The pattern of petroleum being produced in the Middle East and used by Western industrial countries, and the importance of low petroleum prices to the Western economies, made U.S. action almost certain. As one U.S. official put it, American intervention against Iraq was "an easy call. Even a dolt understands [that] we need oil. It's nice to talk about standing up for freedom, but Kuwait and Saudi Arabia are not exactly democracies, and if their principal export were oranges [we] would have [just] issued a statement."[54] The Persian Gulf countries export oil, of course, not oranges, and, as Secretary of State Baker told a congressional committee, since "the economic lifeline of the industrial world runs from the gulf, . . . we cannot permit a dictator . . . to sit astride that economic lifeline."[55]

Second, the industrialized countries, with the United States in the lead, wish to maintain a regional balance of power in the Middle East. The industrialized countries are loath to allow any single power—Nasserite Egyptian, Iranian, Iraqi, or Soviet—to control the region and be in position to cut off oil supplies or dictate their prices. During the Iran-Iraq War in the 1980s, when Iran threatened to win and achieve regional dominance, the United States sided tacitly with Iraq to thwart Iran. Soon thereafter, the Iraqi invasion of Kuwait threatened to catapult Iraq to regional dominance. The United States and its allies then moved to curb Iraq's power. The U.S. interest in maintaining a balance of power in the region also accounted for several actions once the war began. The decision of President Bush to end the war quickly—thus leaving Saddam Hussein in power with some of his military intact—was predicated in part on the U.S. wish to avoid having Iraq dismembered among Kurds, Shiite Muslims, and Sunni Muslims or otherwise destroying Iraq's power completely. That outcome would have enhanced the power of Iran. In fact, some months after the war was over, Washington warned Tehran not to try to take advantage of Iraq's weakness. As one U.S. official said at the time, "signals have to be sent to the Iranians that [Iraqi weakness] is not an opportunity to make mischief or take advantage of the situation."[56]

Third, the gulf crisis showed that while countries are still the most important actors in the international system, other actors are becoming more significant. The United Nations and other international organizations are one type of actor. One example of the significance of the UN is the conscious effort made by U.S. officials to build multilateral support and to achieve UN support for what was essentially an American war with Iraq. Much of the talk about cooperation in a new world order

Many countries and leaders look to the world's most powerful country, the United States, for leadership. This was demonstrated in September 1995 when Yasser Arafat, chairman of the Palestine Liberation Organization, and Yitzhak Rabin, prime minister of Israel, met at the White House to sign a historic peace accord and to receive the imprimatur of the United States, symbolized by President Bill Clinton, who beams as the two former enemies shake hands. It is also a mark of the central role of the United States in international affairs that in November 1995 a solemn President Clinton, as the most important political guest, stood in the front row of leaders from around the world who had gathered in Jerusalem to mourn Rabin, who had been assassinated.

is still rhetoric, but the United States is becoming increasingly reluctant to take unilateral military action. In an earlier time the United States might have acted alone in the Persian Gulf. In 1990, however, Washington sought global condemnation of Iraq's invasion of Kuwait. On November 29, 1990, the UN Security Council passed Resolution 678, authorizing military action against Iraq if it did not withdraw from Kuwait by January 15, 1991. Iraq did not, and U.S.–led UN forces enforced Resolution 678.

Moreover, 29 nations sent armed forces of some kind to the gulf region to participate in the U.S.–led military effort. Extensive funds flowed as well from several other countries, most notably Germany ($6.6 billion) and Japan ($10.7 billion), to support the UN–authorized forces.

Fourth, the change in international system poles—the fact that the Soviet Union was in its death throes—created an international situation in which the United States could act. The USSR had been a major supporter of Iraq, and U.S. intervention would have been much more perilous if a healthy Soviet Union had backed Saddam Hussein. But the Soviets were consumed with their own problems and needed U.S. financial assistance. So they became a tacit U.S. ally in the war, and the United States intervened without fear of confronting the Soviets. The decline of Soviet influence in the Middle

East also changed the American perception that Israel is an indispensable ally in the region and has given American policy makers somewhat stronger tools to lever Israel in desired directions in Middle East peace talks and on other issues of importance.

Indeed, it can be argued that the Persian Gulf events were the first that pressed the United States to take the lead in its new status as the world's sole superpower. Beyond its immense military power, the United States was, and remains, the only country with the international status to lead in such a dangerous enterprise. American leadership can also be pivotal in promoting peace through diplomacy. This was demonstrated in 1995, when the Palestine Liberation Organization (PLO) chairman Yasser Arafat and Israeli prime minister Yitzhak Rabin met on the White House lawn to sign their historic peace accord as a beaming President Bill Clinton looked on. The fact that the Palestinians and Israelis came to Washington to sign the pact "tells you something," one expert on the Middle East commented. "In a world where there is only one superpower, leaders and countries that are taking risks find they have a psychological and political need to make sure it meets with U.S. approval and support."[57]

At the same time, however, factors including multipolarity, the increased aversion to using force (especially unilateral force) in the international system, and the American focus on domestic problems have created an atmosphere in which the United States finds it harder to lead in the international system. The United States, along with all other countries, is struggling to find its role in the new system. Critics have pummeled President Clinton for lack of policy consistency, but they have been less forthcoming about what the outlines of an overall policy strategy for the United States might be. Given the momentous changes that the international system is experiencing, it may be that demanding such a strategic theme may be premature. "I've often asked, 'Does this administration have a coherent, well-planned and clearly articulated foreign policy?' And my response to that question has been that if they do, they ought to be locked up," Representative David R. Obey (D-WI) mused.[58] Even some of Clinton's partisan opponents have been willing to admit that policy criticism is vastly easier than policy formation. "Nobody's gotten it right yet, not Bush, not Clinton," conceded Republican senator Mitch McConnell (KY). "It's easy to jump on the president," he added. "I've done that on a variety of issues. But frankly, I don't have any clearer idea of how to proceed from here than I believe [Clinton] does.[59]

The United States: Still a Most Unrevolutionary Country

The collapse of the Soviet Union and the resulting relative enhancement of U.S. power brought the momentary illusion of a near full circle to post–World War II events. The United States in late 1945 stood astride the world with its enemies in ruins, with its atomic superpower status indisputable, and with an intact economic plant and a civilian population that generated half the world's GNP. Americans struggled to maintain this status quo but could not. The flush of victory in the desert in 1991 brought new thoughts of a unipolar moment, with the United States as the unchallenged international Goliath. It was, however, only for a moment, if that. Still, the United States has continued to seek to preserve the status quo, to preserve an international system in which U.S. power and status are still unparalleled.

In an era of massive change to the international system, there have been many opportunities for the United States to move away from its status quo orientation. The U.S. response, in the main, has been to cling to the past. Especially through the

1980s, this status quo orientation was based in part on traditional cold war attitudes and fear that change was synonymous with gains by the communists. More importantly, the U.S. policy of status quo preservation has emphasized resisting two trends in the international system. One is the relative decline of U.S. power. Americans bemoan the burden of world leadership, but they also enjoy and benefit from it. The U.S. leadership position among the Western industrial powers has slipped, and Americans have struggled to hold onto it. Second, and more generally, the sway of Western political leadership, which the United States champions, has ebbed. African, Asian, and other countries have their own cultural concepts of equity and legality and are demanding that their values be incorporated in the operation of the international system. These demands often challenge U.S. power and American values. The world's geostrategic center has long been roughly parallel to the area encompassed by the countries of NATO, but that focus is beginning to fragment and to become more diverse as countries such as China, India, and Japan assume a more assertive international role and as other countries such as Brazil, Nigeria, and Syria also take on greater regional, even international, roles.

The 1980s: Struggling with a Faltering Status Quo

Compared with his predecessors and his successors, President Jimmy Carter was relatively open to change. He reemphasized the UN, pressed for human rights reforms in South Africa and elsewhere, and supported the Law of the Sea Treaty to regulate and share use of the oceans' resources. Carter's openness to new ideas was evident in his negotiation of the Panama Canal treaties and his initial willingness to deal with the new Sandinista regime in Nicaragua. Still, even Carter frequently defended the status quo, as illustrated by the Carter Doctrine's pledge to defend the Persian Gulf oil supplies if necessary.

Ronald Reagan believed in old-fashioned American values, including the virtue of American dominance. Reagan (1990:266) rejected "the notion that America was no longer the world power it had once been," and he pledged that the United States "would never accept second place." He responded to East-West issues as a cold warrior, and his views, coupled with Soviet actions in Afghanistan and elsewhere, temporarily rekindled an earlier era of U.S.–USSR enmity (Johnson, 1991). President Reagan, like most of his post–World War II presidential predecessors, also believed that communist subversion, rather than social unrest, bred in poverty and oppression, was at the root of revolution and other forms of political unrest in the less developed countries. Therefore he opposed change, except where rightist rebels were attempting to overthrow leftist regimes. For example, Secretary of State Alexander M. Haig Jr. condemned the rebel movement in impoverished El Salvador as "a textbook case of indirect armed aggression by Communist power through Cuba" (Jentleson, 1990:177). Similarly, suspicions that the largest black South African organization, the African National Congress (ANC), had communist leanings and wanted to create anarchy to seize power colored the Reagan administration's reaction to the struggle of black South Africans to end apartheid. Instead of seeing that the ANC favored sanctions against South Africa in order to end racism, Reagan believed that Nelson Mandela's aim was to create "disruption . . . from massive unemployment and hunger and desperation of the people" so that the ANC "could then rise out of all that disruption and seize control" (Jentleson, 1990:160).

The 1990s: Defining a New World Order in the American Image

During the cold war, the status quo gave Americans a great degree of economic, political, and cultural leadership in the world. Much of this remains, but U.S. dominance is less pronounced. In the 1990s, the United States no longer needs—or is needed by others—to protect the international system against another antagonistic superpower. The end of the superpower rivalry has increased the relative power of countries such as Japan and Germany, and U.S. leaders must grapple with the desire of these and other emerging powers in the international system to participate more authoritatively in making international decisions. The end of the cold war also increased concern about the ability of some countries (such as Iran, Iraq, Libya, and North Korea) to threaten the established industrialized powers through such means as terrorism and the development or purchase of nuclear weapons or other advanced military technology.

Given these changes, one example of how the United States has attempted to preserve the status quo in the 1990s relates to its nuclear weapons policy. That encompasses two aspects: first, U.S. acquisition of nuclear weapons by current nonnuclear weapons countries and, second, U.S. nuclear disarmament policy. In the first realm, the United States has steadfastly opposed nuclear proliferation. The Clinton administration led the drive to persuade North Korea to give up its weapons program in 1994. Washington put sanctions on Iran in response to its alleged nuclear weapons program and pressed Beijing and Moscow not to supply nuclear technology to Iran and other countries. Using what Under Secretary of State for Arms Control and International Security Lynn Davis called "full-court press," the United States worked hard in the spring of 1995 to gain enough signatories to extend the Nonproliferation Treaty (NPT) indefinitely, instead relying on the five-year renewals of the treaty that had been performed until then.[60] Whatever the value of the NPT, one of its ramifications is that it seeks to maintain the nuclear weapons status quo throughout the world by allowing the present nuclear powers to keep their weapons while preventing non-weapons states from developing them. Some countries objected to the indefinite extension of the NPT on the grounds that it preserved the dominance of the current nuclear powers. The government of India, for one, condemned the idea of an unlimited extension of the NPT without a pledge by the current nuclear powers to disarm as "perpetuating nuclear discrimination" and as conferring "legitimacy of double standards."[61]

India's charge leads to the second aspect of U.S. policy—Washington's stand on nuclear disarmament. A series of treaties with the Soviets and, later, the Russians, are in the process of vastly reducing the U.S. nuclear arsenal, but Washington had not been willing to consider seriously the subject of true nuclear disarmament. For example, Secretary of State Baker rejected one such call by Russia's president Yeltsin with the argument, "I am not prepared to walk away from the concept of nuclear deterrence that has kept the peace for more than 40 years . . . [or] to subscribe to the philosophy of denuclearization."[62] The United States has also continued to upgrade its nuclear weapons system, including work on building a limited antiballistic missile defense system. Furthermore, Washington retains the option of being the first to use nuclear weapons. When China pledged in 1994 not to be the first to use nuclear weapons and called on the United States to join it in that pledge, the Clinton administration declined to issue such an assurance.

The status quo impulse is evident in other ways. There is a growing norm in the international system that countries should act in cooperation with others rather than unilaterally and that they should work toward the good of the so-called global village rather than following narrow national interests. Rhetorically, President Bush supported creation of a **new world order** in the post–cold war system. The idea is that the international system would be based on international law and would rely on international organizations such as the United Nations to settle international conflicts. Such a system would exist in contrast to the current, largely anarchic, system, which is based primarily on military and economic power relationships among states and only secondarily on cooperation and international law.

In practice, however, the United States would have to share international power with others in this new world order and to suppress its historic foreign policy unilateralism in favor of multilateralism and respect for the opinions of other international actors. In many ways, the new world order would demand the subordination of narrow U.S. interests and initiatives in favor of collective interests and action. The new world order would also require American policy makers to participate more genuinely in the activities of international organizations rather than usually trying to manipulate the organizations to take actions that favor American interests.

American adherence to what Bush envisioned remained uncertain. Bush himself was a traditionalist who, one conservative columnist wrote with some accuracy, had a "preference for any established order abroad . . . [a] preference for order before freedom."[63] That view was echoed by another conservative analyst who argued that the Bush "administration prefers dictators to democrats [because] for Bush the central value of the New World Order is order. Empires are better at it than newborn democracies. . . . Dictators are better at it than democrats."[64]

President Clinton's commitment to moving toward a new world order has been mixed. During his presidential election effort and his first year as president, Clinton seemed to lean toward change. He faulted President Bush for his "eagerness to defend potentates and dictators," and for having a "nostalgic" wish "for a world of times past," dominated by what "is sometimes described as power politics, to distinguish it from what some contend is sentimentalism and idealism [in] foreign policy."[65] And as president, Clinton has sought frequently to support the UN and to obtain UN support for U.S. policy preferences. Whatever Clinton's instincts, however, U.S. support of multilateralism was diminished by the Republican legislative victory in 1994. The House GOP's "Contract with America" would, for example, truncate U.S. support of multilateral UN peacekeeping efforts by banning U.S. troops from serving in such an effort under a commander from another UN country and also by slashing U.S. financial support. During his June 1995 meeting with the other G-7 leaders in Canada, President Clinton was clearly ill at ease because of his inability at that point to assure them that the United States would help pay for (much less participate in) an increase in French and British (UN) forces in Bosnia to prevent a recurrence of the hostage-taking of UN peacekeepers that the Bosnian Serbs had perpetrated a few weeks earlier. The other leaders at the conference were mostly diplomatic about the American step back from the world stage. Prime Minister of Great Britain John Major, for instance, commented that "I think practicing politicians sitting around the table [here at the G-7 summit] know there are frustrations that inhibit them from doing what they most want to do."[66] Still, a more accurate sense may well have been reflected in the candid comment of one Canadian diplomat attending the meeting that "the Europeans and Japanese don't take [Clinton] seriously anymore." Or, as the *Toronto Globe* put it a bit more moderately, events have shown "Again and again that [Clinton] is a diminished leader."[67]

Certainly the United States shares common interests with its allies and with the global village. The question is whether Americans are really willing to share decision making with the Europeans, the Japanese, and others on issues that affect American concerns. Even more broadly, will the United States follow the decisions of global will as expressed in the United Nations when that will runs counter to American wishes? Many observers doubt that American exceptionalism and messianism—to be discussed in detail in the next chapter—will permit the country to share leadership gracefully. Americans have traditionally believed their country to be the city on the hill, providing an ideal of democracy and liberty for all to emulate. More recently, Americans have also become used to being king of the hill—or a least their bipolar half of it. Some people, especially in other countries, suspect that residual racism will inhibit Americans' willingness to share leadership with Africans, Arabs, Asians, and others. One doubtful Japanese foreign ministry official observed that "the American approach to Japan comes across as an attempt to create a spiritual colony of the United States on Japanese soil."[68] So ultimately, the characteristics of continued U.S. power in the world depend in part on the country's willingness to move beyond its traditional status quo orientation. The new world order would be very different from the cold war international system. That system was familiar and was led by the United States. And while it was not always conflict free, some feel that Americans will soon miss the days of a bipolar world (Mearsheimer, 1990). Nonetheless, bipolarity is gone at least for the moment, and this forces the United States to struggle with its status quo tradition in a non-status quo international system.

SUMMARY

1. Over the past 40 years the international system has changed from a bipolar world to more of a multipolar world. The fall of the Soviet Union and the peaceful democratic revolutions in Eastern Europe were stark representations of this changing system. But even before the fall of the Soviet Union in 1989, the changing system was manifesting itself in American foreign policy in Nixon's opening to China in the 1970s and increasing tensions with American allies during the 1970s and 1980s.

2. The Nixon administration used the policy of détente to encourage Soviet cooperation in a variety of policy areas. Kissinger's détente policy sought to elicit Soviet cooperation by offering a number of carrots (such as sales of grain) and linking those carrots to Soviet cooperative efforts in other policy areas, such as conflicts in the less developed countries.

3. In response to the Soviet invasion of Afghanistan, President Carter enunciated the Carter Doctrine, which explicitly put the Soviets on notice that the Persian Gulf was a strategic American interest and the United States would protect it militarily if required. The change in Carter's approach to the Soviet Union was more generally a result of the increasing disillusionment with détente in the United States in the late 1970s.

4. The early 1980s witnessed a reversion to cold war bipolar politics with the election of Ronald Reagan. As part of his hard-line anticommunist stance, Reagan defined the Reagan Doctrine as an American pledge to supply anticommunist forces throughout the world.

5. The 1990s produced dramatic changes, as U.S. leaders and citizens tried to adjust to an international system largely freed from cold war rivalries. The new challenges facing the United States are increasingly economic, political, and military situations, which arise on a regional basis and for which there are no clear blueprints to guide actions.

Chapter Four

POLITICAL CULTURE: THE DOMESTIC SETTING

I'm a yankee doodle dandy, a yankee doodle do or die" goes the famous lyric by George M. Cohan, "a real, live nephew [or, presumably, niece] of my Uncle Sam, born on the 4th of July." The sentiment is corny, but Cohan's musical ditty reflects the cultural distinctiveness and the patriotism that most Americans feel. By extension, it also touches on the fact that to a significant degree the way that Americans conduct themselves politically is culturally based (Payne, 1995; Bartels, 1994; Neuman, Just, & Crigler, 1992). There are differing estimations of political culture's impact on policy, with some scholars believing that political culture "has often been more important in shaping American foreign policy than external realities" (Dallek, 1983:283).[1]

UNDERSTANDING
POLITICAL CULTURE

The concept of **political culture** begins with the fact that individuals differ from one another socially and politically because of the variety of circumstances in which they grew up and live: variations such as what they were taught by their parents, and the other experiences and contacts that have shaped their individual lives. Similarly, collections of individuals in societies are also products of their past (Bruening, 1995; Hudson, 1995). Historical experiences, traditional ways of looking at the world, long-standing norms, and so on provide the mental "map" or "software" that a society uses to interpret political reality (Henrikson, 1991; Hofstede, 1991). What this means is that any society, including the American people, shares at least some common values (norms) about what is good and bad. A nation also shares many perceptions (mental images) about itself and others (Said, 1993). These core values and perceptions combine to form a nation's distinct political culture (Bathurst, 1993). All political cultures differ at least somewhat. Therefore, insofar as the political culture of Americans is unique because of the American experience, then American political culture provides a distinct setting that helps shape U.S. foreign policy (Citrin, Haas, Mute, & Reingold, 1994).

Before detailing how U.S. foreign policy reflects American political culture, a few qualifiers are necessary. One is that political culture should not be confused with the idea of innate national character, which does not exist. Political culture is learned. A second caveat is that political culture is about the way the "average American" feels. You, of course, may find that you do not share some of the values and perceptions discussed in the following pages. That does not invalidate the concept of political culture because what is being discussed is how most Americans feel most of the time, and not—to paraphrase Abraham Lincoln—how all of the people feel all of the time.

Third, political culture changes, although usually slowly. Events are one factor that shifts cultural attitudes. We will see, for example, that important shifts have occurred during the last two decades. The war in Vietnam marked an important turning point in some cultural attitudes. Some changes had to do with the experience of the war itself (Engelhardt, 1995). Other shifts came from vastly increased cultural contacts, economic interdependence, and other dramatic alterations in the way people and countries interact that have occurred in the last two decades (Gurr & Harff, 1994; Gottlieb, 1993). Therefore, many of the aspects of political culture discussed below will be divided into early and recent sections demarcated by the war in Vietnam.

Fourth, any single element of political culture is but one piece in the vast puzzle of foreign policy making. The various elements of political culture interact with one another and with the many other influential factors that will be discussed throughout this book. Sometimes political culture elements reinforce each other. At other times, elements of political culture clash with each other. There is, for example, a long and strong strain of isolationism among Americans. There is also a long history of expansionism that carried Americans outward from the Atlantic seaboard's 13 colonies, across the continent to the Pacific, then outward into the Pacific Ocean, the Caribbean Sea, and eventually to the far reaches of the world.

With these four qualifiers in mind, what is it that we should look for in describing American political culture? The answer, one scholar writes, is to seek "a relatively coherent, emotionally charged, and conceptually interlocking set of . . . core foreign-policy ideas [that] reflect the self-image of those who espoused them and to define a relationship with the world [that is] consonant with that self-image" (Hunt, 1987:14). These ideas or images create various visions for Americans: who they are and what they value; who others are or should be culturally and how to relate to them; the degree to which Americans are part of and should involve themselves in the international system. These images are the cultural setting of American foreign policy because, another analyst comments, when values have been a strong component of foreign policy, then "outcomes, even unpleasant ones, [have] always mattered less than the vision" (Vlahos, 1991:64). To explore these visions, we will adopt three major classifications of images: (1) Americans' self-image and their values; (2) Americans' images of and interaction with others; and (3) Americans' images of the proper U.S. role in the world.

THE AMERICAN SELF-IMAGE AND VALUES

The first set of perceptions and values that influence U.S. foreign policy is based on how Americans view themselves and on the norms that are central to the American "way of life." First we will deal with exceptionalism, that is, how Americans see themselves and their political system. Then we will turn to American norms, including moralism and liberalism.

Exceptionalism

Americans have been and remain self-assured that they, as a people, and their political culture are admirable and unique. This is termed **American exceptionalism**—the notion that the United States is not just different from, but is better than, other countries (Brilmayer, 1994). This sense of superiority can be traced back to the first European colonists in the New World. They found a land of incredible physical bounty. The new settlers were apt to view this natural cornucopia as a gift from God. Many Americans believed themselves to be the new chosen people in a modern land of milk and honey. There was, of course, a native population. But like the Canaanites of the first land of milk and honey, the existing population was soon subjected to the newcomers' vision of a greater good (DeConde, 1992).

The success that Americans had subduing the native population, surviving a civil war between North and South, securing the continent, and establishing a prosperous and democratic nation all served to reinforce the sense of exceptionalism. With all this in place by the end of the 1800s, Americans turned their view outward, convinced that they were destined to bring the assumed bounties of the exceptional American way of life to others. In accordance with a spirit of messianism discussed below, Americans justified the Spanish-American War and World War I partly in terms of bringing the benefits of American ideals and institutions to others. World War II and the Korean War were, similarly, partly perceived by Americans as defensive reactions to assaults on American political values by antithetical ideologies, Nazism, and Communism, respectively. American resistance to and ultimate triumph over such evils were to be expected.

More recently, the years since the Vietnam War have slightly weakened the American sense of exceptionalism. The loss in Vietnam, the Watergate scandal and

Margaret Scott, *Hartford Courant*

A sense of American exceptionalism is one aspect of political culture that influences the nature of U.S. foreign policy. This drawing depicts a number of symbols of Americans' pride in their history, in themselves as a people, and in their democratic government. The stars and stripes, the Statue of Liberty, the signers of the Declaration of Independence and the Constitution, and Uncle Sam himself (not to mention the apple pie he is carrying) are all part of the image that Americans have of themselves and their country. This sense of exceptionalism joins with messianism, paternalism, and other aspects of American political culture, disposing many Americans to judge other people and countries by how closely they conform to the "American way." Americans also often try to convert others to becoming more like themselves.

other disclosures of government abuse, economic woes, the holding of U.S. hostages by Iran, and other events all sapped American self-assurance in the 1970s.

The passage of time, however, and the swaggering presidency of Ronald Reagan helped restore in the 1980s some of Americans' former soaring sense of exceptionalism. He assured Americans that "this anointed land was set apart in an uncommon way, [by a] divine plan [for] people from every corner of the earth who have a special love of faith and freedom" (Lundestad, 1990:17). Self-assurance soon got an even greater boost from the military victory in the Persian Gulf War and the decline of the Soviet Union and its sphere of influence. Some of the strength of this attitude is evident in Figure 4.1, which shows the high percentages of Americans who say they are proud to be an American, who consider themselves very patriotic, who believe that the United States has the best system of government in the world, and who say they would rather live in the United States than anywhere else in the world. There is also evidence that nationalism remains strong among supposedly disaffected young Americans (Bruner et al., 1993). Thus, the sense of American exceptionalism is likely to persist (Lind, 1995).

Moralism

The exceptionalist view of America also engendered a moralistic bent among Americans (Johnston, 1995). Early American political culture was strongly influenced by the Puritans and other strict Protestant denominations that evolved from the stern Calvinist tradition of Switzerland. These Protestants believed they were among the "elect" who had been given the opportunity to create a new type of society in America, a kingdom of God where actions were based on righteousness rather than on power politics, or realpolitik. They also believed that European governments were driven by immoral expediency and that only Americans could be relied on to do the right thing. This tradition spawned the American penchant for political **moralism**, or the need to justify political agendas and actions in moral terms and to judge outcomes against a set of values. As Henry Kissinger has observed, "Americans have never been comfortable acknowledging openly their own selfish interests. Whether fighting world wars or local conflicts, U.S. leaders [have] always claimed to be struggling in the name of principle, not interest."[2] As such, moral considerations and arguments have sometimes been a cause of U.S. policy. At other times they have been merely a

FIGURE 4.1   American Patriotic Attitudes

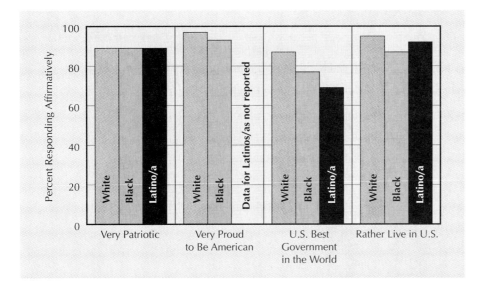

Data source: *The Public Perspective,* March/April 1992, pp. 8–9.

Americans believe that their country is exceptional. This figure shows that across demographic groups Americans are strongly attached to their country and believe it to be the best.

rationalization to make self-interested U.S. policies more palatable domestically (Bril-mayer, 1994; McElroy, 1992). There were and are, for instance, many pragmatic reasons for helping people in economically less fortunate countries. Yet selling the idea of foreign assistance to the American public was easier when using rhetoric, such as President John F. Kennedy's reference to the *Divine Comedy* to warn listeners that "Dante once said that the hottest places in hell are reserved for those who in a period of moral crisis maintain their neutrality."[3]

The Vietnam War affected American moralism in two ways. One was to assault Americans' sense of their own morality. Early critics charged that U.S. intervention in Vietnam was immoral. They saw the war in Vietnam as a civil conflict and rejected the U.S. official rationale that the war was necessary to contain communism. Dissenters also were appalled by a superpower assaulting a small, less developed country. As the war dragged on, television starkly brought home the morality issue to more and more Americans. Graphic images from Vietnam not only portrayed the death and suffering of American soldiers; television also brought pictures of the suffering and death that the war, including the action of U.S. forces, inflicted on defenseless civilians throughout the Indochina region.

Second, Americans had morally justified a great many dubious practices in the name of the crusade against atheistic, totalitarian communism. After Vietnam, a combination of their own spiritual exhaustion and the ebbing of the bipolar world left Americans less convinced that communism (as distinct from the Soviet Union) was either threatening or an unmitigated evil.

The moral backlash manifested itself in several ways. First, the practice of overt or covert intervention in other countries became less acceptable to many Americans.

The Central Intelligence Agency (CIA) came under particular scrutiny and was criticized widely for having masterminded the Phoenix project, which led to the assassination of perhaps 20,000 South Vietnamese communist rebel leaders, for the agency's involvement in plotting that led to the overthrow and assassination of Chile's elected leftist president Salvador Allende in 1973, and for other unsavory or illegal activities (Andrew, 1995; Merrill, 1994; Reisman & Baker, 1992). There was also considerable domestic opposition to using subversion to overthrow the Sandinistas' leftist government in Nicaragua.

It can also be said, however, that public opinion about subversion is selective. There was little opposition, for example, to the CIA's program to smuggle weapons to resistance forces after the Soviets invaded Afghanistan in 1979. More recently, a 1994 survey found that more Americans favored than opposed using covert operations to try to weaken or overthrow unfriendly governments (Rielly, 1995).

Since Vietnam there have been only a few foreign concerns that have excited American moral fervor (Gamson, 1992). The Iran hostage crisis (1979–1980) is one of the events that outraged the American public. The televised images of blindfolded Americans being led from the embassy in Tehran and jostled by angry Iranian crowds, the pictures of Iranians burning the American flag, and the characterization of the United States as the "Great Satan" by Iran's leader, the Ayatollah Khomeini, created a sense of frustrated moral anger. Almost all the American hostages were private citizens, which intensified the American reaction. The most notable example of moral fervor resulted from the widespread characterization of Saddam Hussein as an Arab Hitler, outrage over Iraq's holding foreigners hostage, and horror over the Iraqi army's brutal treatment of the Kuwaitis. As it turned out, these images were somewhat overdrawn and were orchestrated in part to galvanize American support for action. Americans, for example, were horrified by the testimony of a Kuwaiti teenager, identified only as Nayirah. She told Congress and the cameras that before escaping from Kuwait she had seen Iraqi soldiers take Kuwaiti babies from incubators and leave the infants on the floor to die. Later investigation showed the story to be almost surely false; the mysterious teenager turned out to be Nayirah al-Sabah, a relative of the emir of Kuwait and the daughter of the country's ambassador to the United States.[4] Regardless of the truthfulness of these images, they helped contribute to a public moral fervor in support of American participation in the war. There was a vigorous postwar debate among intellectuals about the war's morality (Campbell, 1993a; DeCosse, 1992; Geyer & Green, 1992; Fox, 1991; Johnson & Weigel, 1991). That did not change the mind of the average American, though, with 67 percent of all Americans believing retrospectively that the Persian Gulf War was a just war (Richman, 1995).

Liberalism

The dominant American political ideology of liberalism is intimately connected to the twin themes of moralism and idealism. This is *not* the same liberalism as the contemporary stance of Democrats who favor increased levels of government involvement in society. Indeed, classic liberalism is, in some ways, quite the opposite. Based in part on the writings of English political philosopher John Locke, especially his *Two Treatises on Civil Government* (1689), classic **liberalism** involves the belief in or commitment "to individual liberty and the protection of private property; to limited government, the rule of law, natural rights, the perfectibility of human institutions, and to the possibility of human progress" (Dumbrell, 1990:6). The impact of these Lockean themes on U.S. foreign policy can be seen by examining individual rights and democracy, capitalism, and legalism.

Individual Rights and Democracy

The Declaration of Independence proclaimed that all people are "endowed with certain unalienable rights" including "liberty." The notion that the rights of the individual supersede the rights of the government was, and in many countries remains, a revolutionary idea. The Constitution's Bill of Rights seeks to guarantee these principles. In fact, most elements of the liberal political ideology are so widely held in American political culture that most Americans take them for granted and deny that they think in ideological terms at all.

Early Human Rights and Democracy   One way that liberalism has affected U.S. foreign policy is to create American antagonism toward authoritarian governments that oppress the civil rights and liberties of others (Smith, 1994). Part of Woodrow Wilson's decision to intervene repeatedly in Mexico and various Caribbean countries was based on his determination, as he said about Haiti in 1916, "to insist on constitutional government there" and to "see that a real government is elected which we can support" (Dallek, 1983:67). Decades later, this sentiment helped to motivate the anticommunist impulse. As Secretary of State John Foster Dulles told Congress in 1953, the "enslaved" people in communist countries "deserve to be free." Americans, therefore, "must always have in mind the liberation of these captive people" (Graebner, 1964:805). Yet, anticommunism also seemingly gave license for American policy makers to ignore the abuses of rightist anticommunist dictators. While most cold war–era presidents may not have condoned dictatorships, they often preferred a friendly authoritarian rightist regime to an unfriendly totalitarian communist regime. That principle guided American foreign policy for much of the cold war period.

Recent Human Rights and Democracy   Americans continue to believe in the principle of individual rights and **democracy** and to judge others by American standards (Smith, 1994). In addition to the strong degree to which Americans value democracy as a concept, there is also the more pragmatic assumption by American leaders and others that there is a connection between a government that is democratic and one that is stable and friendly. "We ought to be promoting the democratic impulses around the world," Bill Clinton has commented; "Democracies are our partners. They don't go to war with each other. They're reliable friends in the future."[5] That belief is one of the motives behind Clinton's support of foreign aid for Russia. As he put it, American efforts to "enhance our own security and prosperity . . . lie with Russian reform and with Russian reformers like Boris Yeltsin." Lest anyone underestimate the stakes, Clinton went on to worry about Yugoslavia-like strife "in a nation [Russia] spanning 11 time zones and armed with a vast arsenal of nuclear weapons."[6] The belief that democracies are friendlier also helped shape Clinton's decision to use force if necessary to overthrow Haiti's military junta. "History has taught us that preserving democracy in our own hemisphere strengthens American security and prosperity," the president told Americans during a nationally televised address.[7]

Americans give liberal ideals strong rhetorical support. Presidents Jimmy Carter and Bill Clinton both spoke strongly in favor of such goals, but both found that as president they often had to compromise their ideals to world realities. Symbolizing their shared orientation, former president Carter and future president Clinton are seen here in August 1992 working together in Atlanta, Georgia, to construct low-income housing as part of the Habitat for Humanity program.

There are also supporters of liberal policies who contend that promoting human rights and democracy strengthens the United States because "the attraction of [others to] democratic ideals has created a pro-American public opinion in many countries." These advocates concede that "the enduring worldwide identification of the United States with the cause of human liberty and of responsible human democratic government may rest on imperfect historical foundations." Nevertheless, the proponents of international liberalism assert, American ideals are "a real force in world affairs and an asset that other countries have sought and failed to acquire" (Mead, 1995:16).

Despite the place of **human rights** and democracy in the American values system, the application of these standards to U.S. foreign policy has remained mixed. Studies of U.S. foreign aid extending back into the cold war years reveal only a limited relationship between a positive human rights record in a country and whether or not it receives U.S. aid (Hook, 1995; Poe, 1990). This inconsistency relates in part to the double standard that led to supporting anticommunist governments even if they were oppressive. Also, the closer that support of the democratic ideal brings Americans to a foreign intervention, the less support there is. A 1993 poll found, for instance, that 77 percent of Americans thought it was important to promote and defend human rights in other countries (Waller & Ide, 1995). Contrast this, though, to a 1994 poll that found only 26 percent of Americans would agree that "helping to bring a democratic form of government to other countries" should be a "very important" U.S. foreign policy goal (Rielly, 1995:82). In an even more direct situation, a majority of Americans opposed the U.S. intervention in Haiti to restore democracy or for any other reason. Thus Americans support human rights but are loath to use force to implement them.

Some analysts even dismiss American support of human rights and democracy as mere rhetorical window dressing. Certainly, all presidents have regularly turned a blind eye to abuses. President Carter was the most sincere of all post–Vietnam era presidents about human rights issues. Yet he ignored these concerns in Iran, South Korea, and elsewhere when U.S. strategic interests argued for the support of an oppressive regime. President Reagan condemned the abuses of left-wing governments, such as Nicaragua's, while ignoring them in El Salvador and other places that had rightist regimes. The practice of the Bush administration was similar, with much more interest in strategic factors in China and elsewhere than in the human and political rights records of these governments. Clinton took a strong stand on a number of human rights issues during the 1992 presidential campaign. Presidents, however, often find themselves less willing once in office to act strongly on democractic and human rights issues than they once thought they would be. Clinton has not been an exception, as the box on pages 98–99 shows.

Still, those who dismiss the American wish to support democracy and human rights as mere window dressing would be wrong (Lumsdaine, 1993). Such standards seldom are the only reason for policy, but they are regularly part of the policy debate. The United States did intervene in Haiti in part to restore democracy and end the abuses there. "I know that the United States cannot, indeed we should not be the world's policeman," Clinton reasoned about his threat to invade Haiti. "But when brutality occurs close to our shore . . . we have a responsibility to act."[8] Liberal instincts have also continued to be a part of U.S. relations with Beijing and Moscow. The Clinton administration has downplayed human rights abuses in China and has continued its most-favored-nation (MFN) trade status, but criticism of that country persists. The State Department's own 1994 annual human rights report, for one, detailed what it characterized as continuing "widespread and well-documented human rights abuses in China, in violation of internationally accepted norms, stemming both from the authorities' intolerance of dissent and the inadequacy of legal safeguards for freedom of speech, association, and religion."[9] Given this record, Clinton has been embarrassed by the image, one diplomat said, that China took advantage of the president, "just pocketed" the MFN renewal, and reneged on its human rights pledges.[10] With 62 percent of Americans saying that encouraging human rights in China was more important than trade, as one 1994 poll found, and 60 percent saying that the United States should require China to show more progress before renewing MFN, the president is vulnerable to political attack on the issue.[11]

Such considerations are also part of the debate over U.S. relations with Russia. The criticism that Clinton received for visiting Moscow in May 1995 amid the brutal suppression of the revolt in Chechnya led the president to support a resolution by the G-7 leaders during their June summit meeting in Canada that called on Russia to use negotiations, not force, to settle the dispute. That precipitated such an apoplectic, 10-minute outburst by Russia's president, who was present at the meeting, that Senator Robert Dole (R-KS) commented incredulously, "I thought I was watching *Saturday Night Live,* but it turned out to be Boris Yeltsin."[12]

It is also important to note that the distance between human rights rhetoric and U.S. foreign policy practice rests partly on the slowly growing American cognizance of differences in cultural values found in the world (Kaufman, 1991). Americans, for example, emphasize individual rights (as compared to communal values) much more than do many other societies. As one study noted, "The United States has painfully discovered that American and international versions of human rights are not the same" (Forsythe, 1990:435).

Capitalism

Also synonymous with U.S. political culture is the belief in *laissez-faire* capitalism, which like liberalism focuses on the free will of the individual. The identification of **capitalism** with American growth and prosperity dates back to the age of industrialization and the widespread acceptance of the belief that "private property, profit,

Bill Clinton: Liberal Candidate, Pragmatic President

More than any other single approach, a stress on the liberal values of promoting democracy and human rights characterized the effort of presidential candidate Bill Clinton to distinguish his foreign policy views from those of President George Bush. Addressing the Los Angeles World Affairs Council, Clinton accused Bush of having "abdicated leadership" in the world in an attempt to "prop up yesterday's status quo." Rhetorically circumnavigating the globe, Clinton told his listeners,

> From the Baltics to Beijing, from Sarajevo to South Africa, President [Bush] has sided with the status quo instead of democratic change, with familiar tyrants rather than those who would overthrow them—and with the old geography of repression rather than with the new map of freedom.[1]

Clinton promised that he would "assert a new vision for our [U.S.] role in the world" and would "summon all of our strengths, our economic power, our values and—when necessary—our military might in the service of our new vision." He called for "a response to Serbian aggression in Bosnia"[2] and said that the United States should "take the lead in seeking UN Security Council authorization for air strikes" against the forces besieging the Bosnian Muslims.[3] Clinton also attacked Bush's policy toward China, declaring that "our nation has a higher purpose than to coddle dictators and to stand aside from the global movements toward democracy."[4]

Closer to home, Clinton said that the refusal of the Bush administration to allow Haitian boat people into the United States was "cruel" and violated U.S. political asylum laws.[5] Clinton carried his liberal view of U.S. policy to the steps of the Capitol, where he delivered his inaugural address. He pledged to use U.S. diplomacy and force, if necessary, to act not only "when our vital interests are challenged," but also when "the will and conscience of the international community is defied." The new president's suggestion that American power might be applied to future conflicts on behalf of such ideals led one columnist to wonder if a new "Clinton Doctrine" existed.[6]

Despite such clarion calls, Clinton soon tempered his idealistic campaign positions with presidential pragmatism. On the campaign trail, Clinton called for significant defense spending cuts; in the White House Clinton has not departed radically from the plans of the Bush Administration with regard to defense spending levels and the structure of U.S. military forces (Davis, 1995). Candidate Clinton may have campaigned for U.S. support of Bosnian independence, but President Clinton eventually agreed, in the peace plan signed in Dayton, Ohio, to the de facto partition of Bosnia into two semiautonomous parts.

and the free market were the keys to ensuring the happiness of people by providing them with abundance" (Spanier & Hook, 1995:13).

The belief in capitalism reinforces the American emphasis on trade discussed in chapters 2 and 3 and has a marked impact on U.S. policy. One ramification is that capitalism is antithetical to communism, and that helped define the Soviet Union, China, and other communist countries as alien and threatening, especially during the height of the cold war. Even democracies like India that practice variations of mild socialism were suspect during this period. Furthermore, American faith in capitalism combined with U.S. economic dominance after World War II to help shape many of the international economic agreements and organizations, such as the IMF and the GATT, that continue to regulate the global economy.

All the post–Vietnam era administrations, especially those of presidents Reagan and Bush, have promoted capitalism and, by extension, liberal economic practices.

In another shift, Clinton laid aside his campaign stridency about China and the renewal of its most-favored-nation (MFN) trade status. The prediction of a German diplomat that "if Clinton tries to make the Chinese pariahs, it will only mean the American influence in Beijing will diminish" seemed reasonable to now-president Clinton.[7] He renewed China's MFN status in June 1993. The following year, Clinton not only renewed China's MFN status, he "delinked" trade from China's human rights policy. The pragmatic reality, then, is that U.S.–China relations have continued largely as they had during the belabored Bush administration. "Universal principles of freedom and human rights belong to all, the peoples of Asia no less than others," proclaimed Assistant Secretary of State Winston Lord. But, he explained with pragmatic mitigation, "We must weigh geopolitical, economic and other factors" in making a policy decision on China.[8]

Clinton also continued Bush's policy of either returning Haitian refugees to their country or interning them at the U.S. naval base at Guantanamo Bay, Cuba. "Maybe I was too harsh in my criticism" of President Bush, Clinton said when a reporter asked him to explain his about-face.[9] Clinton then went to court to support his predecessor's policy. When a suit to end the ban on Haitian immigration that had been originally brought against the Bush administration reached the Supreme Court in March 1993, it was Clinton's deputy solicitor-general, Maureen Mahoney, who defended the government's policy and, who, compounding the irony, told the court, "The President is determined that in order to prevent a mass migration . . . a policy of direct repatriation [of refugees to Haiti] must continue."[10] As Stanley Hoffman (1995:159) summarized Clinton's first two years in office, "pragmatism is more visible than Wilsonianism."

Certainly Clinton abandoned some liberal positions that he took as a candidate. It is also true, though, that his leanings toward international liberalism resemble those of Jimmy Carter and are the strongest in the White House since Carter's term. On several instances, Clinton did exert pressure to support democracy. With Carter's help, he negotiated the removal of the top generals from Haiti and the return to power of democratically elected President Jean-Bertrand Aristide.[11] Among other actions, he used diplomatic pressure to oppose the attempt of the president of Honduras to disband the legislature, and to press the military leader of Nigeria to surrender power. After years of wavering, Clinton declared he would "do the right thing" and announced in November 1995 that he was ordering U.S. troops into Bosnia. Still, as Carter did and as most new presidents do, Clinton learned that the world, presidential responsibility, and prudent policy look very different when seated in the Oval Office from how they appear

The governments of the once-communist countries in Eastern Europe and the former Soviet Union have been encouraged to practice "shock capitalism," a process of freeing up prices and markets quickly. To a degree, U.S. aid and willingness to support these countries for membership in such international financial institutions as the IMF have depended on how quickly and completely the governments adopted capitalism. The Bush administration, for example, forgave over half of Poland's debt to the U.S. government as a reward for market reforms.

The policy of promoting shock capitalism, predictably, created shocks. Whatever the long-term benefits, the short-term impact was to send many of the former countries into near economic chaos and to undermine political stability (Murrell, 1992). In part because of the economic dislocation caused by the shift from socialism to capitalism, industrial output in Russia and other former communist countries dropped sharply, unemployment soared, and inflation reached hypervelocity. Domestic political

100

CHAPTER 4
Political
Culture:
The Domestic
Setting

opposition to the new democratic regimes mounted. That left Russian president Boris Yeltsin, for one, hanging "by a thread," according to one expert (Mandelbaum, 1993:19). The West was especially alarmed by the elections in Russia in December 1993 that gave the neofascist Liberal Democratic Party (LDP), headed by Vladimir V. Zhirinovsky, the largest number of seats in Russia's parliament, the Duma. Faced with such realities, the United States and other countries have eased up on their demands for quick conversion to capitalism, and aid began to flow to Russia and other such countries with less stringent requirements for economic reform. The most recent elections in December 1995 reduced the LDP's representation in the Duma, but the first place finish of the resurgent Communist Party left future U.S.–Russian relations up in the air.

Legalism

Another trait of American political culture and values based on the principles of liberalism espoused by Locke is an emphasis on the rule of law. This is **legalism**, an orientation that emphasizes organizations, rules, agreements, procedures, and other such formal structures to judge and govern conduct. Americans are one of the world's most legalistic people. There were in 1993 some 864,000 lawyers in the United States (a 27 percent increase since 1987 alone), and with 5 percent of the world's population, the United States has nearly 70 percent of its lawyers!

Legalism influences U.S. foreign policy in many ways. Many U.S. political leaders and diplomats are attorneys, and their training and mind-set carry over from their law offices to their public positions. Secretary of State Warren Christopher, for example, is a man of distinction, but no one suggested that he brought a grand world vision to office. "He's a lawyer's lawyer, a case-by-case man," a former colleague in government said; Christopher practices "diplomacy as though it were a contract that needed a bit more work before it was ready for a signature," a critic commented.[13] Even the secretary's assistants are boggled by his precision. One aide tells of Christopher's approach to the bowl of M&Ms frequently found on Air Force One. Most people grab a handful of the small candies; but not Christopher. According to the aide, he takes just one, places it on his yellow legal pad on the conference table, where the M&M "just lies there and wobbles for the longest time until you wonder, 'Is he going to eat it with a knife and fork?' Finally the secretary of state consumes the bit of candy and returns to work, making Christopher one of the few people "who really eats just *one* M&M," the aide concluded wonderingly.[14]

The legalistic approach is common among Americans, who tend to rely on laws, treaties, and other legal documents far more than do most other nations. There is, diplomat and scholar George Kennan (1951:44) noted, a "pronounced American tendency to transplant legal concepts from the domestic to the international field: to believe that international society could—and should—operate on the basis of general contractual obligations."

Since many other societies do not stress the rule of law so strongly, the American emphasis on legalism can get in the way of resolving international problems effectively. From the 1940s on, the United States has placed a great deal of emphasis on working toward relatively free trade through agreements and organizations like GATT. While much of the groundwork for these efforts was being laid at the end of World War II, U.S. negotiator Dean Acheson (1969:83) remembered his British counterpart, the famous economist John Maynard Keynes, complaining that the United States was "a lawyer-ridden land," and expressing the belief that "the *Mayflower* . . . must have been entirely filled with lawyers." Economic relations are, of course, very political and not just contractual, and the U.S. legalistic approach to such issues has helped cause friction when, perhaps, a less strict insistence on living up to the letter of the law might have eased tensions.

Legalism also sometimes causes Americans to confuse superficial process for substance. When Americans evaluate another country's political system, for instance, they tend to stress such procedural matters as elections and to ignore equality and other substantive concerns. Senate Foreign Relations Committee chairman J. William Fulbright (1964:67) cogently observed that Americans "are inclined to confuse freedom and democracy, which [are] moral principles," with the way the American system works, that is, "with capitalism, federalism, and the two-party system, which are not moral principles but simply the preferred and accepted practices of the American peoples."

As in all the areas of political culture, Americans are prone to tempering legalism when circumstances dictate. Recent presidents have been less than enthusiastic about some legalistic solutions proposed by others. Reagan, for example, refused to have the United States appear before the UN–affiliated International Court of Justice (ICJ) in a case brought by Nicaragua alleging U.S. aggression. When the ICJ heard the case anyway and found against the United States, President Reagan rejected the court's findings as an intrusion on U.S. sovereignty.

There are some important points to reiterate before leaving this discussion of how Americans perceive themselves and their country and before turning to how they view other people. One point is that any single aspect of political culture, even all of political culture, is just a part of what motivates U.S. foreign policy. Aspects of political culture—idealism and pragmatism, for instance—sometimes clash with one another or with other forces, such as economic interests, in U.S. policy making. Thus political culture provides just one clue as to what prompts policy. What one might expect as policy, given American political culture, and what occurs may be at odds also because of the complexity of the factors that determine U.S. foreign policy. Second, keep in mind that political culture is dynamic. As a measure of what most Americans feel most of the time, political culture evolves with time and as the population changes. As the country moves into the twenty-first century, the American self-image will continue to evolve (Kennedy, 1993). The growing multicultural nature of the population and the changing political power structure resulting from the empowerment of African Americans, Latin Americans, Asian Americans, and others—will alter political culture as the perceptions of each of these cultural groups are woven into the fabric of the American self-image.

AMERICAN IMAGES OF AND INTERACTION WITH OTHERS

Having completed our review of how Americans see themselves and what their values are, we can turn to a second vision, or set of images, that Americans have. These images center on how Americans have historically viewed and related to other countries and cultures. These perceptions are another product of the nation's political culture that influences U.S. foreign policy. The U.S. historical and cultural experience has helped shape five interrelated attitudes that determine the American view of others. First we will discuss messianism, the urge to spread American values around the world. Then we will take up a series of

102

CHAPTER 4
Political
Culture:
The Domestic
Setting

specific and often contradictory impulses. Idealism is at the positive end of the spectrum of American attitudes. Racism is at the negative end. Pragmatism serves, for good or ill, to mute American messianism.

Messianism

American exceptionalism and the norms of moralism and liberalism combine to create a fourth trait of American political culture: **messianism**. There is a missionary urge to remake the world in the American image, to ensure that other societies "increasingly come to resemble the U.S. model" based on the idea that American values and institutions are the "best for all nations" (Cingranelli, 1993:9). Even if that were true, messianism has also created a paternalistic element in U.S. policy. This causes the United States sometimes to feel at liberty to act like a strict, well-meaning parent: telling others what is good for them and seeing that they do it—whether they like it or not. In this sense, Americans are apt to see themselves as wise counselors. Others often perceive Americans as condescending bullies who are guilty of **cultural imperialism**—the imposition of your cultural values and way of life on others.

Proclamations of the American mission predate the republic. "We [Americans] have it in our power," Thomas Paine wrote in *Common Sense* (1776), "to begin the world over again" based on principles of liberty and equality (Clark, 1990). During the nineteenth century, Americans generally focused this mission inward. A member of Congress remarked in 1812 that "it appears that the Author of Nature has marked our limits in the south by the Gulf of Mexico, and on the north by the regions of the eternal frost" (Cingranelli, 1993:92). In 1845, newspaperman John L. O'Sullivan boldly asserted that Americans had a "manifest destiny to overspread the continent allotted by Providence" (LaFeber, 1989:91). The **Manifest Destiny** doctrine was used to justify the physical and cultural conquest of much of the North American continent and its Native Americans, Mexicans, people of French heritage, and others. Americans rarely considered the thought that others might object to American values being imposed on them.

Early International Messianism

Once the continent was largely settled, those who wished to spread the American way of life turned their gaze beyond U.S. borders. This orientation began in the 1890s and was sometimes called the "new manifest destiny." There was a debate, however. What was the best way to project American values outward? The answer has long divided Americans into two camps: those who favor passive messianism and those who favor active messianism (Muravchik, 1992).

Passive messianism is based on the idea that the best way to convert others to the American way is to be so righteous that others will voluntarily follow and emulate Americans. This is sometimes called the "city on the hill" approach, a concept expressed in a lay sermon delivered in 1630 by Massachusetts governor John Winthrop. Using an image from the Sermon on the Mount in the New Testament, Winthrop told his Puritan congregation, in the style and spelling of the time, to follow high morals, "for wee must Considr that wee shall be as a Citty upon a Hill, the eies of all the people are upon us" (Paterson & Merrill, 1995:29).[15]

Throughout U.S. history, many Americans have supported this conversion-by-example-only approach. Secretary of State John Quincy Adams wrote in 1823, for example, that Americans should pray for the success of liberty in other countries but should not go "abroad in search of monsters to destroy" lest the country become entangled "beyond the power of extrication" and see the "fundamental maxims" of U.S. policy change "from liberty to force" (Clifford, 1989:15).

Active messianism has, however, frequently clashed with its passive sibling. Rejecting the efficacy of uplifting others by example only, those who favor active messianism are willing to use coercion when necessary to accomplish their goals. The result, especially since the 1890s, has been repeated U.S. interventions abroad to promote liberty, democracy, free enterprise, or some other manifestation of the American way (Schraeder, 1992). After the Spanish-American War (1898), for instance, President William McKinley decided to annex the Philippines. The islands, he explained, were a gift from the deity. Thus, it was Americans' duty "to take them all, and to educate the Filipinos, and uplift and civilize and Christianize them, and by God's grace do the very best we could by them, as our fellow-men for whom Christ also died" (Morgan, 1965:96).

Americans learned to soften their religious imagery, but they still felt the urge to save those who believed in the American way and to convert those who had not yet come to the light. President Woodrow Wilson asked Congress for a declaration of war (1917) against Germany in order to do "battle with this natural foe of liberty. . . . The world must be made safe for democracy."

Minneapolis Tribune in *Literary Digest,* 1901

Paternalistic messianism and racism are two traits of American political culture that are evident in this cartoon. The United States acquired several territories and established protectorates over others, including Cuba, as a result of the Spanish-American War of 1898. Americans preferred to attribute their expansion to high motives—such as civilizing Cubans, Filipinos, Puerto Ricans, and others—rather than to imperialism. This cartoon depicts General Leonard Wood, who served as U.S. military governor of Cuba (1899–1902) scrubbing a wailing, racially caricaturized Cuban. The caption to the 1901 drawing read, "If General Wood Is Unpopular with Cuba, We Can Guess the Reason."

After World War II, the American exceptionalist and messianic tradition was evident less augustly in the smug proclamation of Senator Kenneth Wherry (R-NE) that U.S. aid could take Shanghai, the greatest city in China's ancient and exquisite civilization, and "with God's help . . . lift [it] up and up, ever up, until it is just like Kansas City" (LaFeber, 1976:84).

Recent Messianism: A Retreat to the Hill

Americans still believe that their country should promote its values (Kerry, 1990). One poll found, for example, that 62 percent of respondents agreed that Americans should "do all that we can to make the world safe for democracy" (Myers, 1989:300).

104

CHAPTER 4
Political
Culture:
The Domestic
Setting

The messianic impulse has, for one, strongly influenced American attitudes and policy toward postcommunist Russia (Cohen, 1993). Foreign aid has been used as a carrot to press Russians to continue on the path toward democracy and capitalism. As noted earlier, however, the shift has caused difficulties in Russia, and there has been a marked backlash by Russians who believe the Yeltsin government has gone too far in caving in to foreign demands. One expert on Russian politics warns that Americans should be wary of their urge to reform Russia because they "lack the fight, wisdom, and power to convert Russia into an American replica," and because "wise policies require realistic perceptions, not missionary assumptions, about what has been happening in post-Communist Russia."[16]

Messianism also plays a role in U.S. relations with China. Americans have long had a missionary urge toward China based on the romanticism of China-trade clipper ships in the 1800s, Christian missionary efforts among the Chinese, the sense that the Hay Notes and the "Open Door" policy saved China from imperial division at the turn of the century, and a self-image of America as China's protector against the Japanese during World War II. China's adoption of communism and its continued refusal to accede to some values that Americans support vex Americans. As one U.S. expert on Asia explained, "The great impetus for Americans . . . is a missionary impetus—wanting China to change, and there's a frustration that China hasn't changed the way we wanted it to."[17] This combination of messianism and frustration creates, according to another Sinologist, "tremendous mood swings . . . going from the exaggerated rosy picture of China that Americans [sometimes] have . . . to the exaggerated, depressed picture that they have [at other times], and now we're in the bottom of the swing."[18]

There are even critics who charge that some American women have become messianic feminists. One study quotes the view of Marketa Spinkova, a Czech journalist, who wrote that "the Americans act like missionaries—as if there is something wrong with us, with Czech women, if we don't believe we are victims. . . . [T]hey act as if we are backward." Spinkova went on to write that when rebuffed, American feminists "cannot believe I mean it. . . . [T]he Americans don't care much about what the Czechs have to say. They came here to save us" (Elshtain, 1995:544).

While the struggle between the passive and active messianic approaches continues among Americans, active messianism has weakened on balance. The burdens of the Vietnam War and other cold war conflicts, and angry "Yanqui go home" chants in many less developed regions, buffeted and chastened Americans, and the trend against activist messianism has intensified in the post–cold war 1990s. Now, more Americans are apt to agree with diplomat and scholar George Kennan (1995:125) that "the best way for a larger country to help smaller ones is surely by the power of example." Respondents to a 1994 survey indicated, for example, that of 16 possible foreign policy goals that might be adjudged very important, promoting and defending human rights in other countries finished thirteenth, and helping to bring a democratic form of government to other countries ranked fourteenth (Rielly, 1995). In short, Americans are still apt to believe that others would improve themselves by adopting American ideals. But Americans are, for now, reluctant to bear the burden of their country being an active missionary and are content to have it be a more passive city on the hill.

Idealism

The exceptionalist notion of America as a grand experiment and its repudiation of the European tradition that were so central to the founding of the republic led to idealism in American political culture. Early American leaders associated Europe with "power politics," with what today would be called **realism** (Holsti, 1995; Waltz, 1995). Realists tend to be skeptics about human nature and to accept the inevitability of aggressive behavior among states. Stemming from this, realist doctrine contends that states must take care of their interests and should pursue them by any means necessary, including the use of force. In short, realism urges countries to manage their power prudently, particularly their economic and military power. When national power interests conflict, violence often results (Rosenthal, 1991).

Many early American leaders thought, or at least hoped, that the quest for national power did not necessarily have to be the driving force behind foreign policy. Instead, these leaders were idealists and had a different vision, an image of the way the world should be. A belief that it is desirable and possible to create a peaceful and prosperous global society is the essence of **idealism** (Kegley, 1995). To idealists, peace and harmony are the natural states of humankind. Violence and conflict represent human failures that can be overcome because humans are rational beings who can change their behavior.

Early Idealism

Making the world a kinder, gentler place could be done in two ways. One was the passive messianic approach discussed earlier. This lead-by-example approach remained highly popular throughout the nineteenth century because of limited U.S. power and because of the country's internal focus prior to the closing of the frontier. The more activist messianic path led to involvement in international politics in order to promote a more utopian world. Actions in this direction became much more common in the twentieth century as American economic and military strength and assertiveness grew (LaFeber, 1993).

One way this has influenced U.S. policy has been to create a desire to seek ways to create a more peaceful world. The legalist tendency to seek treaties led to early U.S. participation in various disarmament conferences, including those in The Hague (1899, 1907), Washington (1922), Geneva (1927), and London (1930, 1935). Secretary of State Frank B. Kellogg joined with French foreign minister Aristide Briand to draft the laudable, if ultimately ineffective, Kellogg-Briand Treaty (1927), by which 62 signatory countries renounced war.

Idealism, interacting with the legalist orientation in favor of formal constitutional structures, also prompted the United States to take the lead in establishing international organizations such as the League of Nations (1919) and the United Nations (1945). Ironically, isolationism—another trait of American political culture, which we shall discuss presently—kept the United States out of the League. Undaunted, Franklin D. Roosevelt sought to establish the United Nations as an organization to promote global order and the preservation of peace. In a prerecorded speech broadcast the day after his death on April 12, 1945, FDR told Americans that "more than an end to war, we want an end to the beginnings of all wars," and

106

CHAPTER 4
Political
Culture:
The Domestic
Setting

that the sole barrier to "our realization of tomorrow will be our doubts of today." Therefore, he counseled, "Let us move forward with strong and active faith."

Another aspect of idealism that has been long-standing, albeit inconsistent, is U.S. opposition to imperialism and colonialism. Due to its own colonial heritage, the rhetoric of U.S. foreign policy was solidly anti-imperial. Even when Americans acted imperialistically in Latin America and elsewhere, they felt a need to justify themselves with the soothing balm of anti-imperial rhetoric. Possession of Guam, Puerto Rico, and the Philippines after the Spanish-American War was justifiable, Americans rationalized, because as a former colony itself the United States would not exploit its own colonial subjects.

American idealism has also promoted a less aggressive quality that is evident in private and public generosity, including more than $200 billion in foreign aid over the last 50 years. Despite some grumbling about the cost of aid programs, the United States since 1945 has been by far the largest international aid donor. The desire to achieve political goals through the use of foreign aid motivated some Americans, but liberal, humanitarian impulses motivated others.

Recent Idealism

Idealism continues to play a role in the post-Vietnam era. It is also the case that, as in earlier times, idealism is sometimes self-serving and is often subordinated to realpolitik concerns (Hoffmann, 1995). Idealism is more frequently and strongly voiced by policy advocates outside the executive branch, but it influences policy by acting as a moral standard that decision makers cannot easily ignore and a basis for public support that policy makers often need to be successful (Muravchik, 1992).

South Africa provides one example of U.S. idealism at work. During the 1980s, the White House tended to view the future of South Africa in geostrategic terms. President Reagan wanted to persuade the white government gently, through a policy of "constructive engagement," to end apartheid. Many Americans disagreed strongly with the president's views. Protesters on college campuses and elsewhere successfully pressured U.S. companies to disinvest in South Africa. Idealists wanted even stronger, legally binding measures. Overriding a presidential veto, Congress mandated economic sanctions against South Africa in 1986 (Hill, 1993). The sanctions imposed by the United States and others worked. South Africa held its first all-race election in 1994, and Nelson Mandela was elected the country's first black president.

Idealism has also helped moderate the frustration that the United States has frequently felt with the United Nations (Gregg, 1993). This sentiment also tempers the antiforeign aid feeling among Americans. This has led, among other things, to limiting the drive by congressional Republicans to cut U.S. funding for the UN, its programs, and its associated agencies. One study found that 78 percent of the American public favored U.S. membership in the UN, and 80 percent agreed that a "very" or "somewhat" important U.S. foreign policy goal should be strengthening the UN (Alger, 1990). In the same vein, another survey found that the percentage of those who rated strengthening the UN a very important U.S. goal had actually increased between 1990 and 1994 by 7 percent to 51 percent (Rielly, 1995).

Idealism further works to soften the reluctance of Americans to intervene abroad. A 1994 survey found that 79 percent of Americans were willing to countenance use of the U.S. military to "provide humanitarian aid when it's needed" (Richman,

United States Interventions in the Caribbean and Central America

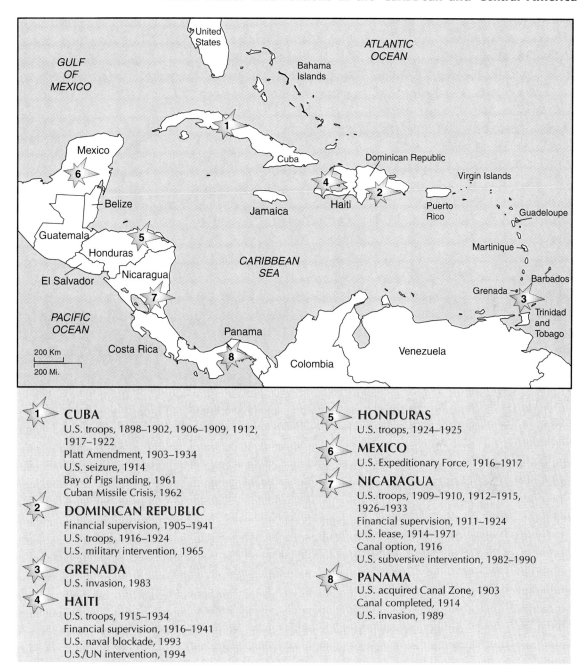

CUBA
U.S. troops, 1898–1902, 1906–1909, 1912, 1917–1922
Platt Amendment, 1903–1934
U.S. seizure, 1914
Bay of Pigs landing, 1961
Cuban Missile Crisis, 1962

DOMINICAN REPUBLIC
Financial supervision, 1905–1941
U.S. troops, 1916–1924
U.S. military intervention, 1965

GRENADA
U.S. invasion, 1983

HAITI
U.S. troops, 1915–1934
Financial supervision, 1916–1941
U.S. naval blockade, 1993
U.S./UN intervention, 1994

HONDURAS
U.S. troops, 1924–1925

MEXICO
U.S. Expeditionary Force, 1916–1917

NICARAGUA
U.S. troops, 1909–1910, 1912–1915, 1926–1933
Financial supervision, 1911–1924
U.S. lease, 1914–1971
Canal option, 1916
U.S. subversive intervention, 1982–1990

PANAMA
U.S. acquired Canal Zone, 1903
Canal completed, 1914
U.S. invasion, 1989

The United States has intervened regularly in the Caribbean and Central America in support of U.S. interests and to force the countries in the region to conduct themselves in a manner acceptable to Americans. This political culture trait of paternalism has joined other traits such as messianism and exceptionalism to promote such interventions. The sense that the region is a U.S. sphere of influence has convinced many Americans that they have a right and a duty to police the people and countries to the south.

107

108

CHAPTER 4
Political
Culture:
The Domestic
Setting

1995:45). Putting theory into practice, 81 percent of Americans supported the move to use troops to ease starvation in Somalia. Americans were less willing to have their forces pursue political ends. Only 44 percent were willing to have U.S. troops remain as long as necessary to ensure peace in Somalia.[19] It was not surprising, then, when the public's support of the U.S. effort plummeted once the main thrust of U.S. policy changed from humanitarian aid to trying to force a political settlement in Somalia. Soon fighting broke out between U.S forces on one side and various Somali factions on the other, American troops began to be killed, wounded, and captured, and American opinion turned against U.S. involvement (Haass, 1994).

Racism

There is an even uglier element of superiority in American political culture. Exceptionalism has also spawned **racism**—in this case, the sense of superiority felt by WASPs (White Anglo-Saxon Protestants) toward peoples of other races and even toward non-European Caucasians.

Early Racism

The colonists brought racism with them to the New World and wasted little time applying it. Because European immigrants typically saw Native Americans as "savages," few invading whites apparently felt any remorse in displacing and almost exterminating the indigenous population. The colonists also imported black Africans as slaves.

White Americans justified their actions by using an explicit hierarchy of peoples based on skin color and general appearance. It was common in the 1800s to believe in a social order in which:

> Those with the lightest skin were positioned on the highest rung of the hierarchy, and those with the darkest skin were relegated to the lowest. In between fell the "yellow" Mongolians and Malays, the "red" American Indian, and the racially mixed Latino. Each color implied a level of physical, mental, and moral development, with white Americans setting themselves up as the unquestioned standard of measurement. (Hunt, 1987: 48)

Historic racism became even more virulent when justified by **Social Darwinism.** Charles Darwin's theory of evolution in his *Origin of the Species* (1859) held that species survived and progressed through a natural selection of the fittest members. Small minds distorted this idea to justify racism and the oppression of others as a natural "law of the jungle" based on the survival of the fittest. Americans used Social Darwinism to rationalize such policies as taking ownership of the Hawaiian Islands, the Philippines, Puerto Rico, Guam, and the Panama Canal Zone and intervening in Cuba, China, and Central America. The United States was justified, one senator proclaimed, because, "God has been preparing [Americans] for a thousand years. . . . He has made us the master organizers of the world . . . that we may administer government among the savage and senile peoples. Were it not for such a force as this, the world would lapse into barbarism and night" (Snyder, 1977:279).

Racial attitudes have also long created disdain among Americans toward countries inhabited by people of color. "Dear me, think of it! Niggers speaking French," an incredulous Secretary of State William Jennings Bryan (1913–1915) once remarked about Haitians.[20] The persistence of such attitudes was evident over a half century later in President Nixon's remark to his chief of staff, H. R. Haldeman, that "you have to face the fact that the whole problem [with Africa] is really the blacks." Haldeman relates that the president went on to assert "that there has never in history been an adequate black nation, and they are the only race of which this is true. Africa is hopeless."[21] Racism may have also led to errors such as underestimating the skill and tenacity of the Vietnamese who withstood the world's most powerful military machine for a decade. Other examples could be cited but are not necessary to make the point that racism has influenced U.S. foreign policy.

Racism since Vietnam

Racist influence on U.S. policy has not vanished. Immigration is one policy issue that provides evidence about American attitudes. A national poll in 1993 that asked Americans whether emigration from certain countries and regions should be made "easier" or "more difficult" revealed data that indicated that the race of the prospective immigrants influences American preferences.[22] Of those respondents expressing an opinion, half thought that it should be easier for (generally white) people from Eastern Europe to come to the United States. Of the respondents 73 percent, by contrast, thought that it should be more difficult for (mostly black) Haitians to immigrate; 59 percent favored making immigration more difficult for Africans; and 65 percent wished to make entry into the United States more difficult for Asians. Another survey found that when people where asked whether certain immigrant groups have benefited the United States or created problems, the percent of those answering "benefited" declined in rough proportion to how dark someone's skin was. The Irish drew a positive evaluation from 75 percent of respondents; Poles got a 65 percent positive rating. Asians did less well, with Chinese, Koreans, and Vietnamese getting positive ratings of 59 percent, 53 percent, and 41 percent, respectively. Latinos/as* did even more poorly (Mexicans, 29 percent; Cubans, 24 percent), and largely African-heritage Haitians finished last (19 percent).[23]

There are tinges of racism in U.S. attitudes toward and relations with other countries. The attitudes of some Americans about relations with the Japanese, for example, are affected by racial bias. The public debate over the multicausal reasons for and solutions to the trade deficit has sparked a simplistic anti-Japanese attitude among some Americans. This has been reciprocated by similar views of Americans among some Japanese. While some accusations of protectionism leveled against Japan are true, similar charges can be made against the European Union (EU) and its mostly white inhabitants. European protectionism, however, gets much less publicity and has sparked almost no Europe-bashing by Americans. Japan-bashing, by unhappy contrast, quickly led to Japanese American–bashing so worrisome that, in February 1992, the U.S. Commission on Civil Rights issued a report decrying the rise of attacks on all Asian Americans and pointing out that "political leaders contribute to the problem

*This text uses "Latino/a" and "Latinos/as" to refer to Americans of Latin American heritage. Latino is no less gender specific than is statesman or congressman. The foreign language original Latino does not change or lessen its male-dominant connotation. As one Latina pointed out to one of the authors, Latino is sexist because if the 100 most able Latina executives were holding a conference, and a Latino janitor came in to empty the trash, you would have to say "there were 101 Latinos in the room."

Comments by prominent Americans that are or seem to be racist harm U.S. relations with other countries. Senator Ernest Hollings told U.S. workers recently that the Japanese should remember that the atomic bombs dropped on Hiroshima and Nagasaki in 1945 were "Made in America." When many aghast Japanese and Americans protested against what was, at the least, racial insensitivity, Hollings replied that he had only been joking. Few laughed.

when they unthinkingly lash out at Japan as the cause of the United States' economic difficulties."[24]

In an age of almost instant global communications, the spate of anti-Asian feeling in the United States is damaging the U.S. image all over Asia and elsewhere. A poll taken in early 1992 indicated that 41 percent of the Japanese believe that the word "prejudiced" aptly describes Americans.[25] Moreover, an increasing number of Japanese see the United States as unfriendly and even as a security threat.[26] If the Pearl Harbor analogy is festering in the minds of some Americans, the Hiroshima analogy has been planted in the minds of some Japanese. The growth of that image was further encouraged in 1992 by Senator Ernest F. Hollings (D-SC). Speaking just four days after the civil rights commission report on Japan-bashing, which he apparently had not read, a campaigning Hollings told voters that his response to Japanese criticism of American workers was that they "should draw a mushroom cloud and put underneath it: 'Made in America by lazy and illiterate Americans and tested in Japan.' "[27] Hollings later protested, "I made a joke." The Japanese were not amused. The senator seemed to learn little from the furor over his remarks. At the end of 1993, Hollings once again gave racial offense when he commented about African leaders attending the GATT negotiations in Geneva, Switzerland, because "these potentates from down in Africa, you know—rather than eating each other, they'd just come up and get a good square meal in Geneva."[28] Africans and black Americans were not amused.

Evidence and charges of bias in U.S. foreign policy based on race and ethnicity also arose over attitudes toward the Balkans, Iraq, Somalia, Haiti, and South Africa. With regard to South Africa, a study on American attitudes toward sanctions aimed at ending apartheid found that "the mass public primarily uses a racial belief system [general attitudes about U.S. domestic racial relations] to structure its attitudes toward South Africa" (Hill, 1993:207). The United States finally placed sanctions on South Africa, but it took many years to reach that point. Similarly, UN secretary-general Boutros Boutros-Ghali and some other critics alleged that racism was part of the reason that the United States (and European countries) waited so long to address the warfare and starvation that was killing hundreds of thousands of black Somalis. Stung by such criticism and by the horrors occurring in Somalia, the United States did finally intervene. The 1994 U.S. intervention in Haiti was similarly delayed by racial indifference, according to critics of the Bush and Clinton administrations. Then, critics further charge, attitudes about moving against Haiti took on an even more negative turn when tidal waves of fleeing black Haitians began to come ashore in Florida. Given the earlier cited data about American attitudes about black immigrants, the inflow of Haitians created tremendous pressure on Clinton to act. The threatened invasion of Haiti was necessary, he told Americans, because without it "we will continue to face the threat of a mass exodus of refugees and its constant threat to stability in our region and control of our borders."[29]

At about the same time, many Muslims were disturbed by the American and European willingness to take military action against Iraqis in 1992 and 1993 (to enforce the no-fly zone over southern Iraq or to punish Iraq for its alleged attempt to assassinate former president Bush) when compared with the reluctance to take strong military action to stop the slaughter of Bosnian Muslims by Serbian Christians.

Outgoing secretary of state Lawrence S. Eagleburger reported a "constant undercurrent in a lot of the Muslim world" that the "West doesn't care about preventing [atrocities] against Muslims [in the Balkans] but we will go out of our way to hit the Iraqis when they do things."[30] That undercurrent was evident once again when Clinton ordered the attack of U.S. cruise missiles on Baghdad in response to a plot to kill Bush. "I wish," said Egypt's foreign minister, Amr Moussa, that "the position of American policies were as strict toward the crimes that the Serbs carry out" against Muslims in Bosnia as they are toward the Iraqis.[31]

Furthermore, there is a still small but growing criticism that moralism and racism are combining under the guise of humanitarianism to usher in a new age of colonialism. One British commentator sees "an unmistakable pattern of U.S. intervention, legitimized by the UN," in which the advocates of "old imperialism, and of the new [imperialism] retain credibility, using and twisting words like 'morality' and 'humanitarianism.'" These, despite their "semantic mask," are "the essence of imperialism, and the antithesis of true internationalism" (Pilger, 1993). Former intelligence agent and novelist John le Carré has made much the same point, suggesting that a "new period of altruistic white colonialism is upon us." It could be an era, his interviewer added to le Carré's comment, of *Pax Americana Moralistica.*[32]

Pragmatism

For all of American messianic impulses, there is another American political culture trait that often moderates, even negates, the influence of these values. That trait is pragmatism. **Pragmatism** means problems are dealt with on a case-by-case basis rather than with an eye to long-term planning. By the same token, pragmatists judge policies based on whether they solve the problem rather than by what is ideologically, even ethically, desirable (Bostdorff & Goldzwig, 1994).

When evaluating pragmatism, messianism, idealism, and other aspects of political culture, you should keep two qualifiers in mind. First, the attitudes of most people are shaped to some degree by all of these aspects of political culture simultaneously. Thus, the aspects may set up clashing, countervailing, even mutually negating internal urges. Second, there are lesser and greater degrees to which an individual or a nation holds the various aspects of political culture. This strength of conviction both varies among people and changes over time.

Within the limits of the cautions, it is possible to say, however, that there is a strong pragmatic element in American political culture. It is an orientation that comes from the early rejection of Europe's traditions. Even more, American pragmatism stems from the experience of expanding and building a country—from the settlers and pioneers who used whatever resources and means were necessary to populate the largely empty continent and to construct an industrial country.

Pragmatism influences foreign policy in several ways. It relieves policy makers and the public from facing vexing questions of cosmic-level truths. As such, pragmatism means that U.S. foreign policy tends to react to problems rather than to anticipate them. Pragmatism often also means favoring short-term solutions over long-term goals, a strategy that makes for policy that can be quite inconsistent. The pragmatic streak is one cause behind the frequent characterization of U.S. foreign relations as more of a series of *ad hoc* reactions than as planned and consistent. "As a nation of short-term pragmatists accustomed to dealing with the future only when it has become the

112

CHAPTER 4
Political
Culture:
The Domestic
Setting

present, we find it hard to regard future trends as serious realities," former Defense Department official Townsend Hoopes has observed. The result, in his estimation, is that "we have not achieved the capacity to treat as real and urgent—as demanding action today—problems which appear in critical dimension only at some future date. Yet failure to achieve this new habit of mind is likely to prove fatal" (Acheson, 1969:770).[33]

Pragmatism also, as noted, can sometimes lead Americans to ignore the more idealistic impulses of liberalism. A classic example involved President Franklin D. Roosevelt and his willingness to aid the Dominican Republic's ruthless dictator, Rafael Trujillo. "The man's an SOB!" an FDR aide objected. "Ah yes," Roosevelt agreed, "but he's our SOB."

Early Pragmatism

Americans have always applied pragmatism to limit foreign policy based on idealistic principles. An early example occurred in the 1790s when the French were at war with the British. France had aided the Americans militarily against the British during the American Revolutionary War. The two countries signed an alliance in 1778. Fifteen years later France was at war in the aftermath of the French Revolution of 1789. The dethroned king, Louis XVI, was guillotined on January 21, 1793. On February 1 the monarchies of Great Britain, Holland, and Spain joined those of Prussia and Austria in their ongoing war to end French democracy and restore the Bourbon dynasty to the throne in Paris. The French appealed to the United States to honor the alliance of 1778 and come to the aid of France's effort to end monarchism and establish democracy.

Some Americans argued that the United States should aid France. Secretary of State Thomas Jefferson wrote that France "changes her government, declares it shall be a Republic" and deserves help. Even more, Jefferson continued, treaties between countries "are obligatory on them by the same moral law which obliges individuals to observe their compacts" (Graebner, 1964:55). Other Americans disagreed. They said that the treaty had been signed with monarchical France. Opponents of American aid reasoned that democratic France was a different country from monarchical France; therefore, the treaty was invalid. Even more important, according to Secretary of the Treasury Alexander Hamilton, "the mischiefs and perils to which the United States would expose" itself by going to war with Great Britain and its allies would far outweigh any of the benefits. "Self-preservation is the first duty of a nation," Hamilton argued pragmatically. Since the Americans were weaker militarily than the British, Hamilton contended that avoiding war with them was "an obvious dictate of reason, with which the common sense and common practice of mankind coincide" (Graebner, 1964:59). In the end, Hamilton's pragmatism prevailed over Jefferson's idealism; President George Washington issued a proclamation of neutrality on April 22, 1793.

Recent Pragmatism

Americans still have a pronounced pragmatic streak, and it continues to conflict often with their other, more idealistic values (Russell, 1990). As in Washington's time, pragmatism has usually prevailed when it conflicted with idealism, especially when short- and long-term interests are involved (von Vorys, 1990).

The Reagan administration, for example, sought pragmatically to free American hostages by selling weapons to Iran in the mid-1980s. Although Reagan had been adamant about not negotiating with terrorists, he agreed to supply weapons to Iran in the hope that it would persuade the pro-Iranian Islamic fundamentalists holding the hostages in Lebanon to release them. Then, taking pragmatism beyond the boundary of legality, National Security Council aide lieutenant colonel Oliver North and other officials funneled the funds generated from the weapons sales through Swiss bank accounts to the Contras in Nicaragua. The transfer was illegal because Congress had passed, over administration objections, the Boland Amendments, cutting off military aid to the Contras (Draper, 1991).

The Bush administration was particularly pragmatic (Duffy & Goodgame, 1992; Schneider, 1992). "I'm more interested in the game than in philosophy," Secretary of State Baker remarked.[34] Bush had the same pragmatic orientation. Indeed he rejected the "vision thing," as he called it. "You could say that Ronald Reagan had a 'vision' in that he talked about a shining city on top of a hill," a former Bush aide observed, but "Bush doesn't see it that way. He has a much more practical approach."[35]

Reflecting the tendency of pragmatists to concentrate on the present, critics charge that the Bush administration reacted poorly to the collapse of communist regimes in Eastern Europe and to the Soviet Union itself. At one point of turmoil in the dying USSR, the *Washington Post* featured a picture of the president fishing at his home in Kennebunkport, Maine, and a story that began, "It was another 'wouldn't-be-prudent' day at the summer White House."[36] The irony, the *Post* related, was that the president seemed to be doing an impression of *Saturday Night Live* comedian Dana Carvey doing one of his biting impressions of George Bush trying to avoid doing anything imprudent. A typical Bush quote—in this case when asked about the rivalry of Gorbachev and Russian president Boris Yeltsin for power—was: "Let them sort it out." "Virtually everything the president has had to say since the coup failed has amounted to 'No comment yet,' " the paper concluded.

Once in office, Bill Clinton, as mentioned earlier, discovered that it was far easier to act based on pragmatism than on idealism (Hoffmann, 1995; Drew, 1994). Whereas he was prone to making idealistic pronouncements during the 1992 campaign, after two years in office he was cautioning against "simplistic solutions that sound good on bumper stickers but that would have tragic consequences" and answering the persistent criticism that his policy lacked a theme by pleading, "I'm doing the best I can with some fairly intractable problems."[37] President Clinton's rhetoric and record were reviewed further in the box on pages 98–99.

THE AMERICAN IMAGE OF THE U.S. ROLE IN THE WORLD

The third category of political culture images that affects U.S. foreign policy relates to how and how much Americans want to interact with the rest of the world. The impulses toward isolationism and internationalism will provide the framework for examining the American images of the U.S. role in the world.

Scholars characterize the roles of isolationism and internationalism in U.S. foreign policy in three ways. The first might be labeled the *dramatic shift theory*. This

114

CHAPTER 4
Political
Culture:
The Domestic
Setting

represents the often-heard view that Americans began as isolationists, then, about the time of the end of World War II, shifted to internationalism. The essence of this approach is that there was a dramatic shift from isolationism to internationalism when the United States became a superpower in the 1940s.

Cycle theory is the second approach. This idea is propounded by some scholars who see a regular pattern, a cycle, to the ebb and flow of U.S. involvement in the world (Klingberg, 1990). Those who believe that cycles occur suggest, for example, that societal "mood" swings and the accompanying periods of introversion and extroversion may be caused by political, economic, or societal factors.

A third approach to evaluating the impact of isolationism and internationalism on U.S. foreign policy can be labeled *ambivalence theory*. This view governs the analysis here. Ambivalence theory suggests that isolationism and internationalism have both existed as important political culture factors from the earliest days of American history and remain as contradictory impulses. These countervailing urges have interacted to create an ambivalence toward the world. It should be noted that the view of American attitudes based on the interaction of isolationism and internationalism does not reject the dramatic-shift idea that American attitudes changed markedly during World War II and the coming of the cold war. There certainly was a profound change in both American attitudes and policy, as we shall see presently. It is also the case, as cycle theory suggests, that there has been an ebb and flow throughout U.S. history in the respective strengths of isolationism and internationalism. Where the ambivalence theory differs from either the dramatic shift or the cyclic theory is in the desire of the United States to face outward and to face inward simultaneously. The ensuing tension created between the two views explains much about the course of American foreign policy.

Early Isolationism

Early U.S. foreign policy was predominantly, but far from exclusively, isolationist. President George Washington used his Farewell Address to warn of the dangers inherent in tying the country's future too closely to any particular European power. "The great rule of conduct for us in regard to foreign nations," he told Americans in 1796, is to extend "our commercial relations" with them while having "as little *political* connection as possible." In essence, Washington went on, "it is our true policy to steer clear of permanent alliance with any portion of the foreign world."

The Origins of Isolationism

Several points should be made about the origins and nature of traditional American **isolationism**—the belief that the country should avoid getting involved in the *political* affairs of other countries. First, while Washington's advice came to symbolize isolationism, the president's warning did not cause it. Indeed, American isolationism stemmed in part from early American exceptionalism and thus is older than the United States itself, as reflected in Winthrop's city-on-the-hill sermon in 1630.

Second, neither Washington's advice nor historical American isolationism should be interpreted as ignoring the outside world. The first president advocated commercial and other cordial diplomatic contacts. Washington was even willing to concede that "we may safely trust to temporary alliances for extraordinary emergencies."

Third, geography played an important role. Vast oceans flank the continent to the east and west, the impassable North Pole lies beyond peaceable Canada to the north, and the balmy Caribbean provides a buffer to the south. Washington valued the measure of distance and protection for the new republic that geography provided; he believed that the United States' "detached and distant situation invites and enables us to pursue a different [politically independent] course."

Fourth, Washington's advice was motivated by his realpolitik evaluation of the relative weakness of the young United States. The Atlantic Ocean and the Caribbean Sea provided potential attack routes for, as well as barriers to, stronger European powers. Furthermore, the new country was not alone on the continent, and for many years the powerful presence of the British and the French proved particularly troublesome. The survival of the United States was not certain in 1796, and Washington wisely opposed foreign alliances because they might bring war, defeat, and renewed foreign subjugation.

Fifth, isolationism stems from the fact that the energies of the society were mostly turned inward. The major goal was to ensure the political survival and success of the country and its democratic experiment and to take full advantage of the country's remarkable economic bounty by remaining relatively unchallenged by serious competitors. There was a need to avoid foreign drains on the country's resources caused by foreign adventures so that Americans' energies could be devoted to domestic development and expansion. Three of the many factors that worked to keep the country focused inward during all or part of the 1800s were settling and developing the frontier, the political preservation of the Union, and industrialization.

Isolationism, Security, and Antimilitary Sentiment

After the War of 1812, there was never again an immediate threat of military invasion to the continental United States. Moreover, the civilian populace has not directly suffered the trauma of war since the Civil War, which Americans inflicted on themselves. This has created a sense of physical security that combines with the political culture's antimilitary feeling to promote isolationism and to be, in turn, reinforced by isolationism.

This antimilitary tradition stemmed in part from the colonial reaction to the king's army. That fear and dislike carried over to suspicion of a large U.S. military. This was expressed in the Second Amendment's establishment of state militias and the Third Amendment's ban on unlawful quartering of troops in civilian houses. Antimilitarism also resulted from a resistance to paying the cost of a large military establishment. After World War I, for example, isolationist senator William E. Borah called for naval disarmament because arms expenditures create only "sheer waste and sterility" and because of "what these armament expenditures and the taxes thereby imposed mean to the business of the future" (Graebner, 1964:508). This contention, from a slightly different angle, sounds much akin to the "peace dividend" argument of today over what to do with money saved from reductions in defense spending in the post–cold war period.

The traditional outcome of this antimilitary tradition was skimpy expenditures on military preparedness between wars. Armies and navies were raised once war broke out, then largely dismantled when peace was restored. Even after World War I erupted in Europe, for example, the United States resisted expanding its small army

116

CHAPTER 4
Political
Culture:
The Domestic
Setting

and navy. When, in January 1917, Germany had to decide whether or not to risk war with the still-neutral United States by resuming submarine attacks, the Germans decided to attack. Even if the Americans declared war, the confident German naval minister predicted, "From a military standpoint, America's entrance is as nothing" (Paterson, Clifford, & Hagan, 1995:96).

It should also be noted that Americans' antimilitary tradition not only promoted isolationism, but that isolationism in turn promoted the antimilitary feelings. One frequent argument is that creating military power tempts the possessor to use it. Furthermore, lack of preparedness can be used as a reason to advocate isolationism. Aviation hero Charles Lindbergh, for one, argued that since "the United States is not prepared to wage war in Europe successfully," it should stay out of World War II (Graebner, 1964:604).

Isolationism Begins to Ebb

It is sometimes said that World War II was the turning point when the United States stopped being isolationist and became internationalist. That is not true. Instead, isolationism began to ebb, and it and internationalism struggled for predominance beginning in the later part of the 1800s. Still, for most of their first century, Americans were occupied with acquiring, settling, and developing the territories that eventually comprised the 50 states. Fulfilling the Manifest Destiny doctrine, the American republic moved rapidly west and south, more than quadrupling its territory to become one of the world's largest countries by 1900. There was also a rapid rise in population fed by a flood of immigrants. Each decennial census during the 1800s found the population an average of more than 30 percent larger than ten years earlier; a small country of 5.3 million Americans in 1800 became a huge country of 76.2 million people a century later.

Domestic political trauma also riveted the country's attention and energy. Rising tension over slavery, states' rights, and the preservation of the union exploded into the Civil War (1861–1865) and reverberated through the Reconstruction Era (to 1876) and beyond. During the 1870s normalcy began to return, and the government's interest refocused on economic growth and expansion. Waterways, roads, railroads, the telegraph, and the telephone united the country into a truly national marketplace. Giant American enterprises fueled U.S. economic growth, with the GNP more than doubling in less than 30 years.

This growth of American wealth and power began to erode the grip of isolationism, but it remained powerful for decades more. For example, despite the urging of President Wilson, the Senate rejected the Treaty of Versailles at the end of World War I and thus forestalled U.S. entry into the League of Nations. Isolationism inhibited early U.S. assistance to Great Britain and others in their struggle against Nazi Germany as Congress passed the Neutrality Acts (1935–1937).

The growing threat of a German victory gradually enabled Franklin Roosevelt to persuade Congress to ease neutrality legislation. Then Japanese bombs falling on Pearl Harbor in 1941 brought the United States into the war. At the end of World War II the growth of U.S. economic and military power and the collapse or marked decline in strength of most of the older powers left the United States an international power by default. Isolationists in Congress and the country attempted briefly to reassert themselves after the war, but they were routed by the seeming threat of world communism and the needs of the containment doctrine formulated to save the free world. Isolationism did not vanish and has, in fact, recently revived. But with the advent of the cold war, isolationism became a faint echo of the past.

Internationalism

We have detailed U.S. international involvement, but it is worth repeating that despite the isolationist tradition, U.S. history has always included interactions with other countries. Beginning in the late 1800s, that international contact evolved into growing internationalism. Here the definition of **internationalism** is important. It denotes the U.S. perception that it has a stake in the general shape of the international political system and the country's willingness to get actively involved on a regular basis in world political affairs.

The 1890s saw the beginning of true internationalism for the United States. Symbolically, the frontier was closed. But America's expansive energy was not to be bounded, and it hurtled outward toward its "new manifest destiny" of overseas expansion. Messianic American exceptionalism, bolstered by virulent racism, helped justify U.S. imperialist internationalism. President Theodore Roosevelt epitomized this approach. He exhibited an exuberant nationalism, corresponded regularly with naval-expansion advocate Alfred Mahan, and practiced Social Darwinist racism. When feeling benevolent, Roosevelt expressed the urge to take up the "white-man's burden" and tutor "backward" peoples in good government; when belligerent, he justified aggressive intervention on the grounds that "all the great masterful races have been fighting races" (Paterson, Clifford, & Hagan, 1995:66).

As discussed in chapters 2 and 3, trade was another factor promoting U.S. internationalism. The importance of commerce helped involve the United States in World War I, for example. Similarly, the growth of the U.S. economy during the twentieth century increasingly tempted the United States to expand its diplomatic horizons. The country no longer ignored the world, and the world refused to ignore the United States.

The early twentieth century also saw ideology begin to draw the United States into greater international activity. American opposition to communism began long before the cold war. Between 1918 and 1919, the United States sent 14,000 troops into the Soviet Union in a vain, thinly disguised allied attempt to quash Lenin's new regime. Not only did communism reject such basic American concepts as democracy, capitalism, and the belief in God, but the revolutionary ideology also promised global expansion, thereby threatening U.S. economic interests around the world (Iriye, 1993). Anticommunism became the guiding force of U.S. military doctrine after World War II. During the doctrine's heyday, U.S. troops were stationed or fought on every continent except Antarctica.

Recent Internationalism and Isolationism

The war in Vietnam created doubts in the minds of many Americans about the containment doctrine. As the war dragged on, an ever greater and more vocal number of Americans objected to the war's social, political, and financial costs. Socially, the war eventually cost the lives of tens of thousands of Americans and perhaps millions of Vietnamese. Politically, it traumatized the body politic, giving rise to an antiwar movement of epic proportions and significantly undermining Americans' faith in their government. Financially, the war cost approximately $149 billion to fight and consumed about 14 percent of the GNP during the years it was waged. Most Americans did not think that containing communism in Vietnam was worth such sacrifices (Ambrose, 1991). By extension, stopping communism in many other places was not worth American blood and wealth either (Di Leo, 1991). Still, Americans were not ready to abandon anticommunism totally; they looked for new approaches. One was the 1969 Nixon Doctrine, which pledged the United States to arm others to fight communism if they provided the troops to be put in harm's way (Hooglund, 1992). This same approach was adopted by Ronald Reagan. The Reagan Doctrine extended U.S. assistance to rebel forces seeking to overthrow communist regimes.

Even more, the war in Vietnam was the first in a series of major events, culminating with the collapse of the Soviet Union and the end of the cold war, that brought the entire internationalist thrust of U.S. policy into question. The fragmentation of the bipolar structure and the other shifts in the international system discussed in chapter 3 left Americans less sure about why they should continue to play a strong international role.

The result is that American attitudes toward internationalism and isolationism have been mixed in the years since Vietnam. As we shall see in the following sections, the United States is still solidly internationalist. That orientation is supported by nearly all American leaders and by about two-thirds of the public. Yet we shall also see that there are strong pressures to curb the level of U.S. internationalist activity. Furthermore the isolationist-internationalist debate is complicated by a related conflict between those who favor a unilateralist approach to foreign policy and those who favor a multilateralist approach.

Prevailing Internationalism

American attitudes and U.S. policy continue to fall well toward the internationalist end of the internationalist-isolationist spectrum. Surveys demonstrate that between 1974 and 1994, the public consistently supported an active U.S. role in world affairs. The level of public support averaged 62 percent and never dropped below 54 percent. At 65 percent in 1994, public internationalist sentiment was higher than at any time since 1974, when it was 66 percent. Not only that, 73 percent of Americans expressed the belief in 1994 that the United States will play a greater role in the future than it does now. American leaders are even more determinedly internationalist. Their support for internationalism during the 1974–1994 period averaged a nearly unanimous 97 percent (Rielly, 1995). Furthermore, as we will discuss in the chapter on interest groups, Americans enjoy both the prestige and some of the fruits of global leadership, and there are many American groups that support a vigorous U.S. international presence based on their group's interests.

Foreign policy reflects these attitudes and interests, and the United States has continued on its internationalist course with only slight moderation. Presidents supported by their executive branch officials have usually been among the most committed internationalists. Jimmy Carter saw the United States as only one of a number of important states in a multipolar world and rejected the notion that Americans could or should dictate solutions to major world problems. Still, he wanted to play the role of peacemaker and champion of human rights and democracy in the world and actively engaged the country in the pursuit of these ends. Carter pushed for a second strategic arms limitation talks (SALT II) agreement with the Soviets, tried to improve the U.S. image in Latin America by transferring control of the Panama Canal to the Panamanians, and furthered the Middle East peace process by getting Egypt and Israel to agree to the Camp David Accords. World events, particularly the Soviet invasion of Afghanistan, made Carter's policy of accommodation seem weak, and Ronald Reagan rode this public perception into the White House. Reagan was also a strong internationalist, but his view of the world as conflict-ridden and bipolar made him determined to assert U.S. international leadership in a way very different from Carter's. Not surprisingly, U.S. foreign policy behavior became more aggressive, as detailed in chapter 3. Like all recent presidents, Reagan also supported the concept of free trade and investment and other internationalist economic policies. While in practice U.S. trade barriers increased during the 1980s because of domestic pressures, Reagan (1990:241) was still able to assert that "I am a free-trader. . . . I believed that once we started down the road to protectionism, there would be no way to turn back, no way of telling where it would end. I'd learned that during the Great Depression, when [in 1931] Congress passed the [restrictive and economically disastrous] Smoot-Hawley Tariff Act." President Bush followed the internationalist path of his modern predecessors. He continued the strong U.S. commitment to NATO and other alliances, asserted U.S. leadership in dealing with the West's response to the Soviet Union's demise, used U.S. troops in Panama and the Persian Gulf, and denounced pressures to lessen the U.S. global role as examples of "the ignorance that inspires people to hide from the rest of the world, wishing our problems away instead of creating solutions."[38] Bush also continued the long-standing U.S. liberal internationalist attitude toward relatively unencumbered trade, investment, and other forms of international economic interchange. His summary view was that "economic isolationism is a bankrupt notion."[39] President Clinton has continued to follow the internationalist path of all post–World War II chief executives. Despite his announced intention of concentrating on domestic priorities, Clinton has pushed the North American Free Trade Agreement (NAFTA) through Congress and pledged to help create the Free Trade Agreement of the Americas (FTAA); he led the United States in its support of the new GATT agreement and the creation of the WTO; he dispatched U.S. ground troops to Haiti, Macedonia, and Bosnia; he ordered U.S. air strikes in Iraq; he confronted North Korea over its nuclear weapons program; he extended U.S. aid to Russia, Ukraine, Kazakhstan, and other former Soviet republics; he helped broker a ceasefire in Northern Ireland; and he has otherwise thoroughly involved himself in the role, albeit in a somewhat restrained manner, of world leader.

Isolationist Pressures

While American attitudes and U.S. policy remain internationalist, it would be myopic not to see that both attitudes and policy have retreated somewhat toward a less pronounced internationalist stance. Many observers believe that the United States will swing away from internationalism because of the lack of consensus about what the U.S. role should be and because of the ambivalence within the general public about internationalism. "Clinton wants to retain the American presence abroad," one British observer noted, "but the question is, 'Will he be allowed to by the electorate and Congress?'"[40] At least one French analyst has answered *non* to that question.

120

André Fountaine, chief editorial writer for *Le Monde,* wrote that "a country that is deprived of its enemies falls back on its internal problems." While "the United States won the cold war," Fountaine added, "it paid too high a price for victory. It no longer has the money or the public backing to play a prominent role abroad."[41] Some American commentators agree with their European counterparts. Commenting on the lack of a great cause on which American opinion leaders agree and behind which the American public can unite, one commentator quipped, "We have a foreign policy today in the shape of a doughnut—lots of peripheral interests, but nothing in the middle."[42]

It is also evident that, as Fountaine suggested, the United States has, in part, fallen "back on its internal problems." Without an immediate and obvious international threat, the American political agenda is dominated even more than usual by economic problems and other domestic issues. Foreign policy was so tangential to the 1992 presidential election that during the campaign the chief diplomatic correspondent of the *New York Times* complained that he has so little to do that he felt "like the Maytag repairman."[43] Indicative of this domestic focus, a 1994 survey found that the public felt the top three issues facing the country were all domestic ones: crime, unemployment, and health care. When members of the public were asked to name their top foreign policy goals, five of the top six goals named had a strong domestic orientation: stopping the flow of illegal drugs into the country (85 percent), protecting American jobs (83 percent), reducing illegal immigration (72 percent), securing adequate energy supplies (62 percent), and reducing the trade deficit (59 percent). The only purely internationalist goal to place near the top was stopping nuclear proliferation (82 percent) (Rielly, 1995). The upshot is that the advocacy of unabated internationalism by Presidents Bush and Clinton put them each in a position akin to that of a band leader desperately trying to lead a marching band made up of citizens who are not sure they wish to follow.

Policy is not immune to these attitudes. Since the end of the Vietnam era, presidents have more often than not found their internationalist policy preferences opposed by the public. President Reagan, for one, discovered this to be true fairly early in the post-Vietnam period. The Reagan administration's support of the rightist Contra rebels in Nicaragua met strong domestic opposition. A majority of Americans disagreed with the president's belief that communism was so evil that virtually any action to forestall its expansion was acceptable. And an overwhelming majority, including more than 80 percent of all conservatives, rejected the idea that either a communist government in Nicaragua or aid by Nicaragua to other communist movements (as in El Salvador) was sufficient cause to attack Nicaragua (Secrest, Brunk, & Tamashiro, 1991). Moreover, there was widespread public outcry when it was revealed that the CIA had produced for the Contras a manual that encouraged the assassination of local Sandinista leaders and had also participated in the mining of Nicaraguan ports (Holt, 1995).

More recently, foreign aid has been under great pressure. Congress appropriated approximately $14 billion in 1995 for foreign aid. That figure is 22 percent less than the approximately $18 billion appropriated in 1985. If one figures in the effects of approximately 45 percent inflation over a decade, the drop in real dollars is even more pronounced. Moreover, when one examines potential conflict issues, the effects of flagging U.S. internationalism are even more dramatic.

Throughout President Clinton's first years in office, indications that he might deploy U.S. ground forces to Bosnia regularly set off firestorms of opposition. The

Republican Party's top elected officials and most of its presidential hopefuls rushed to condemn any U.S. military involvement in Bosnia. Former secretary of state James Baker testified before a congressional committee at one point that, "this is a 'slippery slope' in capital letters. This is exactly the type of 'mission creep' that led to disaster in Somalia."[44] When, in fact, Clinton did finally send troops into Bosnia, the public and Congress were not enthusiastic. More than 200 members of the House signed a letter to Clinton on December 6, 1995, written by Representative Bob Inglis (R-SC) that said simply, "We urge you not to send troops to Bosnia." As Representative Mark Souder (R-IN) explained his motivation, "Bosnia is dwarfing everything else. My constituents are just irate about it. The phone calls and mail coming in are six times heavier than normal, and the opposition is almost unanimous."[45]

Even the executive branch seems less certain than it once was about the exact extent of U.S. international involvement. Some of Clinton's strongest foreign policy initiatives have been in the realm of foreign trade, which has strong domestic overtones. Sometimes Clinton has vigorously promoted economic cooperation, as in NAFTA, the FTAA, and the GATT. He has also been confrontational, using threatened or applied sanctions to win concessions from China and Japan, among others, on economic issues. Where it comes to applying U.S. military power, Clinton has been much less certain. He could be described fairly from early in his tenure as something of a hawk on using force in Haiti and Bosnia (Scolnick, 1995). Yet, as noted, strong congressional and public opposition caused Clinton to delay following his predilections. Many other examples of public and congressional restraints on U.S. internationalist foreign policy could be cited, but that is not necessary to iterate the point that American attitudes and U.S. policy are less internationalist than they once were. The term "globocop" has been used popularly to disparage the idea that the United States should try to act like the world police officer. Instead, as one quip goes, many Americans now lean toward the role of "globoGarbo," a reference to actress Greta Garbo's famous phrase, "I want to be alone."

An important question is this: Are those who want to restrain U.S. internationalist policy trying to reinstitute isolationism? Few commentators admit to the still unfashionable title of isolationist, but many advocate policies that would move the United States in that direction. Commentator Alan Tonelson (1991:35), whose work has been touted by Newt Gingrich, has asserted, for example, that U.S. victories in the Persian Gulf War and the cold war "brought few benefits to the home front; indeed they seem scarcely relevant to the daily life and pressing concerns of most Americans today," and that the continued internationalist emphasis is "at once bizarre and dangerous." And another analyst writes, "The time has come to ask how much America's investment in the United Nations is worth. The short answer is: not very much."[46]

Such attitudes alarm some Americans, including presidents. George Bush expressed his concern about them in one of his last major foreign policy speeches. The president told a Texas A&M University gathering to beware of isolationism. "From some quarters we hear the voices sounding retreat. 'We've carried the burden too long,' they say, . . . 'we've done our part; now it's someone else's turn.' " Responding to such urging would be "disastrous," Bush warned. "The alternative to American leadership is not more security for our country but less."[47] The Clinton administration has also vigorously denounced what it sees as lurking isolationism. "Domestic renewal is an overdue tonic, [but] isolationism and protectionism are still poison," the president has said.[48] Many foreign leaders are also concerned. When, in a December 1995

122

CHAPTER 4
Political
Culture:
The Domestic
Setting

interview, a reporter asked President Jacques Chirac of France about U.S.–France relations, he replied, "I will not hide the fact that I am worried about the isolationism of the current American Congress . . . [T]his alarming tendency . . . is very dangerous for the whole world."[49]

Perhaps Bush, Clinton, and Chirac are correct. But the term isolationist is imprecise, and many to whom it is applied would object to being so characterized. Most Republican leaders would be among those who object. A greater percentage of Republicans than Democrats supported passage of both NAFTA and the GATT in Congress. Furthermore, the GOP leaders in both chambers avow internationalist ideas. Speaker of the House Gingrich has said that Americans must be "prepared to say bluntly and without much debate [that] we will lead the human race." One reason for this commitment, the Speaker continued, is that "if we don't lead the planet, there is no leader on the planet. We're the only military power that matters."[50] Senate Republican leader Dole specifically rejects the call of those who "argue that America should not get involved in the world." He characterizes isolationists as those "on the Left who believe America will corrupt the world, and on the Right who believe the world will corrupt America." The isolationists are correct in saying that "there are no serious and immediate threats to vital American interests," Dole concedes, but he counsels that "while that may be true now, retreat from the world is the surest way to invite the emergence of such threats in the future." Therefore, the senator concludes, the United States, "as the only global power, must lead. . . . on the full range of political, diplomatic, economic, and military issues confronting the world" (Dole, 1995:7).[51]

Clinton administration officials do not accept such protestations of internationalist commitment. National security adviser Anthony Lake, for one, calls the Republicans "back-door isolationists," who "cast themselves as the true guardians of American power," but who are really "agents of American retreat."[52] And during his speech celebrating the fiftieth anniversary of the signing of the UN Charter, President Clinton coined the phrase "new isolationists" for those who are critical of U.S. involvement in the multilateral activities of the UN and other international organizations, and he warned of the danger of following the beguiling "siren song" of these unilateralists.[53]

Unilateralism versus Multilateralism

One way to begin to evaluate the debate between the White House and the Republican congressional leadership is to understand that it does not involve just the extent of international involvement. To a significant degree, it also involves the goals and methods of U.S. involvement. To an extent, the two camps are more likely to divide along realism (a Republican tendency) versus idealism (a Democratic tendency) and on unilateralism (a Republican tendency) versus multilateralism (a Democratic tendency).

The realist versus idealist debate has been reviewed extensively in earlier parts of this book and need not be analyzed fully again here. The essence of the debate is the nature of the American national interest. Democrats are more likely to favor the values associated with liberalism discussed above and to argue that promoting democracy, ending human rights abuses, and generally cooperating globally on a social, economic, and political level are in the long-term American national interest. Republicans are more likely to favor overseas involvement only when it can be shown to have a demonstrable and immediate benefit to the United States.

The **unilateralist** versus **multilateralist** debate is a second dimension of the current foreign policy debate on when and how the United States should take action abroad. The dispute is over whether the United States should mostly undertake international activity alone (unilateralist) or in cooperation (multilateralist) with other countries and, especially, as part of the efforts of international organizations, such as the UN. Another part of this issue is whether the United States should undertake international action as a result of unilateral U.S. decisions or only after multilateral agreements. Referring to this divide, one congressional source has commented that "there's no question that there's a fight for the soul of foreign policy between Congress and the Clinton administration over the question of engagement abroad."[54]

The debate was joined in a recent issue of the journal *Foreign Policy*. Taking the unilateralist view, Senator Dole (1995:8) argued that "international organizations . . . will not protect American interests. Only America can do that." Dole objected to relying on a multilateralist approach because international organizations will "at best, practice policymaking at the lowest common denominator, finding a course that is the least objectionable to the most members"; because international organizations too often "reflect a consensus that opposes American interests or does not reflect American principles and ideals"; and because "even gaining support for an American position can involve deals or trade-offs that are not in America's long-term interests." Moreover, Dole claimed that multilateralism threatens U.S. involvement in the world and U.S. security because "subcontracting American foreign policy and subordinating American sovereignty encourage and strengthen isolationist forces at home and embolden our adversaries abroad."

President Bill Clinton and Senate majority leader Robert Dole disagree on numerous issues, including whether the United States should pursue a multilateralist or a unilateralist foreign policy. As a multilateralist, Clinton thinks that seeking common goals through cooperation with others through such multilateral organizations as the UN and NATO should be the hallmark of U.S. foreign policy. Dole favors a unilateralist approach. He believes that cooperation leads to the subordination of U.S. interests and that the United States should act alone when necessary to ensure that the country achieves its self-interested goals. Some critics charge that such disputes are undercutting U.S. influence in the world, symbolized here by Clinton and Dole riding an escalator downward.

Responding from the multilateralist perspective, Secretary of State Christopher (1995) maintained that U.S. leadership requires that Americans "galvanize the support of allies, friends, and international institutions in achieving common objectives." Not trying to do so, the secretary of state contends, is "naive" and forces the United States

124

CHAPTER 4
Political
Culture:
The Domestic
Setting

to choose between acting alone and doing nothing during humanitarian and political crises.[55] President Clinton made a similar argument at ceremonies commemorating the fiftieth anniversary of the founding of the United Nations. "So I say, especially to the opponents of the United Nations here in the United States," the president said at the end of his address, "turning our back on the UN and going it alone will lead to far more economic, political, and military burdens on our people in the future."[56]

Public Attitudes on U.S. Involvement Abroad

Before concluding this discussion of the relative strengths of internationalism and isolationism, and the related themes of unilateralism and multilateralism, it is important to examine public attitudes because there is also considerable debate about whether or not the public is isolationist. Taking the view that the public is isolationist, one analyst argues that "The public is more self-centered; it wants a foreign policy directed to improving things here in the United States." Replies another analyst, "That's a bum rap. The public has not flagged for a moment in its commitments to the country's leadership responsibilities."[57] In fact, this divergence of informed opinion is indicative of the public's ambivalence, and what any individual survey finds about the public's mood rests somewhat on how you ask the question.

Since World War II, as mentioned earlier, polls have revealed that a majority of Americans have consistently favored an active involvement in foreign affairs. That support stood at about a two-thirds level in 1994. Yet it is prudent to be cautious about such general expressions of internationalism. One reason is that the public's support for general, nonpolicy-specific statements of internationalism may reflect national pride more than policy preference. When survey questions probe specific policy views, they find that the public's support for internationalist policies has dropped off considerably from what it once was (Wittkopf, 1993). The war in Vietnam caused many Americans to question what seemed to be a U.S. attempt to police the world, to establish a *Pax Americana*. Then the collapse of the communist threat eliminated the containment doctrine that had long furnished the rationale for heavy overseas commitments and spending. After surveying American attitudes, one analyst concluded that "the biggest foreign policy problems facing the United States, according to the public, are America's getting involved in the affairs of other countries, too much foreign aid being sent to other countries, and immigration" (Rielly, 1995:81). Other factors have also undermined internationalism. Support for economic protectionism has strengthened among Americans, for example, because of their concerns about the foreign trade deficits and about the loss of jobs when U.S. companies move their operations overseas or when imports undercut American products and the workers who make them.

A second reason to be cautious about the public's general support of internationalism is that, in some respects, it has declined since the end of the Vietnam War era. Idealist goals have particularly suffered. One analyst concludes that "support for many of the more humanitarian goals among both the public and leaders has declined to the lowest level in two decades" (Rielly, 1995:81). When compared with 1974, for instance, there had been a 33 point drop in public support for protecting weak countries against foreign aggression, a 24 point drop in support for promoting and defending human rights elsewhere, and a 19 point drop in support for improving the standard of living in less developed countries.

A third reason to be cautious about the public's general support of internationalism is that public attitudes reflect the traditional American ambivalence about international involvement, especially without a clearly defined and obviously threatening enemy. Clinton has been roundly criticized for what opponents call vacillation. Insofar as that is true, though, it is partly a reflection of the times. Characterizing them succinctly, national security adviser Anthony Lake pointed out that the Clinton administration is the first since Truman's that "has not had a single defining issue against which it could define itself."[58] Moreover, it can be said that Clinton's lack of consistency reflects public ambivalence between wanting the United States to be the leader and not wanting to pay the price of leadership, between wanting to right wrongs and not wanting to bear the burdens of the good Samaritan. To note just one bit of evidence of this public ambivalence, one 1994 survey found what seems to be a profoundly isolationist public. Only 41 percent of the public endorsed the idea of even defending the security of established U.S. allies (Rielly, 1995). Yet another survey the same year disclosed that 59 percent of Americans would "definitely" or "probably" favor fighting if close U.S. allies were attacked (Richman, 1995).

Fourth, what is often portrayed as isolationism in the public is often more a matter of public resistance to multilateralism, not to international involvement (Chittick, Billingsley, & Travis, 1995). Many Americans are uncomfortable with the diminution of sovereignty that is an inherent part of the growth of interdependence and the international organizations (such as the UN, the WTO, and the IMF) that help try to regulate the increasingly intermeshed global enterprise. "In some groups of Americans, there is a distinct fear of loss of U.S. sovereignty," the ranking Democrat on the House International Relations Committee, Representative Lee Hamilton (D-IN), points out. "In many of my public meetings people have gotten up to attack what they call the New World Order."[59]

Here again, though, American attitudes reflect ambivalence caused by clashing aspects of political culture and by the public desire for both continued U.S. leadership and a return to a seemingly simpler, less entangled time. As such, even while Americans resist the loss of sovereignty that the United Nations and other aspects of the new international system entail, Americans also continue to support the UN. That was evident in a survey taken on the eve of the UN's fiftieth anniversary in June 1995. Of those polled, 76 percent expressed a very or mostly favorable view of the UN; that was a better rating than that of the U.S. Congress (53 percent). Furthermore, 62 percent of the respondents said the United States should cooperate with the UN. That is a decline from the 77 percent who favored cooperation in 1991, but it is higher than the mere 46 percent who wanted to cooperate in 1976.[60]

What can be safely said, then, about the public is that the mix of attitudes among Americans and the realities of the modern international system mean that the country is not likely to retreat to a fortress-America stance. Moreover, even if isolationist sentiment increases in the years ahead, the United States will continue to play a central, if less expansive, role in international relations because its global role is required by the demands of economic interdependence and military contingencies. In other words, isolationism may persist as a force in American foreign policy, but its effects on policy will be limited by world realities and by the web of international commitments propagated by American policy makers over the past 50 years.

1. Every country's foreign policy is partly a product of its political culture—long-standing patterns of societal beliefs, values, and traditions. Political culture can change but normally does so only slowly.

2. American political culture can be divided into Americans' views of self, views of others, and views of what they see as the proper role of the United States in the world.

3. American views of self are based on major themes including exceptionalism, moralism, and liberalism. Exceptionalism refers to the typical American belief that Americans are not just different from, but are better than, other people. Moralism refers to the traditional American need to justify political agendas and actions in moral terms and for outcomes to be judged against some normative set of values. Liberalism refers to the dominant U.S. political ideology, including an emphasis on individual rights and democracy, capitalism, and legalism.

4. American views of others are dominated by messianism, idealism, racism, and pragmatism. Messianism refers to the American desire to remake the world in the American image. Idealism presumes peace and harmony to be the natural states of humankind and rejects power-seeking as the basis of human or international relations. Racism is evident in cases where U.S. responses to situations involving other racial or ethnic groups appear to be harsher or less sympathetic than those involving white societies. Pragmatism refers to the tendency to approach problems on a case-by-case basis, thereby avoiding ideological standards or a reexamination of deeply held societal values.

5. The American image of the appropriate U.S. role in the world has been a result of an ambivalence between isolationism and internationalism. Initially more isolationist than internationalist, the United States tried to maintain economic and diplomatic relations with other countries while avoiding involvement in their political and military struggles. From the latter 1800s until the outbreak of World War II, the strength of the isolationist and internationalist impulses shifted back and forth with some frequency. World War II brought a predominantly internationalist course to American attitudes and policy. The loss of the war in Vietnam caused many Americans to veer back toward isolationism. Moreover, the demise of the Soviet Union and with it the threat of international communism ended one of the greatest single impetuses behind U.S. post–World War II international involvement. This has hampered the selling of internationalism by presidents to the somewhat isolationist American people. It is probable, however, that the global importance of the United States and the international commitments made over the last 50 years will combine to keep the country a major player in the international system.

Chapter Five

THE HUMAN SETTING

Foreign policy is made by humans! "Well, of course," you might say. "Everybody knows that!" You would be right— but only so far. Everybody does know that the presidents, cabinet officers, legislative leaders, and others who make foreign policy decisions are humans. Yet we pay little attention to how the human condition limits the ability of policy makers to reach perfectly rational decisions. Just as decision makers are constrained by the system and by the societal settings in which they operate, so too are decision makers limited by the fact that they are humans, not machines. There may come a time when we humans can emulate the emotionless, computer-like decision making of *Star Trek*'s Mr. Data. But at least for now we humans are neither dispassionate nor omniscient. Therefore, we need to explore how policy is affected by people acting and interacting as emotional, intellectually limited humans (Ripley, 1993).

127

To accomplish this, our examination of the human factor in foreign policy making is divided into three major parts. The first is an overview of the characteristics of human decision making. The second part involves a discussion on the impact of making decisions within organizational settings. The third part is an exploration of how idiosyncratic factors affect decisions.

HUMAN DECISION MAKING

Approaches to the general study of human decision making range from analyses of the biological and psychological nature of how the human species makes decisions through studies of the cognitive limitations of humans during the specific steps involved in discrete decisions.

Decision Making: The Human Species

There are myriad theories about the biological and psychological nature of humankind as decision makers. We cannot begin to detail all the theories here, but it is important to understand that some analysts believe that political decisions, like other kinds, are driven in part by deep-seated factors in humankind's genes and psychic makeup. To focus our look at these two factors, we will concentrate on how biology and psychology may affect attitudes and actions involving conflict.

Biological Factors

Human biology is one possible explanation of human conflict behavior. The study of biopolitics, or sociobiology, analyzes the interrelationship between biology and politics. Within that field, the subspecialty of ethology centers on the idea that human behavior is based in part on traits that are traceable to the fact that humans are animals. Political ethologists, therefore, study animal behavior in such areas as conflict and social organization and compare their observations to human behavior.

Territory and Aggression   Ethologists believe, for example, that animals fight instinctively to gain or protect territory that they feel is necessary for their survival or breeding. Robert Ardrey's *The Territorial Imperative* (1961) is a classic ethological study.

While scholars differ sharply about the impact of biopolitical factors, history shows that territory is also a frequent cause of human warfare. One study of 182 wars in the world between 1945 and 1989 found that "more than one-half the conflicts [52 percent] had a territorial dimension: either gaining or maintaining control over strategically significant pieces of real estate . . . or over the precise demarcation of boundaries" (K. Holsti, 1991:282). Moreover, after studying more than three centuries of conflict dating back to the Peace of Westphalia that ended the Thirty Years' War in 1648, Holsti (p. 283) concluded that the territorial "aspect of international conflict remains fairly constant through all the periods of this study."

Given U.S. power and geographic isolation from other powers strong enough to threaten its territory, the territorial factor has not been present in twentieth-century American conflicts. During the first century of U.S. history, by contrast, territory was a regular cause of American wars, including the War of 1812 and the Mexican War.

This does not prove that the urge to dominate the continent and the willingness to fight to achieve that goal were based, all or in part, on animal instinct. Moreover, territoriality, insofar as it exists, may be based on the search for security and not on instinctive aggressiveness. In any case, one has to wonder if territoriality does not stir humans to political action. To cite just one example, the war with Mexico (1846–1848) was precipitated by American and Mexican moves and countermoves into a strip of disputed land between the Nueces River and Rio Grande, a barren, dry territory in which neither Mexico nor independent Texas (1836–1845) had shown much interest.

Gender and Aggression   A variation on the belief that human biology motivates conflict behavior in certain circumstances holds that gender differences are a factor (Brandes, 1994; Togeby, 1994; Howes & Stevenson, 1993; Conover & Sapiro, 1993; Tickner, 1992). There is considerable dispute over the roles of instinctive (genetic) versus learned (socialization) behavior, but the idea that war may be partly the result of males' propensity for aggressive behavior is attracting considerable study. Some scholars suggest that many women and men have very different views of power, national security, and other political concepts and practices, and most survey data bears this view out. For example, one recent survey of American attitudes toward using military

Studies that compare the attitudes of men and women to war have found that women are less likely than men to advocate the use of force. It is, therefore, possible to argue that U.S. foreign policy would be less bellicose than it sometimes is if more women held high policy making positions. The gender differences on war are represented by Jeannette Rankin. The first woman to be elected to Congress (as a Republican from Montana in 1916), Representative Rankin also was the only member of Congress to vote against U.S. entry into both World War I in 1917 and World War II in 1941.

force concluded that "perhaps the most dramatic division [in the willingness to use violence] is along gender lines, with men consistently more willing than women to use troops in various circumstances—often the difference is nearly 20 percentage points" (Rielly, 1995:88).

Furthermore, those women who do achieve high positions in the foreign policy making structure often have attitudes and experiences that are quite different from those of their male counterparts (McGlen & Sarkees, 1993). Such views are often labeled the feminist perspective, although the studies that constitute its literature are not written exclusively by women. *The feminist approach* addresses, among other things, the role of women in politics and the ways that more female participation in politics would change processes and policies. In the area of national security, one feminist scholar argues that "from the masculine perspective, peace for the most part has meant the absence of war and the prevention of armed conflict" (Reardon,

129

1990:137) . She calls this masculine view "negative peace." Women, Reardon continues, are more likely to stress "positive peace," that is, "conditions of social justice, economic equity and ecological balance." There are male scholars who agree. One contends, for instance, that there are "remarkable parallels in male [including human] primate behavior," such as "power seeking" and the "struggle for power" (Schubert, 1993:29). For this reason, he concludes, there are "compelling practical policy implications" associated with women playing a greater leadership role in U.S. foreign and national security policy.

Psychological Factors

There are many theories about mass political psychology. Frustration-aggression analysis, to cite one, might help explain human aggressive behavior. This approach holds that when people (and other animals) get frustrated, they strike out. The old adage about "even a trapped rat will fight" is based on frustration-aggression theory. One could make an argument, for instance, that U.S. behavior in the early 1980s exhibited frustration-aggression traits. The late 1960s and 1970s were, overall, a dismal time for Americans. Urban and anti–Vietnam War violence rocked the country; assassins shot Martin Luther King Jr., Robert F. Kennedy, and other prominent Americans; the economy sagged; inflation heated up; Cambodians seized American seamen; Iranians held American diplomatic personnel hostage. Americans were frustrated and angry by 1980. It may well be that Ronald Reagan's promise to pursue an assertive foreign policy helped propel him into the White House because it resonated the public's frustrated anger. Indeed, his subsequent military forays against Libya, Grenada, and other countries were also an outgrowth of pent-up emotion and were popular with most Americans.

Decision Making: Cognitive Limits

Whatever one thinks of the validity of biological and psychological approaches to decision making, there is no doubt that humans cannot make perfectly rational decisions. Such perfect rationality would involve gathering all possible information, listening to varying expert opinions on the situation and possible responses, considering all possible responses (including the costs and benefits of each), calculating the national interest, selecting the best course of action, and overseeing its implementation. These criteria are beyond human abilities.

One limit is that complete information is not available. Often, for example, decision makers do not know, and perhaps cannot know, what is in the mind of an opposing country's decision makers. Second, even if perfect information were available, it would be an avalanche of material that would overwhelm the human ability to read, much less comprehend, it. Indeed, people have neither the intellectual nor the emotional capacity to know and evaluate the totality of even what information is available regarding a policy question and to process the information in a completely dispassionate way. Recognizing that perfectly rational decisions do not exist, political scientists try to understand decision making within the limits of what is possible physically, intellectually, and emotionally for humans (Hybel, 1993; Sylvan, Ostrom & Gannon, 1993). Therefore, one central factor in decision making is how policy makers deal with poor information, lack of enough training and general knowledge to evaluate existing information, unclear or conflicting standards to evaluate goals, inability to foresee exactly the outcome of policy choices, and other cognitive barriers to making purely rational decisions.

There are several closely related concepts that behavioral scientists use to describe decision making within human limits. One is *cybernetics,* which describes the way that humans (and other living organisms and machines) organize and process information, values, and other inputs into the decision making process. Another important idea is *cognitively limited decision making.* This involves making choices within the limits of what you know rather than the universe of all applicable information. Even more expressively, these limits necessarily mean that decisions are based on *bounded rationality* and are made in an imperfect decision making environment characterized by "structured uncertainty."

The Nature of Cognitive Limits

One study that reviewed the research on cognitive decision making suggests that scholars have come to three main conclusions. They are that "(1) individuals are selective information processors, (2) they have limited cognitive capabilities, and (3) they often use some sort of heuristic or mental aid to handle decision problems" (Powell, Dyson, & Purkitt, 1987:208). A heuristic aid is a mental tool or frame of reference (perception) to help organize and evaluate information and options. *Belief systems* are one such heuristic device. For example, one common belief system shared by many U.S. decision makers—and indeed by much of the American public—during the cold war went as follows: democracy and free enterprise are good, totalitarianism and communism are bad, therefore the Soviet Union is not to be trusted. This belief system made it easy for decision makers to interpret Soviet proposals and actions as being designed for world ideological and political conquest. Other heuristic images will be discussed in this chapter's later section on perceptions.

The Impact of Cognitive Limits

There are many results from the intellectual and emotional limits of human decision makers. A short discussion of a few impacts should suffice to indicate their importance.

Accepting conventional wisdom is one impact. It is easier to buy into prevailing interpretations than to think through a problem anew. During the height of the cold war, the conventional wisdom was that communism was a monolith and that leaders of communist countries and movements were driven by ideology, not nationalism. This view affected U.S. policy toward the fighting in Vietnam. "We totally underestimated the nationalist aspect of Ho Chi Minh's movement. We saw him first as a Communist and only second as a Vietnamese nationalist," former secretary of defense Robert S. McNamara has recalled. "Such ill-founded judgments were accepted without debate," he recalls; "we failed to analyze our assumptions critically, then or later. The foundations of our decision making were gravely flawed."[1]

Seeking cognitive consistency is another impact. During the U.S. involvement in the war in Vietnam, there were analyses that argued that the United States could not prevail militarily or would find it too costly to do so. Yet it was very difficult for top decision makers to believe simultaneously (1) that the United States was a superpower

© 1995 Markstein—*Milwaukee Journal Sentinel*

Decision makers are far from omniscient. Instead, they have many cognitive limits that constrain their ability to make purely rational decisions. Former secretary of defense Robert McNamara admitted in his 1995 memoirs that he and other officials in the administration of President Lyndon Johnson had made many errors attributable to shared cognitive limits. These errors led to the long and draining U.S. involvement in the Vietnam War. Unfortunately for the U.S. soldiers who died in Vietnam, whose names are inscribed on the Vietnam War Memorial in Washington, D.C., McNamara's newfound wisdom came 3 decades too late to save their lives.

and (2) that it could be defeated by a much smaller, lightly armed opponent. Much of this analysis about the limits of U.S. power never reached decision makers, as we will see presently. And even what did get to the top political leaders was largely discounted by them because they found it difficult to believe both (1) and (2) with cognitive consistency.

Incrementalism is a third result of cognitive limits (Bendor, 1995). Policy decisions seldom send a country in a radically new direction. Instead, decision makers usually accept past policy as a given and make only small changes. Even though thinking within the executive branch about recognizing China had begun to change by the mid-1960s, it took a decade and a half and many small steps before relations between the United States and China were fully normalized in 1979. *Satisficing* is yet another impact of cognitive limits. This means that decision makers tend to adopt the first policy option that they find minimally acceptable rather than continuing to search for the optimal solution. Moreover, once a policy course is selected, sheer momentum makes it hard to reverse it, even in the face of doubts or negative results (Lebovic, 1994).

Wishful thinking is the last impact of cognitive limits that we will mention. Decision makers are apt to believe that whatever they have decided will work—no matter what the objective odds may be. During the debate over whether to support a Cuban exile invasion of Cuba at the Bay of Pigs in 1961, advisers told President John Kennedy that there was a "fair chance" that the invasion would succeed and would topple Cuban president Fidel Castro (Neustadt & May, 1986:142). That characterization of a fair chance, it later came to light, was based on a State Department estimate that the odds were 3 to 1 *against* success. "We were guilty of wishful thinking," CIA official Richard Drain later admitted. "We did not like Castro, and we were convinced he had to go. There was the belief that as a result Castro could not stay in power if the U.S. put its hand to it" (Vandenbroucke, 1991:118).

Similarly, President Carter decided in 1980 to try a military rescue of the American hostages in Tehran despite a CIA estimate that at least 60 percent of the hostages would be killed in the attempt. The reason Carter acted anyway, one scholar observes, is that the "key decisionmakers simply did not realistically appraise the plan for the rescue mission" (Smith, 1984:118). Instead, the president's chief of staff, Hamilton Jordan, later wrote, the White House "couldn't even contemplate failure. . . . I couldn't get my mind off the helicopters lifting off the embassy grounds with the hostages. I wanted desperately for this Godforsaken crisis to be over and done with" (Vandenbroucke, 1991:419).

As you will see, the general characteristics of decision making are also often evident in the organizational and idiosyncratic aspects of decision making. It is to these subjects that we can now turn our attention.

DECISIONS IN ORGANIZATIONAL SETTINGS

Most foreign policy decisions are made within an organizational setting. This means that individual policy makers hold positions in a formal organization and that policy makers interact with one another within formal and informal structures (David, Carrol, & Selden, 1993). To examine this, we will look at two factors: role definition and small group decisions.

Role Definition

The concept of **role** means that the way people act is determined partly by the jobs they hold (Ripley, 1993). Role is often equated to bureaucratic self-interest because officials frequently adopt the role of promoting their agency's welfare. But role is more subtle than just bureaucratic position because people define the same job in different ways. Cabinet officers, for example, are presidential appointees who, arguably, should adopt the president's perspective in running their departments. At the same time, it is also appropriate for cabinet officers to represent their departments' interests and views within the administration. Many officials appointed by the president begin by supporting the White House view but quickly wind up being converted to their agency's bureaucratic perspective. This is called "going native" in Washington. When he was appointed in 1988, James Baker acknowledged that the State Department "tends to capture you if you're not careful." Baker said he would be "very careful," because "I want to be the President's man at the State Department, instead of the State Department's man at the White House."[2]

The president's role is defined both by each individual's own views and by the views of the greater society. Presidents, for instance, like to act presidential, which is generally defined as active, decisive, and confident. Most of us like presidents to play this assured role too, and this expectation creates further role pressure on the chief executive. Jimmy Carter was sent back to Plains, Georgia, in part because Americans doubted his grit. Before the U.S. invasion of Panama and the Persian Gulf War, George Bush was derided in the media for being a wimp. Similarly, once inaugurated, Bill Clinton was soon being attacked by the media and others for lack of focus and for indecision. "That Sinking Feeling: Is Clinton Up to the Job?" asked the title of a *Time* magazine article after the president's first four months in office.[3] It was a view reflected by the public. Polls showed that Clinton's public approval rating had plummeted to 36 percent. That was 28 percent below Carter's after four months in office and the lowest by far of any president at that point in office (next was Gerald Ford at 36 percent; best was Harry Truman at 92 percent).[4] Whether accurate or not, this image continued to dog Clinton and to threaten his reelection. Three surveys between January 1994 and January 1995 that asked Americans whether they approved or disapproved of the way Clinton was handling foreign affairs averaged only a 43.3 percent approval rating, with the president never gaining majority approval.[5]

Yet the strong, active role may not always be best. Secretary of State Dean Rusk (1990:137), who served in the Kennedy and Johnson administrations, has remembered that "we tended then—and now—to exaggerate the necessity to take action. Given time, many problems work themselves out or disappear." This expectation of an assertive role pushed Jimmy Carter to try to rescue Americans being held hostage in Iran. Even though the attempt endangered the hostages, National Security Council (NSC) adviser Zbigniew Brzezinski told Carter that "your greater responsibility is to protect the honor and dignity of our country" by taking action. This advice contrasted sharply with Secretary of State Cyrus Vance's counsel to wait and negotiate. "Cy's calm approach sounded good," White House chief of staff Hamilton Jordan explained, "but Zbig's tough approach felt good" (Glad, 1989:47, 48). Carter agreed. "I am the president of a great country," he fretted; "I would like to continue to be patient, but it is very difficult to do so" (Vandenbroucke, 1991:366). Too difficult, as it turned out. Action carried the day; the raid moved toward its abortive end (Moens, 1991; Cogan, 1990).

Small Group Decisions

Political scientists, business organization experts, and other students of group dynamics have long recognized that making decisions in a small-group setting creates many pressures on the participants that can significantly affect policy (Stern & Sundelius, 1994). Sometimes policy making groups provide a setting where information is exchanged and persuasive arguments are made that result in reasoned policy decisions (Mulcahy 1995; Barrett, 1993). Groups may, however, also provide an opportunity for one or more members to manipulate the discussion so as to achieve a policy goal (Maoz, 1991). Those who favor a status quo policy often rely on standard operating procedures and may, for example, push for a quick decision in order to prevent those who would prefer a more innovative policy from gathering new information and providing alternative analyses.

The group decisional setting is also fertile ground for **groupthink**. It can occur in the Oval Office, bureaucratic conference rooms, congressional chambers, or anywhere else policy makers meet. The term groupthink was coined by scholars to describe the pressure to achieve consensus within a small, face-to-face decisional group (Janis, 1982, 1972). Practioners have also come to adopt the term because it captures the essence of what they have experienced. Writing recently, General Colin L. Powell recalls that "our senior officers knew the [Vietnam] war was going badly. Yet they bowed to groupthink pressures and kept up the pretenses" that the United States was winning the war.[6] When leaders give in to groupthink pressure, they tend to seek consensus among subordinates so that the leader can feel reassured. Subordinates tend to avoid contradicting the leader or even the prevailing opinion of the group in order to avoid becoming outsiders. Scholars do not contend that these things always happen, merely that group settings are fertile grounds for the groupthink syndrome to take hold. Just a few of the negative results that may occur from groupthink are:

Discordant information is discounted. Small groups seeking consensus are apt to consider information that fits into established assumptions about what is true. Groups also tend only to accept information that supports what they intend to do. The Bay of Pigs operation in 1961 failed disastrously when the CIA–backed invasion of Cuba by expatriates was quickly demolished by Fidel Castro's military. Inadequate U.S.

support of the rebels was one of the many reasons why the invasion collapsed. Military logistics experts knew that the poor support level endangered the operation, but the White House did not want to hear that advice. One member of the Joint Chiefs of Staff (JCS) later recalled trying to tell this to President Kennedy, who shot back: "This is a CIA operation, it is not a military operation. You will not become involved in this" (Vandenbroucke, 1991:62). Assistant Secretary of State Thomas Mann also opposed the operation on the grounds that, among others, it would not work. He too was ignored. Mann has recalled that the impact of a memo of opposition that he wrote to the president was tantamount to "nothing at all. . . . It was like a stone falling in the water" (Gleijeses, 1995:25).

Subordinates do not dissent. Groupthink inhibits individuals from voicing doubts for fear they will lose favor with their boss. Potential dissenters may also keep their own counsel because they worry that they will be considered misinformed or even foolish by other members of the decisional group. The doubting JCS member during the Bay of Pigs operation later regretted that he and other military advisers "didn't speak out loudly enough . . . didn't pound the table." Why not be forceful? Well, the admiral explained, "You couldn't expect us [the JCS] . . . to say this plan is no damn good, you ought to call it off; that's not the way you do things in government" (Vandenbroucke, 1991:64). Assistant Secretary of State Mann was also passive when the final decision came. "I do have a recollection of a meeting in the Department of State at which President Kennedy asked each of those present to vote for or against the proposed operation," Mann has written. "As everyone present expressed support, I did the same. I did this because I did not wish to leave the impression that I would not support whatever the president decided to do" (Gleijeses, 1995:32).

Dissenters are excluded. Group members often fear that if they dissent they may lose their reputation, be excluded from the inner circle of decision makers, or be forced from office. This is not paranoia; it happens. In 1979 the Carter administration decided to attempt the rescue of U.S. hostages being held in Iran's capital, Tehran. The goal was laudable, but the effort's chance of success was nearly zero. Secretary of State Cyrus Vance opposed the raid. Carter and the rest of his inner circle knew of Vance's opposition. What Carter and his inner circle did to avoid Vance's dissent was to meet on a day when Vance was out of town. Predictably, the group's decision was to proceed with the raid. When Vance returned and insisted courageously on having his say, the secretary was treated shabbily. He stated his case and was ignored. Vance had obviously been "traumatized" and weakened "by his Vietnam experience," sneered NSC adviser Zbigniew Brzezinski. Vance's dissent left the president doubting his secretary of state's emotional health. "Vance has been extremely despondent . . . deeply troubled and heavily burdened," Carter confided to his diary. The mission proceeded. It failed miserably. Vance had been right. Was he vindicated, listened to with new respect within the administration? No; to the contrary, the ignored Vance soon resigned under pressure. In his place Carter appointed a new secretary of state whom the president described as "more statesmanlike" than Vance had been (Glad, 1989:50–56).

The decision of the Clinton administration to reverse existing U.S. policy and begin to return Cuban boat people to their country was another decision that was made in a process that, one analysis noted, "excluded officials who were likely to object." "We wanted to keep this to a very small circle," an administration official explained.[7]

Policy options are not fully evaluated. Rational decision making envisions that all policy options are carefully considered. The principal architects of U.S. foreign policy in the Clinton administration soon developed a reputation for amicable cooperation. Within a year, national security adviser Anthony Lake had come to worry about the lack of conflicts. "I think there is a danger," Lake said, "that when people work well together you can take the edge off options [to develop] 'group-think' [with] not enough options reaching the president."[8] One example of not enough options being considered occurred during the 1990–1991 Persian Gulf crisis. President Bush and his small cadre of advisers gave little or no credence to any options other than (1) immediate and total Iraqi withdrawal from Kuwait or (2) war. Negotiations were never considered and economic sanctions received only lip service. When Iraq held fast, war became inevitable. That may have occurred anyway, but the point is that we will never know because Bush never tried negotiations and never gave sanctions a chance.

This "either-or" approach of Bush occurred in part because the limited circle of presidential advisers either agreed with his confrontational inclinations or were unwilling to challenge the determined president. Even at the time, much less in retrospect, this limited focus worried experienced observers. Former national security adviser Zbigniew Brzezinski expressed concern during the Gulf crisis about "the very narrow decision-making process" at work in the Bush White House. Without "alternative strategic perspectives [presented] very directly at the highest level," Brzezinski warned, a "danger" exists of having Oval Office views "reinforced rather than examined."[9]

The use of long-term economic sanctions to pressure Iraq to withdraw was not, for example, considered seriously by the White House. Such sanctions were imposed by the UN, but Bush and most of his inner circle never really believed in them. This attitude contrasted with that of other experienced practitioners who favored giving economic sanctions a year or more to work before resorting to war. Former Joint Chiefs of Staff (JCS) chairmen Admiral William Crowe and General David Jones both advocated waiting. So did former defense secretaries Robert McNamara and James Schlesinger. Their views were aired during testimony before Congress, not, however, in the Oval Office. There are even some indications that Bush's JCS chairman, General Colin Powell, also favored trying long-term sanctions before moving to war. But Secretary of Defense Richard Cheney told Powell that the president was not disposed to continue sanctions. Still, after considerable hesitation, the general tentatively made his case to the White House. Bush, Cheney, Secretary of State James Baker, and NSC adviser Brent Scowcroft listened in stony silence. They asked no questions, made no comments. When Powell was finished, the president dismissed him with a cursory, "I don't think there's time politically for that strategy" (Woodward, 1991:42). Powell retreated in the face of potential presidential scorn. Two options remained: an Iraqi diplomatic capitulation or war.

The specific examples of groupthink that we have been examining are further supported by scholarship that proves the intuitive view that groupthink results in poor policy. One key study found that good decisional processes yielded successful policy. Three scholars studied the

General Colin Powell, while chairman of the Joint Chiefs of Staff, briefs the press during the Persian Gulf War. Powell reportedly opposed abandoning economic sanctions and moving quickly to war with Iraq. It is symptomatic of groupthink that he hesitated to voice his concerns to President Bush and that, when the general did, Bush and his advisers dismissed them out of hand.

decisional processes at work during 19 crisis decisions (Herek, Janis, & Huth, 1987). The way in which each decision was made was examined to see if there was evidence of one or more of seven symptoms of defective decision making. These flaws are roughly equivalent to the specific characteristics of groupthink discussed above. The three scholars found that eight of the decision making processes were "high-quality," with evidence of zero defects or only one defect. Four decisional processes were "medium-quality" (two or three defects), and seven were "poor-quality" (four or more defects). The scholars then asked a panel of experts to assign a rating of "success" or "failure" to each of the 19 policy decisions based on the experts' evaluation of whether the policies had accomplished their respective goals. Where the experts disagreed, a "mixed" rating was assigned to the policy. The results showed that policy arrived at through "high-quality" decision making process enjoyed a 75 percent success rate. "Medium-quality" decisional process yielded policies that were judged a success in only 50 percent of the cases. "Poor-quality" decisional process resulted in policy that never worked; that is, there was a zero percent success rate. Like most provocative research, the study has been criticized (Purkitt, 1990). Nevertheless, the challenges have not overturned the overall empirical conclusion that good decision making processes—including divergent, multiple-advocacy discussion and criticism of planning—increase the chances for successful policy.

IDIOSYNCRATIC HUMAN DECISIONS

Another implication of the fact that humans make decisions imperfectly is that the uniquely individual characteristics—the personality and other idiosyncratic traits—of each decision maker enhance the impact of the human element on policy.

We will in the following sections look at how these individual factors influence decisions. The focus will be on the president. Remember, though, that presidents are only an example here. All decision makers are affected by their idiosyncratic traits. These traits include perceptions, personality, emotions, and mental and physical health. They combine to establish leadership style.

Perceptions

All of us, presidents included, view the world through the prism of preexisting experiences, images, and values. Thus there is an objective reality and a subjective (perceived) reality. Perceptions create an **operational reality** because decision makers take action based on what they *think* is real rather than what *is* real. During the Cuban missile crisis, the Soviets claimed that their missiles were being sent to Cuba to protect the island country from U.S. invasion. The United States viewed the missiles as a form of Soviet aggression. Whatever reality may have been, the contradictory (mis)perceptions almost took the world into a nuclear war (Sylvan & Thorson, 1990). As Secretary of Defense Robert McNamara later commented, both American and Soviet decision makers were "captives of our perceptions and misperceptions."[10] Indeed, from a broader perspective, whatever the true natures of communism and communist countries like the Soviet Union were during the cold war, the American perception of them as intractably hostile—even evil—governed U.S. policy. Some critics argue that U.S. policy makers overreacted to perceived communist threats during the cold war, thereby leading to unnecessary conflict (McCalla, 1992).

Perceptions range from the general to the specific. Belief systems are at the general end of the range of perceptions that affect leaders. A *belief system* is a complex set of established and deeply held ideas that individuals use to interpret their surroundings, other people, and events. As such, perceptions are analogous to a lens through which we view the world and which subtly or significantly distorts our images. A national belief system can influence the political culture of a society, as discussed in chapter 4. More important to our discussion here, individuals also have their own belief systems. In the case of presidents and other top decision makers, the individual's belief system can affect policy. One way to classify belief systems is to divide them into four elements: (1) beliefs about what works and what the possibilities (cooperation, inevitable conflict) are, (2) beliefs about the aims and character of the other main actors, including allies and opponents, (3) beliefs about what the international role of the United States should be, and (4) beliefs about how the United States should apply military force and other instruments of foreign policy in pursuit of its own and global interests (Spear & Williams, 1988).

It is possible to use categories (1) and (4) to illustrate the belief systems and policies of Jimmy Carter and Ronald Reagan. Carter is an idealist who (1) believes that long-term peace is possible and who (4) is adverse to using military force. It is hardly surprising then, that he used force only once (the hostage rescue mission in Iran) during his presidency. Nor is it surprising that he has more recently continued to try to promote peaceful resolutions to crises by traveling to Bosnia, North Korea, and Haiti. "The critical element of conflict resolution," Carter has said of his belief system, is "the willingness to resist recriminations" and the "patience to allow the [the other side] to understand that there is nothing on the table except a mutual effort to reach some sort of agreement." Carter's fundamental standard is "I'll talk with anybody who wants to talk about peace . . . however odious they are" (Wooten, 1995:33). By contrast, Ronald Reagan's belief system was very different. He viewed the Soviet leaders as evil-minded and dismissed attempts to negotiate with them as "a one-way street" (Paterson & Merrill, 1995:713). Based on this (1) perception, Reagan declined to meet directly with Soviet leaders during his entire first term. Reagan also saw the (4) use of military force much differently than did Carter. "I know that all of you want peace, and so do I," Reagan told Americans; the way to best achieve that is "to rely on the specter of retaliation, on mutual threat" (Paterson & Merrill, 1995:714). The impact of this belief system is evident in the 14 different instances of using military force that Reagan reported to Congress under the provision of the War Powers Resolution (Collier, 1991).

Another perceptual trait is to use past events as *historical analogies* to guide reactions to current events. President Bush saw an analogy between the Persian Gulf crisis in 1990 and 1991 and the rise of Adolf Hitler, the Munich Conference of 1938 (when Great Britain and France appeased German demands for part of Czechoslovakia), and other events associated with the coming of World War II. The lesson of Munich that Bush incorporated into his belief system was that appeasing the aggression of dictators signals weakness that only leads to further aggression. Therefore, negotiating with Iraq was an unacceptable equivalent to the appeasement of Germany (Northcutt, 1992). "If history teaches us anything," President Bush instructed Americans in his August 8, 1990, address to the nation, "it is that we must resist aggression.

. . . Appeasement does not work. As was the case in the 1930s, we see in Saddam Hussein an aggressive dictator threatening his neighbors."

Not everyone agreed; Iraq had some understandable grievances. While they did not justify Iraq's invading Kuwait, some were dismayed that the president refused to even consider them (Karsh & Rautsi, 1991). One Defense Department specialist in Arab affairs bemoaned the fact that "the president has left no wiggle room for Saddam Hussein, only bleak choices."[11] A State Department official agreed, saying that 85 percent of the agency's Middle East experts "think our course of action in the Persian Gulf is terrible." The president has "put himself in a box and has no way out because he refuses to negotiate," the official despaired.[12] But Bush angrily rejected such criticisms. "Everybody wants me to compromise," he snapped at a reporter, "There's not going to be a compromise with this man [Saddam]."[13]

Moreover, Bush seemed to seek reinforcement of the historical analogy that helped shape his perceptions. As the crisis progressed, the president's bedside reading was Martin Gilbert's *A Complete History of World War II.* At one point, he referred to the atrocities committed by Germany's SS "Death's Head" Regiment in Poland. "I'm about 200 pages into a 950-page . . . history of World War II," Bush told a reporter; "and the reason I made reference to the Death's Head Regiment is that it very clearly spelled out what happened [then and is now happening in Kuwait]."[14] At another juncture, Bush attended a play at Ford's Theater. The drama *Black Eagles* was about the gallantry of African American airmen during World War II. Bush returned to the White House after the play and met with his war council. A last-minute attempt by Soviet president Mikhail Gorbachev to broker a compromise was dismissed out of hand. Wavering at the eleventh hour was not the stuff of heroic black eagles.

Before leaving the impact of historical analogies, it must be pointed out that they have another role. In addition to helping shape policy, as the Munich analogy did for Bush, the lessons of history can also be used merely to justify policy preferences based on such factors as ideology. A recent study of the debates in Congress over authorizing the impending war with Iraq found that members who supported the war tended to use the Munich analogy, while members who opposed the war tended to use the Vietnam analogy to argue against involvement. Factors such as age (with older members citing Munich and younger members citing Vietnam) provided less explanation, however, than did foreign policy ideology and party membership. This led the study to conclude that analogies were used to "legitimize, not [to] drive, the policy choice of members of Congress" (Taylor & Rourke, 1995:466).

Personality

Like all humans, presidents are influenced by their basic personalities (Renshon, 1993). Unlike most humans, presidents can affect foreign policy directly. Therefore, presidential personalities can play a role in the foreign policy process.

There have been numerous studies of personality and leadership style. One by James Barber (1985) classifies presidential personality along two scales: *active-passive* and *positive-negative.* Barber's study is far from definitive, but it does provide a well-known and provocative approach to evaluating political personalities. According to Barber, active presidents are high-energy doers who define change and innovation as synonymous with success; passive presidents are conservators who want to avoid conflict and to preserve the status quo. Positive presidents are extroverts who like their job and accept the rough-and-tumble of politics; negative presidents are introverts who feel that they are duty-bound to carry the burdens of office. Combining the two scales, you get four basic personality types: active-positive (Kennedy, Ford, Carter, Bush, Clinton); active-negative (Johnson, Nixon); passive-positive (Reagan); and passive-negative (Eisenhower).

These personality types can affect policy in a number of ways. Barber, like most scholars, favors the active-positive president. That style has its drawbacks, however. One, as we saw earlier, is that an activist president may move forward when waiting would be wiser. Activist presidents also may get overly involved in the details of policy making and implementation. This can result in their flitting from policy issue to policy issue without ever giving any one the attention needed to ensure a clear decision and full implementation. Activists may, additionally, spend so much time with the details of an issue that decisions are delayed. These administrative weaknesses detract from a president's ability to move policy forward, as will be discussed in chapter 8. Passive presidents may not control policy or their staffs closely enough, as the example of the Iran-Contra affair and the renegade bureaucracy that operated under Reagan indicate.

A drawback of positive presidents is that they may like their job too much and may let considerations such as getting reelected overly influence decisions. In the same way, positive presidents are apt to be too eager to please others. One concern about President Clinton, for example, was expressed by an aide who worried that "the will to please is so prevalent that it is interfering with his effectiveness."[15] Negative presidents feel angry and betrayed when they are criticized. This makes them especially likely to reject dissenting advice and to retreat into a shrinking circle of obsequious advisers. In extreme cases such as during the Nixon administration, negative personalities feel justified in flouting the law, smearing opponents, and committing other abuses of office.

Several recent studies have focused on President Bush. One characterized him as a "compulsive" personality type, an achiever with a "need for new challenges and an emphasis on action over words" (Swansbrough, 1991:30, 21). The analyst argued that compulsive traits are a mixture of strengths, such as organizational skills, and weaknesses, including lack of vision, inflexibility, and the stifling of subordinates. Another scholar combined the concepts of political culture, role, and personality to analyze what he termed George Bush's "macho presidential style." According to this scholar, the "sexist political system" in the United States has pressured almost all presidents to adopt the "real man, never feminine" role: competitive, sports-minded, decisive, unemotional, aggressive (Orman, 1991:4, 16). He suggested, moreover, that Bush's personality readily adopted and reinforced the role and made the president try to be the "quintessential real man."

Analysts are also beginning to study the political psychology of President Clinton. It is a common observation, for example, that Clinton often abandons his positions or seeks compromise when faced with strong opposition. In their efforts to understand this trait, scholars of political psychology will be fascinated by Clinton's recollection in late 1995 of the impact of a dysfunctional family during his childhood. The president remembers his stepfather as often abusing his mother. In one incident when he was 5 years old, Clinton's stepfather fired a shot at, and barely missed, the future president's mother. "I remember that incident vividly, like it was yesterday," the president says. Clinton avers that "I don't believe in psychobabble" but adds that "I have to be acutely aware that I grew up as a peacemaker, always trying to minimize the disruption."[16]

In the political psychology studies that have been done of Clinton, most scholars lean toward classifying Clinton as an active-positive president (Greenstein, 1995). Clinton characterizes himself as "almost compulsively overactive," and scholars agree that he falls near the extreme active end of Barber's active-passive scale (Renshon, 1995:59). Clinton seems also to fall toward the positive end of Barber's positive-negative scale, but scholars are less certain about this. There are enough presidential outbursts, such as Clinton's angry lament that "no matter how much I do, it's never good enough" during one interview, that have overtones of the negative approach and make it possible that Clinton is a "masked active-negative" (Renshon, 1995:60).

Another study of political psychology characterized presidents according to levels of motivation for achievement (willingness to take moderate risks, but unwillingness to take high risks, to achieve excellent results), affiliation (concern for warm, friendly relations), and power (concern for impact and prestige). The study finds that "Clinton's motive profile is high achievement, perhaps slightly less high affiliation, and moderate power." The president's particularly high achievement motive, the study worries, may mean that when Clinton fails to achieve many of his goals, "the inherent frustration of politics may in the end overwhelm his aspirations" and drive him "down the bitter paths trod" by presidents Johnson, Nixon, and others (Winter, 1995:115, 128).

Whatever Bill Clinton or any other president may be psychologically, it is important to put the impact of personality into context. Any presidential decision is based on many factors. Yet personality traits are classifiable to a degree, and the types of personality that individuals have can help us to understand what they do and to predict what they might do.

Some scholars believe that a combination of American political culture, role, and personality frequently leads presidents to try to appear and act "macho." Pictures abound of presidents posing valorously in tank turrets, sitting in he-man postures on horses, or engaged in other stereotypically manly pursuits. President George Bush managed to get quite a few symbols of his masculinity into this one photo opportunity. He is clad in military camouflage pants, has on an aviator's jacket (complete with wings), is wearing a military cap emblazoned with USS *Bluefish,* and is holding up a suitably conquered bluefish impaled on a gaff. Given the distance between the president's hands, compared to the less extensive length of the fish, it appears that the president may be engaged in another common male trait: exaggerating his conquests.

Emotions

Presidents like to picture themselves as defenders of the national interest and international peace when they announce policy. Decisions are frequently based on such lofty considerations, but it is also true that decisions are sometimes partly a product of a president's emotions. Anger, ego, and ambition are just three emotions that influence policy making.

We like to think of presidents calmly deciding important policy, but sometimes they get mad. Jimmy Carter was angry at the Iranians. His wife, Rosalyn, remembers that when he saw news reports about the hostages, "I could always tell by the grim set in his chin and the vein that throbbed in his temple that Jimmy was filled with anger." When Iranians studying in the United States picketed in front of his home, Carter could hardly contain himself. "I may have to sit here and bite my lip . . . and look impotent, but I am not going to have those bastards humiliating our country in front of the White House," he fumed to an aide. "If I wasn't President, I'd be out on the streets myself and would probably take a swing at any Khomeini demonstrator I could get my hands on" (Vandenbroucke, 1991:364, 358).

Presidential egos can also affect policy. It is impossible to prove empirically that there is a relationship between the charge of wimp that once dogged George Bush and his subsequent decisions to use military force against Panama and Iraq. It is equally hard for a careful student of foreign policy to ignore the possibility. Eighteen months after *Newsweek* had pinned the wimp label on him, Bush was still fuming. "You're talking to the wimp," the president sarcastically told a Hollywood celebrity crowd in June 1991. "You're talking to the guy that had a cover of a national magazine, that I'll never forgive, put that label on me."[17] Given such reactions and some of the earlier commentary, it seems reasonable to think that Bush's wounded pride pressed him to grasp the sword and ignore the olive branch during confrontations with Panama and Iraq.

Once the sword has been grasped, ego can also make it hard to put it down. Lyndon Johnson was determined not to be "the first American president to lose a war" (Burke & Greenstein, 1989:87). Similarly, an aide rapidly scrawled abbreviations to record Richard Nixon saying about Vietnam ("VN") (Genovese, 1990:117):

VN—enemy Misjudges 2 things
    -the time—has 3 yrs + 9 mo
    -the man—won't be 1st P to lose war

Ambition is a third aspect of the many emotions that sometimes influence presidential decisions. Presidents are politicians; that is how they get to be president. They worry about their reelection and their party's fortunes. Presidents and their advisers routinely, even angrily, deny that partisan considerations had anything to do with critical foreign policy decisions. When a reporter made such a suggestion to President Bush during the crisis with Iraq, he lambasted the journalist for stooping to the "ultimate of cynicism and indecency."[18] Yet the same George Bush once mused that if a president mishandled a foreign policy crisis, then, no matter how well he performed otherwise, "you're probably out of there the next time."[19]

It is not an indictment but a fact of democratic political life to say that electoral considerations enter, consciously or subconsciously, into the calculations of White House decision makers and other political actors. President John F. Kennedy's decision to support the attempt of Cuban exiles to invade their homeland at the Bay of Pigs was partly spurred by partisan politics. Kennedy had heaped scorn, during the 1960 campaign, on the administration of Dwight Eisenhower and its vice president, Richard M. Nixon, the GOP nominee. "If you can't stand up to Castro, how can you be expected to stand up to Khrushchev?" Kennedy asked of Eisenhower and Nixon. That language came back to haunt Kennedy. Despite reservations about the plan, Kennedy decided to go ahead because, as his national security adviser, McGeorge Bundy pointed out, "If we didn't . . . the Republicans would have said: "We were all set to beat Castro, and this chicken, this antsy-pantsy bunch of liberals. . . . There would have been a political risk in not going through with the operation" (Gleijeses, 1995:25, 26).

Partisan politics sometimes even influences crisis decisions. The Cuban missile crisis brought the United States nearer to nuclear war than at any time before or since, and the approaching congressional elections and the president's general political standing and future electoral chances were part of the motivation to confront the Soviets (Hershberg, 1990). Kennedy and the Democrats were loath to subject themselves to the repeated Republican charge of being soft on communism. "I'll be quite frank," Kennedy's defense secretary Robert McNamara interjected during one crisis meeting, "I don't think there is a military problem here. . . . This is a domestic, political problem" (Purkitt, 1990:22). McNamara tentatively suggested doing nothing, but he was ignored. Confrontation with the Soviets and nuclear peril followed because the missiles in Cuba not only threatened the United States, they also could have vaporized the Democrats' fortunes in the approaching congressional elections and destroyed Kennedy's reelection chances for 1964.

Mental and Physical Health

It is easy to forget the impact of poor physical health and psychological pressures on decision makers, but the ravages can be intense. Wars, for one, can claw at the spirit and self-image of policy makers. Chapter 13 on public opinion will relate, for example, the intense and sometimes intimate attacks by opponents of the war in Vietnam on Secretary of Defense Robert S. McNamara. The secretary finally turned against the war and was eased out of office by President Lyndon B. Johnson. McNamara, the president later explained, had come under such pressure from people "telling him that the war was terrible and immoral . . . [that] he felt he was a murderer. . . . I was afraid he might have a nervous breakdown. He was just short of cracking up" (Kearns, 1976:321). Some analysts consider Johnson's characterization as an uncharitable rationalization of his efforts to rid his Cabinet of opponents to the war, and no one would claim that McNamara was mentally ill. Yet it is facile to dismiss the president's comments out of hand, and the post-Vietnam conversion of McNamara to a fervent dove and his anguished memoir of the Vietnam era bear testimony to the strong impact of the war on his psyche.

Other wartime policy makers have become even more despondent over their roles, however justified. James V. Forrestal, who served as secretary of the navy during the latter part of World War II was so war-weary and depressed that he committed suicide while in office. Just before his death, Forrestal closed out his diary with the words of another warrior from the "Chorus of Ajax" by Sophocles. Forrestal's final mortal notation read:

Comfortless, nameless, hopeless save
In the dark prospect of the yawning grave.[20]

No president has suffered indisputable mental illness, but there have been times when a president's health probably has affected foreign policy (Park, 1994). Woodrow

Wilson's refusal to compromise with the Senate led to its rejection of the Treaty of Versailles after World War I. There is medical speculation that the president suffered from cerebral arteriosclerosis, a condition that is characterized by increased egocentricity, intransigence, and other characteristics that Wilson displayed (Saunders, 1994). Physician Edwin Weinstein has concluded, for one, that "there is a great deal of evidence that Wilson suffered from progressive cerebral vascular disease which affected his behavior," causing, among other symptoms, "memory loss and other cognitive impairments, emotional disturbances, and a denial syndrome" (Link, 1988:635).

At the end of World War II, Franklin Roosevelt had astronomical blood pressure and was dying. It may be that his poor health limited his ability to negotiate effectively with Joseph Stalin at the Yalta Conference in February 1945. In recent years, Richard Nixon provided perhaps the most worrisome behavior. He is reputed to have had a fondness for martinis and other concoctions, and his adviser Henry Kissinger joked to aides that Nixon was "my drunken friend" (Schulzinger, 1989:32). As the pressures of the anti–Vietnam War protests and then the Watergate investigation grew, Nixon sometimes displayed erratic behavior. Toward the end of his term, according to one historian, aides were so worried that the president might become "completely unhinged" that White House chief of staff Alexander Haig "told armed forces commanders to check with him before action on unusual orders" (Schulzinger, 1989:178).

The Impact of Idiosyncratic Factors on Policy

Dissecting the idiosyncrasies of presidential and other policy makers is fascinating stuff, but we need to ask how influential such factors are. Personality provides an illustration of the impact of one idiosyncratic trait. Some, such as Stoessinger (1985: xv), believe that "a leader's *personality* is a decisive element in the making of foreign policy." Most political scientists, however, would be less categorical. There are even some observers who reject such concerns as "psychobabble." George Bush expressed this view when he dismissed this "latest thing in politics [which] is to stretch you out on some kind of psychoanalytical couch to figure out what makes you tick" (Swansbrough, 1991:1). The truth is that the impact of personality usually lies somewhere between decisive element and psychobabble. Who makes foreign policy varies, as the next chapter's discussion of policy making models elaborates. The president is only one, albeit an important one, of many inputs into the foreign policy process. We shall see, for example, that the role of the central political leader (and thus the leader's personality) will be stronger in a crisis situation than in calmer times. A second limit to personality study is both the validity of the categories and the placing of presidents in them. According to the studies cited, Bush was an active-positive, pragmatic, compulsive, extroverted, low-dominance, and macho personality type. If you read these studies, you might find that you would disagree with where they place specific presidents. It would also be an interesting exercise to take one of these studies and, with several classmates, try to analyze the current president. Are all your personality classifications of President Clinton in agreement?

SUMMARY

1. Human beings and the way they make decisions—based on their being part of the human species, based on how decisions are made in organizational settings, and based on individual traits—are an important part of the foreign policy process.

2. The analysis of how the biological and psychological nature of humankind affects decisions is one aspect of the human setting of foreign policy making.

3. Even if biological and psychological factors are not present in decision making, it is important to realize that decisions are not, and cannot be, perfectly rational. All decision makers labor within the cognitive limits of what humans can know and can process physically and intellectually.

4. Decision making is also affected by how it is conducted within organizational settings.

5. Decision makers in organizational settings adopt roles based on their positions and on how that effects their expectations and the expectations of those around them about the proper attitudes and behaviors of someone in that position.

6. Organizational settings may also create pressures, such as the urge not to dissent, among participants in small-group decision making situations. Such pressures are often referred to as groupthink.

7. Individual decision makers are also subject to a wide array of idiosyncratic traits that affect their policy choices. These traits include perceptions, specific personality type, emotions, and mental and physical health. Such traits combine to establish a decision maker's leadership style.

Chapter Six

THE THEORY OF FOREIGN POLICY PROCESSES

Chapters 2 through 5 demonstrated that U.S. policy makers are often not free to calculate all options coolly and to make any decision they wish. They are, in fact, hemmed in by system realities, by societal pressures, and by the always less-than-ideally-rational nature of human decision making. These three levels of policy constraints are very important, but, to restate an important point, their influence does not mean that policy is foreordained.

Indeed, decision makers frequently have a great deal of latitude when making policy. One reason is that the United States is the world's most powerful country. It is, therefore, less restricted than most countries by the international system. Also, many Americans are often willing to grant the president and the executive branch more leeway to decide foreign policy than domestic policy.

The substantial freedom that leaders have to make foreign policy leads us back to an important point made in chapter 1. Process helps determine substance; that is, who decides policy influences what will be decided. It is, therefore, more than just intellectual curiosity that prompts us to explore the decision making process.

This chapter begins the task of examining how policy is made within the governmental structure. To that end, we will discuss models, situations, types of policy, perceptions, and other concepts that help establish a framework for examining and understanding how policy is made. Because of this chapter's concentrated theoretical exposition, you may find it more abstract than the other chapters. "Hang in there," is our advice to you. Even for most professors, the "lights, camera, action!" of events are more exciting than the remote realm of theory. But theory is necessary because it allows us to move beyond seeing every event, every decision process, and every policy as a unique occurrence. Theory helps us to understand how events fit general patterns, to see how decisions are alike or dissimilar, and to estimate the chances that a given set of circumstances and interactions will lead to a predictable policy. In a lecture at the University of Connecticut, scholar James Rosenau once said that whenever he examines something, he always asks himself, "Of what is this an instance?" It is an excellent question, the essence of political science and, indeed, at the heart of most scholarship.

Before we begin to look at foreign policy decisions and to ask of what they are an instance, there is some bad news. There is no single foreign policy process (Schraeder, 1994; Scott, 1995; Gibson, 1992). That is too bad because if there were just one way that foreign policy was made, it would be easier for authors to explain, professors to teach, and students to study. The reality is, however, that there are several foreign policy processes. Understanding how they work and when they operate is this chapter's goal. The first step is to examine policy making models. After that we will turn to variables such as situations and types of policy to explain why different models operate in different circumstances. These discussions lead to the construction of a basic, four-cell matrix to help you understand when and how the models of the various foreign policy processes operate.

POLICY MAKING MODELS

One way that political scientists explain how policy is made is by creating models of the policy process. A **model** is an intellectual construct that represents what something is like or how it works. These scholarly models are distant cousins of the plastic or wooden models of ships, planes, and other things that kids and some adults build for recreation. Think about ship models. Most of us never get beyond the five- or ten-dollar Revell kits of, say, the three-masted frigate USS *Constitution*. These kits have a few dozen pieces; they are not hard to build; and when the model is finished we actually do have something that resembles Old Ironsides, as the ship is affectionately known. Of course, the model neither works nor has all the intricate detail of the real *Constitution*. Still, if you built the model and later came upon the actual *Constitution* while visiting Boston, you would recognize the ship.

This analogy goes only so far, however. Politics is vastly more complex and dynamic than any ship, even a nuclear submarine, and building intellectual models is much more difficult than putting together ship models. For this reason, scholars have not yet agreed on the various efforts to construct policy making models (Gibson, 1994; Bendor & Hammond, 1992; Allison, 1971). It would be possible, therefore, to write a lengthy book discussing all the intricate foreign policy making models that students of government have suggested. But for our needs here, we will synthesize the thoughts of these scholars and explore four basic models: (1) the presidential model, (2) the political model, (3) the administrative model, and (4) the subgovernment model.

When you are reading about these models, think about how each one represents the policy process and about how the models differ from one another. Do not worry yet about which model best represents reality. There is still disagreement among leading political scientists on this issue. In fact, the point of view of this book is, to paraphrase Lincoln, that all of these models are right some of the time, but none of these models are right all of the time.

The Presidential Model

One classic description of the foreign policy process is the "rational actor model." Our presidential model resembles the rational actor model in many ways, but we chose another name because rational actor implies an idealized view of policy making. Such a perfectly rational approach to making policy does not, and cannot, exist, as we noted in the last chapter. The reality is that all humans struggle with intellectual and emotional limitations in their attempts to be well-informed and objective. Saying that the ideal cannot be real does not mean, however, that the opposite extreme is the case. Political leaders rarely ignore all information and advice and make decisions based solely on subjective opinions and highly emotional criteria. Instead, almost every decision is the result of some mix of fact and fancy, information and ignorance, objectivity and subjectivity. Thus, it is the decision making recipe, so to speak, that political scientists try to explain.

From the perspective of this realistic understanding of rationality, there are many political scientists who contend that a rational actor model does operate, especially during times of crisis.

At these times public opinion, interest groups, the media, and legislators are most likely to expect and to rally behind executive leadership, thereby creating a level of at least temporary national unity. The presidential model represents this view that an executive-centered, rational pursuit of the national interest does operate, within the context of human limits, in the foreign policy process.

As its name indicates, the presidential model focuses on the president and his immediate, high-level advisers in the White House and the Cabinet. President Harry Truman had a sign on his desk that read "The Buck Stops Here," and President John Kennedy once pictured himself as a matador alone in the ring facing the bull. Such images have an element of truth. Often the presidential model operates in times of seeming national peril. Whether it is Dwight Eisenhower's 1954 decision not to commit American combat units to Vietnam or Lyndon Johnson's 1965 decision to commit American combat units to Vietnam, sometimes the president has the final word.

At other times, the presidential model involves strategic issues that, while important to the country, do not substantially capture the nation's attention. One such matter involved the renewal of the Nuclear Nonproliferation Treaty (NPT) in 1995. This treaty, which went into effect initially in 1970 and had to be renewed after 25 years, pledges nonnuclear signatories of the NPT not to acquire nuclear weapons. Signatories that have nuclear weapons promise not to give nuclear weapons or the technology to build them to nonnuclear countries. The United States, most other nuclear powers, and some other countries took the position that the NPT should be renewed indefinitely. Some nonnuclear countries objected on the grounds that the treaty gives the current nuclear powers a monopoly on weapons of mass destruction. The dissenting countries wanted to put the treaty on a renewal cycle as short as five years in order to put pressure on the nuclear countries to reduce or eliminate their nuclear arsenals. Other issues arose, including objections from several Arab countries that Israel, a non-signatory of the NPT, had nuclear weapons. The Arab states wanted the conference considering renewal to call on Israel to "accede without delay" to the NPT.[1]

The U.S. administration mounted a major diplomatic effort to eliminate the potential roadblocks to a renewed, unconditional, and permanent NPT. President Clinton met in Washington with President Hosni Mubarak of Egypt and won his agreement to the NPT. The United States sponsored a successful resolution in the UN Security Council that makes any threat by a nuclear country against a nonnuclear signatory of the NPT a priority issue before the UN. To supplement that, Secretary of State Warren Christopher stated publicly that "The United States reaffirms that it will not use nuclear weapons against nonnuclear weapon states party to [the NPT] except in the case of an invasion of the United States" or a few other extreme situations.[2] As the conference moved toward a climax, President Clinton sent a personal message to the heads of a number of hesitant governments telling them that the United States would find it hard to understand why friendly nations that received U.S. help would frustrate U.S. goals. Mexico, which was receiving substantial U.S. funds to support the peso, was just one of the targets of pressure. The pressure was so intense that Ambassador Adolfo Taylhardt of Colombia, who had been supporting a limited renewal, resigned as his country's delegate to the conference when Caracas caved in to the American pressure and changed its position. Mexico also fell into line, and a rueful Miguel Marin-Bosch, the deputy head of the Mexican delegation, credited the "impressive" American campaign for its success in getting the NPT renewed indefinitely, as occurred in June 1995.[3] The point here is that for all its importance, the NPT and its renewal were little noted in the United States, and American policy was set almost exclusively in accordance with the presidential model.

It is important to stress again that the presidential model recognizes that rational decision making is limited by many factors. These include the realities that information is usually incomplete or inaccurate; that political leaders are often substantially dependent on bureaucratic subordinates for information, analysis, and advice; that no human being is physically or intellectually capable of omniscience; that Washington is a very political, often intensively partisan, place; and that what constitutes the national interest is arguable (Purkitt, 1990). Still, this model argues that decision makers try to formulate policy based on a reasonable analysis of international circumstances and an estimation of their country's national interest. As one recent study put it, "presidents appear to respond mostly to the rhythms of international events and not domestic politics when making foreign policy" (Lindsay, Sayrs, & Steger, 1992:20).

System-level analysts are essentially presidential-model theorists. They believe that national policy making is executive-centered and that decision makers attempt to make rationally calculated choices based on their country's national interest and to achieve that interest within the confines of system realities. You are adopting the presidential model, for example, if you think that (1) President Bush intervened in the Persian Gulf because he believed that Iraq's conquest of Kuwait and threat to Saudi Arabia and other oil-producing states in the region threatened the economic vitality of the United States and other industrialized countries; and that (2) all things considered, the president believed that using military force rather than diplomacy or economic sanctions was the best course of action. Note that you do not have to agree with Bush's decisions, only that there was a certain logic to them.

The Political Model

"Nothing ever gets settled in this town," Secretary of State George Shultz once complained. "It's a seething debating society in which the debate never stops, in which people never give up, including me."[4] Without knowing it, Reagan's chief diplomat neatly summed up the political model.

The political model views foreign policy making as part of a diverse, multiple actor process that is much broader than envisioned by the presidential model. The president and his political appointees, the bureaucracy, Congress, interest groups, and even the public are all relevant in the policy process. This model also assumes that there are shifting alliances among all the various elements and, as Shultz observed, that decisions are often not clear-cut, but rather part of an ongoing process.

The political model primarily involves foreign policy concerns that are not an immediate crisis but that attract wide and often intense interest among a broad array of political actors. Because of the breadth and intensity of interest, the president and other political leaders also focus on the issue at hand. As you will see, this contrasts with the narrower interest and decisional focus in the administrative and subgovernment models discussed next. Because of the breadth and intensity of debate, general societal and specific electoral considerations play an important role in determining policy, and the president's partisan and national-interest leadership roles intertwine (Evans, Jacobson, & Putnam, 1993; Mintz, 1993). The upshot of this, maintains a former State Department official, is that "policy making is politics" in which foreign policy making often mixes in a significant element of domestic considerations that have little to do with such lofty concepts as national interest or geostrategic theory (Hilsman, 1990:75). Or, as Harry Truman once observed pithily, "A statesman is a dead politician" (Rose, 1988:227).

An illustration of the conflictive nature of a great deal of foreign policy making, and thus of the political model, is provided by the donnybrook set off by the signing of the North American Free Trade Agreement (NAFTA) by President Bush in 1992 and its submission to Congress by President Clinton in 1993. Both Republican president Bush and Democratic president Clinton supported the agreement. In fact, when Clinton kicked off the campaign to persuade Congress to agree to NAFTA, every living president—both Republican and Democrat—endorsed the agreement, and Presidents Bush, Carter, and Ford joined Clinton at the White House to demonstrate their support. Most business groups also supported NAFTA, and a majority of economists and other trade experts in government, academia, and private enterprise added their voices to the pro-NAFTA chorus. Operating from their generally pro-business stance, Republican members of Congress also endorsed NAFTA. The old adage that politics creates

The controversy over whether or not the United States should join the North American Free Trade Agreement (NAFTA) is a good example of an issue that is decided according to the political model. As a so-called intermestic issue, which included elements of both *inter*national and do*mestic* policy, NAFTA sparked activity by many members of Congress and many interest groups. It also affected many individuals, including these protesting California workers.

strange bedfellows was confirmed anew by NAFTA, which cast President Clinton and the Republican leader in the Senate and soon-to-be presidential primary contestant Robert Dole of Kansas as allies. Dole vowed to "stand out front with the president" to get NAFTA passed over the opposition of Richard Gephardt (D-IN), the Democratic majority leader in the House of Representatives, and most other congressional Democrats.[5]

Those who supported NAFTA stressed the broad political and economic impact of the agreement, arguing that in the long run it would benefit Americans as well as Mexicans. Supporters also argued that NAFTA was part of the new world order of mutually advantageous economic interdependence, and that the United States would be left behind in a competitive economic world if it did not agree to the pact. "When you live in a time of change, the only way to recover your security and to broaden your horizons is to adapt to the change, to embrace it, to move it forward," Clinton told an audience at the White House.[6] "The supporters tend to deal with NAFTA on a more intellectual level," one pollster commented accurately.[7]

Labor unions, many environmental groups, those who tend toward isolationism, those who claim to represent common folks, and those in Congress who support such groups lined up against NAFTA. This alignment created its own set of odd bedfellows, with such conservatives as presidential hopefuls H. Ross Perot and neo-isolationist Republican Patrick J. Buchanan joining such liberals as civil rights leader and onetime Democratic presidential hopeful Jesse L. Jackson and consumer advocate Ralph Nader in opposition to NAFTA.

Labor unions were the most powerful organized source of opposition based on their increasing concern about policies that allow the "export" of American jobs overseas. As Thomas Donahue (1991:91), secretary-treasurer of the AFL-CIO, wrote, "among those who would suffer most from a NAFTA are industrial workers in the United States. It would pave the way for tens of thousands of their jobs to be exported to Mexico, and it would bump hundreds of thousands down the economic ladder to underemployment and low wages." The Reverend Jackson was especially concerned that those most threatened by job losses would be the lowest wage workers, many of whom are minority group members. Some environmentalists, led by such groups as the Sierra Club, also opposed NAFTA, arguing that damage to the environment would occur as a result of increased production in Mexico. Environmentalists fear that not only will the environment suffer from increased production by existing Mexican companies, but that NAFTA will give American and Canadian firms an incentive to move south in order to lower their costs by avoiding stricter environmental laws at home. From a related perspective, Nader fretted that NAFTA would require the United States to accept products from Mexico that had been produced under less strict consumer safety standards. The point of view that is leery of international interdependence and the concomitant diminution of U.S. sovereignty was represented by Buchanan, Perot, and others and was captured in Perot's paperback book entitled *Save Your Job, Save Our Country: Why NAFTA Has to Be Stopped—Now!* For one reason or the other, the public was also wary of NAFTA, and polls consistently showed that a plurality of Americans opposed the pact.

Faced with this opposition, the president headed an impressive drive to persuade Congress to accede to the agreement. In an attempt to ease constituency pressures on Congress, Clinton garnered support from luminaries such as former secretary of state Henry Kissinger and a host of Nobel Prize–winning economists. "If NAFTA fails, the relationship with Mexico will be damaged for the foreseeable future," intoned Kissinger.[8] Clinton dispatched Vice President Al Gore to the Larry King show on CNN to debate the NAFTA issue with detractor H. Ross Perot. The president also applied the individual touch. Two weeks before the scheduled vote in Congress, the White House invited 13 undecided legislators for a personal and, Clinton hoped, persuasive private dinner with the president and the first lady.

The president also utilized his ability to make pork barrel concessions. Florida representatives sought greater protection against a surge of citrus fruit, juice, and similar products from Mexico; Louisiana legislators asked for similar advantages for sugar; other farm-state representatives objected to a potential deluge of Mexican vegetables. The White House responded by instituting procedures to prevent a flood of Mexican oranges, sugarcane, cantaloupes, and other such products. "We've got teams of [administration] shoppers prowling the halls of Congress," commented Senator Byron L. Dorgan (D-ND); "The message is, 'If we're willing to help you, are you willing to help us?' It's not a subtle message."[9] To get the vote of Representative Eddie Bernice Johnson (D-TX), for instance, Clinton reportedly agreed to expand the production of the Air Force's C-17 cargo plane produced in her district at the Dallas plant of the McDonnell Douglas Corporation. Depending on the final cost of the C-17, the report estimated that the expense to win the vote of Congresswoman Johnson was between $700 million and $1.4 billion.[10] Representative David E. Bonior (D-MI), one leader of the opposition to NAFTA, complained that "there are a lot of deals being made by the White House. They're porking it [NAFTA] down and loading it up."[11]

The end result of this tumultuous political battle was that President Clinton was successful in getting Congress to agree to NAFTA. It was first approved in the House of Representatives by a narrow 234 to 200 vote. As further testimony to the unusual political coalition that formed around NAFTA, 102 Democrats voted for it, while 156 voted against it. President Clinton got his strongest support from the 132 Republicans who voted for NAFTA. Only 43 Republicans voted against the president in the House. The measure then passed the Senate easily, and President Clinton signed it into law.

Before we move on, there are a couple of important observations to make about the political model and its relationship to the main theme of this text, democracy. One point is that the process in this model is the most broadly democratic. The national debate is almost quintessentially American—a political free-for-all. If you think back to chapter 1, it is what de Tocqueville and other critics of democratic foreign policy deplore and what proponents of democratic foreign policy applaud. Critics can accurately note the partisan sniping and the negative stereotyping of Mexicans that, in part, accompanied the NAFTA debate and wonder reasonably if this is any way to deal with an important country that is also a neighbor. But proponents of extended democracy can point out with equal accuracy that presidents are apt to focus too intently on strategic considerations, that domestic concerns are also legitimate, and that opposition helps balance domestic and international concerns in the White House. Thus, while it is easy to condemn this form of democratic policy making, it is not synonymous with policy failure. Truly, extended democracy is messy, but therein often lies balance and progress. It is also worth reiterating James Madison's view that he did not draft the Constitution to create a neat process. Rather, he believed that the conflict among the branches of government and among interest groups (or "factions," as he called them) was the counterweight needed to avoid hasty or ill-advised decisions or the possibility of any one branch or faction dominating and eroding the American democratic system.

The Administrative Model

The administrative model argues that policy is frequently made by the State Department, the Defense Department, the Central Intelligence Agency, and other such bureaucratic units of government and the officials who staff them. Sometimes one agency controls a decision; often several agencies bargain and compromise.

Before laying out the administrative model, we should distinguish it from two other classic policy making models: the bureaucratic model and the organizational process model. The administrative model combines elements of both. The bureaucracy (the executive branch agencies and their staffs) is influential in almost all aspects of foreign policy making. Its strong role in the gathering, dissemination, and analysis of information, for example, influences presidential decisions in that model. The presidential model encompasses that indirect role, whereas the administrative model focuses on instances when policy is decided directly by one or more agencies below the White House and Cabinet levels. The administrative model similarly incorporates the organizational process model's emphasis on the use of **standard operating** procedures (SOPs) to decide policy. An SOP is an already existing plan or set of procedures that an agency uses in a new situation, sometimes without bothering to evaluate how appropriate the SOP is to the new situation or revising the SOP to fit the peculiarities of the new situation. Thus, when SOPs determine bureaucratic decisions or the advice that bureaucrats give to political leaders, we include such instances in our administrative model.

The power of agencies that underlie the administrative model rests on the scope and complexity of foreign policy. Scope relates to the myriad international issues and interactions in which the national government is involved. Complexity represents the complicated nature of foreign policy and the specialized knowledge and experience necessary to deal with the host of diplomatic, military, economic, and other U.S. foreign policy concerns. How scope and complexity empower the bureaucracy will be discussed in detail in chapter 10. For here though, we can say that the two factors combine to make foreign policy such an immense and complicated subject that the president and his handful of appointed advisers have an intellectually and physically difficult time understanding and keeping track of events, issues, options, and decisions. Reflecting this, virtually every president has bemoaned his inability to gain control of the bureaucracy he is supposed to command. This frustration was emphasized by a 1975 government study of the foreign policy process. Any notion of the president's role, the study cautioned, "that implies that he can make the most important decisions is naive. He doesn't have the understanding. He doesn't have the information. He doesn't have the analysis. If he had all three, he would still lack the power and persistence" (Holland, 1991:8). This view of extreme dependency by leaders on their staff is synonymous with **technocracy**—a government by technical experts. It is an overstatement to label the foreign policy process as technocratic, but it does tell you something about bureaucratic power within the government.

The strategic nuclear doctrine of the United States is one example of an important policy that is determined extensively by the administrative policy model. One aspect of strategic nuclear doctrine, weapons procurement, is partly driven by the calculations of the various military services based on their own needs and perceptions of strategic requirements (Demchak, 1991). The decision to try to develop many kinds of weapons is also the result of the initiatives of military and civilian Defense Department bureaucrats, scientists, and other technocrats. "Most of the action the United States takes in the area of research and development has to do with one or two types of activities," one Defense Department director of defense research and engineering explained. "Either we see from the field of science and technology some new possibilities, which we think we ought to exploit, or we see threats on the horizon, possible threats, usually not something the enemy has done, but something we thought ourselves he might do, [and which] we must therefore be prepared for" (Kurth, 1989:29).

The planning for different nuclear-crisis scenarios and, in each contingency, when to launch nuclear weapons, what targets to attack, and other little-known, but potentially apocalyptic, nuclear-weapons options are also made substantially within the bureaucracy. President, and former five-star general, Dwight Eisenhower admitted once that he had little knowledge of exactly what U.S. military commanders had planned for specific contingencies. Subsequent presidents, with fewer military credentials, have certainly not had detailed knowledge either. What is more, the Defense Department specialists resist attempts to delve into their domain. National security adviser Henry Kissinger (1979:216) has recalled that soon after President Richard Nixon came into

Many matters that are decided according to the administrative model are routine. But not all are. This B-2, or Stealth, bomber is part of the strategic nuclear weapons delivery system of the United States. The use of this force could someday determine life or death for all Americans, and perhaps for everyone in the world. The president, of course, would decide when to launch a nuclear attack. Most of the details of strategic nuclear doctrine, such as targeting, are determined by a small group of uniformed and civilian technical experts (technocrats) within the Pentagon. These technocrats have been called the Wizards of Armageddon.

office he directed the Pentagon to "devise strategies to meet contingencies other than all-out nuclear challenge." "But," Kissinger continues, "our military establishment resists intrusion into strategic doctrine even when it comes from [the] White House." Kissinger (p. 217) relates that former defense secretary Robert McNamara (in the administrations of John Kennedy and Lyndon Johnson) told him that he had tried for seven years to get the military to give the president more nuclear options and "had finally given up." Kissinger reports, "I was determined to do better." But he then tells a tale of woe of bureaucratic resistance. "So it happened, that a specific presidential directive . . . was never answered satisfactorily in the eight years I served in Washington," Kissinger concedes finally. "The response was always short of being insubordinate but also short of being useful. Despite semiannual reminders it [the requested report] was listed as incomplete on the books when we left office."

Although U.S nuclear doctrine did become gradually more flexible, it is also accurate to say that the Pentagon's strategic nuclear doctrine never did fully move away from its massive nuclear-war focus. The nuclear war-fighting plan (Strategic Integrated Operational Plan-7, SIOP-7) that went into operation in 1989 during the waning days of the cold war envisioned such massive operations, including launching 120 warheads against Moscow, that one critic was moved to condemn SIOP-7 as not "strategy," but "pathology."[12] In the same way, when President George Bush took almost 1,000 nuclear warheads and bombs off alert in response to the end of the cold war, the military subtly countered these decreases by increasing the time U.S. strategic-missile-carrying submarines spent on alert at sea from 44 percent in the 1980s to 58 percent in 1992. There has been an approximate 32 percent reduction of U.S. nuclear forces on alert since the 1980s; yet the current war-fighting plan (SIOP-8, effective October 1, 1993) still requires high alert levels and readiness for a massive nuclear strike. "It is time for President Clinton to focus on this problem," another critic has urged.[13]

The administration has done that to a degree and has agreed with the Russians, for instance, to cease reprogramming its missiles for targets in each other's country. Yet in other ways, the bureaucratic juggernaut plows forward. President Carter tried to halt the Air Force's manned bomber program by killing the B-1 bomber, but it survived to fly. More recently, the B-2 bomber program, which costs about $1 billion each, has come under attack. Senator and former Navy pilot and admiral John McCain (R-AZ) fires salvos at the B-2 as "a relic of the cold war . . . that could cost the American people over the next 10 years. The simple fact," according to the senator, "is that we don't need more strategic bombers to meet the likely threats of the future."[14] Yet the Air Force armada is projected to reach at least 20 of the costly and, some say, superfluous planes.

To cite just one last example of the administrative impact on U.S. defense policy, the military continues to favor developing and testing new types of nuclear weapons. Among these are relatively small nuclear weapons with the explosive power of about 10 to 100 tons of TNT that could be delivered by plane, missile, or artillery against tactical targets. Dubbed "micro-nukes," these weapons have set off a strong debate. What is small is of course relative. At an explosive power of 10 tons of TNT, a micro-nuke would be 10 times the size of the explosive power of the largest conventional bombs or warheads used by the United States during the Persian Gulf War, but only 1/500th the size of the B-61 nuclear warhead, the smallest currently in the U.S. inventory. Advocates argue that micro-nukes could be used to protect U.S. deployed forces abroad, to enable the military to attack enemy leaders ensconced in bunkers (as Saddam Hussein was in 1991), and to discourage proliferation by potential new nuclear states by creating the ability to destroy nuclear-weapons production facilities. In any case, one Air Force officer reasoned, "We have to research these things. If we don't someone else will, and use them against us." Offering a dissenting view, one analyst characterized the advocates of micro-nukes as "nuclear zealots [who] couldn't care less that the cold war is over."[15]

The Subgovernment Model

Within the broad interaction among the many actors in American policy making, there is a process that focuses on **subgovernments** (McCool, 1989). This term represents the idea that many decisions are made by bureaucratic substructures cooperating, conflicting, or compromising with other bureaucratic elements, with specific interest groups, and with members of Congress.

The subgovernment model begins with the proposition that there are some foreign policy concerns broad enough to spark more than just bureaucratic activity (the administrative model), yet not vital or wide-ranging enough either to be considered and decided primarily by top political leaders (the presidential model) or to be debated widely and intensely by Congress, interest groups, and the public (the political model). What the subgovernment model focuses on are those issues that, while not critical or of general concern, are still important to a limited number of bureaucratic units, interest groups, and members of Congress. Thus the policy debate is confined to and decided within a small subset (a subgovernment) of political actors that have interest in a particular issue. As Secretary of State Dean Acheson (1969:15) once described his department's organization, "Bureaucratic power had come to rest in the division chiefs. . . . The heads of all these divisions, like barons in a feudal system . . . were constantly at odds, if not at war." Thus the major departments are not unitary actors, but often shells containing many subunits. These subunits, each with its own policy preferences, compete with one another and form alliances with similarly competing interest groups and members of Congress.

Particularly when the subgovernment model relates to defense issues, it focuses on the trilateral image of a bureaucratic-interest group-congressional alliance that is often referred to as an **iron triangle** (Adams, 1988). This is an extension of the idea of the military-industrial complex from an alliance between the Pentagon and industry to a coalition that also includes members of Congress who have military bases or defense contractors and workers in their states or districts. There was, for example, a decision in 1991 to continue limits on the importation of ball bearings into the United States. It was little noted by the president, Congress, and the public. The decision was, however, of considerable concern to (1) bureaucracies such as the Defense Department because of the role of ball bearings in national defense and the Commerce Department because of trade implications, to (2) companies and workers in areas such as central Connecticut that produced ball bearings, and to (3) members of Congress, such as Barbara Kennelly and Nancy Johnson, who represent those areas.

It is important to note that this discussion of the defense-related iron triangle does not mean that the subgovernment model applies only to national security issues. To the contrary, there are many trilateral alliance systems. Issues about tariffs and quotas on the import and export of agricultural goods, for example, involve what could be dubbed a green triangle composed of the Agriculture Department, farmers and agricultural-based businesses, and farm-state representatives. Even fish can be of interest to some subgovernment actors. In 1993, for example, the United States agreed to pay fishermen from Greenland some $800,000 to halt commercial Atlantic salmon fishing for two years. The payments to the Greenlanders were the result of the joint efforts of the U.S. Department of the Interior, legislators from the state of Connecticut and some other Atlantic coastal states, and such interest groups as the Atlantic Salmon Federation and the National Fish and Wildlife Foundation. The object of the agreement was to decrease the pressure on salmon stocks from overfishing, thereby increasing the number of salmon in Connecticut rivers and along the Connecticut coast to provide sport and perhaps even future commercial fishing opportunities. It was an issue that did not capture the attention of President Clinton, the leadership of Congress, or the national media and public opinion. Yet to people like Secretary of the Interior Bruce Babbitt, Connecticut's U.S. senator Joseph Lieberman, and National Fish and Wildlife Foundation executive director Amos Eno, it was an issue of importance.

Discord between Canada and the United States over salmon fishing rights in the Pacific provides another example of subgovernments at work. One recent attempt by Canada to charge a toll on U.S. fishing boats traveling through Canadian waters did not greatly stir the legislators or the people of Kansas, but it did galvanize American west coast fishermen, their legislators, and others affected by the Canadian initiative. "Ludicrous," protested Alaska's Republican senator Frank H. Murkowski, who called on the U.S. Coast Guard to provide warships to protect American fishing boats from Canadian patrols. That suggestion moved Canada's minister of fisheries, Brian Tobin, to call Murkowski the "equivalent of a gnat flying around the horse. . . . All you have to do is give a swish of your tail and it usually vamooses."[16] Fortunately, it can be reported that the tempest in a Pacific teacup abated, and bureaucrats from U.S. and Canadian ministries went back to negotiating a solution under the watchful eye of affected interest groups and their congressional and parliamentary supporters on both sides of the U.S.–Canadian border, the longest without fortifications in the world. In this prevailing calm, the point can be made again that there are many issues that do not attract wide notice but that do intensely interest a narrow range of actors. These issues are apt to be decided within an ad hoc subgovernment that coalesces to deal with the specific issue.

APPLYING THE POLICY MODELS

Given the reality that there are multiple policy processes that can each be replicated by a model, the question is: When does one or another of the models apply? Part of the answer was suggested in the section on the four models that you have just concluded. This section's goal is to add to that answer by pointing out that different processes are determined, in part, by the nature of the international situation, by the nature of the policy concern (issue area), and by the differing perceptions (definitions) of both the situation and the issue area.

Types of Situations

One factor that affects how foreign policy decisions are made is the international context of the issue or event that requires a policy response. There have been various efforts to classify situations. Two ideas that are helpful here are (1) the distinction between crisis and noncrisis situations and (2) the distinction between status quo and non–status quo situations.

Crisis and noncrisis situations are distinguished by three factors. The most important of these is the level of threat. The greater the level of threat, especially if there is a chance of military hostilities, the more intense the crisis. Additionally, a situation that has a limited response time and/or one that is a surprise can also increase the sense of crisis. Most scholars agree that during an acute crisis situation the president and a small circle of advisers, most or all of whom are members of the executive branch, will be the focus of decision making (James & Oneal, 1991). The process will most closely resemble the presidential model. During a crisis, Congress, interest groups, and the public tend to look to the president to lead, and they will tend to back whatever policy he chooses. This support, which is discussed fully in chapter 13, is especially likely and pronounced during the initial stages of the crisis, but support often wanes if the confrontation drags on. Noncrisis situations are much more likely to involve a wider range of political actors in the bureaucracy, Congress, interest groups, and elements of the public and to conform to one of the other three models. As we will discuss in the next section on issues, the nature of the issue will help determine how noncrisis situations are processed.

Mike Keefe, *USA Today*

Whether the foreign policy of a country is incremental and conforms with the status quo or is innovative and occurs in a non–status quo situation is one situational variable that influences how decisions are made and the policy model that most closely represents that process. After many years in which the bipolar, cold war world was the status quo, the United States is now faced with a new situation in which it is the sole superpower in an international system where military power is less applicable and acceptable. Like the superman in the cartoon, the superpower United States is having to reorient its thinking about its proper role in a dramatically changed international system.

Status quo and non–status quo situations also evoke different processes. There is an inertia in government that causes most situations to be analyzed as part of the familiar state of world affairs. As a result, decisions are apt to resemble earlier decisions; bureaucratic policy recommendations and policy implementation are likely to follow standard operating procedures. This results in **incremental policy**, which, at best, evolves slowly in a series of minor steps. After studying arms control policy, for example, one scholar found little innovative thinking and concluded that while "it is an old cliché that the future is merely a repetition of the past . . . public policy relies heavily on precedent" (Diehl, 1991:597).

Especially when status quo policy is supported by consensus, there tends to be little debate and policy is confined largely to the executive branch. This tendency can be illustrated clearly by the anticommunist consensus that existed in the United States during most of the cold war period. Consensus meant that the containment doctrine and its specific policy manifestations sparked relatively little controversy, even if they meant war. When, for example, President Lyndon Johnson asked Congress to authorize military action in the Vietnam region, legislators asked few questions about the president's less-than-candid portrayal of unprovoked attacks on U.S. warships by North Vietnamese naval craft. Instead, Congress quickly passed the 1964 Tonkin Gulf Resolution, authorizing the president to take whatever action he deemed appropriate to protect U.S. interests in the gulf region. The vote was unanimous in the House of Representatives; there were only two dissenting votes in the Senate. Seven years of war followed.

Non–status quo situations are, by contrast, likely to be marked by much more debate among a wider range of political actors. A non–status quo situation occurs when the country is faced with circumstances that diverge markedly from the previous state of affairs and that call for fundamental change—for *innovative policy*. One such shift occurred just after World War II. Instead of reverting to its quasi-isolationist, prewar stance, the United States became a superpower with a global presence in a bipolar world that pitted the United States against a powerful Soviet Union. There were several years of spirited debate over the fundamental course of U.S. policy before the cold war consensus emerged.

Now the world order has changed dramatically again. The Soviet Union has collapsed; the bipolar world has fragmented. In this new, non–status quo situation, there is, once again, a policy making struggle under way over the nature and extent of U.S international interests and commitments. The important thing to note is the parallels between the two non–status quo eras. Entirely new global situations faced the United States in each era; the old standards of conduct seemed no longer relevant. Despite what seemed to be victory (over the Axis powers in 1945, over the Soviet Union in 1991), there was no peace. Soon after 1945, Americans faced cold war confrontations in such places as Berlin and a hot war in Korea. Soon after 1991, U.S. troops were deployed to or near, and sometimes were fighting and dying in, the Persian Gulf, the Balkans, Somalia, and Haiti. Americans during both eras felt threatened by an ungrateful ally. Surely, the perceived political-military threat from the Soviet Union in the late 1940s was more alarming to Americans than is the present sense of economic threat from Japan and Europe (in the form of the European Union) in the 1990s. Still Americans were anxious at the very moments when they might have been congratulating themselves on being triumphant. Congress during both non–status quo eras was more active and influential than normal. In both eras, isolationism and internationalism struggled for dominance. President Truman (1955:97) "could never quite forget the strong hold which isolationism had gained over our country," and he worried that it would revive. President Bush became the first president since Truman to feel compelled to urge citizens to shun a "retreat into isolationism."[17] President Clinton has repeatedly echoed that call.

In a major foreign policy speech delivered in October 1995, the president cautioned against the "isolationist backlash, which is present in both parties." Taking up the related unilateral-multilateral debate, Clinton spoke out in favor of multilateralism, urging that "we need the wisdom to work with the United Nations." As for unilateralism, Clinton derided it as "a disguised form of isolationism" and "not a viable option." Clinton went on to rebuke those who clamor for a simple, overarching policy to address a complex world and to advocate a policy of broad, pragmatic U.S. engagement with world issues and actors. As he put it, "We have to drop the abstractions and dogma and pursue, based on trial and error and persistent experimentation, a policy that advances our values of freedom and democracy, peace and security."[18]

Types of Issue Areas

The policy making process is also affected by the subject it is addressing. This means that foreign policy could be broken down into a number of **issue areas** based on how various issues affected society. While there is still no scholarly consensus about precisely how to categorize types of policy, there have been important ideas and research that enhance our understanding of the policy process. These advances include distinguishing foreign, domestic, and intermestic policy; differentiating types of foreign policy; and recognizing the impact of perceptions on policy categories.

Foreign, Domestic, and Intermestic Policy

President Kennedy once distinguished types of policy by remarking that "domestic policy can only defeat us; foreign policy can kill us" (Schlesinger, 1967:395). Despite the hyperbole, Kennedy's point does underline differences among fundamental types of policy. One reason for making such distinctions is to make it possible to decide which policies to study in a foreign policy text and which policies are not applicable. As we will see presently, differentiating between what is foreign policy and what is not is often controversial. Distinguishing types of policy is also important because some scholars believe that the difference in the potential impact noted by Kennedy and the sense that foreign policy pits "us" (Americans) versus "them" (others) persuade Americans to allow the president considerable latitude in conducting foreign policy.

The Two Presidencies Thesis Based on the distinction between foreign and domestic policy, Aaron Wildavsky (1966:7) argued in an article, "The Two Presidencies," that "since World War II, presidents have had much greater success in controlling the nation's defense and foreign policies than in dominating its domestic policies." It was an important article; political scientists continue to argue about its validity (Parsons, 1994; Shull, 1991; Renka & Jones, 1991; Bond & Fleisher, 1990).

At the risk of oversimplifying the debate over if and when Wildavsky's two presidencies thesis is valid, it is clear that Wildavsky's thesis was too categorical. Yes, the president often does exercise greater control over foreign policy than over domestic policy. This is because the president has extensive constitutional foreign policy authority and also because, as has been said earlier, Congress and the public frequently are more willing to accept presidential leadership in foreign rather than in domestic policy. But, no, presidential dominance is not always evident. Instead, presidential authority varies according to the situation, the issue, and other political circumstances. One way to begin to resolve these variations and to revise the two presidencies thesis is to acknowledge that the dichotomy between foreign and domestic issues is too simplistic. We need to recognize that domestic policy and foreign policy often overlap.

Intermestic Issues Policy concerns that fall into the area of overlap between domestic and foreign policy are called intermestic issues. The term combines the words *inter*national and do*mestic,* thereby denoting the intersection of those two types of policy. There is wide agreement that, along with the growth of global interdependence, there has been an intertwining of international and domestic affairs (Parry, 1993). This reality has assumed a particular importance in the rhetoric of the Clinton administration. Just after his election, Clinton declared that "My first foreign policy priority will be to restore America's economic vitality."[19] Elaborating on that theme, Secretary of State–designate Warren M. Christopher observed that in facing global challenges, Americans "must remain cognizant that a great power requires not only military might but a powerful economy at home, an economy prepared for global competition." That means, Christopher continued, that "foreign policy and domestic policy must be addressed simultaneously, not sequentially, or else neither will be successful for very long."[20] Christopher might also have added that the line between what is a foreign policy issue and what is a domestic policy issue is becoming less clear as national and international circumstances and activities become increasingly linked.

This does not mean that there are no differences; some issues still are clearly foreign or domestic. But there is also a broadly overlapping border between the two policy realms. Foreign trade policy is a classic example of an intermestic issue (Gibson, 1995; Lohmann & O'Halloran, 1994; Nolan & Quinn, 1994; Verdier, 1994; Mayer, 1992). The intermestic nature of trade, one scholar explains, is based on the fact that it "brings together domestic, economic, national security, and foreign policy considerations. It is an arena that not only engages a multitude of actors, governmental and nongovernmental, but one which embraces a host of considerations, competing values, and unending tensions." Therefore, the scholar continues, trade policy often sparks a political free-for-all, in which "both branches see themselves as having large stakes in the outcomes" (Porter, 1988:170)

Recognizing the existence of intermestic issues has several advantages. One is to highlight the perceptual differences among political actors, especially the president and Congress. As one political scientist comments in his study of trade policy making, "Intermestic issues invite presidential initiatives because they lie partially in the traditionally presidential realm of foreign affairs" (Barilleaux, 1988:25). Yet, the scholar continues, "as far as Congress is concerned, intermestic issues are domestic issues, because the immediate concerns of members and their constituents are [local impacts]." For this reason, the president loses much of his traditional foreign policy authority when dealing with intermestic issues because they are processed much like domestic issues.

One study that examined the success of Ronald Reagan's policy preferences, dividing them into international, intermestic, and domestic issues, reached a similar conclusion (Rourke & Carter, 1989). On what that study called pure foreign policy issues, Reagan's preferred programs had a 74.9 percent success rate in Congress. Domestic policy was successful only 54.9 percent of the time; and intermestic policy was only slightly more successful at 56 percent, as is evident in Figure 6.1. As you look at this figure, there are three things you should notice. One is that the president's foreign policy success, compared to his domestic success, was, on average, 21 percent higher in the Senate and 30 percent higher in the House. Second, the president's intermestic policy success rate tended to parallel domestic policy more closely than it did foreign policy, especially in the more constituent-oriented House. Third, all three success rates in both houses generally declined over time, except for the last year. Then there was a foreign and an intermestic jump (from a very low level) in the House. It might be noted also that during the 1981–1986 period, the Republicans held the majority in the Senate, which helps account for the Republican Reagan's higher success rate in that chamber.

The international-intermestic-domestic division helps us to narrow which policies are in the realm of foreign policy analysis. International and intermestic policy should both be considered part of foreign policy. But there is evidence that the two types of policy are processed differently, with the president more powerful in international than in intermestic policy making. This distinction is only part of the key to understanding the operation of the presidential, political, administrative, and subgovernment models. Therefore, the next step is to distinguish between international and intermestic issues.

FIGURE 6.1

Presidential Success Rates in Congress
and Types of Issues

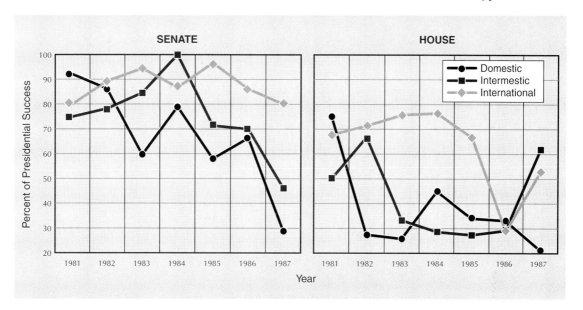

Source: Rourke and Carter, 1989.

A president's ability to persuade Congress to agree to presidential proposals varies according to the type of policy. This figure shows the success rates that President Reagan had in the Senate and in the House of Representatives from 1981 through 1987 for pure international, intermestic, and domestic proposals. Notice that the success rate for pure international proposals was higher in both houses than the success rate for the other two types of policies. Also see that the patterns of success for intermestic and domestic issues are somewhat alike in the House and in the Senate. That is because Congress is likely to treat an intermestic issue much like a domestic issue, even if the president tends to view the issue as one of international relations.

Distinguishing International and Intermestic Issues   The key to telling which issue is international and which is intermestic is *perceived domestic stakes*. When the public or specific groups believe that they will be affected by a policy, they tend to become more active politically and to move the issue into the intermestic realm.

Some of the earliest work on issue areas suggested that foreign policy making processes would vary according to whether an issue area had a tangible impact on society. These studies reasoned that tangible concerns (territory) or instruments (foreign aid) would tend to activate Congress, interest groups, and public opinion more than intangible goals (prestige) and instruments (diplomacy). Also relevant are studies that have examined defense policy making with an eye to constructing issue areas. More than one study has found that the weapons acquisition process involves different, changing stakes that, in turn, cause corresponding changes in the involved decision making actors and the nature of the process. One approach is to distinguish between strategic issues (overseas deployment and use of forces) and structural issues (weapons contracts, base closings).

While such studies were on the right track, they underestimated the ability of some intangible issues to activate various political actors. Ethnic and other subnational

163

groups are frequently activated, for example, by U.S. policy toward countries with which they identify. Greek Americans, Jewish Americans, and Irish Americans are just a few examples of these groups. Too strong a focus on tangibility also fails to explain why so many Americans (of all races) pressed Washington to enact sanctions against the white regime in South Africa or are so concerned about continuing to grant favorable trade privileges to the oppressive regime in China.

The placement of issues into the international or intermestic categories goes a long way to explain which models operate and when, but there is another dimension: intensity.

High Prominence and Low Prominence Issues

The degree of prominence that an issue has within the political system affects the decision making process. Prominence is determined by (1) how widely an issue is debated within the political system and by (2) the intensity of the debate. The wider and more intense the controversy over an issue, the more it will involve a multiplicity of political actors and higher-level decision makers. Like many political phenomena, intensity has a significant perceptual component. For example, the United States has ongoing trade difficulties with both the European Union (EU) and Japan. Measured by economic size and potential, the EU is an even stronger competitor than is Japan. Yet public concern and debate over relations with Japan are much more intense than they are over relations with the EU.

One of the earliest efforts to categorize foreign policy along the lines of intensity argued that policy would be processed by the executive in something like our presidential model during very intense situations (such as crises), called "the pole of power" (Wolfers, 1962). Low-intensity, noncrisis issues that had little or no domestic impact ("the pole of indifference") would be processed according to our administrative model. In between the two extremes, by implication, policy would be handled by the political model or by the subgovernment model, depending on the breadth and intensity of the domestic interests involved.

It is difficult to predetermine which situations and issues are likely to spark an intense reaction and which are not, but there are some clues. As we noted in the earlier discussion of situations, *military crises* almost always are high on the intensity scale. Intensity is governed also by the *immediacy and intensity of impact*. The trade issue with Japan has existed for a long time, but it was brought to the forefront of the **political agenda** (issues being widely and intensely discussed) by the prolonged and sharp recession in the United States in the early 1990s. A sagging gross national product, weak domestic sales, massive layoffs, high unemployment, and general economic anxiety set off an intense American reaction to the flood of Japanese imports.

There are also some issues that evoke an intense reaction within a narrower element of American society. One cause is *emotional involvement*. Emotions may be sparked by national pride, such as the American reaction to the widespread perception that Japan is taking advantage of the United States. The Clinton administration threatened Japan with sanctions in 1995 unless Japan made substantial and quantifiable concessions that would allow more U.S. auto parts to be sold in Japan. "We're not going to blink," declared Vice President Al Gore. Yet blink is what the administration did. When an agreement was reached in June, its vague clauses made it "a complete cave[in]," according to one former U.S. trade negotiator, and "unenforceable, nonbinding—in short, virtually empty," according to Senator Dole.[21] Even the administration had difficulty putting a good face on the agreement. "We all looked over the precipice" of a confrontation with Japan, one senior U.S. official said, "and discovered we couldn't see the bottom. The sanctions were a big risk. So we took what we had in hand."[22]

Contravened values may also cause an emotional reaction, in the way that the apartheid policies of South Africa eventually brought economic sanctions against that country. Cultural group identification is yet another factor that may foster emotional involvement among specific elements of society. African Americans, for example, were particularly active on the question of South Africa, and they also were strongly involved in U.S. policy toward Haiti and the Haitian refugee issue.

Symmetry is another key to intensity. The degree to which any group feels that it is being unfairly burdened or that others are being unfairly rewarded will increase the intensity of that group's efforts. Policies that impact the society *symmetrically* (with gains and burdens shared equally) are often less divisive and intense than policies that impact society *asymmetrically* (with some groups and individuals emerging winners and others losers). Furthermore, intense conflict tends to involve higher levels of decision makers and wider debate (the political model). A limited war such as Vietnam is one type of issue area that asymmetrically burdened part of a society, in this case, young adults.

Asymmetry can also help the varying intensity of reaction within a society even when an issue is on the political agenda. Most Americans, for instance, are concerned about the economy and about Japanese economic competition. Yet many Americans care only a little and may still go out and buy a Mitsubishi car or a Sony CD player. Other Americans, such as members of the United Auto Workers union, are apt to care a lot because they are bearing the asymmetrical brunt of sagging domestic auto sales.

A closely related factor that provides another intensity indicator is the difference between *zero-sum* and *non–zero-sum* policies. A zero-sum policy implies that its impacts must balance, with pluses and minuses equaling zero. The only way for some to gain is for others to lose. Therefore, zero-sum policies are not only asymmetrical but they also cause one group to benefit at the expense of another. By contrast, non–zero-sum policy assumes that benefits can be added either for everyone (symmetrical) or that benefits are possible for some without burdening others (asymmetrical). Budget decisions, for example, that reduce defense expenditures (causing defense worker layoffs) while increasing education spending (and jobs and scholarships in that field) could well pit defense workers and companies against students and education professionals, creating an intense zero-sum struggle for the finite budget resources (Chan & Mintz, 1992).

We can say, then, that issues that are perceived as having intermestic impact, especially intermestic issues that spark an intense interest, are likely to fall within the political or subgovernment models, where the president and the rest of the executive branch constitute only one player in a multi-actor process and are less powerful. Because how an issue is perceived has such an important bearing on how it is processed, there is frequently an important debate over how to define the situation and the issue.

Defining Situations and Issue Areas

One of the problems with much of the work on how situations and issue areas affect the foreign policy process is that it is the scholars who decide into which category a particular policy matter fits. Sometimes this approach is not satisfactory because different policy makers may perceive the same situation or issue differently. These varying perceptions are important in determining situations and issue areas. As such, a decision maker's perception, his or her "definition of situation," influences how an issue will be processed.

Applying these ideas, research suggests that because Congress is sometimes perplexed by the complexity of foreign policy, its members often analyze foreign issues in terms of domestic impact, which they understand better. Trade policy, for example, involves several possible issue area interpretations but is addressed by Congress as an intermestic issue. A related insight is that the perception of an issue may change, thereby changing its issue area definition.

Because the definition of situation can change, one strategy to gain victory in a policy struggle is to define the issue in an advantageous way (Bostdorff, 1993). An example of how this can occur is evident in the struggle over the definition of the issue of whether or not to sell AWACS (Airborne Warning and Control System) radar planes to Saudi Arabia during the Reagan administration. In this case, President Reagan won a victory in the Senate partly by stressing that a negative vote would destabilize the Middle East and the president's leadership credibility. "How can I convince foreign leaders that I'm in command when I can't sell five airplanes" to the Saudis, Reagan asked Senator Edward Zorinski (D-NE). The senator had no reply; he changed his vote and supported the AWACS sale.

Reagan's strategy of changing the definition of the issue from intermestic policy (based on heavy lobbying by economic groups and by Jewish Americans) to a matter of presidential prestige and U.S. security worked on other senators too. Iowa Republican Roger Jepsen had tears in his eyes as he explained that he had decided to vote for AWACS because "A vote for the sale is a vote for my president and his successful conduct of foreign policy" (Bard, 1987:60). Most senators were not swayed, but given the close outcome, which the president won by a scant four votes, just a few senators were enough. The vote, said defeated lobbyist Thomas Dine, director of the American Israel Public Affairs Committee, was "a vote of confidence in President Reagan himself," a response to his "appeal that if the sale were defeated, his effectiveness would be impaired" (Bard, 1987:58).

Thus the political *struggle over definition* is extremely important. How a situation or an issue is defined is a key to how it is processed. This, in turn, may affect what is decided. If an issue is defined as falling exclusively in the foreign policy (especially national security) area, then the president is likely to have a stronger policy making hand. Presidents may even try to create a sense of crisis in order to gain the upper hand in the policy process (Bostdorff, 1991). Alternately, if the policy definition includes strong domestic considerations, then Congress, interest groups, and other factors will play an increased role. One might suppose, for example, that U.S. accession to the Genocide Convention (1948) and other international treaties on human rights would fall within the foreign policy realm. Yet some American groups worried that the prohibitions in these treaties against genocide and other crimes would be used to condemn U.S. treatment of its indigenous people, black citizens, and others (Kaufman, 1991). Such concerns moved the perception of these treaties into the intermestic realm. The Genocide Convention was submitted to the Senate in 1949. The treaty was not ratified until 1986, some 37 years later.

FIGURE 6.2   **Policy Model Matrix**

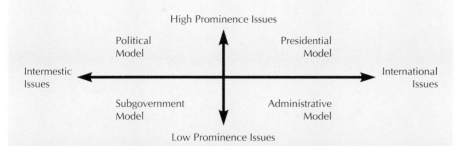

Vertical axis: *High prominence:* circumstances with some combination of crisis, non–status quo situations, asymmetrical impact, zero-sum impact. *Low prominence:* circumstances with some combination of noncrisis, status quo situations, symmetrical impact, non–zero-sum impact.

Horizontal axis: *International issues:* policies with no or minor perceived domestic impact. Actors and disputes mostly within the government. *Intermestic issues:* policies with significant perceived domestic impact. Diverse, multiple actors involved.

The number and intensity of the characteristics found in Table 6.1 (p. 168) will determine whether a policy has high or low prominence and whether it is treated as an intermestic or an international issue. The issue's placement on these two axes indicates which policy making model will best describe the policy process for that issue. This figure is discussed below.

Creating a Model Matrix

"Whew!" you must be saying to yourselves. "Models, situations, intermestic issues, intensity, zero-sum, asymmetry—help!" Certainly it is all hard to keep straight. Still, it is important to do so. Figure 6.2 above and Tables 6.1 and 6.2 will help. Figure 6.2 depicts a four-cell matrix of the policy making models. The horizontal axis is based on international and intermestic policy; the vertical axis is based on high and low prominence.

Although Figure 6.2 provides a quick view of our four models, further detail is needed. This is provided by Tables 6.1 and 6.2. The first, Table 6.1, shows the four models and the situation and issue characteristics common to each. Providing an example of each variable here is not necessary to make the point that which characteristics define a policy question will determine the model by which it is processed. The NAFTA debate, for example, fell squarely into the political model because NAFTA fit almost all the parameters of what works to place an issue within the framework of that particular model. The debate occurred during a *noncrisis* situation. The stakes involved with NAFTA were quintessentially *intermestic*. Internationally, political and economic relations with Mexico were at issue, as was competition with the European Union, and the general international stance of the United States. Domestically, opponents claimed that NAFTA would cost American jobs and would harm the environment due to increases in pollution that would spread to the United States from discharges by environmentally underregulated Mexican factories. Proponents of NAFTA claimed that more jobs would be gained than would be lost, that American consumers would benefit from more and less expensive products, and that Mexican

TABLE 6.1

Foreign Policy Making Models and
Their Characteristics

Models/ Characteristics	Presidential	Political	Administrative	Subgovernment
Situation	crisis	noncrisis	noncrisis	noncrisis
Situation	non–status quo	non–status quo	status quo	status quo
Emotional involvement	strong	strong	weak	weak
Symmetry	symmetrical	asymmetrical	symmetrical	asymmetrical
Gain/loss sum	zero-sum	zero-sum	non–zero-sum	zero-sum
Issue type	international	intermestic	international	intermestic

The degree to which a policy is perceived to have a variety of characteristics will determine the policy process represented by the four policy making models.

prosperity would stem the massive illegal Mexican immigration into the southwestern United States.

Similarly, the fact that there would be distinct economic winners (banking and other service industries, for example) and losers (such as American factory workers) made the stakes in NAFTA *asymmetrical*. A closely related view by U.S. labor unions was that NAFTA was a *zero-sum* policy: if Mexican workers gained, American workers inevitably lost. Finally, the move toward NAFTA also represented a *non–status quo* situation, a trait that tends to increase issue prominence. It encapsulated the controversy over the shift from national-based economics to regional- or even global-based economics. "I don't think there is an issue," commented one public opinion analyst, "that quite so distinctly separates those who think they will succeed in the new world order from those who see themselves as victims of changing economic structure."[23]

Remember two things about placing policy matters in models. One is that *you do not need all the characteristics* listed under any one model for that model to operate. Rather, the more of the characteristics that you have, and the more profound (such as the intensity of a crisis) they are, then the more the process will tend toward that model. Second, *some of the characteristics are based on perception*. Therefore, the struggle over definition will determine their nature. In short, nothing in real-life politics is ever as neatly divided as this or any other categorization scheme. So use Tables 6.1 and 6.2 as intellectual road maps, but stay alert for curves and bumps in the road.

Before leaving this explanation of our four models of the foreign policy process, let us restate a few important points about them. One is that policy making is a complex and dynamic process. A decision may fall well within one of the models, and the process will strongly exhibit the decision making characteristics of that model. Or a decision may fall near the border of two models and begin to exhibit some characteristics of each. Indeed, there is sometimes a struggle over how to define an issue because the perception of the nature of an issue will change the decision making dynamics (the model) and may well influence what policy is adopted. Most important, the models reflect the reality that policy is not decided in a single way. The next five chapters will look at the policy roles played by the major policy making actors: the

TABLE 6.2   Models and Roles of Policy Making Actors

Models/Actors	Presidential	Political	Administrative	Subgovernment
Presidency	policy maker	contestant	ratifier	uninvolved/ ratifier
Bureaucracy	inform, advise	contestant	policy maker	contestant/ ratifier
Congress	supporter	contestant	uninvolved	limited contestant
Interest group	supporter	contestant	uninvolved	limited contestant
The public	supporter	wide influence	uninvolved	narrow influence

The roles of the policy actors vary according to the model by which any given policy is processed.

presidency, Congress, the media, interest groups, and public opinion. An ongoing theme of these chapters is that the policy making roles of these players are not constant. Instead, they vary, and the policy models help explain when and why variations occur. There will be considerable further commentary on the models in the five policy-actor chapters, so it is wise for you to have a firm grasp on this chapter's discussion before proceeding.

·

SUMMARY

1. There is no single U.S. foreign policy process. Instead, the way that foreign policy is made can be divided into four general processes represented by models.

2. The four models are: the presidential, the political, the administrative, and the subgovernment.

3. The presidential model focuses on the president and his immediate, high-level advisers in the White House and the Cabinet. This model envisions policy being made according to rational decisions, within cognitive boundaries, about the national interest.

4. The political model views policy making as part of a diverse, multiple actor process extending beyond top executive branch decision makers to include lower-level agencies, Congress, interest groups, and the public.

5. The administrative model represents policy as being made by the State Department, the Defense Department, and other bureaucratic units and the personnel who work at those agencies.

6. The subgovernment model portrays policy resulting as an outcome of interaction among specific and limited elements drawn from agencies, members of Congress, and interest groups. Only those bureaucratic units, legislators, and interest groups with a special interest in a specific policy issue are involved in making policy related to that issue.

7. Which policy model operates and when is a function of the type of situation and the nature of the issue involved.

8. Based on the situation and the issue, foreign policy can range along two scales: from pure international to intermestic; from high prominence to low prominence. The models (and scale positions) are: presidential model (international / high prominence); political model (intermestic / high prominence); administrative model (international / low prominence); subgovernment model (intermestic / low prominence).

Chapter Seven

THE PRESIDENCY

Politics is about power. So wrote Florentine statesman Niccolò Machiavelli in his classic discourse, *The Prince* (1519). Machiavelli portrayed power as an end in itself, divorced from morality or justice. The art of governing successfully, he advised the princes of his day and the future, is synonymous with acquiring, retaining, and expanding power.

    Machiavelli's starkly realpolitik advice is unsettling because he ignores as irrelevant the question of what, if anything, princes should attempt to accomplish beyond attaining and exercising power. Yet he does have a point: without power even a benevolent prince can accomplish little or nothing. Machiavelli also saw correctly that princes, whether spurred by the desire to do good deeds or driven by a cynical lust for control, almost universally seek power. The study of politics is, therefore, involved intimately with power.

The prince of our day in the United States is, of course, the president. In what has been called "a modern version of Machiavelli's Renaissance study of power,"[1] Richard Neustadt's *Presidential Power* (1960:8) advises presidents that "the search for personal influence is at the center of the job of being President." Following Machiavelli's and Neustadt's strictures, this chapter will focus on the president's foreign policy making power. Our analysis of presidential power will approach its subject from the perspective of formal and informal presidential power to see the means by which presidents and their immediate advisers attempt to attain their ends. This does not always mean coercive power, the power to command. It also includes persuasive power, the power to lead. Presidents can sometimes issue orders successfully; more often they must try to persuade others to follow. An inherent part of discussing the use of power is to discuss restraints, and so we will also examine the formal and informal restraints on presidential power.

Before we take up presidential power, it is appropriate to review some earlier commentary. Recall from chapter 1 that presidents have increasingly asserted exclusive prerogatives in many areas of foreign policy—especially where the use of force is involved. That chapter also discussed ways that White House decisions are affected by group decision making processes and by the idiosyncrasies of policy makers. Chapter 6 extended this discussion, noting the limits on rationality and the role of partisan politics in the foreign policy process. The chapter also added to the discussion in chapter 1 of group decision making, roles, and the impact of idiosyncratic factors on policy. The point is that presidents and their advisers are people, and it is important to keep that in mind while reading this chapter's commentary on the nature and exercise of and restraints on presidential power.

THE SOURCES OF PRESIDENTIAL POWER: FORMAL AND INFORMAL

The presidency is one office, but it fulfills two roles: head of government and head of state. The *head of government* role involves the ongoing operation of the government. The president's authority as head of government is derived primarily from formal powers, those that endow the office with extensive and specific constitutional and statutory authority. The *head of state* role involves the president's symbolic function as the chief American, something of the anthropomorphization of the United States and a symbolic projection of the American people. This role gives presidents immense status and persuasive power. As such, informal powers are the primary source of the president's authority as head of state. This symbolic authority has been enhanced even more by U.S. world leadership.

Some perspective on the power that accrues to the president because these two roles are unified can be gained from thinking about other political systems. Many countries separate the two functions (Prindle, 1991). Great Britain, for instance, has a prime minister (head of government) and a monarch (head of state). British prime ministers are powerful leaders, but they do not have the symbolic status for the British that U.S. presidents have for Americans. In Great Britain this symbolic role is fulfilled by Queen Elizabeth II. Many other countries divide power between a prime minister, premier, or chancellor (on the one hand) and a president (on the other); and in those cases, neither official has as much combined legal and symbolic authority as the U.S. president.

FORMAL PRESIDENTIAL POWER AND RESTRAINTS

The Constitution is the primary source of the powers of and restraints on the presidency. Constitutional powers include those that the document assigns specifically to the presidency (see the box on pp. 176–177), those that can be inferred (implied powers) from the often terse phraseology of the Constitution, and those that have been established through political and judicial precedents over two centuries of U.S. political and constitutional history. Statutory powers, authority granted to the president by legislative acts of Congress, also add to the presidency's formal powers.

Formal Presidential Powers

Our discussion of formal presidential powers will group them into three roles: commander in chief, head diplomat, and chief executive and law enforcement officer.

Commander in Chief

The language in Article II of the Constitution that designates the president as commander in chief establishes the most portentous of all presidential powers. There are two different functions that come from the role of commander in chief. One is operational control of the military in the field, the other is the presidential war power.

Operational Control   The president's role as commander in chief, Alexander Hamilton wrote in *Federalist* No. 69, "would amount to nothing more than the supreme command and direction of the military and naval forces, as the first general and admiral of the Confederacy." As we shall see, he vastly underestimated what would occur in his assumption of a modest, "nothing more than" role for the president. But Hamilton's language does underscore the indisputable role of the president as chief general and admiral.

Presidents do not put on a uniform and go off to command the troops. Or at least they have not done so since 1794 when George Washington led 15,000 troops to Pennsylvania against the Whiskey Rebellion dissidents, who were refusing to pay the federal excise tax on their product. More commonly, presidents use their operational control authority to make strategic and tactical military decisions (Dawson, 1994). Franklin D. Roosevelt's decision during World War II to emphasize the European over the Pacific theater and his decision to invade Europe eastward through France rather than northward from the eastern Mediterranean both later had important political impacts on the postwar world. The wisdom of Harry S. Truman's momentous decision to order atomic attacks on Hiroshima and Nagasaki remains controversial more than a half century later. John F. Kennedy issued orders involving specific naval tactics during the Cuban missile crisis blockade. Lyndon Johnson planned bombing targets during Vietnam, and he and Richard Nixon attempted to use escalations and pauses as a diplomatic tool to coerce or entice North Vietnam to agree to U.S. terms to end the war. George Bush was strongly involved in the tactics of the Persian Gulf War. Among other moves, the long air bombardment of Iraqi positions before the ground assault was dictated, in part, by the president's desire to avoid heavy U.S. casualties and a possible Vietnam-syndrome reaction by the American public. President

Clinton has also made several notable operational control decisions. He was instrumental in deciding on the level of U.S. (as part of NATO) air strikes against Bosnian Serb targets in the forceful response that, in part, finally resulted in a cease-fire in October 1995 and in December the formal signing of a peace accord in Paris, the beginning of peace talks. Clinton was also involved in planning for the deployment of some 20,000 U.S. troops to Bosnia as part of the NATO peacekeeping force.

The president's operational authority under the Constitution has never been challenged successfully. But politics sometimes creates pressure on the president to turn the war over to his military commanders to win victory at whatever price. At times during the wars in Korea (1950–1953) and Vietnam (1964–1975), the frustration of stalemate put pressure on the president to escalate the conflicts by, respectively, bombing or invading China and invading North Vietnam. The presidents involved avoided this dramatic step. In Truman's case in Korea, however, the U.S. commander, General of the Army Douglas MacArthur, pressed to extend the Korean War to the Chinese mainland and tried to undermine President Truman's authority by complaining to Congress about having to fight without being given a chance to win. In one of his finer moments, Truman fired the old soldier, who then faded away into history.

Presidential War Power   Alexander Hamilton argued in *Federalist* No. 69 that Article II of the Constitution gave the president less military power than was possessed by the governor of New York. This insight would undoubtedly surprise New York's current governor and virtually everyone else. In fact, the president's commander-in-chief power far exceeds Hamilton's image. Most important, the president's authority extends to the initiation of **presidential wars**. We will refer to this authority as the presidential or president's "war power," specifically referring to the power of the president to decide unilaterally when and if, not just how, U.S. military forces will be used. There are also a number of powers, often called "emergency powers," that accrue to the president during wars or other international or domestic crises, which will be discussed later.

The issue of when the president can use military force without a supporting declaration of war or without Congress authorizing force (an undeclared war) by means of a joint resolution or some other legislative act is of such consequence and controversy that a small library of books has been written on the subject.[2]

The constitutional basis of the question rests on the uncertain relationship between the language in Article I that states that "Congress shall have the power . . . To declare war" and Article II's declaration that "The president shall be Commander in Chief of the Army and Navy of the United States." There is little doubt that a president can and should respond to a military attack on the United States, its forces, or its territories without waiting for Congress. Beyond this point of immediate defense, the president's war power becomes extremely murky from a constitutional perspective. Whatever the Framers of the Constitution may or may not have intended, in practice the decision to use military force has gravitated into the hands of the president because of expediency, because of the presidential urge to accumulate power, and because of the frequent willingness of Congress and the public to acquiesce to executive authority in times of crisis.

The president's war power grew slowly during the first 150 years of U.S. history, then accelerated after World War II. Prior to that, presidents had almost always consulted with Congress and asked for some sort of authorization. When North Korea invaded South Korea in 1950, President Truman took a new course and ordered U.S. troops to war on his own claimed authority. It was an act, one scholar has recently written, that "violated the U.S. Constitution and the UN Participation Act of 1945" authority (Fisher, 1995c:37). Be that as it may, the State Department argued at the time that legislative action was not needed, because "The President, as Commander in Chief of the Armed Forces of the United States, has full control over the use thereof."[3] Furthermore, Secretary of State Dean Acheson (1969:415) later argued, Truman's unilateral decision was designed not just to repel the North Korean invasion, but to protect the presidency from "the slightest loss of power or prestige" by going to Congress and thereby establishing "a precedent in derogation of presidential power to send our forces into battle."

This practice of self-proclaimed presidential war power has become commonplace. At one point during congressional attempts to force U.S. withdrawals from the Vietnam War by repealing the Tonkin Gulf Resolution, President Johnson's under secretary of state, Nicholas de B. Katzenbach, dismissed the Constitution's declaration of war language as "outmoded phraseology" (LaFaber, 1981:103; Ely, 1993). In retrospect, Robert McNamara, the then–secretary of defense, no longer believes that Article I of the Constitution is obsolete. He asks rhetorically whether "the Johnson administration [was] justified in basing its subsequent military actions in Vietnam . . . on the Tonkin Gulf Resolution." McNamara's reply is, "Absolutely not," because "Congress never intended it to be used as a basis for such action, and still less did the country see it so."[4]

In response to Vietnam and the general excesses of the so-called imperial presidency, Congress passed the War Powers Resolution (WPR) in 1973. This measure attempted to limit when the president can unilaterally commit U.S. forces to war without congressional authorization. The WPR also sought to otherwise specify rules for the respective roles of the president and Congress with regard to the initiation and continuance of military activity in times of crisis or actual combat. We will explore the WPR further in chapter 8, but for here the key is that the resolution has done little to restrain the president (Nathan, 1993).

The failure of the WPR has been repeatedly demonstrated since its passage. Presidents have often committed U.S. forces to combat without seeking congressional authorization. Even in the few instances when they have asked Congress for support, presidents have only done so grudgingly. When, for example, President Ronald Reagan sent troops to Lebanon in 1983, Secretary of State George Shultz told Congress that, irrespective of its views and the WPR, the president "of course is going to do what he thinks best in the interests of the country."[5] As it turned out, political considerations persuaded Reagan to sign a measure applying the WPR to the Lebanon situation, but he simultaneously proclaimed that "my signing [should not] be viewed as any acknowledgment that [my] constitutional authority can be . . . infringed by statute" or that "congressional authorization . . . [is] required" (Katzman, 1990:59).

Reagan's view of congressional support as nice but not necessary carried over to the next administration. President Bush acted without formal legislative support when he ordered the U.S. invasion of Panama in December 1989 (Burgin, 1992). Similarly, the U.S. decision to go to war against Iraq in 1991 was dominated by Bush and a relative handful of White House advisers. He refused to ask Congress for support until the last possible moment. "I cannot consult with 535 strong-willed individuals," Bush asserted; "nor does my responsibility under the Constitution compel me to do that."[6] The president believed, a White House aide explained, that "people should leave him alone to do what he decides is best."[7]

Bush did finally ask Congress whether it agreed that war with Iraq was appropriate, but he waited to do so for five months and until just a week before the war began. The president's delay was based on his desire to ensure that he would get legislative support, his wish to demonstrate national unity, and his concern to cover his political posterior if the war went badly. It is important to note, though, that the president took the position that congressional consent was not legally necessary to begin the war. When Bush did belatedly ask Congress to support a war against Iraq, he told legislators that he was "determined to do whatever is necessary to protect America's security," and he asked Congress only to "join with me in this task." What if Congress had turned the president down? One cannot tell for certain what the president would have done in that unlikely event; but his attitude about congressional approval was clear when he told an aide, "I don't need it [congressional approval]" (Glennon, 1991b:84).

President Bush also added a new and debatable dimension to the president's war power (Franck & Patel, 1992; Glennon, 1991a). Speaking at Princeton University in May 1991, Bush argued that the president was free to commit U.S. forces without congressional approval in cases when military action was authorized by the United Nations. As he put it, "I felt that after studying the question that I had the inherent power to commit our forces to battle after the UN resolution [on Iraq]."[8]

President Clinton has followed the path of his predecessors by asserting the war power authority of his office and disdaining the WPR by sending U.S. forces to Bosnia in late 1995 and ordering other actions. The Clinton chapter in this constitutional saga is told in the box on the next two pages.

Presidents claim that as commander in chief they have the unilateral right to decide if and when to send U.S. forces into combat or other perilous situations. When Iraq invaded Kuwait in 1990, the United States was not attacked, nor did the United States have a defense treaty with Kuwait. Yet President George Bush decided that he had the authority to send Staff Sergeant Karyl Gibson, pictured here filling sandbags in Saudi Arabia, and 500,000 other American troops halfway around the world. Five months after Bush sent U.S. forces to the Persian Gulf, he asked Congress to pass a symbolic, nonbinding resolution of support.

Presidential Peace Power A final noteworthy aspect of the president's military authority is the commander in chief's power to end hostilities and *declare peace*. The Constitution is silent on this process; but, by inference and practice, the peace power falls entirely within the president's discretion. This is not normally controversial: Americans are glad the war is over. There can be criticism, though, as illustrated by the end of the Persian Gulf War and the subsequent criticism of President Bush for

175

(Continued on page 178)

William Jefferson Clinton and the War Power

It did not take long for the 42nd president, William Jefferson Clinton, to begin acting presidential. As a private citizen he had opposed the war in Vietnam and had been ambivalent about the 1991 war against Iraq. But once in the White House, Clinton soon asserted that as commander in chief he had the authority to decide unilaterally to order American troops into action. One of the president's namesakes, Thomas Jefferson, would not have been surprised. "War," the third president wrote in 1788, "is the moment when the energy of a single [monarchical] hand shows itself in the most seducing form."[1]

For Clinton, the siren song of power called to him to take unilateral action in Iraq, Somalia, Haiti, and the Balkans. Over time he asserted his claimed authority as commander in chief with increasing vigor. Two things remained constant, however, in each of these situations: a majority of Americans opposed Clinton's policy and Clinton acted without obtaining the formal consent of Congress.

Clinton's exercise of unilateral authority in the Persian Gulf occurred in June 1993 in response to an alleged plot by Iraq to assassinate former President Bush during his April visit to Kuwait. A poll in May found only 35 percent of Americans in favor of retaliation.[2] Nevertheless, Clinton declared that "a firm and commensurate response was essential to protect our sovereignty" and ordered a U.S. cruise missile strike against Iraqi targets.[3] Not only did the president disregard public opinion, but he ignored Congress despite the fact that more than two months had elapsed between discovery of the alleged assassination plot and the U.S. response.

In Somalia, Clinton used his authority as commander in chief to expand the military's mission from delivering humanitarian relief to conducting more offensive operations against one of the Somali factions after it had attacked Pakistani UN peacekeepers in June 1993. Clinton pronounced the change in mission "an appropriate response to what happened."[4] Perhaps, but it led to more conflict, including an October clash in which 18 American soldiers died. Public and legislative opinion rebelled against the course of action Clinton had unilaterally chosen, and the domestic uproar finally persuaded Clinton to announce that he would withdraw U.S. forces within 6

months. Still, he refused to concede that Congress had any legal say in the matter. The president "must make the ultimate decision, " Clinton declared.[5] He also successfully opposed several legislative resolutions to mandate withdrawal on the grounds that they would, he wrote, "unduly restrict the ability of the President to make foreign policy and to exercise his authority to make foreign policy."[6]

Clinton's exercise of his war power in Iraq and Somalia were mere warm-ups compared to his decision to invade Haiti in order to overthrow its military junta. Public opinion polls demonstrated that Americans consistently opposed using force to restore democracy in Haiti. One survey found that 56 percent of those respondents with an opinion agreed that "nothing the U.S. could accomplish in Haiti is worth the death of even one U.S. soldier."[7] Congressional opposition was also strong. Both houses passed measures pressing Clinton to seek legislative authorization before an invasion. The administration rejected this view. Secretary of State Warren Christopher argued the legal case, saying that Clinton had "a constitutional prerogative" to act and could do so on his "own constitutional authority." President Clinton took the father-knows-best approach. "I know [the impending invasion] is unpopular," he told a national audience. "I know the timing is unpopular. I know the whole thing is unpopular. But I believe it is the right thing."[8] Once again, regardless of what the American people and Congress thought, Clinton ordered U.S. forces into action; war was averted only when the military junta there surrendered its power.

With unilateral military actions in Iraq, Somalia, and Haiti under his belt, Clinton was ready in November 1995 to decide on behalf of all Americans whether or not the country should commit, as he put it, "our most precious resource—the men and women of our armed forces" to face the danger lurking in Bosnia.[9]

Clinton had long declared his willingness to send U.S. ground forces into Bosnia, but he had been inhibited by staunch domestic opposition, among other factors. Nevertheless, Clinton had found other ways to intervene militarily in the Balkans. In May 1993 he dispatched 300 U.S. ground troops to Macedonia to join the 700 UN troops already in that former Yugoslav province who were ready to protect it from a

Serbian or Greek attack. President Clinton also ordered U.S. Navy and Air Force warplanes into an increasing series of attacks against Bosnian Serb positions.

Then, Clinton decided to take the big step and send in ground forces. "For three years, I refused to commit our troops to war," he told a journalist; "but almost from the beginning of my presidency I said I thought we should be part of preserving a peace agreement."[10] The motivations of the president were complex and are discussed elsewhere in this text. What is important here is that Clinton made yet another unilateral decision to put American troops in harm's way. Furthermore, two familiar patterns were emerged. First, most Americans did not support intervention. Second, Clinton asserted that he, not Congress, had the war power.

On the evening of November 27, 1995, Clinton spoke to the nation. "The United States will contribute . . . about 20,000 soldiers" to peacekeeping in Bosnia, the president declared, because, "It is the right thing to do." He asked "all Americans . . . [and] every member of Congress . . . to make the choice for peace" by supporting the intervention.[11] What Clinton might have said more accurately is that he was asking all Americans and every member of Congress to acquiesce to a choice that he had already made. The president might also have added that the troops were going to Bosnia whether or not the majority of Americans and Congress wanted them to go. Underlining the now full development of Clinton's willingness to claim that he, and he alone, should and could decide, his spokesman Michael McCurry told reporters that "President Clinton may have understood the power of the presidency intellectually in the beginning, but he feels it viscerally now."[12]

Americans were not persuaded that the president's brain or intestines were correct. A poll that asked whether Clinton "should have to get congressional approval in advance" or whether "this is a decision he can make for himself as commander in chief, even if Congress does not approve," found that 60 percent of respondents believed that the president "needs approval," while only 37 percent said that he "can decide for himself," and 4 percent did not know.[13] Nor were Americans persuaded that their troops should go to Bosnia. Even after Clinton's address, only a thin plurality, not a majority, of the public rallied to support the move. Then, as the emotion of Clinton's plea for support faded, public opinion turned sharply against the intervention. Ten days after the address, one survey revealed that 38 percent of Americans approved and 58 percent disapproved of Clinton's decision.[14] A week later, another poll found that only 36 percent of respondents agreed that it was "the right thing" to send U.S. troops to Bosnia; 58 percent thought it was the wrong thing to do.[15]

The President was undeterred by public opinion. Clinton also made it clear that he would not be blocked by Congress. He said he would welcome "an expression of support by Congress" but added that, whether or not he received it, he would insist on "maintaining the constitutional authority of the presidency."[16] To dispel any doubt about what the president meant, Secretary of State Christopher announced that the president could not be "bound" by any resolution, either of support or opposition, and "would retain his constitutional power" to deploy troops.[17] Backing up words with action, Clinton did not even wait for Congress to enact the legally meaningless, nice-but-not-necessary resolutions that passed on December 13. Instead, on December 2 he signed the order sending American troops into Bosnia.

The point here is not to think about whether you favored or opposed U.S. intervention in the Persian Gulf, Somalia, Haiti, or Bosnia. The issue is the process by which the United States goes to war. Clinton is among those who believe that U.S. foreign policy is served and U.S. democracy is not offended by the president's making determination of if and when to go to war. Others disagree. They believe that it is both wise and constitutional to require formal congressional consent before sending U.S. forces into war or hostile situations. "We happen to have a Constitution that clearly states where the war-declaring power is located," one critic of presidential wars has written recently. Furthermore, the scholar continued, "The framers of the Constitution deliberately set up a system of checks and balances precisely in order to prevent Presidents from acting on their own. We cannot pretend that [the framers] were right and at the same time claim that in the case of declaring war Presidents should have no checks and balances" (Draper, 1995: 40).

Thus, as it has for most of U.S. history, the issue of the president's war power continues to be controversial. Whether or not the practice of a unilateral presidential war power violates both the Constitution and prudent policy making and, if so, what should be done, is a matter for you, the reader, to decide.

(Continued from page 175)

ordering one of his field commanders, General H. Norman Schwarzkopf, to end operations against Iraq before the general's forces could fully destroy the Republican Guard and other elements of the Iraqi army or, as some people wanted, capture Baghdad and depose Saddam Hussein. The president had a variety of strategic motives, including wanting to preserve Iraq as a counterweight to Iran in the region (Jentleson, 1994). Bush also wanted a quick victory with few American casualties. "We need to have an end. People want that," he told aides. "They are going to want to know we won and [that] the kids can come home. We do not want to screw this up with a sloppy muddled ending."[9] And so, for good or ill, the ground war ended after just 100 hours, and Saddam Hussein and his Republican Guard survived, battered but alive.

Head Diplomat

There are two specific constitutional clauses that support the president's status as chief U.S. diplomat. One clause provides that the president "shall have the power . . . to make treaties." The other stipulates that the president "shall receive Ambassadors and other public Ministers." Beyond these, there is a general sense gained from the Constitution as a whole that the delegates in 1787 intended the president to be the focus of U.S. diplomatic activity.

The Power to Make International Agreements The U.S. Constitution's power-to-make-treaties language establishes the president and presidential appointees as the only officials who can negotiate authoritatively with another government. In fact, after an American Quaker named George Logan went to Paris in 1798 to negotiate with the French in the hope of avoiding conflict (which later ensued) with the United States, Congress passed "An Act to Prevent Usurpation of Executive Functions," generally called the Logan Act. This statute makes it illegal for anyone to negotiate in the name of the United States without the president's authorization. The Logan Act has seldom been applied, though, despite the fact that it is not entirely unusual for members of Congress and even private citizens to hold diplomatic discussions with foreign governments. Such unauthorized contacts may cause confusion or create helpful dialogue, but only the president can legally negotiate a treaty.

One implication of the president's treaty power is that no agreement can be reached without presidential concurrence, since the president initiates all negotiations and must sign a treaty before presenting it to the Senate for ratification. President Bush, for example, refused to sign the international biodiversity treaty at the UN–sponsored "Earth Summit" in Rio de Janeiro in June 1992. Bush did sign the global warming treaty, but only after rejecting timetables for U.S. cuts in the emission of carbon dioxide into the atmosphere. Whatever environmentalists may have wanted, the president's rejection of the biodiversity treaty was absolute. Final, that is, until the next president. President Clinton chose Earth Day, April 21, 1993, to sign the biodiversity treaty and to disclaim the U.S. reservations to the global warming treaty. "For too long we have been told that we have to choose between the economy and the environment," Clinton told a crowd during the signing at the U.S. Botanical Gardens in Washington, D.C. "I'm here today in the hope that we can together take a different course of action to offer a new set of challenges to our people."[10] Then, with the stroke of the pen, Clinton turned U.S. refusal into U.S. agreement and sent the treaties to the Senate for ratification.

The Constitution's authors also provided a check on the president's treaty power. After a president signs a treaty, it must be submitted to the Senate and ratified by a vote of two-thirds of the senators before it becomes law. There is a good deal of controversy about how effective this congressional check is. One can point out that the Senate does sometimes reject an important treaty, such as the Treaty of Versailles in 1919. In the same breath, one can also note that historically the Senate has rejected only about 1 of every 75 treaties it has considered, and that rate has declined since World War II. One reason for senatorial reticence is that by the time the Senate receives a treaty, long negotiations have often taken place and the president has made a symbolic act of commitment by signing the document, often with considerable public fanfare. Since the Senate itself cannot change the treaty, legislators are put in the uncomfortable position of being obstructionists and of embarrassing the president and the country if they reject the treaty. If a president lobbies well, then he is likely to be successful. That is true even for unpopular agreements, such as the Panama Canal Treaties (1978), negotiated by President Jimmy Carter. These treaties transferred to Panama the operation, control, and (in most cases) defense of the canal by the year 2000. The treaties were initially opposed strongly by legislators and public opinion, but Carter's skillful efforts shepherded them successfully through the Senate (Strong, 1991).

Treaties are not as safe as statistics seem to indicate, though, and the concern about national and presidential embarrassment can also work to enhance Senate power in a subtle way. Presidents often negotiate treaties with one eye on the Senate, and some of a treaty's provisions may be designed to head off anticipated senatorial distress. Also, it is not uncommon for a treaty to be left pending or to be withdrawn from consideration if the Senate might defeat it. Such a quiet demise was, for example, the fate of the Strategic Arms Limitation Talks (SALT) II Treaty in 1980. Some critics charged that the treaty disadvantaged the United States. Opposition in the Senate was further inflamed by the Soviet intervention in Afghanistan. The Carter administration decided finally to withdraw the treaty from consideration rather than endure the ignominy of defeat. As one U.S. arms negotiator put it, "SALT II was dead in the water," and its withdrawal by Carter was "just an easy way for him to recognize the obvious: SALT didn't have a chance" (Caldwell, 1990:3).

Before we leave our discussion of treaties, it is important to note that presidents have two important powers related to existing treaties. One is the power to cancel them; the other is the power to interpret them. The Constitution says nothing about how a treaty is abrogated, and the issue did not come to a head until the presidency of Jimmy Carter. In 1978, he announced that he would recognize the People's Republic of China (the mainland) and terminate the Mutual Defense Treaty of 1955 with Nationalist China (Taiwan) as of January 1, 1980. Many senators objected because they opposed what they said was "abandoning" Taiwan or because they wanted to defend legislative prerogatives. The Senate, therefore, passed by a 59 to 35 vote a resolution asserting in essence that since the Senate ratified the treaties, those pacts could not be ended without Senate approval. When President Carter ignored this move, a number of senators led by Barry Goldwater (R-AZ) filed suit. A lower federal court heard the suit and ruled for Goldwater, but the Supreme Court in *Goldwater v. Carter* (1979) dismissed the suit by a vote of 7 to 2 on the grounds that it was a political question and therefore outside of the federal courts' jurisdiction.[11] Thus, the Supreme Court did not rule on the substance of the suit, but the Court's action had the effect of upholding presidential power.

In addition to making treaties, presidents may also negotiate **executive agreements**. Such agreements are meant to settle minor government-to-government matters and do not require Senate action. Some executive agreements are made pursuant to a treaty or other legislation and involve the details of treaty or legislative implementation. Presidents make other executive agreements under their broad, if vague, executive authority. In either case, the line between minor adjustments and major policy initiatives is unclear, and the ability to bypass the Senate makes it tempting for presidents to use the method to achieve policy accords with other countries.

The Vietnam peace accord was, for example, accomplished by executive agreement. More recently, what appears to be an informal defensive alliance with Saudi Arabia, Kuwait, and other countries in the Persian Gulf region has been established by an executive agreement allowing U.S. forces to use military installations and to position armaments and logistics support on the Arabian peninsula. After visiting the region in May 1991, Secretary of Defense Richard Cheney alluded to "a broad agreement" and a "significantly enhanced willingness on the part of many governments . . . to cooperate on security arrangements." Cheney rejected the notion of telling the American people what these arrangements committed the United States to do and with whom. "It's still the Middle East," the secretary demurred. "Therefore a certain amount of discretion is required in terms of what you say publicly about arrangements in any given locale."[12]

As an overall phenomenon, the growth of executive agreements, both absolutely and in proportion to treaties, is detailed in Table 7.1. As you can see, the average number of treaties per year has not increased during the last century, while the average number of executive agreements per year has risen dramatically. The ratio of treaties to executive agreements has similarly skyrocketed. Congress tried to restrain what it considered the president's excessive use of executive agreement; but as Table 7.1 figures show and as we will discuss further in chapter 8, the effort has not been successful.

Beyond formal treaties and executive agreements, there is a broad range of tacit, often murky actions that can be termed "presidential commitments." We noted in chapter 1 the long line of understandings—beginning with President Truman's letter to Saudi Arabia's king in 1947 and including the Carter Doctrine that the United States would defend the Gulf—that laid the groundwork for the U.S. intervention in that region. Arms agreements are also frequently upheld by such tacit commitments. Ronald Reagan abided by the SALT II Treaty with the Soviets for most of his time in office and even accused the Soviets of cheating on it. This occurred despite the fact that the treaty had not been ratified and therefore did not legally exist, and despite the fact that he had denounced it while a candidate for the presidency in 1980.

A more recent presidential commitment that gives some pause involves Ukraine, a former Soviet republic. When the USSR collapsed, Ukraine inherited 176 multiple-warhead strategic nuclear missiles. Ukrainian leaders balked at giving up their missiles in line with treaties negotiated by the United States with the USSR and with Russia. As part of the effort of the Bush and Clinton administrations that finally resulted in 1994 in Ukraine's agreement to give up the weapons over three years, Bush gave Ukraine written security guarantees, which would become effective after Ukraine's denuclearization. What was promised remained a secret from the American people, but when leaving Washington with the document, Ukrainian deputy foreign minister Boris Tarasiuk exalted that "the United States has finally seen our view and understood our fears of the potential threat from Russia."[13]

TABLE 7.1	Treaties and Executive Agreements, 1789–1992		
Period (Years)	Average Number of Treaties per Year	Average Number of Executive Agreements per Year	Ratio of Treaties to Executive Agreements
First Century (1789–1889)	2.8	2.7	1:1
Early Modern Presidency (1890–1932)	13.5	25.1	1:2
Modern Presidency (1933–1960)	13.0	132.1	1:10
Imperial Presidency (1961–1974)	15.1	247.2	1:16
Post-Imperial Presidency (1975–1992)	16.1	351.6	1:22

Data source: McKenna (1994), p. 245.

The average number of executive agreements, both absolutely and compared to treaties, has increased sharply over time.

The Power of Diplomatic Recognition   The constitutional clause that says the president shall "receive Ambassadors and other public Ministers" implies that presidents are solely responsible for determining whether or not the United States recognizes other countries. This is because receiving a foreign diplomat's credentials is tantamount to diplomatic recognition of the government that the diplomat represents. By extension, presidents can also break diplomatic relations. Granting recognition to a new government or even a new country is normally routine. Sometimes, though, recognition has important legal and symbolic ramifications. President Truman's quick recognition of Israel in 1948, for example, allowed the new state to purchase U.S. weapons to defend itself and also gave a psychological boost to the beleaguered Israelis. Nonrecognition can also be important politically, as illustrated by the refusal of the United States to recognize the Soviet government between 1918 and 1933. Washington also did not recognize the Chinese Communist government between 1949 and 1979. At that point President Carter further demonstrated the power of his office when he decided to shift U.S. recognition from Taiwan (Nationalist China, where the remnants of the old Chinese government had fled in 1949) to the mainland. Presidents can also break diplomatic relations with countries, as the United States has with Libya and some other countries, to show disapproval of their governments.

The case of Vietnam is the best recent illustration of the president's power of recognition. The United States never established diplomatic relations with North Vietnam after it was created in 1954, and Washington had no relations with Vietnam after the country was unified in 1975. President Clinton moved to change this, but he did so cautiously because of domestic political considerations. Vietnam's communist government and human rights policies, lingering American bitterness over the war, and the issue of U.S. soldiers still listed as missing in action (MIA) were all problems. So was Clinton's earlier opposition to the war in Vietnam and the fact that some critics charge that he dodged the draft to avoid serving there.

As a first step, and supported strongly by U.S. business interested in trade with Vietnam and by supportive congressional resolutions, Clinton ended the U.S. economic embargo in 1994. Then in 1995 the White House gave signals that it would normalize relations with Vietnam. The danger of political attack was partially defused by the support for recognition of such Vietnam veterans in Congress as Republican senator John McCain of Arizona (a former prisoner of war). "For the sake of America, maybe it's time we ended the war, McCain said; "normalization would be an important part of the healing process."[14] Public opinion also supported the move by a margin of 61 percent in favor, 27 percent opposed, and 13 percent unsure.[15] With his political flanks at least partially covered, the president took the podium outside the White House on July 11, 1995, and announced that he would take the final step and recognize Vietnam. It was a speech and ceremony calculated to provide further political armor. Behind the president stood McCain and several other senators who had served in Vietnam and retired chairman of the Joint Chiefs of Staff, General John Vessy. Clinton declared that his action "offers us the opportunity to bind up our own wounds," thus paralleling the words of Abraham Lincoln's second inaugural address: "Let us strive . . . to bind up the nation's wounds." Clinton also evoked the Bible. "Let this moment, in the words of the Scripture," he intoned, "be a time to heal and a time to build" (Ecclesiastes, 3:1–3: "To every thing there is a season, . . . a time to heal; . . . and a time to build up").[16]

There was, of course, criticism of the president's action. The Last Firebase, a group of Vietnam veterans and relatives of MIAs, issued a statement that "today will forever be known by America's veterans as Black Tuesday." Senate Republican leader Robert Dole added his criticism, saying it was "a strategic, diplomatic, and moral mistake to grant Vietnam the stamp of approval." Some members of Congress tried to block recognition by introducing bills that would have tried to require the president to certify that Vietnam had been fully forthcoming on accounting for those who are still listed as missing in action or by denying funds to build a U.S. embassy in Hanoi. Such opinions and actions could do nothing, however, to prevent the president from exercising an authority that is clearly his under the Constitution.

General Diplomatic Power   The president's diplomatic power is greater than the sum of its constitutional parts. Because presidents serve as both head of government and as head of state, they represent the United States. Precisely summarizing the extent of this authority is difficult, but one indication of its basis and importance can be gained from a Supreme Court decision written by Justice George Sutherland in the *Curtiss-Wright Export Corporation* (1936) case.[17] The aircraft manufacturer contested the president's authority to embargo the sale of arms to the then-warring countries of Paraguay and Bolivia. The Court found that not only had Congress given the president proper statutory authority to do so, but—even more importantly—that:

> We are not dealing alone with the authority vested in the President by the exertion of legislative power, but with such an authority plus the very delicate, plenary, and exclusive power of the President as the sole organ of the federal

government in the field of international relations. It is quite apparent that . . . in the maintenance of our international relations . . . [Congress] must accord to the President a degree of discretion which would not be admissible were domestic affairs alone involved.

Presidents decide, for example, how U.S. representatives will vote in international organizations. Often these votes are significant. When the UN Security Council moved in 1995 to condemn the expropriation by Israel of land owned by Arabs in Jerusalem, the vote was 14 to 1 in favor of the resolution. Because the single dissenting vote was cast by the United States, however, the resolution was defeated by the first veto cast by Washington in five years. Presidents can also proclaim U.S. neutrality when other countries are at war or tilt in favor of one combatant or another. When two U.S. allies, Great Britain and Argentina, clashed over the Falkland Islands in 1982, the Reagan administration professed neutrality but allowed London to communicate with its fleet via U.S. satellites and provided intelligence information to the British from U.S. orbiting spy stations.

Presidents can also interject the United States into a wide variety of international and even domestic matters in other countries. This is evident in recent decisions by President Clinton regarding Northern Ireland (Ulster) and Taiwan. The Irish issue involved the long struggle of Irish Catholics in Ulster in order to achieve equality with the Protestants in that part of the United Kingdom or perhaps even become associated in some way with the Irish Republic. Beginning in 1994, Washington began official contacts with Sinn Fein, the political wing of the Irish Republican Army (IRA) in the north, in an effort to end the fighting. Talks between Sinn Fein and the British government, in part with U.S. encouragement, led to new peace initiatives, including an IRA agreement to begin talks on laying down its arms. This favorable movement was closely coupled with a decision by Clinton to direct the State Department to grant an entry visa to Gerry Adams, head of Sinn Fein. Indeed the IRA peace initiative and the visa decision both came on the same day in March 1995. Adams's trip had two important elements. The first was that he was, for the first time, allowed to raise money in the United States to support the IRA cause. Second, the increasing acceptance of the IRA as a legitimate movement was demonstrated when the president invited Adams to attend a St. Patrick's Day reception at the White House.

Clinton's moves had several international and domestic motives and ramifications. First, Clinton hoped to ameliorate the long and bloody struggle in Northern Ireland. Second, the president was under domestic pressure from many Irish Americans, including Senators Edward Kennedy and Daniel Patrick Moynihan, to allow Adams to visit and raise money in the United States. Third, the move offended London. Prime Minister John Major expressed his dismay, and the British press reported events under headlines such as "Clinton caught in the Irish embrace."[18] Most scathingly, and reflecting the British position that the IRA is a terrorist organization, former prime minister Margaret Thatcher condemned Clinton's decision to have Adams visit the White House. It was, she said, the "equivalent of having the prime minister of England invite the Oklahoma City bombers to [the prime minister's residence at] 10 Downing Street to congratulate them on a job well done."[19] Despite such views, Clinton has continued to press both sides to reach peace. When talks faltered, Clinton traveled to London, Ulster, and Dublin in a successful example of personal diplomacy that resulted in new compromises between the two contending parties.

Presidents possess extensive diplomatic power. President Clinton took a major diplomatic step when in March 1995 he decided to grant an entry visa to Gerry Adams, head of Sinn Fein, the political arm of the underground Irish Republican Army. The visa and the president's invitation to Adams to attend a St. Patrick's Day reception at the White House demonstrated U.S. acceptance of the IRA as a legitimate movement. Clinton was spurred by his desire to help end the struggle in Ulster and by the heavy pressure from many Irish Americans, including Senator Edward Kennedy, pictured here with Adams, to allow the Sinn Fein leader to visit and raise money in the United States.

Another presidential decision to allow a politically sensitive visit to the United States was potentially of even greater import. Taiwan exists in a diplomatic twilight zone. It functions in most ways like a country. Yet it is claimed by China as a province, and it is not recognized by other countries as sovereign because Beijing will not have diplomatic relations with any country that recognizes Taiwan as independent. Washington had switched its recognition in 1979, as noted earlier. There has been stress at times between Beijing and Washington over the sale of U.S. weapons to Taiwan, but relations over the Taiwan issue took a major downturn in 1995. The president of Taiwan, Lee Teng-hui, let it be known that he would like to visit the United States to attend a class reunion at his alma mater, Cornell University, where he had received a doctorate in agricultural economics in 1968.

To avoid any implication of recognition of Taiwan, no Taiwanese president had been allowed to visit the United States since 1979. Indeed on an occasion in 1994 when the plane of the Taiwanese president had needed to refuel in Hawaii, he had not even been allowed to get off the aircraft temporarily. Clinton, however, reversed U.S. policy for several reasons. One was his embarrassed rancor over having delinked China's human rights policy and its trade relations with the United States only to have Beijing's treatment of political dissidents become more severe. This left Clinton vulnerable to domestic political attack. "The president does not want to be too closely associated with China, and that view is permeating a certain amount of policymaking," one analyst commented.[20] Congress was a second and related factor. The Senate and House passed nonbinding resolutions by the respective votes of 97 to 1 and 396 to 0 calling on the president to grant the visa. The move in Congress reflected support for the democratization of Taiwan's government and dismay with various policies of China. Faced with the possibility that Congress might even pass resolutions calling on the president to grant recognition to Taiwan, Clinton decided to issue the permit. "The Taiwan issue is very important symbolically for China and we have to manage it very carefully," a State Department official said. Nevertheless, Clinton decided to risk Beijing's ire because "there was a desire . . . to pre-empt new binding legislation that could hurt our relations with China."[21]

It is important to see the ramifications of Clinton's decision to avoid the mistake of viewing the visa decision as a tempest in a Chinese teapot. Whatever President Lee's collegiate spirit, the proposed trip also was clearly part of Taiwan's diplomatic effort to regain recognition as a sovereign state. China is very emotional on that issue; it considers moves to recognize Taiwan roughly the same way Americans would react to Beijing's recognizing the native Hawaiian independence effort. Predictably, then, Beijing was outraged by Clinton's decision to grant Lee a visa. Beijing recalled its ambassador to "report on his work in view of the current [plummeting] state of Sino–U.S. relations."[22] And the U.S. ambassador was summoned to China's Foreign Ministry and read a statement that warned that "if the United States clings to its erroneous decision" to grant Lee a visa, "it will inevitably cause severe damage to Sino–U.S. relations."[23] China also took a number of steps that many observers saw as retaliation for the U.S. move. Within days Beijing authorized the sale of M-11 ballistic missiles to Pakistan and took several other steps to signal that it might not cooperate on the nonproliferation of nuclear arms and ballistic missile technology. China also cracked down very publicly on human rights activists, including the arrest of visiting Chinese American Harry Wu in July 1995 for espionage and subversion. Wu was finally released in a tacit trade for Hillary Rodham Clinton's agreement to visit China and address the UN–sponsored conference on women in Beijing. The charges could, however, have carried the death penalty. Yet new strains in U.S.–China relations occurred in December 1995 when a Chinese court sentenced democracy advocate Wei Jingsheng to 14 years in prison for sedition. The Clinton Administration moved back toward linking China's human rights policy with economic relations by threatening to block the admission of China into the World Trade Organization until Beijing eased its domestic oppression.

Presidents can also use their general diplomatic power sometimes to persuade other countries to do what it is legally impossible or politically unwise for the U.S. administration to do. Congress prohibited the Reagan administration from giving aid to the Contra rebels in Nicaragua. Quite apart from the patently illegal activities headed up by Lieutenant Colonel Oliver North to supply the Contras, what the administration could do legally was to encourage several countries, ranging from Bahrain (in the Persian Gulf) to Honduras, to aid the Contras. A White House document obtained by special investigators and leaked recently to the press records then–vice president Bush urging Honduran president José Azcona Hoyo to "tell the [Honduran] military to work out ways to assure a supplied front [the Contras]." "We, President Reagan and I," Bush went on, "hope we can work very quietly and discreetly with you. It can be done with deniability."[24]

Chief Executive Officer

There are a number of sometimes vague clauses in Article II that serve as a foundation for the president's role as the country's chief executive officer. One relatively specific constitutional clause empowers the president to "appoint Ambassadors . . . [and most] other officers of the United States." Beyond that, the president's executive authority rests on the Constitution's provision that "The executive Power shall be vested in a President of the United States." The president can also claim the title of chief law enforcement officer by virtue of the language that "he shall take care that the laws be faithfully executed." Another legal power is "to grant reprieves and pardons for offenses against the United States." To illustrate a few aspects of the executive power, we will examine the president's appointment power, the discretionary authority granted to the president by Congress, and the president's general executive authority.

The *appointment power* enables the president to name the entire upper ranks of both the foreign and the defense establishments. By extension, the president can also fire these officials at will. The most obvious strength to derive from this power is the ability of the president to appoint officials who will reflect his views and carry out his policy faithfully. President Clinton's relations with General Colin L. Powell, chairman of the Joint Chiefs of Staff (JCS), were, for example, less than ideal. Powell disagreed with Clinton's plan to slash the defense budget and his desire to include homosexuals in the military and to expand the combat role of women. The general was also leery of the commander in chief's inclination to commit U.S. troops in Bosnia and other global hot spots. When Powell's term in office expired in late 1993, he did not ask for, nor did Clinton offer, reappointment. Instead, the president named General John Shalikashvili to the post. Shalikashvili brought more than military experience as NATO commander to the job. His qualifications included an expressed sympathy with the president's views. "I am very comfortable with the compromise policy to allow gays in the services," the general told reporters. "I feel great about women in the military," he added.[25] During his confirmation hearings the general also supported Clinton on Bosnia. He told senators that the "alternative" to not acting in the Balkans "is also very expensive." "There is a likelihood that fighting . . . will reach a sort of final crescendo. . . . Women and children and old people will pay an awful price if there is not a peace settlement."[26] The general's confirmation as Powell's replacement left the president more firmly in control of the Pentagon. Less than two years later, U.S. troops were taking up positions in the snow of a frigid Balkan winter.

There are also important restraints on the president's power of appointment. One limit is that the president appoints less than 2 percent of all State Department personnel and less than 1 percent of the Defense Department staff. The vast majority of people in both departments are civil servants; and as chapter 9 on bureaucracy will point out, presidents are regularly frustrated by their inability to control the bureaucracy tightly.

A second restraint is that most presidential appointments must be confirmed by a majority vote in the Senate. Like its treaty ratification authority, the effectiveness of the Senate's ability to check the president through confirmation is debatable. Senators reject national security appointments submitted by the president even less frequently than treaties. Between 1945 and 1974, for instance, the Senate confirmed 99.8 percent of all major diplomatic and military appointments (Edwards, 1980). This does not imply a cowed Congress so much as a persistent attitude, expressed in 1949 by powerful senator Arthur Vandenberg, that "Mr. [Dean] Acheson would not have been my choice [as secretary of state, but] as a general rule, I would let [the president] have his own way in choosing his personal advisors" (Rourke, 1983:186).

Still, presidents are not always successful in wielding their power to appoint. There are cases where an important nominee is rejected outright. John Tower, President Bush's initial nominee for secretary of defense, provides an example. A former Republican senator from Texas whose acerbic personality had rankled many senators, Tower also earned Senate rejection after confirmation hearings produced testimony that he abused both alcohol and women. More frequently, like unpopular treaties, nominations that draw strong opposition are likely to die quietly. The White House regularly leaks prospective lists of nominees, and a name may be dropped if there is a strong negative reaction in Congress or from the press and the public. Nominees under fire during their confirmation hearings also often withdraw their own names. President Clinton, for example, nominated Morton Halperin to fill the newly created post of assistant secretary of defense for democracy and peacekeeping. Halperin's nomination was attacked by conservative senators who characterized the nominee as an extreme liberal who had opposed the war in Vietnam and who had too adamantly criticized U.S. intelligence operations. After his nomination languished in the Senate Armed Services Committee throughout the 1993 legislative session, Halperin faced the inevitable and in January 1994 asked the president to withdraw his name from further consideration.

Discretionary authority is a second aspect of the president's many executive powers. Some of this authority is inherent in the position of chief executive. Presidents can issue formal *executive orders* and other directives to their appointees. Presidents also have a significant degree of discretionary authority over expenditures, although the Budget Impoundment and Control Act of 1974 restrained that authority in response to President Nixon's overly cavalier actions regarding the use or nonuse of appropriated funds. Presidents Reagan and Bush, for example, withheld U.S. funding for the UN Fund for Population Activities and for International Planned Parenthood on the grounds that the two organizations support abortion. President Clinton reversed that U.S. policy.

The president's power to exercise executive discretion is also regularly enhanced by statutory authority. Congress often passes legislation that establishes general policy guidelines but grants the president great discretion about when and how to apply policy. Sometimes this is a rational response by Congress to the fact that it cannot anticipate changes or micromanage policy. Sometimes giving discretionary authority to the president is a way of avoiding responsibility and political risk. Congress has, for example, delegated considerable authority to the president to set tariffs and make other trade decisions. One reason, as one study explains it, is because legislators recognize the importance of relatively free trade but also "realize that they are unable to resist the protectionist pressure of special interest groups. . . . They choose to bind their hand by delegating policy making authority to the President . . . who is less susceptible to protectionist pressures" (Lohmann & O'Halloran, 1994:597).

Over the years, Congress has also enacted a host of legislation granting the president discretionary power to deal with threats to the national security. Not only that, but it is usually the president who gets to declare that an emergency exists. During the period of congressional assertiveness after Vietnam and Watergate, some 470 such emergency acts were discovered to exist. Congress passed legislation to rein in these grants of power, but like most of the other reforms of the era, its effectiveness has fallen short of its intent. In 1986, to cite just one example, President Reagan declared a national emergency and imposed a trade embargo on Nicaragua on the grounds that the leftist-led country threatened the national security of the United States. The peril to the United States from the small, impoverished country to the south, with a population about the size of Connecticut's, was not as clear to many Americans as it seemed to Mr. Reagan.

During the Clinton administration, the president has similarly used his discretionary powers to apply economic sanctions to what he has portrayed as security threats. Clinton issued an executive order in January 1995, for example, that froze the U.S. financial assets of a number of Middle Eastern groups and individuals that the White House portrayed as associated with terrorism. Then in April, the president ordered a ban on all U.S. investment in and trade with Iran. Speaking to the World Jewish Congress in New York City, the president explained that "to do nothing more as Iran continues its pursuit of nuclear weapons would be disastrous." Moreover, Clinton continued, "to stand pat in the face of overwhelming evidence of Tehran's support for terrorists would threaten to darken the dawn of peace between Israel and her neighbors."[27]

There is also a wide range of *general executive authority* available to the president. During and after the Iran-Iraq war (1980–1988), the U.S. administration "tilted" toward Iraq. Much of what was done was accomplished by the president's executive authority (Jentleson, 1994). Less than a year before its invasion of Kuwait, Iraq had applied for $1 billion in U.S. commodity loan guarantees to buy U.S. agricultural products. Despite vigorous objections within the executive branch, President Bush issued a presidential order, National Security Decision 26, in October 1989, directing that the loan guarantees be granted to Iraq. This allowed Iraq to buy food on credit and to use its own scarce monetary reserves to buy weapons. One source was the United States. The increase in Iraqi purchases of U.S. dual-use technology (equipment such as advanced computers that have both military and civilian uses) led the U.S. Department of Commerce to propose increased restrictions on such Iraqi purchases. In April 1990, just four months before Iraq's aggression, the White House quashed the Department of Commerce's proposal. "The president does not want to single out Iraq," Under Secretary of State Robert Kimmitt told a high-level, interdepartmental decision making group.[28] Technology with potential military use continued to flow to Iraq.

Presidents can also use their discretionary authority to extend economic help. When the value of Mexico's peso collapsed in December 1994, President Clinton's desire to assist Mexico faced opposition in Congress and was opposed by a majority of the public. Representative Helen Chenoweth (R-ID), for one, wondered why "we're giving loans to Mexico" when "Idaho farmers and ranchers have problems getting loans."[29] Unwilling to ask Congress to appropriate the necessary funds, Clinton chose to use various discretionary funds controlled by the Treasury Department to cobble together a $20 billion package for Mexico. The president was also able to persuade the International Monetary Fund (where the United States has the most votes and is the biggest contributor) to also use its (and indirectly U.S.) funds to help support the peso.

There are also many things, great and small, that a president can do to influence how one or another agency is conducting itself and affecting foreign relations. The Postal Service, for instance, announced in late 1994 that it would issue a stamp commemorating the fiftieth anniversary of the end of World War II showing an atomic

As chief executive, a president has a great deal of discretionary authority for taking action. When the value of the Mexican peso plunged in December 1994, President Clinton feared that economic chaos in Mexico would harm U.S. economic interests. He was also concerned with Mexico's political stability because of evidence of long-standing discontent, such as these Zapatista rebel troops, who are parading in the city of La Realidad in southern Mexico in October 1995. When it became apparent that Congress would not fund a bailout financial package for Mexico, Clinton used $20 billion in discretionary funds, controlled by the Treasury Department and by the U.S. Export Import Bank, in order to aid Mexico.

mushroom cloud and bearing the inscription "Atomic bombs hasten the war's end." Not surprisingly, the stamp offended the Japanese. Even the pilot of the B-29 that dropped the bomb on Nagasaki called the stamp "too heavy-handed." Soon, the Postal Service saw the light. Postmaster General Marvin Runyon announced that the stamp would be scrapped because of "the importance of U.S.–Japan relations at this critical time" and because "President Clinton conveyed his views that it was appropriate to do so."[30]

A final element of the president's general executive authority that should be mentioned is his ability "to grant reprieves and pardons for offenses against the United States." The *power to pardon* occasionally touches on foreign policy. For example, Jimmy Carter pardoned those who had dodged the draft during the Vietnam War. And President Bush pardoned six former officials convicted or accused of perjury and other crimes related to the Iran-Contra affair and its cover-up. Former secretary of defense Caspar Weinberger was the most prominent of the six men. Bush termed Weinberger "a true American patriot," who had "rendered long and extraordinary service to our country." Moreover, the president reasoned, he was pardoning Weinberger and the others because of a "profoundly troubling development in the political and legal climate of our country: the criminalization of policy differences."[31] Others viewed Bush's action less charitably. "The pardons maintain the appearance of an

Iran-Contra cover-up, suggest presidential approval of violations of law, and condone ill-founded foreign policy decisions," charged House Democratic Leader Richard A. Gephardt (D-MO).

Formal Restraints on Presidential Powers

There are a variety of constitutional restraints on the president. Some of these, such as the requirement that the Senate ratify treaties and confirm appointments, have already been detailed. Beyond these, presidential tenure is finite. Presidents are elected for only four years and can serve only two terms. Presidents can also be removed from office by impeachment and conviction by Congress for "high crimes and misdemeanors." Legislators have never formally removed a president, but Richard Nixon's pressured resignation from office was an example of this check in action. The powers of Congress to pass laws and to control the spending of money, both discussed in chapter 8, provide further restraints on the White House. Presidents can, of course, veto measures passed by Congress, but Congress itself can override a veto by a two-thirds vote of each chamber.

The third branch of government, the courts, also provides a check on the president (Franck, 1992). They can reject presidential actions as unconstitutional. There are a few cases where the courts have done so in the realm of foreign affairs, but judges have most often been reluctant to restrict the president's foreign policy authority (Silverstein, 1994). One reason, illustrated by the *Curtiss-Wright* case, is that the courts are apt to grant the president wide discretion in foreign affairs. Second, the courts have frequently declared, as in *Goldwater v. Carter* and other cases, that disputes over power between Congress and the president are political questions that are nonjusticiable. This judicial reluctance to intervene in the executive-legislative power struggle has been especially obvious in the war powers dispute. As scholar Thomas Franck (1991:67) puts it, "Fearing the 'political thicket' of foreign affairs, nimble judges have twisted and turned to avoid ruling on the constitutionality of U.S. involvements in Grenada, Panama, and . . . [elsewhere] even after fighting stopped." In another case, Ron Dellums (D-CA) and 53 other representatives asked the courts in November 1990 to enjoin the president from ordering a U.S. attack on Iraqi forces without a declaration of war by Congress. "I would remind the chief executive that he is President George Bush and not King George," Dellums declared.[32] Federal District Court judge Harold Greene dismissed the suit. The judge did not invoke the political question doctrine, but he did rule that "It would be both premature and presumptuous for the Court to render a decision on the issue" when Congress itself had not objected to the president's past or potential actions.[33] Thus, arguing that Congress had ducked the issue, the court did likewise, and the buildup to war proceeded.

INFORMAL PRESIDENTIAL POWER AND RESTRAINTS

Making foreign policy is a political as well as a legal process. Because of this, one could spend a lifetime reading the Constitution, statutory law, and court decisions and never fully understand the foreign policy powers of and restraints on the president. Supplementing these legal bases of power, there is a wide and important range of informal powers and restraints that help determine the president's foreign policy role.

Informal Presidential Powers

The president's role as head of state is the primary source of the office's informal powers. This role puts the president at the emotional center of the American polity. The danger of war, advancements in communications technology, and the complexity of world affairs have further augmented the president's informal powers. We will examine these by looking at presidential prestige, at public and congressional expectations of presidential leadership, and at the presidency as the focus of political attention and a presumed source of superior information and expertise.

Presidential Prestige

The presidency is an awesome office. As head of state, the president is more than just the chief U.S. political officer; he is the chief American. This is especially true in foreign affairs. Domestic political disputes and elections resemble family affairs, and the president's head-of-state status is muted. Many Americans take great pleasure in joking about, even deriding, the president. President Clinton's calorically catastrophic craving for pizzas and Big Macs, along with other aspects of his demeanor, have certainly been capitalized on by professional and amateur comedians. Such jesting is often the norm until a crisis arises or some other situation occurs that creates a reaction of we (Americans) versus they (anyone else). Then the president becomes the chief "we," and the immense prestige of the office comes into full play.

The *power to persuade* is a pivotal aspect of presidential power (Craig & Smith, 1994). Many presidents have lamented the necessity to persuade and their frequent lack of ability to command. Harry Truman once complained, "I sit here all day trying to persuade people to do the things they ought to have sense enough to do without my persuading them. . . . That's all [that] the powers of the President amount to" (Neustadt, 1960:9). Seconding this view, Dwight Eisenhower observed that a president "does not lead by hitting people over the head. . . . [Leadership is] *persuasion*—and *conciliation*—and *education*. It's long, slow tough work" (Cunliffe, 1987:278).

Fortunately for presidents, their office adds prestige to the other persuasive tools, such as logic and political favors, that they can wield. Following the theme of the imperial presidency, some scholars and politicians have even drawn a close parallel between the persuasive authority of a monarch and that of the president. Senate Foreign Relations Committee chairman J. William Fulbright (D-AR) noted that a "psychological barrier" exists that makes it difficult to dispute foreign policy with the president at the White House, to "contradict kings in their palaces" (Lynne & McClure, 1973:131). This advantage sometimes allows a president to gain cooperation even when a member of Congress is in doubt about the substance of a policy. During a pitched battle in 1981 between the Reagan administration, which desired to sell Airborne Warning and Control System (AWACS) aircraft to Saudi Arabia, and those in Congress and the country who opposed the move, the president prevailed because, in part, he utilized prestige in the realm of foreign policy. Following a talk with Reagan about the issue, for example, Senator John Glenn (D-OH) commented that "after sitting down with the most powerful person in the free world, maybe the whole world . . . when the President says 'I need your help,' that's a rather potent argument" (Bard, 1987:59).

Expectations of Presidential Leadership

As we have noted on several occasions, when discussing the growth of presidential power, American attitudes toward the presidency and the office's powers are ambivalent. Especially in recent years, Americans have been disillusioned with the institutions of government, including the presidency. There have also been times of marked reaction against presidential power following periods of excesses. The most recent of these was in the mid-1970s after Vietnam and Watergate. Yet it is also true that the public and Congress look to the president for leadership and complain when it is not forthcoming.

This expectation is especially strong in times of crisis. During virtually every crisis since World War II, the president's popularity has jumped significantly. This is called the **rally effect** or the "rally 'round the chief (or flag) syndrome," and its effects are shown in Table 7.2.

The rally effect evident in Table 7.2 also influences Congress. Some members are swept up—just like the public—in the emotions of rallying behind the chief during times of crisis. Other members realize that even if they disagree with the president, it is politically unwise for members to criticize him when his public opinion standing is high. Thus, while the rally effect is frequently short-lived, the upsurge of support usually gives the president the political leverage he needs to take the initiative. Then, once the president commits the country to action, it is difficult or impossible to change course. This helps explain the rush to war in Vietnam in 1964. Public and congressional sentiment rallied behind President Johnson after his dramatic assertion that North Vietnamese patrol craft had attacked U.S. warships in the Tonkin Gulf. Playing on that emotion, Johnson stampeded Congress into approving the Tonkin Gulf Resolution, which gave him broad war power. As Senator Fulbright (1972:194) characterized what happened, Congress acted as a "legislature which does not hesitate to defeat or override the executive on domestic legislation . . . but which reverts to a kind of tribal loyalty to the 'chief' when war is involved."

The Persian Gulf War provides even more recent evidence of both the rally effect and its ephemeral nature. Immediately after Bush announced in August 1990 that he would send troops to the gulf, 75 percent of Americans polled supported Operation Desert Shield. Congress also strongly rallied behind the president, with legislators passing a post hoc resolution supporting Bush's move to defend Saudia Arabia by ratios of 13 to 1 in the House and 32 to 1 in the Senate.

Then, as the confrontation dragged on into late fall, public support dropped. Some 62 percent of Americans said that they supported the president, but 50 percent said they had "some" or "a lot of reservations."[34] Congress mirrored these views, and the president hesitated to ask for congressional support because, he admitted, "I'm not sure . . . [what] mood Congress is in."[35] Finally, as war became virtually inevitable in early January, the patriotic rally effect took hold again. As Congress considered whether to support the president's imminent strike against Iraq, a swell of popular patriotism helped convince those members who were wavering to vote for war. "If war is more likely, more [members of Congress] want to be behind the President," explained veteran Representative Lee Hamilton (D-IN), who voted against the war.[36] Most members of both houses voted their convictions, but in the end the rally effect swayed enough votes to pass the resolution for war comfortably in the House (250–183) and narrowly in the Senate (52–47).

TABLE 7.2   **The Rally Effect**

President	Year	Incident	Percentage Changes in Presidents' Approval Ratings*
Johnson	1965	U.S. intervention in Dominican Republic	+7
Johnson	1965	U.S. ground troops enter Vietnam War	+6
Johnson	1968	North Korea seizes USS *Pueblo*	+7
Ford	1975	Cambodia seizes SS *Mayaquez*	+13
Carter	1980	Mission to rescue hostages in Iran fails	+10
Reagan	1983	U.S. invades Grenada	+4
Bush	1989	U.S. invades Panama	+9
Bush	1990	Iraq invades Kuwait	+14
Clinton	1993	U.S. bombs Iraq	+11
Clinton	1995	U.S. troops enter Haiti	+9
Clinton	1995	U.S. troops enter Bosnia	+2

*Figures rounded to nearest percent.

Data sources: Rose (1988:282) for Johnson, Ford, and Carter; *Gallup Poll Monthly,* December 1983, August 1987, January 1990, August 1990 for Reagan and Bush; *World Opinion Update,* July 1993, and *New York Times,* September 21, 1994, and December 13, 1995, for Clinton.

During true crises, as distinguished from merely important foreign events and situations, public support of the president almost always increases at least briefly.

President Clinton's effort to rally public support in favor of deploying troops to Bosnia proved successful but only weakly so. A poll taken 3 weeks before Clinton's national address on November 27, 1995, found that 49 percent of respondents were opposed to, 47 percent were in favor of, and 4 percent were undecided about sending U.S. ground forces to Bosnia. Another survey taken immediately after the president's speech revealed a narrow plurality in favor of sending troops. Notably, the change was caused by a decline in opposition and an increase in uncertainty rather than by an increase in support for Clinton. The new poll recorded 46 percent of Americans in favor of the deployment, 40 percent opposed, and 14 percent undecided.

The tepid nature of the rally effect was also evident in Congress. On December 13, 1995, the House and the Senate passed a series of resolutions backing the deployment and defeated other resolutions condemning it. The House, which had a few weeks earlier voted 243 to 171 to deny funds for a deployment to Bosnia, reversed itself by a narrow 218 to 210 vote. Mixed feelings were also evident in two votes in the Senate. In one vote, the Senate passed by the wide margin of 69 to 30 a resolution acquiescing to the deployment. The second vote saw the Senate narrowly defeat (47 to 52) a resolution sponsored by Senator Kay Bailey (R-TX) that deplored Clinton's decision. What can be said about the uncertain swings by public opinion and congressional sentiment from opposition to, then to support of the president's plan is that the ability of the president to create a rally effect survives, but has been greatly weakened in the postwar era.

Focus of Attention, Information, and Expertise

A third source of informal presidential power is the president's ability to command the attention of the American people. Part of the public's attention to what the president says and does is based on the impressive formal powers of the office. Beyond that, the head-of-state role endows the president with something like royal status. As such, the personal lives of presidents, their families, and even the activity of their pets attract public interest and press coverage that is akin to the focus on Queen Elizabeth II, Prince Charles and Princess Diana, and the other "royals," as they are called in Great Britain.

Americans' fascination with presidential pets provides a telling symptom of the attention paid to America's de facto royals. *Millie's Book,* the ostensible autobiography of George and Barbara Bush's presidential spaniel, spent four months on the national best-seller lists, earned over $889,176 in royalties, and accounted for 67 percent of George and Barbara Bush's 1991 income. With the coming of the Clinton administration, not only did the generation and the political party controlling the White House change, so did the species of pet. Socks, the Clinton family cat, became an instant celebrity, pursued by what otherwise appeared to be adult news photographers. Merchandisers rushed to capitalize on "Socksmania."[37] The hottest item, reported Pam Gibson, owner of the Cat's Meow shop in Portland, Oregon, was a T-shirt emblazoned with a picture of Socks at the White House and the advice, MOVE OVER MILLIE.

The combination of formal power and popular fascination enables the president to command political debate. Congress comes in a distant second. One study that examined the lead stories on ABC, CBS, and NBC during four selected years (1975, 1979, 1981, 1985) found that the president received a total of 3,935 minutes of coverage compared to Congress's 243 minutes of coverage—a 16-to-1 ratio. When the focus is on foreign policy, the imbalance became even more lopsided (Gilbert, 1989). During the four years of the study, stories by the three networks that discussed the president's foreign policy position totaled 2,057 minutes; Congress received only 87 minutes—a ratio of 24 to 1.

Modern technology has provided other advantages to presidents. Franklin Roosevelt used radio effectively through his "fireside chats" and other radio talks. Now presidents use an even more personal medium, television, to bring themselves into American living rooms. Eisenhower was the first to do so, and since then (through 1987) presidents have made 215 televised addresses and held (through 1989) 518 televised press conferences (Gilbert, 1989).

This focus of attention combines with the assumption that the White House commands superior information and analytical expertise to give presidents several advantages. One is the ability to *set the political agenda.* This means that, at least to a significant degree, the president is able to focus attention on a particular issue. President Bush provided one estimate of how important the ability to set the political agenda is when he told a college audience that "the real power of the presidency lies in a president's ability to frame, through action, through example, through encouragement, what we as a nation must do."[38] In chapter 12 on the media we will see that this does not mean that only the president establishes the political agenda. In particular, presidents do not have much negative agenda power; that is, they cannot prevent issues from being debated. But presidents do have a powerful positive ability to bring an issue to the forefront.

Furthermore, the ability to utilize the focus of attention gives presidents the upper hand in *defining the situation*. As noted in chapter 5, this means the ability to cast an issue in terms that are favorable to you (Stuckey, 1992). One reason the Reagan administration was able to persuade the Senate not to block the sale of AWACS to Saudi Arabia in 1981 was that the president and his legislative lobbyists successfully redefined the situation from an intermestic issue, which included strong opposition to the sale by Jewish American groups, to a purer international issue, which involved U.S. and presidential credibility far beyond the immediate controversy. This tactic moved the issue in the minds of some senators from the political model to the presidential model and made just enough of a difference to allow the president to prevail.

As the focus of attention, the president

The degree to which the public and the press focus on the president gives him an immense advantage in dominating political communications. Indeed, presidents are treated to some degree like royalty, with much attention being paid to their families and even their pets. Socks, the presidential cat, became an instant celebrity and was pursued, as is evident in this photograph, by a host of seemingly adult journalists.

and the White House are also able to *manipulate information* to a certain degree. Global communications and other technological advances have increased the flow of information available to Congress and the public. But presidents still frequently have an informational advantage because of their access to reports by the intelligence agencies, the military, and other bureaucratic and overseas sources. Sometimes this means that presidents may have better information; it also means, to a degree, that what Americans know is what the administration tells them.

Presidents have repeatedly suppressed or manipulated information to achieve their purposes. Information is power. Presidents often control policy by keeping events or information secret. Sometimes presidents even invoke *executive privilege* and refuse to tell Congress or anyone else what is occurring or has occurred. President Nixon and Henry Kissinger, his national security adviser, maneuvered in secret through several foreign governments to establish relations with China. Secrecy was necessary, the two thought, to avoid opposition in Congress, the State Department and other agencies, and the public. "This resulted in the odd situation," a recent biography of Kissinger points out, "in which the Foreign Ministries of China, Pakistan, Romania, and the Soviet Union knew about the American initiative to China, but the U.S. State Department did not."[39]

Presidents also manipulate information at times by disclosing only the part that fits their policy preference. Franklin Roosevelt galvanized anti-German opinion among Americans in September 1940 by telling them on the radio that German "rattlesnakes" were guilty of "piracy" because a U-boat had attacked the USS *Greer* "without warning"

(Jones, 1988:426). What FDR did not tell Americans was that the *Greer* had been shadowing the German submarine and radioing its position to British patrol bombers. Lyndon Johnson similarly riveted Americans with his description of North Vietnam's unprovoked attack on the USS *Maddox* and USS *C. Turner Joy* while they were peacefully patrolling in international waters. Johnson did not tell Americans that the U.S. warships had been supporting South Vietnamese raiding parties along North Vietnam's coast or that the Navy doubted whether some of the purported attacks on the two U.S. destroyers had actually occurred.

The crisis that arose after the Cambodians seized a U.S. merchant ship, the SS *Mayaguez,* and its small crew in May 1975 and held them on an island provides a pointed example of both defining the situation and manipulating information. The *Mayaguez* was, by itself, of marginal importance, but it gave the Ford administration a chance to reassert U.S. power and prestige after a decade of frustration and defeat in Vietnam and elsewhere.[40] The mood in the White House, as one senior official described it, was "that one too many feathers had been plucked from the eagle's tail, and that we could not allow such harassment from a rinky-dinky country." Despite the fact that there was uncertainty about whether the seizure had been ordered by the Communist government or undertaken by a local commander, Ford presented the incident to the country as a calculated act, and the rally effect took hold. "Those bastards," Speaker of the House Tip O'Neill exploded, "we can't let them get away with this."

The Cambodians did not get away with it. The Ford administration acted forcibly not only to rescue the crew but also, as Ford put it, to demonstrate that the United States was not a "helpless giant." Far beyond what was necessary to rescue the crew, the White House authorized the bombing of the Cambodian mainland. The administration justified the attacks on the grounds of military necessity, but, as a defense department official later confessed, "I invented . . . the rationale that the mainland bombing helped by disorienting the Cambodians. I said this to Congress. . . . Nobody in the military felt that the mainland bombing was necessary."

At their worst, presidents and their staffs can dominate information by lying or by not reporting it even when they are legally required to do so. An example is the sale of weapons to Iran during the Reagan administration and the use of some of the funds to aid the Contra rebels in Nicaragua. Reagan authorized the sales in January 1986 by a procedure called a "finding," which carries the legal requirement that Congress be informed. Yet Secretary of State George Shultz has written in his memoirs that "CIA director Bill Casey had been told, presumably by the president, not to brief Congress on it."[41] Subsequently, when information about what became known as Iran-Contragate leaked, numerous high-ranking administration officials were charged with lying to Congress about the affair and other felonies. Some were convicted, and some escaped punishment through legal maneuvers (including a presidential pardon by President Bush).

Informal Restraints on Presidential Power

To a significant degree, the informal powers that the political system giveth to a president, the political system can also taketh away. Some of the informal political restraints on presidents have been examined during the description of policy models in chapter 6. Other informal restraints will be discussed as part of the explanation for the medium- and short-term fluctuations in relative presidential power that are examined in chapter 9. In one way or another, most of these restraints stem from two factors: public opinion and the physical and intellectual limitations of the president.

Public Opinion

Public opinion is frequently an important factor in presidential decision making. It is true that presidents can and sometimes do ignore public opinion. Furthermore, as we have noted, presidents have a significant ability to mold public opinion. Yet the reality is that presidents are apt to be swayed by public opinion.

Sometimes, public opinion can push the president to act. This was the case once the United States had confronted Iraq in the Persian Gulf in 1990. "If a stalemate is the best we have six months from now," one official worried in August, "why wouldn't the American people wonder why we're still [in the Middle East]."[42] "I think holding public opinion . . . is very difficult to do," Bush agreed; "I think there is a ticking of the clock."[43] The ticking told the president that he had to act quickly in order to avoid losing public support during a drawn-out stalemate.

At other times, public opinion can restrain a president. The barrier of public opinion is certainly one of the reasons that for almost 3 years until late 1995 President Clinton repeatedly backed off pronouncements that seemed to presage a more active military role for U.S. forces in Bosnia. Similarly, the inclination of President Reagan and his secretary of state, Alexander M. Haig, to intervene militarily in Central America to defeat leftist rebels in El Salvador was deterred in part by a reluctant public that was firmly opposed to another Vietnam War—full of jungles, guerrillas, American deaths, and frustration. "The White House did not appreciate how rapidly El Salvador would take off in the minds of the press as a Vietnam," a presidential aide remarked (Paterson, Clifford, & Hagan, 1995b:523). Direct intervention never came.

There are several reasons why presidents often defer to public opinion. One reason is that presidents are politicians. Most individuals who finally get to the White House do so after a career in the political system. This partisan path to the Rose Garden conditions them to react to concerns about their own reelection, their party's fortunes in congressional races, and how they will be judged by history. Such factors were repeatedly evident in the decision of the Kennedy administration to risk nuclear war in order to force Soviet missiles out of Cuba in 1962. Robert Kennedy (1969:25), in his later recounting of the Cuban missile crisis, set the scene with the comment, "It was election time." He meant that political considerations had pressed the White House to do something. "Have you considered the very real possibility," one presidential adviser wrote to another, "that if we allow Cuba to complete installation and operational readiness of missile bases, the next House of Representatives is likely to have a Republican majority?" (Sorensen, 1965:688). Later, when the crisis had abated, President Kennedy wondered aloud to his brother if there was any way the nuclear confrontation could have been avoided. "I just don't think there was any other choice," brother Robert replied, "and not only that, if you hadn't acted you would have been impeached." "That's what I think," agreed the president, "I would have been impeached" (Kennedy, 1969:67).

A second reason that presidents pay heed to public opinion is their desire for consensus before taking action. Oval Office occupants are prone to believe that public support increases their chances of international success. President Kennedy was elected by a razor-thin margin and without a majority of the popular vote. He therefore believed, an aide later recalled, that since "the country was narrowly divided, that it was terribly important to have as much national unity as possible on foreign policy questions" (Rourke, 1983:103).

A third reason that presidents desire popular support is that they believe public approval will intimidate political opponents and will improve the chances of winning battles with Congress. Dwight Eisenhower, for one, was convinced that "my influence in the next four years . . . is going to be determined by how popular I am with the multitudes. . . . Strength can be marshaled on both sides of the aisle [in Congress] only if it is generally believed that I am in a position to go to the people over their heads" (Neal, 1978:380).

Physical and Intellectual Limits

It may seem obvious to say that the president is just one person, while the government is a huge organization and the world is a vast and complicated political system. Yet we sometimes forget that. The reality of the lone official in a complex, sometimes byzantine, environment of national and international politics means that the time and energy that a president can devote to any one issue are limited. Not only that, but physical limits restrict to a very few the issues that a president can even address. Most of what the government does in the realm of foreign policy receives little or no presidential attention.

Certainly, presidents focus on the most critical issues. But even in these situations, the intellectual limits of a president restrain what a president can reasonably decide, at least without seeming rash and acting on instinct rather than knowledge. Think for a moment about what you would ask for if you were to write a help-wanted ad for a president. In addition to all the personal qualities such as charisma and honesty, you might also want an expert in defense, economics, law, geography, history, and a variety of other subjects. No one possesses all of these qualifications, and some presidents do not possess any of these. This is not the fault of presidents; it is a function of the position.

The result of every president's physical and intellectual limitations is that the chief executive is heavily dependent on advisers, technical experts, and other bureaucratic actors to supply and interpret information, to recommend policy, and implement it. The president's reliance on advisers is often particularly strong in the sometimes dangerous, often unfamiliar, realm of foreign affairs. "If someone comes in and tells me this or that about the minimum wage bill," President Kennedy once observed, "I have no hesitation in overruling them. But you always assume that the military and intelligence people have some special skill not available to ordinary mortals" (Vandenbroucke, 1991:114). The point is that while we may often think of presidents as omniscient and omnipotent, they are not. To the contrary, they are significantly constrained by their political environment and by the limits of their own minds and bodies.

SUMMARY

1. The president possesses two bases of power and restraints. Formal powers and restraints are found in the Constitution and in legislative acts. Informal powers and restraints are based on the prestige of the presidency and on precedent.

2. The role of commander in chief is one important presidential power. The president's operational control of the military is relatively noncontroversial. The president's war power authority to utilize forces without a congressional declaration of war or other authorization is very controversial. The president also has the peace power.

3. The president's formal powers also make him the head diplomat. Presidents have the power to make international treaties (subject to Senate ratification) and, more controversially, the power to make executive agreements and presidential commitments. Presidents also have the power of diplomatic recognition and a wide range of general diplomatic authority.

4. Other of the president's formal powers derive from his position as chief executive. This authority includes the powers of appointment, discretionary authority, and the ability to grant pardons and reprieves.

5. Formal restraints include the need to have the Senate ratify treaties and confirm appointments, the limits to presidential tenure, court decisions, and the need for the president to ask Congress for money.

6. Informal presidential powers are derived from presidential prestige, public and congressional expectations of presidential leadership, the focus on the presidency in the political system, and the presumed superiority of information and expertise in the executive branch.

7. Informal restraints on the presidency include public opinion and the physical and intellectual limitations of the president.

Chapter Eight

CONGRESS

Congress, like the presidency, is a complex and dynamic political institution. The legislative branch joins the executive branch as the second major player in the struggle for foreign policy control. Also, like the presidency, Congress draws its power from both formal and informal sources and from the skill and willingness of legislators to use the authority at their command. This makes for somewhat of an improvisational play, and the historical script that Congress has written for itself has been inconsistent, with representatives sometimes playing a lead role and at other times being mere members of the chorus. It is a story that might well be dubbed, with apologies to Charles Dickens, A Tale of Two Congresses.

A TALE OF TWO CONGRESSES

There are, in a sense, two congresses in Washington. The first congress, which we will call *Congress Combative,* possesses and uses imposing constitutional powers that enable it to influence, sometimes even determine, foreign policy. The second congress, styled *Congress Compliant,* has the same constitutional powers but frequently does not use them.

These two congresses are, of course, legally just one: the United States Congress. In practice, however, Congress has two political personalities based on a power gap and a process inconsistency. The *power gap* relates to the difference between the constitutional powers that Congress possesses and the degree to which it uses those powers. The *process inconsistency* focuses on the range of congressional activity and impact, which vary from near irrelevant passivity to meaningful assertiveness in the foreign policy process. There is an invitation to struggle that, according to the classic interpretation of the vague and overlapping distribution of power noted earlier, has been issued to the presidency and Congress. Sometimes Congress accepts that invitation; sometimes it declines to join the policy battle. This chapter begins with two tales of Congress: one of Congress combative helping to force an end to the U.S. involvement in Vietnam, the second of Congress compliant docilely following the president's march to war in the Persian Gulf. These tales are followed by an exploration of the causes of the power gap and process inconsistency by examining the formal constitutional and informal political powers of and restraints on Congress. Then chapter 9 will continue the analysis by focusing on the fluctuations in the relative power of the president and Congress.

Congress Combative: Getting out of Vietnam

Congress acted like the proverbial lamb when it voted almost unanimously for the Tonkin Gulf Resolution in 1964; but it soon began to transform itself into a policy lion. Congressional opposition to the Americanization of the war in Vietnam grew steadily as the conflict dragged on. Some members were appalled by the loss of life on both sides. The war's economic costs in terms of budget reductions of domestic programs also motivated Congress. "I think we should express less interest in South Asia and more in South St. Louis," Senator Stuart Symington (D-MO) exclaimed (Rourke, 1983:229). Electoral considerations were a third factor. Democrats during Lyndon Johnson's presidency and Republicans during Richard Nixon's tenure worried that the war's unpopularity would put them at risk. "The Democratic Party will be hurt by the war," Senate majority leader Mike Mansfield (D-MT) told President Johnson in 1966; "if 6 percent or 7 percent [of usual Democratic voters] are unhappy enough to vote Republican in protest in November think what it will do to Democratic candidates for Congress" (Rourke, 1983:223).

It is difficult to get out of war, especially in the face of a determined president who wants peace only with victory (or, at least, without obvious defeat). But the mounting din of opposition from Congress and the public helped to reverse the U.S. course slowly. Both Presidents Johnson and Nixon were determined not to be the first president to lose a war, but each in his own way failed. The American military was rocked in February 1968 by a communist offensive during Tet (the Vietnamese lunar new year); the president was pounded by an increasingly combative Congress at home. Johnson decided not to seek reelection in 1968 rather than try to fend off communist thrusts in Vietnam and electoral challenges at home led by Senators Eugene McCarthy (D-MN) and Robert Kennedy (D-NY).

Nixon fared little better. The antiwar outcry in Congress mounted; public demonstrations became more frequent, larger, and more volatile. The "Domestic Travail" is how national security adviser Henry Kissinger (1979:509) labeled the explosion of dissent in his memoirs. American college campuses, in particular, were aflame—sometimes literally. Among other tragedies, protesting students at Jackson State University in Mississippi and at Kent State University in Ohio were shot to death when they clashed with law enforcement officials and with National Guard troops. Kissinger (p. 513) later commented that by 1970 it was clear that legislative "opponents of the war would introduce one amendment after another, forcing the Administration into unending rear-guard actions to preserve a minimum of flexibility for negotiations" with North Vietnam.

Nixon and Kissinger came to understand that they had to act relatively quickly to make the best deal possible with Hanoi because, as Kissinger (p. 1042) put it, "the day when Congress would legislate a deadline [to end the war] was clearly approaching." Aides recall Kissinger muttering, "We'll never get through another session of Congress without their giving the farm away" (Walters, 1978:517). President Nixon (1978:209) told South Vietnam's president Nguyen Van Thieu that if they, the presidents, could not end the war, Congress would. Just as Congress reconvened in January 1973, the tortured negotiations to end U.S. involvement in an anguished war finally succeeded. Washington and Hanoi agreed to withdraw their troops from South Vietnam. The reasons behind the U.S. agreement to withdraw were complex, but the point here is that Congress was an important factor in the events. Congress would not have let the war go on much longer. Nixon and Kissinger knew that. And so U.S. involvement ended.

The drama was not quite over, though. In 1975 pressure arose for a U.S. encore performance in Southeast Asia. The U.S. position was that the settlement meant that North Vietnam would not use its forces directly to overthrow the Saigon government. This was wishful thinking; the ambiguous peace accords did not long deter Hanoi's government from seeking the independence and national unity it had fought for against successive Japanese, French, and American armies. Rather, the 1972 Paris Peace Accords provided only a "decent interval," as one CIA official called it, for the United States to get out of Indochina (Snepp, 1978).

The decent interval ended in early 1975. North Vietnam's forces crossed the demilitarized zone and routed South Vietnam's army. President Gerald R. Ford, who had assumed office in August 1974, and his secretary of state, Henry Kissinger, felt betrayed by what they saw as North Vietnam's perfidy and by Congress's opposition to renewed U.S. military reaction. Ford and Kissinger, in the estimate of one historian, believed that U.S. prestige would suffer greatly if U.S. inaction in the face of South Vietnam's downfall came "under pressure from a disillusioned Congress and public." Moreover, the account continues, Ford and Kissinger believed that congressional intransigence "represented something far more significant. . . . It was in fact a defiant assault on executive prerogatives in foreign affairs" (Schulzinger, 1989:193).

The administration pressed to reenter. "We do not have an enforceable legal obligation [to help] South Vietnam," Kissinger told Congress, "but we do have a moral and political obligation" (Schulzinger, 1989:193). Congress refused to budge, however, and there was little Ford and Kissinger could do without violating the law and risking constitutional crisis. Congress had used its appropriations power in several acts to, as one bill specified, prohibit spending money "to finance the involvement of United States military forces in hostilities in or over or off the shores of North Vietnam, South Vietnam, Laos, or Cambodia, unless specifically authorized hereafter by Congress."[1]

Without U.S. support, South Vietnam's fate was sealed. Saigon fell in April 1975; at last, the war was OVER. Almost 20 years after the fact, Kissinger was still frustrated by events. "When Congress eliminated our leverage, we were trapped in the classic nightmare of every statesman," Kissinger told a congressional committee. "We had nothing to back up our tough words but more tough words. Under such conditions, we had no bargaining power [with Hanoi] left."[2]

Congress often complies with presidential initiatives during times of crisis. Even though many in Congress had deep reservations about going to war against Iraq, many legislators felt that they had little choice but to support the president. Congress passed several symbolic resolutions of support for the president's policy. "WAR" read the headlines just days later in this Rock Falls, Illinois, diner.

Congress Compliant: Getting into the Persian Gulf

It was a different Congress that contemplated war in 1991. It was not until January 10—more than five months after President Bush had ordered the first of a half-million U.S. troops into the Persian Gulf region—that Congress began debate on a resolution authorizing military action to drive Iraq's forces out of Kuwait. The stakes were enormous. Senate president pro tempore Robert C. Byrd (D-WV) declared gravely that his vote was the most important and troubling of the 12,822 votes he had cast during his 38 years in Congress. Speaker of the House of Representatives Thomas S. Foley (D-WA) reported somberly that in his 26 years in the Congress, he had never seen his chamber's membership "more serious nor more determined to speak its heart and mind."[3] One by one, three hundred members of the House and 94 senators stepped to the podium. Many expressed anguish. "We are left to make judgments while doubt sits like a raven on our shoulders and taunts us," worried Senator William Cohen (R-ME) in an allusion to Edgar Allan Poe's dark, poetic tale "The Raven" (1845).

Some members not only urged a vote against war, they called on their colleagues to make courageous, individual decisions rather than simply following the president's lead. Robert Kerrey (D-NE), who had lost a leg and won a Congressional Medal of Honor in Vietnam, asked his Senate colleagues, "consider what a farce we would be perpetrating if the U.S. Congress did not exercise an independent judgment about war." "Are we . . . supposed to go to war simply because the President thinks we should and [has put us] . . . in the position of having to back him up?"[4] Senator Edward Kennedy (D-MA) recalled the last-minute vote of Senator Edmund Ross of Kansas that saved embattled President Andrew Johnson from removal from office in

1868. It was an act that had been lauded in brother John Kennedy's Pulitzer Prize–winning book, *Profiles in Courage* (1956). "When the Senate roll call is called tomorrow," the last Kennedy brother asked, "who will be Senator Edmund Ross and cast the single vote that saves us all from war?"[5]

Other members of Congress had a different view of the war and what constituted courage. Will Congress be "a tower of strength or . . . a tower of Babel," House minority leader Robert Michel (R-IL) asked his colleagues. Do not "cop out. . . . rally around the chief and give him the support he deserves," the congressional leader urged.[6] Remember this, Toby Roth (R-WI) told House members: "There is only one person who is elected by all the people." Some members say "Don't vote with the president," Roth went on, but "who should we vote with, Saddam Hussein?"[7] It was an unfair, but politically potent, question.

In the end, the impulse to rally around the chief and the implication that failing to do so was tantamount to near treason were too strong for some in Congress to withstand. "I suspect that 75 percent or more of those who will vote for the use of force desperately do not want it to be used, and a significant number will vote for it only because they want to prevent the President from being reversed," Senator Kerrey predicted during the debate. "That really means that this vote to grant [the president] the use of force may very well carry . . . only because some will succumb to the very box the President has put us in."[8] The senator was correct. Most members did vote their hearts and minds, but some who wavered chose to back the president in the name of unity or to escape the charge that they had sided with Saddam Hussein. Congress authorized action. Soon U.S. warplanes streaked northward from their bases in Saudi Arabia toward targets in Iraq and Kuwait. "WAR," read the headlines.

A Tale of Two Congresses: Thinking about the Differences

These two differing tales of Congress's role in getting the United States out of war in Vietnam and Congress's role in getting into war in the Persian Gulf illustrate many of the factors that we will discuss in this and the next chapter. One is that Congress has formidable constitutional powers. Congressional legislative and appropriations authority helped press the administration to end the U.S role in Vietnam and not to renew it. Second, the Persian Gulf War vote demonstrated that there is a frequent gap between the formal powers of Congress and its willingness to use those powers. Congress could have rejected the president's call to war. But Congress did not; it was almost afraid to do so. Third, the first two points demonstrate the inconsistency of Congress's role in the foreign policy process. The assertive authority that Congress wielded in the early 1970s had faded by the early 1990s. This was further demonstrated by a series of skirmishes between President Bill Clinton and Congress over his authority as commander in chief. These were discussed in the box "William Jefferson Clinton and the War Power" on pages 176–177 in chapter 7. In the end, Congress backed away from formally restraining the president, although legislative and public protests over armed interventions in the Balkans, Haiti, and Somalia did, arguably, have an impact on Clinton's policies, as we discuss further presently.

This reluctance and inconsistency that characterize Congress's exercise of its formal authority are part of the dilemma of democratic participation in U.S. foreign policy making. The Constitution created Congress to represent the public's interests in the policy making process. Congress was also designed to check and balance the executive branch. And there are plenty of opportunities for Congress to represent and to check and balance. Yet sometimes the legislative branch does not fulfill these duties.

With regard to the Persian Gulf crisis, the question here is whether Congress, for all its expressed agony of conscience, counted for much in the decision to go to war. Yes, the democratic process was served legally: Congress voted formally to authorize war against Iraq. But was there *meaningful* democratic participation in this policy choice? The answer to this question provides a basis for a great deal of insight into the role of Congress in the foreign policy process.

The point that many commentators have made is that by January 8, when President Bush asked for the congressional authorization, there were nearly as many U.S. troops in the Middle East as there had been in Vietnam during the height of that war. Could Congress, at that late date, have voted realistically not to act? The members could have legally done so, but politically they could not. Legislators knew that a negative vote would make the country look like a "paper tiger": willing to threaten, afraid to act. The blow to the country's military and diplomatic prestige would have been incalculable. In effect, Bush had forced Congress to back up his prior actions. As one extended news magazine headline read, "The President says he can take America to war without asking Congress. The lawmakers disagree—but most would rather not take a public stand at all."[9] Or, as the title of a journal article put it, "War Leaves Congress on the Sidelines."[10] For meaningful democratic participation in this case, Congress should have taken a vote early in the crisis. An early vote in support of the president might well have strengthened his hand in the confrontation with Iraq; a negative vote would not have irretrievably damaged the country's prestige.

Does this mean that Congress is impotent? Absolutely not! Despite all the media attention given to presidents when they make foreign policy pronouncements, sign treaties, or attend important summit conferences, sooner or later virtually every foreign policy initiative will require some congressional action to authorize, fund, or otherwise implement it. These actions relate to its formal, constitutional legislative powers. Congress also possesses informal powers that allow it to influence foreign policy. Moreover, the end of the cold war, the rise of intermestic affairs, and structural reforms in Congress lead some scholars to predict that Congress will play a newly invigorated role in the future (Lindsay, 1993). It is, therefore, important to understand Congress's foreign policy role. The first step toward this goal is to examine formal and informal powers and restraints.

THE SOURCES OF CONGRESSIONAL POWER: FORMAL AND INFORMAL

Congress has a wide range of powers at its disposal to influence foreign policy. As with the powers of the presidency, these legislative powers have both formal and informal sources. First, we can take up the formal powers of Congress.

Congress's Formal Powers

The bases of Congress's formal powers, like those of the presidency, are the Constitution and statutory law. Article I of the Constitution spells out the formal powers of Congress relative to foreign policy. The list is impressive, as shown in the box in chapter 1 entitled "The Constitution and Foreign Policy," and includes the powers to tax, impose tariffs and otherwise regulate foreign commerce, declare war, raise and support military forces, regulate immigration, confirm diplomatic and military nominations, and ratify treaties. Congress also has the constitutional authority "To make all laws which shall be necessary and proper to carrying into execution the foregoing powers, and all other powers vested by this Constitution in the government of the United States, or in any department or officer thereof." This "necessary and proper" clause is also often called the "elastic" clause because it provides Congress with the authority to regulate a wide range of matters that stretch beyond those specifically covered in the Constitution. This range of powers and the tenor of debate among the delegates to the Constitutional Convention in 1787 led to the conclusion, as one scholar has put it, that the Constitution "expressly divided foreign affairs powers among the three branches of government, with *Congress,* not the president, being granted the dominant role" (Koh, 1990:75).[11] Many of these powers will be discussed separately, but you should understand that in practice they—as most of the factors discussed in this book—interact powerfully and subtly. Because of the system of checks and balances in the Constitution, *compromise* is often the outcome of policy struggles between Congress and the president. Several such compromises will be discussed in the sections that follow.

It is possible to group the ways in which Congress's formal powers operate in three ways: legal mandates, institutional manipulation, and indirect influence. The operation of the first of these, *legal mandates,* is the most obvious. Through its powers of legislation and appropriations, Congress can legally require or bar certain actions by legislative mandate or by funding or denying funds to a program.

Institutional manipulation is a second, and somewhat more circuitous, way that Congress attempts to control policy. There is, in the study of American government, a relatively recent approach called "new institutionalism." What those who take this approach contend is that Congress sometimes tries to influence policy by creating agencies, mandating bureaucratic procedures, and making other institutional arrangements in an attempt to ensure that the way the legislative branch operates is more likely to result in decisions that are in accord with legislative preferences (Wirls, 1991).

One scholar suggests that Congress utilizes five different strategies to manipulate executive institutions. First, Congress can create new institutions within the executive branch that will be "more sympathetic" to legislative preferences (Lindsay, 1994:285). Congress, for example, directed the State Department to create a bureau for South Asia in order to give more attention to the Indian subcontinent. Second, Congress inserts legislative vetoes that, in limited circumstances, give legislators the authority to block an action taken by the president. Much more about this will be said presently. Third, Congress may change procedures to ensure that it, some agency, or even a private group is included in decisions. The Trade Act of 1974, for instance, mandates that business and other private interests be consulted by the executive branch during trade talks. Fourth, legislators may specify new procedures for the executive to follow. To use another trade example, the Omnibus Trade and Competitiveness Act of 1988 made it mandatory, rather than discretionary, for the U.S International Trade Commission to investigate complaints about certain types of unfair trade practices by other countries. The fifth type of institutional manipulation is to impose reporting requirements on legislative agencies. Current laws require various agencies to submit to

Congress some 600 reports, which "are designed to keep Congress abreast of executive branch behavior and thereby give members . . . the opportunity to mobilize against policies they dislike" (Lindsay, 1994:287).

Indirect influence based on Congress's formal powers is a third way that legislators attempt to influence policy. This means that even if a president can act unilaterally, or pressure Congress to pass or defeat some measure, the victory may not be worth the cost because it so aggravates Congress or expends so much of the president's political capital that other programs are put at risk. Indirect influence also works through what is termed "anticipated reaction." Sometimes just the threat of congressional legislation is enough to affect policy. What one scholar has labeled the "cry and sigh syndrome" is evident, for example, in trade policy. What occurs is that interest groups that have been harmed by trade cry out for relief. Their legislators threaten to pass protectionist acts. The president then takes some moderate executive measures to lessen the negative impacts. Finally, the interest groups and concerned legislators sigh with relief (Pastor, 1980).

Presidents who are faced with strong legislative pressures often modify their policy somewhat to defuse objections. Sometimes, presidents retreat. The Kennedy administration, for example, contemplated the possibility of seating mainland China in the United Nations. President Kennedy could have directed his ambassador to the UN to change the U.S. position, but news that the White House was even studying the possibility set off a political firestorm in Congress. The House passed a resolution against the idea by a 395 to 0 vote, and the Senate also went on record against seating China in the UN. Congress could not have stopped the president from making the move, but legislators threatened to dismantle the president's foreign aid program. Not surprisingly, the White House retreated. President Johnson tried again a few years later. He even considered extending diplomatic recognition to mainland China, which he also could have done unilaterally. In the end, though, Johnson did not try to begin to normalize relations with China. The problem, national security assistant McGeorge Bundy explained, was that nobody in the White House was willing to tell the president "Damn the torpedoes! Go ahead! . . . Congressional reaction was always . . . [assumed] to be high, you couldn't do it" (Rourke, 1983:143).

Congress continues to use indirect pressure as a vehicle to influence the White House's policy on China. When the issue of Taiwan's president, Lee Teng-hui, attending his class reunion at Cornell University arose in 1995, as related in the last chapter, the U.S. administration indicated initially that it would not permit the trip. To do so, said a State Department spokesperson, would offend China and, therefore, have "serious consequences for United States foreign policy." Indirect legislative influence soon changed that position. The Senate, by a vote of 97 to 1, and the House, by a vote of 360 to 0, passed resolutions calling on President Clinton to allow President Lee to visit the United States. Those resolutions were nonbinding, but the administration feared they would presage other congressional actions, such as resolutions calling for establishing diplomatic relations with Taiwan, that would spark a violent reaction by Beijing. "The congressional mood was a very serious problem," Secretary of State Christopher later commented; "I pressed [Congress] on the Taiwan situation several times, [but] I failed to persuade anyone that I talked to."[12] The result was that the White House did an about-face: Lee received a visa. In a testament to the cause of Clinton's switch, the government of Taiwan said that it "certainly appreciates the friendship and support of members of Congress."[13]

Members of Congress tend to be more protectionist in their attitudes than presidents. So when imports undercut U.S. business and the jobs of workers, they and their representatives in Congress cry out for relief through tariffs, quotas, or other trade barriers. Congress holds hearings to allow interest groups to bemoan allegedly unfair foreign competition, and representatives introduce strong measures to impose trade sanctions. If put into law, however, such actions might set off retaliation from other countries and spark an escalating trade war. No one, especially the president, wants that, so presidents use their congressionally granted discretionary authority to adjust tariffs or quotas. Or presidents may demand trade concessions from other countries, warning that without concessions they will be unable to control Congress. The other countries usually agree to the "voluntary" concessions, at which point Congress sighs with relief and drops the issue. A recent example of an apparently similar process at work is the renewed economic pressure on Iran by the Clinton administration. Notwithstanding legitimate administrative concerns about Iran's nuclear weapons program and financial support of international terrorist groups, many Washington insiders think that the 1995 push to get more of America's allies to apply economic sanctions against Iran was due to fears that congressional efforts to punish Iran would be even more severe.

The point here, which is worth reiterating occasionally, is that while policy making has many facets, it is an interconnected whole. After a policy struggle, most or all of the legislative and executive combatants remain on the field ready to contest the next issue. Winning political battles may exhaust too much of any one actor's political ammunition, create lingering hard feelings among those defeated, and leave the winner vulnerable to retaliation in subsequent political battles. Therefore, you should read the sections that follow while keeping in mind the larger policy making puzzle into which they fit.

Declaring War

Since the Constitution was written soon after the Revolutionary War, it is not surprising that most of the specific powers given to Congress in the foreign affairs realm dealt with war and military issues. On the face of it, the Constitution gives to Congress the responsibility for both preparing the nation's defenses and initiating warfare. But reality differs considerably from theory (Jackson, 1993). In later sections on appropriations and other formal powers, we will review Congress's input into structuring the military, but here it is appropriate to review the congressional role in making the most important of all military choices, the decision to go to war.

One clue to Congress's role in deciding on war is that there has not been a formal declaration of war since 1941. We have already examined several instances, such as President Truman's ordering U.S. troops into the Korean War (1950), where presidents order American forces into action without a declaration of war or other formal expression of congressional support. There have been several resolutions, such as the Persian Gulf Resolutions (1991), that authorized military action, but they cover only a small percentage of the times that force has been employed. Moreover, in the case of some authorizing resolutions, such as the Tonkin Gulf Resolution (1964), presidents have carried the war far beyond what was intended by Congress.

The almost unanimous support in Congress for the president's Vietnam War initiative was the lowest point of legislative influence during the imperial presidency

The War Powers Resolution

Public Law 93-148
93rd Congress, H.J. Res 542
November 7, 1973
The War Powers Resolution took several steps. It:

1. *Defined when the president can act unilaterally:* The WPR asserted that "the constitutional powers of the President as Commander in Chief to introduce United States Armed Forces into hostilities, or into situations where imminent involvement in hostilities is clearly indicated by the circumstances, are exercised only pursuant to (1) a declaration of war, (2) specific statutory authorization, or (3) a national emergency created by an attack on the United States, its territories or its possessions, or its armed forces." Note that situations (1) and (2) are *after* congressional action. The WPR states that the only time a president may act unilaterally are those situations covered under (3).

2. *Mandated consultation and reporting:* The WPR mandated that "The President in every possible instance shall consult with Congress before introducing United States Armed Forces into hostilities or into situations where imminent involvement in hostilities is clearly indicated . . . [and continue to consult] until United States Armed Forces are no longer engaged in hostilities." The WPR also directed the president to report to Congress within 48 hours of beginning hostilities or sending U.S. troops into imminent danger.

3. *Limited the length of military action:* Presumably the president should not take action except under the three situations above. Even in those circumstances, the WPR says that unless the president receives specific congressional authorization within 60 days to continue the hostilities, they must cease. The president could declare that 30 days are needed to withdraw in an orderly way, thereby extending the military action to a maximum of 90 days.

4. *Specified congressional action:* Even before 60 days are up, the WPR says that except under situations (1), (2), and (3), "such forces shall be removed [from combat] by the President if the Congress so directs by concurrent resolution."

era. Soon antiwar sentiment began to grow in Congress; public unrest further strengthened legislative sentiment. Congress became combative. It repealed the Tonkin Gulf Resolution, pressed numerous antiwar efforts, and in 1973 enacted the **War Powers Resolution** (WPR) in an attempt to limit the president's unilateral ability to deploy U.S. forces into dangerous areas or order them into combat. The provisions of the War Powers Resolution are detailed in the box of the same name.

From the beginning of the WPR's development soon after the invasion of Cambodia, the Nixon administration reacted strongly to this threat to the president's policy prerogatives. An internal White House memorandum in May 1970 characterized the various congressional efforts to end the Vietnam War and to constrain the president's war power as "a historic assault upon the constitutional powers of the Presidency." The memo predicted that "unless we meet this assault directly and rebuff it, we will have presided over a constitutional revolution."[14]

The details of the ensuing struggle over passage of the WPR are long and complex, but in the end the White House lost. The WPR was enacted by Congress. President Nixon vetoed the joint resolution on two grounds: that it was unwise policy and that it violated the president's constitutional authority as commander in chief. Congress was not persuaded. It overrode the president's veto by the necessary two-thirds vote in each house, and the WPR became law.

TABLE 8.1   Selected Incidents Relevant to the War Powers Resolution

President	Year	Place	Action
Ford	1975	Cambodia	Rescued American crew of the USS *Mayaguez*
Carter	1980	Iran	Attempted to rescue American hostages in Tehran
Reagan	1981	Libya	Shot down Libyan warplanes over Gulf of Sidra
Reagan	1982	Lebanon	Deployed troops as part of multinational force
Reagan	1983	Grenada	Toppled leftist government
Reagan	1986	Libya	Engaged Libyan ships and shore batteries
Reagan	1986–1988	Persian Gulf	Multiple orders to engage Iranian naval and air forces and armed oil-drilling platforms
Bush	1989	Philippines	Provided air support to suppress rebellion
Bush	1989	Panama	Invaded to topple and arrest Manuel Noriega
Bush	1990	Saudi Arabia	Deployed troops in Desert Shield
Bush	1991	Kuwait	Launched Operation Desert Storm to force Iraqi forces to withdraw from Kuwait
Bush	1992	Somalia	Started Operation Restore Hope to provide relief
Clinton	1993	Balkans	Authorized U.S. participation in enforcing no-fly zone over Bosnia-Herzegovina
Clinton	1993	Macedonia	Ground troops join UN forces
Clinton	1993	Iraq	Baghdad attacked by cruise missiles in retaliation for alleged Iraqi plot to assassinate George Bush
Clinton	1993	Haiti	Naval forces enforce UN blockade of Haiti
Clinton	1994	Persian Gulf	Deployed forces to counter Iraqi troop movements near Kuwaiti border
Clinton	1994	Rwanda	Ground forces dispatched to provide security for relief flights and supplies at airport in Kigali
Clinton	1994	Haiti	Occupied after military junta ceded power
Clinton	1994–1996	Bosnia	Multiple orders to U.S. air and, finally, ground forces to intervene in Bosnia

Data sources: U.S. Congressional Research Service (1991 and 1988); Blechman (1990); Glennon (1991b); authors.

Whatever the intent of the WPR or the wisdom of Congress in enacting it, what is certain is that the resolution has been largely ignored by presidents and members of Congress alike. There are various tallies, depending on whether one counts a series of distinct actions in a region or ongoing crisis, of the number of separate instances since the passage of the War Powers Resolution in which the president ordered U.S. forces into combat or otherwise into harm's way. The Congressional Research Service had identified 45 from the passage of the WPR through 1993 (Collier, 1994), and there were several further instances during 1994 and 1995. Of all these military actions, only five were authorized by Congress. Moreover, three of the authorizations (Lebanon, 1983; Desert Shield, 1990; Haiti, 1994) came after the event, and the other two (Desert Storm, 1991; Bosnia, 1995) left Congress little choice but to concur. Table 8.1 lists the most significant of the earlier presidential actions and the actions taken by Presidents Bush and Clinton.

The war making power typifies congressional action in those cases that fit the presidential policy making model. Although some exceptions may be found, Congress most often acquiesces to the president's policy position, acts only after the most important decisions have already been made, or simply does nothing at all.

The WPR has failed to accomplish its purpose for numerous reasons (Deering, 1991). The act contains significant legal loopholes, and it does not give Congress a dependable and constitutionally acceptable method of enforcing its provisions (Thurber, 1991). The most important weakness of the WPR, however, is political. Presidents consistently ignore it. Congress, with equal regularity, declines to enforce it. One might expect that Congress would resist additions to the president's power, since such increases often mean relative decreases in congressional authority. Sometimes this expectation is fulfilled, and there are many in Congress who criticize presidential power and policy and who urge their own institution to assert itself. Most members, however, are unwilling to demand that the president seek legislative authorization for a coming war (Blechman, 1990).

Like his predecessors, President Clinton has paid little heed to the WPR, as Table 8.1 and the box, "William Jefferson Clinton and the War Power" in chapter 7 attest. The response of Congress to Clinton's assertions of presidential prerogative has been to watch fitfully from the sidelines. Legislators often complain, but they seldom take formal action to restrain the president's war power. And even when Congress does enact a restriction, the law usually grants the president a degree of discretion that allows him to ignore the statute if he wishes (Fisher, 1995a).

Congress has been the source of loud warnings about becoming involved in Bosnia, but at several junctures Congress has declined to assert itself. The unwillingness of Congress to challenge the president legally was evident, for instance, in Haiti. As the crisis mounted, the press speculated that any attempt by the president to win congressional authorization to act would fail. Yet, legislators also avoided taking action to block what they reportedly opposed. In August 1994, for example, the Senate voted by a lopsided 65 to 34 to kill an amendment that demanded that the president get congressional approval before sending U.S. troops into Haiti. The next month, American troops were sent to Haiti without either congressional approval or consultation.

Something of the same pattern reoccurred the following year as the possibility that Clinton would send U.S. ground forces into Bosnia came to a head. Congress began bravely enough. As if auditioning for a part in "Congress Combative," legislators insisted that the president get congressional approval before sending U.S. troops to Bosnia. The House of Representatives, by an overwhelming margin of 315 to 103, passed a resolution in late October stating that the United States should not send troops to Bosnia without congressional approval. In mid-November, the House acted again. This time it passed by a vote of 243 to 171 legislation that would prevent any funds from being spent to send U.S. peacekeeping troops to Bosnia. The Senate did not join the House in this action, but some senators cautioned that it might.

Once the president announced on November 27 that he would send troops, many legislators shifted predictably to a "Congress Compliant" posture. The president stated clearly that any action that Congress took would have no legal impact. Given that, some members argued, as did Senator Russell Feingold (D-WS), that by avoiding any legally binding action on Bosnia, Congress was ceding its role and ducking its responsibility."[15] Many opponents of intervention felt pressured, however, to support the United States and its troops, if not the president. Senator McCain (R-AZ) argued that while "this is not something I want to do," it is necessary to vote to support the deployment because "the president has the constitutional authority to do this, and I want to do everything I can to minimize the loss of life and to insure that the peace agreement is lasting." The leader of the loyal opposition in the Senate, Robert Dole (R-KS), raised the standard of bipartisanship to explain his support of the president and his willingness to concede that Clinton had the authority to send the troops with or without the approval of Congress. "It wasn't easy," Dole said of his decision. "I knew the easy way out was to go out and trash everything . . . , but I've been around here long enough to know that at this point we shouldn't be so partisan."[16]

Other legislators voted to support the deployment because they realized they were in a trap, just like the one that had occurred in the Persian Gulf crisis. There and in the Balkans, the president had staked American prestige on U.S. military action. Congress could go along or be accused of demolishing U.S. credibility and, in the case of Bosnia, of wrecking the peace process. During Senate debate, Mitch McConnell (R-KY) likened the pressure to support the president's announced commitment as akin to a "shotgun wedding" requiring the Senate to act with "honor and accountability" in response to "an unfortunate mistake" by the president.[17] So, in the end, Congress did the "right thing." On December 13, 1995, it passed a series of nonbinding resolutions, wedding itself reluctantly to intervention in Bosnia.

The key question to ask here is why Congress is so reluctant to insist that its authority under the Constitution and the provisions of the WPR be upheld. There are two primary causes: partisan politics and deference to presidential authority.

Partisan politics make legislators wary of making definitive foreign policy and having to answer to the voters. "They're afraid they'll be wrong in three weeks. No one wants to go on the line," observed Senator Joseph R. Biden (D-DE) of his colleagues during debate about Haiti. Based on this queasiness, explained Representative Lee H. Hamilton (D-IN), "the preferred stance is to let the president make the decisions and, if it all goes well, praise him, and if it doesn't, criticize him."[18] The same sentiment was evident in the Bosnia votes. "If the commander in chief wants to hang himself, who are we to take his rope away?" asked one Republican congressional staff member.[19]

Partisan politics also makes legislators reluctant to criticize a president of their own party. The position of the Democrat's party leader, George Mitchell of Maine, in the Senate provides an apt example. During the Persian Gulf crisis, with Republican George Bush in the White House, Mitchell insisted that the president had "no authority, acting alone, to commit the United States to war." The Constitution, the Senate majority leader said, "clearly invests that grave responsibility in Congress and Congress alone." Three years later, with the issue of Haiti and with Democrat Bill Clinton in the Oval Office, the senator had come to a new interpretation of the Constitution.[20] "It's not legal or necessary" for the president to seek congressional authorization, Mitchell told a reporter.[21]

Moreover, even when a president of the opposing party is in the White House, legislators are reluctant to vote restraints that might set a precedent binding the next candidate of their own party to become president. "You've got to ask, How would I vote if my guy was in the White House?" was how Republican senator Conrad Burns of Montana explained his vote not to limit Democratic president Bill Clinton on Haiti.[22] In a similar way, some senators and other members of Congress have presidential ambitions and are reluctant to vote restraints that would limit them if they succeeded in capturing the presidency.

Deference to presidential authority is the second factor that makes Congress reluctant to insist on its constitutional and statutory authority. Many members of Congress doubt their institution's ability to make foreign policy. "This is the world's champion forum for nit-picking, second guessing, and should-have-been dones," majority leader George Mitchell said of the Senate.[23] This view, among others, disposes many legislators to support broad presidential authority. Even with a Democrat in the White House, Senate majority leader Dole introduced the Peace Powers Act. Dole's bill, among other things, would have repealed the WPR. The powerful Speaker of the House, Newt Gingrich, also favored repeal of the WPR on the grounds that "We live in an instantaneous age where there are times, such as the Oklahoma City bombing, when you need a commander in chief."[24]

Opponents of the repeal argued that democracy demanded that the president be reined in. "Every president finds Congress inconvenient," Representative Toby Roth observed accurately, "but we're a democracy, not a monarchy."[25] Speaker Gingrich noted similarly that many legislators "didn't want [to do] something that strengthened the president's hand."[26] In the end, a slim majority voted to preserve the WPR for its symbolic value, if nothing else. The House defeated its version of the Dole bill by a vote of 217 to 201 with, ironically, most Repub-

After much congressional sound and fury in opposition to sending U.S. troops to Bosnia, legislators lapsed into the role of Congress Compliant once President Clinton announced that he would send troops there. The November 1995 arrival in Bosnia of the first U.S. troops, including this American reconnaissance patrol with its young Bosnian escort, came well before Congress passed its symbolic but legally meaningless resolutions of support in mid-December.

licans voting for the measure that would have enhanced President Clinton's power and most Democrats voting against it. In a final twist and tribute to the convoluted rules of the blame game in Washington, some Republican sponsors criticized President Clinton for not coming out in support of repeal. "Clinton was no help," was the grumpy evaluation of repeal supporter Representative Henry Hyde (R-IL).[27]

Ratification and Confirmation

The Constitution also grants Congress, specifically the Senate, authority to ratify or reject treaties signed by the president and the ability to confirm or reject nominations made by the president. Treaties require a two-thirds ratification; nominations require majority confirmation. As the previous chapter noted, the Senate rarely rejects either treaties or nominations. Yet these discussions also indicated that the Senate's role is often more subtle than can be measured by simply tallying outright rejections of presidential proposals.

Ratification   The Senate usually ratifies treaties submitted to it by the president. This does not mean, however, that the Senate is without influence (Pitsvada, 1991). Congress's impact on the treaty process is evident in several ways. One is that presidents sometimes withdraw treaties from Senate consideration rather than have them defeated. This is what happened to the SALT II Treaty, as we saw in chapter 7. The Senate may also delay or modify treaties that the administration wishes to conclude. President Johnson explored the idea of negotiating a new canal treaty with Panama in 1967, but the move sparked a vehement negative reaction by many senators. As a result, one senator wrote, the administration "pulled back its horns . . . realizing [it] would probably get clobbered in the Senate" (Rourke, 1983:273).

The issue simmered for another decade before President Carter pressed the Senate to ratify a treaty turning over control of the canal to Panama. A majority of senators were skeptical of the treaty, as was public opinion. This time, however, the Senate merely modified it (Skidmore, 1993). Senators proposed 145 amendments, 26 reservations, 18 understandings, and 3 declarations. Most of these failed or had no legal effect, but an amendment proposed by Senator Dennis DeConcini (D-AZ) was important. It reserved for the United States the right to intervene militarily if necessary to keep the canal open. Even though the amendment offended Panama by violating its sovereignty and by requiring negotiations to be reopened, the administration decided not to fight DeConcini's effort. The amendment was adopted; Panama was forced to swallow its pride; and the treaty was renegotiated to conform with the Senate's demands (Strong, 1991).

Another issue dealing with the ratification process, discussed in chapter 7, is the use of executive agreements. During the period of legislative fervor that led to passage of the WPR, Congress also moved to rein in the president's ability to make executive agreements, especially secret ones. The 1972 **Executive Agreements Act** (the so-called Case-Zablocki Act) required presidents to inform Congress of agreements made with other countries within 60 days of the agreement's implementation. While Congress could not change these agreements, the idea was that members would at least know if international commitments had been made.

Like the WPR, the Executive Agreements Act has proven to be more impressive on paper than in practice. The most significant flaw is that presidents simply ignore it and have made many important executive agreements—some formal, others tacit—that have not been transmitted to Congress. President Reagan, for instance, agreed in 1982 to cooperate with the Vatican to bring down the communist government in Poland and to pressure the Soviets not to intervene to save it. Among other things, this effort included warnings by Washington to Moscow that intervention would bring serious repercussions. As far as can be determined, members of Congress, just like the American public, learned about this only when the story was unveiled in a news magazine a decade later.

The executive agreement that President Clinton concluded with North Korea in late 1994 serves as an example of the ongoing importance of this diplomatic practice. In return for halting its efforts to acquire nuclear weapons, North Korea will receive a variety of incentives including up to nearly 139 million gallons of petroleum annually. Much of the approximately $62 million cost of the fuel aid will be paid by the United States. There was congressional grumbling over the agreement, with, for one, Senator Frank Murkowski (D-AK) objecting, "We have given away the store. I don't know what we have gotten in return other than promises." Some legislators even threatened to try to use Congress's appropriations power to derail the agreement. Such grousing was mostly political posturing, however. Most members heeded the warning of South Korean foreign minister Hang Sung Joo, that "any change of the accord would lead to uncontrollable instability on the Korean peninsula. . . . even though [the accord] must not be renegotiated or scrapped."[28] Moreover, Clinton sidestepped the need to ask Congress to appropriate funds by using his discretionary executive authority to reallocate Defense Department funds in order to begin transfer of the promised petroleum to North Korea.

Before leaving our discussion of ratification, it should be noted that the House of Representatives has become part of the ratifying process for some foreign agreements that involve trade and other matters of international economic interchange. Because U.S. adherence to the North American Free Trade Agreement (NAFTA), the General Agreement on Tariffs and Trade (GATT), and other such treaties requires so much implementing legislation that must be passed by both houses of Congress, the House has been able to insist that it be included in the approval process. This extraconstitutional process treats U.S. final agreement to NAFTA, GATT, and other such treaties as "non-self-executing congressional-executive agreements," matters that fall under the Omnibus Trade and Competitiveness Act of 1988 and, therefore, under Congress's constitutional power to regulate interstate and foreign commerce (Twombly, 1995). As such, this aspect of the House's role comes properly under its general legislative authority and is discussed in that section below.

Confirmation   The Senate must also approve presidential nominations for most posts involving diplomatic and military functions. Normally, the Senate takes the attitude that the president should be free to name executive officials. The extent of this willingness to let presidents have whomever they wish was evident, for example, when President Reagan nominated William Clark to serve as deputy secretary of state. Clark was a longtime Reagan associate, whom Reagan had appointed to the California Supreme Court when he was governor of that state. At his confirmation hearings, Clark demonstrated such scant knowledge of international politics or even world geography that he actually apologized to the members of the Foreign Relations Committee for his ignorance. Apparently, Clark's sole qualification for this office was his personal loyalty to Reagan. This trait qualified him to keep an eye on Secretary of State Alexander Haig, who was not a Reagan loyalist. Derisive comments on Clark's nomination were widespread in the United States and abroad, but the Senate voted to confirm Clark anyway.

For all its willingness to confirm, sometimes a nomination is defeated. The Senate refused in 1989 to accept Texas senator John Tower as defense secretary because of his abuse of alcohol and women. The Senate also plays a subtle, but important, role when nominations are withdrawn because of legislative opposition. Robert Pastor asked President Clinton to withdraw his nomination as U.S. ambassador to Panama because Senate Foreign Relations Committee chairman Jesse Helms (R-NC) had made it clear that Pastor's name would never come up for a vote. Pastor, a scholar in Latin American affairs, had served as National Security Council staff member during the Carter administration, and Helms blamed him for helping negotiate the Panama Canal Treaties, for supposedly ignoring the arming of El Salvador's leftist rebels by Nicaragua, and, in general, for what the senator described with considerable hyperbole as "presid[ing] over one of the most disastrous and humiliating periods in the U.S.

involvement in Latin America."[29] Another Clinton nominee, Morton Halperin, withdrew his nomination, in this case as assistant secretary of state for democracy and peacekeeping, when the Senate refused to act on it, again because of the assertion of Helms and others that Halperin's background was ultraliberal.

The confirmation process can also serve to warn nominees that following certain policies will lead to trouble in Congress and that to win confirmation, the nominee needs to forswear those policies. The nomination of Strobe Talbott as deputy secretary of state by President Clinton alarmed some legislators because of what Talbott had written as a journalist with *Time* magazine. He had commented in a 1985 article, for instance, that Israel was "well on its way to becoming not just a dubious asset but also a downright liability to American security interests." In another, later article, Talbott had criticized U.S. efforts to transform the Russian economy rapidly from socialism to capitalism on the grounds that it was a "prescription for hyperinflation and economic collapse."[30] Talbott was forced to recant these and other former views during his confirmation hearing. The chastened nominee told his Senate inquisitors, for instance, that "I do want to set the record straight on the question of my views of Israel as a strategic asset. On that I have simply changed my opinion."[31]

At other times the Senate helps create a vacancy. R. James Woolsey abruptly resigned as CIA director in 1995 after concerted congressional attacks on his performance. Many in the Senate found him overly protective of the CIA's budget, unwilling to force the CIA to redefine its purpose in a post–cold war environment, and far too lenient in reprimanding CIA supervisors responsible for the Aldrich Ames spy disaster. Once he resigned, the Senate unanimously approved his replacement, former deputy defense secretary John Deutch.[32] Furthermore, the Senate affects who gets nominated. Ironically, one reason Woolsey had been initially selected by Clinton to head the embattled CIA was because the nominee was known as the congressional "Republicans' favorite Democrat" because of his conservative views on defense.[33] In short, senatorial sentiments help shape presidential foreign policy making teams in a variety of direct and indirect ways.

Legislation

The power to legislate, to enact statutory law, is one of the two great pillars of Congress's power, and Congress can use that power to affect foreign policy. There are, as noted in the initial discussion of Congress's formal powers, several ways that it exercises its authority: legal mandates, institutional manipulation, and indirect pressure. These apply to legislative power as well as to the appropriations power that we will analyze presently. Yet, despite these multiple paths of influence, it is difficult to define precisely the impact of Congress's legislative power because it seldom takes the form of specific policy requirements that represent a clear defeat of a president's preferred policy and a clear substitution of congressional policy. Also, the impact of the legislative power is inconsistent. While it is true, for example, that 22 percent of all laws passed by Congress between 1947 and 1990 dealt with foreign policy, it is also true that half of those acts dealt with just two, highly intermestic topics—military matters and foreign economic relations (Emery & Deering, 1995).

It is also true, as indicated earlier, that the president has considerable ability to persuade Congress to enact foreign policy legislation favored by the White House. It is further the case, as the history of the WPR illustrates, that presidents can sometimes

The increased assertiveness and importance of Congress in the foreign policy process during the post–cold war era was enhanced when the Republicans took control of Congress beginning in January 1995. One indication of the increased authority of Congress has been the rise in the number of foreign leaders who have visited Capitol Hill while in Washington, D.C. This attention to Congress is depicted here: Prime Minister John Major of Great Britain, on the right, is talking with the Republicans' new Speaker of the House, Newt Gingrich.

undermine legislative mandates successfully. Moreover, the machinations of the Reagan administration to supply arms to the Contra rebels in Nicaragua despite specific prohibitions by Congress in the form of the Boland Amendments show that the executive can sometimes even engage in illegal acts to follow a policy despite contrary statutory law.

Overall Operation of Legislative Power It would be an error, though, to imagine that Congress's legislative authority is not a powerful tool. American presidents and even foreign leaders recognize the potential that exists, and they court Congress to promote, change, or block legislative action. After the Republicans captured both houses of Congress in the 1994 elections, foreign governments were understandably anxious to learn what that would mean for U.S. foreign policy. Speaking at a news conference in Manila with the Philippine president, Fidel Ramos, at his side, President Clinton sought to assure Ramos and other foreign leaders that "I don't expect [Republican control of Congress] will have any impact on our foreign policy." The reason, Clinton told himself and others with probably unfounded optimism, is that "I'm convinced that what I am doing is in the interest of all the American people without regard to party and is supported by leaders of both parties in the United States Congress."[34] In another forum, Secretary of State Christopher also took pains to assure the world that there would be no fundamental change. "Whatever the outcome of the mid-term elections," Christopher told the Korean-American Friendship

Society, "there is a strong continuity in American foreign policy. I want to assure this international audience that we intend to go forward in the spirit of bipartisanship and continuity."[35]

Perhaps, but foreign leaders have dramatically increased their visits to Congress just to ensure that the lines of communication are open to what they perceive as a branch of government that may well increase its challenges to presidential policy. During the first half of 1995 alone, for example, those who traveled to Washington to lobby Congress included Bosnian prime minister Haris Silajdzic, British prime minister John Major, Egyptian president Hosni Mubarak, Pakistani prime minister Benazir Bhutto, French "first lady" Danielle Mitterrand, Turkish foreign minister Erdal Inonu, and French foreign minister Alain Juppé. It is also important to note that Congress does not only affect policy when it modifies what presidents desire. Often presidents are opposed by elements within their own administration, by interest groups, and by a significant percentage of public opinion. In some such cases, Congress can act to signal its support of a presidential initiative. The desire of the White House to normalize relations with Vietnam was encouraged by various congressional calls to do so, most significantly the Senate's January 1995 resolution calling for lifting the economic embargo against Vietnam. With almost half of all Senate Republicans voting for the measure, Clinton gained a degree of insularity from partisan criticism. A week later the president ended the embargo, and when no firestorm of opposition erupted, he established full diplomatic relations with Hanoi six months later.

In the realm of legal mandates, just one indication of how seldom Congress legally forces a profound change can be seen in the somewhat breathless reaction of the press to the July 1995 votes by the Senate and House to force an end to the U.S. arms embargo on Bosnia. The *New York Times* characterized it as a "rare direct assault on a president's foreign policy" and noted that "over the past two decades, the two branches of government have clashed often over the president's handling of foreign conflicts, but the cases where [Congress] directly undercut a president were exceptional."[36]

Even these votes, which so amazed observers, were not, however, the stunning defeat of presidential authority that they seemed to be. In the first place, even though the margins of both votes (Senate: 69–29; House: 298–128) were greater than the two-thirds needed to override a presidential veto, Clinton vowed to exercise that option. Second, some legislators seemed to support the resolution more as a way of pressing Clinton to make a firm policy than as a method to take control of foreign policy. Senators of both parties seemed almost to plead with Clinton to find a firm policy so that they could change their vote and uphold an expected veto. "I don't think a veto can be overridden if the president calls his party to action and says, 'Here is what the policy is,' " said Republican William S. Cohen of Maine. "For me, this was not the final vote," added Democrat Kent Conrad of North Dakota. "It's conceivable I would support a presidential veto if between now and then there was an effective policy."[37] Other votes could be changed by the president's arguing that congressional support of the president was vital to a successful foreign policy. After meeting with Clinton just before the initial House vote, Representative David Obey changed his mind and voted against lifting the embargo in part, he said, because "it seems to me that the most important thing at this point is for us to be together. We ought to grant the president the time he needs."[38]

Third, the bill contained several escape clauses. These included language stating that the president would not be required to end U.S. participation in the arms embargo until 3 months after UN peacekeeping forces withdrew from Bosnia or the Bosnian government requested their withdrawal. Neither contingency was immediately probable. Furthermore, even if the Bosnians made such a request, and even after the 3-month waiting period, the president could institute unlimited 30-day delays in lifting the embargo, pending the safe withdrawal of UN forces.

Perhaps most importantly, Congress did not attempt to override Clinton's veto. Charges on the battlefield in Bosnia and the convening of the peace talks in Ohio persuaded Congress to follow the president's lead.

The fact that Congress did not force arms sales to Bosnia does not mean, however, that the bill did not have an impact. To the contrary, the move to lift the embargo had real policy importance that illustrates the indirect influence of the legislative power. The Senate's action on the arms embargo put the president on notice that unless he did something to help the Bosnian Muslims, he might lose control of U.S. policy direction. That is one of the reasons that Clinton authorized U.S. participation in a much tougher policy of NATO air strikes against Bosnian Serb positions. The pressure on Clinton also helps explain why the United States began to support, perhaps encourage, Croatia to come to the aid of the Bosnian Muslims.

Indirect legislative influence that modified the influence, the direction, and the tone of U.S. foreign policy has also been evident on a number of other fronts during the Clinton presidency. Many of the foreign policy clauses of the so-called Contract with America that Republican candidates for the House signed in 1994 were included in the GOP-sponsored National Security Revitalization Act of 1995. This bill would, among other things, prohibit in most circumstances placing U.S. military forces under UN commanders. It also would deduct the U.S. costs of peacekeeping operations from its UN dues, would direct the defense secretary to speed the development of a ballistic missile defense (BMD) system, and would foster the early enlargement of NATO to include Poland, Hungary, Slovakia, and the Czech Republic. While the bill's fate is uncertain at this point, several factors highlight the give and take by which legislative initiatives usually influence, rather than take control of, policy. One factor is that the bill takes the typical tack of including escape clauses for the president. The president could, for instance, allow American troops to serve in a UN force commanded by a foreign general by certifying to Congress that U.S. national security required it. A second factor is the president's veto power. Two days before the legislation passed the House in February 1995, President Clinton sent a letter to Speaker Gingrich condemning the bill as containing "numerous flawed provisions that are simply unacceptable."[39] Amid the fervor of newly acquired power, the GOP-dominated House passed the bill anyway, but Clinton's warning served notice on the Senate that a presidential veto was certain unless it made changes in the House version. At this juncture, months later, the face of the bill is unresolved as it languishes in the Senate. It is almost certain, however, that the Senate will moderate the provisions of the House bill or that the president will veto the measure entirely.

This does not mean that the National Security Revitalization Act of 1995, enacted or not, will not have its impact. The Republicans' discontent with the UN has already been reflected to a degree in Clinton's policy. The president and his foreign policy lieutenants have said in a number of forums that the UN must act vigorously to reform some of its structures and operations, and they have also spoken of strict limitations on U.S. participation in UN peacekeeping missions. The discontent that lingers from U.S. involvement in the UN operation in Somalia is one of the reasons that the Clinton administration has assiduously kept U.S. forces separate from the UN forces in Bosnia. The administration has also included money for a BMD system in its budget and has continued negotiations with the NATO allies and with several East European countries aimed at bringing them into some type of association, if not full alliance, with NATO. The point is that even if the National Security Revitalization Act were to be passed by the Senate and signed by the president, it would almost certainly not be in anything like the form in which it was passed by the House. Yet it has influenced policy as Clinton has taken actions aimed at lessening the pressure to pass the bill by partially accommodating some of the views behind it.

Institutional manipulation through legislative action has also occurred during the Clinton administration. One way that Senator Helms and others in Congress are attempting to cut the foreign aid program, to moderate what some legislators see as too much eagerness to cut U.S. nuclear weapons, and to affect some other policies, is by dismantling or merging the Agency of International Development (AID), the Arms Control and Disarmament Agency (ACDA), the United States Information Agency (USIA), and other agencies into the State Department. The move is based on the Washington reality that an independent agency with direct access to the president has more authority and money than it probably would have if it were subordinate to a larger agency, in this case the State Department. Senator Helms claims that the U.S. foreign policy making structure is "a mess" and that his plan would "be good for the country and be good for the taxpayers." Brian Atwood, the head of AID, retorts that Helms's plan is "mischievous" and "designed more to pursue an isolationist foreign policy than it is to do something constructive."[40] The fate of the Helms institutional initiative is, at this writing, uncertain. It is probable, however, that, as is most often the case in the crucible of Washington maneuvering, the Helms bill will not pass or will be substantially modified, that all or most of the agencies will survive, but that compromise in legislative language or executive changes made in anticipated reaction will modify both the operation and the responsibility of some of the affected bureaucratic units.

The Legislative Power and Arms Sales: A Case Study To reiterate a key point, perhaps the most frequent pattern occurs when Congress uses its legislative power to force the administration to compromise. In order to give substance to this generality, we can cite one issue: the sale of military equipment to the Middle East, especially Saudi Arabia, during the 1980s. Recall that in chapter 7 we saw that President Reagan persuaded Congress not to block the sale of AWACS aircraft to Saudi Arabia in 1981. That was certainly a presidential victory, but the extended story of military sales to countries in the Middle East reveals a much more complex interaction between the executive and Congress. Among the things you will see in the saga are Congress using its legislative authority to shape policy, many legislative-executive compromises, Congress declining to strengthen its authority, and President Reagan using his emergency authority to do what Congress opposed (Jentleson, 1990). This case study is also a fine example of the political model and later of the presidential model of foreign policy making in action.

A preliminary step that led to the executive-congressional battle throughout the 1980s was a decision by the Carter administration in 1977 to sell 60 F-15 Eagle warplanes to Saudi Arabia. According to the Arms Export Control Act of 1976, Congress could block military sales worth $25 million or more if both houses voted by concurrent resolution against the sale within 30 days. As noted, concurrent resolutions do not have to be signed by the president and therefore are not subject to veto. This process is called a **legislative veto**, by which Congress gave the executive discretion to perform certain acts but reserved the ability (by either a one-house, simple resolution or a two-house, concurrent resolution) to block the action within a specific period. Since simple and concurrent resolutions do not have the force of law, the Supreme Court overturned their use of legislative vetoes in *Immigration and Naturalization Service (INS) v. Chadha* (1983) and several other cases. Until 1983, though, military sales were subject to legislative veto (Silverstein, 1994; Gibson, 1992; Mann, 1990).

In the matter of F-15 Eagle fighters sold to Saudi Arabia in 1977, Carter's move touched off a political donnybrook that has been repeated whenever the administration has proposed to sell military hardware to Arab countries. Several powerful domestic groups became involved. Weapons manufacturers and unions with employees in that industry favored the sale; Jewish Americans, primarily represented by the American Israel Public Affairs Committee (AIPAC), opposed the sale. Those in Congress who sympathized with these groups could not block the sale, but their vociferous opposition did force delay of the sale for almost a year. When Carter finally moved ahead with the sale, he packaged it with the sale of 90 F-15s and F-16s to Israel. Still Congress resisted, and it forced the administration to increase by 20 planes the sale to Israel and to delete several key weapons systems, such as bomb racks, from the planes going to Saudi Arabia. The Saudis also had to promise not to base their Eagles within operational range of Israel. Needless to say, the Saudis were offended.

With the Middle East becoming increasingly unstable in the aftermath of the 1979 Iranian revolution that brought the Ayatollah Khomeini to power, Carter moved tentatively in 1980 to sell the deleted F-15 equipment to the Saudis. But an angry letter signed by 68 senators and 178 representatives persuaded the president to back off.

In February 1981, President Reagan once again also tried to send the deleted F-15 equipment to the Saudis and also to sell them five AWACS and eight KC-707 refueling tankers. Intense congressional opposition caused Reagan to delay submitting the proposed sale for six months. The president's effort to ease opposition failed, however, and when he did submit the proposal, the House disapproved it by a lopsided 310 to 11 margin. The battle then turned to the Senate. There the administration eked out a 52 to 48 victory. One part of achieving that, however, involved addressing senatorial concern that the Saudis might feed intelligence information from the AWACS to Syria. This forced Reagan to agree that the planes would have joint American-Saudi crews. The Saudis were again offended. It is also worth noting that two Republican senators, Charles Percy of Illinois and Roger Jepsen of Iowa, who provided key support for the sale, were defeated in the following elections. Whatever the exact causes of their defeat, the conventional wisdom in Washington was that angry Jewish Americans had worked successfully to defeat the two senators. They represented electoral deaths that surviving members of Congress contemplated somberly.

The issue of arms for Saudi Arabia arose anew in 1984 when Reagan proposed to sell 1,200 Stinger antiaircraft missiles to the Saudis. Opposition in Congress forced the president to retreat, but he countered the following year by using discretionary authority under one of the many emergency powers granted over the years by Congress to send 400 Stingers to Saudi Arabia. Congress was not pleased, and that, in part, persuaded Reagan to delay a proposal to sell yet another 40 F-15s to the Saudis. This time, the offended and frustrated Saudis gave up on their American allies and turned to the British to buy $4 billion worth of Tornado fighters.

The bell sounded in 1986 for a new round of legislative-executive struggle over arms sales to Saudi Arabia. A key change in the process stemmed from the *Chadha* case. Reacting to the Court's decision, Congress amended the Arms Export Control Act to provide for a legislative veto by a constitutionally acceptable joint resolution. Still, the administration moved cautiously in the face of congressional opposition. A preliminary move in 1986 to sell attack helicopters, advanced F-15 avionics equipment, and modern M-1 tanks to the Saudis was dropped in the face of congressional opposition. The Saudis were offended yet again. Reagan tried to soften the blow by offering the Saudis 2,600 tactical missiles in a $354 million package. Congress moved to block the sale by votes of 73 to 22 in the Senate and 356 to 62 in the House, more than two-thirds in each chamber. Reagan vetoed the joint resolution. But fearing he would be overridden, the president offered to drop 800 of the most advanced missiles from the deal. That was just enough, and the Senate failed to override the veto by a one-vote margin.

By this time the situation in the Persian Gulf was truly alarming. The Iran-Iraq war was raging and had expanded to include Iranian attacks on Kuwait and on oil tankers in the gulf and threats against Saudi Arabia. All this affected arms sales to the Arab countries. The heightened sense of danger helped move the issue perceptually from the political toward the presidential model. Members of Congress were less willing to oppose the president. Therefore, they resorted to a degree of subterfuge to untangle the Gordian knot of their concern about Israeli security and Jewish American voters, on the one hand, and the president's ongoing argument, on the other hand, that arming Saudi Arabia would enhance security in the gulf. What Congress did was to continue to oppose sales to the Saudis (thereby meeting one concern) while knowing full well that the president would veto any prohibitive joint resolution and could probably not be overridden (thereby letting the arms sale go forward and meeting the other concern).

Amid these conundrums, Congress also declined to take greater control over arms sales. Several members introduced legislation in January 1987 that would have revoked the president's discretionary authority to sell arms subject to legislative veto. Instead, the legislation specified that no sale could go forward without congressional approval. If any of the bills had been adopted, Congress could have barred any sale simply by not acting. That would have put Congress very much in the driver's seat. It was authority that most members did not really want. The bills died in Congress without a vote.

The next legislative twist occurred beginning in late 1987 when the Reagan administration proposed selling Maverick missiles, F-15s, and a variety of other sophisticated equipment to the Saudis. More than two-thirds of the Senate voiced opposition, and the White House dropped the Mavericks from the package. The move was a deception, however, and everyone knew it. The deletion of the missiles meant that Congress could refrain from blocking the sale while claiming that the weapons most threatening to Israel had been deleted. But Reagan had announced that he would use his emergency authority to provide Mavericks to the Saudis in the event of a crisis (which already clearly existed). As a result, Congress could say that it had blocked the Mavericks, and Saudi Arabia could get the Mavericks.

The Saudi arms-sales case illustrates the typical nature of congressional foreign policy legislation. The final results represented compromises. Despite congressional opposition, the administration kept the various sales alive and was able to send considerable advanced U.S. weaponry to the Saudis. Still, the opponents were able to limit both the types and amount of weapons sent to the Saudis. Opponents also partially offset the impact of the arms sales to Saudi Arabia by linking them to increased arms sales to Israel. Thus both the administration and its congressional critics could claim victory, even if neither was satisfied fully with the final outcome.

Appropriations

The appropriations power is the second great pillar of Congress's formal authority. Article I, Section 9, of the Constitution directs that "No Money shall be drawn from the Treasury, but in Consequence of Appropriations made by Law." This means that no federal official, including the president, can legally spend money unless it has been appropriated by Congress. Since almost everything the government does eventually requires some sort of financing, and since Congress has the sole power to provide the money, the power of the purse is, in theory, perhaps the most momentous policy making tool that Congress possesses. For this reason, and even though only 10 percent of the foreign policy laws passed by Congress are appropriations bills, the appropriations power is potentially potent (Emery & Deering, 1995; Stockton, 1995; Thurber, 1991).

Yet, as we have seen repeatedly, having power and using it are two decidedly different things. Congress's appropriations power, like its legislative power, can be exercised through legal mandates, institutional manipulation, and indirect pressure. But also like the legislative power, the exercise of the appropriations authority by Congress to try to control foreign policy is restrained and inconsistent. And even when it is used, it most often results in compromises with the executive branch rather than decisive victories or defeats for either of the two branches. Thus, the pivotal issue about the appropriations power, like all congressional authority, is the degree to which Congress uses it to influence the course of U.S. foreign policy.

Overall Operation of the Appropriations Power The Republican Congress that came to power in 1995 has sought to use the power of the purse in a number of ways. House GOP members, in particular, have moved to slash foreign aid, to reduce U.S. funding of the UN and its programs, to reduce the staff levels and programs of the USIA and even the State Department, and, in general, to cut spending and to limit some aspects of U.S. overseas involvement.

While these measures are still pending, the original proposals are being modified by the need for compromise and by the realization by some Republicans that what made good campaign rhetoric for a minority party in 1994 does not make good policy for a congressional majority party in 1995. Speaker Gingrich reportedly pressed House Republicans in private to pass the foreign aid bill on the grounds that it projects "American power and presence around the globe in a nonmilitary way at a cost of one cent on the federal dollar." That change of heart, explained a Gingrich spokesperson, came about because the Republicans are "reorienting as a majority governing party." The spokesperson noted that "there are old instincts that occur when you are in the minority that mean there are certain things [like foreign aid] that you don't vote for." Now, with the Republicans in the majority and the Democrats in the minority, "those things are reversed in this case for both parties."[41] The administration is also doing its part of compromising. For example, Secretary of State

Christopher moved to head off more sweeping reductions proposed in Congress by announcing in May 1995 that he would cut some 500 jobs at the State Department, a reduction of a little less than two percent of the department's staff of 260,000.

For all of these thrusts and parries, the vast monetary bulk of appropriations related to U.S. international relations are involved with such national security affairs as funding U.S. military forces, giving military aid, and supporting intervention activities by the CIA. Therefore, this general category of national security provides a good focus for discussing the role of Congress's appropriations power. National security is a complex policy realm in which the policy making process conforms in various circumstances to each of the four policy models described in chapter 6. Sometimes, especially during crises, national security policy is determined according to the presidential model. This is discussed or illustrated at various points throughout this book. At other times, national security policy is determined by uniformed and civilian professionals within the Department of Defense in line with the administrative model. Because national security spending involves hundreds of billions of dollars each year, however, a great deal of policy is formulated according to the political model or the subgovernment model. In these two models, Congress or its subdivisions are major policy players.

One aspect of determining national security policy involves overall funding levels, numbers of personnel, specific weapons systems, and other factors that determine the general configuration of U.S. military forces. The defense budget is widely construed as competing directly with funding for domestic programs, contributing to the budget deficit, or affecting tax rates. As such, the defense budget is a matter of significant interest to Congress. There are occasions when Congress forces the administration to spend more than it wants or funds a program that the Department of Defense does not support. In 1992, for example, Congress ignored the administration's decision to cut the Seawolf submarine program. Instead Congress voted to build at least one more multibillion-dollar boat and to preserve jobs and the operation of the Electric Boat shipbuilding yard at Groton, Connecticut, at least for a while. And in 1995, Congress appeared poised to fund more B-2 bombers than the administration had requested in its budget and, indeed, to increase marginally the overall defense budget.

Such examples are exceptions, though. In most circumstances, because of the president's veto and administrative discretionary authority, Congress finds it much easier to cut the executive's defense budget than to expand it. Table 8.2 shows the annual percentage changes made by Congress in the administration's defense spending requests. It is evident that Congress has cut the defense budget far more often than it has expanded defense spending. Using a shift of 5 percent or more in the president's budget request to denote a significant change, we can see that Congress made significant changes in 21 of 49 years, or 43 percent of the time. Table 8.2 also shows that the frequency of significant changes has increased from 35 percent between FY1947 and FY1969 to 46 percent from FY1970 through FY1995. This increase is indicative of the breakdown of the cold war consensus that began during the Vietnam War. Note that the funds in Table 8.2 are expressed in *real dollars*, not *current dollars*, for successive *fiscal years*.

There are several subsidiary points evident in Table 8.2. One is that Congress is most likely to make significant changes in the president's request during times when there is no consensus on fundamental foreign policy direction. This relates to the difference in congressional activity during status quo and non–status quo situations,

TABLE 8.2   Congressional Changes in Major Defense Spending Requests Expressed in Billions of FY1987 Dollars: Fiscal Years 1947–1995

FY	Request	Appro-priated	Percent Change	FY	Request	Appro-priated	Percent Change
1947	$123.3	95.7	-22.4	1972	232.6	223.2	-4.1
1948	84.2	65.2	-22.6	1973	217.1	202.9	-6.5
1949	90.3	82.0	-9.3	1974	209.6	197.4	-5.8
1950	97.4	95.1	-2.3	1975	200.3	188.6	-5.8
1951	365.3	367.6	+0.6	1976	210.4	191.9	-8.8
1952	431.5	418.7	-3.0	1977	211.5	204.7	-3.2
1953	340.4	300.4	-11.8	1978	209.5	201.5	-3.8
1954	219.4	209.7	-4.4	1979	208.4	204.0	-2.1
1955	183.7	175.4	-4.5	1980	199.4	197.3	-1.1
1956	175.3	178.0	+1.6	1981	224.5	229.7	+2.3
1957	188.6	193.9	+2.9	1982	251.6	247.6	-1.6
1958	199.0	185.3	-6.8	1983	296.0	274.0	-7.4
1959	185.4	196.9	+6.2	1984	299.8	284.7	-5.0
1960	194.6	193.7	-0.5	1985	329.0	306.4	-6.9
1961	191.9	194.2	+1.2	1986	334.8	308.5	-7.9
1962	202.3	220.9	+9.2	1987	336.1	300.5	-10.6
1963	219.6	219.1	-0.2	1988	315.9	299.0	-5.4
1964	238.5	215.9	-9.5	1989	292.4	291.6	-0.3
1965	215.4	211.1	-2.0	1990	266.9	266.8	-0.0
1966	245.8	251.5	+2.3	1991	265.2	248.2	-6.4
1967	280.6	281.3	+0.3	1992	240.4	239.5	-0.4
1968	292.2	282.1	-3.4	1993	216.7	210.9	-2.7
1969	285.2	264.8	-7.2	1994	188.7	188.4	-0.2
1970	255.3	235.6	-7.7	1995	185.9	185.1	-0.4
1971	218.3	211.3	-3.2				

Real dollars is a measure that lets you calculate changes in growth while controlling for inflation. *Current dollars* are the dollars we actually use. They measure the value of something today. However, a dollar today will not purchase as much as a dollar did 10 years ago. Since inflation reduces the value of dollars, comparing the current dollar figures from different years does not accurately measure the values represented in those different years. Using *real dollars* allows you to measure value with the effects of inflation removed. The most common way is to convert amounts into a single base year, in this case FY1987 dollars.

Also note the term *fiscal year* (FY). This is the government's budget year. Through FY1976, the fiscal year ran from July 1 through June 30. In FY1977 this was changed to begin on October 1 and end on September 30. Thus, FY1995 ran from October 1, 1994, through September 30, 1995.

Sources: Historical Tables, Budget of the U.S. Government, FY1996, pp. 82–88; *Congressional Quarterly Almanacs, 1946–1992; Congressional Quarterly Weekly Report,* 1995, p. 2379.

as discussed in chapter 6. During the period immediately after World War II, the situation was non–status quo. There was little consensus, as internationalists struggled with rearguard isolationists over the extent of U.S. global involvement. Also, the defense budget had to compete with domestic needs that had been pent up during the many years of World War II military spending. These factors led to major defense budget cuts by Congress in fiscal years 1947, 1948, and 1949. The cold war consensus of the 1950s and most of the 1960s saw only two years (FY1953 at the end of the Korean War, and FY1958) in which there were significant cuts. By FY1969, however, dissent over Vietnam was in full voice and the cold war consensus was rapidly crumbling. The result was 5 percent or more congressional cuts to Defense Department requests in 6 of the next 10 years (FY1969–1978). The Soviet invasion of Afghanistan in 1979, the election of Ronald Reagan, and other events temporarily revived the cold war consensus between FY1979 and FY1982. But the consensus soon dissolved again, and Congress made significant cuts in seven of the next nine (1983–1991) fiscal years. Then, starting in FY1992, the percentage of congressional cuts declined below the significant level.

Currently, discord over the defense budget is probable as long as the Republicans control Congress and the Democrats control the White House. Many Republicans contend that Clinton has gone too far in cutting defense, and they want to increase the Pentagon's budget. This could lead to a reversal of the most common pattern found throughout most of the last two decades and see Congress increasing rather than decreasing defense spending. The looming realities of huge budget deficits and the president's veto power make it unlikely, however, that any such increases will reach the significant 5 percent threshold. The FY1996 budget, for instance, saw President Clinton submit a defense spending request of $257.3 billion. The House budget authorized $267 billion (a 3.8 percent increase), and the Senate budget allocated $263.7 billion (a 2.5 percent increase), almost certainly meaning a final increase of about 3 percent when the compromise bill is agreed to by the two chambers.

The intermestic nature of defense spending adds another significant factor to the attitude of Congress toward it. Legislators believe that defense spending competes with domestic programs for budget funds. This resulted in one pattern evident after the Vietnam War: stronger opposition to defense spending (as well as to foreign intervention and military aid) among legislators from the manufacturing belt than among those from the sun belt. The reason, one scholar suggested, was that "in an era when much of the Northeast was experiencing hard economic times . . . political representatives and interest groups from this region saw political advantage in stressing the domestic 'opportunity cost'—economic and social—of military [spending and use] . . . [and sometimes] sought to redistribute military outlays to . . . the manufacturing belt" (Trubowitz, 1992:185).

It is also true, however, that defense spending can help local economies, and Congress's power to appropriate defense funds helps determine which defense contractors and their workers will prosper and which will perish economically. This fact creates tremendous constituent pressure on Congress and leads to determined efforts by individual legislators to promote or save one weapons system or another or one military base or another that would benefit their district or state. Congress has reacted in part to these pressures by delegating the authority to make these decisions. Congress created the Base Closing Commission and gave it the authority to decide which bases to keep open or which to close and where to locate many military functions. The commission's decision cannot be changed in part, only rejected in its entirety by the president or by legislative action. That is unlikely, as was proven when the commission ordered massive and painful cuts in 1995. Even though these cuts most severely affected California, with the largest congressional delegation and the largest number of electoral votes for presidential elections, neither Congress nor Clinton was willing to open a political Pandora's box by rejecting the commission report.

Still, a great deal of maneuvering on the defense budget does occur within Congress and between it and the executive, and these shifts play a role in determining

TABLE 8.3 Examples of Weapons Systems Terminated or Protected by Congress in the 1990s

Year	Weapon System	Reason for Termination
1990	Navy F-14 fighter	Obsolete; cost
1993	Navy A/F-X ground attack plane	High cost
1993	Air Force MRF small fighter	High cost

Year	Weapon System	Reason for Protection
1990	Marine Corps V-22 Osprey aircraft	Mission effectiveness; Marine Corps support
1992	Army M-1 tank upgrades	Cost savings
1992	Army Bradley troop carriers	Need for greater numbers
1992	Army Scout helicopters	Need for greater numbers
1992	Navy small aircraft carrier	Need for more
1992	Navy Seawolf submarine	Adverse local economic impact
1994	Army Apache attack helicopter	Maintain production line
1995	B-2 bomber	Adverse local economic impact

Sources: Carter (1991); *Congressional Quarterly Almanacs,* 1991–1994; *Congressional Quarterly Weekly Reports,* 1995.

Congress sometimes terminates or protects weapons systems against the wishes of the executive branch.

U.S. capabilities and, therefore, policy. One way to recognize this impact is to examine which weapons systems Congress has terminated or has protected against the administration's wishes. These decisions, shown in Table 8.3, have tremendous economic impacts on the local communities around the factories where these weapons are made or the military installations where they are used. They also help dictate what the United States can or cannot do in the national security realm.

Yet another way to see the impact of Congress through defense appropriations is to examine the way legislators used them to influence arms control policy during the Reagan administration. When Reagan became president he was skeptical about arms control negotiations with the Soviets. Many members of Congress disagreed, but there was little that they could do directly to make Reagan negotiate with the Soviets. Nevertheless, Congress was able to use the power of the purse as a source of indirect influence on arms control.

Congress began a process that has been termed "appropriating arms control" by funding fewer weapons and tests (Blechman, 1990). Such efforts included limiting the administration to acquiring 50 ten-warhead MX missiles rather than the 100 it wanted; forcing the administration to continue research and development of the Midgetman missile, a single-warhead missile thought to be less destabilizing to the nuclear balance than the MX; and stopping the funding of the administration's anti-satellite weapons program. The House also passed a nuclear freeze resolution in 1983 that would have ended further development of nuclear weapons. Several attempts to get the Senate to pass the resolution failed, but the effort and the widespread debate in the country helped pressure Reagan to negotiate more diligently with the Soviets. The Intermediate-range Nuclear Forces Treaty was concluded in 1987, and significant progress was made toward the eventual signing of the first Strategic Arms Reduction Talks Treaty in 1991.

Congress also addressed conventional arms control matters. In 1973 and 1974, Congress passed amendments limiting the number of U.S. troops stationed in Europe as part of NATO. Such actions and general pressure on the defense budget were factors in the successful conclusion of the Conventional Forces in Europe (CFE) Treaty of 1990.

There is even evidence that the stands of Congress on arms control also may have affected the position of the Soviets. Ironically, it may have worked in the opposite way from what Congress had intended. One study found that the Soviets were more apt to make concessions at the bargaining table when Congress supported the president on key defense votes and were less likely to make concessions when Congress did not meet presidential requests (Morrow, 1991).

Congress occasionally also uses its appropriations power to influence national security policy. When Turkey invaded Cyprus in 1974, for example, Congress terminated U.S. military aid to Turkey. Congress has also tried to use the appropriations power to control covert operations by the CIA. The **Hughes-Ryan Amendment** (1974) requires the president to inform Congress of covert operations. One result of this new flow of information was a decision by Congress to pass the **Clark Amendment** (1975), which terminated financial support for CIA operations in Angola (Reisman & Baker, 1992).

The Appropriations Power and Nicaragua: A Case Study   The subtleties of the appropriations power can best be understood by examining a specific case, and, to that end, the struggle during the 1980s over aid to the Contra rebels in Nicaragua provides an apt illustration. The leftist Sandinista government of President Daniel Ortega Saavedra came to power in 1979 when it overthrew the right-wing dictatorship of Anastasio Somoza Debayle. President Carter adopted a moderate stand toward the Sandinistas, but President Reagan used his executive authority to cut off U.S. aid to Nicaragua; to direct the CIA to provide arms, training, and money to the various anticommunist groups collectively known as the Contras; and to ban trade with Nicaragua. The involvement of the CIA grew quickly to include flying supply missions into Nicaragua and attaching mines to piers in Nicaraguan ports.

Congress was initially compliant. Some of the administration's efforts were reported to the congressional committees that oversee intelligence activities, and they approved the expenditure of $19 million to support the Contras. The full Congress appropriated Contra aid in 1983. Stories in the media, however, about increasingly direct U.S. involvement worried many legislators. For a while the administration denied direct involvement, but the extensive activities could not be kept secret. Among other things, the Sandinista government brought a successful case before the UN's International Court of Justice (ICJ) accusing the United States of conducting aggressive war against Nicaragua. Many members of Congress agreed with Nicaragua. "I am pissed off! It's an act of war," arch-conservative senator Barry Goldwater (R-AZ) upbraided CIA director William J. Casey over the agency's subversive activity (Paterson, Clifford, & Hagan, 1995b:525).

As domestic and international criticism of Reagan's policy mounted, Congress moved to try to take control. As early as 1982 Congress barred the expenditure of funds to topple the Ortega government. This legislative action came in the form of an amendment to a larger appropriations bill sponsored by Representative Edward Boland (D-MA), chairman of the House Intelligence Committee. As such, the prohibition and several similar amendments that ensued are commonly referred to as the **Boland Amendments**. The administration sought to avoid such restrictions by claiming that aid to the Contras was not intended to overthrow the Ortega regime, merely to force a political settlement. Congress then moved in 1984 to close this loophole by passing another of the Boland Amendments. This one prohibited any new funding of Contra military activities for any reason.

Reagan continued to press for aid to the Contras, however, and Congress wavered back and forth during the next few years. Many legislators opposed U.S. intervention as unwarranted and because of worries that U.S. troops might eventually follow U.S. funds into Central America. Yet even in the waning days of the cold war, members did not want to seem soft on the reputedly communist-leaning Sandinistas. In 1986, for example, Congress once again passed Contra aid after a poorly timed trip by President Ortega to Moscow. The aid was restricted, however, to nonlethal purposes. The president pressed to remove the restrictions, and his battle with anti-aid members of Congress continued to sway back and forth (Leogrande & Brenner, 1993). In 1987 alone, the Senate cast more than two dozen votes on the issue. Generally, though, it can be said that Congress progressively allowed less and less money for the Contras and put more and more restrictions on it (Moreno, 1990).

The administration tried other ploys to fund the Contras. It persuaded other countries to send funds. As discussed earlier, administration officials also hatched a plot whereby weapons were sold to Iran to try to gain the release of hostages in Lebanon. The funds from the weapons sales were then diverted illegally to the Contras through secret Swiss bank accounts. This activity, coordinated by National Security Council (NSC) staff member Lieutenant Colonel Oliver North, became known as the Iran-Contra scandal (or Irangate or Iran-Contragate).

Congress moved on several fronts also. Rumors of the illegal funding sparked a congressional investigation in 1987. A special prosecutor was also appointed, and criminal charges were eventually brought against North, national security adviser Admiral John Poindexter, and others. Members of Congress also became directly involved in seeking a diplomatic settlement in Central America, including the civil war raging in El Salvador. Senator Christopher Dodd (D-CT) traveled to Nicaragua and held talks with Ortega. House Speaker Jim Wright (D-TX) followed up on a peace plan offered by Costa Rican president Oscar Arias Sanchez. His effort had been scorned by the White House; the same year Arias received the Nobel Peace Prize for his contribution. The House Speaker worked with Arias, Nicaraguan officials, and others in Central America in his attempt to find a settlement. The White House howled in protest against Wright's interference, but the effort went forward. Central American presidents met in 1989 and formulated their own peace plan (Wright, 1993).

Reagan was succeeded as U.S. president by the less ideological George Bush. He recognized that he would never get Congress to give significant military funds to the Contras. Soviet support for Nicaragua was also drying up. Mutually exhausted and largely out of money, the Sandinistas and the Contras agreed to abide by elections supervised by the UN. In April 1990, to almost everyone's surprise, a coalition of parties called *Uno* defeated the Sandinistas, and Violeta Barrios de Chamorro became president of Nicaragua.

The story of aid to the Contras is instructive in several ways. It demonstrates a number of congressional powers, including appropriations and investigation (covered further below). The struggle over aid also demonstrates some of the ways that a president can get around Congress, legally and illegally. The aid saga also demonstrates the informal power of Congress to be in contact with foreign leaders. Whether or not Speaker Wright had any constitutional authority to negotiate, he did, and those negotiations hastened the arrival of peace in the region. Finally, the battle over Contra aid in the 1980s clearly illustrates the compromises, the split decisions, that frequently characterize the struggle between the president and Congress over a policy. The Reagan administration got a good deal of what it wanted. Hundreds of millions of dollars flowed to the Contras, the Sandinistas were weakened by the armed Contras and by the U.S. economic boycott, and eventually the Ortega government fell. Still, the Contras did not overthrow the Sandinistas. Instead, it was events—the end of the cold war—that spelled an end to the Ortega government more than anything the Reagan White House did. It is impossible to know what might have happened if the Contras had received all the support that Reagan might have supplied them without congressional restraints. This much is certain, though: Congress played an important role. Aid to the Contras was increasingly diminished and restricted. In the final analysis the Contras did not win; most of them were not a direct part of the Chamorro coalition; and they, like the Sandinistas, had to settle for a decision by ballots rather than bullets.

Investigation and Oversight

Yet another important congressional power, which some scholars describe as "one of the most potent," is the authority to ask questions, to demand information, and to monitor operations of the government and its policies in general (Johnson, Gelles, & Kuzenski, 1992:137). This authority can be divided into two broad categories: investigation and oversight.

Investigation   There is no specific constitutional clause that grants investigative authority to Congress, but it is established firmly in precedent. As early as 1792, the House of Representatives appointed a committee and empowered its members to "call for such persons, papers, and records, as may be necessary to assist their inquiries" into the defeat of U.S. troops during a 1790 campaign against Indians in the Ohio Territory.[42] This power of **investigation** includes requiring testimony before legislators and the transmission of information to Congress (Davis, 1992a). Investigations are backed up by the power to subpoena witnesses and records, by the power to issue contempt citations in the case of refusal to testify or produce records, and by potential imprisonment by congressional action for recalcitrant citizens and executive officials. This punitive step has never been taken against an executive branch official, although it has been threatened.

The need for Congress to press an often reluctant executive branch for information results from two executive claims: *secrecy* and *executive privilege*. The executive branch classifies more than a million documents a year by stamping them with "top secret" or other such designations. Sometimes this information is disclosed to leaders or specific committees of Congress; sometimes the information is never revealed. Furthermore, administrations regularly complain that Congress leaks information to the press. During the 1992 investigation of U.S. aid to Iraq just before the Persian Gulf War, the Justice Department notified House Banking Committee chairman Henry B. Gonzales (D-TX) that the committee would not receive any further documents relating to U.S.–supported commercial loans to Iraq and other forms of American assistance if the chairman persisted in publishing some of the information in the *Congressional Record*. Inasmuch as the Iraqis and the banks knew all about the loans, it is clear that the U.S. administration's stand was based at least in part on the desire to avoid political embarrassment during an election year.

In a more recent case, the Senate Intelligence Committee held hearings in 1995 regarding allegations that the CIA continued to support the Guatemalan army even after U.S. aid to Guatemala was suspended amid allegations that the army was murdering civilians and executing prisoners. This story did not become public knowledge until Robert Torricelli (D-NJ), a member of the House Intelligence Committee, revealed the information. Such disclosures are, however, controversial. Speaker of the House Gingrich told reporters that "Torricelli should resign" for disclosing secret information; Torricelli retorted that "Speaker Gingrich's criticism of my telling the truth indicates his complicity in a conspiracy of silence."[43] Whatever the merits of the argument, the Senate Intelligence Committee began hearings regarding the CIA's performance and the administration's handling of the matter. The Clinton administration also began an investigation into the matter, the details of which will be elucidated in chapter 10.

The White House also regularly invokes executive privilege to claim that internal communications within the executive branch are not subject to congressional examination. Similarly, White House staff members are not subject to being questioned by Congress. This practice rests on the separation of powers doctrine and the idea that each branch's internal processes are its own exclusive concern. In the abstract, executive privilege is an accepted constitutional principle. The controversy is over where executive privilege legitimately ends and where its misuse by the executive (to shield information from Congress and the public) begins. During the hearings on prewar aid to Iraq, for example, the White House refused to allow two presidential assistants, Richard Haass and Stephen Danzansky, who were involved in the aid effort, to testify before the House Banking Committee.

Oversight The overall authority of Congress to monitor the operations of executive departments and agencies is termed **oversight**. It is a more comprehensive power than investigation. The tools of oversight range from mandatory reports that bureaucratic units must send to Congress to relatively informal visits by and letters and phone calls from members of Congress and their staffs.

While investigation and oversight have long existed, attempts by Congress to increase its foreign policy role during the Vietnam-Watergate era have led to the increased use of these techniques. The Senate Foreign Relations Committee held extensive hearings on the Vietnam War, for example. These sessions provided a high-visibility forum for antiwar views and arguably helped move public opinion against (and the United States eventually out of) the war. As one study summarizes these changes, before the Vietnam-Watergate era, the foreign policy committees of Congress passed "shorter laws with more open-ended authorizations." Since then, "not only are the laws much longer and more complex, but the language is different. The laws are detailed, the tone is aggressive, and authorization is specifically determined. There is greater in-depth explanation of intent" (Emery & Deering, 1995:13). In other words, trust in the executive branch is in short supply on Capitol Hill.

The legislative trend of requiring more and more information from the executive branch has continued. In some policy arenas, the number of reports and the details required therein raise charges of congressional **micromanagement**. This term refers to the belief, usually expressed by administrative officials, that members of Congress have crossed the line separating basic policy making (which is their legitimate function) from the day-to-day management and implementation of policy (which bureaucrats see as their legitimate function). As you can guess, micromanagement is a very subjective phenomenon, one that lies in the eye of the beholder. A bureaucrat's example of micromanagement may be a legislator's example of prudent oversight. An example of such detailed congressional oversight can be found in the area of defense appropriations. The number of mandatory annual financial reports from the Defense Department to the congressional Appropriations and Armed Services Committees jumped from 36 in 1970 to 719 in 1988 (Carter, 1994). Discounting weekends and holidays, this means that the Pentagon must send three required financial reports to some congressional committee or subcommittee every workday.

Trying to oversee administrative actions regarding routine appropriations matters is one thing; trying to oversee actions that the administration seeks to keep secret is another. Congressional oversight of covert operations is a difficult business at best. Beginning in 1974, Congress became increasingly alarmed about secret CIA activities. Many members considered some of these intelligence operations to be questionable both politically and ethically. Members were also distressed at often having to find out about them by reading the newspapers. Perhaps more than any other incident, Congress was alarmed when the *New York Times* disclosed that the CIA had participated in plotting the military overthrow in 1973 of the popularly elected, socialist government of Chile's president Salvadore Allende Gossens. The fact that Allende died during the coup raised the specter of CIA involvement in the assassination of a foreign head of government. Hardly anyone believed the new Chilean junta's story that Allende had killed himself. Congress responded by passing the aforementioned Hughes-Ryan and Clark Amendments, launching several committee investigations of the CIA, creating new intelligence oversight committees in each chamber, and requiring the president to inform eight different congressional committees of any new covert intelligence operations. Executive branch officials complained that informing so many committees was burdensome and an invitation to leaks. By 1980 most in Congress agreed, and the **Intelligence Oversight Act** of that year reduced the reporting requirement to just the Senate and House Intelligence Committees. Restricting information even more, prior notice in extraordinary circumstances can now be provided to just eight individuals, the so-called Gang of Eight: the chairmen and ranking minority members of the two Intelligence Committees, the House Speaker and minority leader, and the majority and minority leaders of the Senate (Holt, 1995).

The efforts to improve oversight have had mixed results. On the one hand, Congress has gained a greater role than it had before the mid-1970s. Hearings such as the Iran-Contra probe have helped Congress to assert its role in the foreign policy process and expose executive attempts to preempt that role (Cole, 1994). Most covert activities have been reported to the oversight committees. And in a few cases, such as a CIA plan to overthrow the leftist government of Suriname in 1983, the committees have been able to block or alter administration plans. On the other hand, the Iran-Contra affair and the U.S.–Vatican efforts to overthrow the government of Poland show the limits on how much Congress can influence a president determined to conduct covert operations (Koh, 1990). It is still very hard for Congress to discover information that the executive does not want it to know. As one member of Congress put it, "you have to be pretty smart to know what the question is that will get the answer you are seeking" (Lindsay, 1990:14).

Congress, for example, did not know of the NSC's illegal diversion of funds to the Contras until reports in newspapers in the Middle East revealed the Iranian part of the operation. Another incident involving Nicaragua was revealed when CIA director William Casey was fulfilling the letter of the law prescribed by the Hughes-Ryan Amendment: In the middle of an hour-long presentation to the Senate Intelligence Committee, Casey made a veiled reference to the planting of explosives in Nicaragua's harbors by his agency. When a member asked him directly if what he had said meant that the CIA was mining harbors, Casey said no. Technically he was correct; the CIA was attaching mines to piers in the harbors, not mining the harbors themselves.

Instances where the executive branch persuades a friendly government to conduct covert activity on its behalf, often in exchange for increased aid or some other favor, are even more difficult for Congress to monitor. This was another method the Reagan administration used to subvert the intent of the Boland Amendment. Congress tried to improve its oversight of this tactic in 1990 by enacting legislation that required the president to inform Congress whenever the executive branch asked a private individual or another government to conduct covert operations on behalf of the United States. President Bush vetoed the measure, however, on the constitutional grounds that it "purports to regulate diplomacy by the president," thereby violating his constitutional authority to negotiate with foreign governments. Bush also rejected the measure on policy grounds, claiming that it would "seriously impair the conduct of our nation's foreign policy."[44] It was just one of several bills that Bush vetoed because, in part, they would have increased Congress's role. However, President Clinton did not veto the Intelligence Authorization Act for Fiscal Year 1994, which required the CIA director to submit annual *declassified* reports to Congress noting both the intelligence community's successes and failures over the past year as well as areas requiring more intelligence attention in the upcoming year. To no one's great surprise, CIA director Woolsey dragged his feet in terms of submitting such declassified reports to Congress. Thus, the oversight process by Congress remains something of a cat-and-mouse game in Washington.

Formal Restraints on Congress

Most of the formal restraints on Congress have all been identified and illustrated in earlier discussions. Several such restraints deserve mention again. One is the president's ability to *veto* legislation. Since George Washington came to office, presidents have vetoed over 1,500 bills; Congress has overridden those vetoes only about 7 percent of the time. More than 1,000 other bills have died by the so-called pocket veto—when Congress passed them and adjourned and then the president refused to sign them, thereby killing the measures. Congress is also restrained by its own *organization.* It is divided into two houses, and its members are elected independent of the control of any national party or congressional caucus. The impact of this organization will be discussed more fully in the next chapter, but the effect is to make it very difficult for Congress to act with speed or unanimity of purpose. In a sense Congress is also restrained by its *limited roles.* The Constitution grants Congress many powers, but it lacks the power to take direct action. Congress can legislate, appropriate, and investigate; but the president can command the military, negotiate with foreign leaders, establish or break diplomatic relations, and take other direct actions. Finally, Congress is also restrained by *judicial review.* The courts can declare actions taken by Congress, as well as those of the president, to be unconstitutional. The judiciary's rejection of the legislative veto process in the *Chadha* case is an example.

INFORMAL POWERS AND CONSTRAINTS

The powers of, and restraints on, Congress, like those of the president, cannot be determined by examining the Constitution and statutory law alone. Congressional powers also derive from, and are limited by, the institution's position within the political system.

Informal Powers

The *power of dissent*—the standing to criticize presidential policy and to advocate alternatives—is the principal informal power of Congress. This ability is rooted in Congress's formal powers, but it goes beyond that. Congress can play a role in setting the political agenda, that is, in deciding what issues are being debated in the political system. Congress also serves as the source of policy alternatives, and this role increases when, as occurred after the 1994 elections, Congress and the White House are controlled by different political parties.

It must be acknowledged, of course, that Congress is at a distinct disadvantage compared to the president as the two struggle for the political spotlight. Congress receives much less coverage by the media than does the president. With Republican control of Congress, the overwhelming attention that the media pays to the president compared to Congress has probably lessened somewhat. The assertive personality of Newt Gingrich, the possibility of Robert Dole being the 1996 Republican presidential nominee, and the often controversial, even outlandish statements of Senate Foreign Relations Committee chairman Jesse Helms have also increased media attention on Congress and, to a degree, its foreign policy views, as discussed in the box entitled, "The GOP Worldview: Newt, Bob, Jesse, and Ben" on pages 236–237. Furthermore, members of Congress are much less well known and frequently less respected by the public than is the president. Nevertheless, it is also the case that Congress provides a public platform for policy discussion inside and outside the chambers that is the single most visible alternative to the president's use of speeches, press conferences, and other public forums to promote his policy views.

Congressional dissent, especially when it comes from the majority party in Congress about the policy of a president of the other party, has an impact partly because of possible legislation or other formal congressional action. There is, however, also an informal aspect to this congressional power of criticism and advocacy. Members of

Congress have access to the media because of their institutional standing. Because the media is especially attracted to controversy, congressional criticism of the president receives at least some attention by the press. This airing of controversy, in turn, has an impact on public opinion, although the specifics are hard to trace.

Congressional dissent also sometimes worries presidents and makes them alter policy in the search for compromise or consensus. Presidents do not always seek consensus, but they prefer to have it if possible. As Kennedy presidential assistant Theodore Sorensen (1963:114) put it, "In the White House, as everywhere, the squeaky wheel gets the grease."

Informal Constraints

More than any single factor, Congress is restrained by the *expectation of presidential foreign policy leadership* that members share with the public. This frequently noted factor rests on the attitude of many that in the "we" versus "they" realm of foreign policy, the chief "we"—that is, the president—should be followed or at least given the benefit of the doubt. Many in Congress and the public accept the idea that dissent at home will

The Republican leadership in Congress differs markedly from the Democratic leadership in the White House, as discussed in the box, "The GOP Worldview: Newt, Bob, Jesse, and Ben." Perhaps the most provocative Republican foreign policy leader is Senator Jesse Helms of North Carolina, pictured here on the left talking with Secretary of State Warren Christopher. Among other differences: Christopher has urged Congress to appropriate considerable foreign aid; Senator Helms claims that funding foreign aid is akin to throwing money down a "rat hole."

weaken the strength of the country's diplomatic stance abroad. Conversely, many believe that bipartisan unity increases the chances of international success. As we have seen, the White House understands that some in Congress value bipartisanship and has been able to use this belief in the value of bipartisanship to its benefit by browbeating opponents into line. "Now the way to do that," former secretary of state Dean Acheson once explained, "is to say that politics stops at the seaboard—and anyone who denies that postulate is a son-of-a-bitch or a crook and not a true patriot. Now, if people will swallow that then you're off to the races" (Paterson, 1979:17).

The tendency of Congress to defer to the president in the field of foreign policy has also led most members of Congress to devote almost all of their attention to domestic affairs. This is the policy realm where members have had considerable experience and are more likely to have a policy impact. Legislators also believe that their work and stands on domestic issues will enhance their chances for reelection more than efforts on foreign policy issues. In a sense, then, the tightest informal restraint on Congress is Congress. It cannot be what it does not aspire to be.

The GOP Worldview: Newt, Bob, Jesse, and Ben

When the votes were counted after the 1994 congressional election, observers concluded that U.S. foreign policy making was about to become a great deal more contentious. The Republicans had captured control of Congress. Beginning in January 1995, a great deal of Congress's foreign policy power came into the hands of four Republicans: Speaker Newt Gingrich (GA); Senate majority leader Robert Dole (KS); Senate Foreign Relations Committee chairman Jesse Helms (NC); and chairman of the House International Relations Committee, Benjamin Gilman (NY). Each of the legislators differs to one degree or another with the foreign policy of President Clinton. Moreover, they were all anxious to place their stamp on policy after many frustrating years in the minority. The House Republicans were also determined to enact the foreign policy clauses of the Contract with America on which they had campaigned.

It did not take long for the barrage of verbal bombs and legislative bills to begin. Measured in vitriol, Helms was the chief cannoneer. He had amassed, as one reporter put it, a "list of pet hates" including "foreign treaties, foreign aid, many foreign countries, and most of the striped-pants experts at the State Department."[1] According to a former senior State Department official in the Reagan administration, Helms "genuinely believes that there are certain people in this world who represent Satan. . . . He sees evil in such things as the United Nations."[2] From this perspective, Helms lashed out at the sins he saw, and news publications were soon running articles with such titles as "Quotes from Chairman Helms." Among the more notable: Much of foreign aid is "going down foreign rat holes;" there should be a "surgical" operation to decapitate Fidel Castro; the Israel-Syria peace process is a "fraud"; Haitian president Jean Bertrand Aristide is "a murderer."[3] Such remarks were decidedly undiplomatic, but Helms and his supporters defended them as forthright. "He's scary because he shoots straight," said a Helms aide.[4]

Perhaps, but one Helms fusillade in November 1994 was so wildly fired that it nearly killed his chances of becoming chairman of the Committee on Foreign Relations. A journalist asked Helms whether he thought Clinton was "up to the job" of com-

mander in chief. "No, I do not," the senator replied, "and neither do the people in the armed forces." That observation paled in comparison to his comment three days later on November 22, the anniversary of the assassination of President John F. Kennedy. Helms said that the president was so unpopular in North Carolina because of his supposed draft-dodging during the Vietnam War, his support of having homosexuals in the military, and his defense budget cuts that "Mr. Clinton had better watch out if he comes down here. He better have a bodyguard." Whatever prompted the senator's salvo, the return fire questioned everything from his grasp of constitutional relationship to his sanity; it was so devastating that he was forced to retreat. "I made a mistake . . . which I shall not repeat," he soon admitted.[5]

Speaker Gingrich's initiation into a position of true power in the foreign policy arena was equally quotable, if less acerbic. Critics have called his style "grenade-throwing," and he did toss some explosive ideas about in the early going. These included suggesting international recognition of Taiwan and its membership in the UN. Other things that Gingrich advocated, such as defense spending restraints while pursuing a strong national defense, seemed puzzling. "I'm a hawk, but I'm a cheap hawk," Gingrich commented in an unsuccessful attempt to clear up what to most seemed contradictory stands.[6]

While Gingrich's comments were less bombastic than those of Helms, they made more of an impact because of the widespread perception that the new Speaker had taken command of policy making in Washington. One indication was the cover of Germany's widely read magazine, *Der Spiegel,* which featured a photo of Gingrich encaptioned "America's Surrogate President?" The president himself gave further substance to the Speaker's power when Clinton was moved to observe during a press conference that he, as president, was still "relevant" in Washington.

The arrival of the new and powerful Speaker and the other Republicans on the scene also unsettled the diplomatic community. "The [foreign diplomats] who troop into my office are scared to death of " Gingrich," one senior administration official was heard to comment. "Newt represents thoughts and behavior they're not accustomed to. Shooting from the hip and diplomacy do not fit together naturally." This purported lack of fit has led to a variety of responses. "Listening to the Speaker is very stimulating business," commented British foreign secretary Douglas Hurd with exemplary English restraint. Other foreign observers were less reticent about the Speaker. One Hong Kong daily newspaper, *Wen Wei Po,* described Gingrich as "notorious for speaking nonsense," and Iranian officials portrayed the Speaker as lacking "mental balance" and being an "imbecile."[7]

The remaining two legislative members of the congressional foreign quadrumvirate, Senator Dole and Representative Gilman, have been less acute in their public remarks. The Senator has longer experience than his colleagues near the pinnacle of power, including an earlier stint as majority leader. His predilections make him a politician who values pragmatic compromise rather than principled stalemate; he is, as one biography subtitle portrays him, "The Republicans' Man for All Seasons" (Thompson, 1994). Moreover, as does Gingrich, Dole both believes in presidential prerogative in foreign policy and, as a potential president himself, is wary of restricting the current president in ways that might bind him if he should attain the Oval Office. That almost certainly was why he supported President Clinton's authority to decide unilaterally to dispatch U.S. troops to Bosnia.

Gilman is the least well known of the GOP foreign policy team. He criticizes Clinton's foreign policy leadership as projecting "instead of a strong steady signal, . . . a series of waving notes sounded by an uncertain trumpet."[8] Apart from such thematic rhetoric, though, Gilman is, by Helms's standards, a moderate who supports the Israel-Syria peace talks and is less critical of the UN than is his Senate counterpart.

For all the attention paid to Helms, Gingrich, and the others, and while their impact on foreign policy is still uncertain, it will be less than the exaggerated post-1994 election reports that elevated the Speaker to surrogate president. Despite some shaky moments, Bill Clinton is still the most relevant foreign policy player in Washington, if not in the world.

Several factors promote this. Helms lost considerable credibility due to his ill-founded remarks, and his rhetorical profile has been much lower since. Dole clearly repudiated Helms for his remarks on Clinton, saying that "In my view the president's welcome to any state."[9] Gingrich added his voice of rebuke, declaring that "All Americans welcome and honor the presidency."[10] Moreover, Dole does not support many of Helms's strong positions. And beyond this, the chairman is further restrained by moderate Republicans on his committee, including Dole's Kansas colleague Nancy Kassenbaum and Indiana's Richard Lugar (a former chairman of the committee). On top of all this, the Senate is usually a more deliberate body than the House, and most of the foreign policy clauses of the Contract with America that were passed in the lower chamber remained stalled in various Senate committees throughout 1995. It may be worth noting what a former committee staff member said about Senator Helms, "He will pitch a fit and make a stink about a lot of things, but on the big things, he rarely prevails."[11]

Gingrich's impact on foreign policy is more problematic. His chief of staff has compared him to stalwart Winston Churchill, Egypt's courageous Anwar Sadat, and has even suggested that "Newt is a tad like Gandhi."[12] Happily, the Speaker is a bit less impressed with himself. He has learned that those in power often need to speak with more care, and, in some cases, he has backed away from policy pronouncements that proved too provocative. For instance he now says, "I don't think we should recognize Taiwan." Moreover, Gingrich has learned to heed the limitations of his experience and interests. "I don't do foreign policy," he concedes, estimating that the percentage of the time he spends on domestic policy compared to foreign policy is "ninety-ten." About his foreign policy role the Speaker says, "I don't know. . . . I'm still learning. I don't mind saying that on the record."[13] That is well, because as John Kennedy wrote in a speech he meant to deliver in Dallas on November 22, 1963, "Leadership and learning are indispensable to each other."

1. At times, the U.S. Congress acts as if it were two different organizations. There is *Congress Combative,* aggressively using its powers. At other times we see *Congress Compliant,* shying away from using its powers.

2. The combative Congress is well illustrated by its role in forcing U.S. presidents to end American participation in the Vietnam War. The compliant Congress is illustrated by the lack of *meaningful* congressional involvement in the decision to commit U.S. forces to liberate Kuwait.

3. The formal foreign policy powers granted to Congress by the Constitution are impressive and include the power to declare war, to ratify treaties by a two-thirds vote of the Senate, to confirm the appointment of high executive branch officials by a majority Senate vote, to enact the legislation that becomes the law of the land, and to appropriate the money necessary for the government to operate. Although not explicitly granted in the Constitution, the powers to conduct investigations and to oversee the actions of the executive branch date back to the earliest days of the republic. But Congress utilizes each of these formal powers inconsistently.

4. Congress has been reluctant to use its power to declare war. As a result, presidents have gradually assumed more and more of the war power. Congress tried in 1973 to recapture its war making powers by passing the War Powers Resolution. But it has been routinely ignored by presidents, and few in Congress have been willing to try to enforce it.

5. The Senate's role in ratifying treaties also presents a mixed picture. Treaties are usually ratified, but they are often shaped to the Senate's liking in order to facilitate ratification. Often presidents rely on executive agreements with other regimes rather than face the uncertainties of the Senate ratification process.

6. Senate confirmation of appointments reveals a similar process in which the legislative role may be fairly subtle. While most nominees get approved, presidents take senatorial sentiments into account when making nominations to important foreign policy posts.

7. In policy making, Congress has two great pillars of authority. The first is the power to legislate, by which Congress can establish policy if it wishes.

8. The second source of congressional authority is the power to appropriate the money needed for government operations.

9. As an extension of the legislative and appropriations power, Congress has power to investigate. This often leads it into clashes with the president, who will often try to avoid congressional scrutiny by classifying information as secret or invoking executive privilege.

10. In addition to these formal powers, Congress has formal restraints. Presidents can veto legislation. Also, Congress is limited by the fragmentation of power within it and by the fact that the judiciary may rule its actions unconstitutional.

11. Informally, Congress enjoys the power of dissent, the role of institutional critic of the administration. Congress is also restrained informally by its own expectation that it is the president's job, not Congress's, to be the leader in foreign policy.

Chapter Nine

THE PRESIDENT AND CONGRESS

The old adage that some things are equal to more than the sum of their parts holds true for the foreign policy process. In the last two chapters, we looked at two institutional actors: the presidency and Congress. To understand the roles of these institutions, however, it is necessary to do more than just consider their respective formal and informal powers and the restraints on them in isolation. As the previous two chapters illustrate, much of what happens in the foreign policy process cannot be explained adequately by focusing on either branch in isolation. Presidents make treaties; the Senate can modify, delay, or defeat them. Presidents appoint executive officials; the Senate can reject nominations. Presidents have wide discretionary authority as chief executives to make program and spending decisions; Congress can pass specific legislation and has the power of the purse. Even when it legislates and appropriates, Congress may face a presidential veto. Moreover, once a program is enacted, the discretion that the executive has to implement it may modify congressional intent. For these reasons, this chapter will focus on the foreign policy making interaction between the presidency and Congress.

The reality of presidential and congressional foreign policy power is that the vast majority of it falls in the realm of what are called *shared powers*. These powers involve the interaction of the president, Congress, and other participants in the foreign policy process, especially when one or more of these actors have the legal authority to involve themselves. As we shall see, shared power is a complex subject that varies greatly over time and circumstance. Congress, as we have seen, possesses no unilateral power. In fact, as one scholar has observed, "To study one branch of government in isolation from the others is usually an exercise in make-believe" (Fisher, 1993:ix).

HISTORICAL SHIFTS IN FOREIGN POLICY POWER

Some aspects of shared power in areas such as treaties and appointments have already been examined. These discussions, however, do not fully capture the ebb and flow of presidential and congressional foreign policy power. As we have noted repeatedly, legal authority and the actual ability to do things are different. Some of this variation is accounted for by the informal powers and restraints discussed in the previous two chapters. These variations and others make it clear to those who study the foreign policy process that *power is dynamic.* Who can do what, and when they can do it, is not constant. Rather, power changes in two ways. First, there have been changes related to the overall growth (or decline) of power exercised by the president, Congress, or any other actor in the foreign policy process over the course of U.S. history. Second, there have been and continue to be shifts in the balance of relative power among the actors or coalitions of actors. Inasmuch as political power is a key determinant of which policy is adopted, this chapter will begin by reviewing the history of the growth of the overall and relative foreign policy power of the president and of Congress. Then the chapter will turn its focus to the specific dynamics of the relative power between the president and Congress.

Overall Growth of Foreign Policy Power

One of the most striking aspects of U.S. political history is the rapid growth in the size of the federal government and the scope of its activity. Washington now spends considerably more each day than it spent the year that Franklin Roosevelt first took office in 1933! The original 4 Cabinet departments have increased to 14. Each represents a new or increased area of federal activity; more than half of these agencies did not exist when FDR became president. This expansion of the scope of governmental activity has involved international as well as domestic activity, and the result is that the overall foreign policy activity and authority of both the president and Congress have expanded over the years.

The Overall Growth of Presidential Power

When George Washington assumed the presidency, the United States was a weak country with only limited diplomatic activity. This changed slowly, and then during the twentieth century, and particularly since World War II, the United States became a world power. As U.S. power and international activity expanded, there were parallel increases in the foreign policy activity and power of the president. One can imagine that President Washington would be amazed and awed by the mighty military machine at the president's command and by the billions of dollars in aid, trade incentives, and other economic instruments that a modern president can utilize to pursue foreign policy goals.

George Washington would also be surprised by the range of presidential action in foreign policy. Interdependence among countries has increased the scope of presidential power. Bill Clinton and other recent presidents have been able, for example, to use the lure of most-favored-nation trade status or the strong influence of the United States on such international economic organizations as the IMF to attempt to affect the foreign and even domestic policy of Russia, China, and many other countries.

Technology has also vastly enhanced presidential power. Modern communications and travel, combined with the U.S. global role, have involved modern presidents much more closely in the ongoing diplomatic process. When Woodrow Wilson sailed to France for the Versailles Conference in 1919, it was the first time in the 130 years of the presidency that a chief executive had ventured overseas while in office. Richard Nixon went on his first official visit to Europe after only 33 days as president. George Bush raised the personal diplomacy of presidents to new levels. He departed for Asia soon after his inauguration; he held 135 meetings with foreign leaders in Washington or foreign capitals during his first year in office; and he made such a regular practice of picking up the telephone and calling other countries' leaders that his style was dubbed "Rolodex diplomacy." Even Bill Clinton, who began his term in office trying to deemphasize foreign policy, was rapidly caught up in the regular interaction of international leaders. Within a day of his election, Clinton was in phone contact with Russian president Boris N. Yeltsin and other leaders, and the president-elect met with the president of Mexico. During the first 90 days of his presidency, the British and Israeli prime ministers and several other leaders journeyed to Washington to meet with Clinton. He, in turn, flew to Vancouver, Canada, to meet with Russia's president and with Canada's prime minister. Since then, Clinton has become a regular world traveler, visiting France, Great Britain, Italy, Russia, Belarus, the Czech Republic, Japan, South Korea, Israel, Jordan, Syria, Indonesia, Ireland, and other countries. The flow of other heads of government, foreign ministers, and other foreign officials through the White House is almost continuous.

The Overall Growth of Congressional Power

The foreign policy power of Congress has also grown. One indication of this growth is the sharp rise in congressional activity. Representative Joseph Martin (R-MA), who served as Speaker of the House (1947–1949, 1953–1955), captured the changes in his autobiography, *My First Fifty Years in Politics*. When he arrived in Washington in the 1920s, Martin (1978:49) recalled, "foreign affairs were an inconsequential problem in Congress." "For one week" in that earlier era, he remembered, "the House

Advances in communications and transportation technology have increased presidential power over the course of U.S. history. Presidents are able to exercise much more control over diplomacy because they can now negotiate personally by telephone and meet easily with foreign leaders. This ability to act, literally, as the chief U.S. diplomat is illustrated here. In September 1995 President Clinton, in the center, met at the White House with, from left to right, King Hussein of Jordan, Prime Minister Yitzhak Rabin of Israel, Chairman Yasser Arafat of the Palestine Liberation Organization, and President Hosni Mubarak of Egypt. Just six weeks later, President Clinton traveled to the Middle East to attend the funeral of the assassinated prime minister Rabin.

Foreign Affairs Committee debated to the exclusion of all other matters the question of authorizing a $20,000 appropriation for an international poultry show in Tulsa. This item, which we finally approved, was about the most important issue that came before the committee in the whole session." Over the years, according to Martin, the atmosphere changed because of "the immense pressure that came with the Depression, World War II, [the war in] Korea, and the cold war." By the time Martin left Congress it was making decisions on multibillion-dollar foreign aid packages, defense budgets in the hundreds of billions of dollars, important alliance and arms control treaties, and a host of other weighty foreign policy issues. In fact, just the foreign aid budget alone means that the now renamed House International Relations Committee authorizes funds at a rate of more than $20,000 a minute. It is unlikely, then, that a mere $20,000 appropriation would even be mentioned, much less debated for a week.

Shifts in the Relative Power: The President and Congress

The fact that over time the foreign policy powers of both the president and Congress have increased significantly does not mean that they have expanded equally. In fact they have not. Even though Congress is arguably the most powerful legislature in the world, presidential power during this century has grown even faster than has the power of Congress (Pfiffner, 1991). The reasons are myriad for the differing growth rates, but the Constitution provides a good beginning to understand the uneven historical growth of relative power. While chapter 7 detailed some of the reasons for the growth in presidential power, the sources for the relative weakness of Congress compared to the presidency have yet to be explored.

The Constitution: An Invitation to Struggle

The decision of the delegates to the Constitutional Convention in Philadelphia in 1787 to establish and empower Congress in Article I and to create and enable the executive branch in Article II was not random choice. The order reflected what the majority of delegates expected and desired the relative standing of the two institutions to be. Under the first U.S. constitution (the Articles of Confederation), there was no executive at all. That arrangement did not work well. The delegates who drafted the second U.S. constitution wished to create an executive with some strength. At the same time, however, the Philadelphia delegates took pains to avoid the impression that they were creating the equivalent of an American monarch.

The Constitution contains many countervailing powers, called checks and balances, between the branches of government. It is also true that the Constitution is often vague as to the meaning of its clauses. The combination of countervailing powers and vagueness has created what one scholar called "an invitation to struggle." The president and Congress have struggled for power throughout U.S. history.

The intended constitutional order that placed Congress in the preeminent position did not, however, continue unchanged for very long. There are several reasons. One is that the main body of the Constitution is short and often vague because, among other reasons, the delegates were frequently unable to agree on specifics. It is for this reason that the Constitution has been called a "bundle of compromises."

A second reason for change in the relative power of the legislative and executive branches is that the delegates created a system of checks and balances. These were designed to prevent any branch from seizing total power. The checks and balances did that. At the same time, though, they also created a tension between the branches and an ebb and flow of authority as the upper hand shifted back and forth between the presidency and Congress.

Experience is a third cause of change in constitutional usage. This was anticipated by the delegates. According to James Madison, writing in *Federalist* No. 37, "All new laws, though penned with the greatest technical skill and passed on the fullest and most mature deliberations are considered as more or less obscure and equivocal until their meaning be liquidated and ascertained by a series of particular discussions and adjudications."

The delegates' desire to avoid creating a president that could aspire to monarchical power, on the one hand, and their desire to avoid the deficiencies of the Articles of Confederation by establishing a viable and vigorous executive, on the other hand, led the Constitution's drafters to equivocate in the language of Article II. Presidential scholar Edwin Corwin (1957:3) has characterized this article as "the most loosely drawn chapter of the Constitution." We will see, for example, that the designation of the president as commander in chief, especially in relation to the language in Article I that specifies that it is Congress that declares war, remains a source of uncertainty and conflict within the constitutional system. The result of the compromises, imprecision, and checks and balances in the Constitution, Corwin has suggested, was to create an "invitation to struggle." It was a challenge that was soon met and that has continued during a 200-year-old battle for political power (Skownokek, 1993).

Relative Power Shifts: 1787 to World War II

During the first century of U.S. constitutional history, the relative power of the presidency and Congress ebbed and flowed. Congress normally dominated. There were, however, strong presidents, such as Thomas Jefferson, Andrew Jackson, and Abraham Lincoln, who asserted their office's authority forcefully. There were also times of crisis, such as the Civil War, that added important precedents to presidential power. Even strong presidents, though, had trouble controlling Congress consistently. The first three presidents, Washington, Adams, and Jefferson, left office bruised, battered, and bitter over their feuds with Congress concerning foreign affairs. Then, after each strong president or time of peril, normalcy returned.

What is normal began to change, however. The balance of power shifted slowly toward a permanently stronger presidency. When Theodore Roosevelt became president in 1901, the United States was evolving into a truly powerful and internationally active country. These changes gave presidents more opportunities to assert themselves on a wider range of foreign policy issues.

Roosevelt epitomized many of the changes in presidential attitudes that would help shape that office's role in the years to come. First, he was an aggressive internationalist. "The increasing interdependence and complexity of international political and economic relations render it incumbent on all civilized and orderly powers to insist on the proper policing of the world," he told Congress in 1902 (Jones, 1988:277).

Second, Roosevelt advocated expanded presidential power. He proclaimed the so-called *stewardship theory*. The president argued that as the only official chosen by all the people, each president "was a steward of the people bound actively and affirmatively to do all he could for the people" (Edwards & Wayne, 1985:7). Moreover, Roosevelt asserted that his power was not limited to what the Constitution specifically said a president *could do*. Instead, he held that presidents had the authority to do anything that the Constitution did not specify that they *could not do*.

Roosevelt combined internationalism and broad presidential authority to play a foreign policy role that was unprecedented, especially in peacetime. When, for instance, the Senate refused to ratify a treaty he had negotiated with the Dominican Republic, Roosevelt signed an executive agreement putting the proposed treaty's provisions into effect. Over the objection of Congress, Roosevelt dispatched the fleet on an around-the-world cruise to demonstrate U.S. power. He engineered the Panamanian revolution and began building the canal there, sponsored the Algeciras Conference to resolve a dispute between France and Germany over Morocco, and hosted the Portsmouth (New Hampshire) Conference that ended the Russo-Japanese War. All of this and more, Roosevelt boasted, he had done "without consultation with anyone, for when a matter is of capital importance, it is well to have it handled by one man only" (Paterson, Clifford, & Hagan, 1995a:251).

The principles of internationalism and broad presidential power were not, however, established firmly by Roosevelt. Some presidents were restrained. Not surprisingly, for a man who was happier as chief justice of the Supreme Court than he had been as president, William Howard Taft rejected the stewardship theory on the grounds that legitimate presidential authority could come only from a "specific grant of power . . . either in the federal Constitution or in an act of Congress" (Edwards & Wayne, 1985:7).

By contrast, Woodrow Wilson was both an internationalist and a proponent of broad presidential power. He took the position that the new reality of U.S. strength meant that the country would "henceforth, be one of the great powers of the world." This status, Wilson continued, meant that the president would be "of necessity" a global leader. "We have but begun to see the presidential office in this light," he concluded, "but it is the light which will more and more beat upon it, and more and more determine its character and effect upon the politics of the nation" (Link, 1965:8).

Wilson's views did not, however, prevail immediately. After World War I, the country reverted for 2 decades to general isolationism. Wilson's effort to include the country in the League of Nations was defeated when the Senate rejected the Treaty of Versailles. The relative foreign policy power of the president ebbed, while that of Congress flowed during the terms of Presidents Warren Harding, Calvin Coolidge, and Herbert Hoover.

Foreign Policy Power: World War II through Vietnam

There was a distinct change in the foreign policy roles of the president and Congress in the period between the U.S. entry into World War II and Vietnam (Biggs, 1991). The early and closely fought contests over power between the president and Congress quieted. Presidential strength grew. When Franklin D. Roosevelt entered office in 1933, Congress was a guardian of the relatively isolationist U.S. stance during the interwar years. As the threat from Germany and the other Axis powers grew in the aftermath of the outbreak of World War II in 1939, FDR edged cautiously toward more and more overt aid to Great Britain and other beleaguered allied powers. Still, it took the bombing of Pearl Harbor by Japan, more than two years later, to overcome congressional resistance to American participation in the war.

World War II and the cold war ushered in a new era of foreign policy making. Cowed by continuing crisis and by self-doubt and caught up in the anticommunist consensus, Congress willingly let the president make unilateral decisions and even granted him emergency and other discretionary powers to act alone. As a result, the president gained permanent preeminence in the foreign policy process. There is, as we shall see, considerable debate about the extent of presidential dominance. But there can be little doubt that during the 1940s, 1950s, and 1960s, relative power flowed toward the White House and away from Capitol Hill. Congress has regained some of its former role since then, but the president remains the key actor.

Increased Congressional Deference Fear, a congressional inferiority complex, and the anticommunist consensus are the three main factors that persuaded Congress to acquiesce to increased presidential authority. *Fear* of communism linked with the military might of the Soviet Union was the first factor that produced bipartisan congressional deference to the president. It is difficult for students today to grasp the anxiety that gripped Americans, especially from the late 1940s into the 1960s. Americans feared that the Soviet Union—with its massive conventional and nuclear arms, with its allies stretching from East Germany to China, and with its alien communist ideology—could eventually encircle and endanger the United States. "After World War II, Senator J. William Fulbright (D-AR) later remembered, "we were sold on the idea that Stalin was out to dominate the world." Once the Soviets exploded their first atomic bomb in 1949, the perceived peril of immediate nuclear destruction intensified American fear to, at times, near hysteria levels. In line with the presidential model discussed in chapter 6, most members of Congress believed that only the president could supply the decisive, quick decisions necessary to counter this perceived global communist danger.

This anxiety played an especially important part in enhancing the president's role as commander in chief and his ability to use military force without a declaration of war or other congressional authorization. Even beyond purely military questions, however, the urge for bipartisan cooperation was enhanced by the popular theory that foreign policy success required that "politics stop at the water's edge." The "yielding of some of our democratic control of foreign affairs is the price that we may have to pay for greater physical security" is how one eminent diplomatic historian explained it at the time (Paterson, Clifford, & Hagan, 1995b:303, 305).[1]

A congressional *inferiority complex* was the second reason for increased legislative deference during the cold war era. The close identification of foreign policy with national security policy during the cold war led many in Congress to feel that they did not have the institutional expertise to challenge information or advice that was available to the president through experts in the Departments of Defense and State, the Central Intelligence Agency (CIA), the National Security Council (NSC), and other specialized agencies. All too typically, when Lyndon Johnson sent the U.S. military to the Dominican Republic to protect the military junta there against a supposed communist rebel threat, one member of Congress lamented that he could not protest because he did not know "what is really going on. . . . What do you say," the legislator asked, "when they [executive branch officials] say the Dominican Republic is being taken over by Communists? I looked at 58 names [of supposed communists] too, but they meant nothing to me" (Fenno, 1973:30).

The anticommunist *consensus* among Americans that Soviet-led communism was evil and a terrible threat that the United States was compelled to confront everywhere is the third factor that propagated increased congressional deference. There was general support among legislators and the American public for the containment doctrine. Recall from the models discussed in chapter 6 that status quo situations in which policy is incremental tend to favor policy making by either the presidential or the administrative model. Thus, as long as the status quo, anticommunist consensus held together, and as long as the president followed incremental containment policies, most members of Congress had little reason to challenge them. Members of both political parties in Congress rallied behind the anticommunist policies of Presidents Truman, Eisenhower, and Kennedy. This produced an era (from the 1940s into the 1960s) of at least limited **bipartisanship**, in which Democrats and Republicans often cooperated on foreign policy within the boundaries of the anticommunist consensus.

Debate over the Degree of Congressional Deference While scholars agree that Congress was unusually deferential to the executive branch between World War II and the Vietnam War, they disagree over how much of a back seat Congress took. This varying estimate of the degree of deference affects, in turn, evaluations of how radical a change occurred during and after the Vietnam War when Congress reasserted its authority. The greater the earlier deference, the more significant the post-Vietnam change. The two schools of thought can be respectively termed the conventional wisdom and the revisionist points of view.

The *conventional wisdom* view is held by scholars who contend that Congress was deeply deferential during the era of bipartisanship that lasted from the 1940s through the late 1960s. Such scholars regard the period after World War II as an era of virtually unrestrained presidential control of foreign policy. Writing near the end of this period, Aaron Wildavsky (1966) formulated the theory of the two presidencies, as discussed in chapter 6, that depicted two distinctly different presidencies: a domestic presidency, in which the president had to fight Congress tooth and nail for control of policy, and a foreign policy presidency, in which the president got virtually anything he wanted from Congress. Studies confirmed Wildavsky's thesis and also found that, overall, presidents had a higher success rate with Congress during this quarter century than they had before it, or have had since then (Carter, 1986). The Tonkin Gulf Resolution (1964) symbolized the deference of Congress during this period. With just two dissenting votes, Congress authorized the president to take whatever action he deemed necessary to protect American interests in Southeast Asia. The Vietnam War followed; Congress later regretted and repealed the resolution.

This photograph of President Clinton and his reflected image symbolizes the "theory of the two presidencies." This theory, which scholars continue to debate, suggests that the president has considerably more power to make foreign policy than to make domestic policy.

Scholars who propound the *revisionist interpretation* contend that the conventional wisdom about Congress during the cold war underestimates the role that legislators continued to play and oversimplifies the complex interactions between the two branches. According to this view, there were factors that restrained Congress. But revisionists maintain that it is inaccurate to characterize Congress as a passive player in the foreign policy process during the period from the end of World War II through the war in Vietnam.

Revisionists point to instances in this period when congressional desires and actions had important consequences on foreign policy. After World War II, for example, Congress favored giving aid to the regime of Spain's Generalissimo Francisco Franco. Truman was bitterly opposed to supporting Spain because the Franco government was fascist and, while officially neutral, had tilted toward the Axis powers during World War II. What mattered to many members of Congress, however, was that Franco was a staunch anticommunist. Therefore, Congress sought to give foreign aid to Spain in return for its allowing the establishment of U.S. air and naval bases to help contain possible Soviet military expansion in Europe. Despite Truman's active opposition, Congress kept pushing until the administration gave in and made the bases-for-aid deal.

The marked anticommunist sentiment in Congress also played a subtle role in getting the United States involved in the Vietnam War. During the late 1950s, many members in Congress pressed the Eisenhower administration to abandon its policy of "massive retaliation," which relied on nuclear weapons to help contain communist expansion. The House and Senate Armed Services Committees became forums for those endorsing a more flexible approach to national security that would include, among other things, more counterinsurgency and irregular warfare capabilities designed to fight and defeat communist insurgencies in less developed countries (Carter, 1991). This new capability, in turn, paved the way for President Kennedy to test flexible response by sending thousands of U.S. military advisers to South Vietnam (Lomperis, 1993). Attacks on those advisers led to larger numbers of U.S. troops, who took on an increasingly direct combat role, which led to more American casualties, to more troops, and so on in a bloody spiral.

The Vietnam Era of Congressional Resurgence

Whatever the exact balance of executive-legislative foreign policy making power, it shifted anew during the period marked by the U.S. armed intervention in the war in Vietnam (1964–1973) and by the disclosures of illegal activity by the president (the Watergate scandal) that forced the resignation of Richard Nixon in 1974. During this period, Congress asserted its authority with increasing vigor. Based on their differing views of the degree of earlier congressional deference, scholars of the conventional wisdom and revisionist schools of thought would disagree on whether the upsurge in legislative activism was, respectively, revolutionary or incremental. All would agree, however, that congressional activity and influence in the foreign policy process increased.

Events in the international system and shifts in the attitudes of Americans combined to bring about change. By the mid-1960s, the cold war consensus was beginning to fragment. Both superpowers had been frightened by the 1962 Cuban missile crisis. Each sought to reduce tensions with the other thereafter, and the fruits of this effort included a period of "détente" extending from the mid-1960s to the mid-1970s. If the United States and the USSR could get along, Americans began to wonder why it was necessary to fight communist expansion in Vietnam? Furthermore, the increasingly obvious split between the USSR and China ended the myth of the unified, global communist threat. The easing of anticommunist fervor also made Americans more sensitive to the corrupt and abusive nature of the various South Vietnamese regimes that the United States was trying to support.

The horror of the war in Vietnam also became more personal to most Americans than any previous war because for the first time television brought the images of death and destruction into American living rooms. The mounting death toll of U.S. troops was the primary concern that turned many Americans against the war, but the devastation of Indochina and its people also strengthened the opposition of many. Frustration was yet another factor that added to the mounting antiwar sentiment. As the war ground on, it became ever more obvious that victory was nowhere in sight, despite dispatching a half-million troops to South Vietnam and despite expending uncountable tons of ordnance on North and South Vietnam. Administration officials assured the public that the end of the war, the light at the end of the tunnel, was visible. Antiwar protesters answered that the light at the end of the tunnel was a train coming from the other direction.

The Vietnam War's impact on American politics was profound. It forced President Johnson to announce that he would not seek reelection in 1968. The war also weakened Americans' faith in the presidency. Members of Congress and many other citizens felt that Presidents Johnson and Nixon and some of their respective staff members had misused their powers, had sometimes lied to gain congressional and public support, and had made serious policy mistakes. If the executive branch was capable of such malevolence and malfeasance, there was no longer any political reason for members of Congress to defer to it. Then President Nixon fell victim to his own character flaws. Watergate came to symbolize a host of illegal and unethical activities being directed by the White House. Not only was Nixon forced to resign, but the presidency itself fell into considerable disrepute.

All of this reinforced the impact of the easing of the cold war and the anxieties associated with it. The improving relations between the United States and both the Soviet Union and China lessened Congress's sense of danger and increased legislative assertiveness. The result of war and of the ebbing of the bipolar era undermined the cold war consensus, thus further emboldening Congress. Ronald Reagan tried to resurrect the consensus briefly during the early 1980s, but the effort was short-lived and—in the end—unsuccessful. In the meantime, a reassertive Congress had set out to reclaim at least some of its rightful role in foreign policy making.

Foreign Policy Power after Vietnam

During the 1970s, Congress acted strongly to reinvigorate its role in the foreign policy process. Congressional challenges to executive branch primacy were initially related to the war in Indochina (Briggs, 1991). In 1970 Congress repealed the Tonkin Gulf Resolution and passed the Cooper-Church Amendment forbidding U.S. combat activities in Cambodia. The War Powers Resolution followed in 1973.

Congressional challenges to the president soon spread to other issues. The year 1974 saw Congress cut off arms shipments to Turkey over the president's objections; pass the previously mentioned Jackson-Vanik Amendment, linking most-favored-nation trade status to the Soviet Union's willingness to allow more Jews to emigrate; and enact the Hughes-Ryan Amendment, forcing the president to inform congressional intelligence committees of covert operations. Congress approved the Clark Amendment in 1976 prohibiting the CIA from assisting anti-Marxist factions in the Angolan Civil War. In 1978 the Senate nearly scuttled the Panama Canal Neutrality Treaty by insisting on the U.S. right to reopen the canal by force if it were shut down in the future. The first of the Boland Amendments was passed in 1982, prohibiting the use of government funds for the purpose of overthrowing the government of Nicaragua. A final example came in 1986 when Congress overrode a presidential veto and imposed economic sanctions on the government of South Africa.

All of these, and other actions that are discussed in chapter 8, placed congressional restrictions on presidential activity, increased the requirements for the executive to report to Congress, and otherwise tried to narrow the relative power gap between the president and Congress (Adler, 1988). Furthermore, as explained in chapter 1, scholars, the press, and the public greeted the changes as needed reforms in light of the abuses of executive authority associated with the Vietnam War and the Watergate scandal. So strong was the congressional resurgence that it seemed to some scholars at the time as a "revolution that will not be unmade" (Franck & Weisband, 1979:6).

Such estimates of a permanent, radical shift in the balance of foreign policy power between the executive branch and Congress proved to be overstated for three reasons. First, since the role of Congress during the 1950s and 1960s was not quite as weak as some scholars estimate, the shift in the 1970s was not quite as large as it seemed to some observers. Second, many of the actions taken by Congress during the 1970s have proven to be little more than symbolic gestures that have done little in practice to restrain the executive. The earlier discussions of the War Powers Resolution show clearly, for example, that Congress has failed, for the most part, in its attempt to restrain the president's war powers. The Executive Agreements Act has also been largely ignored. Evidence indicates that the executive branch has violated the Hughes-Ryan Amendment on more than one occasion, and the Clark Amendment was repealed. Third, the level of congressional activism has waned somewhat from its peak in the 1970s (Hinckley, 1994; Peterson, 1994a).

There were several reasons for the ebb of congressional assertiveness from its high-tide mark. Congress's activism in the 1970s assuaged its institutional ego, and the intensity of the political reaction to Vietnam and Watergate faded with time. Members of Congress, as well as the country in general, reacted negatively to the rather tepid leadership of Presidents Gerald Ford and Jimmy Carter, and the urge for stronger executive leadership reemerged. Ronald Reagan provided it, and Congress returned to its dominant domestic focus.

None of this means that Congress has lapsed into inactivity or irrelevance in the foreign policy process. One important lesson that can be drawn from examining the history of, and the unresolved scholarly debates about, the ebb and flow of relative power exercised by Congress and the president is that congressional-executive interactions on foreign policy are not easily measured or categorized. As Figure 9.1 shows, congressional foreign policy behavior over time sometimes complies with what the president wishes to do and sometimes rejects it. At other times, Congress resists executive initiatives or takes independent action. In these cases, compromise with the executive on foreign policy direction is a common outcome. It is evident that compliant behavior had declined markedly by the Kennedy administration and ebbed even further by the Reagan years, while rejection, resistance, and independence have fluctuated less uniformly. What can be said about the patterns during the Vietnam and post-Vietnam periods is that they show a Congress that wants to play a significant role in foreign policy making, sometimes challenges an administration, yet does not try to take fundamental foreign policy responsibility away from the president.

In general, then, the pattern of congressional activity since the presidency of Franklin Roosevelt can be said to be (1) secondary to that of the president, yet (2) of continuing importance, while (3) ebbing and flowing substantially relative to presidential power. Given these shifts, the next significant question is: What factors determine the respective levels of congressional and executive activity and influence in

FIGURE 9.1   Congressional Foreign Policy Behavior Types by Administrations, 1946–1982

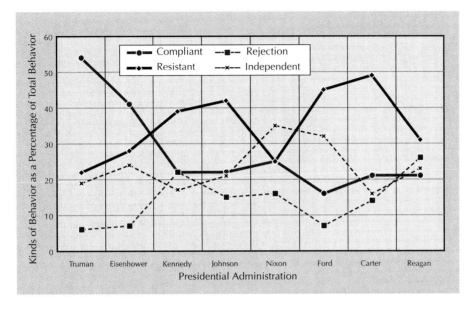

Source: Carter (1986), Table 2.

This figure shows how congressional foreign policy behavior has exhibited both acquiescence and assertiveness over the years. On some issues, Congress gives the president exactly what he wants; on others, Congress resists or rejects the president's proposals; on yet other issues, Congress sets policy independently.

foreign policy making? Before answering this question, however, it is worthwhile to note that the courts also have a say in the foreign policy process. That role is discussed briefly in the box "The Courts and Foreign Policy."

FACTORS THAT DETERMINE SHIFTS OF RELATIVE POWER

Before examining the determinants of the relative power of the president and Congress, it is important to stress that foreign policy making is often a very political process. It is important to remember that, contrary to the popular image of a dominant presidency, the president's power rises and falls over time and according to issues and situations. Presidents themselves often bemoan the limits of their office and sometimes use an image of prison or some other form of servitude to depict their sense of being trapped rather than in charge. George Washington compared his feelings of taking up the seat of power as "not unlike those of a culprit who is going to the place of execution." Woodrow Wilson characterized the president as "a superior kind of slave," and his successor, Warren G. Harding, once exclaimed, "The White House is a prison. . . . I am in jail."[2] The current White

(Continued on next page)

The Courts and Foreign Policy

Compared to the presidency and Congress, the courts have played a relatively limited role in foreign policy. During most of American history they have tried to avoid becoming embroiled in the struggle for foreign policy power between the president and Congress. The courts have frequently ruled that they lacked jurisdiction. This has usually served to uphold the president. When the courts have made decisions, they have sometimes restrained presidential power; much more often they have favored the executive.

Perhaps the most frequently quoted example of the judiciary's attitude came in 1936, when the U.S. Supreme Court issued the decision in *United States v. Curtiss-Wright Export Corporation*. The Court upheld the right of the president to embargo the sale of weapons to warring countries in saying that the president should be the "sole organ of the federal government" in the realm of foreign affairs, due to the national security dangers involved, the need for secrecy, his access to confidential information, his access to diplomatic and other forms of expertise, and his lone ability to speak or listen for the nation as a whole. Without specific constitutional authorization to the contrary, the president would get the benefit of the doubt (Franck, 1991:70). That wording, in itself, had little legal impact. Yet for much of the cold war era to follow, this decision was acceptable to many in Congress, who either agreed with presidential foreign policy actions or did not care to share the responsibility for making such decisions.

Since 1936, judicial intrusions into foreign policy making have been decided largely on *procedural grounds*. Some of those have inconvenienced the president, while others have frustrated members of Congress. In 1952 during the Korean War, President Truman was denied the right to seize strike-bound steel mills in *Youngstown Sheet & Tube v. Sawyer*. A specific procedure for handling national strikes had been established in the Taft-Hartley Act of 1947. The Supreme Court said that the president did not have the unilateral power to change that procedure just because the country was at war.

In most other instances, the courts have sided with presidents. In 1979, the Supreme Court ruled in *Goldwater v. Carter* that the president had the right to terminate a treaty with the Republic of China (Taiwan), because the Senate had not specified a role for itself in the termination process when it gave its original consent to the treaty. In 1983 the Supreme Court ruled in *Immigration and Naturalization Service v.*

House resident, Bill Clinton, often feels the same way, calling the executive mansion "the crown jewel of the federal penal system."[3]

Statutory law and the Constitution count in determining presidential and congressional power, but so do the myriad electoral and other pressures that make up the political environment in Washington. This means that neither the president nor Congress often operates in a political vacuum where they can ignore each other—or, for that matter, the bureaucracy, interest groups, and public opinion. Sometimes, during a crisis, a president exercises the near unilateral authority that approximates the presidential model. In other cases, policy making occurs largely with the bureaucracy according to the administrative model. What is more common, though, is a pluralistic policy process that resembles either the political model or the subgovernment model, depending on the specific circumstances. In these cases, the nature of the process and the details of the policy adopted will partly reflect the dynamics of the power relationship of the two branches. The factors that govern this dynamic relationship between the president and Congress include, for each, (1) policy focus, (2) institutional strength, (3) political standing, (4) situation and issue, and (5) public opinion and partisanship.

Chadha that Congress could no longer use a concurrent resolution to stop executive action. While not invalidating the War Powers Resolution and other laws relying on the use of such a legislative veto, this decision made them more difficult to implement (Gibson, 1992; Koh, 1990). Moreover, the courts have refused on numerous occasions to hear challenges that presidential wars are illegal without congressional authorization. In each case, the courts have ruled that the matter is a political, not a judicial, issue. In another area the Supreme Court said in *McNary v. Haitian Centers Council* (1993) that the Coast Guard could intercept Haitian refugees at sea and return them to Haiti without an asylum hearing. This decision endorsed a Bush administration policy, reluctantly enforced by the Clinton administration, that had angered the Congressional Black Caucus, the NAACP, and other human rights groups. In its decision, the Court said that legal rights due refugees under international law did not bind the United States if the refugees never reached U.S. territory or territorial waters.

Even when lower courts have sought to restrain the president, the court of appeals or the Supreme Court has usually deferred or denied the restrictions.

A federal district court judge ruled in 1993 that President Clinton could not send the North American Free Trade Agreement to Congress until an environmental impact statement was provided, as required by the National Environmental Policy Act. Nevertheless, the administration was able to submit the legislation after a successful appeal. Similarly, Clinton's proposed "don't ask, don't tell" compromise policy regarding gay persons in the military was rejected by a district court judge, only to be validated by the Supreme Court as too broad a finding given the original case before the district court. The policy went into effect.

It is safe to say that the courts have been consistent for over 200 years in dealing with interbranch disputes regarding foreign policy. Simply put, the courts will probably not side with Congress until it stops delegating broad foreign policy roles to the executive branch and, instead, enacts decisive, unambiguous legislation that puts its constitutional prerogatives into operation. When Congress fails to be precise in protecting its own foreign policy prerogatives (or when there are loopholes in statutes), the judicial benefit of doubt shifts in favor of the executive branch (Silverstein, 1994). Recent cases seem to bear out this conclusion.

Policy Focus

One key factor that determines relative power is the difference in the policy focus of the president compared to that of Congress. What we will see is that presidents tend to stress their foreign policy role, while Congress is more comfortable with a domestic policy orientation (Gibson, 1992).

The President: Foreign Policy Focus

Twentieth-century presidents have devoted increasing amounts of their time and effort to what can be called the foreign policy presidency, in contrast to the domestic policy presidency. Furthermore, as noted, the accession of the assertive Franklin Roosevelt to the Oval Office, the crisis of World War II, the perceived peril of the cold war, and the emergence of the United States as a superpower combined to reorient U.S. foreign policy toward internationalism and vastly to enhance the foreign policy power of the president. The president's foreign policy preeminence was, and is, secure.

253

Concentrating on Foreign Policy   It is common for chief executives to concentrate on foreign policy. A study of presidential State of the Union addresses between 1953 and 1989 found that of all policy issues, foreign policy and domestic economic policy combined for about two-thirds of the presidents' remarks during these addresses. Of the two focal points, however, foreign policy took up, on average, 40 percent of the State of the Union addresses compared to 25 percent for economic policy. Moreover, during the 37 speeches, economic policy received more emphasis in only 10 of the addresses. There is also evidence that many presidents develop more foreign policy orientation as their years in the White House go by. Various analyses of presidential speeches show that with the exception of Gerald Ford, each president from Eisenhower through Reagan spent more of his time addressing foreign affairs during his last year in office than during his first. An analysis of Ronald Reagan's speeches, for example, shows that he spoke more and more on foreign policy and less and less on domestic policy during each succeeding year of his presidency (Cohen, 1995; Stuckey, 1990).

Presidents explain their focus on foreign policy in similar terms that include their sense of satisfaction at being world leaders and their ability to use broad powers to address global problems, especially when compared to their frustration with the fewer powers they have to address more parochial national issues. President Kennedy estimated that he spent 80 percent of his first year in office on foreign policy issues. Part of the reason he did so, the president observed scatologically, is that "foreign affairs is the only important issue for a president to handle. . . . I mean, who gives a shit [what the] . . . minimum wage is . . . in comparison to something like the Bay of Pigs?" (Rose, 1988:215). George Bush echoed that sentiment. As he put it during the Persian Gulf crisis in 1990, "When you get a problem with the complexities that the Middle East has now, . . . I enjoy trying to put the coalition together." Such heady duties, Bush continued, are very different from the task of discussing tax policy with members of Congress. "I can't say I just rejoice every time I go up [to Congress] and talk [about] taxes," the president lamented.[4]

Even presidents who say that they want to emphasize domestic affairs are soon enmeshed in foreign policy. That is what happened to Lyndon Johnson. Similarly, Bill Clinton entered the presidency vowing to concentrate on domestic policy, especially the economy. A week before his inauguration, Clinton told reporters that existing foreign issues, such as Somalia, "cannot distract us from the urgent domestic mission, and it will not."[5] The fact that the former Arkansas governor had little foreign policy experience added to that domestic orientation. Clinton "does not have that same well of knowledge to draw on [for foreign policy] that he does in domestic policy. Don't underestimate how raw he is," a staff member commented.[6] Clinton's domestic orientation was further strengthened by public opinion. One poll showed that when asked, "In his first months in office, what should Clinton spend more time on?" 76 percent of Americans replied "domestic and economic problems" and only 14 percent said "foreign affairs."[7] Furthermore, according to one study, Clinton's domestic bent means that insofar as he does address foreign issues, "intermestic . . . issues such as immigration or trade with a high level of domestic political content will receive most of the president's attention" (McKenney, 1995:16).

Whatever Clinton and the public may have thought they wanted, foreign policy soon captures every president's attention. By his second month in office, the president found that fighting in Bosnia-Herzegovina, instability in Russia, and other international issues were consuming increasing amounts of his time and energy. During March 1993, as he prepared for his first meeting with Boris Yeltsin, aides reported that Clinton was spending up to 50 percent of his day studying the Russian situation and bombarding them with demands for information. Foreign policy staff members were "tearing their hair out," according to one White House official. "With George Bush, the [policy] briefing books were 15 pages. The briefing books for Clinton are up to 100 pages."[8] The aide also noted that in the previous few weeks the president had talked to 30 foreign leaders about Russia and other international issues. A year later, another White House account of the president's attention to foreign policy claimed that between his inauguration and the end of April 1994, Clinton had held 153 conversations with foreign leaders, and that in just one 2-week period that April he had participated in more than 50 phone calls, meetings, and briefings involving foreign policy.[9]

During an interview after almost 2 years in office, Clinton explained some of the reasons behind his greater attention to foreign policy. A reporter asked Clinton if he concurred with President Bush's view that foreign policy was more fun than domestic policy. Clinton demurred but added, "If 'more fun' means you have more control, and you can do it [make policy] with less interference and static in Congress, to that extent of course that's true." For domestic policy, the president continued, he was but "one of a zillion decision makers" including Congress, interest groups, and others. That, Clinton implied, makes it hard to get things done. By comparison, he said, "foreign policy has a certain satisfaction when you can be active and you can achieve a result."[10]

Defending and Expanding Presidential Prerogatives   The frustration in domestic policy and the relative exhilaration of leadership in foreign policy also prompt presidents to defend and try to expand the prerogatives of their office. While this is especially true during times of tension, the quest for greater executive power extends to all policy areas. Even on a controversial issue such as whether to restrict trade with China in light of its human rights abuses, the White House has argued that it alone should decide. As one Bush administration official put it, "We really and firmly believe that the leadership on this issue must come from the executive branch . . . from the president . . . as commander in chief."[11]

Clinton has followed the path of his predecessors in defending the presidency's assumed prerogatives vigorously. During Clinton's initial year in office, Congress challenged the president and tried to place restrictions on U.S. involvement in those three countries. "When you have a president who is new in foreign affairs and a secretary of state who is cautious," observed Senator Paul Simon (D-IL), "Congress fills the vacuum."[12] Clinton counterattacked to defend his power. "I think that, clearly, the Constitution leaves to the president, for good and sufficient reasons, the ultimate decision-making authority," he declared.[13] That attitude, as earlier commentary herein has detailed, has continued throughout Clinton's presidency.

Not surprisingly, the lower echelons of the executive branch reflect presidential attitudes. During the Persian Gulf crisis, a White House staff member was bemoaning presumed congressional meddling. Don't worry about Congress, a colleague counseled, "we'll phone them just after the first bombs have been dropped" (Salinger & Laurent, 1991:176). Even worse, executive assertiveness can lead to the tactics of NSC aide Lieutenant Colonel Oliver North and others in the secret and illegal activities that constituted the Iran-Contragate scandal. When Congress investigated, North and other high officials lied under oath. To them it was all justified. The "fickle, vacillating, unpredictable, on-again-off-again policy" of Congress, North said, compelled him to take control (Crabb & Holt, 1989:187). His boss, NSC head Admiral John Poindexter, agreed. "The President has the constitutional right, and in fact the constitutional mandate, to conduct foreign policy," Poindexter sweepingly claimed, "I simply didn't want any outside interference from Congress" (Jervis, 1990:37).

The pervasiveness of this attitude has been confirmed by one study of what presidents do when faced with a choice between political (and democratic) accountability and the expediency of unilateral executive decisions in both crisis and noncrisis situations. The scholar concluded that when faced with a choice between democracy and self-defined expediency, "All presidents who faced this conflict in the cases examined here . . . chose to stress expediency over accountability" (Barilleaux, 1988:11).

Congress: Domestic Policy Focus

The orientation of Congress is quite different from that of the president. While presidents usually gravitate toward foreign policy, members of Congress tend to be attracted to domestic policy. As noted in the last chapter, Speaker of the House Newt Gingrich has estimated that he spends 90 percent of his time on domestic policy, leaving just 10 percent for foreign policy. Still, Congress, like the president, is jealous of its institutional prerogatives and may rise to defend them against presidential intrusions (Fascell, 1991).

There are numerous reasons why Congress tends to turn its attention inward and is generally willing to leave external relations to the president. First, as discussed earlier, many members believe that the president should dominate foreign policy. Second, many legislators doubt that Congress can make sound foreign policy. "Congress is very good at acting in a negative fashion," Senator John McCain (R-AZ) pointed out in a debate over Bosnia, but "it is almost incapable of policy formulation."[14] A third reason that relatively few members of Congress focus on foreign policy is that the president's formal and informal strengths in foreign policy make it more difficult for Congress to contest foreign policy issues with the executive branch. "The preferred stance" of members, observes Representative Lee Hamilton (D-IN), "is to let the president make the decisions and, if it goes well, praise him, and if it doesn't, criticize him."[15]

The fourth and most important reason for the domestic policy focus of Congress is that most members concentrate on the issues that directly and obviously impact their constituents. These high-profile constituency issues are generally domestic issues such as social security, welfare, farm subsidies, and, of course, taxes. This orientation by members of Congress is related to the fact that it is normally domestic issues, not foreign policy concerns, that influence a member's chance of reelection. "There is almost no political sex appeal to issues like Bosnia," says Senator Richard Lugar (R-IN). "For those who get involved it's strictly pro bono service."[16] In fact, some members are afraid that paying too much attention to foreign policy is a liability with voters (Burgin, 1991). When the Republicans captured the Senate in 1994, the new majority leader, Robert Dole, reportedly had a difficult time finding enough Republicans willing to serve on the Foreign Relations Committee. One senator described his service on the committee as "a political liability." "In my election campaign last fall," the senator explained, "the main thing they used against me was my interest in foreign relations. [My opponent said that] I was more interested in what happened to the people of Abyssinia and Afghanistan than in what happened to the good people of my state" (Fenno, 1973:161). By the same token those foreign policy issues that do draw significant congressional attention are likely to be intermestic issues that do markedly affect legislators' constituents. The North American Free Trade Agreement (NAFTA) was such an intermestic issue, with many legislators worried more about its impact on local jobs than on global trade. "It's very simple," said Representative John Conyers (D-MI), expressing the view of many. "If we could retrain and employ anybody that's legitimately displaced because of NAFTA, if I [could] argue that NAFTA's a job-gainer," then, Conyers said, he would vote for NAFTA.[17]

It should be added, before leaving this discussion of the congressional focus on domestic policy, that the commentary does not mean that some members do not have a high level of interest in foreign affairs. There are members who are interested and active regularly. Many motivations affect individual senators and representatives. Some are truly interested in foreign policy. Others may become involved for more personal reasons. For example, members of Congress who have presidential ambitions often seek seats on their chamber's foreign policy committee, make foreign trips, and speak out on foreign affairs so that they can gain international experience and seem more presidential. Such foreign affairs interest by individuals sometimes may even have an impact if they control a leadership position in Congress. Usually, though, such activity fails to generate the wide support throughout Congress required to challenge the executive successfully.

Institutional Strengths

The respective institutional strengths of the presidency and of Congress also influence the dynamic power relationship between the two branches. The strength of any organization—whether a sports team, a business, Congress, or the presidency—is based in part on a combination of two factors: first, the suitability of the organization to its tasks and, second, the skills of the organization's members and leaders.

Basic Structure

The basic institutional structure of the legislative and executive branches tends to favor the president over Congress in foreign policy making. The executive branch is hierarchically organized. The president and his relatively small staff of immediate advisers can make rapid decisions and can issue orders to the operational elements of the government over which he has authority. President Clinton, for instance, could decide to support the UN sanctions against Haiti and order the military to deploy ships to the Haitian coast and to ready ground-combat forces for use if required. Such is not the case in Congress. "Structurally in Congress," Senator Kent Conrad (D-ND) has observed, "there is no place were you have the ability to really communicate with your colleagues on the question of an overall plan or strategy for the country."[18] Instead, Congress is divided into two equal, sometimes feuding chambers. The House and Senate are further divided into a combined total of approximately 250 committees and subcommittees. Beyond that, there are 535 independent-minded members of Congress and approximately 12,000 staff members. To pass a law, it takes a majority of both the 435-member House and the 100-member Senate. "Even when the . . . president calls on us to do something," Representative Dennis Eckart (D-OH) has noted with discouragement, "you've got to get hundreds of people to sign off on it. That's difficult."[19]

There are, for example, numerous committees that deal with foreign affairs. Using the House of Representatives as an example, some of those committees, such as the National Security, the Intelligence, and the International Relations committees, are obvious. But there are many others. The Ways and Means Committee is involved in tariffs, which also involve the Commerce Committee, which (if what is being imported or exported is foodstuffs) also involves the Agriculture Committee. Anything that requires the expenditure of funds also brings in the Appropriations Committee. The committee list could go on, since each committee is further splintered into numerous subcommittees. Each has its own chairperson and staff. Sometimes they squabble over which committee or subcommittee should have jurisdiction over a piece of legislation. More often these turf battles are avoided by having more than one committee or subcommittee involved in an issue. Because of the highly complex and heavy workload of Congress and because of its balkanized structure, each of the many internal subunits may be very influential on certain foreign policy issues. This overlapping authority creates a process in which different groups often contest for control of the issue. The result is that the authority of Congress is weakened because it so often speaks with so many and such discordant voices. This disarray stands in contrast to the executive branch, which at least usually gives the appearance of speaking with one voice, that of the president.

Much of this loss of influence by Congress has been self-imposed. During the 1970s, Congress instituted a number of internal changes designed to lessen the authority of legislative leaders (such as the Speaker, the majority and minority leaders, and committee chairpersons) and to increase the autonomy of subcommittees and the authority of individual members. This made the two chambers more democratic in one way. But by fragmenting legislative power even more than it had been, it decreased the ability of Congress to provide a democratic counterweight to the executive branch.

This self-inflicted debilitation has been reversed somewhat in recent years, especially in the House (Sinclair, 1992). The Republican electoral triumph in 1994 and the subsequent elevation of Newt Gingrich to the post of Speaker of the House has further increased the strength of leadership in Congress. It is too early to tell, however, if the initial power that Gingrich wielded in the House will persist. Moving Congress forward quickly and in one direction has been compared with trying to herd cats, and even after six months there was evidence that the Speaker's authority had slipped somewhat. Moreover, both Speaker Gingrich and Senate majority leader Dole support broad presidential authority in foreign policy. It is symbolic of the views and authority of the two most important leaders in Congress that they both supported the 1995 attempt to repeal the War Powers Resolution, yet the measure failed to pass the House, in part because 20 percent of House Republicans voted against repeal. With the measure failing by only 16 votes (217–201), the 44 GOP votes were more than the margin that determined the outcome.

Indeed, it can be argued that the nature of representation itself puts Congress at a disadvantage when dealing with the presidency. Making decisions in a group where everyone involved has a voice in the decision is a slow process. Since members of Congress represent different constituencies and usually hold divergent views, and since there is only limited leadership authority in Congress, reaching a collective decision is difficult and time-consuming. As such, there is a degree of tension between being broadly representative, on the one hand, and making expeditious decisions, on the other (Aldrich, 1991). With the exception of those rare foreign policy issues on which there is general societal agreement, members must consider the trade-off between the goals of representing constituents and the ability of Congress to be an effective policy making institution. Thus, the more representative Congress is, the slower its policy making becomes, and the more it loses ground to the presidency.

Professional Skills

Institutional strength also depends on the professional skills of an organization's members and leaders. Recent leaders of Congress have generally not demonstrated the skills of such earlier legislative leaders as the powerful Speaker of the House Sam Rayburn, who presided over his chamber almost continually from 1940 through 1961. Even the current Speaker, Newt Gingrich, for all the media attention accorded him, does not wield the power that Rayburn did when he would summon junior legislators to sessions in his office, known as the Board of Education, and over "bourbon and branchwater" supposedly tell them that "if you want to get along, go along."

Similarly, the professional skills of a president play an important role in determining the strength of the presidency. Inasmuch as the president can command others to do things less often than we imagine, he relies heavily on persuasion to lead. The president's power to persuade relies in substantial part on his professional skills in three areas: those of the public president, the political president, and the administrative president. His ability to project a commanding public presence, his ability to maneuver effectively on the complex political playing field, and his ability to organize and administer the executive branch play pivotal parts in determining whether a president will succeed or fail in persuading others to follow. Jimmy Carter and Ronald Reagan provide good examples of how the three skill areas affect a president's relative power.

Public President It is important for the chief executive to be a skilled public president. This means being able to project a confident, imposing, and otherwise impressive image during speeches, press conferences, and other public appearances (Bostdorff, 1993).

Jimmy Carter's public president image was damaged by a nagging public perception that he lacked the aura of a president. There were many reasons, including Carter's informal, "down-home" image. Before becoming president, he was largely an unknown figure who had served just one term as governor of Georgia. In fact, only a few years before his inauguration he had stumped a panel trying to guess his name and occupation on the nighttime television program *What's My Line?* The outsider showed through when President Carter rode occasionally in a subcompact Ford Pinto instead of the presidential limousine. He ordered the Marine band to stop playing "Hail to the Chief" when he appeared at formal occasions; carried his suitcase off Air Force One; and appeared on television for a national address wearing a cardigan sweater. The public did not like it, and polls throughout the Carter years showed that the public never really did consider him to be a forceful leader.

Ronald Reagan's effective utilization of his background in broadcasting and acting to enhance his public president image contrasts with Carter's poor image. Polls regularly showed that the public liked Reagan as a person more than it supported his policies. Even when policy misfortune struck Reagan, it never seemed to stick to him. This earned for him the sobriquet "Teflon president" and added to his ability to gain political leverage over Congress (Mouw & MacKuen, 1992).

President Clinton's public image is closer to that of Carter than to that of Reagan. Like Carter, Clinton was a little-known southern governor. Clinton has also projected a "down-home" persona, beginning one radio talk show session during the 1992 campaign with the greeting, "This is Bubba." Clinton frequently allows himself to be photographed in very informal dress and situations, which, some observers say, detract from the dignity of his office. All presidents are the butt of jokes, but Clinton and those around him have often provided willing accomplices. He and his wife joke publicly about his weight problem. Hillary Clinton has told television audiences about her efforts to get the commander in chief to eat fewer cheeseburgers and about his refusal to eat tofu. Husband Bill has depicted himself to reporters as being "a lot like Baby Huey. I'm fat. I'm ugly. But if you push me down, I keep coming back."[20] Perhaps the president's most memorable moment in this vein came when he appeared on MTV and took questions from a youthful audience. One woman asked the president what sort of underwear he wears: boxer or jockey shorts. Instead of ignoring the juvenile query, Clinton quasi-dignified the question with the answer: jockey shorts.

There are other similar stories, but they are not necessary to make the point that Clinton's informality has detracted from his ability to command the awe that can work to a president's advantage. The problem with President Clinton, comments one presidential scholar, is that "he's too plebeian. He's everyperson. . . . He's reduced the presidency to his size rather than gain[ed] in size from the office." Concurs another student of the presidency, "I must say, I have never seen a president have as much trouble learning to be president [as Clinton has]. . . . Going on MTV, you may pick up 5 percent of the vote, but going on MTV and talking about your underwear, you may lose 12 percent of respect."[21]

Political President   To be successful, the occupant of the Oval Office must also be a skilled political president who knows well the workings of government and how to bargain, reward, threaten, and otherwise manipulate the complex political relationships that exist within the nation's capital (Kerbel, 1991). Here again, Carter and Reagan provide contrast.

Carter's outsider credentials and his anti-Washington rhetoric during the election weakened his presidency by alienating many of the politicians he had to work with once elected. During a campaign stop on a South Dakota farm, a wag asked Carter if some of the cattle in the field reminded him of legislators. "No," he quipped, the cows "are more intelligent" (Caldwell, 1989:3). Legislators were not amused. If Carter had been willing to be a political cowherd he might have done better, but he rejected that role as unnecessary. "Fundamentally, he seemed to believe that if a decision was correct it would sell itself," recalled a National Security Council staff member (Caldwell, 1990:4). As such, Carter rejected using political trade-offs to win the support of legislators. This stand hindered the legislative liaison staff, according to one member, by leaving it "no longer in a position to discuss a sewage treatment plant [for a representative's district] in the context of [the representative's] foreign aid vote" (Fisher, 1981:50).

Carter's staff was also poorly equipped to deal with the political maneuvering in Washington. Many of his key aides served with him in Georgia and had no Washington experience. For example, Georgian Frank Moore, who directed the congressional relations office, was dismissed by one senior Senate staff member as "the worst White House congressional liaison I have ever dealt with" (Caldwell, 1990:7). Similar estimates existed about much of the rest of the president's staff. The Carter people "don't know anything about Congress, and they don't like Congress," one Democratic legislator lamented (Caldwell, 1989:3). Many staff errors were sophomoric. Speaker of the House Tip O'Neill asked Carter's chief of staff, Hamilton Jordan, to provide tickets for an inaugural gala at the Kennedy Center. The Speaker's family were exiled to the last row in the second balcony. That and a series of unanswered phone calls from O'Neill to Jordan moved the Speaker to caricaturize Carter's chief aide as "Hannibal Jerken."

The legislative skills of the Reagan White House again contrasted with those of the Carter administration (Conti, 1995). One of Reagan's first foreign policy tests involved his proposal to sell five AWACS to Saudi Arabia. That proposal seemed doomed in Congress but was saved when, in the estimate of one study, Reagan "snatched victory from the jaws of defeat" by a skilled and intense lobbying campaign (Bard, 1988:583). The tactics of the White House ranged from personal presidential appeals to legislators' patriotism to threats that "pork-barrel" projects and federal job appointments to benefit constituents depended on their AWACS vote. After leaving an Oval Office session with Reagan, one senator moaned that he needed "to go to the Capitol physician first to get my arm put back in the socket." The pressure was so intense that just before a key Foreign Relations Committee vote, Senator Edward Zorinski (D-NE) sought surcease by refusing to accept a phone call from Reagan. "[I just did not] want to get caught with the Gipper in the locker at half time," the besieged Zorinski explained (Bard, 1987:60). Senator Edward Kennedy (D-MA), who opposed the sale, howled about the pressure, patronage, and pork to no avail. "In my 19 years up here I have never seen such 180 degree turns on the part of so many Senators," Kennedy grumbled as the Senate voted not to kill the AWACS sale (Bard, 1988: 594).

President Clinton's long years of dealing with the Arkansas legislature afforded him substantial experience in persuading legislators to follow his lead. But Little Rock is not Washington and at first Clinton stumbled in his legislative efforts at the national level. After Clinton's first 100 days in office, an assistant worried that "the President's losing his touch. He can't get the modulation right. He's not quite sure how to use his power to press for what he wants and how to preserve it when bending is the wiser course."[22]

Unlike Carter, however, Clinton adjusted his touch and began to get the modulation right. Media reports tend to portray the president as politically inept, but objective data presents a different picture. Figure 9.2 shows Clinton's legislative batting average during his first 2 years in office compared with those of his nine immediate predecessors. Clinton ranks only behind Lyndon Johnson in the percentage of time Congress passed legislation he favored. Like most data, however, such statistics tell only part of a story, and these do not necessarily mean that Clinton was the second most skillful president in the last 45 years. Like most of the presidents rated here, Clinton had the luxury during his first 2 years of dealing with a Congress in which both houses were controlled by his own party. Nixon, Ford, and Bush faced an opposition Congress, with Democrats in control

FIGURE 9.2

Presidential Legislative Success during
the First 2 Years in Office

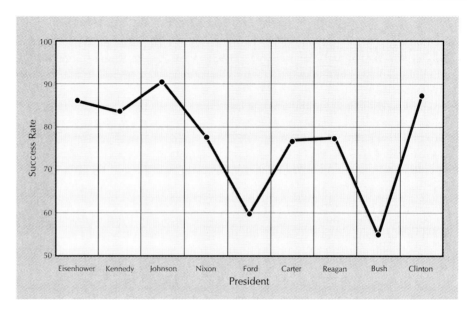

Data Source: Time, October 24, 1994, based on data from the *Congressional Quarterly.*

This figure shows the success of presidents in getting Congress to enact legislation that is supported by each president indicated during his first 2 years in office. As the data shows, Clinton ranks second in his so-called presidential batting average, having only been exceeded by Lyndon Johnson. For all the frequent negative commentary about Clinton, his substantial success rate indicates that he is adept at political maneuvering in Washington.

of both houses, and Reagan had to deal with a split Congress, with the Democrats a majority in the House. Also from this perspective, Carter's relatively low success rate while working with a Congress in which the Democrats held an approximate two-to-one edge is an indication of his poor political skills.

Two of President Clinton's 1993 efforts to win congressional support for his initiatives illustrate his political skills. One was the president's effort to enact the North American Free Trade Agreement (NAFTA). The details of this effort were related in chapter 6 and need not be repeated here, but the bottom line is that Clinton eventually prevailed. The legislation authorizing NAFTA passed the Senate easily and, after a pitched battle, moved through the House of Representatives by a narrow 10-vote margin. In the aftermath, one of the administration's legislative strategists paid homage to the example provided by another skilled political president. "We learned something from Ronald Reagan, finally," the aide said. The lesson was that "You need to be right on more than the merits of the case; you need to be right on the presentation. We started to do better," the aide continued, "when we got off statistics and cast it more broadly as a shining city on the hill, you know—as a choice between the future and the past, optimism and pessimism, hope and fear, embracing the modern world and trying to hide from it." It was a heartening victory for the Clinton White House, especially in light of its earlier missteps. As one Democratic legislator put it, "The gang that couldn't shoot straight must have been taking a lot of target practice over the summer."[23]

Clinton was also able in 1993 to get Congress to pass a $2.5 billion aid package for Russia. There were elements of the president's lobbying effort that raised images of President Harry S. Truman's successful effort to get Congress to pass the Truman Plan, an anti-Soviet foreign aid package for Greece and Turkey in 1947. The 80th Congress was just as reluctant to appropriate foreign aid in 1947 as the 103rd Congress was in 1993. To get an aid package enacted, Truman relied on various strategies. One was early consultations with opposition Republican leaders in Congress. Another was casting the aid as a national security issue and presenting dire predictions of the consequences if Congress failed to fund the program. During a meeting between Truman and his lieutenants with congressional leaders, Under Secretary of State Dean G. Acheson (1969:219) told the legislators that Greece and Turkey were overripe for a communist takeover, and "like apples in a barrel infected by one rotten one, . . . it could carry infection to Africa through Asia Minor . . . to Europe." Only the United States could forestall this political cancer by inoculating the threatened countries with curative aid dollars. The key GOP leader on foreign policy, Senator Arthur H. Vandenburg, replied to Acheson's grim diagnosis by turning to Truman and telling him, "Mr. President, if you will say that to the Congress and the country, I will support you and I believe that most of its members will do the same."

Taking the same tack 46 years later, President Clinton met with congressional leaders to warn them of the ills that would befall the United States and the world if Russia was not given foreign aid. In what one aide depicted as "an extemporaneous, passionate speech," Clinton told the legislators that a destitute Russia was an unstable Russia and an unstable Russia was a dangerous Russia. The congressional response, as one participant has recalled, was typified by then–House minority whip Newt Gingrich, who told Clinton that "this was one of the great, defining moments of our time; that it could not be a partisan issue; and that if the President were willing to commit to this personally and make the case to the public, Republicans in Congress would stand by him" (Rosner, 1995:23). Just as had occurred in 1947, the president's depiction of national peril gave a tinge of crisis to the foreign aid question and moved the issue toward the presidential model. That gave the president the advantage, just as it had in 1947. In both years, a foreign aid program that many thought doomed was resuscitated and moved through Congress by similarly large margins. The respective House and Senate votes were 287–107 and 67–23 in 1947 and 309–111 and 88–10 in 1993.

Administrative President To be a strong chief executive the president must also be a skilled administrator. This means possessing decision making and organizational skills necessary to make policy decisively and to organize and control both the immediate presidential staff and the extensive bureaucracy (Barrett, 1993; Haney, 1992).

Carter's weaknesses as administrative president were another factor that detracted from his power. Among other things, he became so absorbed in details that he pondered too long and decided too late and too tentatively. National security adviser Zbigniew Brzezinski has recalled that when Carter approached a policy decision he sometimes vacillated "by simply sticking with it too long. At times, I thought he was like a sculptor who did not know when to throw away his chisel" (Hargrove, 1988:116). The result was that, for instance, the president had trouble handling the very divergent policy views of Brzezinski and Secretary of State Cyrus Vance (Carrol, 1992). As one study puts it, Carter allowed "great policy competition" among his advisers that, because of the president's weaknesses, "in the end . . . overpowered him" (Moens, 1990:180).

At the other end of the continuum of paying too much and too little attention to detail, President Reagan lost power in the realm of the administrative presidency because of the increasing awareness in Washington and the country that he was grossly inattentive. National security adviser William Clark has said of Reagan, "I don't think I have had an in-depth, one-on-one, private conversation that existed for more than three minutes with him—on any subject. That might shock you. We had our own code of communication. I knew where he wanted to go. . . ."[24] This process of reading the chief's mind by the staff eventually led to the bizarre, sometimes illegal, staff machinations of Oliver North and others during the Iran-Contra scandal.

Dwight Eisenhower's management style was a happy median between Carter's micromanagement and Reagan's laissez-faire approach. One study of decision making in the Eisenhower White House during a 1954 crisis in Vietnam, which threatened to bring the United States into the war on the side of France, characterized the president as "wary of defining the situation as a crisis or of making a quick decision"; as "an experienced military planner, calling for future analysis and deliberation"; as "establishing a range of advisory groups"; and as encouraging decision making group "participants to express their own view freely." These traits, the study concludes, contributed to Eisenhower "thinking of long-term consequences and overall costs and benefits." Eisenhower decided against intervention (Burke & Greenstein, 1989:91).

President Clinton entered office with some observers worrying that he had much the same administrative style as Carter. Clinton admits to being a policy "wonk," someone who revels in the intricacies of policy. "I lean toward getting into the details of policy," the president acknowledged.[25] One ramification of that preference is that Clinton favors listening to a multitude of policy views. David Gergen—who served in the White House under Clinton and three Republican presidents, has commented that "Staffs are a reflection of the desires of the person in the center. The person, this president [Clinton], likes a staff in which many diverse views are expressed."[26] To a degree such an approach is good. Past a point, however, it leads to confusion and lack of decision, and there are many critics who say that Clinton is well beyond that point (Drew, 1994; Woodward, 1994).

Clinton's focus on detail also means that he delegates authority poorly (Greenstein, 1995). One Clinton official describes the approach as "almost a throwback to the days when presidents did everything themselves." Another official adds, Clinton "tries to keep all these balls in the air. He could get away with it in Little Rock. He's smart enough to pull it off in that town. But here [in Washington]? He's not that smart."[27]

Perhaps the strongest criticism of Clinton in this area is that his penchant for delving into great detail and to listening at great length to competing opinions detracts from his ability to move from debate to decision and, even once decisions are made, to stand by them. Such commentary from Republicans might be dismissed as partisan, but the same charges come from Clinton's own staff and from other Democrats and supporters. For example, one Clinton adviser says of his boss, "he's fairly slow, he's fairly indecisive, and he is easily sidetracked."[28] When another aide was asked what administrative model Clinton followed, he laughed and replied, "Well, you aren't going to find it in *Presidential Quarterly*. You aren't going to find it period. It's the Bill Clinton model." This includes holding policy making sessions with so many people that they "could be held in Yankee stadium."[29] Clinton "can have a 10-minute meeting in two hours," grumbles another aide.[30] The result is that decisions are slow and subject to multiple reversals. "I think most of us learned some time ago," says Representative David Obey (D-WI), "that if you don't like the president's position on a particular issue, you simply need to wait a few weeks."[31]

Clinton seems to recognize that becoming too focused on policy details and trying to accomplish too many things simultaneously is a misuse of his time and political capital. In September 1992 a reporter asked him what he thought he had learned during his first six months in office. "Well, first, I think I've learned to focus . . . my energies. . . . A president is not America's chief mechanic. You know I didn't get hired to fix everything. . . . I got hired to do what I'm now trying to do, to set forth a vision."[32] The president also made a number of staff

Tribune Media Services: Reprinted by permission.

The individual skills, administrative and other, of a president are one of the factors that determine presidential power in the short term. For most of his first term, President Clinton was weakened by the image, demonstrated in this editorial cartoon, that he neither made decisions effectively nor maintained a steady policy once a decision had been reached.

changes, including appointing Washington insider Leon Panetta as chief of staff, in an attempt to bring some discipline to the White House. Whatever Clinton's intention and efforts, others do not think that he can change his basic approach. The president persists in wanting to oversee details. "There's been a modest improvement," says one official, "but I wouldn't make too much of it. We have a hard time deciding what not to take to [Clinton] because he wants to do everything."[33] Even more pessimistically, one long-time House Democrat has commented, "God knows he's trying," but "I'm reluctantly coming to the conclusion that [Clinton] has the dreaded Carter disease—no focus, no continuity, confusing motion with accomplishment."[34]

Political Standing

The respective strengths of the president and Congress also depend on their political standing. This factor involves public confidence in the two institutions and in the individuals elected to the executive and legislative branches.

Political Standing of the President

"A statesman is a dead politician," Harry Truman once quipped (Rose, 1988:267). By inference, live presidents are politicians. And since politicians are often unpopular, every president experiences rises and falls of public support (Nice, 1992). These shifts in presidential popularity, especially if dramatic and sustained, affect a president's ability to dominate the political agenda and his short-term political clout with Congress and other foreign policy actors (Cohen, 1995). One group of scholars has focused on the importance of the president's standing and called it the "politics of prestige." As they explain it, "The politics of prestige pertains to the fact that public evaluations of presidential performance have become a core ingredient of presidential power as well as a key determinant of an administration's effectiveness" (Marra, Ostrom, & Simon, 1990:589). This means that when a president is popular, many opponents in Congress and elsewhere are reluctant to oppose executive initiatives. Furthermore, studies show that in the mass media age, presidents increasingly use television addresses and other techniques to gain the public's support and "when they [successfully] mobilize public support, presidents are able to enhance the prospects of their policy proposals" (Mouw & MacKuen, 1992:98).

By contrast, a decline in a president's popularity often equates to a diminished ability to persuade others to follow. The Vietnam-related free fall of Lyndon Johnson's public standing was so disabling politically that one assistant secretary of state commented in 1967 that "the change in the Congressional mood . . . is remarkable. It doesn't do much good now, and it can often do harm, to say the President is personally interested in a piece of legislation" (Frankel, 1968:117).

The dramatic drop in President Clinton's popularity during his first 100 days in office had similar effects on Capitol Hill. Only 38 percent of Americans polled in May 1993 said they thought Clinton was "a strong and decisive leader," a drop from 67 percent in February.[35] Clinton was in trouble. Republicans were eager to challenge him, and Democrats no longer feared his wrath. His domestic program was stalled, and pundits were widely predicting that his presidency in terms of effectiveness was all but over. Even the president was dispirited, feeling "sadness and disappointment and anxiousness" over his drop in the polls, according to the White House chief of staff.[36]

Clinton's public standing has ebbed and flowed, but it has generally been relatively low and has weakened his ability to dominate the foreign policy process. Some of Clinton's difficulties have stemmed from the public's estimate of his professional ability; some are caused by reactions to persistent allegations regarding the president's earlier financial dealings, draft record, and sexual conduct. One survey found that 72 percent of Americans thought that "questions about Bill Clinton's character" either "seriously" or "somewhat" hurt his ability to be an effective moral leader.[37] More generally, after two years in office, polls found that 47 percent of respondents rated Clinton's performance favorably. This was better than some recent presidents (Ford, 45 percent; Carter, 43 percent; Reagan, 37 percent) at their 2-year mark. A Gallup Poll analysis pointed out, though, that the 47 percent favorable evaluation was unusually high for Clinton and that "between his initial rating and his 2-year rating, Clinton received the lowest rating of any president at similar points in their presidency."[38] The public's evaluation of Clinton's specific foreign policy skills has varied much like the public's overall estimate of his ability. A series of polls in 1993 found that an average of only 43 percent of the public would say they "approve" of Clinton's handling of foreign policy.[39] In January 1994, 57 percent of respondents to one poll answered yes when asked, "Is Clinton doing a good job handling foreign policy?"[40] By May, though, when a survey asked whether "President Clinton [has] been a strong or weak leader when making foreign policy decisions," only 41 percent replied strong, while 51 percent answered weak. It is interesting to note that at the end of 1995, Clinton's favorable rating in public opinion moved further upward, reaching 55 percent in December. Political commentators speculated that a major factor was Clinton's effort to be more decisive, even if, as was the case with Bosnia, his specific decisions did not have the public's support.

It should also be remembered that the presidency itself rises and falls in the public estimate. As indicated earlier, for example, one cause of the upswing of congressional activity and influence in the mid-1970s was the decline of the prestige of the presidency in the aftermath of the disastrous war in Vietnam and the scandals of the Watergate burglary and cover-up. By 1975 the percentage of Americans expressing a great deal of confidence in the presidency had declined to 13 percent.[41] Ronald Reagan's tenure at first witnessed an increase in public confidence in the office. The Iran-Contra scandal, however, and widespread public belief that the president's advisers (and perhaps the president himself) had broken the law and were lying to cover it up once again sullied the image of the office. The passage of time and new presidents have partially erased the stains in the public's mind, but the public's ambivalence about the presidency is reflected by the mere 26 percent that expressed a great deal of confidence in the presidency in 1991. At least part of the reason for this declining estimate, some analysts believe, is that there is a gap between rising public expectations of what the president and the rest of government should do and what they possibly can do (Pika & Thomas, 1992). If public expectations are beyond what is possible, then presidential (and congressional) failure become a self-fulfilling prophecy. In a circular way, the presidency's diminished standing has created other dynamics that further erode the office's leadership capability. When Clinton scheduled a prime-time news conference in April 1995, only CBS, of the major over-the-air television networks, opted to interrupt its normal programming to carry the event. Executives at ABC decided that it was more important for the public to view a rerun of a *Home Improvement* episode, and NBC chose not to preempt *Frasier* for Clinton. "You can look at the news coverage of speeches and press conferences as a fairly good index of power in a society," commented one scholar. "The networks were voting with their feet. They're saying [that] the presidency is not as powerful as it was, especially under this president."[42]

The Political Standing of Congress

It might be that such public doubts would harm presidential foreign policy authority even more if it were not for the fact that while the public's estimate of all presidents, and even the presidency, rises and falls, the public standing of Congress is uniformly low. This works to Congress's disadvantage. In addition to public confidence in the two institutions, the reputation of congressional leaders and presidents influences relative power. Yearly polls from 1973 through 1991 reveal that the percentage of respondents saying that they had "a lot of confidence" in the leaders of Congress ranged from a high of only 24 percent (1973) to a low of 9 percent (1980). Congress's average confidence rating was 15 percent.[43] These figures are even more unfavorable when compared with those of presidents. The 10 presidents from Franklin Roosevelt through George Bush enjoyed on average a 56 percent approval rating during their respective years in office. Roosevelt's was highest at 75 percent; Kennedy's was a close second at 71 percent. Four presidents (Truman, Nixon, Ford, and Carter) averaged under 50 percent, with Truman having the lowest average at 41 percent.[44] Thus, even when a president's standing in the polls is low, it is usually higher than that of the leaders of Congress, and a 1994 survey showed that while a plurality of the public thought that the role of Congress in the foreign policy process was about right, the percentage of respondents who said that Congress's role is too strong had increased 6 percentage points to 28 percent compared to responses four years earlier (Rielly, 1995).

Situations and Issues

The discussion of the presidential, political, administrative, and subgovernment models in chapter 6 stressed the point that the strengths and roles of the various foreign policy making actors shift according to a number of variables. The situation and the nature of the issue are two of the important variables.

With regard to *situation,* recall that Congress defers to presidents during crises, especially acute ones such as the Persian Gulf confrontation (Nacos, 1994). Congress also tends to be less active in noncrisis, status quo situations, when foreign policy decisions are incremental, following previous policy within the accepted consensus. Non–status quo situations, when Americans lack consensus on basic policy direction, are accompanied by greater congressional activism. The immediate post–World War II period and the current post–cold war period are examples of two important times of non–status quo situations.

As occurred in the late 1940s when the bipolar system came into being, there are now once again significant splits within the United States over the fundamental course of foreign policy in a dramatically changed world. "You know," President Clinton remarked to a panel of experts while preparing for a trip to Europe, "the problem is that in this post–cold war period, the lines just aren't as clear as they were before." Yes, "Mr. President," an adviser replied, "That is your fate. You will just have to get used to dealing with ambiguity."[45] The effect of this ambiguity, in the words of one recent study, is that "the broad cold war consensus of the postwar era is now defunct and undertakings suggestive of the cold war are extremely contentious, generating huge partisan and ideological splits" among policy makers and other opinion leaders (Holsti & Rosenau, 1990:592).

What has emerged in place of the cold war consensus is a split among several incompatible foreign policy orientations, to be discussed in chapter 13. Since no single foreign policy orientation commands majority support in the public or Congress, the president must seek to build coalitions behind major foreign policy initiatives. This lack of consensus thrusts policy into the realm of the political model, where presidential authority is reduced and there is a more conflictual process that involves compromise and increased influence for more and more divergent foreign policy actors.

The *nature of the issue* also plays a strong role in determining the level of congressional interest and activity in it. As noted earlier, Congress is oriented more toward domestic policy than toward international affairs. Still, the dividing line between foreign and domestic policy is frequently not neat. Intermestic policy is the term we use to designate policy with both important foreign and domestic ramifications. The upshot is that Congress will be more active on intermestic issues, such as trade legislation, and less active on pure foreign policy issues, such as nuclear nonproliferation (Brown, 1994). The rise in the number and impact of intermestic issues is one cause of the increased attention of Congress to foreign policy in recent years. As Representative Jim Leach (R-IA) put it, "Increasingly all foreign policy issues are becoming domestic issues. As a reflection of the public input, Congress is demanding and playing a greater role."[46]

There are some factors, however, that limit this broad statement about intermestic affairs and increased congressional activism. First, which policies will be intermestic and which will be foreign is impossible to predict precisely, because the presence or absence of significant domestic impact is often in the eyes of the beholder. Trade policy, with its multiple domestic economic ramifications, seems to be a clear intermestic policy, and legislators tend to address it in that light. "Much congressional interest in trade policy issues," one study noted, "revolves around the implications for particular industries," with an eye to providing "opportunities for individual industries to protect their interests in international trade" (Porter, 1988:179). That has created a situation, as Ambassador Robert Strauss explained, in which "during my tenure as Special Trade Representative, I spent as much time negotiating with domestic constituents (both industry and labor) and members of the U.S. Congress as I did negotiating with our foreign trading partners" (Lindsay, 1991:10).

In contrast to the perception of trade legislation as a domestic issue, the White House is more apt to see it in terms of strategic relations with other countries. These divergent views of the two branches often set off a struggle over the definition of the issue. Presidents who can focus the policy debate on strategic issues are more likely to predominate than if the focus is on domestic ramifications. As a result of this definitional struggle and the inescapable constraints on U.S. policy in an increasingly interdependent world, presidents have in some ways gained more say in trade and some other intermestic issues that were once dominated by Congress (Peterson, 1994b). The fact that Congress agreed with hardly a murmur to the latest revision of the General Agreement on Tariffs and Trade and the creation of the World Trade Organization is evidence of legislators' willingness to grant leadership to the president on issues with strong domestic impacts.

Policy that creates an emotional response in the public or a segment of the public is also apt to be processed as intermestic. The strong interest of American Jews in U.S. policy toward Israel is an example. Also, as noted in chapter 6, a policy that has a negative and an asymmetrical impact on one part of the population is likely to evoke an emotional response. Part, but not all, of the reason that American students were so active against the Vietnam War was that it was their generation that was being sent to Indochina to fight, sometimes to be wounded, and sometimes to die.

Public Opinion and Partisanship

Yet another factor that affects congressional activity in foreign policy relates to the closely connected considerations of public opinion and partisanship. Is there strong public opinion on an issue? What are the electoral stakes of an issue? These questions are intertwined with such matters as political standing and the nature of the issue discussed earlier. Public opinion and electoral stakes are such key determinants, however, that they merit separate examination.

Public Opinion

Because Congress is an elected institution, its assertiveness in pursuing an important foreign policy role depends on congressional perceptions of public opinion. Members of Congress are significantly influenced by their perceptions of strong public opinion on an issue (Bartels, 1991; Overby, 1991; Arnold, 1990; Peterson, 1990).

The four policy making models described earlier relate to this phenomenon. When dealing with pure foreign policy issues, Congress tends to be less active and influential, often because the public is either uninterested or supports the president. When addressing intermestic issues, Congress is much more involved because the public is more often interested in them and also is often less supportive of the president's policy position (Rourke & Carter, 1989). Thus, congressional activity tends to be greatest on political and subgovernment issues and least on presidential and administrative issues.

One reason that foreign aid has often fared so poorly in Congress is that its members are sensitive to the public's general hostility to what many people see as a foreign giveaway program. Some members have made a virtual career out of opposing foreign aid. Representative Otto Passman (D-LA) spent years attacking the program as chairman of the subcommittee that oversaw foreign aid. "Son," the elderly Passman once told a State Department official, "I don't smoke and I don't drink. My only pleasure in life is kicking the shit out of the foreign aid program" (Immerman, 1992:146).

The public's antipathy toward foreign aid is so strong that even those members of Congress who do recognize the need for an aid program are wary of voting for it. During a debate over U.S. funding of UN peacekeeping operations, Senator James Sasser (D-TN) fretted that "we are in a dilemma here. Many of us [in Congress] recognize the importance of . . . peacekeeping . . . and recognize our responsibility to pay our share. But . . . our constituents are saying that they have borne the burden as long as they intend to."[47] During consideration of the 1993 aid bill for Russia, a parallel complaint was heard from Senator Patrick Leahy (D-VT), who worried that after Congress had voted down a jobs bill for Americans, "Now we are going to be asked to vote . . . for a job program for Russians" (Rosner, 1995:18).

The public opinion that influences legislators can be part of a national trend or can be much more localized. Senators and representatives regularly become active on policy and favor certain positions based on the impact on their states and districts. For example, various efforts to close military bases have predictably brought members of Congress to the defense of their districts' interests. "The current situation in Congress," Defense Secretary Les Aspin observed cogently, "is not a split between hawks and doves, between liberals and conservatives, between Democrats and Republicans. It's between those [legislators] that have military bases and facilities in their districts and those who don't."[48]

Thus, if the public does not seem to care about a foreign policy issue, members of Congress are freer to follow their own policy preferences, cues given by other legislative actors, or cues given by the president. The resulting congressional reaction may be active or passive, depending on the situation. By contrast, strong and widespread public opinion usually prompts serious congressional attention to the matter at hand (Russett, 1990). Presidents at this point may or may not get what they want from Congress, but the congressional role in the decision process is an important one (Friedberg, 1992).

Partisanship

Congress is an institution organized around partisan lines. Party identification, party differences, and the party's welfare count a great deal. This is intensified by the fact that party control of Congress and of the White House brings significant benefits to members in terms of their institutional power, such as being a committee chairperson.

Party control of one or both of the elected branches also increases the ability of members to pass legislation that they favor. This ability benefits a member's district or state, thereby increasing the chances that the member will be reelected. The House National Security Committee, for example, added some $500 million to the FY1996 defense spending authorization bill to fund pork barrel projects such as new squash courts for the Puget Sound Naval Shipyard. About 80 percent of the added budget fat was earmarked for districts of the committee's members. Presidents can also help members of their party by larding the budget with helpful projects. The benefits of control of Congress and the White House mean, therefore, that members sometimes take foreign policy stands that are based on party loyalty.

It would be an error, though, to view the positions of most legislators as determined solely by partisan support or antipathy. Disagreements based on ideological differences or constituent interests are almost surely a more important source of debate. Policy disputes in this sense are the essence of democracy. What is hard to determine is when differences between the two parties are based on narrow partisanship and when they are based on broader ideological and constituent concerns.

What can be said is that ideology, such as a member's liberal or conservative philosophy, is the single best predictor of congressional voting (Leogrande & Brenner, 1993; McCormick & Wittkopf, 1992; Bond & Fleisher, 1990). This is even true, albeit less so, for strongly intermestic, constituency-relevant issues such as trade, on which constituency impact also plays a strong role in determining a member's stand (Lutz, 1991). Democrats in Congress, for example, do not cast liberal votes because they are Democrats. Instead, they are Democrats and (as Democrats) vote similarly because they are liberals. This partisan bent helps shape legislators' constituency orientations. As one study put it, research indicates that on economic and foreign policy issues, legislators "vote in a manner consistent with the preferences of their own-party constituents and, to a lesser extent, with the preferences of independent constituents" (Shapiro et al., 1990:616). The views of constituents who identify with the opposition party are much less important, since they are unlikely to vote for the legislator anyway.

Moreover, there is evidence, according to one study, that because "liberal Republicans and conservative Democrats have become more and more scarce in Congress, cleavages on foreign and defense policy have increasingly coincided with party line" (Lindsay & Ripley, 1992:429). As foreign policy making becomes more partisan, members of the opposition party in Congress become less likely to vote for the president's foreign policy proposals. Opposition party voting for presidential foreign policy proposals has decreased steadily since the Johnson administration. One reason, according to James Meernik (1993:585), is that after the "conflict [in Vietnam], consensus broke down and was replaced with much more conflictual voting behavior" in Congress.

Thus, political parties count a great deal, but they are not the primary source as such of congressional voting. Virtually every time that members take up any issue, such partisan matters as to which party they belong, which party controls their chamber or Congress in general, which party controls the White House, and possible electoral repercussions are never far from members' minds. But constituent impact and general ideological orientations are also prominent considerations.

The varying impact of trade and constituency is evident in the votes during the 103rd Congress (1993–1994) on general foreign policy and on trade. On foreign policy, Democrats in the House and Senate voted, respectively, for Democratic president Clinton's policy positions 76 percent and 80 percent of the time. House and Senate Republicans had an identical support score of only 35 percent. Trade was a different story altogether. Here the president's internationalist preference for free trade lined up better with the interests of business, which tends to support Republicans, and ran counter to the interests of unions, which tend to support Democrats. The result was that on trade issues, the support scores for Clinton were only 52 percent for House Democrats and 64 percent for Senate Democrats. Clinton actually received more support from Republicans, with scores of 72 percent in the House and 74 percent in the Senate (Rosner, 1995).

SUMMARY

1. The foreign policy process is influenced strongly by the interaction between the presidency and Congress, as well as the respective powers of those two institutions. The Constitution is a fluid, often vague document that has provided to the president and Congress "an invitation to struggle" over power.

2. The absolute power of both the president and Congress has grown. But the relative power of the presidency has grown more rapidly than that of Congress. The growth of presidential power has accelerated during this century and has been especially rapid since the presidency of Franklin Roosevelt.

3. Congressional deference to the president after World War II was reversed to a substantial degree by the events surrounding the Vietnam War, Watergate, and the decline of the cold war consensus. The efforts of Congress to reassert itself have been only partially successful, and the president remains the normally dominant foreign policy maker.

4. There are a number of factors that determine shifts in the relative power of the presidency and Congress over time.

5. Policy focus is one factor. Presidents tend to focus on foreign policy. Members of Congress are more apt to focus on domestic policy.

6. Another factor is organizational strength. The fragmentation of Congress tends to lessen its impact on foreign policy. The strength of the presidency varies depending on the administrative skills of the president and his chief subordinates.

7. The political standing of the president (and the presidency) and Congress also helps determine the respective influence of the two contestants in the struggle for power. The public's esteem of Congress is normally quite low, which harms that institution. The public standing of the president varies greatly depending on how the public perceives the president personally and what it thinks of the president's policies.

8. Situations and issues also have an impact on the relative power of the two institutions. Crises, status quo, and pure international issues are areas in which presidential strength is maximized. Intermestic issues, non–status quo issues, and noncrisis situations are more likely to evoke congressional activity.

9. Partisanship also influences the relations between the president and Congress. Efforts to attain partisanship advantage sometimes lead members of Congress to oppose policy favored by the president. Partisanship is especially likely on issues in which the public or significant interest groups are in opposition. Partisanship is also especially likely when the president's standing is low in the public opinion polls.

Chapter Ten

If you were to ask Americans, "Who makes THE BUREAUCRACY

foreign policy?" most people would probably start with the president. Some might throw in some comments about Congress or public opinion. Few Americans would be apt to mention the vast supporting cast of permanent professional workers called civil servants or bureaucrats who make up over 99 percent of the government.

By contrast, you would get very different answers to your question if you were to ask presidents about the bureaucracy or—more likely—if you read their comments. You would discover that these supposedly powerful chief executives, these commanders in chief, are frequently frustrated by and antagonistic toward the bureaucracy they suppos-edly control.

273

Franklin D. Roosevelt led the United States to victory over the Axis powers during World War II, but he was often less successful dealing with the U.S. Navy. Trying to change the Navy, Roosevelt complained, was like "punching a feather bed. You punch it with your right and you punch it with your left until you are finally exhausted, and then you find the damn bed is just as you left it before you started punching" (DiClerico, 1979:107). John Kennedy felt much the same. Once when a visitor to the Oval Office suggested a course of policy, the president replied, "I agree with you, but I don't know if the government will" (Rose, 1988:162). President Nixon fumed saltily to aides about the bureaucratic "sons-of-bitches that kick us in the ass. [It is] the little boys over in State particularly, that are against us [and] Defense . . . particularly" (Sherrill, 1979:217). President Ronald Reagan fared little better. "One of the hardest things about being president," he wrote, "is to know that down there, underneath, is a permanent structure that's resisting everything you're doing" (Rourke, 1990:131). Moreover, presidents are not alone in this view. One survey of elected officials found that 57 percent of them agreed that "elected officials have lost control over bureaucrats, who really run the country," and eighty percent agreed with the milder statement that the federal government had become "too bureaucratic" (Hummel & Isaak, 1986:226). To presidents and other political leaders, then, the permanent structure "underneath," as Reagan put it, is a formidable political actor.

The last three chapters examined the central, and well-publicized, role played by the president and his close advisers and the prominent, though inconsistent, role played by Congress. This chapter will explore the significant, albeit lower profile, role that the bureaucracy plays in the foreign policy process. It is a role that has expanded since World War II as the United States has held the center stage in world affairs and has become more enmeshed in global interdependence. As a result, top-level decision makers in the executive branch and Congress have found their time and expertise strained, leaving the political leaders less able to control policy making and to manage the geographically widespread and substantively diverse details of American foreign policy.

Yet we will also see in this chapter that the presidential statements railing against bureaucratic power are somewhat hyperbolic, that the power of the bureaucracy ebbs and flows depending on many variables, and that bureaucrats often themselves feel constrained. Still, bureaucrats are sometimes important policy makers. For us to begin to understand this complexity, it is important to consider the general role of bureaucracy in the U.S. political system, the cast of bureaucratic players, the factors that determine the policy preferences of different units and individuals in the bureaucracy, and the powers of and limits on the bureaucracy's role in the foreign policy process.

BUREAUCRACY AND THE POLITICAL SYSTEM

Our first task in this chapter is to gain an overview of bureaucracy and the part it plays in the American political system. This includes reviewing what our policy making models say about the role of the bureaucracy and then considering the issue of the interplay between bureaucratic power and democracy.

Bureaucracy and the Policy Making Models

It is important to reiterate or make several related points that are important to understanding the foreign policy process and the role of bureaucracies in it. First, the bureaucracy is but one of the many potent actors in the process. Second, the policy role of the bureaucracy and every actor in the U.S. foreign policy process varies. For certain issues and in certain situations, bureaucratic actors will be the most important actors in the system, while at other times they will be peripheral to the policy process. In particular, the bureaucracy does not play as visible a role in the foreign policy process as do other governmental institutions.

Yet, third, it can also be said that more than any other actor, the bureaucracy is involved in almost all policy. Even if a particular policy decision does not involve the bureaucracy, it is the bureaucracy that will usually carry out those decisions. It can be dangerous, however, to assume that the policy will be implemented as intended because all bureaucracies have agendas and interests of their own that may be different from the agendas and interests of the officials who made the original decisions. Even though the extent of the bureaucracy varies across the four policy models, it is almost always a factor.

During a crisis, for example, decision making tends to be focused around the White House and correspond to the *presidential model*. Nevertheless, the president and other political leaders are heavily dependent on the bureaucracy to provide information and analysis. It may also be that the decision makers themselves are rooted in the bureaucracy. At the time of the Persian Gulf crisis in 1990–1991, three of the key decision makers were national security adviser Brent Scowcroft, his deputy Robert Gates, and chairman of the Joint Chiefs of Staff Colin Powell. Scowcroft is a retired Air Force general, Gates had a career in the Central Intelligence Agency (CIA) and later became its director, and Powell had decades of military service. They were all serving in politically appointed positions; each also had strong bureaucratic ties.

Bureaucratic elements are very much involved in issues and situations that generate a policy process that corresponds to the *political model*. The military, for example, is heavily involved in issues such as defense-spending reductions, the service of homosexuals in uniform, and other issues that are being broadly debated in society. The administrative units can supply information to one side or another, leak information to the press, try to galvanize supporters in Congress and the public, and take a variety of other actions to promote the position favored by the bureaucrats.

The bureaucratic role in the subgovernment and administrative models is even stronger. In the presidential and political models, bureaucratic influence is usually indirect. Bureaucrats ordinarily do not hold the top political leadership positions where decisions are made. In the *subgovernment model,* by comparison, bureaucrats are stronger because they are operating in a much smaller, less prominent policy making universe. On issues that spark the attention of a relatively narrow spectrum of administrative units, members of Congress, and interest groups, bureaucrats are able to make decisions in the absence of any interest in or input from top political leaders.

Matters that fall within the *administrative model* are, by definition, within the decision making realm of the bureaucracy. Each year, for instance, the UN General Assembly adopts nearly 400 resolutions. The United States votes on each; and each represents a policy stand by the country. Nevertheless, you probably cannot identify many of those positions; hardly anyone else can either. A few of the votes are decided on by the president or the secretary of state; most are on matters that excite little general interest among the political leaders, interest groups, or the public. Policy therefore is decided at Foggy Bottom, the name given to an area in Washington where the State Department is located.

A few more comments are in order before leaving this discussion of how bureaucracies fit into our policy making models. One is to note that in all of the models, there may be a high level of *bureaucratic competition,* with various bureaucracies opposed to one another. During the early 1980s, for instance, the State Department favored the grain embargo placed on the Soviet Union in retaliation for its invasion of Afghanistan. The Agriculture Department opposed the embargo and worked successfully with farm groups and farm-state members of Congress to overturn this ban on trade.

Bureaucratic competition has a number of implications for foreign policy. Inconsistency is one potential impact. As different parts of the bureaucracy compete for power and control, policy may shift depending on which agency has the upper hand on a given aspect of policy. Lack of perceived reliability is a second impact of bureaucratic competition. The bureaucracy is but one of the many potent actors in the policy process. When bureaucratic struggles become public, as they often do through leaks and investigative reporting by the press, others in the world may question the stability and consistency of American policy choice. Third, bureaucratic competition also creates doubts about whether or not the decisions are actually being carried out in the manner intended by the president and Congress. If a bureaucracy does not agree with a policy decision to begin with, there are legitimate concerns about the willingness of the bureaucrats to carry out the policy enthusiastically or even to implement it in accordance with the intent of the decision makers.

Yet it would be wrong to suggest that bureaucratic competition is always negative. Bureaucrats are often experts in their fields and have their own ideas about what policy should be. Also, interest groups are, to a degree, represented by associated agencies (such as farmers and the Department of Agriculture). This makes agencies a channel of input for interest groups, an access that arguably serves to promote democratic debate.

A further summary comment about the bureaucracy's fit within the policy models is that we must be careful not to attribute too great a role in foreign policy decision making to career officials. As one scholar points out, too much emphasis on bureaucratic politics obscures the power of the president, undermines assumptions about the efficacy of democracy, and offers our leaders a convenient excuse for failure when failure does occur (Krasner, 1988). It is, therefore, appropriate to think of bureaucratic politics as one piece in the foreign policy puzzle. Bureaucratic power is most prominent in the more mundane administrative and subgovernment models; it is less influential in the presidential and political models.

Bureaucracy and Democracy: Accountable to Whom?

A thematic question that we are pondering in this book asks how democratic foreign policy is and ought to be. The role of the permanent, nonelected bureaucracy in the policy process is a key part of this issue. There are, as chapter 1 discussed, observers who believe that too many democratic foreign policy cooks spoil the foreign policy broth. Career officials are apt to believe that only they—not transitory elected officials or the whims of public opinion—can provide the expertise and continuity necessary to successful foreign policy. Some scholars agree that the bureaucrats provide stability to foreign policy process because of the length of their time in office and their institutional background (Aberbach, Mezger, & Rockman, 1991).

Conventional wisdom holds that governmental officials in democracies are held accountable to the public for their actions. This is more or less true for elected officials and those appointed officials, such as the secretaries of state and defense, whose time in office is dependent on the confidence and tenure of the president. Democratic theory becomes a good deal murkier when we consider bureaucracies.

The power and accountability of bureaucrats in a democratic system is important because few of the people in government are political leaders whose time in power is directly or indirectly dependent on voters and elections. A handful of others are permanent employees (such as senior military officers or foreign service officers who become ambassadors or even assistant secretaries of state) who reach high decision making levels and, as such, might be considered political leaders. Thus the line between bureaucrat and political leader is imprecise and permeable. That lack of finite clarity should not, however, disguise the fact that almost everyone in the government is someone whom few people have ever heard of and whom even fewer people have had a say in choosing and evaluating. Furthermore, it is even often unclear who made a decision. As one former assistant secretary of state has noted, "Responsibility for decision [in government] is as fluid and restless as quicksilver, and there seems to be neither a person nor an organization on whom it can be fixed." Instead, the official continued, the decision is made anonymously within "the labyrinth of governmental machinery," hidden under "layers and layers of bureaucracy" (Johnson, 1989:7). This anonymity and insularity raise some troubling questions for a democracy, a matter that we will address in a later section.

The accountability of bureaucrats is important because they administer an annual federal budget of approximately $1.5 trillion, accounting for about 30 percent of the GDP (gross domestic product) and costing about $6,000 per citizen. Such numbers are not mere curiosities. As we shall see, the size, scope, and complexity of the federal government and its programs, including foreign and national security affairs, are significant factors that empower the bureaucracy.

It is important to say at the outset that there is no implication here that career officials constitute some sort of dark, subterranean cabal to undermine U.S. interests, democracy, or the authority of elected officials. That is far from the truth. According to a recent study, State Department personnel and National Security Council staff members are "much more attentive to public opinion—as *they* operationally define it—than was previously thought" (Powlick, 1995b: 447, emphasis in original). "Contrary to the public mythology," Henry Kissinger (1979:319) has commented about senior military officers, for instance, they "rarely challenge the Commander in Chief; they seek excuses to support, not oppose him" and "to find a military reason" to support policies "they consider barely tolerable."

Some observers would argue that Kissinger was being too charitable, but the fact remains that members of the bureaucracy are seldom in open rebellion against political leaders or are trying consciously to undermine their policy. Conflict within the bureaucracy and between it and political officials is usually much more the result of different perspectives and policy preferences between career and political officeholders than it is a product of bureaucrats conspiring consciously to form policy counter to that espoused by elected officials. It would also be wrong to imagine that bureaucrats regularly or brazenly can ignore with impunity the wishes of elected officials. Bureaucratic accountability, insofar as it exists, occurs through a range of formal and informal limits to administrative power detailed below. The president and Congress exercise control through their shared power to reorganize the bureaucracy, to control its funds, and to determine who holds the top positions in each agency (Wood & Waterman, 1991).

Despite these limits, and whatever the specific inclinations and power of bureaucrats, the notion that they play an authoritative role in the foreign policy process raises serious questions regarding the accountability of foreign policy officials. No one elected these "faceless" officials who play such a significant role in running American foreign policy. Moreover, they generally continue in office no matter how the political preferences of the electorate may change and no matter who occupies the White House or which party controls Congress. This longevity and insularity raise the question: To whom are they accountable? The answer is that bureaucrats are not easily held accountable to the public, since they are neither chosen nor removable by the electoral process. Furthermore, bureaucrats are not easily held accountable by those officials who are elected democratically. This is because bureaucrats serve in office regardless of whether or not they agree with the elected officials and can be dismissed only for gross dereliction of their offices.

There are also difficulties in making evaluations of accountability. One is measuring just how responsive the bureaucrats have been in following policy directives from above (O'Loughlin, 1990). So even if we can say that bureaucrats are at least theoretically accountable to the American public and political leaders for their actions, it is difficult to know for sure whether they are in fact held accountable for their actions.

Notably, many political scandals have involved the accountability issue. The upheaval of the Iran-Contra affair, with the renegade actions of Oliver North and others in the bureaucracy, is a prime example. President Reagan's detached and delegatory leadership style allowed nonelected NSC, CIA, and other officials to implement a set of policies that ran directly counter to legal constraints placed on the administration by Congress in the form of the Boland Amendments. In an unusual twist on the bureaucratic accountability issue, the officials directing the Iran-Contra dealings took active steps to prevent accountability for the president by not telling him what was happening. This preserved the ability of the president to maintain what is called "plausible deniability," to say truthfully that, as far as he knew, no money-for-arms diversion to the rebels in Nicaragua had occurred.

Even more recently, a tale of murders and cover-ups allegedly involving CIA activities in Guatemala underscores the point of accountability. These events are discussed in the box, "The Guatemalan Connection" on pages 280–281.

The issue of accountability and the related issue of bureaucratic responsiveness to political direction are functions of the nature of organization and the civil service system. Increasing accountability and responsiveness is desireable, but the remedies have their own side effects.

Presidents have tried to increase their control of foreign policy, for example, by appointing political allies, rather than career **foreign service officers (FSOs)**, to many ambassadorships and other top diplomatic posts. There are many arguments for and against political compared to career ambassadors (Cohen, 1991). The advantage of political appointees is, of course, that they are loyal to the president, and their views are more likely to parallel those of the president rather than represent the institutional view of the State Department. The frequent disadvantage of political appointees is lack of expertise.

The percentage of career FSO appointments as ambassador has risen from about 50 percent during the Truman administration to about 70 percent during recent presidencies. Moreover, one study has found that while "the better posts in Europe, the Pacific islands and much of the Caribbean may be filled with the political affiliates of the current administration," presidents name FSOs to the "overwhelming majority of . . . posts in areas of conflict, tension, and turmoil" (Pacy & Henderson, 1992:399).

The record of the Clinton administration has followed this general pattern. President Clinton pledged that he too would fill 70 percent of all ambassadorships with career diplomats and that political appointees would be given posts only if they merited them. Clinton met his goal at first. By late June 1993 the president had kept his promise by filling 74 percent of the posts with career officials. Subsequent appointments lowered that percentage, though, to only 59 percent career appointees by April 1994. "The numbers so far are bad," charged F. A. Harris, president of the American Foreign Service Association, which represents current and retired FSOs. "In many cases we're sending people who are doing a C job when we should be sending people who should do an A plus job. The reason is lack of experience."[1]

Critics charge that too often bureaucracies operate with too little accountability to elected leaders. This concern is illustrated by the revelation in 1995 that the CIA had been paying as a spy a Guatemalan colonel who was allegedly responsible for the 1990 murder of a U.S. citizen and the suspected 1992 nonjudicial execution of a rebel Guatemalan leader, Efrain Bamaca Velasquez. Bamaca was also the husband of an American, Jennifer Harbury, who is here holding a picture of her missing husband while conducting a hunger strike outside the Ministry of Justice in Guatemala City. The story of CIA and White House cover-up regarding U.S. policy toward Guatemala is told in the box entitled "The Guatemalan Connection." Congressional investigations and Ms. Harbury's protest helped expose a bureaucracy-directed policy that many Americans found objectionable.

That Clinton, like most presidents, has made numerous political appointments is not the issue. The question is one of qualifications. Some of his appointees have been individuals with long-standing government service and considerable expertise. The appointment of retired admiral William J. Crowe Jr., a former chairman of the Joint Chiefs of Staff with a Ph.D. in political science from Princeton, to the post of American ambassador to the United Kingdom is one example. The appointment of former vice president and senator Walter Mondale as ambassador to Japan is another.

(Continued on the next page)

The Guatemalan Connection

Michael DeVine, an American living in Guatemala was found dead, almost beheaded, on a road outside his village in May 1990. It is unclear why DeVine was executed, but evidence convinced the U.S. ambassador, Thomas F. Strook, that the Guatemalan military was responsible. "We knew that they [the military] had murdered this guy," Strook later recalled. "I was furious," he continued. "Here was a peaceful American citizen being murdered by an army that we are sending aid to.... I just figured that this was something that the average American taxpayer wouldn't stand for."[1]

Another thing that the average American taxpayer would not have stood for was CIA involvement, however indirect, in DeVine's death. Ambassador Strook knew that various Guatemalan military officers were "assets"; that is they were receiving funds from the CIA in return for providing information and for other forms of cooperation. Strook called in the CIA station chief, the agency's top official in Guatemala. "I looked him in the eye and said, 'Are any of your assets involved in this?'" Strook recalls. "And he said no. And I believed him."[2] The ambassador soon found that his trust may have been misplaced. Colonel Julio Roberto Alpírez commanded the special forces base from which the soldiers that probably killed DeVine had come. He had twice attended high-level military schools in the United States; Alpírez was also on the CIA payroll. When Ambassador Strook later learned about the CIA relationship with the colonel, he knew that he had been deceived by the CIA. "If I didn't know about this Alpírez thing," the ambassador conceded, "I'd have gone to my grave thinking that the [CIA] station did a good job."[3]

As a result of the killing of DeVine by the military, the Bush administration in December 1990 ordered a suspension of about $3 million a year in military aid to Guatemala. The CIA had a different view and continued its annual $5 million to $7 million annual "liaison" support for Guatemala's military intelligence operations. The State Department denies that it knew that the liaison aid had continued in contradiction to U.S. official policy. "This raises very serious questions," one State Department official pointed out. "The CIA absolutely knew that the U.S. government was confronting the Guatemalan government.... They knew that it [DeVine's death] was a central issue in U.S.–Guatemalan relations. For them [the CIA] not to have disclosed that [the millions of dollars in liaison aid] to State and to the NSC is a serious issue."[4]

Amazingly, the CIA may not have violated any laws in obscuring its ties to Colonel Alpírez and continuing its unilateral dispatch of foreign aid to Guatemala's military. Unlike formal covert operations, liaison programs neither require presidential authorization nor must the House and Senate intelligence committees be notified.

Suspicions about the part of Alpírez in political executions did not end with the DeVine case. A second incident involved the death while in custody of rebel leader Efrain Bamaca Valasquez, known by the nom de guerre of Comandante Edvardo. He was captured in March 1992. Later, amid reports that he had been tortured and executed, his American wife, Jennifer Harbury, an attorney, asked the U.S. government for information. In November 1994, national security adviser Anthony Lake told Harbury that the government had no information about her husband's death. What Lake should have said was that his part of the government had no information. Harbury turned up the pressure on U.S. and Guatemalan officials by staging a hunger strike outside the Ministry of Justice in Guatemala City. The resulting publicity prompted President Clinton to order an investigation. Information began to surface. Congress learned that the CIA had reports dating back to 1992 on Bamaca's death but had not initially shared those with other agencies, then had resisted disclosing the information. When

Other Clinton appointments have been at least partly a function of patronage, though. At one point early in 1993, Secretary of State Christopher sent a list of four career diplomats to the president for his approval for diplomatic posts. Clinton scribbled a "no" next to each name and added the note, "Where are all our friends?" and returned it to Christopher for further consideration. Numerous so-called FOBs (friends

House Intelligence Committee member Robert Toricelli (D-NJ) released the information, the CIA's acting director, Admiral William Studeman, replied that the agency had not known of the murders of Bamaca and DeVine at the time that the deaths occurred.[5] A subsequent investigation by the CIA inspector general made it clear that Studeman's "at the time" comment was, at best, a razor-thin semantic distinction. The report indicated that the station chief had been reprimanded for not telling his own superiors in the CIA about the connections to Colonel Alpírez, and the station chief was finally removed from his office in February 1992 for that and other transgressions. Among these was not telling the U.S. ambassador, Marilyn McAfee, of a plot by Guatemalan army officers to force her out of the country by launching rumors of indiscreet behavior. It was, the report disclosed, the sixth time in 8 years that a station chief in Latin America had been cashiered by the CIA after having been accused of such activities as lying to superiors, sexual harassment, threatening subordinates with a gun, erroneously shipping tons of cocaine to the United States, and the loss of $1 million due to sloppy bookkeeping.

There are even suggestions, although no firm proof, that the Guatemalan military and the CIA preferred to work with one another and mutually resisted political direction from either of their legal superiors. Vincincio Cerezo, the president of Guatemala from 1986 through 1990, has recalled that "we demanded that Guatemalan officers inform us of issues that they handled with the U.S. intelligence agents, and that they not undertake any operation with them that was not authorized by the Government." While "this was the official policy," former president Cerezo concluded with some understatement, "that doesn't mean that in some cases some officials don't do things that could be considered irregular."[6] From the American side, a report based on the comments of one official familiar with the situation concluded that the actions of the station chief about the plot against Ambassador McAfee and other matters showed that the CIA operative "was showing a stronger affinity for his contacts in the Guatemalan military than he had for the ambassador."[7]

The new DCI, John Deutch, fired two officials involved in the scandal, demoted another, and issued letters of reprimand to seven others in September 1995. Deutch told Congress that his inquiry would continue and that he expected "to find further instances" of CIA wrongdoing.[8] Thus the investigation into the CIA-Alpírez connection continues. "This is the beginning, not the end, of the story," as one intelligence official notes correctly.[9] Discovering all the details of who in the United States knew what and when is not necessary to make some unsettling conclusions about bureaucratic accountability in a democracy. At the very least, the CIA station chief in Guatemala was a renegade who pursued his own foreign policy and did not disclose some or all of what he was doing to his CIA superiors in Washington, much less the State Department, Congress, or the president of the United States. It is also clear that once the CIA learned of the connections with Alpírez and his alleged part in the executions, the agency suppressed the information. In fact, until the uproar generated by Harbury's hunger strike, the CIA's only seeming concession to the concerns being expressed was to remove Alpírez from the payroll, but then only after giving him $44,000 in severance pay. Thus even before the final chapter of the story is written, one is left wondering about accountability in a democracy when agencies, perhaps even individuals, conduct their own foreign policy on behalf of the United States while hiding and, perhaps, even lying about what they are doing.

of Bill) were found. Swanee Grace Hunt was among them. She was named ambassador to Austria. Among Hunt's other qualifications to represent her country was the fact that she had contributed $328,700 to the 1992 Democratic campaign.[2] K. Terry Dornbush's appointment as ambassador to the Netherlands was aided by $253,750's worth of friendship he felt for the Clinton campaign. M. Larry Lawrence ($196,304

There is a controversy over whether political allies of the president or career foreign service officers make better ambassadors. Like most presidents, Clinton has appointed a large number of his supporters to head U.S. embassies. Among her other qualifications, Pamela Harriman's donation of $130,902 to Clinton's presidential campaign helped her gain an appointment as U.S. ambassador to France. Ambassador Harriman, accompanied by General Wesley Clark and Assistant Secretary of State Richard Holbrooke, is seen here leaving the French Foreign Ministry on the Quai d'Orsay.

contribution) went to Switzerland as ambassador; Edward Elliott Elson ($182,714) became ambassador to Denmark; Pamela C. Harriman ($130,902) took up the U.S. ambassadorial post in Paris. Donors in the $25,000 to $100,000 range became ambassadors to such countries and organizations as Belgium, Germany, Sweden, and the United Nations. Some of these appointees (such as Madeleine Albright at the UN and former FSO and assistant secretary of state Richard C. Holbrooke) had expertise as well as money.

The qualifications of some other appointees are less clear. During her confirmation hearing, Ambassador-designate Hunt noted that she had been to Austria several times, that her husband had once studied orchestra conducting in Salzburg, and that her mother-in-law had a doctorate from the University of Vienna. Ambassador-designate Lawrence told senators that he had traveled to Switzerland about 25 times to conduct business negotiations. A supportive Senator John F. Kerry (D-MA) added that Lawrence would be helped in his post by his experience in welcoming prominent people, a job skill acquired by the nominee while hosting the rich and famous (including Bill Clinton) at Hunt's luxurious Hotel del Coronado near San Diego, California, and his personal 17-bedroom, 13-bathroom home. Among other appointments, former Washington Redskins linebacker and car salesman Sidney Williams became ambassador to the Bahamas, and prominent North Carolina fundraiser Jeanette W. Hyde was appointed as ambassador to Barbados. She had told a newspaper that she was hoping for Greece or Switzerland but "would take some little island."[3]

To return to our basic concern with bureaucratic accountability, the dilemma is how to have a bureaucracy that is accountable and responsive while also preserving the expertise of career civil servants and avoiding the obvious dangers of an overly politicized bureaucracy. A final point is that none of this discussion means that bureaucracy or bureaucrats are inherently antidemocratic. Bureaucracy is necessary in a complex government, and most civil servants serve conscientiously and well. Still, they exercise impressive powers, and the degree of their accountability, or lack of it, to political leaders and, by extension, to the people, is an important concern.

THE CAST OF
BUREAUCRATIC PLAYERS

Having discussed the general role and accountability of "bureaucracy" in a democratic political system, we can now turn our attention to the major bureaucratic actors in the U.S. foreign policy process (Prados, 1991). A good beginning point is to note that the term bureaucracy is misleading. Even though we use this collective noun, there is really no such singular thing as *the* bureaucracy. Instead it is better to think of the term in the plural: bureaucracies. There are an almost countless number of departments, agencies, and other administrative units in the government that require almost 600 pages to list in the *United States Government Manual*. Even listing all the agencies would not reveal a true roster of the bureaucracies because most of them are subdivided.

The substructures often have their own views and ways of operating. Secretary of State Dean Acheson (1969:15) has recalled that during his long service in the "ancient and, to outsiders, mysterious" State Department:

> bureaucratic power had come to rest in the division chiefs and the advisers, political, legal, and economic. . . . The heads of all these divisions, like barons in a feudal system . . . were constantly at odds, if not at war. Their frontiers, delimited in some cases by geography and in others by function, were vague and overlapping.

There have been reorganizations and reforms since Acheson's time at the department (1941–1953), but the State Department has become an even more vast and complex organization, as Figure 10.1 shows. Whereas in late 1944, at the height of World War II, the department's top officials numbered just 6 (the secretary of state, the undersecretary, and 4 assistant secretaries), it now numbers 28 (the secretary, deputy secretary, 5 undersecretaries, and 21 assistant secretaries). Surely that size and intricacy necessarily reflect the world; but the characteristics also are today, as in Acheson's time, the stuff of bureaucratic insularity.

Breaking the bureaucracy down even further, we find that its various units and subunits are staffed by about 3 million civilian and 2 million military personnel. This means that 1 in every 50 Americans is a federal worker. As we will discuss later, these individuals have their personal views and operational standards and, thus, the potential for affecting the formulation and conduct of policy. Many analysts believe that such phrases as "the government decided" mask the reality that decisions are really more the product of the struggle between various government agencies.

In the following sections, we will examine the organizational components of the bureaucracy. The executive bureaucracy is made up of several Cabinet-level departments and a number of specialized agencies. We will begin by discussing two key departments: the Departments of State and Defense. We will then move on to two other departments—Treasury and Commerce—that deal with specific aspects of foreign economic policy. This discussion will be followed by examinations of the intelligence community and White House staff.

Executive Departments

Each component of the bureaucracy has resources and capabilities that in theory make its role in the foreign policy process distinct from the role of each of the other components. In reality, as we will see throughout this chapter, these role distinctions have been blurred over the years as international relations issues have become more complex and interwoven and as the bureaucracies themselves have attempted to expand their influence within the system.

The State Department

The State Department is meant to be the primary diplomatic arm of the government. It is charged with providing information for and advising the president and other top decision makers, with negotiating treaties and other international agreements, and with maintaining constant contact with foreign countries through its embassies worldwide. The department is divided organizationally along issue lines (such as the Bureau of Business and Economic Affairs), along regional lines (such as the Bureau of East Asian and Pacific affairs and African affairs), and along administrative lines (such as the Office of Legislative Affairs).

Although the State Department is in theory the leader in foreign policy, in actuality its leadership has ebbed and flowed. The department's exact role depends on several factors. One is the desires of each president. President Kennedy, for instance, wanted to take the lead in foreign policy. That was one of the reasons that he appointed the relatively mild Dean Rusk as secretary of state. The same desire to exercise personal control led Richard Nixon to choose William P. Rogers to be his secretary of state. Henry Kissinger (1979:26) has recalled that Nixon considered Rogers's "unfamiliarity with the subject [of foreign policy] to be an asset because it guaranteed that policy direction would remain in the White House."

A second factor that defines the authority of the State Department is the temperament and skills of the secretary of state, especially relative to the president's national security adviser and other powerful officeholders. Clinton's secretary of state, Warren Christopher, was initially thought to be a weak choice for the job because of his quiet and unassuming demeanor. One foreign policy analyst even commented that "Christopher makes a good number two, but isn't the person you want up-front on foreign affairs."[4] By late 1994 Christopher's stock had fallen so low that there were widely reported rumors that he would resign. These were later confirmed by Colin Powell, who recorded in his memoirs that on December 18 Clinton told him that Christopher would step down and asked the retired general whether he would accept the post of secretary of state. Powell turned the post down because of "the amorphous way the administration handled foreign policy."[5] Christopher stayed on, and

FIGURE 10.1

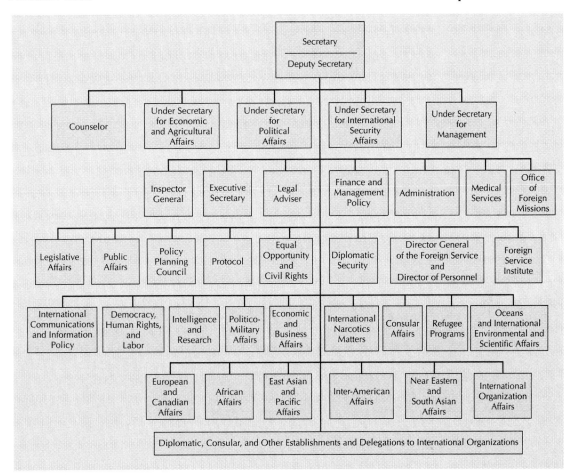

Data source: U.S. Government Manual 1994/95.

The State Department is a highly complex and fragmented organization. It is divided into offices that specialize in regional perspectives on diplomatic issues (such as African Affairs or East Asian and Pacific Affairs), into offices with topical specializations (such as Refugee Programs or Democracy, Human Rights, and Labor), and into offices that specialize in other aspects of diplomacy (such as Diplomatic Security and various administrative offices). The State Department also has offices that specialize in areas covered by other portions of the executive redundancy. For example, Intelligence and Research is also covered by the CIA, Economic and Business Affairs by the Commerce Department, and International Narcotic Matters by the Office of National Drug Control Policy.

over time his low-key style came to command a good deal of respect and confidence within an administration populated by many younger, less-experienced appointees. As 1996 began, Christopher was still secretary of state and rightfully enjoying a good deal of praise for his role in brokering the Bosnian peace settlement, in resuscitating peace talks between Israel and Syria, and other successful diplomatic initiatives.

A third, and longer-term, factor in the varying role of the State Department is based on changes in the global system. As the international system has become increasingly interdependent, as more and more issues have become less distinctly either foreign or domestic and instead have become more intermestic, more and more agencies have come to assume important foreign policy roles. We will see presently, for instance, that in an era of massive economic interchange, the Department of the Treasury, the Department of Commerce, and other such agencies often play pivotal roles in international affairs. Technology, especially the rapid increase in communication and travel, has also changed the global system and the State Department's role. The department no longer clearly dominates the process of gathering and transmitting information about other countries and global issues to the president. When George Hill, who served as the top administrative aide to Secretary of State George Shultz, retired, he told his successor that "I am handing over something that is much more problematic, much less authoritative [than it once was]. You [are] going to have a lot of problems because [the] monopoly [on advising the president is] gone. People are doing things in their own way" (Kux, 1995:25).

The Defense Department

The Defense Department (DoD) is charged with providing and maintaining the military forces to deter and wage war and to protect national security. Since its creation from the combination of the Departments of War, Army, and Navy in 1947, its role has continued to grow to the point where it now plays an active part both in foreign policy formulation and implementation. It possesses the largest budget ($253.5 billion for FY1995) and the largest number of civilian personnel (nearly 900,000 million) of any of the bureaucracies that deal with foreign policy. The department also includes 1.6 million uniformed personnel. Because of the shape of its headquarters building, DoD is often called the Pentagon.

One of the primary policy reasons for the power of the Pentagon in foreign policy making grew out of the need to deter the perceived threat of Soviet aggression during the cold war. Beginning in the late 1940s and early 1950s, and formalized through the creation of NSC-68, discussed in chapter 2, most policy makers thought that the outcome of the cold war confrontation would hinge on the degree to which the United States could militarily contain Soviet influence throughout the world. Operationally, this meant deploying significant numbers of military forces abroad in such places as Germany, Japan, Korea, and the Philippines and the development of a full range of military forces for use in times of conflict. This operational capability and the monopoly on military expertise housed within the department made DoD an increasingly important player in the foreign policy process.

It is certainly true that in the aftermath of the end of the cold war, the defense budget, in terms of real dollars, has shrunk about 39 percent from $301 billion in FY1987 to $185 billion (in 1987 dollars) in FY 1995 (see Table 8.2 on p. 225). Nevertheless, DoD's budget is still larger than that of any other single agency, and members of the Clinton administration have stressed the continued necessity of maintaining a strong military force (Davis, 1995). Moreover, there is pressure from the Republican-controlled Congress to increase the defense budget submitted by Clinton. All this suggests that the Pentagon will remain a power in the foreign policy process in the years ahead.

The Treasury and Commerce Departments

When thinking about who makes foreign policy, there are many bureaucratic units, such as the Departments of Treasury and Commerce, that do not come readily to mind. This is partly because economic affairs have traditionally been low politics and have received less public and media attention than the topics dealt with by State and Defense. The flood tide of global economic and other forms of interdependence is changing that, though, and other executive departments are playing a larger role in the foreign policy process. "Everyone's been saying for a long time that foreign policy is becoming economic, but like everything, it's taken a while for the message to sink in around here," observed Clinton's first secretary of the treasury, Lloyd Bentsen. "It just shows you how important the economic issues are internationally," he continued, "and that's a situation secretaries of state don't work at very much."[6]

On the global stage, the Treasury Department is responsible for U.S. international monetary policy and for concerns about the international debt owed to U.S. banks and other institutions and individuals by many developing countries. In recent years, Treasury has played a large role in helping to coordinate monetary policies among the G-7 countries, as discussed in chapter 3, and in renegotiating debt packages for Mexico, Chile, and others. Treasury was also instrumental in developing the stabilization package offered to Mexico after the severe peso crisis that hit at the end of 1994.

The Commerce Department, overseeing trade and technology issues, is also an increasingly active player, even though the Republican Contract with America targets it for elimination in the years ahead. Under the Clinton administration, Commerce has taken the unprecedented role of promoting U.S. business interests around the world. Jack Shaw, chairman of Hughes Network, credits Ron Brown, Clinton's secretary of commerce, with helping him land a $700 million contract in India for the development of a satellite communications system. "In my 30 years in international communications," Hughes states, "this is the first time that I've felt the U.S. government has truly supported U.S. business." Specifically, the presence of Secretary Brown on Shaw's trip to India enabled his firm to see everyone they wanted to see from top politicians to lower-level bureaucrats that implement the decisions.[7]

There are also any number of other departments and agencies that have some international responsibilities. Among the Cabinet-level departments, the Agriculture Department has an office of International Affairs and Commodity Programs; various elements of the Department of Justice, including the Drug Enforcement Agency and the Immigration and Naturalization Service, have personnel stationed abroad; there is a Bureau of International Affairs in the Labor Department; the Coast Guard and the Bureau of International Affairs and Aviation are part of the Department of Transportation; and the Department of Energy is involved with building nuclear warheads and bombs. Bureaucracies with at least some international activities or national security responsibilities also include numerous independent agencies, such as the Arms Control and Disarmament Agency, the Agency for International Development, the Export-Import Bank, the Federal Maritime Commission, the Inter-American Foundation, the International Trade Commission, the National Aeronautics and Space Administration, the Peace Corps, the Selective Service System, and the United States Information Agency. Detailing the activities of all these departments and agencies is beyond our need here and, indeed, would fill up a good-sized book. A bit more about some of these units is available, however, in Table 10.1.

TABLE 10.1   Bureaucratic Players in American Foreign Policy

Executive Branch Office	Budget	No. of Personnel[1]	Roles and Responsibilities
Executive Office of the President			
National Security Council	$6,000,000	52	To advise the president on foreign policy issues and to help coordinate and integrate the functions of the various executive agencies and departments dealing with national security issues.
Office of the Special Trade Representative	$22,000,000	168	Oversees all U.S. activities pertaining to the multilateral trade negotiations under the General Agreements on Tariffs and Trade; consults outside of the GATT structure with other governments on trade issues; negotiates in the United Nations Conference on Trade and Development (UNCTAD) and at other international discussions regarding international trade.
Office of Management and Budget	$57,000,000	539	General budget creation, oversight, and analysis. The National Security and International Affairs unit, a subdivision, is charged with supervising and analyzing the budget for the various other elements of the foreign policy establishment.
Office of National Drug Control Policy	$53,000,000	28	Advises the president on all aspects of national drug control policy. Deals with international drug trafficking issues.
Office of Science and Technology Policy	$4,000,000	35	Serves as a source of scientific, engineering, and technological analysis and judgment for the president. This office's role was especially prominent during the Reagan administration's Strategic Defense Initiative.
Examples of Executive Departments			
Department of State	$5,718,000,000	25,200	Chief diplomatic arm of the federal government. Aims to promote the long-range security goals of the United States. Negotiates treaties and international agreements; maintains constant contacts with foreign governments through embassies worldwide. Organizationally, it is divided along issue, regional, and functional lines.

Executive Branch Office	Budget	No. of Personnel[1]	Roles and Responsibilities
Department of Defense	$268,000,000,000	868,300[2]	Responsible for providing the military forces needed to deter and wage war and to protect national security. Largest budget and number of employees of foreign policy agencies.
Department of the Treasury	$13,016,000,000[3]	157,300	Responsible for formulating and recommending international financial policy. Most recently, Treasury has played a prominent role in international debt issues and macroeconomic policy coordination among the industrialized countries.
Department of Commerce	$2,915,000,000	36,000	Responsible for international trade and technology policies.
Department of Agriculture	$60,753,000,000	109,800	Oversees international agricultural commerce; promotes American cooperation in the agricultural sectors of developing countries.
Department of Energy	$17,839,000,000	19,800	Oversees many nuclear weapons programs.

Examples of Foreign Policy Agencies

Central Intelligence Agency	$182,000 plus secret budget	N/A	Advises the NSC on intelligence issues in all aspects of the foreign policy process; gathers and analyzes information; conducts covert operations.
Arms Control and Disarmament Agency	$46,000,000	233	Formulates and implements U.S. arms control policy, including the international arms trade.
Agency for International Development	$3,440,000,000	3,900	Administers economic assistance programs.

[1]All personnel figures are 1994 figures.
[2]Department of Defense personnel figure reflects only *civilian* employees and not uniformed military.
[3]Department of Treasury budget figure excludes interest on the public debt, which is included in the Treasury's budget figure published by the Office of Management and Budget. As a result, the $25 billion budget figure for the Treasury, as with the others in this chart, reflects the Treasury's operating budget.

Data source: U.S. Government Manual (1995), Washington, DC: Government Printing Office; *Budget of the United States Government, FY1996* (1995), Washington, DC: Government Printing Office.

There is no such thing as *the* bureaucracy. Instead, there are many departments, agencies, and other government units that are powerful players in the U.S. foreign policy process.

The Intelligence Community

To most people, the Central Intelligence Agency (CIA) is synonymous with the term intelligence community. But the intelligence community comprises a much more diverse set of actors, including the CIA but also such organizations as the National Security Agency, the super-secret agency charged with collecting information from telecommunications and other types of signal intelligence (SIGINT) from around the world.

As the name suggests, however, the *Central* Intelligence Agency was created in 1947 to coordinate intelligence activities throughout the government. Headed by the Director of Central Intelligence (DCI), the DCI is the primary adviser to the president on intelligence issues. The CIA is also charged with information gathering and analysis and some types of covert activities.

During the cold war, the efforts of the intelligence community were primarily focused on gathering information that could be used in U.S. efforts to contain Soviet influence in the world. With the end of the cold war, the intelligence community in general and the CIA in particular have come under increasing pressure to shrink both in terms of budget and personnel. Moreover, CIA personnel have been demoralized by such scandals as the discovery that one of their own, Aldrich Ames, had long spied for the Soviets and by revelations about the CIA's financial support of a Guatemalan military officer known for terrorist tactics who was involved in at least two murders. The credibility of the CIA was further tarnished in late 1995 by the revelation that it had spent over $20 million consulting psychics in an effort to foretell the future. In one instance while Henry Kissinger was secretary of state and en route to Riyadh, Saudi Arabia, a CIA–employed psychic broke into a cold sweat during a seance and screamed, "No! No! No!" He told alarmed agents that he saw a Libyan assassin shooting at Kissinger, missing him, but killing his wife Nancy. The CIA sent a flash warning to the U.S. embassy in Riyadh. When Kissinger and his wife landed, they were rushed into a waiting limousine, which then sped pell-mell to King Faisal's palace. No Libyan assassin materialized, but, according to a retired CIA official, "We almost killed Kissinger" by careening along at speeds of up to 90 miles an hour amid the screeching brakes of startled Saudi drivers and the bleating of panic-stricken Saudi goats.[8]

Some critics, such as Senator Daniel Patrick Moynihan (D-NY), have called for the elimination of the CIA entirely. And David Boren, former chairman of the Senate Intelligence Committee, has asserted that "the CIA has become mainly bureaucratic, protective of itself." Senator Arlen Specter (R-PA), current chairman of the Senate Intelligence Committee, is even more pointed when he says that "there is an aura of incompetence" in the agency today.[9] All these pressures, DCI John Deutch asserts understandably, has left the intelligence community feeling "undervalued, a little picked on" these days.[10]

To relieve outside pressures and improve CIA morale, Deutch has undertaken a radical reorganization of the agency. He replaced the top management soon after taking over in early 1995 and installed Nora Slatkin, a former assistant secretary of the navy, as a chief deputy. It is through her that most personnel will report to the DCI. Having to report through a woman sent shock waves through the male-oriented CIA.

The White House Bureaucracy

Presidents have been frustrated by the growth in the size and power of the bureaucracies and by the difficulty of dealing with the agencies' unwieldy size, their bureaucratic rivalries, and their frequent resistance to direction. As a result, presidents have sought to escape the burden of their own bureaucracies. President Kennedy, for one, mused—perhaps facetiously—that he hoped to establish "a secret office of 30 people or so to run foreign policy while maintaining the State Department as a facade in which people might contentedly carry papers from bureau to bureau" (Nelson & Tilman, 1984:499).

The Executive Office of the President

The method that presidents have chosen to escape dependency on and restraints by the extended federal bureaucracy is to create new, albeit more personal, bureaucracies. Part of the White House bureaucracy includes the president's chief of staff and other immediate aides. A second part is called the Executive Office of the President (EOP). Presidents have met at least part of Kennedy's hope by expanding their own staffs and by creating advisers and support staff that report directly to the White House in an attempt to get around the existing bureaucracies. Over 2,000 people work at the White House on the president's personal staff and in the EOP in such foreign policy–relevant organizations as the Council of Economic Advisers, the Office of National Drug Control Policy, the Office of Science and Technology Policy, and the Office of Management and Budget. To increase coordination of trade policy among the Departments of Agriculture, Commerce, Defense, State, and Treasury, the office of the Special Trade Representative (STR) was established in 1963. The STR reports to the president directly and has a staff that has grown from an initial 30 to over 150 now.

The National Security Council

More than any unit of the EOP, however, the National Security Council (NSC) reflects the growth of the presidential bureaucracy (Crabb & Mulcahy, 1991; Shoemaker, 1991) and is the highest-profile White House foreign policy actor. The creation in 1947 of the NSC came about because of the desire to control or circumvent the bureaucracy. The NSC technically consists of the president, the vice president, and the secretaries of state and defense. It was designed to bring these decision makers together and to provide them with a small, independent staff to coordinate the collection and dissemination of information, analyses, and alternatives. Over the years, the role of the NSC and the size and role of its staff have changed markedly. The NSC itself hardly exists beyond paper, since presidents choose whichever advisers they wish to consult on foreign policy concerns. The real issues center on the evolution of the NSC staff and all the changes that have served to empower it. One change involves the size of the NSC staff. When it was established, the staff numbered 20 professionals. It grew to 85 in the mid-1970s. Since then the NSC professional staff dropped to 55 in 1994. These numbers are somewhat muddled, though, by the frequent "detailing," or assigning, of staff members to the NSC by other agencies.

The creation of the position of special assistant to the president for national security affairs was another significant change for the NSC. This position was not even mentioned in the 1947 act that established the NSC. The NSC administrator was appropriately titled "secretary." The change came in 1953 when President Dwight D. Eisenhower appointed Robert Cutler as a special assistant to coordinate the policies of the diverse agencies within the foreign policy bureaucracy. Cutler played a relatively discreet role. Nevertheless, because of the contact between the president and the special assistant, the importance of the position began to grow. Soon the special assistant was being called the "national security adviser." President Kennedy appointed Harvard dean McGeorge Bundy to the position. A combination of Bundy's good personal relations with the president, the low-key style of Secretary of State Dean Rusk, and Kennedy's inexperience and impatience with administration led to the diminution of the influence of the State Department and the rise of the NSC. Symbolically, common usage of the term NSC changed during the Kennedy years from meaning the formal council members to the national security adviser and the staff.

Since that time, the national security adviser has almost always been a major policy player rather than just an information coordinator. In some administrations, the national security adviser has even overshadowed the secretary of state. President Nixon's national security adviser, Henry Kissinger, was much more influential than Secretary of State William Rogers, whom Kissinger (1979:30) viewed as "an insensitive neophyte who threatened the careful design of our foreign policy." That contrasted with Kissinger's image of himself as being like a "cowboy who leads the wagon train by riding ahead alone on his horse," as he confided indiscreetly to an interviewer. "This amazing, romantic character suits me precisely," Kissinger went on, "because to be alone is part of my style, or, if you like, my character" (Schulzinger, 1989:115). The image of the stocky, bespectacled, German-accented Kissinger as the Lone Ranger was an odd one. Nevertheless, he thought so highly of being alone on the policy prairie that when Nixon appointed Kissinger as secretary of state, he insisted on keeping his position as NSC head, thus avoiding a rival.

Similarly, during the presidency of Jimmy Carter, Zbigniew Brzezinski was widely recognized as the most influential foreign policy adviser to the president. Secretary of State Cyrus Vance was often out of the loop, being excluded, as chapter 5 details for example, from the decision to launch the abortive raid to free the American hostages in Iran. Other national security advisers have played a more modest role. But the office is now far beyond the executive secretary role intended originally, and many observers regard the national security adviser and the NSC as rivals to the secretary of state and the State Department. Moreover, the rivalry is likely to continue. "There's been a persistent tendency for presidents to come into office saying they will give power to the secretary of state and downgrade the NSC," a former staff member has observed. "But it never works that way."[11] Insofar as this is true, it means that the NSC and its staff do not play their intended role of being a neutral coordinator of the flow of information and advice to the president.

A third important change took place in the NSC during the Nixon presidency. Kissinger and the NSC began to take on operational, in contrast to strictly advisory, roles. Kissinger not only dominated the advisory system, but he also engaged in operational functions such as the secret negotiations to arrange for Nixon's trip to China and the also secret negotiations with North Vietnam to end U.S. involvement in the Vietnam War. This operational role has continued sporadically since then. Most notably, the operations involved with the Iran-Contragate scandal, detailed elsewhere, were centered in the NSC, especially on NSC aide Lieutenant Colonel Oliver North.

Even if a national security adviser wants to shun the limelight and play the role of honest broker, there are almost inevitable pressures to step to the forefront. When President Clinton named Anthony Lake as national security adviser at the beginning of his administration, the president chose a man versed in the workings of the NSC.

As a political scientist, Lake had studied and written against what he saw as confusion in U.S. foreign policy resulting from the internecine struggles among the State Department, the NSC, the Defense Department, and other policy making centers (Destler, Gelb, & Lake, 1984). Especial anathemas to Lake were the examples of the infighting between Secretary of State Rogers and national security adviser Kissinger in the Nixon administration as well as between Secretary of State Vance and national security adviser Brzezinski in the Carter administration. Therefore Lake began his term, according to a diplomat who reportedly knows him well, saying to himself daily, "I'm not Kissinger; I'm not Brzezinski."[12]

Given his concerns, Lake was extremely cautious at first about pushing his point of view and, especially, of doing so in public. Indeed, he was so invisible that the caption to a photograph of President Clinton and his advisers that appeared in the *New York Times* labeled the national security adviser an "unidentified" man.[13] The exceedingly restrained nature of Secretary of State Christopher also made him seem invisible. Referring to problems in Haiti, one critic quipped that "none of this would be happening if Warren Christopher were still alive."[14] With Clinton a foreign policy novice, this twin set of vague images created the unsettling impression among some that no one was in charge of foreign policy.

Subsequently, both Lake and Christopher asserted themselves more. One of Lake's motivations was his conviction that the president's foreign policy needed a strong public defense. Another part of Lake's emergence is almost inherent in the office of national security adviser, particularly when the president is not a foreign policy expert. "Because [President Clinton] is not involved in foreign policy as much as other presidents have been," says one White House official, "Tony is in a unique position. He is the only one who sees the president every day. That puts him in a very strong position to be the interpreter" of foreign events. A third factor, some say, is Lake's ambitions. Behind his accommodating exterior, Lake is very competitive. "He likes to play squash," says one colleague, because "there's a lot of disciplined violence."[15] Perhaps most indicative of Lake's attachment to power is that he reportedly chose it over his marriage. Lake decided to stay on as national security adviser despite having promised his wife of 30 years that he would step down after 2 years and restore their family life to relative normalcy outside the pressure of Washington. They were separated in 1995.

Whatever his precise motivations, Lake has come to argue that while his primary responsibility is still to "make sure that the president is getting all points of view," he now also makes his own recommendations "because if you don't have a view, you shouldn't be doing this job."[16]

Before leaving this discussion of the White House bureaucracy, two important issues should be mentioned. One is whether the president's effort to escape the regular bureaucracy by creating a presidential bureaucracy has had a positive effect on the formulation and implementation of American foreign policy. The results are mixed, at best. On the positive side, from the president's point of view, the NSC staff and other White House staffs are more closely tied to and responsive to the president than are the staffs of the State Department and the other main departments and agencies. Without the NSC system the president would be without a means for more direct control over the diverse organizations within the executive branch. On the negative side, the NSC has largely failed to fulfill its original purpose. The NSC staff was created to coordinate the flow of information and advice to the president;

the NSC itself was meant to be the ultimate forum for foreign policy and national security debates and decisions. When the national security adviser is a policy advocate, as he usually is, then he is a rival of the secretary of state and other top decision makers and cannot, by definition, serve the role of honest broker of information and analysis. In this way the NSC is often just one more self-interested bureaucratic player. Thus the lack of coordination often persists, thereby compounding, not easing, the president's problems. "As the size of the White House staff expands," notes Joseph Califano, a senior staff member in both the Johnson and Carter administrations, "the ability of the President to maintain taut control is weakened" (Rose, 1988:160).

Another drawback to the policy advocacy role of the NSC staff involves secrecy. Even more than most bureaucracies, the NSC is able to shield information from the view of the public, legislators, and even other agencies. The national security adviser is not, like the secretary of state and other Cabinet members, subject to Senate confirmation. Nor are the national security advisers or other NSC staff members (again, unlike the secretaries of state and other departments) required to testify before Congress, although they occasionally do so voluntarily. Similarly, NSC internal documents are normally not available to Congress or the public. Especially when the NSC conducts foreign policy, its ability to operate outside the public and legislative view raises questions about democratic control of foreign policy.

THE BUREAUCRATIC PERSPECTIVE: ONE GOVERNMENT, MANY VIEWS

The structure of the bureaucracy and such issues as bureaucratic accountability would not be important—and this would be a very short book—if all Americans agreed on what policy should be or if the bureaucracy was a dispassionate mechanism that supplied information and advice evenhandedly and carried out policy faithfully according to the wishes of political leaders. None of these things are the case, however. Instead, there are multitudinous opinions about what policy should be. Almost inevitably, the policy preferences of career officials influence the information and advice they supply and how they implement policy. Scholars suggest that the bureaucratic perspective is rooted in such factors as organizational affiliation, personal ambition, and personal evaluation of the domestic and international political climates. Because the bureaucratic interests and outlooks diverge and sometime conflict, these perspectives interact to increase the level of struggle among bureaucrats and between them and political leaders, with each maneuvering in part to influence the policy process in ways that will benefit themselves and the organizations they serve.

For all these reasons, our next major step is to focus our attention on the bureaucratic perspective. The factors that create the bureaucratic perspective on policy making include expertise and ideology, self-interest, organizational standards and culture, and clientism.

Expertise and Political Point of View

The staffs of the Departments of State and Defense, the CIA, and the other foreign policy agencies are experts in their field. These professionals combine substantial

295

The
Bureaucratic
Perspective:
One
Government,
Many Views

education and training in their areas of specialty. This is as it should be. Moreover, given their *expertise,* it is natural for bureaucrats to develop their own opinions about how programs should be structured and operate. Those opinions may, however, differ from the perspectives and policy preferences of elected and appointed political leaders. When this occurs, the professional may try subtly or overtly to change declared policy or to administer policy in such a way as to bring it closer to the professional's view of how things should be done. Kissinger (1979:27) has observed that many of the State Department's career FSOs believe "that a lifetime of service and study has given them insights that transcend the untrained and shallow-rooted views of political appointees." Speaking in a similar way about CIA operatives, one agency insider commented that "they always feel their view is the right view. They're arrogant. They view themselves as a cut above."[17]

From this Olympian perspective, secretaries of state, CIA directors, and other officials are, in the words of one career ambassador, little more than "crusading amateurs" whose "comings and goings" create a "gypsy-encampment atmosphere along the banks of the Potomac" (Rourke, 1990:117). Elected officials fare no better in the estimate of some bureaucrats. When asked his opinion of the members of Congress, one senior civil servant replied, "They're a pretty dumb bunch," especially when compared with "most people in administrative jobs [who] are there because they are trained for the job" (Hummel & Isaak, 1986:224).

The *political point of view* of individual bureaucrats is another factor that influences bureaucrats' perspective. Ideology is one element of this perspective. Like most of us, government professionals have a political point of view. They are liberals, moderates, or conservatives. They may register as Democrats or Republicans or support independent candidates like H. Ross Perot. These ideological, perhaps even partisan, views inevitably affect the perspectives and policy preferences held by administrators.

Demographic composition is another factor that may affect basic political orientation. As we have mentioned, U.S. political leaders in the United States do not accurately reflect the demographic composition of the American people. This is true for the bureaucrats as well. There are relatively few generals and admirals who do not have a European heritage. There are female generals and admirals, but since none of them have combat command experience, none of them serve in the key military policy making posts. Much the same can be said about the State Department, which President Nixon once described as "primarily Ivy League and the Georgetown set," and the CIA, which President Johnson characterized as a bunch "of boys whose families sent them to Princeton but wouldn't let them into the family brokerage business" (Oudes, 1989:448). [18]

Data bears out the demographic narrowness of the State Department and other agencies. The 3,500 or so FSOs who constitute the diplomatic corps and the upper echelons of the department have had a tradition of being white, upper-class, and Ivy League–educated males. During one 11-year period, for example, only 9 of 586 (3.5 percent) FSOs appointed to the second-ranking post (deputy chief of mission) in U.S. embassies were women (Hastedt, 1991). This demographic imbalance is important because ideology influences what officials advocate and decide and how they implement policy. Because political perspective originates in significant part on life experiences, the atypical personal history of white, upper-class males colors their advice, decisions, and policy implementation in a way that does not accurately reflect society.

One reason for the varying points of view between political leaders, the public, and the foreign policy bureaucracy is that the bureaucracy is not demographically representative of the population. Few women, for example, have achieved high policy making posts within the bureaucracy. The U.S. ambassador to the UN, Madeleine K. Albright, shown here testifying before the U.S. Senate, was the only woman that President Clinton appointed to a top foreign policy post.

As with much of the government, the demographic balance is beginning to change. The State Department has made reforms; these were speeded up after an admission by the department in court in 1989 that it had been discriminatory. Other agencies are under similar internal and external pressure. More than 100 female CIA case officers joined together to accuse the agency of denying them promotions and choice assignments. That and the revelation that agent Aldrich Ames's betrayal of the agency to the Soviets had gone undetected for years, in part because he was a member of the "old boy system," have forced the CIA to promise to reform. "We are running intelligence collection against a very diverse world, a world in which there are two genders and lots of people of different kinds of races," Director R. James Woolsey at that time told a congressional committee. "The CIA will do a better job if it's not a white male fraternity."[19] Such bursts of newfound enlightenment are certainly good. Change comes slowly, however, and for many years to come, the views of one group will be overrepresented in the bureaucracy, while the views of other demographic groups will be underrepresented.

Self-Interest

Another factor that accounts for the policy preferences of organizations and individual staff members is self-interest. It is a natural psychological phenomenon for people who invest their professional lives in an organization to become loyal to that organization and to believe that good policy and what is good for the organization are synonymous.

The well-being of an organization is gauged in a number of ways. An organization is healthy if its budget and realm of authority are stable or growing. These standards are both symbolic and have the real effect of allowing an organization to control the purse strings on a large number of foreign policy activities. Organizational status also depends on the number of people who work in an organization. As with large budgets, large numbers of personnel mean that an organization can provide more information and analyses, make more recommendations, conduct more operations, and generally play a more powerful role than rival organizations. In a circular way, more funding and personnel have the further salutary effect of gaining yet new capabilities and responsibilities. This makes the organization increasingly indispensable to the successful conduct of policy and, thus, secures its status. What this all suggests,

297

The
Bureaucratic
Perspective:
One
Government,
Many Views

then, is a reinforcing cycle that yields increasing pressure for growth within the bureaucracy.

For these reasons, bureaucrats tend to fight for missions and programs that will increase (or avoid decreases in) their agency's resources and the realm of responsibility (bureaucratic turf). Organizations will even try to preserve themselves by looking for new tasks after all or most of the rationale for their existence has disappeared. Critics charge that in addition to inflating budgets, such bureaucratic self-interest leads to inefficiency and to an agency's focus on its own welfare rather than its mission. One former chairman of the Joint Chiefs of Staff (JCS), General David C. Jones, has admonished the military for spending too much time "on intramural squabbles for resources" and too little time "on our war fighting capabilities." Along the same line, a retired Army chief of staff has chided the JCS for "logrolling" its resource and strategy recommendations; that is, for achieving consensus by "seeking a lowest common denominator" and "not giving the best military advice" (Rourke, 1990:126). Other analysts, it must be said in fairness, disagree. One study of naval budgets, for example, concluded that "while parochial loyalties have indeed split the Navy and the Navy bureaucracy," the Chief of Naval Operations and other higher officials have been able to referee these disputes, making ideas about naval strategy, not bureaucratic politics, "critical in shaping" the Navy (Rhodes, 1994:40).

Even such studies concede the existence of bureaucratic parochialism, however, and this section looks at institutional self-interest by focusing on the military and intelligence bureaucracies. It is important to remember that they serve only as an example and that self-interest affects the perspectives of all bureaucracies.

Self-Interest: Maintaining and Enhancing Missions and Budgets

One way that policy is affected by bureaucratic self-interest relates to the bureaucratic battle for the relationship between budget resources and an agency's preservation or expansion of its mission. The end of the cold war and the collapse of the Soviet Union ended the rationale on which defense budgets in the hundreds of billions of dollars were constructed. Not surprisingly, the Pentagon did not respond to this turn of events by declaring its job successfully done and recommending that its budget and forces be cut dramatically (Goldman & Diaz, 1993). Instead it scanned the horizon for new foes. A major Defense Department report circulated in 1992 argued that a new military mission should be deterring potential "competitors" from aspiring "to a greater role" or pursuing "a more aggressive posture to protect their legitimate interests." To accomplish this, the report continued, significant budget resources would be required to "sufficiently account for the interests of the advanced industrial nations [presumably Western Europe and Japan] to discourage them from challenging our leadership or seeking to overturn the established political and economic order."[20]

A related Pentagon planning document envisioned several possible areas of conflict, including the Baltic region, Korea, Panama, the Persian Gulf, and the Philippines, and the rise of a new superpower enemy that had the "capability to threaten U.S. interests through global military competition." These possible scenarios meant, the report said, that the United States should maintain a "technological" and "doctrinal" edge and "a credible capability to expand military forces."[21] While contingency planning is certainly appropriate, it was difficult to discount completely the skeptical *New*

York Times headline, "Pentagon Imagines New Enemies in Post–Cold-War Era. Planning for Hypothetical Wars and Big Budgets."[22]

Mission preservation also partly helps explain the Air Force's continuing commitment to manned bombers and its effort to add to its B-2 fleet. With B-2s "I can sustain bomber operations over an extended period of time," declared General John Loh, head of the Air Combat Command.[23] The issue is whether that capability is needed. Many analysts suggest that large manned bombers are obsolete for a variety of reasons. First, the electronically invisible B-2 was designed to penetrate the sophisticated air defense radars of the Soviet Union, which no longer exists. Second, new radar technologies make the B-2's invisibility suspect. The efforts of the Air Force to develop a missile capability for the B-2 to allow it to deliver munitions without coming near its target is a tacit admission of the plane's vulnerability. Third, the need for a heavy bomber is questionable in an age of cruise missiles, smaller war planes that can deliver remote-controlled "smart bombs" precisely, and other attack technologies. Air Force chief of staff General Anthony McPeak has argued that the B-2 is needed because "it's not fun to fly half way around the world and miss your target."[24] The question is whether flying that far is necessary at all when there are other ways to attack distant targets. Fourth, the case for the heavy bomber is even more problematic given a B-2 bomber's price tag: approximately $1 billion per plane. One implicit effect of terminating the B-2, however, would be ending one of the Air Force's traditional main missions: strategic bombing. The backbone of U.S. strategic bombing forces is the aged B-52, the most recent of which were delivered in 1962. The B-1B, which came on line in 1985, has had such an uncertain level of reliability that critics have dubbed it "the flying Edsel," after the ill-fated Ford automobile of an earlier era. Thus with the B-52 twice the age of most readers of this book, and with the B-1B a costly error, termination of the B-2 would mean the end of an Air Force mission, the decline of Air Force budgets, and the reduction of Air Force personnel. No bureaucracy is apt to accept being declared obsolete and being, in essence, disbanded.

The Pentagon has not been alone in being threatened by the loss of its mission. Without a Soviet Union, of what use are the CIA and other intelligence agencies? Whatever others might conjecture, the agencies soon discovered new—or at least increased—threats that required their services. Several directors of Central Intelligence (DCI, the official who heads the CIA and also serves as at least titular coordinator of all intelligence activities) have emphasized the perils and what they should mean for the budget of the intelligence community. Representative Robert Torricelli (D-NJ) recalls that DCI Woolsey "flew into a rage" whenever significant budget cuts were suggested.[25] Any budget reductions were dangerous, Woolsey told Congress, because "the end of the cold war does not mean the end of conflict or the end to threats to our security," and he welcomed the opportunity to tell the legislators of "not fewer than ten issues, ranging from developments in the former Soviet Union to countering the proliferation of weapons of mass destruction, that made it dangerous to cut the CIA's budget."[26]

Self-Interest: Using and Preserving Resources

While it is not surprising that "the typical response of the Defense Department to a problem is to try and obtain an increase in the defense budget," Carter administration national security adviser Zbigniew Brzezinski has commented, it is perplexing

299

The
Bureaucratic
Perspective:
One
Government,
Many Views

that, "at the same time," the Pentagon is "very reluctant to use force once that budget is increased" (Rose, 1988:230).

Brzezinski's comment focuses on a second manifestation of bureaucratic self-interest: using and preserving resources. Sometimes an agency tries to use resources. There is a maxim in the bureaucracy that says you should spend all the money in your budget and perhaps a bit more. The idea is that if you underspend, your executive branch superiors and legislators will think you do not need the money and will give you less for the next budget year. If you overspend, you can hope for a supplemental allocation for this year and can also ask for more next year.

There are other times when a bureaucracy wants to conserve its resources. It is not unusual to hear people talk about the "military mind," with the inference that generals and admirals are itching to go to war to justify their budgets and exercise the troops. There are certainly examples of that mind-set that could be cited. But, overall, it does not reflect reality.

To the contrary, the military leadership is often very reluctant to go to war. Wars chew up soldiers and materiel. Many general officers are fiercely protective of the lives of the people under their commands. These officers also recognize that materiel lost is materiel that they may not be able to replace. Such considerations often make military leaders cautious about committing to battle. Once safely retired from active service, General H. Norman Schwarzkopf castigated "White House hawks" for trying to push him into an early ground offensive against Iraq in 1991. "These were guys who had seen John Wayne in 'The Green Berets,' they'd seen 'Rambo,' they'd seen 'Patton,' and it was easy for them to pound their desks and say: 'By God, we've got to go in there. . . . Gotta punish that son of a bitch!' " "Of course," the general added acerbically, "none of them was going to get shot at."[27]

The experience of the military in Vietnam and its aftermath has made officers especially wary of wars against guerrilla or other irregular forces in situations where using overpowering force to achieve a decisive military victory is not achievable or politically acceptable. Secretary of State Alexander M. Haig Jr., a former Army general himself, has recalled, for instance, that military leaders dissented when he and other civilians in the Reagan administration pressed for military intervention in El Salvador and Nicaragua. The reason, Haig explained, was that the Joint Chiefs of Staff had been "chastened by [being politically undercut in] Vietnam, . . . by the steady decline of respect for the military, . . . and [by] the decline of military budgets" (Taylor & Petraeus, 1987:258).

Organizational self-preservation has continued to be a major factor in military policy preferences. Among other things, it has influenced the reluctance of the military to intervene in Bosnia, Haiti, and Somalia. Moreover, once it is pressed into combat in those countries, the experiences of the military have often reinforced the lessons officers drew from Vietnam. "Madeleine and Tony feel we should get involved in many more things than this building thinks, . . . operations other than war," one Pentagon official said in reference to the disposition of UN ambassador Madeleine Albright and national security adviser Anthony Lake to use U.S. forces as part of UN peacekeeping operations.[28] Colin Powell recalls feeling much the same way during his tenure as chairman of the Joint Chiefs of Staff. According to the general, a frustrated Ambassador Albright asked him during one heated debate over Bosnia, "What's the point of having this superb military that you're always talking about if we can't use it?" Powell related that he thought he "would have an aneurysm." He told Albright that "American G.I.s were not toy soldiers to be moved around on some sort of global game board." Capturing the distrust that many military officers have toward the judgment of their civilian bosses, Powell charges that it is "politicians [who] start wars," while it is the "soldiers [who] fight and die in them."[29]

Such reservations have policy implications. One reason for U.S. hesitancy about getting involved was the disagreement between the president and his generals. The White House desired to use force, but only limited force so as not to create too much domestic opposition. This contrasted sharply with the Pentagon's insistence that if the United States intervened, it had to do so massively. The result was that U.S. policy for several years was an embarrassing mix of occasional stern threats, followed by tepid responses to Serb aggression. As one former DoD official explained it, "The Pentagon does not want to use force and the White House does. So we end up using force gingerly."[30]

Another way that the Pentagon has resisted unwanted uses of its resources is by constructing its budgets so that they include funds for maintaining the armed forces but no funds for using them in a war. During 1994, for example, the military was asked to intervene in Haiti, move forces in response to the Persian Gulf to counter maneuvers by Iraq, house Cuban refugees at the Guantanamo naval base, and fly humanitarian relief to Rwanda. For these, and other activities, the Pentagon came back to Congress in early 1995 with a request for a supplementary appropriation of $2.6 billion. Some members of Congress were stunned. "We appropriate a quarter of a trillion dollars for the military budget, but if we want to actually use the military we have to pay again?" asked an aghast Representative David R. Obey (D-WI). Secretary of Defense William Perry answered such criticism by commenting about how difficult it was to get the "subtlety of this argument across." This, of course, implied that anyone who objected was suffering from a lack of mental acuity. Other challenges were also beaten off. First-year representative Mark W. Neumann (R-WI) suggested that the Pentagon merely drop the least important 1 percent of its projects (roughly equal to the $2.6 billion as a percentage of the $264 billion defense budget). Defense Department officials said that they could do that but that 1 percent would include cutting bases and other facilities and pet projects that were near and dear to the hearts and constituencies of many members of Congress.

The maneuvering over sending troops to Bosnia in December 1995 provides another illustration of the way the military handles the budget and the extra cost of deployment. In an informal, but widely reported deal, the Pentagon agreed not to ask for a supplemental appropriation to fund the $2 billion that Secretary of Defense William J. Perry estimated that the deployment of U.S. forces to Bosnia would cost. The president, in turn, agreed not to veto the defense spending bill passed by Congress, even though the legislation authorized $7 billion more in military spending than the White House had asked for. In a thinly disguised reference to the understanding, Senate majority leader Robert Dole (R-KS) said of Clinton, "He's looking for cooperation in many areas these days, and we'd like to see a two-way street."[31]

To summarize, then, the military's sense of misuse by politicians and its reluctance to be hobbled by political constraints have made it wary of limited interventions. The general and the admiral resent and resist being told by political leaders what the size of their forces should be and what their tactics will be because the officers fear such constraints will result in an unwarranted loss of resources and prestige in a conflict they cannot win. These feelings are clearly evident in a bit of doggerel penned by a retired admiral (Taylor & Petraeus, 1987:254) who lamented:

301

The
Bureaucratic
Perspective:
One
Government,
Many Views

I am not allowed to run the train
  The whistle I can't blow.
I am not allowed to say how fast
  The railroad train can go.
I am not allowed to shoot off steam
  Nor even clang the bell.
But let it jump the goddamn tracks
  And see who catches hell.

Self-Interest: The Personal Element

Self-interest within bureaucracies is not confined to promoting the welfare of the organization. Individuals also are motivated by their professional self-interest. To reiterate an important point, this factor is a trait of almost all humans, not just civil servants. All but a few of the most noble of us sometimes confuse what is good for us with what is good policy.

Self-interest is associated with several concepts discussed at length in chapter 5. These concepts include role and groupthink, in the discussion of "Decisions in Organizational Settings," and ego and ambition, found in the review of the idiosyncratic "Emotions" of decision makers. These factors almost inevitably color the policy preferences of individual decision makers, whether elected or appointed. *Role theory* tells us, for example, that individuals who staff an agency often come to identify with it and to depend upon the success of the organization for their career prospects and personal well-being. This idea is captured by the axiom that "where you stand [on an issue] depends on where [organizationally] you sit."

At an even more specific level associated with the pressure to conform involved with *groupthink*, individuals may try to please the organizational hierarchy by pursuing decisions and ideas that serve self-interest by promoting organizational interests. In this case, where you stand depends not only on where you sit (and want to remain sitting), but on where you might want to sit in the future. For example, one military officer recalls that this factor affected military analyses during the Vietnam War. Writing recently, General Colin L. Powell relates that "our senior officers know the [Vietnam] war was going badly. Yet they bowed to groupthink pressures and kept up the pretenses" that the United States was winning the war.[32]

The crux of this point is that bureaucratic perceptions are fed in part by an individual's desire for professional success. It is normal and laudable for individuals who staff our bureaucracies to strive for success. What may occur, however, is that organizational interests and personal ambition converge to provide a powerful set of incentives for bureaucrats to act in ways that may or may not coincide with the interests of others in the foreign policy process. Understanding this frequent union of agency and personal interests is also important for recognizing the competitive nature of the bureaucratic decision making process. Bureaucrats in one organization must compete with bureaucrats in other organizations to carve out missions for themselves, to gain access to higher levels of government, and to build confidence regarding their own abilities in the minds of the high-level decision makers.

Personal ambition within an organization also may contribute to perceptions and policy. One example comes from the U.S.–supported invasion of Cuba at the Bay of Pigs in 1961. The prime advocate of the invasion was Richard Bissell, the CIA's deputy director for operations. With a reputation for ruthlessness and risk taking, he had risen rapidly in the CIA and hoped to replace Allen Dulles as its director. When John Kennedy replaced Dwight Eisenhower in the White House, Bissell maneuvered to gain the directorship by orchestrating a daring overthrow of the communist regime of Fidel Castro. To ensure that the Kennedy team did not miss the point, Bissell introduced himself to them during a get-acquainted dinner as "your man-eating shark" (Wyden, 1979:95). Bissell moved to link his reputation and credibility with the Bay of Pigs operation. If the operation succeeded, so did he. According to accounts, his ambition drove him to run roughshod over internal CIA dissenters, particularly rivals for the directorship, and to oversell the operation's chances of success to Kennedy and his top advisers (Kessler, 1992; McClintock, 1992). When the Bay of Pigs invasion ended in catastrophe, and after his next assignment (to engineer the assassination of Fidel Castro) also failed, Bissell left government service. It would certainly be hyperbole to assert that the Bay of Pigs happened solely because of Bissell's self-interested drive; it would be equally in error to discount the impact of Bissell's ambition.

Organizational Standards and Culture

You may recall from the discussion of political culture in chapter 4 that a society acquires values and perspectives from historical experience and many other sources. Because new members (say, children) of a society are socialized by older members (such as parents and teachers), the political culture continues and is relatively slow to change. These values form a foundation that colors the fundamental views of the society about what policy should be and how it should be carried out.

Long-standing organizations, including bureaucracies, have some of the traits of a mini-society. They have a relatively stable population (workers); they distinguish themselves from other societies (agencies); they have shared experiences; they have values; they have ways of doing things (standard operating procedures); they preserve their political culture by socializing new members of the agency, recruiting people with similar values, promoting those who share the organizational culture, and ignoring or forcing out those who do not. The bureaucratic culture of the State Department, an internal study conceded, tends to "stifle creativity, discourage risk-taking, and reward conformity" (Rourke, 1990:117). The analogy between the political culture of a nation and the organizational culture of a bureaucracy can be taken only so far. It serves to make the point, though, that it is necessary to understand the agency's organizational routines and its sense of mission in order to understand why any given bureaucracy operates the way it does.

Organizational Routines

One aspect of organizational culture involves the way bureaucracies operate. Whether processing information or conducting operations, agencies most often rely on **standard operating procedures (SOPs)**. One analyst asserts that the decision making process within organizations is based on controlling the level of uncertainty that the organization confronts, with "decisions . . . fragmented into small segments and the segments treated sequentially. The process is dominated by established procedure" (Steinbruner, 1974:71). SOPs, then, provide large organizations with coherence, direction, and clear guidelines for action.

303

The
Bureaucratic
Perspective:
One
Government,
Many Views

SOPs are especially important for organizational coherence and direction when the individual within the organization is faced with ambiguous or broadly defined policy decisions from above. SOPs allow bureaucrats to fit the problem of the moment into a neat formula for action that is based on organizational tradition. In this way, the individual knows that he or she is operating within the parameters of what is considered "safe" for the organization. It is especially important for lower-level bureaucrats to have this guidance since their personal success depends on serving the interests of their organization. Without it, they might be forced into inaction rather than action aimed at serving organizational goals.

Lastly, the bureaucracy at times simply ignores or disobeys the policy directives sent from above. An example involves the Cuban missile crisis of 1962. Secretary of Defense McNamara had ordered that the ships forming the naval blockade line be shifted during the crisis from a position 500 miles off the coast of Cuba to one that was 300 miles off the coast. The intent was to give Khrushchev more time to decide whether he wanted to order approaching Soviet ships to try to break the blockade line. However, the Navy never moved the ships back. To do so would have put them within range of Cuban aircraft attacks, a violation of the Navy's SOP. Since the Navy felt that this directive needlessly put its ships and sailors at risk, it chose not to obey the order.

Sense of Mission

Another part of an agency's culture that helps determine its action is the agency's sense of mission. Organizations have missions to perform, whether they are military forces, intelligence gathering agencies, or diplomatic corps. Some of these missions are established by law or by directives from higher levels of government. Missions can also emerge when organizations are given considerable latitude in defining their own goals. Either way, an organization's mission defines how the career officials that staff the organization perceive the essence of the organization. This essence is the dominant view held within the organization about its missions, the capabilities required to fulfill those missions, and the types of people who should staff the organization to accomplish the missions. The CIA provides valuable insights into how the sense of mission plays a role in shaping the organization's assumption of danger, its emphasis on active covert operations, its subordination of information gathering and analysis functions, and its policy advocacy.

Assumption of Danger   One aspect of the CIA's culture is an assumption of danger, a tendency to view others and their actions as motivated by ill-intent toward the United States. This is not surprising, given the agency's origins in 1947 during the early cold war anxiety. It is an attitude that permeated most of the national security structure. The conventional wisdom became that the world was an intractably perilous jungle inhabited by powerful political carnivores driven to and capable of making a meal of America. This culture and its conventional wisdom have influenced the CIA's output ever since.

Even the CIA now acknowledges, for instance, that it sometimes made serious errors in its estimates about the intentions of the Soviet Union. One error was to inflate Soviet strength. "Every major intelligence failure over the last 20 or 30 years," President Bush's DCI Robert Gates told a reporter, "has been because the analysts tended to accept the conventional wisdom. The problem has not been a lack of dissent by various agencies. The problem has come about when they all signed up to a view that was in fact wrong."[33] According to another DCI, Admiral Stansfield Turner, who served in the Carter administration, the CIA's support of the nuclear buildup was one way that the CIA's acceptance of the conventional wisdom influenced its recommendations. Turner told a post–cold war conference that while the CIA estimates of Soviet nuclear strength were fairly accurate, the agency's interpretation of the information "was not of help to the president. What [the CIA] should have said to him," Turner continued, "was simply two words: too much. We and the Soviets both had too much nuclear firepower to need any more. At some point, threatening more damage is meaningless for deterrence."[34]

Vietnam is another area in which the CIA's culture of suspicion and its acceptance of the cold war conventional wisdom about the danger of communism may have warped the information and advice that the agency transmitted, according to McGeorge Bundy, national security adviser in the Kennedy and Johnson administrations. The "operating world" of the CIA, Bundy told an audience, made it

> a hard boiled, activist, give-us-the-job, anti-communist agency, which believed that confrontation was the nature of the adversary. And so did most of the rest of us to one degree or another. But it meant that you could not expect from the agency a detached assessment where the agency was involved. The most important example of that is Vietnam.

Emphasizing Active Covert Operations   When the CIA was first established, its enunciated mission was to gather information and to provide it with analysis to decision makers. Dean Acheson (1969:214), then undersecretary of state, has recalled that "I had the gravest foreboding about this organization and warned the President that as set up neither he, the National Security Council, nor anyone else would be in a position to know what it was doing or [a position] to control it." Acheson proved prescient. The mission quickly began to change, and the government has struggled to keep track of the CIA ever since.

Soon after it was established, the CIA, with the knowledge of the president, began to conduct active covert political and paramilitary operations. During the 1960s and 1970s alone, the agency conducted 900 large- and medium-size operations and thousands of smaller programs. President Reagan approved an average of 8 covert interventions annually. Many of those, such as in Iran in 1953 and Guatemala in 1954, have been mentioned in previous chapters. Presidents and members of Congress have found it difficult to keep the agency reined in. Early in his first term, President Nixon told Henry Kissinger that "I want a good thinning down on the whole CIA personnel situation, as well as our intelligence activities generally." Toward the end of his term, Nixon was still saying (this time to chief of staff Robert Haldeman) that "one department which particularly needs a housecleaning is the CIA" (Oudes, 1989:179, 448).

The agency adopted the common view during the cold war that it was in a death struggle in which, as one government report warned, "We must learn to subvert, sabotage, and destroy our enemies by more clever, more sophisticated and more effective methods than those used against us" (Johnson, 1991:331). This culture had several impacts on policy. One was that it led to CIA involvement in assassinations

305

The
Bureaucratic
Perspective:
One
Government,
Many Views

and a wide range of other activities that were morally dubious. Second, the death-struggle, anything-goes perception persuaded some in the CIA to conduct independent operations and sometimes to ignore the law. The role of the CIA in the Iran-Contra scandal is a prime example (Reisman & Baker, 1992).

The culture of covert operations also inculcated CIA operatives with a sense of elitism, even hubris. "There was a mysticism, some special ties that only exist in the CIA's Directorate of Operations," one agent has recalled. "Everything's shrouded in secrecy," he continued:

> It's a mist you dip into and hide behind. You believe you have become an elite person in the world of American Government, and the agency encourages that belief from the moment you come in. They make you a believer. You're doing all these exotic things in exotic lands, and people stand in awe of you. There was a camaraderie that doesn't exist in normal life. You felt like you were accomplishing something even when you weren't.[35]
> "God, we had fun!" put in another CIA operative as an amen.[36]

Deemphasizing Information Gathering and Analysis   The stress on the fun of covert operations in the CIA's organizational culture also meant that the agency's intended function of supplying information and analyses suffered. "The agency has a double world, the estimating world and the operating world," McGeorge Bundy has noted, but it is the operations side that has dominated the agency throughout its history.[37] Just one indication of how the CIA has valued its two worlds is that several CIA officials have advanced up the agency ladder through its "operating world" to become DCI. No one from the "estimating world" has ever done so. In this atmosphere, the personnel of the agency that collected and analyzed information became something like second-class citizens, serving in jobs that led to retirement, not in the operations division that led to the top of the agency. The problem with this, as President Nixon put it in a memo to his chief of staff in 1974, is that "the CIA is a muscle-bound bureaucracy, which has completely paralyzed its brain power" (Oudes, 1989:448). Among other things, the relatively scant resources given to information gathering and analysis meant that CIA estimates on such issues as the size and power of the USSR's nuclear arsenal were compiled in part from information supplied by other agencies. Analysts question the accuracy of the estimates of some of these other agencies, such as the Air Force, which was also seeking increased budgets for its ballistic missiles and tended to take the most pessimistic view of Soviet missile strength.

Policy Advocacy and Decision Making   Policy advocacy and decision making were not part of the CIA's (or the rest of the intelligence community's) initial responsibilities. Nevertheless, the CIA (and other intelligence agencies) soon became increasingly involved in the policy process. This perhaps inevitably decreased the CIA's reliability as a provider of unbiased information and analysis because the agency was loathe to supply information that undermined the policies that the CIA favored. By an almost necessary corollary, the policy advocacy role also lessened the confidence in the CIA felt by policy makers, who were aware that the agency had its own agenda. Often, however, leaders found that out too late. President John Kennedy's national security adviser, McGeorge Bundy, observed ruefully that "presidents should have intelligence reports presented . . . [by analysts who are not] advocates" (Vandenbroucke, 1991:85). Bundy's insight came too late; it came after CIA misinformation had helped persuade Kennedy to authorize U.S. support of the calamitous rebel invasion of Cuba at the Bay of Pigs in 1961. Bundy's advice also went for naught; the CIA continued to be both intelligence provider and policy advocate.

This politicization of the agency peaked under William J. Casey, DCI in the Reagan administration. Casey was an adamant cold warrior who pressed his analysts to provide information that would, for example, support his efforts to topple the Nicaraguan government and to undertake other anticommunist programs. "He does not ask us for a review of an issue or a situation," one analyst said of Casey. "He wants material he can use to persuade his colleagues, justify controversial policy, or expand the Agency's involvement in covert action" (Hastedt, 1987:20).

In the long term, such abuses undermined the credibility of the CIA and DCI Casey. "With some of us [senators] at least," Joseph Biden (D-DE) said to a CIA official during a Senate Intelligence Committee hearing, "the utterances of Mr. Casey are not always [believable]. We do not always leap at them to embrace them as being the whole story" (Blechman, 1990:156). This aspect of the CIA has much to do with the role of information as power that will be discussed below.

The abuses of Casey and a cavalcade of assorted scandals have created repeated attempts to rein in the CIA's independence and to "demote" the DCI from policy adviser to the president to a provider of information and analysis. Such efforts have not been long successful. Casey served with Cabinet rank, but his immediate successors did not enjoy that status. This changed when President Clinton appointed John M. Deutch as DCI in 1995 and gave him Cabinet rank. Amid the CIA's Aldrich Ames scandal, the pressured resignation of DCI Woolsey, and the also pressured decision of DCI–designate General Michael P. Carns to withdraw his name from Senate confirmation procedures, President Clinton asked Deutch to take the job as DCI. Deutch, who was serving as deputy secretary of defense, had reportedly turned down the job previously. Desperate to stabilize the CIA, Clinton appealed to the well-respected Deutch to take the post and, as a incentive, agree to elevate it to Cabinet status. That made Deutch a foreign policy principal on par with Secretary of State Christopher and others and once again put the CIA in the contradictory roles of providing neutral information and analysis and being a policy advocate.

Clientism

Yet another source of bureaucratic perspective is "clientism," or "localitis" as it is also sometimes known. Clientism means a tendency to represent the interests of the people and groups that a bureaucrat deals with rather than the government for which he or she works. The State Department is accused frequently of viewing foreign governments as its clients. During a debate over international fishery rights, Senator John Pastore (D-RI) lambasted State Department opposition to tightened controls on foreign fishing near the U.S. coast. "For once in our life [we should] help Americans," Pastore chided:

> What is so bad about that? We bleed for the Russians, we bleed for the Chinese, we bleed for the Japanese. Down there in the State Department, they have an Asian desk, they have an African desk, they have a European desk, but they do not have an American desk. Is it not about time that we had an American desk? (Porter, 1988:189)

307

The
Bureaucratic
Perspective:
One
Government,
Many Views

Pastore's complaint cannot be dismissed as the rantings of a disgruntled legislator grandstanding for his constituents. Former secretary of state Henry Kissinger has a similar view. "Desk officers become advocates for the countries they deal with and not spokesmen of national policy," according to Kissinger (1979:27). "Officers will fight for parochial interests with tenacity and a bureaucratic skill sharpened by decades of struggling for survival."

Other agencies also are subject to clientism. The Department of Agriculture, for example, views farmers as its clients. This made it reasonably predictable that the department would oppose President Carter's 1979 grain embargo to the Soviet Union after its invasion of Afghanistan. During the cold war, the Department of Commerce, which tries to promote the interests of U.S. exporters, predictably fought against strict controls on dual-use (military and nonmilitary applications) technology exports to communist countries. Similarly, Commerce approved licenses for the export of $1.5 billion in dual-use technology to Iraq between 1985 and 1990.

It should be said here that our focus on clientism and other traits that turn a bureaucracy away from its supposed broad focus on the national interest does not mean that agency policy is always influenced by these and other domestic pressures. A recent study of the International Trade Administration (ITA), which can grant protection against unfair trade practices to American industries, concluded, for example, that "domestic factors are not enough to explain the decision-making behavior of the [ITA]," and that "national interest factors" must be added to explain ITA decisions (Hansen & Park, 1995:207).

Furthermore, the clientism of one agency may be offset by the clientism of another agency or even by the different perspective of a subunit. One study of U.S. human rights policy has found, for instance, that the congressionally mandated creation of a Bureau of Human Rights within the State Department meant that the bureau was greeted as an "uninvited interloper," even an "alien creature," and that its mission of highlighting foreign governments' human rights abuses clashed with the department's goal of maintaining amicable relations with its clients, those very same governments. "You can't do human rights without stepping on toes," pointed out one bureau official. "This contrasts," the official continued, with "the nature of the State Department [which] is to pursue a goal of frictionless relations. . . . We . . . are creating friction. . . . The culture [at State] is negotiate and compromise. No ripples, please" (Mackenzie, 1995:272).

To review for a moment, what we have seen in the last several pages is that bureaucracies often have their own perspectives on what proper policy should be. The president's wishes, the law, and national interest are certainly part of the equation. But beyond these, each bureaucracy's perspective is also based on a range of factors rooted in an agency's perceptions of its interests and in its organizational culture. Knowing this is important for understanding that bureaucratic policy preferences are based in part on the agency's particular point of view, not only on an abstract notion of national interest or a reading of the president's desires. To the degree that the bureaucracy possesses power, its policy preferences influence or may even become national policy. Thus it is to the subject of bureaucratic power that we should now turn our attention.

BUREAUCRATIC POWER AND LIMITS: FORMAL AND INFORMAL

Like presidential and congressional power, bureaucratic power has both formal and informal sources. Formal powers are those granted to the bureaucracy by the Constitution and by legislation enacted by Congress. Informal powers are those that stem from the historical evolution of the government's structure and operation or from the ongoing give-and-take of politics. In the same way, there are formal and informal limits on the powers of the bureaucracy. To explore bureaucratic power, we will first examine formal powers and limits. Then we will turn to informal powers and limits.

Formal Powers and Limits

The *formal powers* of the bureaucracy are more implicit than legally explicit. Unlike the president and Congress, the bureaucracy has no explicit foreign policy role given to it by the Constitution. Article II, Section 1, states that "executive power shall be vested in a President of the United States of America," but it says nothing about how that executive power should be organized or implemented. Article II, Section 2, goes on to state that the president "may require the opinion, in writing, of the principal Officer of the Executive Departments upon any Subject relating to the Duties of their respective Offices." More specific to the role played by the bureaucracy, Article II, Section 3, states that the president "shall take Care that the Laws be faithfully executed." This authority to enforce the laws, which includes administrative regulation, is a main source of bureaucratic authority.

The remainder of bureaucratic authority is derived from the bureaucracy's necessary role in implementing legislation enacted by Congress. In Article I, Section 8, Congress is charged with enacting legislation in such areas as regulation of foreign commerce, the provision of an army and a navy, and the creation of regulations governing the armed forces. Clearly then, the Constitution anticipates an administrative structure growing out of both executive and congressional powers. By the very nature of things, that structure has to have a degree of authority to accomplish its tasks. Therefore, the bureaucracy derives part of its role in the execution of American foreign policy from these sections of the Constitution.

Through legislation, Congress creates the statutory power possessed by the bureaucracy in the foreign policy process. When Congress enacts a law that grants foreign aid to Egypt, for example, legislators empower the agency that will administer that aid. In this way, executive agencies such as the Agency for International Development (AID) are given the legal or statutory power to carry out foreign aid programs with the money allocated by Congress.

As mentioned in chapter 8, the use of statutory power by Congress to *delegate authority* to the executive branch has been an expanding phenomenon, especially in the past several decades. Legislators, to a degree, have been overwhelmed by the sheer volume of decisions they face and by the pressures from all sides to adopt favorable policies. In response, Congress has frequently passed general guidelines and has demanded reports from the executive, but it has allowed the president to make detailed policy decisions. Equally overwhelmed presidents have further delegated these decisions to agency heads, who may pass them on to heads of subdivisions. Trade is one example, with Congress now setting general parameters while leaving specific export control, tariff, and other trade decisions to the executive branch. Table 10.1 provides a number of other examples of statutory sources of power for various bureaucratic foreign policy players.

There are also *formal limits* to bureaucratic power. The appropriations and authorization power of Congress controls the bureaucracies' funds, missions, and organization. There have been instances of agencies ignoring the law willfully or inadvertently. But for each of such instances, there are a multitude of instances where the bureaucracy does what it is directed to do. When Congress is displeased or even when it merely wishes to keep tabs on the actions of the executive branch, it can take action, using its powers to investigate, legislate, and appropriate (or withhold) money, as detailed in chapters 8 and 9.

Presidents and politically appointed executive leaders also have many tools at their command to limit agencies. Bureaucrats may resist legal direction, but they seldom openly defy it. When they do, they can be fired or (more likely) reassigned. We have told the story of the Navy, led by the chief of naval operations Admiral George Anderson, resisting the direction of President Kennedy and Secretary of Defense McNamara to alter the Navy's blockade of Cuba. The ax did not fall right then, but soon Anderson was quietly eased out as chief of naval operations and packed off as ambassador to Portugal.

Informal Powers

Although the informal sources of bureaucratic power are hard to detail concretely, they are an important basis of the role that administrators play in the foreign policy process. Bureaucrats exercise informal power in the foreign policy process in four basic ways: (1) by providing information to officials at higher governmental levels; (2) by utilizing their expertise to analyze information and to present policy options to political leaders; (3) by political maneuvering; and (4) by implementing the broad policy decisions made by political leaders. These four areas of power have limits, however, and we will conclude with a brief exploration of informal limits.

Information as Power

"By and large a president's performance in office is as effective as the information . . . he gets," Harry S. Truman once remarked (Edwards & Wayne, 1985:198). What Truman realized is that leaders depend on their bureaucracy to gather information and then to filter and condense the huge mass into a quantity that is manageable.

Most leaders share Truman's sense of dependency. They therefore struggle to gain multiple sources of information because they too are aware that the information that is passed upward through the bureaucratic layers to political leaders may be colored by the organizational culture and policy preferences of the agency that is providing the information. This distortion of information may occur because of a bureaucracy's inadvertent bias, its intentional misrepresentation of facts and analysis, or its keeping secrets (Banks & Weingast, 1992). In any case, the point is that information is power, and it is important for decision makers to understand that the information they receive may not be the truth, the whole truth, and nothing but the truth.

For their part, bureaucracies also realize that information is power. They therefore work hard to dominate the information flow if they can. A now retired State Department official recently recalled what happened in 1963 when he wrote and circulated a memorandum that concluded that "on the basis of available statistical trends, there appears to have been a number of significant and unfavorable changes in the military situation in Vietnam." The Pentagon was outraged by this view, and, in a handwritten note to Secretary of State Dean G. Rusk, Secretary of Defense Robert S. McNamara demanded that "you tell me that it is not the policy of the State Department to issue [independent] military appraisals." Rusk replied in another handwritten note that "it is not the policy of the State Department to issue [independent] military appraisals." Rusk's reply, the author of the offending memo continues, "made it clear that the State Department would acquiesce in the military's demand that State stop issuing independent assessments of the overall military situation in Vietnam. This gave the Pentagon the overwhelming role in producing such analyses and denied top officials data and appraisals that might call the military's official position into question."[38]

Inadvertent Bias Most cases of slanted information are probably the result of organizational culture and other factors discussed earlier that create the bureaucratic perspective. What happens is that as an agency sorts through a mass of information, it tends unconsciously to give the most credibility to, and to pass on, the facts and interpretations that support the agency's perspective.

We noted earlier, for example, that the conventional wisdom of the cold war, intensified by the CIA's organizational culture, led the agency to overestimate the strength of the Soviet Union and its government. That meant that when the Soviet Union began to fall apart, the CIA, as its director Robert Gates conceded, "considerably understated the real burden economically of the Soviet military, underestimated how sick the Soviet economy really was, and dismissed the danger to communist control posed by this illness."[39]

Unwilling to abandon its image of a powerful USSR, the CIA continued to advise President Bush that Soviet president Mikhail S. Gorbachev could hold his country together. The agency also discounted Russian president Boris Yeltsin as "an opportunistic lightweight who drank excessively, behaved erratically, spoke colloquial Russian and was not in Gorbachev's league intellectually or socially."[40] Such an intelligence estimate led U.S. policy to lag events in the USSR substantially, with Bush continuing to support Gorbachev for much longer than most Soviets did.

Intentional Misrepresentation There are also times when the bureaucracy skews information intentionally by either consciously suppressing information that would contradict an agency's policy preferences or by lying. Some would argue that the line between half-truths (partial information suppression) and whole untruths (outright lying) is thin indeed.

In the realm of *filtering information intentionally,* bureaucracies rely on the fact that government is so complex that political leaders do not even know what they do not know. "You have to be pretty smart to know what the question is that will get the answer you are seeking," William Dickenson (R-AL) of the House Armed Services Committee commented. "And I don't think for a minute that the [military] Services knock themselves out trying to help you ask the right questions, unless they are anxious to have you ask the question" (Lindsay, 1990:14).

There is also ample evidence that presidents are not told things for fear of upsetting or compromising them. "You think presidents should be warned," Secretary of State Dean Acheson once observed. "You're wrong," he admonished, "Presidents should be given confidence" (Betts, 1978:77). Henry Kissinger urged Secretary of State William Rogers and Secretary of Defense Melvin Laird to "talk affirmatively to the President [Nixon], stop discouraging him. Above all, don't . . . take big problems to the President" (Ambrose, 1991:32). Ronald Reagan's national security adviser, Admiral John Poindexter, used the same line of "logic" to explain why he did not tell the president that the government was illegally using U.S. funds to buy weapons for the rebels in Nicaragua. "I was convinced that I understood the President's thinking on [this policy] and that . . . he would have approved it," Poindexter later said. Therefore, he continued, "I made a deliberate decision not to ask the President, so that I could insulate him from the decision and provide some future deniability for the President."[41]

Lying also occurs occasionally. Sometimes the issues are relatively minor in terms of foreign policy. A study of the development of Advanced Medium-Range Air-to-Air Missiles (AMRAAM) has found that in order to keep funds flowing from Congress, the Air Force and the contractor developing the missile lied routinely to cover up its skyrocketing costs and other problems. One Air Force civilian official defended the process on the grounds that,

> It's the way the Air Force does business. The Air Force lies; Congress knows we lie. If everyone told the truth, the one liar would have the advantage. Studied lying is necessary to sell the program to Congress. . . . The Navy has some really proficient liars. (Gilmour & Minkoff, 1994:207)

What is most disturbing about this misdirected line of reason is the implication that the practice is a regular part of doing business in Washington. As one former congressional staff member who specialized in defense put it, "The world system is built around, 'Cover it up; don't tell the Hill.'. . . It's just a game; they lie, we know it, and they know we know (Gilmour & Minkoff, 1994:208).

At other times misleading information and counsel may have a major impact on foreign policy. The CIA manipulated the information and advice it gave to President Kennedy about the Bay of Pigs invasion plans in order to ensure that the CIA-backed operation went forward. The CIA's deputy director, Richard Bissell, calmed White House anxiety about the operation by assuring it that even if the rebels could not defeat the Cuban army quickly, Cuba was "guerrilla territory" and that the invaders "had all been trained for guerrilla action." In fact, the CIA had made no plans for a guerrilla operation. "I think all of us committed the error of saying 'there is always the guerrilla option,' without planning it," Bissell later admitted. Thus, the CIA's advice was, in the words of one scholar, "a smokescreen, a lullaby for John Kennedy" (Gleijeses, 1995:36, 39).

The CIA also manufactured misinformation about Vietnam, and it may have prolonged the war. A top CIA official, Richard Helms, who later became DCI, urged the CIA staff to report from the field in ways that would instill confidence in decision makers in Washington. "There's a lot of ways you can write the English language to make it sound like we're moving ahead," was Helms's counsel. Some field agents took that advice to heart. Among them was Ted Shakley, a key CIA operative in Vietnam, who, one of his subordinates has charged, "would report progress [in the war] because it was his job to bring about progress."[42]

In a more recent episode, the CIA admitted that from the mid-1980s into the early 1990s it gave the White House and the Pentagon false information that vastly overestimated the political stability and military strength of the Soviet Union. The CIA reports were based on information by its spies, whom the CIA knew or strongly suspected were double agents. The reasons that this occurred are complex but, at root, involved Aldrich Ames, who had turned over to the Soviet intelligence agency (the KGB) the names of Soviet citizens who were CIA spies. Some of the betrayed spies were executed; others escaped death by becoming double agents who passed on information supplied by the KGB to the CIA. Even after the CIA discovered that some or all of the information was false, it continued to pass it on rather than risk other sources in Moscow that had told the CIA that it was being misled. It was a "mind-boggling" policy, according to Senator Arlen Specter (R-PA), chairman of the Senate Intelligence Committee, and even the DCI, John Deutch, had to admit that his agency's actions constituted "an inexcusable lapse in elementary intelligence practice."[43] The net result is that for seven years the CIA funneled inaccurate information to top U.S. decision makers. Among many outcomes, the inaccurate information was one reason that the Bush administration continued almost until the last to act on the assumption that Soviet president Mikhail Gorbachev could avert the collapse of the Soviet Union. Another impact, according to congressional sources, was that the vastly inflated estimates of Soviet military capabilities led to the funding of expensive U.S. military programs, including the decision to go ahead with the F-22 flight program, which may eventually cost some $73 billion.

Secrecy   Because information is power, it is not surprising to find that bureaucrats are secretive about the information they hold. The more eyes that examine a set of information, the greater the chance of an outcome other than the one that the bureaucracy prefers. In an effort to serve a certain perspective, secrecy is used to protect an agency's monopoly on some pieces of information as well as the analyses that are based on that information.

Each year the government stamps the words "eyes only," "top secret," or some other security designator on about 6 or 7 million documents. The National Archives, which maintains documents more than 30 years old, alone holds some 325 million pages of classified documents, some dating back to World War I. For newer classified documents, there are about 80,000 other depositories controlled by individual agencies and holding untold millions—perhaps billions—more secret pages. The vast majority of these are foreign and national security policy–related documents classified by the Departments of Defense and State and by the CIA. Secrets must, of course, be kept if they contain sensitive technical information, tactical military battle plans, names of undercover agents, or other material that could directly assist an enemy or endanger Americans.

Some secrets in a democracy are appropriate, but many are not, especially when material is classified to protect an agency's or an individual's political flanks rather than national security. Henry Kissinger negotiated secretly with China to begin to normalize relations between Beijing and Washington; he negotiated secretly with North Vietnam to end the Vietnam conflict and secretly offered Hanoi U.S. aid; President Bush secretly sent envoys to China after the Tiananmen Square massacre in 1989 despite his announced freeze on high-level contacts with those Chinese leaders whom the press labeled the "butchers of Beijing." These instances have all been discussed in earlier chapters, and the list could go on. The point is that in each instance, the "other side" knew what was occurring. The secrets, then, were designed to avoid policy objections from Congress, potential naysayers in the bureaucracy, the press, and—ultimately—the American people.

The executive branch makes regular pledges to open up many more of its files to public, democratic scrutiny. It is hard not to be somewhat skeptical about the CIA's sincerity on this issue, especially since one recent study on declassification by the agency's Openness Task Force was itself classified on the grounds that "it must be withheld in its entirety" from Congress and the American people.[44] The Clinton administration renewed the executive branch's rhetorical commitment to reduce secrecy in government. "It is time to re-evaluate the onerous and costly system of security which has led to the overclassification of documents,"[45] President Clinton said as he ordered a wide review of government secrecy rules. Earlier presidential directives aimed at similar issues, however, have been largely ignored by bureaucracies. Forcing the agencies to declassify documents is further complicated by the fact that nobody even knows how many secret archives exist, much less what is in them. "I guess I'm the only person except the President and Vice President who has the right to know that number," said Steven Garfinkle, director of the Information Security Oversight Office, which administers classification/declassification matters. "But," he conceded, "I don't know what it is."[46]

Toles, *Buffalo News*

Information is power, and one way bureaucracies exercise power is by controlling information. Keeping information secret is one technique. The cold war–era mania for government secrecy has eased slightly, allowing the public somewhat greater access to activities of U.S. agencies abroad. One thing that some Americans have discovered is that what the CIA and a number of other government agencies have been doing abroad is not very palatable.

Expertise as Power

Control of the flow of information to higher levels of government is not the only way that bureaucracies use information or exercise power within the foreign policy process. Political leaders are usually policy generalists because of the wide path they take to office and because they focus on a broad range of topics and have many demands on their time. Some political leaders surely do come to office with or develop expertise in one or a small number of issue areas. Most, however, do not.

In such cases, decision makers are usually wary of ignoring the advice of the technical experts, the technocrats. Bureaucrats understand this, and, unintentionally or not, sometimes try to structure their advice and analysis to ensure that political leaders make the "right" decision. Zbigniew Brzezinski suggests that "a basic rule of bureaucratic tactics [is that] one should never obtain the services of an 'impartial' outside consultant regarding an issue that one feels strong about without first making certain in advance that one knows the likely contents of his advice" (Carrol,

313

1992:106). And Henry Kissinger (1979:418) has recalled that "the standard bureau-cratic device" is trying to give a political leader "only one real option." To allow "easy identification," according to Kissinger, the preferred option "is placed in the middle," with a prototypical example being to "confront the policy maker with the choice of (1) nuclear war, (2) present policy, or (3) surrender."

The reluctance of decision makers to ignore the advice of experts is especially strong in matters of national security. "If someone comes in and tells me this or that about the minimum wage bill," President Kennedy once observed, "I have no hesitation in overruling them. But I always assume that the military and intelligence people have some special skill not available to ordinary mortals" (Vandenbroucke, 1991:113).

Kennedy at least had combat experience. Neither President Clinton nor his national security adviser, Anthony Lake, has ever been in the military, which many analysts believe puts them at a disadvantage when dealing with the military. "My feeling," says JCS chairman General Shalikashvili, "is that [the White House] must always be conscious when it comes to making decisions on the use of military power—that the president has not served and that [Lake] has not served."[47]

Lack of expertise also makes it difficult for leaders to judge the need for or capability of such highly technical weapons systems as the B-2 or such complicated matters as military readiness. Faced with a series of annual budget cuts, the military has begun to argue that U.S. forces are slipping in their readiness as training funds are cut. General David M. Maddox, commander of U.S. forces in Europe, disclosed to the press recently that his two main combat units, the First Armored Division and the Third Infantry Division, had slipped from the Army's highest readiness status (C-1) to a less stellar C-2. "Am I proud of it?" a wounded General Maddox asked rhetorically. "I am not," he replied predictably.[48] Just a month earlier, Secretary of Defense William Perry had acknowledged that three divisions stationed in the United States had been downgraded to a worrisome C-3, indicative of significant fighting deficiencies and vulnerabilities. The question one may ask is why the military, which usually touts its valor and strength, tells the world, including all potential U.S. enemies, that American forces are beginning to become shabby at the edges. The answer, according to Lawrence Korb, a former assistant secretary of defense for readiness, is that "readiness is a hot-button political issue, subject to unlimited manipulation." Inasmuch as "even the informed public can't judge" the complicated factors that determine readiness, the analyst continued, "military leaders [have been] quick to grasp the political potential of readiness scares," and they have "skillfully used the issue to help secure a large spending increase." This ploy, Korb charges, is exactly what is behind the current tales of readiness woes by the "nonpolitical admirals and generals . . . [who are] taking us all to the cleaners, using the readiness gap to snatch up precious dollars to defend against a threat that no longer exists."[49]

The expertise-based leverage of the military is further enhanced by the fact that many members of Congress also hold general officers in high esteem. As then-chairman of the House Armed Service Committee Les Aspin noted, "To most Congressmen, defense experts are people in uniform, rather than academics in universities or 'think tanks.' Uniforms are identified with expertise" (Lindsay, 1990:16). This esteem gives the military bureaucracy a great deal of political power. Paul Stockton (1991:153) points out, for instance, that "no arms control treaty has ever been ratified without the support of the [JCS] since they were first appointed in 1947." This leverage over ratification gives the services a powerful voice in the drafting of U.S. treaty proposals.

Political Maneuvering as Power

When we think of bureaucracy, we tend not to think of electoral campaigns because, in a narrow sense, bureaucrats do not run for office. But in a broad sense agencies do very much engage in political maneuvering that takes on much of the cast of an electoral campaign in their search for programs, budgetary resources, and other policy preferences. We can see this through the related actions of agencies to affect public and legislative opinion and to build political alliances.

Affecting Public and Legislative Opinion   One way that the bureaucracy maneuvers politically is by using its information and prestige to try to sway public and legislative opinion. There are many ways to do that. The eagerness of the military to proclaim publicly that the readiness of U.S. forces is slipping is one example of a bureaucracy trying to win public and legislative sentiment over to its side. A year earlier, with the military resisting the desire of the Clinton White House to invade Haiti, the Pentagon became suddenly budget conscious. Taking an unusual tack, DoD experts estimated that invading and securing Haiti would cost American taxpayers $427 million. "It is a significant amount of money," then–deputy secretary of defense John Deutch said with some understatement.[50] This and other bureaucratic public relations campaigns make it important that you, in order to be a sophisticated news analyst, always ask yourself the question: Why is this source telling me this? Question who or what the source is; ask yourself what the source's preferred policy is; ask yourself which policy direction the disclosed information points to.

Building Political Alliances   A second way that a bureaucracy conducts campaigns in favor of its preferred policy is by building alliances. One type of political alliance, known as **iron triangles**, are informal alliances among specific offices in the bureaucracy, congressional subcommittees and legislators, and private business and interest groups that have mutually supportive interests. The three points of the iron triangle ally themselves to fend off threats to their prosperity and political survival. All points of the triangle share information and expertise with one another to serve the common interests of the members of the triangle. A representation of an iron triangle and its relationships is depicted in Figure 10.1. The nature of these trilateral alliances means that an agency such as the Department of Defense that has strong domestic client groups is able to build an iron triangle alliance system more effectively than is an agency such as the Department of State that has limited domestic connections.

One of the strongest iron triangles allies bureaucrats in the Pentagon, legislators with states and districts that have military contractors or bases, and defense contractors and unions representing workers in defense industries. Within the defense-policy iron triangle, defense contractors and bureaucrats have a common interest in larger defense budgets, which translate into more acquisitions and larger staffs for the bureaucracy and into larger contracts and higher profits for the manufacturers. Members of Congress, especially those with defense contractors based in their home states or districts, want to keep their constituents happy by assuring more jobs for the defense contractors. Additionally, the relationships of the triangle are reinforced by the campaign contributions that flow from contractors and unions to help members of Congress get into and stay in office.

FIGURE 10.2 The Iron Triangle

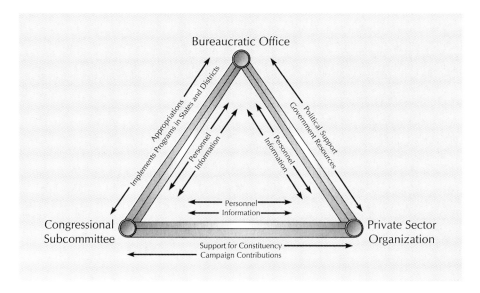

Bargaining takes place within the iron triangle among the various actors involved in the subgovernment model. The actors also often give one another support in a symbiotic relationship. Between the corners of the triangle, information, personnel, and money flow back and forth. The arrows next to the terms along each side of the triangle indicate the direction of the flow of resources inside the iron triangle.

Iron triangles and other alliances affect policy by making it difficult for top decision makers to gain full control of some policy areas. We noted in chapter 8, for instance, that members of Congress ally themselves with contractors and constituents to defend against threatened cuts to military bases or defense contracts in their districts. This is one reason that the military budget is difficult to cut and one reason why the government sometimes funds weapons systems that are of dubious value compared to the vast quantities of money they cost. President Ford's secretary of defense, James Schlesinger, for one, later complained that his responsibilities were "not matched by the power of his office"; and Henry Kissinger agreed that in his time the "White House never achieved the control over defense policy that it did over foreign policy" (Lindsay, 1990:14). Despite numerous efforts to improve the defense acquisition process, the strength of the defense-policy iron triangle remains formidable. A recent report of the General Accounting Office (GAO) on the procurement policies of DoD and other agencies concluded that the processes "through which weapons requirements are determined and systems acquired have often proven costly and inefficient." Furthermore, the report continued, "the 'high stakes' weapons acquisition process has proven vulnerable to fraud, waste, and abuse." Focusing on the causes of the persistent problems, the GAO concluded:

> While there are many reasons for these types of problems, the underlying cause
> of persistent and fundamental problems in DoD's weapons acquisition process
> is a prevailing culture that is dependent on generating and supporting new

weapons acquisitions. The culture is made up of powerful incentives and interests that influence and motivate the behaviors of participants in the process. Participants include the various components of the Department of Defense, the Congress, and industry.[51]

Before leaving this discussion of bureaucratic alliance behavior, it is worth noting that it does not always involve just iron triangle collaborations. *Logrolling alliances* also are formed. One study points out that the JCS is often able to strike a bargain with arms control advocates in the executive and Congress. It is a deal that barters JCS support of an arms control treaty for authorization and funding of weapons systems that the military wants. In this way, development of the Trident ballistic missile submarine was tied to JCS support of the first Strategic Arms Limitations Treaty (SALT I); building the MX intercontinental ballistic missile was linked to JCS endorsement of SALT II; and funding for the B-2 bomber was tied to JCS agreement to the first Strategic Arms Reduction Talks (START I) Treaty. In this most recent instance, for example, General John Chain, commander of the Strategic Air Command (SAC), vowed that if bills pending in Congress to scrap the B-2 were passed, "I will go and testify strongly against support of the START agreement" (Stockton, 1991:155, 153). The B-2 survived, and so did START I.

Implementation as Power

Our discussion of bureaucratic power has, so far, focused attention on the ways that bureaucracies exercise power before decision makers make their policy choices. In addition to these techniques, bureaucratic power is evident after decisions are made. The bureaucracy is charged with *implementing policy,* that is, carrying out the decisions made by the president and other officials and with executing the laws passed by Congress. In many instances, the decisions made and laws passed provide general policy guidelines but do not prescribe specific courses of action in particular instances. In these situations, the creation by the bureaucracy of specific regulations, operating procedures, and other administrative details can have a significant impact on how a policy works. Even when laws or the decisions of political leaders are relatively precise, the very nature of policy implementation means that the choices made by administrators in the field can influence policy substance.

As with information and expertise, the manner in which a bureaucracy implements policy may have unintentional implications for policy substance. To cite an earlier example, the U.S. intervention in Lebanon ended soon after a truck bomb destroyed a barracks there, killing 243 American servicemen. The decisions to house military personnel in a single compound, not to have vehicle barriers, and to have the guards keep their weapons unloaded were all made by officers on the scene following standard operating procedures.

There are other times when bureaucracies implement power in ways that are intended to change the thrust of policy. Two examples from the Cuban missile crisis provide a good illustration. One of these, the story of the resistance of the Navy to the directive of the president and secretary of defense to change the blockade line, was discussed earlier. The other illustration involves U.S. missiles in Turkey. President Kennedy was embarrassed when Soviet leader Khrushchev demanded that the removal of Soviet missiles in Cuba be linked to the removal of U.S. missiles in Turkey. Kennedy had previously issued three directives ordering removal of the missiles, which one assistant secretary of state described as "obsolete, unreliable, inaccurate, and [so] very vulnerable" that they "could be knocked out by a sniper with a telescopic rifle" (Hilsman, 1990:136). "The President believed," Robert Kennedy (1969:73) wrote about the crisis, that "he was President and that his wishes having been made clear, they would be followed and the missiles removed." Wrong! In reality, the U.S. diplomatic and military officials involved with implementing the presidential directive either disagreed or thought it a peripheral concern and did not act. As a result, when the demand from the Soviets came, it put the United States in the position of having to reject it publicly (even while agreeing to it secretly) in order to avoid seeming to abandon Turkey (Cimbala, 1992; Ambrose, 1991). An exasperated Kennedy could not believe that his presidential directive had been ignored. "There's always some SOB who doesn't get the word!" he exploded in the Oval Office (Clifford, 1993:1).

Informal Limits

It would be easy when reading about the various sources of bureaucratic power to imagine the bureaucracy as a sort of Jurassic Park denizen ignoring or terrorizing political leaders. That is not the case. Like all the players in the foreign policy process, bureaucrats have their power; but there are also important limits. In addition to the formal limits detailed above, there are many informal limits to bureaucratic power. Bureaucracies are just one player in a complex foreign policy process and, thus, their influence is diluted. This is especially true for political issues and in situations that are prominent enough to be handled according to the political or presidential models. In these cases, information tends to flow more readily from other sources. It is also true that while political leaders are mostly generalists, some possess their own expertise. President Bush, for one, had a great deal of experience and expertise in foreign policy: He had been U.S. ambassador to the United Nations in the early 1970s, Director of Central Intelligence in the mid-1970s, and head of the Reagan administration's crisis management team.

Furthermore, bureaucracies often oppose, and neutralize, one another. The Defense Department usually opposes sending ground troops into what it sees as political, rather than military, crises; the State Department often pushes to use the military as a tool of U.S. diplomacy.

The ability of bureaucracies to use their informational advantage and expertise is also limited. In the first place, as noted before, political leaders are suspicious of bureaucrats and may reject their counsel because of that doubt. Then–vice president George Bush recorded such an incident in his diary on November 10, 1986. After a meeting with Secretary of State George Shultz, who expressed concern about the dealing of arms to Iran, Bush "walked down" to President Reagan's office "and filled him in on Shultz's concern. . . . The President was alarmed by this. [But] the president is very suspicious of the State Department bureaucracy [and] wondered if perhaps the State Department people were perhaps playing games and trying to undermine policy."[52] Reagan went ahead with the plan despite Shultz's misgivings.

Bureaucratic advice is especially ignored when an administration has already decided on a course of policy. During the late 1980s, the administration supported

Iraq in its war with Iran and tried to win Iraqi moderation after the war through various trade and aid programs. Obviously, Washington failed. In the aftermath of the Persian Gulf War, it became evident that Iraq had been trying to construct nuclear weapons and that the United States had been supplying Iraq with technology and money that were being used in the program. When this scandal broke, President Bush vehemently denied that he had ignored the signs that Iraq was an aggressive country bent on developing a nuclear arsenal and that U.S. policy was to encourage exports to Iraq and to supply Iraq with funds through various U.S. aid programs. "We didn't know that," Bush snapped at reporters at one point in 1992. "The State Department didn't know it" either, he added.[53]

What Bush knew is not yet fully clear. It is certain, however, that the State Department and other agencies did know. Pentagon documents began warning as early as 1985 that exported U.S. technology was possibly being diverted into Iraq's secret nuclear weapons program. "Iraq is a problem country," their memo argued, possessing "many if not all" the elements necessary to reprocess uranium. Therefore, one March 1985 memo recommended that "it makes sense to apply controls to help deter the use of U.S. computers in any such program."[54] Another memo, this one in April 1989 by an official in the Department of Energy, warned that "recent evidence indicates that Iraq has a major effort underway to produce nuclear weapons."[55] Soon thereafter, Frank Lemay, a special assistant to the under secretary of state for economic and agricultural affairs, tried to warn superiors that Iraq was misusing money from a U.S. farm-loan program to buy nuclear-related equipment. Citing preliminary evidence, Lemay warned his bosses in an October 1989 memo that, "if smoke indicates fire, we may be facing a four-alarm blaze in the near future."[56]

The Bush administration ignored the warnings of Lemay and others for a variety of reasons centering on trying to manage Saddam Hussein by proffering him carrots rather than brandishing sticks. One official, who described Lemay's memo as "more bombastic" but no different from similar cautions, conceded that "the issue was brought to the attention of all the big boys and [Secretary of State James] Baker was aware of all the assertions through the huge paper trail. We knew Saddam Hussein wasn't a saint," the official admitted, "but we couldn't cut off a policy based on hunches and assertions." As it turned out, of course, the hunches and assertions were correct. It is also worth noting as a codicil related to the concept of groupthink, that for his insight and forthrightness Lemay wound up being ostracized as a "whistle blower" by his superiors in the State Department. When asked if the charges about shunning Lemay were true, the department's legal adviser, Edwin Williamson, shrugged, "You probably can't have it both ways," that is, be a dissenter and be accepted by your bosses.

In the end, all the powers and limits on the bureaucracy mean that its impact on policy varies widely, just as do the rules of the other policy actors. Issue, situation, and other factors determine how critical the role of the bureaucracy will be.

1. As we focus on the bureaucracy's role in foreign policy decision making, we see that the foreign policy process is even more complex and fragmented than discussed in chapters 7, 8, and 9. Bureaucratic politics and the influence of the bureaucracy over decision making and policy implementation provide further evidence to show that the American foreign policy process is not rational and unified by nature, as it is often caricatured.

2. Although the bureaucracy is involved in all elements of foreign policy, its power varies across the four foreign policy models. The bureaucracy will possess its greatest power in the subgovernment and administrative models. In the presidential and political models, it is more likely that the bureaucracy will be pressured to follow the policy decisions by higher levels of government on the more high-intensity issues.

3. Decision making by the bureaucracy leads one to question the democratic nature of the foreign policy process. In a democracy, policy officials are theoretically accountable to the citizens. Bureaucrats, however, are not elected but make policy decisions in the name of providing greater efficiency to a cumbersome and difficult-to-manage system.

4. Bureaucratic decisions are influenced by many factors, including the expertise held by members of the bureaucracy, personal self-interest of individual bureaucrats, organizational interests based on clientism, secrecy, and defense of turf within the bureaucracy, and organizational routines, or SOPs.

5. Personal ideology originates in life experience and socialization. Most foreign policy bureaucrats are white males. This commonality tends to produce a similar viewpoint. This in turn colors the ways foreign policy decisions are made and implemented.

6. The bureaucracy gains little of its power from the Constitution, although some role is *implied* in Articles I and II. Other formal powers are derived from statutes or laws adopted by Congress and signed by the president that assign specific roles and duties to the bureaucracy.

7. Many other powers are informal and result from one of several factors: (1) the bureaucracy's monopoly on information, (2) the reliance of high-level decision makers on the bureaucracy for analysis of information, (3) political maneuvering, and (4) implementation.

8. The existence of iron triangles in subgovernments provides the bureaucracy with allies in Congress and the private sector that enhance its powers within the system.

Chapter Eleven

Before going on, it is worthwhile to consider how
INTEREST GROUPS

the previous four chapters relate to the next three chapters. Our discussion of the actors in the foreign policy process in the last four chapters concentrated on formal institutional actors: the presidency, Congress, and the executive bureaucracy. These organizations are all legal parts of the government. They therefore play formal roles in deciding and implementing foreign policy. These institutional actors are not, however, the only organized actors involved in making foreign policy. Interest groups and the media are also highly involved. They are nongovernmental organizations and do not have a legal say in making foreign policy. Nevertheless, interest groups and the press play an important part in the policy process because they occupy a position between the formal governmental structures and the people. From this location, these organized, but nongovernmental, actors exercise influence in both directions: they help to shape policy adopted by the government, and they help to inform and form public opinion. The role of interest groups in this interrelationship is discussed in this chapter. The part played by the press will be taken up in chapter 12; the nature and impact of public opinion will be the subject of chapter 13.

INTEREST GROUPS

One of the major theories about how the U.S. political system works is called **pluralism**. In essence, the concept of pluralism refers to the notion that a political society is an amalgam of many different groups, each of which has its own interests. Thus **interest groups** are a pivotal element of political interaction, according to pluralist theory. There is a broad literature on the nature of interest groups (Petracca, 1992). Suffice it to say here, though, that interest groups can be defined as nongovernmental associations of people who have some shared characteristics and who also have a political stake related to that characteristic. Some interest groups, such as business and labor unions, are organized, and individuals join them or have some other form of official affiliation with them. Other groups, such as ethnic groups, are based on involuntary association. That is, they are based on cultural or other types of demographic connections among people. Often interest group activity combines organized and associational groups. Jewish Americans constitute a cultural group; the American-Israel Public Affairs Committee (AIPAC) is an organized group. We will also see presently that not all interest groups that try to influence U.S. policy represent Americans exclusively or even at all. There are transnational groups—such as Amnesty International, foreign corporations, and foreign governments—that operate across national borders. They are active in the United States and in other countries and often engage in the same kinds of lobbying efforts associated with domestic interest groups.

Note that our definition of interest group excludes bureaucratic organizations, those that are part of the government. It is true that bureaucracies pursue their own interests and act like interest groups in many ways. Most Cabinet departments, for example, have congressional liaison and public affairs offices dedicated, respectively, to lobbying Congress on behalf of the department's needs or to reaching out directly to the public in an effort to build grassroots support for the department. But because interest groups are private, nongovernmental associations, such self-interested bureaucratic activity was considered in chapter 10 rather than here. You should, however, keep that activity and the significant symbiosis between the interests of private groups and government agencies (and legislators) through iron triangles and other political alliances in mind when considering the range and importance of interest group activity in this chapter.

There are a number of other preliminary points to note about interest groups. First, the position of interest groups between government and people is important to a democracy. Democratic government demands that policy makers be at least broadly responsive to public policy preferences. Certainly "good government" includes the idea of government officials serving on the basis of their expertise, experience, and intellect. We expect officials to apply their best professional judgment when making foreign policy decisions. Yet if U.S. foreign policy is to be made democratically, policy makers should not base all their decisions on their individual—or even their collective—beliefs and values alone. To do so could result in elitist rule. The groups discussed in this chapter help avoid that possibility, although, as you will see, there are criticisms of the activity of interest groups and other nongovernmental organizations involved in the policy making process.

Second, the levels of activity and influence of interest groups in the foreign policy process vary considerably. A great deal of the variance in activity and influence relates to the *models of the foreign policy process* discussed in chapter 6. The nature of the issue is especially important. Foreign policy issues that also have a domestic impact (and thus are intermestic issues) are apt to stimulate interest group activity. Economic issues such as trade are a prime example. Issues that create an emotional response by one or another element of the society are also intermestic. Greek Americans, for instance, are likely to become active on foreign policy questions involving Greece and to lobby through such organizations as the American Hellenic Institute Public Affairs Committee. An emotional response may also be evoked by an issue that has an asymmetrical impact on society. As noted earlier, one reason that youths are prone to being active on questions of war and peace is that they recognize that it is their age group that will do almost all of the fighting and dying in a war. Thus, to refer again to the four foreign policy making models outlined in chapter 6, interest groups are most likely to be active and influential in issues and situations that are processed according to the political model or the subgovernment model. Groups will play less of a role in the presidential and administrative models.

Third, and a related point about interest group influence, is that the groups vary considerably in their strength. Some groups, such as defense contractors, are highly organized, well-financed, and have excellent political contacts. There is, for example, a military-industrial-congressional complex that operates as an *iron triangle,* as explained in chapter 10. In contrast to the strength of defense contractors and their bureaucratic and elected allies, peace groups have had much greater difficulty getting organized, obtaining funds, and generating political support.

To explore the extent to which pluralism operates in foreign policy making, we will examine the types of interest groups involved, their various activities, and the degree to which they appear to shape U.S. foreign policy.

Types of Interest Groups

Diversity is one indicator of the importance of interest groups. They range from large to small, from liberal to conservative, and from those with a broad focus to those who are concerned with a single issue. Interest groups also address virtually every foreign policy issue that concerns the United States (Skidmore & Hudson, 1992). The discussion of economic, demographic, ideological, single-issue, and transnational groups in the following sections can, therefore, only begin to suggest the diverse scope of types of interest groups.

Economic Groups

Various economic sectors make up what is perhaps the largest and most diverse class of interest groups. Business, agriculture, and labor are major economic sectors with important stakes in foreign policy.

International economic relations have become an increasing focus of U.S. foreign policy in the post–cold war era. One result is that corporations and other economic interest groups with interests overseas are playing a more significant role in making American foreign policy. Presidents are now more likely to base U.S. attitudes toward other countries on economic considerations and to become involved in promoting specific American industries and even particular products. President Clinton has acted as U.S. "salesman in chief," as well as playing more traditional presidential roles such as commander in chief. His global business activity has ranged from efforts such as lobbying Saudi Arabia's king to have his country buy U.S. aircraft to promoting Coca-Cola sales in Russia. Here, in Moscow, the president, first lady Hillary Rodham Clinton, and Michael A. O'Neill, head of Coca-Cola operations in Russia, are all demonstrating that they have had their Coke today.

Business Groups   American business is the leading player in the world economy. In 1994 American businesses exported $697.9 billion in goods and services while importing $804.4 billion in goods and services. Thus the leaders of these companies are vitally concerned about U.S. relations with other countries. Many U.S. companies are **multinational corporations (MNCs)**, companies that have production facilities and other operations in foreign countries. The scale of these MNCs can be astounding. General Motors, the world's largest MNC, produced $154.9 billion in goods and services in 1994. General Electric, Ford, and Exxon corporations were the world's second-, fourth-, and fifth-largest MNCs in that year. Overall, 24 of the world's 50 largest MNCs in 1994 were U.S.–based corporations.

American banks are also heavily involved in foreign commerce. Their ledgers in 1994 showed $217 billion in foreign assets (such as loans to foreigners) and $299 billion in foreign liabilities (such as foreign deposits). These huge financial assets and stakes give the banks both strong leverage and an interest in the economies of other countries and regions. For example, the dramatic fall in value of the Mexican peso in December 1994 diminished the assets of those major U.S. banks, like J. P. Morgan & Company, which held large investments in pesos. The peso debacle also sent the price of many mutual funds that specialize in Latin American stocks and bonds into a nosedive. This adversely affected the portfolios of many American individuals, retirement funds, educational institutions, and even state and local agencies that invest in such securities. Altogether, U.S. short-term losses may well have exceeded $10 billion. More broadly, less developed countries (LDCs) owe U.S. banks about $175 billion on loans taken for development purposes. When a downturn in the world economy and other factors in the 1980s made it virtually impossible for Argentina, Brazil, Mexico, and several other LDCs to meet principal and interest payments, a debt crisis arose that threatened the financial stability of both debtor countries and creditor banks. At this point, the debt became a major foreign policy question, with the United States helping to work out the Brady Plan and the other agreements that were reviewed in chapter 3 in order to ease the financial peril.

Broad-based business organizations (such as the National Association of Manufacturers and the U.S. Chamber of Commerce) and specific industry associations (such as the National Cotton Council and the American Petroleum Institute) are another type of business-based interest group. They often press the government for policies that promote an improved business climate for them. Oil-exploration companies and others persuaded the administration not to ratify the UN–sponsored Law of the Sea Treaty, until it was modified in 1994 to protect U.S. companies that mine the ocean's floors from having to aid poor countries by paying royalties on the wealth the companies extract from international waters. Other U.S. groups successfully lobbied the Clinton administration in February 1994, for example, to normalize trade relations with Vietnam in 1994 and then, in 1995, to establish full diplomatic relations with Hanoi. As auto accessories executive Heinz Precher, who is also chairman of the President's Export Council, put it, "We cannot watch from the tailgate as other nations get their fair share of trade in Vietnam, a big nation of 66 million people that needs to buy many things."[1]

Individual corporations also press for their preferred foreign policy objectives. Defense contractors provide a good example (Mayer, 1991). Lockheed, the largest U.S. defense contractor, had military sales of $14.4 billion in 1994; McDonnell Douglas came in second with military sales of $9.2 billion, while Hughes Electronics came in third at $6.3 billion. Due to the end of the cold war and subsequent reductions in U.S. defense spending, defense production in 1994 was only 71 percent of the level it had reached in 1987. Still, that amounted to new orders worth $78.5 billion. These corporations have fought hard (and often against one another) to keep sales up.

One way to keep arms sales up is to sell more abroad; by 1994 foreign sales represented about 20 percent of U.S. defense contractors' total business. By any measure, U.S. corporations now dominate the global arms market. Since 1989 U.S. corporations have sold more weapons abroad than the rest of the world combined—$82.4 billion versus $66.8 billion, respectively. By 1994 the U.S. share of the annual arms market was 70 percent. In 1993 alone, U.S. defense contractors sold $22.3 billion in arms abroad. Russia came in second at $2.8 billion. From 1990 to 1993, Saudi Arabia purchased the most U.S. weapons—$30.4 billion. Taiwan came in second at $7.8 billion. Egypt ($4.4 billion) and Kuwait ($3.8 billion) came next, and South Korea ($3.7 billion) rounded out the top five.

Critics of such sales charge that they make volatile regions even more dangerous. American arms merchants take a very different view. "There are good and compelling reasons why the United States should encourage the export of U.S.–made weapons to friendly nations around the globe," argues John McDonnell, head of McDonnell Douglas. Such sales, he reasons, "serve U.S. strategic interests" and "help to shore up the U.S. industrial base at a time of declining spending."[2] McDonnell might also add that sales such as the 1994 agreement by Israel to buy 20 F-15s for $2 billion are also very good for his company. In fact, foreign sales are the only thing currently keeping the production lines alive for the F-15 and for other military hardware, such as General Dynamics's M1-A2 tank. The Clinton administration recognized this economic reality in 1994 by including the health of U.S. defense contractors, along with broader foreign policy goals, as formal considerations when deciding whether to approve arms sales abroad. "We will work with you to help you find buyers for your products in the world market place," Secretary of Commerce Ron Brown told a gathering of weaponsmakers; "and then we will work to help you close the deal."[3]

Agricultural Groups   Many Americans think of agriculture as the individual farmer atop a tractor or the lone rancher herding the stray calf back to its mother. Most of American agriculture does not fit this idyllic image. Instead, much of it is better thought of as "agribusiness," which (along with such associated industries as forest products and fisheries) produces hundreds of billions of products annually. Agricultural interest groups include associations, such as the American Farm Bureau Federation and the National Farmers Union, and agricultural corporations, including both such well-known names as General Mills and the Dole Food Company and such lesser-known but huge corporations as Archer-Daniels-Midland and Cargill. The prosperity of agribusiness is heavily linked to foreign affairs. During 1994, foods, feeds, and beverages accounted for $42 billion in U.S. exports and $31 billion in U.S. imports.

Like other economic groups, agribusiness is concerned about general trade relations. A range of disputes between the United States and the European Union (EU) over Europe's heavy subsidization of its farmers was one factor that long delayed the finalization of the extension of the General Agreement on Tariffs and Trade (GATT). It should be added, though, that some U.S. producers enjoy their own subsidization and other forms of protection. American sugar producers are shielded by rules that limit imports and limit domestic production. Inasmuch as world sugar prices are lower than the prices of domestically produced sugar, the U.S. General Accounting Office (GAO) estimates that this policy costs American consumers an extra $1.4 billion a year. From a foreign policy point of view, it also means that countries in the Caribbean and elsewhere are denied full access to U.S. markets. This inhibits their economic growth and, some say, is one reason for their continuing poverty and associated political instability.

Agricultural interest groups were also a strong player in the Clinton administration's effort to get Congress to consent to the North American Free Trade Agreement (NAFTA). To ease domestic opposition, President Clinton pressed Mexico to agree to increased protection under NAFTA for agricultural products ranging from beef, sugar, and wheat to cucumbers and peanut butter. The $275 million cucumber industry, for example, won a pledge that the United States would reimpose tariffs at the existing 6.6 cents per kilogram (3 cents a pound) if NAFTA drove down the price that U.S. cucumber growers could reap from their product. Such concessions to agricultural interests swung legislators from Florida, Oklahoma, and other states behind NAFTA.

Anti-NAFTA forces protested the president's wheeling and dealing. Perhaps thinking of the then-approaching holiday season, opposition leader David E. Bonior (D-MI) labeled Clinton's efforts "NAFTA Claus time at the White House."[4] Perhaps, but the presents helped, and all through the House, and Senate too, not enough legislators were stirring to keep NAFTA from coming about.

Trade relations, as such, are not agriculture's only concern. The United States uses trade as a diplomatic weapon, and that can strongly affect farmers and ranchers. American growers of wheat and other grains were harmed in 1980 when President Carter shut off sales to one of their most important customers by imposing economic sanctions on the Soviet Union in retaliation for its invasion of Afghanistan. A decade later, the economic sanctions that President Bush placed against Iraq in retaliation for its invasion of Kuwait harmed U.S. rice growers, among other economic groups. The rice farmers lost a customer, which had, the year before, taken 25 percent of all U.S. rice exports, or about $143 billion worth of rice.

Labor Unions   Associations of workers are a third type of important economic group. In a world where jobs, wages, and working conditions are increasingly influenced by the ability to export and by competition from imports, American workers and their unions are ever more concerned with foreign affairs.

Businesses and labor unions are often at odds over such domestic issues as contracts and labor laws. Management and labor are often united on foreign policy issues. Both the auto companies and their workers have, for example, pressed Washington to limit the import of foreign cars. Defense contractors and their unions have joined together to lobby against drastic defense spending cuts and to press for government approval of foreign sales. When the American-Israel Public Affairs Committee (AIPAC) and other interest groups opposed the sale of F-15s to Saudi Arabia, an opposing coalition of interest groups formed to push for the sale. Named "U.S. Jobs Now," the coalition included, among others, jet-maker McDonnell Douglas, engine-maker Pratt & Whitney, and the International Association of Machinists and Aerospace Workers, which represents workers at both corporations.

There are also times when labor unions and businesses are not aligned. Labor unions are, for one, increasingly concerned about policies that allow the "export" of American jobs overseas. On this basis, many unions opposed both NAFTA and the new GATT agreement.

Demographic Groups

The idea of the "average American" is a myth. Instead, Americans are a diverse people of different ages and gender, of various socioeconomic statuses, and of a multitude of ethnic, racial, and other heritages. Many demographic categories, such as being left-handed, are not related to foreign policy or, indeed, to politics. There are, however, other demographic categories for which at least some foreign policy issues are important. One key to interest group activity is its *perceived salience*, or its relevance to politics. This may be evoked by the impact of a policy. We have already noted that military-aged youth are apt to have their sense of group identity and their sense of the salience of that group to foreign policy raised during times of war.

Kinship identification also engenders perceived salience. For instance, issues that involve countries or people with whom various ethnic, racial, or religious groups of Americans feel linked are apt to create interest group activity. Whether they are based on gender (female), religion (Jewish Americans), ethnicity (Cuban Americans), or race (African Americans), these social heritage groups often play an important role in the foreign policy process.

Gender   Women make up a demographic group that is beginning to see salience in foreign policy issues and is beginning to play a role in those issues (Jeffreys-Jones, 1995). One factor, which will be addressed in chapter 13, is that, on average, women have different views on some policy issues, such as war, than do men. A second factor is that the increasing participation and power of women in national political systems and in international organizations is bringing their views to the forefront. Third, the rising feminist consciousness around the world has worked to help all women see that they have common concerns with women in other countries and to encourage these women to work together toward shared goals.

Women's groups have been important in structuring U.S. policy regarding various international organizations and related matters. The United Nations Conference on Population and Development that met in Cairo, Egypt, in September 1994 was an important meeting that focused on women's reproductive rights and similar issues. The United States was among the more than 170 countries that sent delegates. Numerous private groups, such as the New York–based International Women's Health Coalition, attended a parallel meeting in Cairo of nongovernmental organizations (NGOs) and were also influential in forming their home governments' positions at the Cairo Conference. To a significant degree, commented the chief U.S. delegate, Under Secretary of State Timothy E. Wirth, it was "women's groups that really drove" the relatively strong U.S. stand promoting the availability of birth control and recognizing unsafe abortions as a health crisis for women in many parts of the globe.[5] Similarly, groups that focus on women's issues played an important role in the UN's Fourth World Conference on Women, which met in Beijing, China, in September 1995. The U.S. delegation was headed by Ambassador Madeleine K. Albright, and U.S.–based interest groups both attended a parallel conference for NGOs and had an input in the stands taken by Ambassador Albright.

Other good examples of the growing activism and influence of women center on the issue of domestic and other forms of violence against them. One indication of activism is the Violence against Women Act (1994), which allows immigrant women to leave their abusive husbands without risking deportation. Then, in 1995, the Immigration and Naturalization Service (INS) amended its guidelines to make the United States the second country (after Canada) to recognize rape, domestic abuse, and other violence directed mostly at women as potential grounds in political asylum cases. "This is a major shift in both the commitment of the agency and its understanding of the way that the asylum claims of refugee women differ from those of men," commented Michele Beasley, a member of the Women's Commission for Refugee Women and Children, a private group that helped draft the new INS guidelines.[6]

From the same perspective, the State Department now includes a country's treatment of its women in its annual human rights report. "We felt not enough attention was being paid to the women's situation in many countries," explains Deputy Assistant Secretary of State for Human Rights Nancy Ely-Raphel. "You only have to look at our country. We're slowly moving ahead on these issues, and we want to push that around the world."[7]

Religion   Various religious tenets and a sense of religious kinship are also important spurs to interest group activity. With respect to the Cairo Conference, not all American interest groups favored strong abortion rights language and some other stands favored by most women's groups. The American Roman Catholic hierarchy and its supporters, the Southern Baptist Convention, and some other Protestant groups were among those that pressed the Clinton administration to moderate the early drafts of the Cairo Conference declaration. One change that this pressure helped bring about was U.S.–sponsored language in the final declaration that, while it supported safe abortions, did so only "in circumstances in which abortion is legal," and which further declared that "in no case should abortion be promoted as a method of family planning."[8]

Jewish Americans are also an active and effective religious demographic group. Indeed, some people argue that the reason U.S. support of Israel has been so consistent is because Jewish Americans and the organized groups that represent them have played a dominant role in shaping U.S. policy toward Israel. Other observers claim that such a characterization is overdrawn. To address this controversy, the box entitled "The Jewish Lobby: David or Goliath?" on pages 330–332 examines the strength of Jewish Americans as a foreign policy interest group.

Ethnicity   There is an old saying about something being "as American as apple pie." Perhaps, but any attempt to equate apple pie with Americans must recognize that there are many varieties of apples in the pie. The American nation is a society with a multiethnic heritage, and there are numerous Americans who are sympathetic toward their ancestral homelands and who work in favor of policies that favor those countries and the ethnic kinfolk who reside there (Shain, 1995). Armenian Americans are one such group. They have helped make Armenia the second largest (after Israel) per capita recipient of U.S. foreign aid, at $36 per Armenian in 1995. Irish Americans provide another example. They were influential in persuading the Clinton administration to become more heavily involved in the peace process in Northern Ireland and, as explained in chapter 7, to invite Gerry Adams, head of Sinn Fein, to attend a 1995 St. Patrick's Day reception at the White House, and to have Clinton visit Ulster in late 1995. Irish Americans also have been successful in ensuring favorable treatment of Irish immigration. They and several other ethnic interest groups combined to press Congress to enact a law in 1991 allowing an extra 40,000 immigrants from 34 designated countries to enter the United States. Instead of approximately 3 percent of the quota being allocated to each of the 34 countries, however, several American groups were successful in gaining favorable treatment for the country of their heritage. The Irish came out the most advantaged, with the law reserving a minimum of 40 percent of the quota for Irish-born applicants. The influence of Polish Americans was also evident in the law's provision of about 18 percent of the immigration slots for Polish-born applicants.

Immigration issues, it should be noted, do not only pit demographic groups against each other in battles over the relative size of their slice of the legal immigration pie. Other interest groups get involved over the size of the pie itself. Rising public concern over the number of legal immigrants allowed increased after 1991. Based on a recommendation by President Clinton's Commission on Immigration Reform, a bill to reduce the number of legal immigrants by 30 percent was introduced in the House of Representatives in June 1995. Some interest groups (such as the Federation for

(Continued on page 332)

The Jewish Lobby: David or Goliath?

There is a long-standing debate about the impact of Jewish Americans on U.S. foreign policy. Some believe that Jewish interest groups constitute a formidable Goliath that intimidates U.S. decision makers (Ball & Ball, 1992). Senator J. William Fulbright (D-AR), chairman of the Senate Foreign Relations Committee, told a reporter in 1969 that "we . . . do everything possible to support Israel because we have an extremely active and powerful Zionist [pro-Israel] group in this country" (Rourke, 1983:262). He even guessed that Israel's prime minister had more support in the U.S. Congress than in Israel's parliament, the Knesset. Others disagree. "Jewish lobby? There is no such thing," exclaimed Senator Jacob Javits (R-NY) (Lanquette, 1978:748). To Javits, the Jewish lobby effort would conform more closely to the image of a David, reluctant to fight and facing powerful opponents.

The status of Israel has been the principal focus of foreign policy interest for Jewish Americans. One issue has been the sale of weapons to Israel and Arab countries in the Middle East, as detailed in earlier chapters. Other issues include such matters as U.S. foreign aid to Israel and questions regarding the status of Jews and Palestinians in the West Bank (land captured by Israel from Jordan during a war in 1967). Jewish Americans have also been active on issues that involve Jews outside of Israel. One notable example occurred in 1974 when American Jewish groups successfully urged Congress to pass the Jackson-Vanik Amendment, which suspended the Soviet Union's most-favored-nation trade status until Moscow eased restrictions on the emigration of Soviet Jews.

Even though only about 3 percent of all Americans are Jewish, they have played an important role for several reasons. One is that they are well organized, being represented by a number of organizations, such as the Anti-Defamation League of B'nai B'rith, which try to coordinate their activities through the Conference of Presidents of Major Jewish Organizations (CPMJO). More than any of these, the advocacy of pro-Israeli policy is associated with the American-Israel Public Affairs Committee (AIPAC). Additionally, one scholar writes, "Jewish strength in America arises from the thousands of individual Jews

who are prepared to express their sentiments to politicians and officials" and to be politically active in a number of other ways such as voting in high numbers, giving their time to work for candidates, and contributing to political campaigns (Spiegel, 1987:24).

For all its strength, the impact of the so-called Jewish lobby has to be put into context. Three points are important. First, while there is no doubt that Jewish domestic political clout has had an important impact on U.S. policy, it is also true that other factors have played a significant part. A sense of moral outrage and concern is one. Polls show that Americans strongly support the existence of Israel. The long discrimination and periodic violence against Jewish people in Europe and elsewhere, symbolized horrifically by the Holocaust at the hands of the Nazis, have convinced most Americans that Jews deserve and need their own homeland. National security policy has also promoted strong U.S. support for Israel. During the cold war successive American administrations saw Israel as a strong and dependable ally against Soviet intrusion into the vital Middle East (Clifford, 1991; Organski, 1990).

Second, the success of the pro-Israel interest effort in the United States has been mixed (Goldberg, 1990). The discussion in chapters 6, 7, and 8 about the controversy over selling AWACS aircraft and other military equipment to Arab countries demonstrated that AIPAC and similar groups were able to delay and modify, but not defeat, a policy decided upon by the White House. Washington has also pushed Israel toward granting ever greater rights, even autonomy, to Arabs in Gaza and the West Bank Palestinians, to restrict the settlement of Jews in the West Bank, and to follow other moderating steps. Despite vigorous protests from some Jewish American groups, for example, President Bush withheld U.S. financial backing for loans to Israel to build housing to accommodate Jews coming into Israel from the former Soviet republics and Eastern Europe. The U.S. loan-guarantee was not forthcoming until Israel agreed not to use the money to build new housing in the West Bank. In short, it "is easy to exaggerate the magnitude and impact of Jewish money, votes, and organization" (Schoenbaum, 1993:5). President Clinton has also sometimes ignored Jewish American wishes and sometimes even changed their view. The administration decided in 1994 not to veto a UN Security Council resolution calling on Israel to grant Palestinians greater security and stating that Jerusalem is part of the occupied West Bank, not a part of Israel. That position set off such strong protests from among Jewish Americans that Secretary of State Christopher called Lester Pollack, chairman of the CPMJO, to assure him that U.S. support of Israel had not lessened and that the lack of a veto was only designed not to rankle the Arabs unnecessarily. The assurances were enough to mollify Pollack and others. "The consensus view among Jewish groups," Pollack observed, is now "that if the resolution facilitates the prompt resumption of negotiations" by the PLO, "the community would accept the results."[1]

Third, Jewish Americans are not always a unified political group. Most of them support the existence of Israel. That does not mean, however, that they are unified in their support of specific Israeli policies. Especially in recent years, significant splits have developed within the American Jewish community (and in Israel, as well) about a number of issues related to Israel's attempt to achieve peace by recognizing the legitimacy of the Palestine Liberation Organization (PLO) and by allowing the PLO and other Palestinians to gain at least limited control over the Gaza region and parts of the West Bank. When Senator Jesse Helms (R-NC) sponsored legislation in 1995 to bar U.S. aid to the PLO in the aftermath of the Israeli–PLO peace accord, the Zionist Organization of America and some other Jewish American groups sided with the senator. What made this remarkable was that the government of Israel favored the aid, as did most Jewish American groups and the Clinton administration. Representatives from both Jewish American camps lobbied Congress, and the infighting became of such concern that Prime Minister Rabin met personally with Jewish American leaders and admonished them about the perils of divisiveness to Israel's cause. "Never before have we witnessed an attempt by U.S. Jews to pressure Congress against the policies of a legitimate, democratically elected government," Rabin told the meeting.[2]

Another recent issue that divides Jewish Americans involves whether the United States should move its embassy from Tel Aviv to Jerusalem. President Clinton opposes the move on the grounds that it will needlessly outrage Arabs and harm the peace process in the region. Senator Robert Dole (R-KS) sponsored legislation to force Clinton to move the embassy. Israel claims Jerusalem as its capital but has not pressed Washington to move its embassy and, indeed, may agree with Clinton's reasoning. Within this complex set of circumstances, Jewish Americans have been divided. Supporting the move, the executive director of AIPAC argued that "it is the absolute right of every sovereign state to designate its own capital." Other Jewish groups favor the shift but urged Congress to go slow. And Senator Dianne Feinstein (D-CA), a Jewish American, announced that she opposed the Dole effort on the grounds that it would "collapse" the peace effort. Dole even found that being pro-Israel can backfire politically. Some charge that his advocacy of the move was connected with his presidential ambitions. The *Forward*, a Jewish newspaper in New York, editorialized that Dole's effort to be a "champion of Israel would be laughable were it not so blatant a play for position in the coming [presidential] primaries."[3] In the end, in October 1995 Congress approved legislation that ostensibly would force the transfer of the U.S. embassy in Israel from Tel Aviv to Israel. The legislative action was, argued Representative Lee Hamilton (D-IN), a "classic congressional foreign policy maneuver," by which the representatives and senators "get the domestic political advantage" of appealing to voters who support the move and "the president gets the responsibility" for dealing with the diplomatic damage the move would cause in relations with the surrounding Arab states.[4] Even though the administration condemned the legislation, Clinton chose not to veto it. One reason was that the margins of passage (374–37 in the House, 93–5 in the Senate) were so lopsided that it was almost certain that Congress would have overridden the veto. More important, the bill did not really force the move. Instead, in another traditional congressional maneuver, legislators passed a headline-grabbing bill that seemed to do much, but which left the president a loophole that meant that the bill would accomplish nothing. In this case the escape clause allowed the president to delay the move if, in his estimation, it would threaten U.S. security by disrupting the peace negotiations between Israel and its neighbors. Since that is exactly what Clinton had said the bill would do, it came as no surprise to Congress, the White House, Israeli leaders, or Arab leaders that the U.S. embassy continues to be in Tel Aviv.

There are even times when the majority of American Jews oppose Israeli policy. With regard to the housing loan-guarantee issue, for instance, a survey of Jewish leaders found that a majority disagreed with Israel's government and, instead, backed a freeze on building houses for Jewish settlers in the West Bank in return for U.S. financial backing. Jewish American leaders also differed on two associated issues with the conservative government of Prime Minister Yitzhak Shamir that was in power at that time. An overwhelming 88 percent of Jewish American leaders favored "territorial compromise" with the Arabs in exchange for peace guarantees, and a strong 79 percent said they could eventually accept a Palestinian state.[5]

It appears, then, that instead of automatically following Israel's leadership, Jewish Americans have their own views on the course that Israel should follow. They are, according to one analyst, more "dovish" than are the conservative elements in Israel and more in tune with the more liberal political view of Prime Minister Yitzhak Rabin and the Labor Party government, which assumed office in mid-1992.

What American Jewish citizens want, the analysis concludes, is an "Israel that makes them feel good, that reflects their liberal outlook and values" (Marcus, 1990:557, 548).

Thus the idea of a single-minded, nearly invincible Jewish lobby is mostly fiction. Jewish Americans have lobbied on behalf of their emotional homeland; but so have Americans of Cuban, Greek, Irish, Polish, and other heritages. Sometimes American Jews have been nearly united in their support of a specific Israeli position; sometimes they have been divided. Sometimes American policy has followed the preferences of the majority of Jewish Americans; sometimes American policy has disappointed many in the Jewish community. Surely the effort on behalf of Israel usually is strongly supported by almost all American Jews. But the usually favorable attitude of the United States has also been based on Israel's strategic position in the pivotal Middle East and on widespread sympathy for and support of Israel among a broad range of Americans (Guth & Fraser, 1993). Thus, there are many reasons for U.S. support of Israel. The pro-Israel lobby may be a David, waging a skillful campaign, but it is not a Goliath, larger and seemingly more powerful than any challenger on the policy battleground.

(Continued from page 329)

American Immigration Reform) typically support efforts to reduce immigration, while others (like the National Immigration Law Center) generally oppose them.

Joining Irish Americans and other ethnic groups that have long played a role, various Spanish-heritage groups have begun to become more active and influential. Cuban Americans have been particularly effective. The Cuban American community, centered in Florida and operating through such organizations as the Cuban American National Foundation and the Cuban-American National Alliance, strongly opposes the communist government of Fidel Castro in Cuba and is generally more conservative than the overall U.S. population or other Latino/a American groups.

A surge of Cuban boat people arriving in Florida in 1994 put the Clinton administration in a difficult spot, caught between countervailing pressures from Florida. The governor of Florida and others called on Clinton to end the U.S. policy that admitted Cubans almost automatically as political refugees.

In August 1994 American ships began taking Cuban refugees who had been picked up at sea to the U.S. naval base at Guantanamo Bay in Cuba for screening on whether they should be granted political asylum or be returned to Cuba. That pleased some Floridians but outraged Cuban Americans living there and elsewhere. It also led to the buildup of over 20,000 Cubans at the base and a worry, a top U.S. military officer said, that "civil disturbance was clearly an option." Trying to avoid that, and the politically explosive image of U.S. troops in action against Cuban refugees, the Clinton administration decided in May 1995 to admit the Cubans to the United States. But to avoid a backlash by Floridians, and after high-level talks in New York between U.S. and Cuban (UN-based) diplomats, Clinton decreed that all future Cuban boat people would be returned to Cuba. This step by Clinton, Jorge Mas Canosa, head of the Cuban-American National Foundation, told a congressional committee, amounted to an "indefensible and morally bankrupt collaboration with the criminal regime of Fidel Castro."[9]

Hoping to offset the anger of Cuban Americans, Clinton also chose to maintain, and even slightly tighten, economic sanctions against Castro's Cuba despite the criticism of Senator Christopher Dodd (D-CT) and others in his party for being "unwilling to examine and explore alternatives" toward Cuba in the post–cold war era. The president's unyielding stance is caused in part, according to one observer, by the fact that Clinton knows that "if he had gotten 25 percent of the Cuban American vote, he would've won Florida in the [1992 presidential] election." As such, Clinton's policy on Cuba is "a straightforward political calculation" aimed at winning Florida in the 1996 election.[10]

Puerto Ricans living in the continental United States have been less active on pure foreign policy issues, as such, because their traditional homeland is a U.S. commonwealth and all Puerto Ricans are U.S. citizens. Intermestic issues are another matter. Puerto Ricans were active on both sides of the debate over whether Congress should pass NAFTA. Governor Pedro J. Rosselló of Puerto Rico and many other politicians on the island supported NAFTA on the grounds that it would open markets in Mexico to products produced in Puerto Rico. However, all Puerto Rican–heritage members of Congress opposed NAFTA because of the negative impact they feared that the agreement would have on their constituents in the continental United States. Mexican Americans were similarly split over the NAFTA issue. Those with an emotional identification with Mexico favored the trade agreement. Those without a strong emotional attachment to Mexico opposed it, again fearing a loss of jobs.

Race African Americans are another of the demographic groups that are beginning to play a more significant role in the foreign policy making process (Normandy, 1994). The abomination of apartheid in South Africa was the issue that first galvanized African American activism in the foreign policy realm. The treatment of South Africa's black population by the country's whites was an indignity to which American blacks could relate. Beginning in 1984, Randall Robinson, the executive director to the lobbying group TransAfrica, and other leaders were instrumental in persuading the U.S. government to tighten its sanctions aimed at ending South Africa's racist system and to release South African black leader Nelson Mandela from jail (Normandy, 1994). One impact of these efforts was that in 1986 Congress overrode President Reagan's veto and imposed strict economic sanctions on South Africa. Such actions were also adopted by most other countries. As a result, South Africa outlawed its apartheid system and negotiated a new constitution that led to the election of a multiracial government led by President Nelson Mandela.

A more recent and race-related issue that also activated African Americans involved Haiti. They were offended by what they saw as U.S. unwillingness to take strong action to ease the plight of black Haitians. Clinton's policy of returning Haitian

The United States has been called a "melting pot," but numerous societal groups have retained a strong demographic identity and are concerned with U.S. foreign policy that involves ancestral homelands and other issues about their demographic kin in other countries. For example, African Americans have been or are active on such matters as ending apartheid and white rule in South Africa, promoting democracy in Nigeria, and improving political and economic conditions in Haiti. The Black Caucus in Congress brought significant and ultimately successful pressure on President Clinton to topple the military junta in Haiti and to restore President Jean-Bertrand Aristide to his office. A key African American in this effort was the chairman of the Black Caucus, Representative Kweisi Mfume (D-MD), shown here to the left of President Aristide. In December 1995, Mfume resigned from Congress to take up the post of president of the NAACP.

refugees to their homeland without an asylum hearing was particularly offensive, especially when contrasted with the willingness to allow generally lighter-skinned, Spanish-heritage Cuban refugees into the country. African Americans took several effective actions. Randall Robinson staged a highly publicized, 27-day fast in 1994 to protest Clinton's refugee policy. That policy changed, with Haitians being taken to the U.S. naval base at Guantanamo Bay, Cuba, for interviews, possibly leading to granting political asylum. The thought of large numbers of Haitians being allowed to come to the United States in turn triggered others to press Clinton to unseat the military junta in Haiti rather than encourage a renewed tidal wave of refugees.

African Americans strongly supported the move to oust the junta. They lobbied successfully to have William H. Gray III, a former African American member of Congress, named as Clinton's special adviser on Haiti. With more than 40 members, the Congressional Black Caucus worked to get Clinton to act against the junta. Members such as Donald M. Payne (D-NJ) contrasted Clinton's hesitancy to move to help blacks with Reagan's willingness to invade Grenada and Bush's intervention in Panama and asserted that "race has something to do with it."[11] Representative Kweisi Mfume (D-MD), the caucus chairman, denounced Clinton for fostering "a policy of anarchy, one that changes by the moment." Such criticisms had their effect. Clinton decided to force the junta out; Jean-Bertrand Aristide was restored to the presidential palace in Port-au-Prince. Representative Payne commented modestly that he thought the caucus may have "played a role in changing policy." Other sources gave the group's efforts higher marks. "The basic components of the black caucus approach . . . all . . . have been adopted," commented one State Department official.[12]

In 1995 the attention of African American leaders switched back to Africa. The issue was Nigeria and its corrupt military regime. Apart from the issue as such, what is significant about this African American effort is that it does not involve any issues of overt or alleged racism, as did South Africa and Haiti. Instead, Robinson and TransAfrica began a series of demonstrations to call attention to the human rights abuses of black Nigerians by Nigeria's black military regime.[13] "We must isolate Nigeria, politically, socially, and economically in the same way we were able to isolate South Africa and Haiti," Robinson urged. Joining in the effort were other well-known

African Americans, including poet Maya Angelou, entertainers Danny Glover, Bryant Gumbel, and Quincy Jones, athlete Sugar Ray Leonard, and the Reverend Jesse Jackson. The Nigerian issue, and especially the military regime's tolerance of—allegedly participation in—drug trafficking, has also attracted the attention of the Congressional Black Caucus. Representative Payne, for one, argues that the Nigerian regime is an intermestic issue because its "military leaders continue to line their pockets with drug payoffs to transport narcotics through Nigeria to our youth on the streets of every city in the United States."[14]

Another recent African American initiative is to promote more trade and aid ties between the United States and African countries. This effort is being led by the Reverend Leon Sullivan, a Philadelphia veteran of the antiapartheid movement. He organized a May 1995 conference of 1,000 African Americans and 4,000 African government officials, including 20 African presidents and prime ministers, in Dakar, Senegal. Included in the African American delegation attending were such notables as Jesse Jackson, Secretary of Commerce Ron Brown, Mayor Marion Barry of Washington, D.C., and Joseph Lowery, president of the Southern Christian Leadership Conference. "A new movement is being born among African Americans," Sullivan proclaimed. "We're going to build bridges to Africa. We're going to put our skills and training to work to help Africa."[15] Other African American groups and individuals have joined the movement. The National Association for the Advancement of Colored People (NAACP) rejected a proffered contribution of $20,000 by Nigeria, and a group of African American notables wrote a joint letter to President Clinton urging him to ban the import of Nigerian oil. These efforts have not been successful to date, but they are taken seriously by the Nigerian government. Nigerian UN diplomats intervened successfully to downgrade an award ceremony, in which the United Nations Children's Fund honored Randall Robinson for his group's humanitarian efforts, by moving it out of the chamber of the General Assembly to a less august forum. A group of Nigerians also took out full-page ads in various newspapers to denounce Robinson's campaign against their country as nothing but a ploy to gain financing for TransAfrica Forum.

Yet another policy concern issue involving African Americans illustrates how a sense of asymmetrical impact can affect a demographic interest group. African Americans constitute 11 percent of the adult population. Yet in 1990 they made up 21 percent of the military, 25 percent of the troops sent to the Persian Gulf, and 30 percent of the Army, the service that saw the heaviest combat there.[16] Such statistics add to a sense among many African Americans that they are often asked to fight abroad for a country that does not treat them equally at home. These factors may well have been why a smaller percentage of African Americans than of the overall population supported U.S. involvement in the Persian Gulf. One survey found, for example, that 77 percent of whites, but only 49 percent of blacks, supported the war.[17] Thus it was not surprising to find an African American such as Representative Maxine Waters (D-CA) declaring, "It is not anybody's war to fight, most definitely it's not Africa America's war to fight."[18]

Ideological Groups

Ideological groups are formed on the basis of general beliefs or attitudes about politics. There are a wide variety of ideological interest groups. First we will discuss general ideological groups, then we will turn our attention to a specific type of such groups, think tanks.

General Ideological Groups   Ideological interest groups span the spectrum of political thought. There are *conservative groups* like the American Conservative Union, Americans for Constitutional Action, the American Security Council, the John Birch Society, and the National Conservative Political Action Committee. Groups like these favor policies such as limited foreign involvement and a strong national defense. In the late 1970s and in the 1980s, for example, the Committee on the Present Danger pressed for higher defense spending and a firm stand against the Soviet Union. Ronald Reagan was just one of the many members of his administration who were members of this committee. One of the group's leaders, Paul Nitze, also became Reagan's chief arms control negotiator in the intermediate-range nuclear force talks with the Soviets.

At the other end of the spectrum are *liberal groups* like the Americans for Democratic Action, the Women's International League for Peace and Freedom, and the World Peace through Law Association. Such groups promote a variety of humanitarian policies that emphasize cooperative internationalism. Liberals are more likely than conservatives to be concerned with the needs of the world community; conservatives are apt to rally around an "America first" banner. Conservatives tend to be strong nationalists. They favor unilateral U.S. action in foreign policy and are leery of U.S. involvement in the UN and other multilateral organization and efforts. Liberals have a more globalist perspective. They lean toward multilateralism and are prone to worry somewhat less about always preserving the independence of U.S. actions, especially if international cooperation helps to solve global problems.

The American Communist Party (ACP) represents yet another type of ideological interest group. In this case, some of its past activities can be described as treasonous. The recent declassification of Soviet documents has revealed that during the cold war the ACP conducted espionage on behalf of the Kremlin. The party received funds from Moscow and, in return, tried to penetrate the U.S. government and help spies steal and transmit secrets, including atomic weapons information. According to two scholars who have studied the documents, what they "show is that the American communist movement assisted Soviet intelligence and placed loyalty to the Soviet Union ahead of loyalty to the United States."[19]

Not all ideological groups that affect foreign policy are explicitly political. *Religious organizations,* for example, are properly classified as a type of ideological group when they engage in political activity. Among the important groups are the American Friends Service Committee, the National Conference of Catholic Bishops, and the National Council of Churches. They have, for instance, often taken stands against the use of force as an instrument of U.S. policy, although in some instances (such as the fighting in Bosnia) some prominent religious groups and leaders have urged military intervention. The recent, semisuccessful effort by Roman Catholic and some Protestant groups to drop the idea of abortion as a form of population control at the 1994 Cairo Conference was discussed in the last section. "You're constantly blindsided if you consider religion as neutral or outside world politics," one analyst observed correctly. "Better to understand the place that religion holds in the wider international framework."[20]

Think Tanks   Another set of organizations that displays some characteristics of ideological interest groups are **think tanks**. They are privately funded public policy research centers. The reason that think tanks can be classified as ideological interest groups is that many of these research organizations have an ideological slant.

The Council on Foreign Relations is the most prominent foreign policy think tank. Its point of view is internationalist and, thus, somewhat liberal. Other think tanks span the ideological spectrum. Some examples from left to right are the very liberal Institute for Policy Studies, the left-of-center Ethics and Public Policy Center, the slightly left-of-center Brookings Institution, the centrist Center for Strategic and International Studies, the right-of-center American Enterprise Institute (AEI), and the markedly conservative Heritage Foundation and Cato Institute. Many think tanks are substantial operations. The Heritage Foundation, for instance, employs over 150 staff members and collected about $23 million in tax-free contributions from more than 200,000 donors in 1993.

Colleges and universities are not think tanks as such, although there are some such organizations attached to them. The Hoover Institution on War, Revolution and Peace at Stanford University and the Carter Center at Emory University are among the most well known. It is possible to argue, though, that institutions of higher learning are akin to think tanks insofar as individual professors conduct research and comment on various foreign policy issues. Ideologically, professors are predominantly liberal. One survey found that 56 percent of professors classify themselves as "liberal" or "moderately liberal."[21] Seventeen percent of the professors responding to the poll described themselves as "middle of the road," and 28 percent said they were "moderately conservative" or "conservative." Furthermore, the more prestigious the college or university, the more likely it is that its faculty will be liberal. For example, 70 percent of the faculty both at those liberal arts colleges rated "highly selective" by the Carnegie Commission on Higher Education and at the most notable research universities (those receiving the most grants and awarding the most Ph.D.'s) called themselves liberal or moderately liberal. By comparison, only 46 percent of the faculty at 2-year colleges placed themselves in either of the two liberal categories.

Think tanks play several foreign policy making roles. The Council on Foreign Relations (CFR) provides an example. Think tanks are vehicles for communications among the elite. The CFR brings leaders from various areas of the society together for conferences. It also publishes books, short papers, and *Foreign Affairs,* a quarterly publication of opinion on foreign policy. If your college or town library has only one journal devoted to foreign policy, it probably will be *Foreign Affairs,* which *Time* magazine once described as the most influential journal in America.

Think tanks also serve as policy advocates and as sources of policy expertise (Ricci, 1993). They sponsor research both on the broad directions of future U.S. foreign policy and on very specific policy problems facing the country. The studies are published and circulated with the aim of bringing them to the attention of the media and to those in power in the government. Many techniques are used. The published reports are forwarded to the press and to all appropriate governmental officials, the researchers may personally contact journalists and policy makers in the executive branch and in Congress, and think tank experts may testify in congressional hearings. Think tanks also serve as a source for many of the experts, sometimes derisively labeled "talking heads," who appear on television or who write op-ed pieces for newspapers. Just during the year between June 1992 and June 1993, for instance, the AEI estimates that think tank experts made more than 10,000 media appearances on television and radio and in newspapers and magazines.

One indication of the importance of think tanks is that their number is growing rapidly and has reached about 1,000 such organizations. A key reason for the proliferation of think tanks is the increasing scope and complexity of the political issues that political leaders face (Smith, 1991). But the proliferation of think tanks also has increased the "competition among them to attract the attention of decision makers and contributions of potential donors" (Abelson, 1995:118). All this creates something of a symbiotic relationship between decision makers, who have a need for expertise, and think tanks, which "need to sell" their advice and their publications to political leaders in order to have an impact and justify their existence. As one analyst puts it, "Normative arguments and empirical evidence have, in effect, become unavoidable components of modern policy struggles, and the social science communities have emerged as the principal suppliers of the necessary intellectual ammunition" (Fischer, 1991:348). Such advice is particularly important as "counter-expertise" to those out of power who wish to counter policy advocated by the executive branch and the experts it employs.

A third function of think tanks is to act as recruitment agencies for the government (Dye, 1995). Policy makers have been consistently drawn from the CFR ranks. Among the CFR members appointed to high office during the Clinton administration's first 3 years in power were Secretary of State Warren Christopher, Deputy Secretary of State Clifton Wharton Jr. and his successor, Strobe Talbott, Under Secretary of State Peter Tarnoff, UN ambassador Madeleine Albright, and deputy national security adviser Samuel Berger. Outside the immediate foreign policy realm, CFR membership was on the résumé of five other Cabinet-rank officers, including Secretary of the Interior Bruce Babbitt, Secretary of Health and Human Services Donna Shalala, Secretary of Housing and Urban Development Henry Cisneros, and chairman of the Council of Economic Advisers Laura D'Andrea Tyson. When one party loses power, think tanks supply alternative sources of contacts, influence, and sometimes employment. For example, Richard Perle, a top defense official in the Reagan administration, is with the American Enterprise Institute. Higher education also serves as a recruiting ground: national security adviser Anthony Lake served as a professor at Mount Holyoke College and Ambassador Albright was at Georgetown University.

Issue-Oriented Groups

Some groups restrict their attention to a limited range of issues or even to a single issue. The focus of such groups can be a general issue area, such as care for the environment (Friends of the Earth, Greenpeace, World Wildlife Federation), the need for a strong defense (American Legion and Veterans of Foreign Wars), or the need for arms control (Arms Control Association, Peace Action, Union of Concerned Scientists). The focus can be as narrow as support for a single organization (United Nations Association) or country (National Network in Solidarity with the Nicaraguan People) or as broad as U.S. policy toward a region of the world, like Central America (Council for Inter-American Security) or calls for world government (World Federalists).

Transnational Interest Groups

An important phenomenon of modern international relations is that traditional national borders are becoming less and less important to political activity. There are many **transnational interest groups** operating across borders. These groups span the varieties that we have already discussed.

Some transnational groups have members or associated organizations in many countries. Amnesty International and Greenpeace are two such groups. Another is the International Physicians for the Prevention of Nuclear War, founded in 1980 by American cardiologist Bernard Lown and Soviet cardiologist Yevgeny Chazov. It won the Nobel Peace Prize in 1985.

Although foreign companies and governments have interests in U.S. foreign policy, their lobbying activity raises concerns in the minds of some about undue foreign influence (Rehbein, 1995; Hocking, 1990). Over the past 20 years, about half of all former senior officials in the Office of the U.S. Trade Representative and about a third of those from the International Trade Commission have subsequently become registered foreign agents. A related concern occurs when individuals who once lobbied for foreign interests are appointed to policy making positions or have other insider positions in an administration. President Bush's chief trade negotiator, Carla Hills, was a former lobbyist for Japanese clients. Among the Clinton appointees, Mickey Kantor, who succeeded Hills as chief trade negotiator, came from a firm that represents Japan's NEC corporation. Clinton's secretary of commerce, Ron Brown, was a partner in a law firm that represented the oil sheikdom Abu Dhabi and Japanese television manufacturers. (Brown has also been accused of improprieties with regard to his contacts with Vietnamese businessmen who were trying to get the United States to ease or end its ban on trade and other financial relations with Vietnam.)

Lobbying by transnational or foreign interest groups has jumped dramatically in recent years. In 1978 registered foreign groups spent almost $126 million in lobbying activities in the United States. The top three countries represented by such groups in 1978 were Australia ($12.2 million), Japan ($10.6 million), and Canada ($8 million). By 1991 the total had more than tripled, rising to over $410 million. The top three countries represented in 1991 were Japan ($82.5 million), Colombia ($35.5 million), and Mexico ($34.5 million). Most of the money was spent for trade promotion and other such supposedly nonpolitical activity, but $52 million was spent in 1991 on what one study terms "access to power" (Summary & Summary, 1994). Whatever their ultimate objective, such large expenditures by foreign groups to influence U.S. policy, and particularly the huge sums spent by the Japanese, alarmed many Americans. A 1990 book, *Agents of Influence* written by business analyst Pat Choate, set off a storm of controversy by arguing that "the manipulation [of U.S. policy] by Japanese and other foreign interests has reached the point that it threatens our national sovereignty."[22] Choate focused especially on the regular practice of former top officials going to work as lobbyists for foreign interests. Some observers, such as Chrysler Motors chairman Lee Iacocca, agreed with Choate. Others denounced him for, in the words of one columnist, engaging in "McCarthyism" for "his easy accusations of disloyalty, his imagery of infection in the body politic, [and] his woozy mixture of falsehoods, half truths and exaggerations."[23]

During the 1992 presidential campaign, candidate Clinton charged that under Republican presidents Reagan and Bush, "the last 12 years were nothing less than an extended hunting season for high-priced lobbyists and Washington influence peddlers."[24] Once elected, Clinton imposed new standards on his top political appointees. They had to agree that they would wait at least 5 years after leaving government service before lobbying their former agencies on behalf of a domestic or foreign private client and that they would never lobby the U.S. government on behalf of a foreign government or political party. Enforcing such regulations is difficult, though. There have long been rules that bar a former official from lobbying with regard to a decision in which they "personally and substantially" were part. Yet there are many loopholes. After less than a year as President Clinton's chief congressional lobbyist, Howard Paster resigned in December 1993 to become chairman and chief executive officer of the Hill and Knowlton lobbying firm. Since Paster did not work for an agency as such, he will not be barred from contacting Congress, the State Department, and other centers of policy on behalf of his firm's many foreign clients. These have ranged from countries such as China and Kuwait to companies such as Mazda and the Bank of Credit and Commerce International, whose officers were indicted for felonious activity.

Interest Group Activities

Due to the significance of their involvement, it is important to examine how interest groups attempt to influence foreign policy. We will, therefore, discuss the way they operate in setting the agenda, influencing who serves in government, intervening in decision making, and affecting policy implementation.

Setting the Agenda

An important initial step in the policy process is getting the political system to focus on an issue. This is called agenda setting, as discussed in earlier chapters. The most commonplace ways for interest groups to try to set the political agenda include approaching the media directly with information and urging reporters to follow an issue, presenting research findings to government officials, promoting letter-writing campaigns to government officials, serving on advisory commissions or task forces, and filing suits or engaging in litigation.

A good example of agenda setting is the effort of Greek American groups in 1974 to prompt Congress to cut off military aid to Turkey following its invasion of Cyprus. The Ford administration was reluctant to punish Turkey, a NATO ally sharing a border with the Soviet Union, and wanted to keep the issue off the political agenda. Greek Americans soon changed that. They held protest marches that drew media coverage; issued press releases; bombarded legislators with mail, telegrams, and phone calls; and visited every member of Congress who would see them. The pressure was intense. One senator reported spending 40 to 50 hours on the phone talking to angry Greek American constituents and receiving 300 telegrams a day from Greek Americans. Greek American members of Congress such as Representatives John Brademas (D-IN) and Paul Sarbanes (D-MD) took up the issue and demanded action. The result was that Greek Americans persuaded Congress to take up the issue and to pass an arms embargo against Turkey.

Influencing Who Serves in Government

Another important interest group activity involves attempting to influence who serves in government. This activity includes being involved in elections and trying to influence who is appointed and confirmed for key executive posts.

Electoral activity is one way to determine who makes policy. Presidents and members of Congress must be elected or reelected. This fact sensitizes politicians to interest groups, because they can supply campaign workers, campaign financial contributions, votes, and other types of electoral support. Realizing this, many interest groups are very active in elections. Groups make financial contributions to electoral campaigns, try to sway voters by publicizing candidates' voting records, contribute personnel or supplies to the campaigns of those candidates they wish to see elected, and publicly endorse their favored candidates prior to elections. Most of this activity is conducted by domestic interest groups, but transnational groups are also active. Focusing on campaign finance, for example, one study of the political activities of 119 U.S. subsidiaries of foreign corporations based in 21 other countries found that the companies were represented by 124 political action committees; during 1987 and 1988 these political action committees spent $3,624,000 making 3,818 contributions to candidates for federal office. British firms led the way, spending 27 percent of the total and outdistancing second-place Japanese firms by almost 2.5 to 1 (Mitchell, 1995).

Decisions by politicians about whether or not to respond to pressure from an interest group depend in part on the strength of that group in their electoral district, state, or (for presidential candidates) the country. Other factors are important too. The intensity of group pressure and whether or not there are countervailing group pressures in a politician's constituency are among the variables that influence the degree to which politicians respond to group pressures. Also, the more intense the interest groups are, especially if most important groups within a constituency are on one side of an issue, the more likely it is that the politician will be swayed by interest group pressure.

The likelihood that members of an interest group will vote for (or did vote for) a politician is also important, because politicians tend to be more responsive to the opinions of those who actually voted for them rather than to the constituency as a whole. Jewish Americans, for instance, vote overwhelmingly for Democrats. In 1992, for example, 83 percent of all Jewish voters cast their ballots for Clinton; 79 percent of them voted for the Democrat in congressional elections. Not surprisingly, Republican presidents and legislators have often been less responsive to Jewish lobbying efforts, or more willing to press Israel for concessions, than have been Democratic officeholders and candidates. On the other hand, Cuban Americans typically vote for Republicans. This is one reason Clinton was willing to upset them in May 1995 by forcing future illegal Cuban refugees to go back to Cuba. After all, he was not likely to get the votes of Cuban Americans anyway. In short, elected leaders are far less responsive to the needs of interest groups that have not supported them in the past than they are to those who helped them get elected.

Interest groups also try to influence *executive branch appointments*. When President Clinton began to put his foreign policy team together, a number of choices were influenced by interest groups. Clinton sent a report to Congress on nominees that included Cuban American attorney Mario Baeza as assistant secretary of state for inter-American affairs. Cubans are a racially diverse people, and Baeza, who is black, was promoted by members of the Congressional Black Caucus. Cuban American groups objected to Baeza, claiming that he was too moderate on relations with the Castro government in Havana. By the time Clinton's list wound its way through channels and arrived on Capitol Hill, Baeza's name had a line drawn through it.[25]

Clinton's nomination of several officials who had served in the Carter administration also created some pressures from Jewish American groups. The appointment of Peter Tarnoff as under secretary of state for political affairs (the department's third-ranking position) worried some Jewish Americans who viewed the Carter administration as not particularly sympathetic to Israel. Tarnoff's nomination was approved by the Senate anyway.[26] There were also reports of objections to the nomination of another former Carter official, Warren Christopher, as secretary of state. Some Jewish American representatives argued that they had no objections to Christopher. AIPAC issued a statement that said, "We know of no opposition to him by the mainstream of the pro-Israel community."[27] But other Jewish American leaders did express disquiet. "When you look at the people appointed to the top foreign policy jobs, there is a lingering concern about Carterism," said Abraham Foxman, executive director of the Anti-Defamation League.[28] Clinton quickly recognized the pressure. "I know there is concern out there—I know that I have a problem out there," he told several Jewish members of Congress.[29] Christopher's appointment went through, but the administration was on notice that its attitude toward Israel was suspect.

That did not end the concerns of Jewish Americans. The 1994 nomination of Strobe Talbott as deputy secretary of state once again created concerns for many Jewish Americans. As a *Time* magazine correspondent, Talbott has often been critical of Israel, writing such columns as "How Israel Is Like Iraq," which appeared in October 1990 in the aftermath of Iraq's invasion of Kuwait. Strong protests by many Jewish organizations persuaded Talbott to reconsider his views. Talbott, as discussed in chapter 9, beat a diplomatic retreat during his confirmation hearings. Whereas in 1981 he had termed Israel "an outright liability" to U.S. interests, in 1994 he was sure that "a strong Israel is in America's interest" and that U.S.–Israeli ties should be "unshakable."[30] This epiphany and the strong support of Jewish American senator Howard Metzenbaum (D-OH) assuaged Talbott's critics and he was confirmed.

Intervention in Decision Making

In addition to getting issues on the political agenda and to supporting friendly politicians electorally, interest groups also attempt to influence policy decisions. The groups use a variety of techniques commonly referred to as *lobbying.*

Lobbyists are individuals who present the views of an interest group to government officials. Often these people are paid professionals. Contrary to myth, most *professional lobbying* does not involve electoral threats, promises of campaign contributions, or other arm-twisting techniques. Insofar as such electoral connections exist, they are usually implicit, not explicit. Rather, lobbying involves mostly the presentation of information and argumentation to elected and appointed executive and legislative officials. Lobbyists provide facts and lines of reasoning to decision makers who support their cause to bolster the power of the policy makers' arguments in Congress or within the executive branch. Professional lobbyists also help friendly politicians devise legislative strategies and even write the draft versions of legislation.

Lobbyists also focus on undecided policy makers. For example, the North American Free Trade Agreement touched off a major lobbying effort by interest groups on both sides of the issue. As one congressional aide observed, "For those of us who work for congressmen who are undecided about the issue, seeing lobbyists from one side or the other has become a full-time job."[31]

Grassroots lobbying is another common technique. This approach involves public relations campaigns and other efforts that will activate the public to contact decision makers, to write letters to newspapers, to march in demonstrations, and to take other actions that will bring pressure to bear on Washington. Various interest groups launched a concerted grassroots campaign, for example, when the Bush administration tried to terminate the military's V-22 Osprey aircraft. The plane's builder, Bell Helicopter Textron, and the unions whose members construct the plane joined weekly with military officials and local members of Congress to coordinate their campaign. They worked to get op-ed pieces favoring the aircraft into newspapers around the country. Supporters even landed a prototype of the V-22 on the Capitol's grounds in Washington to attract press coverage. Every congressional district in the country was examined to see if it contained any subcontractors supplying parts for the V-22. Owners of and workers at these subcontractors were urged to participate in a telephone and mail campaign to put pressure on their representatives in Congress to vote to keep funding for the Osprey. The effort worked. Congress insisted that the V-22 continue to receive research and development money, and the project survived.

Affecting Policy Implementation

Interest group activity does not end once policy makers have acted. Instead, interest groups often attempt to influence the chosen policy in obvious or subtle ways. *Monitoring implementation* by the bureaucracy is one technique. Interest groups seek to ensure that the policy is implemented in the most favorable way, whether that means enthusiastic implementation by the executive branch of policies with which a group agrees or a foot-dragging approach toward policies that a group opposes. This concern usually entails monitoring the actions of the executive branch departments and agencies entrusted with carrying out policy makers' decisions and stepping in to help with the implementation wherever possible. Virtually all interest groups stress this last phase of the policy process.

Sometimes interest groups play an even more direct role in policy implementation. One approach is for interest groups to work with the government to implement policy. American oil companies played at least a supportive role in the CIA-sponsored coup that toppled Iranian leftist prime minister Mohammed Mossadegh in 1953 and cemented the power of the young shah of Iran. In an even more direct manner, the United Fruit Company promoted the overthrow of the Arbenz regime in Guatemala by the CIA in 1954. Most notoriously of all, corporations like ITT and Anaconda Copper worked with the CIA to destabilize the economy of Chile and to overthrow the regime of leftist president Salvador Allende in 1973.

On other, rarer occasions, an interest group's efforts to affect policy implementation approaches the point of trying to take over policy. Jorge Mas Canosa heads the Cuban American National Foundation (CANF) and is considered widely to be the most powerful member of the Cuban community in the United States. Among the CANF's earlier successes was to persuade the U.S. government to establish Radio Martí in 1985 and Televisión Martí in 1990. The radio station is probably heard in Cuba, but few Cubans can watch the television station, which broadcasts only between 3:30 a.m. and 8:30 a.m. and which is jammed by the Cuban government. These two broadcast stations are in the Office of Cuba Broadcasting, a subdivision of the Voice of America, which is part of the United States Information Agency (USIA). The legislated mission of the stations is to provide balanced news to the Cuban people. Federal funding through FY1996 has amounted to more than $270 million.

The issue regarding the two Martí stations involves the influence of Mas over their broadcast content. Mas was appointed by President Reagan as head of the

Cuban Americans have used a variety of techniques to influence U.S. policy toward Cuba. There are strong international and domestic pressures on President Clinton to ease the long-standing U.S. effort to maintain the diplomatic and economic isolation of Cuba. But most Cuban Americans oppose any moderation of U.S. policy until Cuba's communist government, headed by President Fidel Castro, holds democratic elections. Clinton's tentative steps to better relations with Cuba or to restrict the ability of Cuban refugees to claim political asylum in the United States have sparked protests such as the one shown here, which blocked the Lincoln Tunnel between New Jersey and New York during a rush hour in May 1995.

advisory board that oversees the two stations, and he continues to hold that position. Critics charge that Mas has pressured the stations to broadcast propaganda and to promote his supposed goal of become the president of Cuba after the Castro government falls. For his part, Mas has refused to comment. But one official of the CANF suggested, "This is all part of a very long-standing campaign of political harassment of the Office of Cuba Broadcasting." The reason, the official continued, is that "Jorge Mas has many political enemies in this town [Washington, D.C.] who may have latched onto this device to take a chunk out of his hide."

Others disagree that there is a vendetta under way. Among those is the U.S. General Accounting Office, which in a 1992 report concluded that Televisión Martí's broadcasts "lacked balance and did not meet established Voice of America standards."[32] Similarly, a preliminary 1995 report by the inspector general of the USIA found that Rolando Bonachea, director of Radio Martí and a longtime associate of Jorge Mas, had fired or sought to oust executives and reporters at the station who refused to follow Mas's direction and had hired replacements that would. The director of audience research was among those dismissed when she found that only 2 percent of Cubans watch Televisión Martí. Some members of Congress supported the move to terminate employees who disclose the station's weaknesses. Representative Christopher H. Smith (R-CO) sponsored legislation to eliminate the posts held by several dissidents. Other legislators disagreed with Smith vehemently. The stations have "been subject to the manipulation and corruption by Jorge Mas Canosa," charged Representative David Skaggs (D-CO). Mas "has had an undue and unlawful affect on an agency of the United States for serving his political ends." Among those ends, critics said, was to attack President Clinton's decision to return many refugees to Cuba and to support congressional Republican plans to tighten the embargo against Cuba. One research analyst at the station found, for instance, that it had broadcast 280 stories in favor of tighter sanctions and only 70 stories against the bill. Critics also say that the stations promoted Mas's aspirations to become the president of Cuba someday by, said one former executive, making "sure that the station reported on Mas 10, 20, 30 times a day."[33] From this perspective, some say, the efforts of Radio and Televisión Martí are aimed more at rallying political support among Cuban Americans than Cubans in their home country.

Litigation is another technique used by interest groups to influence policy implementation. Many groups have, for example, brought legal challenges to what they see as the government's lax enforcement of clauses in U.S. laws that require action against governments that abuse human rights (Tolley, 1991). Interest groups also frequently bring cases before regulatory agencies such as the U.S. International Trade Commission in an effort to influence the implementation of trade and other types of policy (Hansen, 1990).

Evaluating Interest Group Influence

As noted earlier, interest groups are a wide-ranging and important aspect of the American political process. There are difficulties, such as differences in strength, with the role that interest groups play in a democracy. Nevertheless, interest groups are important channels through which citizens, businesses, and groups can present their collective views and demands forcefully to the government. Interest group activity is most likely to seem questionable when it is being conducted on the behalf of others, especially if you disagree with their desires. Such activity is apt to seem proper and wise when it is being conducted on behalf of a policy position you favor.

Interest Groups and the Policy Making Models

It is important to remember that interest groups are just one element of policy making. Sometimes they are important; sometimes they are not, as outlined in the policy making models.

Interest group activity is least likely to be influential during policy making that occurs according to the *presidential model* or the administrative model. In the atmosphere surrounding the Cuban missile crisis of 1962, for example, decision making was concentrated in the White House. The country united behind the president; the few interest groups that did have a view on Cuba either supported John Kennedy or were silent.

Other issues conform more closely to the *administrative model,* with, again, interest groups being absent or silent. The Clinton administration has, for instance, persuaded Khazakhstan to pledge to give up all the nuclear weapons it had inherited from the Soviet Union when it collapsed. There are very few Khazakh Americans, and virtually all Americans would (if they were aware of the issue) support Khazakh nuclear disarmament. President Clinton was certainly involved in the issue, but it was hardly on the front burner of international issues like Bosnia, trade with Japan, NAFTA, Somalia, Russian political and economic reform, renegotiation of the General Agreement on Tariffs and Trade (GATT), and other such prominent issues were. Therefore the U.S. position on negotiations with Khazakhstan about its weapons was largely within the administrative realm of the Departments of Defense and State.

The political and subgovernment models involve much greater interest group activity and influence. The *political model* was evident in U.S. policy making during the effort to negotiate, then gain, legislative support of NAFTA, the debate over whether to use force to topple the military junta in Haiti, and a number of other issues.

The *subgovernment model* is aptly illustrated by defense spending. During the cold war, spending large sums of money on defense seemed noncontroversial, and a defense subgovernment (or iron triangle) evolved, with defense contractors and unions working closely with their representatives in Congress and with Defense Department officials to promote their mutual interests. Not only did defense contractors provide the military with weapons, they also provided about 10 percent of the workforce with jobs during the cold war. The workings of this subgovernment model were illustrated in another policy issue discussed earlier in this chapter, the fate of the V-22 Osprey. The combined effort of businesses, unions, interested members of Congress, and the military to protect the funding for the V-22 Osprey is a classic example of the iron triangle working intensely on an issue that engendered little interest or activity beyond the narrow range of interest groups, constituency-serving legislators, and the bureaucratic agencies directly affected.

The Limits and Dynamics of Interest Group Influence

Even when policy is formulated according to the political and subgovernment models, in which interest groups play a strong role, it is important to note that they seldom determine policy alone or for long. One fact of political life that limits the influence of any one group or alliance of groups is that there is often opposition by other groups and alliances. The political and economic isolation of Cuba and its Castro government, which many Cuban American groups favor, is being challenged by others. American business interests, for one, are anxious to gain access to the Cuban market. "You've got 12 million people [in Cuba] who know names like Snickers, Coca-Cola, and Ford," says John Kavulich, president of the U.S. Cuba Trade and Economic Council. "That's pretty attractive."[34] The White House heard the calls. "Pressure is growing," a Clinton spokesperson admitted; "There's a very high degree of business interest in Cuba."[35]

For all the strength of the so-called military-industrial complex, it is offset to a degree by interest groups that oppose defense spending as such or that wish to reallocate it toward domestic programs. While some specific defense-spending issues are still decided according to the subgovernment model, defense-spending issues have recently shifted increasingly into the realm of the political model. American attitudes about the Vietnam War and, by extension, about defense spending reversed the trend of defense spending, which has declined overall since 1968 in constant dollars. From Fiscal Years 1948–1968, major U.S. defense appropriations increased over 3 percent per year in constant dollar terms. From Fiscal Years 1969–1995, those major

FIGURE 11.1   Defense Industry Jobs Lost in the Ten Largest
Defense Contracting States

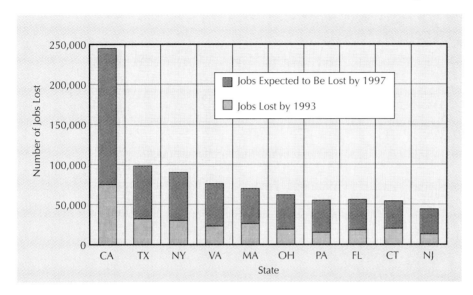

Source: Fortune, February 8, 1993, p. 86.

The billions of dollars spent annually on defense are an important source of money and jobs in many states. The post–cold war defense cuts have threatened businesses and workers in many states and have created strong interest group pressures to minimize the cuts. This figure shows the number of jobs lost and projected to be lost as a result of defense spending cutbacks.

appropriations declined by an average of 1.8 percent per year in terms of constant dollars (see Table 8.2 on p. 225). As the perceived Soviet threat declined, other interest groups came forward to press for more spending for domestic programs funded by cuts in the defense budget. Defense contractors lost anticipated future revenues, for example, when the Strategic Defense Initiative was scaled back, the A-12 attack fighter program was canceled, and the concept of a 600-ship navy was abandoned.

Such defense cuts, in turn, evoked strong counterefforts by defense-oriented interest groups and their legislative and bureaucratic allies. From 1989–1993 a total of 840,000 U.S. workers nationwide lost defense-related jobs, and it did not end there. Figure 11.1 shows that the top 10 defense-spending states alone had lost 271,000 jobs by 1993; the total could go as high as 850,000 by 1997.[36] In short, when interest groups came to represent the other side, the political model was activated, and the defense contractors were less successful than they had previously been in a subgovernment setting.

Sometimes there are even clashes of interests within a broad interest group category, such as business. For example, U.S. corporations that produce copyrighted "intellectual property," such as compact discs or video cassettes, endorsed the Clinton administration's threat in 1995 to place sanctions on China to pressure it to crack down on Chinese companies that produce illegal (pirated) copies. After all, Chinese consumers got to buy pirated copies of *The Lion King* video before Disney began selling authorized copies in North America. On the other hand, Boeing, General

Motors, Ford, and Chrysler were all threatened with a huge loss of business in China if sanctions were instituted. Luckily for the latter group, trade sanctions were avoided when the Chinese agreed to step up their enforcement of rules against unauthorized copying of copyrighted materials.[37]

In sum, interest groups play a highly visible role in U.S. foreign policy making. However, high visibility does not guarantee access to the relevant policy makers, and access does not guarantee influence. Interest groups will have their greatest influence on single issues, when the group position is unchallenged by countervailing pressures, and when the policy making arena is Congress rather than the executive branch.

SUMMARY

1. Beyond the activities of the president, members of Congress, and the executive bureaucracy, other nongovernmental organizations get involved in the making of U.S. foreign policy.

2. Interest groups, nongovernmental associations of people with some shared commonality that has a political stake, occupy an important role in American democracy. According to pluralism, most citizens affect their government through the multiple groups to which they belong. Thus interest groups serve to link the members of the government with the governed.

3. There are a wide variety of types of interest groups. Some are based on economic commonalities, such as business and corporate actors, agricultural actors, and labor unions. Those based on demographic commonalities often involve so-called hyphenate Americans (African Americans, Asian Americans, Latinos/as, Greek Americans, and so on). Organizations based on ideological commonalities may be groups of either a liberal or a conservative slant (like the World Peace Through Law Association or the American Security Council, respectively), or they may be think tanks (like the Council on Foreign Relations or the American Enterprise Institution). Issue-oriented groups revolve around a single issue or a small set of related issues, like the United Nations Association or the Union of Concerned Scientists. Transnational groups have members in more than one country, like Greenpeace or Amnesty International.

4. Interest group activities fall into four major categories. First, they try to help set the agenda of government, in the hope of getting the government to act on the issues they care about. Second, they influence who serves in government by trying to help friendly officials get elected or appointed. Third, they intervene in decision making by lobbying officials who actually make the decisions. Such lobbying may be by direct contact or indirectly through grassroots campaigns back home. Fourth, interest groups try to influence how policies get implemented, by monitoring the implementation process or by getting actively involved in it themselves.

5. Interest group influence varies across the four policy making models. It is highest in the political and subgovernment models, where interest groups are active players in the decision making process. It is lowest in the presidential and administrative models, where interest group influence is indirect at best. However, as the context of a political decision changes, the consideration of an issue can move from one policy making model to another, often changing the roles and influence of interest groups.

Chapter Twelve

THE MEDIA

An axiom of politics is that information is power. Information gives people the ability to know what is happening; information provides the necessary foundation for deciding what policy to favor. By the same logic, those with the ability to control information can control what others know about events. This ability to control what, if anything, the public is told and to provide an analysis—perhaps expert and unbiased, perhaps not—gives those who control information and analysis great influence over the opinions that most citizens have. It follows, then, that the flow of information and analysis—knowledge about what is occurring and why—is a vital aspect of democracy. Without adequate and unbiased information available to the people, democracy is imperiled.

    The mass media plays a pivotal role in this critical flow of information. As you will see in the following section, there are many commentators who laud the press for playing a necessary and proper role in keeping watch over the government, for informing the citizenry about events and officials, and for providing critical commentary. Because "the basis of our government [is] the opinion of the people," Thomas Jefferson wrote in 1787, "were it left to me to decide whether we should have a government without newspapers, or newspapers without a government, I should not hesitate to prefer the latter."[1]

There is, however, another view of the press. Some analysts charge that the press is biased in favor of its own political perspective, is irresponsible in its zealous reporting, is often cozy with politicians, and is harming society by overemphasizing the negative. Jefferson's contemporary, and himself a future president, John Quincy Adams penned in his diary that journalists are "assassins who sit with loaded blunderbusses at the corner of streets and fire them off for hire or for sport at [anyone] they select."[2]

Providing information to the citizenry about the government is not the only role that the media plays. The informational flow also runs in the opposite direction, with the media conveying messages to Washington and to other political centers. Decision makers learn about public opinion and other expressions of political dissent and support through the media. The media also carries images of and commentary about global events, and these help determine what issues will capture the country's political attention. Thus the media, like interest groups, occupies a position between the formal institutions of government (discussed in chapters 7 through 10) and the public (discussed in chapter 13) and is a two-way conduit for information, opinion, and political signals.

To examine the media and its role in the foreign policy making process, we will first explore the nature of the media. Then we will turn our attention to the roles of the media.

THE NATURE OF THE MEDIA

Because the media is a key element in our political process, it is important to understand journalists and news organizations. To do this, we will explore the organization and operation of the media, whether or not it is biased, and the degree to which it is an antagonist or ally of political leaders.

The Media: Organization and Operation

The **mass media**, in its broadest terms, includes radio, television, and printed sources (newspapers, magazines) of information and entertainment. Some movies, television dramas, and other media "entertainment" productions can also have an impact on political opinion. Examples include *The Killing Fields,* and other grotesquely graphic, post-Vietnam movies; *The Day After,* a disturbing 1983 television movie that portrayed a nuclear attack on the United States and the resulting carnage; *Schindler's List,* a film that brought us face to face with some of the horrors of the Holocaust; and *Nixon,* which, even if something of a caricaturization, portrayed the human frailties that sometimes are evident in the White House. Along a somewhat different line, *Free Willie* prompted many Americans to call or write political leaders demanding more protection for whales and other endangered species. For our purposes, however, we will use the term mass media, or simply media, to discuss organizations that convey political news to the public. Even more specifically, we are using the term media to denote those sources of news that (1) have a national distribution and (2) are primary sources of international news. These elements include the major television networks (ABC, CBS, CNN, NBC, and PBS), to a lesser extent, their radio network affiliates, the national wire services (Associated Press and United Press International), a select group of newspapers (such as the *New York Times* and the *Washington Post*), major newspaper chains (such as Gannett and Times Mirror), and weekly news magazines (*Newsweek, Time,* and *U.S. News & World Report*).

There are several points to remember about the organization and operation of the media that impact on the rest of our discussion. First, the media is a business. With few exceptions, television networks, newspapers, and other media channels are businesses that seek to make a profit. The corporate nature of the media leads some critics to charge that what the press reports and the stands that it takes are sometimes influenced by financial concerns rather than solely by newsworthiness.

There are several ways that financial concerns may influence what gets reported. Some critics charge that advertisers, such as U.S.–based multinational corporations, are handled with kid gloves by media moguls who fear the loss of advertising dollars. Another criticism is that competition drives the press to emphasize the sensational and the negative in an effort to increase circulation for the printed media or ratings for the electronic media. These factors determine what publishers and managers can charge for advertising space or time. Charles A. Dana, a prominent nineteenth-century editor, wrote an article in 1882 whose title asked, "What Is News?" The answer, Dana said, was "When a dog bites a man, that is not news, but when a man bites a dog, that is news."[3]

Dana's standard continues to govern a great deal of reporting. War makes better press than peace; scandal sells more papers than good government; "breaking" stories are more compelling than "old" news. CNN, for example, has made its reputation on continuous coverage through the day of such "breaking" stories—whether they are foreign (the arrival of U.S. troops in Bosnia) or domestic (the Oklahoma City bombing, the murder trial of O. J. Simpson). CNN's success has been copied by the other networks, which are now more likely to preempt regular programming to cover a breaking story. The result is that CNN's ratings have fallen, and now the news network is imitating the other networks by using more "talk show" formats to try to regain its audience.

Moreover, some analysts argue that the press has become even more negative and sensationalistic since the upsurge of cynicism that followed the Vietnam and Watergate era in the late 1960s and early 1970s (Soderlund, Wagenberg, & Pemberton, 1994; Nacos, 1990). Don Oberdorfer, a diplomatic correspondent for the *Washington Post* from 1958 to 1993, recalls that when he arrived in Washington "the vast majority of journalists covering national affairs in the capital were trusting and uncritical of the ways of government."[4] "Thirty-five years later," Oberdorfer reports, "many reporters have gone to the other extreme, assuming that nearly every public official statement is a lie or a half-truth until proved otherwise." This cynicism (or perhaps legitimate skepticism), according to Oberdorfer, comes from "a pervasive sense of being manipulated by official spokesmen" using falsehoods and other techniques.

The negative orientation of the press remains strong and is epitomized by a comment by Sam Donaldson of ABC News. "If you send me to cover a pie-baking contest on Mother's Day," Donaldson said, "I'm going to ask dear old Mom why she used artificial sweetener in violation of the rules, and while she's at it, could I see the receipt for the apples to prove that she didn't steal them" (Press & VerBerg, 1988:87).

A second point about the organization and operation of the media is that most international news flows from relatively few media organizations. Only one percent of all newspapers have the money to maintain foreign correspondents. These few newspapers along with the other handful of media channels noted earlier generate the vast majority of international news stories. This reporting may be, in turn, picked up by local print and electronic media that do not have independent sources. The effect is to limit the diversity of information and analysis available (Graber, 1993).

There has been some movement to broaden the U.S. news presence overseas. Recently, both the Associated Press and CNN increased their number of overseas bureaus to record highs at 90 and 20, respectively. Yet such expansions have been offset by other contractions. Many news departments lose money, and over the last decade, the profit-conscious corporate owners of the three commercial television networks dramatically cut back on the number of full-time overseas reporters and camera crews. "As never before, network news divisions rely on freelance video footage and commentary from foreign stringers, some of whom have dubious connections," worries one analyst. "When regular correspondents are used, too often they are 'parachuted' into the latest strife" from which they "air knowing reports via satellite within hours" of arriving (Hoge, 1994:143). Such practices raise questions about how insightful the commentary of such on-the-scene news stars actually is.

Third, television has the broadest impact of the various media channels. Polls from the 1990s indicate that about 50 percent of the public gets its news exclusively from television. Less than 35 percent of the public relies exclusively on newspapers, and just under 20 percent use a variety of sources. The impact of television is intensified by the fact that over half of the public considers television news to be the most trustworthy source of news; less than 25 percent perceive newspapers as most trustworthy; only about 10 percent each see either radio or magazine news sources as most trustworthy (McKenna, 1994). A cautionary note, though, is that those who get their news primarily from television are also less informed and less politically active than those who read the newspapers. Even *who* reads *which* paper is important. Very few Americans read the *New York Times* or the *Washington Post* regularly. The *Post*, for example, is arguably the country's most careful chronicler of the federal government's daily activities. Yet beyond the metropolitan Washington, D.C., area, the paper sells less than 10,000 copies per day, and 6,000 of those copies are sold in just three cities: New York, Baltimore, and Richmond. It is true that the *Post* reaches out by making syndicated stories available to other papers, but it is local editors elsewhere, guided by their perceptions of local preferences, who determine if the *Post's* syndicated stories get printed in their papers. Nevertheless, the *Times* and the *Post* are very influential papers because almost everyone involved in the formal institutions of foreign policy making in Washington reads them (Larson, 1990).

The Media: Neutral or Biased?

"Show me a man who claims he is objective and I'll show you a man with illusions," the great publisher and editor Henry Luce, who founded *Time, Fortune,* and *Life* magazines, once commented about those in his profession.[5] Luce's view stands in contrast to the normal and understandable propensity of journalists to portray themselves as evenhanded purveyors of "All the News That's Fit to Print," as the *New York Times* motto puts it.

It goes without saying that the ability of the press to play a positive part by helping create an informed public in a democracy is compromised severely if journalists slant the news. Yet, there are persistent charges that the media does exactly that. To explore whether the media is biased we can ask two questions. First, do journalists share similar ideological and policy views? Second, if those views are similar, do they color how journalists report and analyze the news?

The first question is easier to answer. There is reasonable evidence that the political views within the media are considerably less diverse than the views held by the public. Editors, reporters, and other media staff tend overwhelmingly to be white, male, liberal Democrats from the northeast or north central parts of the country. On average, only 23 percent of the staff of the most prominent news organizations are women, 3 percent are black, and just 4 percent are Republicans (Graber, 1993). In age, news executives tend to be part of the Vietnam War generation, a group that came of political age during the turmoil and disenchantment spawned by that war and by the Watergate scandal.

Those who defend the media argue that the demographic composition of the newsroom is changing in an attempt to diversify the perspectives of journalists. The effort is "about changing the way we view each other and the way we view the news," *New York Times* publisher Arthur Sulzberger Jr. said to a meeting of 6,000 journalists of African, Asian, Latino/a, and Native American descent.[6]

Change is slow, however, and a continuing imbalance is reflected in the policy preferences held by journalists compared to the general public. Polls in the early 1980s found that journalists were twice as likely to favor economic sanctions against South Africa as was the public and almost twice as likely to oppose U.S. aid to the Contra rebels in Nicaragua. There were similar gaps between the opinions of journalists and the public on the level of the defense budget and on whether to freeze nuclear weapons, with journalists more liberal in both cases (Graber, 1993). Thus journalists appear more liberal and less trusting of U.S. government institutions than the population as a whole.

The second question—Are press reports generally neutral or biased?—is much harder to address. It does not necessarily follow that what the press reports is biased just because journalists tend to have similar political attitudes. Through a conscious, professional pursuit of the truth, journalists may be able to guard against letting their biases influence their reporting. Research on bias in the press is not definitive, especially with regard to specific policy issues. Some scholars argue that the media is neutral until a government policy or leader obviously fails (Berry, 1990). Other studies reach opposite conclusions and find a liberal bias in the press. Studies of the 1968 and 1984 presidential elections, for example, demonstrated that reporting heavily favored Democratic over Republican candidates (McKenna, 1994). A study of the 1992 campaign reaches similar conclusions (Ladd, 1993). Liberal bias in the press was also found by a 1995 study conducted by the nonpartisan Center for Media and Public Affairs (CMPA). It reported that in major newspapers, criticism of Republican policy proposals in the wake of the GOP's victory in the 1994 congressional elections outweighed praise by a two to one margin in editorials and by a three to two margin in news articles. The evening news broadcasts of ABC, CBS, and NBC were even more negative toward Republican proposals, panning them by a 71 percent to 29 percent margin.

The New York Times

New York: **Today**, some sun, windy, a flurry. High 43. Tonight, part cloudy, chilly. Low 33. **Tomorrow**, mainly cloudy. High 46. **Yesterday**, high 54, low 43. Details are on page B16.

VOL.CXLV.... No. 50,253   Copyright © 1995 The New York Times   NEW YORK, WEDNESDAY, NOVEMBER 22, 1995 $1 beyond the greater New York metropolitan area   60 CENTS

ACCORD REACHED TO END THE WAR IN BOSNIA; CLINTON PLEDGES U.S. TROOPS TO KEEP PEACE

The amount of international news reported by the various media sources and the number of people whom those stories reach vary greatly. Compared to television, the print media carries more foreign news and, while its audience is smaller, it is often more influential because its readers tend to be more interested and active in politics than are those who rely on television. Only a tiny percentage of Americans read the *New York Times*. But who does read it includes most policy makers in Washington and other elites throughout the country. Therefore, the amount and tone of the *Times*'s coverage of events in Bosnia or elsewhere play a role in setting the foreign policy agenda and in influencing other aspects of the U.S. foreign policy process.

There is no evidence that journalists, editors, and others slant the news consciously. The causes of the press view are "much more prosaic" (Ladd, 1993:9). One is the tendency of the press to stress the negative. The political studies director of the CMPA argues, for one, that negativism, not bias, is the source of press criticism of the Republicans. "It is not unusual to find a lot of criticism about anyone in politics today," Richard Noyes notes accurately.[7] Another cause of unintended bias is that journalists, with their similar backgrounds and views, tend to approach their work in the same way (Kerbel, 1994). The result of this pattern of relatively homogenous views is that the national media tends to report the same stories in largely the same ways. This is sometimes referred to as "pack journalism."

While criticism of the media as too liberal is commonplace, there are also those who contend that there is a conservative bias in the media that operates in a much more subtle way. Given pack journalism and the role of the press in deciding what is news and what is not (the gatekeeping function discussed below), some charge that the press tends to keep "normal" or "legitimate" messages before the public while suppressing "radical" ideas that threaten widely shared societal perspectives. This view sees the press as a "defender of the status quo" (Davis, 1992b:17). From this perspective, critics charge that economic considerations are a major cause of the self-censorship exercised by the press. Since most media outlets are owned by conglomerate corporations, media personnel choose, either consciously or unconsciously, to veer away from stories that attack general business interests, specific advertisers, or the laissez-faire capitalist system. The result, some analysts believe, is a "tilt to the right of the political spectrum" (Ansolabehere, Behr, & Iyengar, 1993:217).

To a significant degree, then, the direction of media bias lies in the eyes of the beholder. "Psychologists have identified a 'hostile media' phenomenon in which people who call themselves conservative are more likely to view the media as anti-conservative, whereas liberals view the media as pro-conservative" (Ansolabehere, Behr, & Iyengar, 1993:217). Furthermore, another analyst concludes that "group membership does indeed play a role in public perceptions of the fairness or credibility of mass media" (Gunther, 1992:161). In short, the more an individual's group is involved, the

354

more likely it is that the person will think that negative stories about the group or about policy stands that the group favors are the result of media bias.

The Media: Watchdog or Lapdog?

Another important question with regard to the nature of the media is whether journalists are watchdogs who doggedly track down stories or lapdogs who are muzzled and kept on a leash by their political masters in government. The answer is that they are both.

Members of the press and government officials share a mutually schizophrenic relationship. On the one hand, their relationship is often antagonistic. The press probes the government, trying to uncover its secrets, trying to expose its foibles and failures. Politicians and bureaucrats are prone to thinking that the press combines the bloody instincts of predatory sharks and the murky ignobility of bottom-feeding carp. One reflection of this cat-and-mouse game is a book, *Wary Partners: Diplomats and the Media*. As a former journalist and current foreign service officer, the author knows how each profession sees the other and he offers advice to diplomats about how to manage the media and advice to reporters on how to get the information out of diplomats (Pearce, 1995).

On the other hand, the relationship between the press and officialdom is also frequently symbiotic, sometimes even sycophantic. The two groups need each other. The press needs officials to provide it with stories. Officials need the press as a channel to the American people and to the people and governments of other countries.

The Press as Watchdog

The media frequently plays a vital role in bringing information to the public that officials would rather be kept secret. One way to gauge the tenacity of the press in that role is to consider the reactions of presidents to scrutiny. Some presidents accept press criticism and investigative reporting with relative good grace. When one reporter asked John F. Kennedy during a press conference to comment on his treatment by the press, the president evoked a ripple of laughter by telling the journalists, "Well, I am reading more and enjoying it less."[8]

Other presidents have reacted to the press with less humor and patience. One of the most significant examples of the press acting as watchdog involved what became known as the Pentagon Papers. In 1971 Daniel Ellsberg, a National Security Council staff member, "leaked" (made unauthorized disclosures of) copies of a top-secret government study and supporting documents concerning the U.S. entry into and role in the war in Vietnam. The *New York Times* and the *Washington Post* caused a sensation when they published excerpts from the papers. They showed, among other things, that the government had not been completely truthful with Americans about motives and incidents that had led to escalating U.S. involvement in the war.

President Richard M. Nixon and others in his administration were apoplectic. One approach that they tried was to suppress publication of the papers. The Supreme Court rejected the attempt. The Court's view, Justice Hugo L. Black wrote in a concurring opinion in *New York Times Co. v. U.S.; U.S. v. The Washington Post* (1971), was that "in revealing the workings of government that led to the Vietnam War, the newspaper nobly did precisely that which the [Constitution's] Founders hoped and trusted they would do."

Politicians who unduly offend the press can turn the press against themselves and suffer ill effects. The White House press corps, led by senior correspondent Helen Thomas, was upset when President Clinton's first director of communications, George Stephanopoulos, severely restricted access of the press to White House officials and even to the White House press office. This photo shows Thomas and Stephanopoulos in the White House press area in July 1993. Shortly thereafter, Stephanopoulos was reassigned, and a new communications director was appointed by Clinton.

Nixon was not chastened; he sought to retaliate directly against the *Times*. He declared in a memo to his chief of staff, H. R. Haldeman, that "we must take action" in light of what the president termed the "irresponsibility and recklessness" of the *Times* in "deliberately printing classified documents without regard to the national interest" (Oudes, 1989:270). An angry Nixon acted to cut the paper off from its news sources. "Under absolutely no circumstances," Nixon directed, "is anyone on the White House staff on *any subject* to respond to an inquiry from the *New York Times* unless and until I give express permission (and I do not expect to give such permission in the foreseeable future)." Haldeman raised the ante even further. In a White House "action paper" he laid out a plan to "launch an attack." One step was to distance his president from the distressing disclosures in the Pentagon Papers by directing that the White House staff refer to them as "the Kennedy/Johnson papers." Haldeman also thought that condemning journalists as traitors might have good effect and so urged that "we need to get across the feeling of disloyalty on the part of those that publish these papers" (Oudes, 1989:271).

Among presidents, Nixon's periodic crusades against the media were unusual in their intensity, but presidential feelings, ranging from antagonism to frustration, are common. During a 1993 speech, Helen Thomas, the dean of the White House press corps, recalled the attitudes of the presidents toward the press since she had begun covering the White House during the Kennedy administration. She remembered Kennedy's remark (quoted here earlier) about reading more papers but enjoying them less and that Lyndon Johnson's comments on the press were unprintable. Thomas also recalled that Carter seemed to be always praying for deliverance from the press. Reagan was told at one point that a U.S. press helicopter had been fired on in Nicaragua by the leftist Contra rebels. According to Thomas, the president brightened and said it just went to show that there was some good in everyone.[9]

President Clinton's relations with the press have assumed the wary posture of most presidents. Once in office, his press strategy followed his campaign's populist approach that deemphasized meeting directly with the press and emphasized events featuring the president in direct contact with groups and individuals. Clinton's first communications director, George Stephanopoulos, further aggravated the White House press corps by announcing that Clinton would hold fewer press conferences than George Bush had and by banning reporters from the area near the offices of Stephanopoulos and press secretary Dee Dee Myers. "It's a real control thing. Clinton's going over and around reporters," objected Karen Hosler, a *Baltimore Sun* reporter and president of the White House Correspondents Association. Helen Thomas went even further, making an unfavorable comparison of the Clinton to the Nixon White House. "Even in the worst moments of Watergate," Thomas explained, "we were always able to get to the press office. The whole question of where the White House stands is not something that can just be ladled out on their own terms. You have to have access to have information. But all of a sudden, where we've always tread freely, we are the intruders."[10]

According to some observers, reporters retaliated for being shunted to the side. "For dissing the press, presidents pay a price . . . nonlethal but painful," one columnist wrote in the *Washington Post*.[11] He went on to quote the comments of two other columnists in *Time*. The first wrote that "the President and his young staff don't really seem to like journalists very much;" the second wrote in the *Wall Street Journal* that "Mr. Clinton, by most accounts, distrusts the whole kit and caboodle [of the media]." The result, according to yet another columnist, was that "The White House press room has never been as relentlessly petty and mean as it is today . . . the impact on Clinton is clear: He gets even worse press than he deserves."

It would be unfair to lay all the blame for Clinton's press problems on his messengers. The president's message also provided meat for the media grinder. A number of early decisions reversing other decisions or earlier promises promoted media criticism. Clinton retreated from a campaign pledge to open the military fully to gay and lesbian personnel; he reneged on a pledge to seek a middle class tax cut; he nominated Lani Guinier, an African American law professor, as an assistant attorney general to oversee civil rights, then abandoned her to Senate critics who opposed her because she had endorsed such supposedly radical ideas as structuring voting districts to ensure representative numbers of minority members in Congress and state legislatures. When public criticism arose, her nomination was withdrawn against her will.

Whether it was the message or the messenger, the relationship between the White House and the press became so strained that a series of changes began. First, the White House decided to stop televising Stephanopoulos's daily press briefings at the White House because they had become "unnecessarily combative."[12]

Then, in May 1993 Stephanopoulos was removed further from the spotlight by a shift in his position from that of communications director to policy adviser to the president. To try to bolster the president's image, Clinton brought in David Gergen, a veteran political image maker, a so-called spin doctor, who had previously served Republican presidents Nixon, Ford, and Reagan. Almost simultaneously, Mark Gearan, the deputy chief of staff and special assistant to the president, was named to fill the vacant post of communications director. With this new structure in place, Gergen would set the administration's strategy for dealing with a media still viewed as hostile; Gearan would serve a middle management supervisory role and conduct some press briefings; and press secretary Dee Dee Myers would conduct the daily briefings of the White House press corps.

This triumvirate of public relations officials was not noticeably more successful than Stephanopoulos had been. In fact the changes, and the implication that it was the messengers and not the message that was the problem, only served to further antagonize the press. Typically, one senior *New York Times* reporter chastised the White House because its "admissions that policies have failed are as rare as balanced budgets" and because "the Clinton Administration . . . has attributed its troubles to everything but ill-considered policies: poor communication, lack of focus, inadequate staff work, unfortunate timing and conflicts among the president's aides."[13]

Soon a new White House personnel shuffle was under way. The president's chief of staff, Mack McClarty, a man generally considered to be too nice a guy for his job, was replaced as chief of staff by veteran congressman Leon Panetta. Panetta made Mark Gearan his assistant, thereby, in essence, demoting him from his post of communications director. David Gergen was also shunted aside, in his case to an amorphous position as foreign policy adviser, and exiled to an office in the State Department many symbolic blocks away from the White House. Panetta also wanted to "promote" Dee Dee Myers out of the limelight and replace her with State Department press secretary Michael McCurry, but that proved more difficult.

Myers demanded and got a private meeting with Clinton. She told the president that she would quit if she were pushed aside. As the White House's second most visible woman, after Hillary Clinton, the threat by Myers was a serious one. A number of female White House staff members had become increasingly and openly embittered by White House personnel changes that the women believed had systematically demoted women or replaced them with white males. As one put it, "They're perpetuating the role that it's the white boys who make all the decisions. That is sad, because this is the administration that's supposed to look like America."[14]

Rather than risk the political fallout from a Myers resignation, Clinton seemingly made a compromise with Myers. She was retained for a time and even given the additional rank of an assistant to the president, thereby giving her greater access to meetings at which policy decisions were made. The hiatus also gave her time to look for other work. This she soon found. Three months later, at the end of 1994, Myers resigned her post and soon thereafter resurfaced as Mary Matalin's cohost on CNBC's *Equal Time* program. As Panetta wanted all along, Michael D. McCurry assumed the job of press secretary. Larry Speakes, one of Ronald Reagan's press secretaries, commented ruefully on the day that he resigned in 1987 that his job had "probably . . . the most screwing-up potential in the world." This is hyperbole, but not dramatically so, and it is too early to estimate McCurry's chances of long-term survival in his pressure-filled post.[15]

The White House has felt beset in many ways by the press. But perhaps more than any single other thing in the foreign policy realm, the administration has been nettled by the media's persistent characterization of Clinton as indecisive. Even presidential vacations have provided fodder for what the White House sees as unfounded pack journalism. When, for instance, Clinton took a golfing vacation to Wyoming in 1995, the press hastened to report the comment by the golf pro who was trying to improve the presidential game that Clinton's biggest problem was that he thought too hard about his swing, that he suffered from "paralysis by analysis."[16] The president has, for the most part, ignored such characterizations, at least in public. Occasionally, though, his pique has surfaced. At one point after Clinton had been in office for less than a year, a reporter asked him about the widespread impression that he had few convictions. An account of what happened next relates that the president "glared at" the reporter, his "face reddened, and his voice rose to a furious pitch, as he delivered a scalding rebuke" to the hapless journalist. "I have fought for more damn battles here, for more things than any president in the last twenty years," Clinton raged, "and [I] have gotten not one damn bit of credit for it from the knee-jerk liberal press, and I am sick and tired of it, and you can put that in the damn article." The president fumed with a touch of self-pity that "I get up here every day, and I work till late at night" on a wide range of problems, "and you guys [in the media]" still "say . . . 'what else can I hit him about?' So if you [journalists] convince them [the people] I don't have any conviction, that's fine, but it's a damn lie. It's a lie" (Renshon, 1995:59).

Another notable show of presidential pique occurred during a live public forum that featured, among other things, a question telecast from CNN's Christiane Amanpour. Did Clinton think, the veteran war reporter asked the president, that his cautious policy toward Bosnia might undermine his credibility with other potentially hostile leaders. "No," Clinton snapped back at her, "but speeches like that make them take me less seriously than I'd like to be taken."[17]

Yet another display of presidential emotion occurred in October 1995 during a joint press conference that Clinton held with Russia's president, Boris Yeltsin. Both presidents had been in New York City to commemorate the fiftieth anniversary of the founding of the United Nations, and they met at the home of Franklin D. Roosevelt in Hyde Park, New York, to discuss numerous outstanding problems. Especially given U.S.–Russian disagreements on Bosnia, the press had been predicting a difficult session. Yeltsin picked up that theme when a reporter asked him to comment on his talks with Clinton. To paraphrase, Yeltsin, speaking in Russian, said that you reporters have been predicting a disaster. Now, he told the reporters, I can tell you that you are a disaster and that contrary to your dire predictions the talks had been cordial and fruitful. As a translator rendered into English Yeltsin's characterization of the press as a disaster, Clinton began laughing so hard that he had to steady himself against Yeltsin. Wiping his eyes and obviously envying the ability of the Russian president to tell the American press what he thought of them, a guffawing Clinton pleaded with the reporters to make sure that they attributed the quote to the right president.

The Press as Lapdog

The press-as-lapdog image is the tame antithesis of the ferocious watchdog image. Yet this more timid persona also sometimes characterizes the press accurately. The news often reflects the views of the administration, particularly those of the president (Schudson, 1995; McCartney, 1994). One study of all front-page news stories in the *New York Times* and the *Washington Post* found that more than half relied on government sources (Graber, 1993). The percentage of international news stories that depends on the government as the main source of information is almost certainly even higher.

Reliance on government sources for news occurs because it is often the only source readily available to reporters. Moreover, there is tremendous competitive pressure on journalists to get and publish stories quickly. Therefore, to a degree, reporters depend on officials for interviews, briefings, and other sources of information and commentary.

"Beat" reporters (those who cover specific institutions, or beats, such as the White House) are fed news releases and "leaks" by governmental officials, often so close to deadline that there is no time to get opposing viewpoints. Furthermore, reporters who question the accuracy of their sources might be cut out of the "insider" circle in the future, making it hard to compete with those who get the news first from policy makers. "Reporters are suckers for a politician who knows how to work the press," acknowledges one *Washington Post* reporter. "Bare-knuckled press manipulation can work—even when it backfires. Reporters always need a new story line."[18]

It is also the case that a reporter does not disclose who leaked the information. Journalists defend this practice on the grounds that if the sources were made public

One cause of the press-as-lapdog image is that reporters often rely on government sources to provide information, photo opportunities, and other so-called news. This allows officials to manipulate the news by providing image-enhancing material. This photograph, taken in Montana in June 1995 of President Clinton striking a rugged, Old West pose for a herd of journalists covering what they evidently consider to be news, is an example of the willingness of the press to cooperate in an official attempt to project a flattering public image.

the leaks would dry up. It is important to see, however, that the press is withholding important information from the public. Often those who leak information to the press do so to influence public policy. By denying the public the information about who leaked information, the press is limiting the public's ability to evaluate the veracity of the information and the political motivations behind the leak. The result of such practices is that various versions of reality get press time in the guise of news when, in fact, the press, by basing stories on leaks, is often being little more than a channel for the official line or for a dissenting position.

A worrisome scenario occurs when the government successfully manipulates the media into conveying what amounts to domestic political propaganda (Herman, 1993). The technique is to distort the truth by ignoring discomforting facts and relying on simple, vivid, ideologically and culturally popular images when communicating with the press. Then journalists do the easiest thing, which is to report what they have been told. The passive public, looking to resolve new situations in easy terms, completes the cycle either by having its prejudices confirmed once again or by tuning out the drone of politics altogether.

While most observers do not view the press as a mindless propaganda tool of the government, there is still no denying governmental manipulation in some cases

(Roy, 1990). Tight governmental controls on the press during the U.S. military actions in Grenada, Panama, and the Persian Gulf helped ensure highly positive coverage (Davis, 1993). One study argues that a "spiral of silence" occurred in which government control of the news and media acquiescence to that control "served as a barrier to perceiving the war in any way other than as a military-technological event" rather than as a gruesome undertaking in which people by the tens of thousands were being killed. In this way, according to the analysis, the "spiral of silence [served to] prolong . . . support of the [U.S.] president and [to] overwhelm . . . dissent and debate" (Allen et al., 1994:282). Later analyses did reveal significant problems in these military operations, but these shortcomings did not appear until long after the operations were over. There is wide disagreement about whether or not such a near government-press conspiracy occurred during the war, about the impact of the media on public opinion, and about the difficult issues relating to the press covering military operations (Lance & Paletz, 1994; Zaller, 1994a; Zhongdang & Kosicki, 1994; Herman, 1993). These matters are discussed further in the box "The Press Goes to War" on pages 362–364.

The Reagan administration's handling of the Muammar Qaddafi regime in Libya represents another example of the government's ability to manipulate the media. According to Gregory Nokes (1991:34), the Reagan administration "made Muammar Qaddafi and Libya a story" in a "distasteful" effort to focus wrath on Libya in order to "divert attention from [the administration's] failure to deal effectively with more serious problems of terrorism elsewhere." Among its other techniques, the administration conducted a disinformation campaign against the Qaddafi regime that included a now-widely disbelieved story that Libyan terrorists had infiltrated the United States with the aim of assassinating Reagan. The administration also planted false stories in the press alleging that Libyan rebel groups were organizing in efforts to topple Qaddafi and that the United States might help in that effort. Unfounded stories that the United States might invade Libya were also given to the press. The object was to undermine Qaddafi and perhaps frighten Libyans into overthrowing him. The effort was unsuccessful, but when the deceits were exposed, there was considerable embarrassment within both the press (which had gullibly printed the stories) and the White House (which had been guilty of lying). Among other things, Assistant Secretary of State for Public Affairs Bernard Kalb, himself an experienced journalist, said that he had not known the stories were false when he passed them on to the press; he subsequently resigned in protest.

Just as naively reporting disinformation plays into politicians' hands, so too can *not reporting* stories. There are times when press restraints are, of course, laudable. When some reporters gained clues as to the coalition military strategy against Iraq in February 1991, they withheld the story rather than endanger the operation and the troops conducting it. Other instances are more questionable. There are regular charges that the press pulls its punches frequently because of a favored relationship with the president or some other high official.

The most alarming collaboration between press and politicians occurs when the press knowingly allows itself to be used for political ends. At the extreme there have been cases where reporters worked with the CIA. Reports in the mid-1970s indicated that at least 36 and perhaps as many as 50 American journalists had contractual agreements with the CIA (Holt, 1995). The question arises: Were they being paid to share with the CIA what they learned in the course of their journalistic endeavors,

(Continued on page 364)

The Press Goes to War

When a democracy is at war, there is tension between the ideal of a free press keeping the people informed and the reasonable need for military secrecy. The issue is how to balance the two. The 1990–1991 Persian Gulf crisis and war provide a recent and complex illustration of the dilemmas that arise when the country and the press go to war (Thompson, 1991).

Initial press reports during the war were heartstopping. During the first air assault by coalition forces, television broadcast awesome images of anti-aircraft fire exploding over Baghdad as the Iraqis tried to destroy attacking warplanes and cruise missiles. Bernard Shaw and two other CNN reporters who witnessed the attack from their hotel in Baghdad, provided an emotional and vivid account of the action with the constant din of explosions in the background. "It feels like we're in the center of hell," Shaw exclaimed at one point.[1]

As the war continued, the media brought other images of dramatic conflict that riveted Americans. Behind this action there was, however, another struggle going on: the press versus the government (Davis, 1993).

The government restricted press coverage of the war in several ways that exceeded the censorship imposed during World War II or the wars in Korea and Vietnam. The press was required to create "pools" of a limited number of reporters to visit the front and other points of coverage. Other reporters were supposed to draw their commentary from the raw material provided by the pool. Reporters had to be escorted by military officers. All stories were to be submitted to the military for review and possible censorship.

The government said that military security and ensuring the safety hundreds of reporters in the war theater justified the restrictions. Whatever the validity of these reasons, there was another, unstated motive behind restricting the press: maintaining public support of the war. As one White House aide explained, "In earlier wars, even in Vietnam, it took months and years for public opinion to shift [to an antiwar position]. In this age of real-time journalism, our concern is that any major setback or anything that hurts the Administration's credibility could send public support sliding in a matter of weeks."[2] Officials were especially worried about public reaction to images of

Americans dying. Among other restrictions, reporters were barred from photographing the coffins of slain American soldiers. Surveys of public opinion heightened the government's concern. One poll that was taken just 10 days after the war began found that the most frequent reactions on seeing combat on television were sadness (74 percent) and fear (67 percent).[3]

The reactions of the press to the restrictions were complex. One response was to attack the limits as antidemocratic. The heads of several major media organizations wrote Secretary of Defense Richard Cheney charging that the rules "go far beyond what is required to protect troop safety and mission security" and, therefore, "raise the specter of government censorship of a free press."[4] Another press complaint, was that "the [press] pools have not been granted access to things when they are happening."[5] "There's a beast of a war out there, an elephant we're trying to describe," agreed Forrest Sawyer on ABC's *Nightline.* "Based on the information we're given, we're about at the toenail range" (Marder, 1991:3).

Yet despite these complaints, a second response of most of the press was to comply with government restrictions. Pools were established, and journalists mostly abided by the rules. This created a third response: disagreements within the press. The major media channels had permanent members of the pools and tended to dominate coverage. Some reporters felt that this was the reason that the major media channels had agreed to help set up the pools. Frank Aukofer (1991:24), Washington bureau chief of the *Milwaukee Journal,* wrote with "bitter amusement" that the same media executives who had written in protest to Secretary of Defense Cheney were, "for the most part, the same closed little group of collaborators who had helped the Defense Department set up the pools, and had done it to protect their own asses—er, access—while freezing out news organizations not deemed worthy to join their elitist clique."

Many reporters who were not pool members were dissatisfied with the information supplied by reporters in the pool. Carl Nolte of the *San Francisco Chronicle* argued that "if you sit around waiting for the scraps to be fed to you, you're going to get the kind of things a dog gets: leftovers."[6] He and many such journalists sought to evade restrictions and get stories independently. Critics call this "pool busting."

Whether journalists acted independently or relied on pool reports, they were subject to several criticisms. Some of the criticism was contradictory. Detractors claimed, on the one hand, that the press was being too docile and supportive. On the other hand, critics castigated the media for harming the war effort.

We can first review the charges that pool reporters were "pawns of the Pentagon," as Frank Aukofer (1991:24) put it. The general criticism is that the press became a lapdog by acceding to restrictions and by reporting uncritically in order to avoid tighter restrictions. *New York Times* columnist Anthony Lewis, for one, wrote that most of the press was "not a detached observer of the war, much less a critical one, but a clique applauding the American general and politicians in charge" (Marder, 1991:4).

Among other things, critics who said that the press was too compliant charged that restrictions on the press allowed the military to stress events and statistics that reflected well on it. The military, for example, highlighted the success rate of its guided, "smart" bombs, 90 percent of which hit their targets, and gladly gave out footage, taken from attacking U.S. war planes, of the bombs hitting their targets. The networks repeatedly played the laudatory footage. What the government did not discuss (and what reporters did not ask about) was that smart bombs made up only 7 percent of the munitions dropped on the enemy, and that of the remaining 93 percent, some 75 percent, made up of "dumb" bombs, missed their targets. Similarly, television reporters were allowed to take and broadcast numerous pictures of Patriot antimissile missiles hurtling with fiery menace into the night and reportedly destroying incoming Iraqi Scud missiles. Military officials claimed, and the press reported, a 90 percent success rate. Postwar analysis suggests that the success rate may have been as low as 10 percent.

Other criticism of the press came from the opposite direction. It charged journalists with not being sufficiently patriotic. One worry was that the press would compromise military security. H. Joachim Maître (1991:11), a veteran German reporter and professor of journalism, wrote that what journalists who complained about restrictions "ignored and [what] the American public recognized, [is] that the paramount object of war is victory"; and that among the "measures applied to facilitate victory in modern times we find press restrictions, ranging from access limitations to outright censorship of all reporting from the war zone." Maître concluded that "the First Amendment does not provide tools for breaking into the government vault protecting the secrets of national security."

Such worries proved unfounded. For example, some journalists knew of, but never reported, the massive buildup of the coalition forces' left flank prior to the surprise attack on the lightly defended Iraqi right front. The press was also aware that stories of a planned U.S. Marine landing in the northern part of Kuwait were not accurate. Yet the press broadcast the "rumors." This helped hold Iraqi troops in positions designed to repel the amphibious landing that never came. Said a Pentagon official to reporters, "We merely invited you to cover the exercises and you guys did the rest."[7] After the war, General H. Norman Schwarzkopf, who commanded the coalition forces, even thanked the press for this contribution to deceiving the Iraqis.

A more controversial charge against the press was that it allowed itself to be used by Iraq as a propaganda tool. The cable news network, CNN, came under the most criticism because one of its reporters, Peter Arnett, remained in Iraq. CNN aired several stories that upset many Americans. Perhaps the most sensational incident of all was when the Iraqis escorted Arnett to a bombed-out factory. The Iraqis claimed it was a baby formula factory, and a broken sign (in English) bore testament to that claim. The U.S. military said the plant was, in reality, a munitions factory.

There was a torrent of condemnation of CNN's coverage of the war. One critic said CNN should change its name to SNN—Saddam News Network. Even some members of the press were critical. A member of the ABC news staff called the images Iraqi "propaganda" and declared, "At some point you have to draw the line."[8] Doubts also surfaced at CNN. Part of the problem, one CNN producer explained anonymously, is the pressure on the media to report widely and rapidly. "The network isn't interested in analyzing information," the producer said. "It wants to move tonnage." The result, the producer conceded, is that "CNN has really evolved into a potential propaganda tool for the world's powers. If you want to get a message out internationally, CNN is vulnerable to that."[9]

Despite such criticism, most journalists defended both their right to report and the content of their reports. Officials at CNN stressed the public's right to know and the network's repeated warnings to viewers that Iraq was censuring the news. Other media leaders agreed. "It's unpleasant, it's difficult, it's tough, but of course it constitutes news," said former NBC news president Lawrence Grossman in defense of CNN.[10] Well-known journalist Marvin Kalb defended Arnett and CNN on the grounds that both Washington and Baghdad manipulated reporters. Kalb also argued that those worrying about the news from within Iraq underestimated Americans. "I believe," he countered, "the American people are able to absorb and digest Arnett's reporting, the Pentagon's story, chew gum and walk, all at the same time."[11]

Others in the press argued that negative reaction to press reports should not deter journalists. David Halberstam, who won a Pulitzer Prize for his reporting from Vietnam, commented, "It isn't a popularity contest for us, and we shouldn't seek it to be one. The people of this country wouldn't like it very much afterwards if it turns out that [the war] doesn't go well. Then they'll say, 'Well, where was the press?'" Arguing even more aggressively, Sam Donaldson of ABC news snapped during a broadcast that "if people don't like it, I'm sorry, but they really need to know what's happening."[12]

Did the American people like it? Their reviews were mixed. Not surprisingly, given the rally-'round-the-flag emotions evoked by war, American support of the government was unusually high. A national poll during the fighting showed that 78 percent of respondents thought the military was not hiding anything that was embarrassing, and that it was telling everything it could prudently say. Of those with an opinion, some 63 percent also said that the military should tighten its controls of the media. But 37 percent said decisions about what to report should be left to the press. Furthermore, 72 percent thought press coverage of the war was objective, 61 percent said it was mostly accurate.[13] After the war, another poll found that 59 percent of Americans surveyed had increased their respect for the press as a result of its war coverage (Sparrow, 1993). As for CNN specifically, the public was again split. More than 55,000 phone calls, faxes, and letters poured into CNN during the first month of the war. About 60 percent were negative. Polls showed an even closer division in public opinion. Asked about CNN broadcasting news censured by Iraq's government, 51 percent of those with an opinion disapproved; 49 percent approved.[14]

(Continued from page 361)

or were they being paid to color their reports to the American public according to CIA dictates? We will probably never know the answer, but such activities damage the press's credibility. This is a serious matter, given the importance of the press in a democracy.

ROLE OF THE MEDIA

The media plays three important roles in the foreign policy process. These include at least some part in setting the political agenda, conveying information and analysis, and shaping public opinion.

Agenda Setting

One important role that the media plays is to determine which people, regions, and issues will be the focus of the government and the public attention. This process is referred to as setting the **political agenda**. It is a crucial step in the policy making process, because there are always more problems than the government and the public have the time and energy to address. Therefore, by emphasizing one concern or another, the press plays a role in deciding which matters will be addressed by the political systems and which will languish (Flanigan & Zingale, 1991). Also, being told what to think about is very close to being told what to think (Weaver, 1991).

In some cases, there is no question as to events and issues getting on the political agenda. Events such as Iraq's invasion of Kuwait in 1990 are so important or compelling that they must be covered by the media and addressed by the government. Most events and issues, however, depend on media coverage to gain national attention. This is not to say that the media "invents" the agenda. Instead, there is an interactive process in which the media picks up on something of concern to some element of the society, then reports on it, creating more attention, yet more reporting, and so on. Thus, the process of building the political agenda involves information flowing back and forth between press, politicians, and public, thereby increasing an issue's prominence on the political agenda.

Most frequently the media serves as a conduit used by political leaders to set the agenda. With very few exceptions, presidents receive free airtime, usually during prime-time hours, to deliver televised speeches or to hold press conferences. During the Eisenhower through the Reagan years (to 1988), for example, presidents received free airtime to deliver 216 televised speeches. Almost two-thirds of those were during prime time. During the same seven administrations, presidents broadcast 518 press conferences. The amount of routine coverage that the press gives to the president compared to other policy makers also works to the advantage of the White House in setting the agenda. A study of the lead stories aired by ABC, NBC, and CBS during four years (1975, 1979, 1981, 1985) found that the president was featured in 12 times as many lead stories and (measured in time given the story) received 16 times more coverage than Congress. These figures were even more unbalanced for foreign affairs. Presidents were featured in 19 times as many lead stories and received 24 times more coverage than did Congress (Gilbert, 1989). Presidential addresses to the nation, press conferences, and other policy statements are certainly news. It is also important to realize, however, that they are also opportunities for presidents to present their own agenda and political spin. The White House press corps covers everything that happens there, just as do the reporters assigned to the departments of State and Defense. Thus when reporters cover press conferences or are handed news releases, they are being used by the policy makers to get certain messages across to the public. As a former *Washington Post* editor argues, "In just about every important respect, [media-government interactions] continue to favor the government by allowing policy makers, not reporters, to set the news agenda" (Geyelin, 1991:21). As such, the ability to use this access through the media to the public to set the agenda is a key aspect of the president's political skills.

Yet it is also true that the press can play some role in agenda setting. Sometimes this is done simply by the decision of network television anchors to go (or not to go) to the location of the story. That might be to the site of a summit conference, to Berlin as the Wall comes tumbling down, or to Beijing as Chinese troops crack down on students in Tiananmen Square (Kalb, 1991). In other instances, the media can make it difficult for the government to ignore an issue. "If an ominous foreign event is featured on TV news," one White House official observed, "the President and his advisers feel bound to make a response in time for the next evening news program" (Graber, 1993:388). At other times, it is the accumulation of written, verbal, and visual images conveyed by the press to the public that can move in one direction or another. When a mortar shell exploded in a schoolyard in Bosnia, the image of the shattered bodies of the children horrified Americans. Slaughtered shoppers in Sarajevo's central market added to the assault on American sensibilities. A poignant news photo of a young Muslim woman who had fled to the forest and hanged herself when her town had been captured by Serb forces carried, for many Americans, a message that the United States could not just stand by and watch the horrors continue. Such images can affect policy makers on a personal level, as well as through the pressure generated by general public opinion. A daughter of Vice President Al Gore saw the picture of the woman dangling lifeless from the tree and asked him why he was not doing something about the ongoing tragedy in Bosnia. Gore related his daughter's comments to a top-level meeting in the White House. No one had an answer. "Everyone in the room was very, very quiet," an official who was present recalls.[19] It would be an exaggeration to say that this one sad photograph moved Washington to action. Yet it would be an underestimation to imagine that the picture encapsulated thousands of words and other horrific images and helped galvanize the White House. Less than three months later, American troops were in Bosnia.

Even in noncrisis situations, the media can play a role. The media did not let George Bush forget that he had proclaimed himself "the environmental president," thus making it hard for him to explain his initial decision not to attend the 1992 Earth Summit in Rio de Janeiro. Ultimately, he went. The media can even serve as a source of information and analysis that directly informs policy makers and influences both their attention to and evaluation of issues. "I learn more from CNN than I do from the CIA," President Bush commented at one point (Lineberry, Edwards, & Wattenberg, 1994:379).

There is considerable controversy about this aspect of agenda setting. Critics of the press argue that journalists' insatiable appetite for reporting, perhaps overreporting, trouble, and doing that almost instantaneously, creates detrimental pressures on the government to react before it can deliberate carefully. Representative Lee Hamilton (D-IN), a leading congressional expert on foreign policy, claims that television "encourages policy makers to react quickly, perhaps too quickly, to a crisis. It allows the media to set the agenda. It generates pressure for action selectively: why Somalia and not Sudan, why Bosnia and not Nagorno Karabakh." Journalists take a very different view. "If the administration has thought its own foreign policy through, and is prepared and able to argue the merits and defend the consequences of that policy, television and all its technologies can be dealt with," rejoins Ted Koppel, anchor of ABC's *Nightline*. "If on the other hand," Koppel continues, "the foreign policy is ill-conceived and poorly explained, it does not much matter whether the news arrives by satellite or clipper ship. Eventually, the policy will fail."[20]

There are many factors that determine which stories the press will report or largely ignore. This control of the flow of stories is termed **gatekeeping**. The tendency to define what is news in terms of what is unusual, negative, or sensational is one factor. A second involves the ratio of domestic and foreign news that the media reports. Even in the national press, foreign news receives a minority of coverage. Research on the coverage of two newspapers and three television networks, all with foreign correspondents, indicated that for each, the percentage of stories devoted to foreign affairs was low. The newspapers devoted an average of 6.4 percent of their space to international news; such stories averaged 19.8 percent of the airtime on the over-the-air networks (Graber, 1993).

The paucity of international news coverage was confirmed by a study released in November 1995 by the Times Mirror Center for the People and the Press. The study, which examined a variety of national, regional, and local newspaper and television news sources over a four month period, found that newspapers carried the most international stories; television, which is the main source of news for most Americans, carried the fewest international stories. The *New York Times* printed a daily average of 26 international stories; 8 regional newspapers each printed an average of 12 such stories a day. By contrast, the ABC and CNN television networks carried between two and three foreign news stories on an average day. "Local television (from which one-fourth of Americans get most of their news) may be all but ignoring the world," the study continued. It cited one local channel in a major city that carried an average of less than one foreign story per week. The impact of the domestic orientation of the media, the study worried, is that "the overemphasis on U.S.–related stories caters to the self-centered concerns of Americans during this period of rising internationalist sentiment." In this sense, media leaders, who, like other leaders, tend to be more internationalist than is the general public may well be helping to set a less internationalist policy agenda, which is not in accord with their own beliefs.

The Times Mirror Center for the People and the Press study also supported the notion that the press tends to be crisis oriented, especially in its foreign news coverage. According to the report, "Events overwhelmingly drove foreign news coverage, probably more than they do domestic news, since foreign events and disasters must be more dramatic and violent to compete successfully against national news." The upshot of this crisis-oriented reporting was that of 7,061 international news stories that appeared over 4 months, only 9 dealt with agriculture, just 11 with demographics, and a mere 21 with education. This left the report concerned that the American media carries "few international articles that would broaden and educate Americans about the world beyond those hot spots where 'breaking' news—usually about conflict—is occurring."[21]

A third gatekeeping factor involves cultural biases of most of the press and the public. Coverage of instances of genocide provides an appropriate, if distressing,

Media coverage helps set the political agenda and may even influence policy decisions. This photograph of a young Bosnian Muslim woman, who hanged herself when her town was captured by Serb forces, helped bring about U.S. intervention in Bosnia. A daughter of Vice President Al Gore saw this picture and asked her father why the United States was doing nothing to stop the slaughter. He related the story and asked the same question of others in the White House. No one had an answer. Soon thereafter, American forces were on the way to Bosnia.

367

example. How much the media should cover any story is, of course, subjective. But a survey of congressional staff members found that, at least in the opinion of 76 percent of them, the media gives "only sporadic coverage to human rights" stories (Ovsiovitch, 1992:24). One reason this occurs is that cultural biases influence where foreign correspondents are stationed. Compared to world population distribution, Europe has a disproportionate number (about 40 percent) of foreign correspondents working for the American media. Southeast Asia and the Pacific account for just 7 percent of such journalists; sub-Saharan Africa has just 2 percent of these reporters. The *New York Times,* for example, tries to cover all of Asia with half the number of bureaus that it uses to report on much smaller and vastly less populated Western Europe. Only three *Times* bureaus are located in all of sub-Saharan Africa (Graber, 1993). These news bureau locations are important because what limited coverage does exist for these underreported regions usually centers on the area around the news bureaus (Gergen, 1991).

This distribution of journalistic resources shows up in geographic reporting. In July 1990, for example, 60 percent of all foreign news stories on the television networks were about Europe and the Soviet Union. Only 7 percent of all stories were about Southeast Asia and the Pacific and just 8 percent were about sub-Saharan Africa (Graber, 1993:375). Even war receives spotty attention. Bosnia may dominate the news, but seldom if ever does television carry images of most of the other approximately 30 global conflicts in places such as Africa (Angola, Sudan) and southwest Asia (Kashmir, Tajikistan). The 1995 Times Mirror study cited earlier reached a similar conclusion. It found that only 16 of 7,061 stories surveyed were about Australia or the Pacific islands; just 157 stories related to the South Asia subcontinent, which includes India.

The distribution of reporters has ramifications for the political agenda. What happens in Europe gets the most press attention. The genocidal attacks against Muslims in Bosnia-Herzegovina received quick and extensive coverage by the press. Yet, numerically, the worst instance of genocide since World War II occurred in Cambodia during the late 1970s. There the Khmer Rouge government slaughtered over 1 million people through executions, starvation, and forced labor. This tragedy went almost unnoticed and unreported in the United States. Similarly, famine after famine has occurred in Ethiopia, Somalia, and other parts of Africa with relatively little notice or response by the American press, public, or politicians. The horrific conditions in Somalia finally evoked press coverage, but only after a long period of daily images of dying children in televised appeals by Save the Children and other humanitarian organizations, as well as charges by the UN secretary-general and others that the United States and Europe were engaging in tacit racism by ignoring the problem. These forces sparked interest in Somalia, and, quite suddenly, conditions in that country became the daily fare of the printed and televised press. What then occurred, according to one analysis, was that "the crisis in Somalia was made an unavoidable U.S. foreign policy priority through nightly broadcasts flashing graphic scenes of starving, emaciated women and children" (Dobriansky & McCaffery, 1995:102). Soon U.S. forces were on their way to Somalia as part of Operation Restore Hope.

We must return, however, to a fundamental truth. Gatekeeping leads to agenda setting only if the public follows the media's lead. Studies show that the public's willingness to do that is far from ensured. One important factor is the differences in the makeup of the national press and the public. The differences just start with national journalists being better educated and better paid than the average American. Only 5 percent of national journalists see themselves as conservative in their political views, compared to 39 percent of the public. Only 20 percent of national journalists attend church or synagogue regularly, compared to 40 percent of the public. National journalists get most of their news from newspapers, particularly the "prestige press" (like the *New York Times*, the *Washington Post*, and the *Los Angeles Times*); most of the public relies on television. The public trusts their local television news the most; national journalists trust local television news the least.[22]

It is also true that while most of the public does not trust its elected and appointed officials, neither does it give a high level of trust to the press. As a *Chicago Tribune* journalist put it, "No wonder real people are uncomfortable with news people. They don't agree with them on much of anything."[23] That reporter's intuition is confirmed to a degree by recent analyses that question the ability of the media to set the political agenda. According to 54 national surveys covering the 1989–1995 period, only 1 in 4 Americans closely follows most news stories and almost half of the public pay "little or no attention" to the news.[24] Many Americans just tune out the news because they either feel it has very little relevance to their daily lives or they are alienated from the political system and identify the news media as part of that system. Such individuals are more likely to be guided by their personal experiences, or the experiences of people they know, in determining how things "really" are, and they tend to remember the news reports that confirm what they already think (Neuman, Just, & Crigler, 1992).[25]

Another study concludes that the so-called CNN factor, the idea that vivid and sensational real-time televised images drive foreign policy, is actually a myth. Horrific televised images did not produce significant changes in U.S. policy toward the Rwandan refugee crisis, the breakup of Yugoslavia, or the ongoing Bosnian civil war. At best such images may produce the *appearance* of change in U.S. policy, but they do not change its fundamental or strategic aspects. Since the current post–cold war era has left the media as diverse as the rest of the country in its opinions about what the country's foreign policy interests are, the ability of the press to set the agenda is constrained. In this atmosphere of lack of consensus, policy makers have a clear advantage in setting the agenda when they articulate it clearly and consistently (Hadar, 1994; Hoge, 1994).

Information and Analysis

Conveying information and analysis to the public is a second important role of the press. Because most Americans lack familiarity with foreign countries, events, and personalities, the information and analysis that the press passes along about them are especially important.

We have, in the previous sections of this discussion of the media, examined the salient points about the information and analysis that the media conveys. It is worthwhile summarizing them here. First, the press is a primary source of information about foreign affairs for the public and even for many policy makers. Second, international news comprises a small minority of all news. Third, a handful of printed and electronic media organizations dominate gathering and disseminating international news. Fourth, the public gets most of its news from television; but policy makers are apt to rely on a few printed sources, especially the *New York Times* (Gowing, 1994). As one U.S. State Department official put it, "The first thing we do is read the newspaper—the *newspaper*—the *New York Times*. You can't work in the State Department without the *New York Times*" (Graber, 1993:362).

Fifth, since reporters, editors, and other key media staff do not reflect the general public, either demographically or politically, this leads to charges that the information and analysis that the media conveys are biased, although the direction of that bias might depend on who is asked. There are also cultural biases. Europe is covered extensively; the less developed countries of the world are relatively underreported. The press also focuses on the negative or the unusual—man bites dog—stories. Sixth, despite its often critical appraisal of government, the press also serves as a passive conduit for information from government sources. Some of this information is factual and neutral; often the information is slanted (sometimes even falsified) by political sources to manipulate public opinion.

Opinion Shaping

Given the relative unfamiliarity of Americans with things foreign, and the important role of the press in conveying information and analysis, the next important step in examining the role of the media is to explore its impact on public opinion. How opinions are formed is a very difficult phenomenon to isolate. As a result, there is considerable disagreement over the role of the press in shaping public opinion (Schmitt, 1995; Serfaty, 1990).

To some degree, the press does help shape public opinion. One study found that "reported statements and actions by media commentators, allegedly non-partisan 'experts,' opposition party figures, and popular (but not *un*popular) presidents" have the greatest influence on public opinion, while "the impact of other sources [such as interest groups] is negligible" (Jordan & Page, 1992:227). Another analysis also found that changes in the opinions of readers of the *New York Times,* admittedly a small and unrepresentative slice of the public, were more strongly related to the statements of experts and commentators than to the reporting of the events themselves or to the interpretations of those events offered by the president or other administrative officials (Jordan, 1993). Still another study found that the views of people who paid "greater attention to foreign affairs news on television" are "consistently associated with more *positive* opinions of a country" (Semetko et al., 1992:34). In sum, such commentary leads to the conclusion that media decisions regarding what to report, whom to interview, and whose analysis to highlight to determine the meaning of an event do all help shape public opinion on an issue.

Yet it is also the case that the impact of the press on public opinion is limited. That restraint is the result of five factors. First, the press reports relatively little international news. Second, the public pays relatively little attention to what is reported. Third, most individuals resist messages that do not fit their preexisting opinions. Fourth, those who do pay relatively more attention to the media's coverage of international news events are people with higher education and prior knowledge of the relevant issue. Thus their views are more stable (Mondak, 1995). Fifth, the media's point of view is just one source of public information and analysis. Therefore its impact is diluted. As one study suggests, "the public cannot easily be pushed around by any particular source" (Jordan & Page, 1992:237).

In the final analysis, then, the media plays an important, but not controlling, role in the U.S. foreign policy making process. The media serves as a communications channel to link citizens to both the events and issues facing the United States and to their elected and appointed officials. The media may help shape the political agenda, if appropriate government officials do not, and it can help shape public opinion to some degree. Moreover, the press is a two-way conduit, and by conducting and reporting the outcome of public opinion polls, by printing op-ed pieces and letters to the editors, and by covering those who dissent from current policy, the media also carries messages to Washington, D.C., that policy makers receive and sometimes heed. The press is a vital link between the government and the people, and it is to the important matter of public opinion in a democracy that we will now turn our attention.

SUMMARY

1. The mass media, like interest groups, constitutes a set of nongovernmental actors involved in the policy making process. The press in its various forms (newspapers, newsmagazines, radio, and television) provides information to both the citizens and their government officials.

2. Second, we get most of our international news from just a few sources, due to the high costs of such coverage. This means that the original sources of news exercise great influence over what we see, hear, and read, and how events are interpreted.

3. Third, relying on so few sources is especially worrisome if the media exhibits a systematic bias. There is controversy over whether or not it does. It is easy to show that media elites do not reflect the diversity seen in the U.S. public, but bias in operation is less clear-cut. Research suggests that media bias lies in the eye of the beholder, with some seeing it and others not.

4. Fourth, the media can also be seen as the government's watchdog, holding governmental actions up to public scrutiny. It can also be the government's lapdog, reporting what the government wants reported the way it wants it reported. Sometimes the government manipulates the media and sometimes it is the other way around.

5. Like interest groups, the media plays multiple roles in American foreign policy making. It helps set the government's agenda. It provides both information and analysis to the public and government officials alike, and, in doing so, it helps shape opinions.

Chapter Thirteen

PUBLIC OPINION

Why care? Why care what foreign policy is or who makes it? Chapter 1 posed these questions, then responded by making the case that foreign policy is important because foreign policy affects each of us regularly and in important ways. We also saw that we should care about the foreign policy process because *who* makes foreign policy plays an important role in determining *what* gets decided. This is because political leaders, the various political institutions, the public, the multitude of interest groups, and you all often have differing ideas about what policy should be. Therefore, the amount of say that various players have in the policy process helps determine which policy proposals prevail.

    These concerns about who makes policy and what difference that makes are at the core of this book. The theme is democracy: how democratic the U.S. foreign policy process is, how democratic it should be, how democratic Americans want it to be. A good standard for judging the democratic nature of the foreign policy process is the role of "We the people," as the U.S. Constitution begins. This chapter concentrates on the role of we the people and is organized in part according to two other questions that helped structure the first chapter: What is? What ought to be?

"What is" relates in this chapter to the realities of the structure of public opinion, its role in the foreign policy process, and its quality. From this perspective, you will see that public opinion is characterized by diversity rather than by unity. Talking about *the* public is just as misleading as speaking of *the* bureaucracy. You will also see that the impact and the quality of public opinion vary greatly, which can be explained in part through a discussion of what the foreign policy making models tell us about the role of public opinion.

"What ought to be" is, in part, a less empirical, more normative issue. We will discuss the quality of public opinion, using measures such as interest in and knowledge about foreign policy. You will find that there is a debate over whether the public is largely ignorant and inert or aware and active. After examining each viewpoint and its supporting evidence, we will ponder their implications for contracting, maintaining, or expanding the role of the public in the foreign policy process.

WHAT IS: THE STRUCTURE OF PUBLIC OPINION

Studying the nature and role of public opinion is one of the more daunting tasks that political scientists face. There are many reasons for this difficulty. One is that public opinion is multifaceted. There are, as we shall see presently, many publics, not just one public (Yeric & Todd, 1996). A second difficulty is that there are marked ideological cleavages within public opinion. It is appropriate, therefore, to begin by looking at the different publics and at ideological diversity before turning to the role of the public, as such.

A final matter before proceeding with our discussion of public opinion and foreign policy is to define **public opinion**. The term as used here means the opinions held by the wide range of Americans: the people whose names appear in telephone directories and who are called by polling organizations when they conduct random samples using computer-generated phone numbers. It is important to understand that our use of "public" means almost all Americans because you will also find that opinions are not distributed uniformly across the population. Instead, there are divisions in foreign policy beliefs that correlate to a degree with mass and elite status, with membership in a demographic group, and with ideological position.

Opinion Divided: Elites and Masses

One way that some scholars divide the public is to differentiate between the mass and the elite (Cunningham & Moore, 1995). The word **mass** is often used to denote the general public. Frankly, we do not like "mass" and will generally not use it. Mass carries something of a condescending connotation, begging for the derogatory adjective "unwashed" before it. This is because, in part, the mass is distinguished from the supposedly more sophisticated and wiser elite.

Elite is a term to designate the relatively few people in a society who either exercise power directly or who have direct access to policy makers. As such, members of the elite wield power in inordinate proportion to their numbers. The elite extends beyond those people in high political office to include also the upper reaches of all the major societal structures, such as business, labor, academia, organized religion, organized interest groups, and the media. Scholars who believe in elite control contend that the elite shares many demographic, educational, and other similarities that are atypical of the average American; that, therefore, the elite has similar attitudes and shares a basic consensus about the fundamental nature and thrust of the political system; and that the elite controls government and the other major structures that organize and regulate public life. Elite theorists also contend that the members of the elite interact regularly and directly with one another. It is, for example, relatively common and easy for members of the elite to call or visit one another, to meet at their golf clubs, to associate at the reunions of their often Ivy League schools, and otherwise to interact and exercise policy influence on a one-to-one basis. This frequency and intimacy of contact are very different from what is available to most Americans, including most of you who are reading this book.

For our discussion in this section, drawing a distinction between the elite and the general public (the mass) is important because the two groups often disagree on what should be the most important goals of U.S. foreign policy. As shown in Table 13.1, a series of polls indicates that for the most part the public consistently placed intermestic concerns at the top of its list of foreign policy goals, whereas leaders usually placed purer global concerns first. The public's number one foreign policy goal in 1994 was stopping the flow of illegal drugs; protecting American jobs was number two. Elites placed the drug issue fourth. Protecting American jobs did not even make the elite's top five; it finished sixth. That year leaders were most concerned about preventing nuclear proliferation; the issue finished third on the list of public concerns (Farkas, 1995; Rielly, 1995).

These polls and the accompanying commentary do not mean that the public is isolationist. In 1994, 65 percent of the public thought it would be best for the country if we took an "active part" in world affairs, and 73 percent thought the country would play an even greater role in world affairs over the next decade (Rielly, 1995). Americans also continued to support that most international of all organizations, the United Nations, with 65 percent of the respondents to a 1995 survey saying they agreed that "the United States should cooperate fully with the United Nations."[1] A large majority of the public was willing to put such general support into action. Another 1995 poll recorded 86 percent of Americans willing to use U.S. forces to help UN forces withdraw from Bosnia, 66 percent willing to send American troops to help safeguard the relocation of UN forces in Bosnia, and 61 percent willing to have U.S. forces join with UN forces to help maintain the peace and protect relief operations.[2]

Yet it is also true that in some ways the public is more nationalistic than its leaders. The public tends to want to first expend American wealth and energy at home and to be more wary than leaders about overseas involvement. In a 1995 survey, 64 percent of the public agreed that "taking care of people at home is more important than giving aid to foreign countries."[3] The average American is also very cautious about the use, especially the unilateral use, of U.S. troops abroad. Another recent survey found that only a minority of Americans (43 percent) favored taking the lead in "protecting democracy," and a slim 21 percent wanted the United States to be a

TABLE 13.1   **Different Foreign Policy Priorities:**
The Public and Leaders

1986				
Public:		*Leaders:*		
1. Protect American jobs	78%	1. Worldwide arms control	83%	
2. Secure energy supplies	69%	2. Defend allies' security	78%	
3 Worldwide arms control	69%	3. Secure energy supplies	72%	
4. Combat world hunger	63%	4. Combat world hunger	60%	
5. Reduce trade deficit	62%	5. Match Soviet military	59%	

1990				
Public:		*Leaders:*		
1. Protect American jobs	65%	1. Prevent nuclear proliferation	94%	
2. Protect American business	63%	2. Worldwide arms control	80%	
3. Secure energy supplies	61%	3. Aid global environment	72%	
4. Defend allies' security	61%	4. Reduce trade deficit	62%	
5. Prevent nuclear proliferation	59%	5. Secure energy supplies	60%	

1994				
Public		*Leaders*		
1. Stop illegal drugs	85%	1. Prevent nuclear proliferation	90%	
2. Protect American jobs	83%	2. Secure energy supplies	67%	
3. Prevent nuclear proliferation	82%	3. Defend allies' security	60%	
4. Control illegal immigration	72%	4. Stop illegal drugs	57%	
5. Secure energy supplies	62%	5. Maintain superior military	54%	

Data source: Rielly (1995, 1991b, 1987).

The American public and its leaders have different priorities in what they rank as the most important U.S. foreign policy goals. Percentages reflect the percent of people in each category who replied that a given option "should be a very important policy goal of the United States." The top five selected options for each group are shown.

"world policeman, fighting aggression wherever it occurs."[4] With regard to the use of troops, the survey found that only a hypothetical popular revolt against Cuba's Fidel Castro sparked an overwhelming willingness (94 percent) of the public to intervene. Sending troops in two other crises (Russia invades Western Europe; Iraq invades Saudi Arabia) also received majority public support, but only by the narrowest of margins (54 percent and 52 percent, respectively). A majority of the public was not willing to intervene in response to invasions of Israel by Arab forces, South Korea by North Korea, Poland by Russia, or Ukraine by Russia, or in response to a civil war in South Africa. A majority of U.S. leaders favored intervention in all but the last two crises (Rielly, 1995). Moreover, when another 1995 poll changed the hypothetical circumstances for intervening in Bosnia from protecting UN peacekeeping troops to getting actively involved in the civil war, the willingness of Americans to send troops virtually disappeared. Almost two-thirds disagreed with a statement that the "United States has a responsibility to do something about the fighting between Serbs and Bosnians."[5] Just 39 percent of the public was even willing to endorse U.S. air strikes against Serbian positions, and only 28 percent were willing to use U.S. ground forces to help Bosnian Muslims under attack.[6] Just as these polls suggested, when President Clinton finally deployed U.S. troops to Bosnia, public opinion turned quickly against his decision.

What this mix of opinions shows is that, first, there is general support for U.S. international activity. Yet, second, the public also has an intermestic focus and wariness of foreign military involvement. These two sets of attitudes are not wholly antithetical, but they do create some complex policy preferences. Furthermore, while the public's responses depend in part on how questions are asked, results like those above show that there are some clear divisions within the public. This occurs, in part, because there is not just *one* public; instead, many groups make up American society.

Opinion Divided: Demographic Groups

Who counts in the foreign policy process is also important because of opinion differences among demographic groups. Chapter 11, for example, detailed the opinions rooted in the demographic characteristics of many such racial, ethnic, and other demographic American groups.

Gender is another demographic division that has important ramifications for individual policy opinions (Myerson & Northcutt, 1994). Women have many attitudes that differ from those of men (Sylvester, 1994; Peterson & Ronyan, 1993). Moreover, because males have thus far dominated the foreign policy process, gender differences have an impact on national policy decisions (Jeffreys-Jones, 1995; Enloe, 1993; Tickner, 1992). This **gender gap** in public opinion regarding foreign policy, as well as other issues, is evident in a number of ways. According to one study, for example, "In international conflict situations, females may tend to perceive more negative risk, more potential harm, and they also may view such losses as more certain than do males" (Brandes, 1993:5). The result of this attitudinal difference is that women are less apt than men to support the use of force abroad.

The greater willingness of males than females to advocate the use of force holds over time, as a series of polls during war demonstrates. During World War II, a 1944 poll found that 76 percent of the men, but only 64 percent of the women, wanted to continue the war "until the German army is completely defeated." A 1952 Korean War era poll found that 45 percent of men, compared to 33 percent of women, favored doing "whatever is necessary to knock the Communists out of Korea." A 1968 poll indicated that males were 18 percent more likely than females to classify themselves as "hawks" in favor of increasing the U.S. military effort in Vietnam.[7]

The Persian Gulf crisis and war in 1990 and 1991 also proved women to be more restrained about using force than men (Wilcox, Ferrara, & Allsop, 1993). During the initial days of the crisis, 84 percent of men, but only 70 percent of women, thought that sending U.S. forces to Saudi Arabia had been a wise decision.[8] Polls during the first few days of the fighting in January 1991 found that when asked if the costs of war in terms of deaths and other losses would be worth the gains, 69 percent of men thought they were. Just 48 percent of women agreed. Men and women also differed on tactics. Sixty-one percent of men, compared to only 37 percent of women, advocated bombing "all military targets including those in heavily populated [Iraqi] areas."[9]

The public's reaction to the intervention in Bosnia evoked the by now predictable gender difference. One poll found 51 percent of males in favor of the deployment of U.S. troops and 44 percent of women opposed. Somewhat oddly, the stronger support for the intervention by males occurred despite the fact that they were more pessimistic about the possible course of events. Some 54% of males, compared to 46% of females, thought U.S. troops would be "stuck" in Bosnia for a "long time."[10]

Questions about hypothetical conflicts bring similar patterns. A 1990 poll asked men and women about their willingness to commit U.S. combat forces in a series of international crises ranging from a Soviet invasion of Western Europe through civil war in Mexico. On average, a majority (56 percent) of men favored responding with force, but only a minority (45 percent) of women were willing to do so.[11] A similar poll taken in 1994 led to the conclusion that with regard to distinctions among those more and less inclined to use troops, "perhaps the most dramatic division is along gender lines, with men consistently more willing to use troops in various circumstances—often the difference is nearly 20 percentage points" (Rielly, 1995:89).

Even the indirect use of force reveals a gender gap, as shown by the Reagan administration's policy of aiding the Nicaraguan Contras. According to one study (Reiter, 1990:138) "the strongest correlate of that support was gender. . . . Simply stated, women were especially likely to oppose aiding the Contras." Furthermore, in both the 1980 and 1984 presidential campaigns, women were less likely to vote for Ronald Reagan than were men, apparently due to women's fears about Reagan pulling the country into war.

Gender is among the important demographic divisions in public opinion. This woman student demonstrating during the Persian Gulf crisis in 1991 is a symbol of these divisions. On average, women have opinions that are sometimes different from those of men, and they are becoming more active in making those opinions known in the political system.

Other issues are also subject to gender gaps, but they are a good deal narrower than those that exist regarding the use of force. On immigration issues, for example, females in one 1993 poll generally held more negative attitudes regarding immigrant groups to the United States than did males. This gender difference ranged between 2 and 9 percentage points and held for all eight of the nine groups mentioned in the survey. Moreover, females were more likely than males to support initiatives designed to keep illegal immigrants out of the country, such as increases in the number of border patrols or the construction of a wall along the Mexican border. By a factor of 7 percentage points, females were more likely than males to require the use of ID cards for all legal residents of the United States. However, there was one contrary gender-based result. Males were 9 percent more likely than were females to endorse the idea of disallowing the use of school and hospital services to illegal immigrants.[12] Thus it appears that females would go to greater lengths to keep illegal immigrants out of the country than would males. But once illegal immigrants were in the country, females would be less likely than males to support actions perceived as harmful to their quality of life, particularly to that of their children.

Opinion Divided: Ideology

Ideological perspective is a third way to analyze divisions in the foreign policy beliefs and preferences of Americans. Along with elite-mass and demographic differences, ideology helps determine the basic dispositions of individuals and the importance that they attach to particular issues (Jacoby, 1995; Jacoby & Valentine, 1995; Murray, 1993). These fundamental positions, in turn, play an important role in structuring specific policy opinions (Russett, Hartley, & Murray, 1994; Zaller, 1994b; Michalak, 1992).

Ideology has been a consistent determinant of foreign policy preference, although ideological divisions were somewhat muted by the cold war–anticommunist-containment consensus that dominated U.S. foreign policy for many years after World War II. That consensus ebbed and then collapsed, and the country has since been divided over what the U.S. orientation toward the world should be.

There have been many attempts to classify Americans' foreign policy ideology (Kuzma, 1993; Lagon, 1992). To provide a flavor of this work, we will look at three related efforts: (1) liberal-conservative status and political party, (2) isolationism-internationalism and humanitarianism-militarism, and (3) unilateralism-multilateralism.

Liberals, Conservatives, and Political Affiliation

One way to divide up foreign policy opinion by ideology is to use the familiar, albeit somewhat vague, concepts of liberalism and conservatism. Affiliation with a political party fits in with this division because studies show that, on average, more conservative people tend to be Republicans, more liberal people are apt to be Democrats, and Independents (unaffiliated) fall somewhere between the other two ideologically.

One study has shown that policy opinions vary according to philosophical and partisan identification (Holsti & Rosenau, 1990). Using a survey of Americans in leadership positions (elites) taken in 1988, the study found frequent variances among the opinions of conservatives, moderates, and liberals. Many of the splits were closely paralleled by divisions among Republicans, Independents, and Democrats. The average gap in public opinion on foreign policy issues between liberals and conservatives was 32 percent. The average gap between Republicans and Democrats was 27 percent. A related study concluded that there is "a strong and consistent relationship between domestic and foreign policy beliefs" among the leaders they surveyed (Holsti & Rosenau, 1988:248). In other words, domestic liberals are not foreign policy conservatives or vice versa.

This notion is illustrated in another study that concludes that when elites disagree on foreign policy issues, their positions resemble their personal ideology or partisanship. Moreover, this congruence increases as the elites get more information, in which case liberals take increasingly liberal positions and conservatives take increasingly conservative positions. This pattern is found in a recent study of mass public opinion as well (Jacoby & Valentine, 1995). There is, then, a polarization effect through which added information intensifies ideological clustering (Zaller, 1994b).

Isolationism-Internationalism, Realism-Idealism

Another, and more complex, effort to categorize post–cold war ideological divisions is reflected in studies that suggest that foreign policy opinion can be divided between isolationism and internationalism. Then, those who are internationalists can be subdivided according to whether they support cooperative internationalism, militant internationalism, or both cooperative and militant internationalism. (Wittkopf, 1993, 1990). This approach results in four ideological types (Wittkopf, 1994:399):

1. *Isolationists* wish to shun most political involvement in global affairs.

2. *Idealists* (accommodationists, cooperative internationalists) support a U.S. global role that emphasizes humanitarian goals but that shuns the use of violent coercion as a tool of foreign policy.

3. *Realists* (hard-liners, militant internationalists) favor an American world role that stresses national security goals and shun the pursuit of humanitarian goals. They are willing to use military means to achieve these security goals.

4. *Internationalists* (comprehensive internationalists) support both cooperative and militant internationalism.

When one such approach used periodic surveys spanning 16 years (1974–1990) to analyze opinion according to four similar attitudinal divisions, it found that the public was fairly evenly split among the four types. The size of each attitude cluster ranged between 21 and 30 percent of the respondents (Wittkopf, 1990). There were, however, elite-public differences. Compared to the public, elites were less isolationist (by 4–6 percent) and considerably less realist (by 10–14 percent) and were far more idealist (by 27–35 percent) and significantly more internationalist (by 36–55 percent).[13] Other studies have revealed similar clusters in elite attitudes (Russett, 1990). The fact that the public was far less ideologically unified than were elites is not surprising.

The bulk of such findings were based on public opinion during the cold war, which leads to the question of whether the categories and distribution of opinion during that period will hold up in the post–cold war era. The answer is that they do hold up, according to one scholar, whose work leads him to argue that "traditional questions about whether the United States should be involved in the world will continue to differentiate internationalists from isolationists. It also suggests that questions about how to be involved in the world will distinguish realists from idealists" (Wittkopf, 1994:398).

Unilateralism-Multilateralism

A third informative aspect of foreign policy attitudes differentiates *unilateralists,* who argue that the United States should usually act independently to pursue its self-interested foreign policy goals, and *multilateralists,* who maintain that the country should generally try to act in concert with other countries and with international organizations to achieve goals that are in the common good of the international community (Chittick, Billingsley, & Travis, 1995). In another policy area, unilateralists tend to favor bilateral foreign aid giving (the United States giving to a specific country); multilateralists are more likely to support channeling U.S. aid through multilateral financial agencies like the World Bank.

Exploring Ideological Divisions

The debate continues among scholars about how to characterize and measure the ideological divisions that clearly exist. What is important to grasp here is that

Mike Keefe

Two divisions of foreign policy opinion pit isolationists versus internationalists and unilateralists versus multilateralists. As a general rule, Republicans are more likely to be unilateralists or even isolationists. Democrats are apt to claim that either orientation puts the wisdom of the Republican Party, symbolized here by its traditional elephant, in the same category as the ostrich, which, proverbially, sticks its head in the sand in the hope that what it cannot see will not affect it.

specific policy opinions are often rooted in a fundamental ideological framework. Sometimes, the sharp policy disagreements occur along ideological dimensions. For example, one question in a 1990 survey asked respondents whether they favored ending U.S. troops to respond to an invasion of Saudi Arabia by Iraq. Predictably, only a small minority of isolationists (33 percent) and idealists (38 percent) favored a U.S. military response, while a majority of internationalists (82 percent) and realists (73 percent) favored sending American troops. In another area, majorities of idealists, internationalists, and realists say that improving the global environment should be an important U.S. foreign policy goal; only a minority of isolationists support that position (Hinckley & Wittkopf, 1994).[14]

At other times, majorities of all ideologies may be on one side of a question, but with different levels of support and opposition to that policy. When asked whether they prefer U.S. troops to serve under only U.S. commanders or also under UN commanders, even multilateralists favored just U.S. commanders by a wide margin. The 30 percent of multilateralists who were willing also to let U.S. troops serve under UN commanders was far greater, however, than the 12 percent of unilateralists who were willing to countenance such a policy (Hinckley & Wittkopf, 1994).[15]

There are several useful things you can do with this knowledge. One is to examine your own beliefs. A good way to do this is to construct a survey that includes some of the dimensions we have just discussed. Use inductive logic (going from the specific to the general) by creating agree-disagree questions regarding specific policies that would reveal attitudes about the various dimensions. Then analyze your own responses (and those of your friends, perhaps) to see what the responses reveal about your ideologies. This basically replicates the methodology used by several of the studies we have cited.

You can also use the various ideological scales to evaluate the views and policies of current and potential political leaders. Once you know your own ideological position, being aware of a leader's ideological orientation can assist you in deciding whether you favor that person's candidacy for or continuance in office. If, for instance, you are a hard-liner, you probably would not support an accommodationist and might even have doubts about comprehensive internationalists. Few people are absolutely consistent, but it is reasonable to contend, for example, that President Clinton's comprehensive internationalist orientation was evident when he declared during his inaugural address that the United States would not only "protect its vital interests" using "forces when necessary," but would also act when "the will and conscience of the international community is defied."[16] By contrast, Secretary of State Warren Christopher is more solidly in the idealist camp. He has been described by the *New York Times* as someone who "would negotiate endlessly to avoid military confrontation" and characterized by former national security adviser Zbigniew Brzezinski as a man who would shy away from what Brzezinski (a hard-liner) says is "the unavoidable ingredient of force . . . in dealing with realities."[17] Both the president and secretary of state, as chapter 4 discusses, tend to favor the multilateralist approach. The administration sought UN support for the U.S. intervention in Haiti, for example. In another region, one reason for U.S. restraint in Bosnia was the Clinton administration's reluctance to take military action in the face of resistance by the UN and by NATO that lasted until late 1995. By contrast, Senator Robert Dole (R-KS) and most of the other Republicans who announced against Clinton could be described as realists; most also tend toward the unilateralist position, and some, such as Patrick Buchanan, lean toward isolationism.

Another point to think about with respect to the various ideological foundations of opinion is whether they have a sound basis on which to form specific policy opinion. This addresses the issue of quality, which we will take up later. As you will see, there is considerable debate over the quality and, therefore, the proper role of public opinion in the foreign policy process. Before getting to "what ought to be," however, there is another "what is" to explore. That is the question of the role of public opinion.

WHAT IS: THE ROLE OF PUBLIC OPINION

We have frequently noted the impact that American citizens have on the foreign policy process, but we have done so only in relation to other subjects. Chapter 1 outlined various views on public input into foreign policy making; chapter 4 discussed political culture, for instance. The chapters on the presidency and Congress examined public opinion as one of the informal limits to political power. Then, in the two previous chapters, we looked at the roles played by interest groups and the media as two-way intermediaries between the society and its political institutions. We will expand on many of these factors in this chapter during our discussion of the place of the public in the foreign policy process.

What is the role of public opinion? Is the public an actor, or is it merely the audience? There is no single answer to this question. Some analysts minimize public sentiment as a factor in the foreign policy process. This view, especially common in studies from the 1950s–early 1970s, portrays the public as a passive audience that disinterestedly watches U.S. foreign policy unfold and tends to applaud whatever the president and other foreign policy leaders do. Other scholars disagree. Particularly in more recent studies, evidence has been found that public opinion has more significant power in the foreign policy process. This view sees the public not as the audience to the foreign policy drama, but as an important actor that helps determine the story line in an improvisational political play.

Both the views of the public as audience and as actor are partly correct; neither is totally accurate. Clarifying this perplexing statement is the task of the next few pages. What we will do first is to discuss the models of foreign policy making to see what they can tell us about the role of public opinion. You will see that its role varies considerably depending on the issues and the circumstances involved in any given policy question. Then, in a second section, we will examine the formal and informal channels through which public opinion works.

Public Opinion and the Foreign Policy Process Models

As you will recall from chapter 6, the differing ways that foreign policy is decided can be divided into four models. The *presidential model* focuses on the president and his immediate, high-level advisers in the White House and the Cabinet as the nexus of policy making. The *political model* represents foreign policy making as part of a diverse, multiple-actor process, with the president and his political appointees, the bureaucracy, Congress, interest groups, and the public all interacting and having an impact on the policy process. The *administrative model* maintains that policy is often decided within the State Department, the Defense Department, and other such bureaucracies. Sometimes one agency controls a decision; at other times several agencies are involved. The *subgovernment model* represents the process where many issues are debated and decisions made by those bureaucrats, interest groups, and members of Congress who have a particular interest in a specific matter. Thus, the model focuses on issues that are not critical or of general concern but that are still important to a limited number of bureaucratic units, interest groups, and legislators.

You might also want to review chapter 6 to reacquaint yourself with the specific types of issues and policy circumstances that help determine the model by which a policy issue will be decided. The types of issues of concern to us here are pure international versus intermestic policy (which combines elements of *inter*national and do*mestic* issues) such as trade policy. There are two types of relevant situations: (1) crisis and noncrisis situations and (2) status quo and non–status quo situations. A final point of review is to consider once again Figure 6.2 and Tables 6.1 and 6.2.

The Public as a Passive Audience

There are times when the public assumes the stance of an audience, when public opinion plays little role in foreign policy. *Pure international issues,* those that do not affect the public directly or cause an emotional reaction, are apt to generate little public interest or strong opinion. In these cases, policy is processed according to the presidential model or the administrative model. The U.S. Senate in August 1993 overwhelmingly ratified an open-skies treaty with Russia that allows the countries to conduct aerial inspections to verify mutual compliance with arms control treaties. The vast majority of the public had not heard of, much less thought about, the treaty.

Crisis situations are prone to be dealt with according to the presidential model. What normally occurs during a crisis is the "rally 'round the flag effect," a phenomenon discussed extensively in the chapter on the presidency. During a crisis, the public tends to support whatever the president's announced policy is. Furthermore, there is sometimes a "halo effect," by which the president's overall public approval rating temporarily increases, sometimes significantly, during crises (Edwards & Gallup, 1990).

For example in 1993, President Clinton experienced a jump in his approval rating after American forces launched a cruise missile attack against Iraq in June, in retaliation for Baghdad's alleged role in plotting to assassinate former president Bush in April. Clinton's overall public approval rating jumped 11 percentage points, from 39 to 50 percent, and the public approval of the job he was doing in foreign policy increased similarly from 38 to 49 percent.[18] The surge in Clinton's public standing occurred even though a poll taken just a month before the raid showed that only 35 percent of Americans favored retaliation against Iraq.[19]

There are differences among scholars over the exact workings of the rally effect, and some even doubt its existence (Edwards, & Swenson, 1994; Callaghan & Virtanen, 1993; Lian & Oneal, 1993; Brody, 1991). Certainly it is not true that public support of the president during a crisis is unanimous or unwavering. Several factors get involved. First, the public is more likely to rally strongly when immediately threatened, as occurred during the Cuban missile crisis, than when the threat is more remote, as occurred in the recent crisis over Haiti. Most Americans did not feel threatened by the events in that country, and they refused to support sending troops even when the president presented his case in a nationally televised address. The speech had a positive effect, but it was limited to reducing popular opposition to invading Haiti from 73 percent just before the telecast to 60 percent just after it.[20] Even 3 months later, with the intervention an apparent success, 51 percent of the public thought U.S. troops should have stayed out of Haiti.[21] It is a testament to the public that even though it opposed the intervention before, during, and after its occurrence, some people may have been willing to give Clinton grudging credit for having removed the military junta without spilling blood. The month before the action only 34 percent of Americans expressed approval of the way Clinton was handling foreign affairs; less than 3 months after the intervention the public's support of Clinton's conduct of foreign affairs had risen to 40 percent.[22]

Second, rally effects can be like a roller coaster, however, with public support flowing and ebbing over time and according to the intensity of the crisis. The events of the Persian Gulf War created six discernible rallies in the public's approval of President Bush between August 9, 1990, and March 3, 1991, with drop-offs in public approval in between (Mueller, 1994). During the 6-month, August 1990–February 1991 period, the public's overall approval of Bush's performance as president rose and fell between 53 percent and 89 percent, and the public's estimate of the president's handling of foreign policy alternately soared and plunged between a high of 89 percent and a low of 54 percent (Nacos, 1994). The success of the war effort enhanced Bush's image in the public's mind. It also improved the image of the Republican Party among Americans (Norrander & Wilcox, 1993).

Third, the existence or extent of a rally is influenced by the media. The greater and more dramatic the media's coverage of the threatening event, and the more uniformly supportive of the president the media's coverage is, the more the public will rally to the president (Eveland, McLeod, & Signorielli, 1995; Oneal & Bryan, 1993). Fourth, the strength and duration of rallies depend in part on how strongly the president is supported by other elites (Iyengar & Simon, 1994). As one scholar put it, "A rally will last as long as the president's tacit or explicit support-coalition [among elites] persists" (Brody, 1994:212). Fifth, presidents may find that too frequent appeals to patriotism decreases positive public response as the public become "wary and weary after repeated urgings to rally around the flag" (Bennett, 1993:7).

For all these variables, the main point is that crises improve presidential popularity. One series of polls indicates that during crises since 1945, the public's approval of the president has increased by an average of 8 percentage points and that the positive effect has lasted an average of about 10 weeks.[23] Another and similar analysis finds the average increase in public approval to be 3.8 percent and lasts 12 weeks (Burbach, 1995). Moreover, this increased public support can occur even if the president's response to the crisis is ineffective. In 1980, for example, President Jimmy Carter's approval rating increased sharply immediately following the attempt to rescue American hostages held in Iran, even though the rescue mission failed. Similarly, President Kennedy's public approval shot up in the midst of the Bay of Pigs catastrophe in 1961. "The worse I do, the more popular I get," Kennedy quipped incredulously, albeit accurately (Russett & Starr, 1992:247). President Clinton's popularity similarly rose in November 1995, as people seemingly approved of his decisiveness, even if they disapproved of sending U.S. forces to Bosnia.

Presidents are aware of the rally effect and sometimes have tried to capitalize on the public's willingness to be led (Brace & Hinckley, 1992; Marra, Ostrom, & Simon, 1990). The White House has occasionally misled the public by creating an unwarranted crisis atmosphere or by using its control of information to present an inaccurate impression of events. There is even some evidence that presidents have utilized or exacerbated crises in order to shore up sagging support within their party (Morgan & Bickers, 1992). An example discussed in the last chapter focused on the Reagan administration's effort through dubious stories—including those of Libyan terrorists plotting to assassinate the president—to win public backing for action against the government of Muammar Qaddafi. Such shaping of reality may have served presidential interests, but not always the public's (Page & Shapiro, 1992).

Status quo situations are yet another circumstance in which public opinion is not apt to affect policy overtly. What occurs in such cases is that the public supports the existing policy consensus and existing policy direction. Policies that fit with that consensus or with established policy tend to enjoy public support. Indeed, most studies find that the public tends to anchor policy, in the sense that the public usually changes its views on basic policy more slowly than political leaders do.

A primary example of the public supporting status quo and incremental policies relates to the cold war consensus in American foreign policy. This consensus centered on the two fundamental premises that the Soviet Union and international communism represented a profound national security threat, and that the United States had the responsibility to protect itself and the rest of the "Free World" from Soviet and communist expansion. This consensus gave rise to what one scholar has termed a "followership" mind-set, in which the public was content during the cold war to follow the lead of its leaders, so long as foreign policy actions were justified in light of the existing threat (Melanson, 1991).

The Public as an Active Player

The public is not always willing to sit passively and applaud policy. Often the public or segments of it become active and independent players in the foreign policy process (Krosnick & Tehlami, 1995). In such cases, policy is apt to be decided according to the political or the subgovernment model. The political model will govern when a significant element of the public is activated. The subgovernment model will prevail when a narrow range of interest groups and other actors are concerned. Space does not allow a complete review of all the factors that spark public reaction, but three—intermestic issues, noncrisis situations, and non–status quo situations—will serve to illustrate.

Intermestic issues are almost sure to engage the general public or specific groups. The range of issues that, based on their domestic implications, spark a reaction in the American public was detailed in chapter 6 and elsewhere and need not be repeated here. Several points are, however, worth iterating. One is that whether an issue is foreign or has domestic characteristics is a matter of perception, even in times of crisis (James & Hristoulas, 1994). Trade issues, for instance, have routinely been perceived differently by presidents, members of Congress, and the public. Presidents tend to think of trade policy in terms of overall relations with other countries. The public and members of Congress are more apt to evaluate trade relations strictly in terms of what they mean for American jobs and other domestic considerations. Table 13.1, earlier in the chapter, supports this view.

Second, policy that falls unevenly on domestic groups is likely to intensify opinion. It is not surprising that youths and minorities are often less supportive of military action than is the general public. As discussed in chapter 1, young people are the ones most likely to bear the physical brunt of war, and minorities are often more likely to be in combat positions than whites. Thus it is not surprising, as noted in previous chapters, that organized opposition to the war in Vietnam began on college campuses or that opposition to the use of troops in both Vietnam and the Persian Gulf was sharply higher among African Americans than among whites.

Third, the growing interdependence of the world's countries means that more and more issues are likely to fall into the intermestic category (Parry, 1993). President Clinton's remark during his inaugural address that "there is no clear division today between what is foreign and what is domestic" was revealing, if a bit of an overstatement.

Noncrisis situations are circumstances where the public feels a good deal less restrained in its willingness to differ with the president and with existing policy. This category certainly includes trade, diplomatic recognition, and other such day-to-day issues of foreign affairs. The issue of assistance to help stabilize the reeling Mexican economy in early 1995 provides a good example. Even though the press tended to report the financial turmoil as the "peso crisis," only the tiny minority of the population who had direct financial stakes in Mexico felt directly threatened. Therefore, it is hardly surprising that a whopping 81 percent of the public opposed the $40 billion financial aid package that Clinton proposed or that Congress refused to act on it. Even after Clinton used discretionary funds already available to him to help create a multinational loan-guarantee program, a majority of the public still opposed the idea.[24] General foreign aid is another noncrisis issue on which the public differs strongly with presidential preferences. A January 1995 poll found that 75 percent of the public felt too much was being spent on foreign aid, 83 percent believed that most aid failed to reach the people most in need, and 86 percent thought domestic problems should take precedence over foreign aid.[25] It was no wonder then that the House of Representatives later in the year voted to cut Clinton's foreign aid request by 20 percent.[26]

Noncrisis situations, however, are not confined to just such routine matters. They can also include situations that involve confrontation, even military tension, with other countries. Take the Haiti intervention for instance. The issue of Haiti's repressive military regime was a "crisis" for relatively few Americans, primarily those with racial or personal ties to Haiti or those living in south Florida—the destination of Haitian refugees trying to enter the United States. For most Americans, the return of democratic government to Haiti was a laudable goal but not one worth the shedding of American blood. The Clinton administration's effort to talk the Haitian military elites out of power, so that U.S. troops could go ashore there as peacekeepers rather than combatants, had to be influenced by public opinion.

Non–status quo situations and innovative policies also are apt to energize public opinion. Once the cold war consensus broke down, the public became a more important factor as the elite split over basic policy direction and as the public similarly split in its preferences about fundamental policy direction. This ideological divergence is further discussed below, but for now we can say that the lack of consensus, in a world where the status quo ceased to exist along with the Soviet Union, has sparked a deep debate among Americans over the course of foreign policy (Lomperis, 1993). In the new era, one scholar theorizes, the public abandoned its "followership" stance and became more pivotal in what he characterizes as a "fragmentation/swing" situation (Melanson, 1991). From this perspective, elites fragmented in their foreign policy preferences following Vietnam. Disagreement among the elites resonated in similar splits within the public. This lack of consensus has the effect of empowering the public as the various elements of the political leadership appeal to mass sentiment and attempt to win its support to swing policy direction one way or another.

As a result, policy is more likely to be decided according to the political model. During the cold war era, the public would have probably supported the president if he had dispatched troops to a Bosnia being threatened by communist guerrillas. Now the situation is more muddled. By 1995 a majority of the public would support the use of U.S. troops in Bosnia only if they were needed to help with the protection or withdrawal of UN peacekeeping troops (Kull, 1995). However, a majority of the public would oppose the use of troops if their purpose was to punish the Serbs for their aggression in Bosnia or, as it turned out, to be part of the NATO peacekeeping force.[27] In other words, the public would be willing to send U.S. forces against Serbs in some scenarios but not in others.

How Public Opinion Affects Policy

It is clear that public opinion does not have just one persona. Sometimes it plays the role of an audience that watches passively as the president and other leading actors on the foreign policy drama strut and fret their hour upon the stage. Indeed, the audience may not even be paying any attention at all. There are other times, however, when the public joins the action. The citizenry hardly ever takes the starring role. That usually falls to the president. Yet the public can and often does become a marquee actor that changes the ongoing script to suit its liking.

"Well and good," you might say, "but none of this tells me *how* the public influences foreign policy." Your point is well taken, and it is to explaining the "how" that we will now turn our attention. Just as when we discussed the presidency, Congress, the bureaucracy, and other actors, our examination of the impact of public opinion involves power. Also, just like the other actors who are granted a constitutional role, the public's power can be analyzed by dividing it into its formal and informal bases.

Formal Power: The Voters Speak

The ballot box is the source of the public's formal power in foreign policy. The public elects the president and the 535 members of Congress. It would be incorrect to say that most elections are decided on foreign policy issues; they are not. It would be equally erroneous to dismiss foreign policy as an element in the electoral equation. In this section we will examine the direct impact of elections on foreign policy, including how foreign policy affects who gets elected and how who gets elected affects foreign policy. Then, in the section on informal powers, we will explore the indirect, "between elections" role of the public's franchise.

Foreign Policy and Who Gets Elected Politicians normally are strongly motivated by an urge to get reelected. Lyndon Johnson in 1968 was the first and, to date, the only president to decline a reelection bid since Calvin Coolidge declared, "I do not choose to run" in 1928. The overwhelming majority of senators and representatives also repeatedly seek reelection each time their 6- or 2-year terms expire.

Presidential elections are one level at which foreign policy may impact who serves in office. It is difficult to analyze precisely why voters chose as they do and the impact on foreign policy of those choices (Gaubatz, 1995). Some voters may be swayed by the candidates' stances on foreign policy issues. Many react, however, to candidates' stances on any number of domestic issues. Other voters respond emotionally to candidates, reacting to perceptions that one candidate appears more caring, trustworthy, or dependable than the others. Polls throughout the 1980s, for instance, showed that many in the American public had a favorable impression of Ronald Reagan while at the same time having an unfavorable impression of many of Reagan's policy stances (Sobel, 1993). Even who turns out or does not has some bearing on elections and subsequent policy, since those who do not vote are apt to be a bit more liberal on a range of foreign policy issues than those who do vote (Gant & Lyons, 1993). Such complexities, though, do not diminish the fact that foreign policy issues can at times determine how voters choose in presidential elections (Jackman & Miller, 1995).

Sometimes foreign policy has a strong impact. Dwight Eisenhower's 1952 victory was significantly aided by his pledge to "go to Korea," thereby promising an end to the war there. His 1956 landslide reelection was due in large part to the public's belief that he could stand firm regarding U.S. interests abroad without necessarily bringing the country closer to a war with the Soviet Union (Boyd, 1993). In other circumstances, those who support a candidate's foreign policy may provide the margin of victory. One political analyst noted, for example, that while only approximately 22 percent of voters cited foreign and defense policy as their primary concern, of that 22 percent, almost 80 percent voted for George Bush, not for Michael Dukakis, in 1988.[28]

THE AMERICAN
PEOPLE ARE
BEHIND ME!

BOSNIAN
CRUSADE

Americans elected Bill Clinton as president in part because of his emphasis on domestic issues. Over time, however, Clinton has increasingly turned his attention to foreign affairs. Many Americans do not support the extent of the president's internationalist orientation. In this editorial cartoon, the intervention in Bosnia is portrayed as one of the president's internationalist policies about which the American public has serious doubts.

Such cases are the exception, however, and most often foreign affairs plays a lesser role in presidential elections. The 1992 presidential race provides a good example. If the election had been decided solely on foreign policy, Bush would have been reelected. An August 1992 poll found 58 percent of the respondents expressing confidence that Bush could deal wisely with an international crisis; only 28 percent expressed similar confidence in Clinton.[29] An October poll found that 61 percent of all voters thought that, compared to the other candidates, Bill Clinton and H. Ross Perot, "George Bush is more likely to do a better job of handling U.S. foreign policy."[30] Other polls confirmed the Bush advantage in foreign policy.

As it turned out, though, it was Clinton, not Bush, who delivered the inaugural address on January 20, 1993. This reality reflected the dominance of domestic issues in the campaign. It was conducted amid an economic recession. One study comparing the impact of the public's estimate of Bush's foreign policy performance and his economic policy performance has shown that from November 1989 through October 1991, the president's foreign policy was consistently the more important factor in determining his public approval ratings. Then beginning in November and continuing through the election, it was Bush's economic policy performance that was just as consistently the more important factor in determining his public approval ratings (Edwards, Mitchell, & Welch, 1995). With other polls indicating that as few as 15 percent of respondents felt that Bush would bring about any real economic change, and 63 percent saying that Clinton could, the incumbent's electoral fate was all but sealed.[31]

Not only did Bush lose, but it may be that the presidential success he claimed may have cost him the election. Bush claimed that he and other Republican presidents had "won the cold war" by keeping the pressure on the Soviets over the years. Whether or not it is true, there is little doubt that these Republican commanders in chief may have weakened their party's chances of capturing and holding the White House. Throughout most of the cold war years, voters tended to prefer Republicans on foreign policy, while preferring Democrats on domestic policy. The end of the cold war drained much of the fear from the U.S. foreign policy equation and lessened the voters' perceived need for a president who could manage foreign policy in a dangerous world. Without a formidable foe, Americans could concentrate on domestic issues. There is some truth to the comment made during the campaign that in the old days, foreign policy "literally vetoed" some candidates because of the perception that "if you couldn't handle foreign policy, you couldn't handle the presidency."[32] Given the virtually unanimous poll results showing that most Americans had a poor estimate of Bill Clinton's ability to handle foreign policy, it is clear that domestic, not foreign, policy decided the 1992 election.

It is also the case that even when foreign policy is an important issue, elections rarely feature sharp differences among the candidates over the goals of foreign policy. In the two elections during the Vietnam War (1964 and 1968), for instance, both major candidates vowed to end the war. In short, foreign policy issues in an election year rarely split the public into competing groups. Nor do dramatic policy changes typically follow the election of a new president (Dixon & Gaarder, 1992). Even when a new president tries to change policy in accordance with his campaign pledges, he often finds it politically unwise or impossible to do so. This was true for Clinton's initial policies on Haitian immigration, intervention in Bosnia, and several other stands. Thus while presidential victors may proclaim that the public has provided them with a **mandate,** an endorsement of their foreign policy proposals, such mandates are hard to discern in the analysis of the presidential vote and later presidential policy.

Yet foreign policy issues do not have to dominate presidential campaigns in order to be important factors (Popkin, 1991; Ornstein & Schmitt, 1990). There are always some voters, and usually large percentages of them, to whom foreign policy issues are important. That means that foreign policy is often a factor and, in a close race, it may play a significant role in deciding who stays in Washington and who returns home. For some voters, foreign policy is a determinant of their choice for president (Nincic & Hinckley, 1991:350; Wilcox & Allsop, 1991). Others make retrospective judgments, basing their vote on how the prior administration performed on foreign policy and other issues. The 1988 race was arguably a referendum on the Reagan years that benefited Bush (Abramson, Aldrich, & Rohde, 1990). Still other voters are swayed by the image of foreign policy leadership and competence that a candidate projects. Jimmy Carter labored under a weak image in 1980 that was significantly enhanced by the drawn-out Iranian hostage situation. In 1988, Michael Dukakis's apparent discomfort with foreign policy issues seemed to contribute to his poor image of national leadership potential. Thus while foreign policy is usually not the overriding factor in a presidential race, it is also rarely as much of a nonfactor as it was in 1992.

A final way foreign policy can affect presidential elections is through public perceptions of each party. For example, in eight of the nine elections between 1952 and 1984, public views on foreign policy helped Republican candidates to capture or hold the White House. In each case, these candidates benefited from the public perception that Republicans were more likely to keep the country out of war. The lone exception was 1964 when Lyndon Johnson benefited from public fears that Barry Goldwater might be too willing to use nuclear weapons in Vietnam or future conflicts.

Congressional elections can also be affected by foreign policy, either directly or indirectly. Direct effects occur when legislators run afoul of influential interest groups with clear foreign policy stands. Several chairmen of the Senate Foreign Relations Committee, for example, have been driven from office in part because of their foreign policy activity. These include Senators Tom Connally (D-TX), Walter George (D-GA), J. William Fulbright (D-AK), Frank Church (D-ID), and Charles Percy (R-IL). In the most recent case, Percy ran afoul of Jewish constituents and others sympathetic toward Israel because of his endorsement of dealing more openly with the Palestine Liberation Organization (PLO) and his public pressure on the government of Israel to moderate its stand. There is also some evidence from a study that examined votes on decisions to go to war from the War of 1812 through the Persian Gulf War that legislators who vote against conflict are less likely to be returned to office in the next election. This did not occur after the Persian Gulf War. Almost an equal percentage of those legislators who voted for and against the authorizing resolutions were reelected (Regens, Gaddie, & Lockerbie, 1995).

Congressional elections may also be affected indirectly as a result of the public's reaction to either a presidential candidate's foreign policy stances or the foreign policy actions of an incumbent president. Popular presidential candidates produce more votes for that party's congressional candidates; an unpopular candidate may not only lose, but also take other members down to defeat (Campbell, 1993b). Similarly, in midterm elections, when the presidency is not at stake, members of the president's party may be affected by how the public reacts to the job being done by the president. The 1994 midterm elections saw Democrats lose control of both chambers of Congress to the Republicans for the first time since the 1950s. While a number of political factors combined to produce this dramatic change in Congress, Clinton's performance as president over the prior 2 years had to play some part. During virtually all of 1994, Clinton's handling of foreign affairs got low grades from the public. His approval rate stayed in the low 40 percent range for virtually the entire year, and at times a clear majority of the public disapproved of his handling of foreign policy in the months leading up to the November elections.[33] Public dissatisfaction with Clinton's policies regarding Bosnia, Haiti, Chinese and Japanese trade, gay males and lesbians in the military, and other such matters cannot be discounted when considering the partisan change in Congress in 1994.

Who Gets Elected and Foreign Policy   Just as foreign policy can and does affect elections, so too do elections and the electoral cycle affect foreign policy (Nincic, 1990). Elections change the officeholders, and that change may produce foreign policy shifts. It is true, as noted, that the winning candidate's campaign positions are not always converted into policy. Presidents often find that they must alter or abandon foreign policy stands that they took as candidates. These course corrections are due to changed international circumstances, public and congressional opposition, or the different way the world looks when sitting in the Oval Office compared to standing on the campaign stump.

Nevertheless, electoral outcomes can affect foreign policy. Dwight Eisenhower vowed in 1952 to get the country out of the Korean War if elected. He did. In 1960 John Kennedy vowed to change Eisenhower's strategic military doctrine emphasizing the use of nuclear weapons. Once elected, Kennedy and his advisers instituted the flexible response doctrine, calling for a full range of military options from low-level conventional forces to strategic nuclear options. Emphasis on the development of counterinsurgency forces under the flexible response doctrine helped pave the way for U.S. participation in the Vietnam War. Jimmy Carter vowed in 1976 to reinject morality into the making of foreign policy. At least during his first 2 years, he did so with his human rights policy. In 1980 Ronald Reagan vowed he would not be afraid to use force to protect U.S. interests; he subsequently used force against Grenada, Lebanon, and Libya. And during the 1992 campaign, Clinton advocated taking stronger action against both the military junta in Haiti and the Bosnian Serbs. Those things did not happen quickly, but eventually they did occur. Electing a new president, then, sometimes does alter the style, and some of the substance, of U.S. foreign policy.

Furthermore, elections change the partisan makeup of Congress. Which political party controls Congress is very important because **bipartisanship**, the idea that presidents should be able to count on foreign policy support from both Republicans and Democrats in Congress, has been increasingly rare since the 1940s. Despite all the overheated rhetoric that "politics stops at the water's edge," and that "the nation must speak with one voice in foreign policy," there has usually been very little bipartisan agreement on foreign policy. Significant foreign policy differences often exist between the two parties, and foreign policy can often pit the interests of one region of the country against another (Trubowitz, 1992; McCormick & Wittkopf, 1990).

Beginning in the 1950s, foreign policy became an increasingly partisan subject in Congress and was especially contentious during the Reagan years. Many Democrats no longer viewed the world in cold war terms. Thus they strongly opposed such Reagan policies as arming the Nicaraguan Contras and spending billions of dollars on the Strategic Defense Initiative. Partisanship has remained pronounced, if somewhat less markedly so, during the Bush and Clinton presidencies. If the U.S. intervention in Bosnia that began in November 1995 were to fail or result in an unacceptable level of U.S. casualties, then the 1996 elections might feature an attack on "Mr. Clinton's war" just as the 1952 election saw criticism of "Mr. Truman's war" in Korea. Presidents can generally expect to face tough partisan opposition. For many foreign policy issues, the opposition party in Congress, particularly in the House of Representatives, will find reasons to object to presidential foreign policy positions.

Informal Power: Politicians Anticipate

There is a much more subtle, informal role played by public opinion than can be ascertained by merely examining electoral results. Public sentiments affect presidents and legislators as they try to formulate policy between elections.

Anticipated reaction by officials to the potential impact of public opinion strengthens the role of the citizenry's views in the foreign policy process. What this means is that for a variety of reasons, both elected and appointed officials calculate what public opinion is or may be as they make their policy choices. The executive branch officials gauge public opinion based on their interactions with or reading of (in order of influence) legislators, the media, public opinion polls, interest groups, and elites (Powlick, 1995b). In this sense, mass public opinions and beliefs help establish informal parameters, limits beyond which the public is unlikely to support policy options (Radway, 1993; Stimson, 1991). This parameter-setting function works because, as one scholar argues, "Policymakers in liberal democracies do not decide against an overwhelming public consensus" (Risse-Kappen, 1991:510).

It also may be that advances in the ability to know what the public thinks are having an increasing impact on policy. Opinion polling has become an industry in its own right. It is difficult to pick up a paper or view or listen to a newscast without being told how Americans feel about one or more issues or individuals. The result, according to one scholar, is that "public opinion polls have become an agenda-setting instrument and are used by virtually all political participants" (Hinckley, 1992:138).

Two questions are relevant to analyzing this informal power based on anticipation. One is why elected and appointed officials anticipate public opinion. The second is how that anticipation affects policy.

Why Officials Gauge and Anticipate Public Opinion   Presidents are expected to lead, but they are also expected to follow public opinion to one degree or another. A variety of factors determine where on the scale between leading and following any president falls. Truman and some other presidents have been "more willing than others to place their convictions, or at least their policy goals, before their popularity" (Reingold, 1994:756). Other presidents tend to be followers. Two scholars have written of President Clinton, for example, that "overall we find that [he] emphasized responsiveness to the public's wishes—as he had during the campaign—over efforts to direct the public" (Jacobs & Shapiro, 1995:197). There are any number of reasons why elected and appointed officials pay attention to foreign policy. Some of the more important factors include the electoral impulse, the norm of democracy, the belief that public standing affects political power, and the belief that public support and policy success are linked.

The *electoral impulse* persuades elected officials that they should keep a close eye on public sentiment. Those appointed officials whose terms in office depend on the continuance of their president or their political party are similarly persuaded. As a senator in the 1950s, Lyndon Johnson had watched Democrats get blamed for "losing China" to communism. A decade later as president, he did not want to be responsible for "losing Vietnam" to communism. Whatever reservations he had, Johnson felt he had to pursue the war to prevent later partisan accusations that he had done too little to protect freedom there. "Hence," one scholar writes, the president *"followed* public opinion by *leading* it into a war that neither he nor the public wanted" (Zaller, 1994b:250).

Members of Congress also attempt to read public opinion. During the heyday of the cold war consensus, legislators may have been relatively free from constituency pressures on foreign policy issues, but those times are long gone. Now defense, trade, and economic issues affect jobs here at home, regional issues mobilize constituents with racial or family ties to the area, and immigration issues seem to upset everyone. For contentious issues, legislators determine the range of opinion among their constituents and often work to place themselves at a safe, centrist position. Elected officeholders are especially sensitive to the views of their party's constituents because they form the core of support that legislators need for reelection (Burgin, 1991; Shapiro et al., 1990). If opinion shifts on an issue, legislators frequently shift their stances as well, trying not to run afoul of what the folks back home think about the matter (Herrera, Herrera, & Smith, 1992).

The Persian Gulf War illustrates such an interplay between executive and legislative attempts to both read and lead public opinion. When opinion polls showed that segments of the public were beginning to think of a reliance on economic sanctions against Iraq as a "do nothing" policy, President Bush escalated to more active military options. Bush was already being accused of having a do-nothing response to the ongoing domestic recession, so he could ill afford to be accused of a lack of leadership in foreign policy too. Similarly, congressional Democrats who wanted to give sanctions more time to work or who opposed the military option were reluctant to risk challenging Bush's leadership and falling afoul of the rally 'round the chief syndrome. Thus, as one scholar notes, "both parties were . . . active agents in shaping public opinion, but they took care to lead toward goals the public would ultimately approve; or . . . to avoid leading toward goals the public would not approve. In both cases, the threat of electoral retribution gave pause to the wielders of power" (Zaller, 1994b:271). Later, anticipation of public opinion helped shorten the war. General

Colin Powell has recalled in his 1995 memoir that the president told him, "We're starting to pick up some undesirable public and political baggage with all those scenes of carnage. . . . Why not end [the war]?"[34]

The point is that both executive and legislative officials constantly calculate the potential electoral effect of their actions and the possible advantage that the other party may try to seize from any misstep. Opposition party members of Congress are often suspicious of presidential motives and maneuvers. The "October surprise" is one such tactic. One variation is the possibility that a president might launch a major initiative, especially a public-rallying crisis, just before the November elections. Or a president might suppress potentially upsetting information until after the election. George Bush signed an order on October 31, 1990, to double U.S. troop strength in the Persian Gulf in preparation for the offensive against Iraq. Yet he did not tell congressional leaders of his directive when he met with them that day. Bush would surely claim, but it would be difficult to believe, that it was mere coincidence that he did not reveal his order to the public until November 6—the day after the congressional elections. Surprise!

The *norm of democracy* is a second reason why officials pay attention to public opinion. Officials are apt to believe, just as you probably do, that public opinion should count at least to some degree in a democracy. It would be naive and erroneous to imagine that presidents or their advisers see themselves as bound by public opinion. It is not accurate to argue that political leaders disdain democracy and put up with it only because they must. Instead, what one finds is that they try to balance what is sometimes an uncomfortable fit in the meaning behind the two words, democratic leader. "No president is obliged to abide by the dictates of public opinion," President Kennedy's special assistant, Theodore Sorensen, asserted. Yet, he continued, the president also "has a responsibility" to "respect it . . . to woo it, and win it" (Goldstein, 1984:176). President Gerald Ford similarly attested to the attempt to balance the role of leader and servant of the people when he observed that "a president ought to listen to the people, but he cannot make hard decisions just by reading the polls once a week" (Edwards & Wayne, 1985:97).

The norm of democracy is even held by appointed officials. Studies that examined the attitudes of appointed officials in the State Department and on the National Security Council (NSC) staff during the Reagan, Bush, and Clinton administrations found a widespread belief among them that it was necessary and desirable to take public opinion into account because foreign policy could not be successful without public acceptance. It is also the case, however, that officials within and between administrations varied considerably in their views on how responsive to public opinion they should be. During the Reagan administration, for example, some members of the NSC staff were not adverse to ignoring public opinion that did not support the administration's preferred policy on such issues as the arming of the Contra rebels in Nicaragua. State Department and NSC staff members appointed by Clinton acknowledge that public support of foreign policy is important, but that they see their job as providing expert advice to the president. If public opinion opposes the administration's policies, then the staff members believe it is their job to help the president educate and lead public opinion to support Clinton. If they cannot persuade the public to see the wisdom of the president's policy, then the staff members feel that the responsibility for deciding whether or not to modify the policy is properly the realm of elected, not appointed officials (Powlick, 1991, 1995a, 1995b).

The belief that popularity affects political power is a third reason that political leaders pay attention to public opinion. Presidents strive to be popular with the public in part because they are convinced that they can use that popularity as leverage to get their proposals passed by Congress. Just after he began his second term, President Eisenhower predicted that "my influence in the next four years" will depend on "how popular I am with the multitudes. . . . Strength can be marshaled on both sides of the aisle only if it is generally believed that I am in a position to go to the people over their heads" (Neal, 1978:380). In the same vein, when President Johnson (1971:443) reviewed his decades of experience in Washington he concluded that "presidential popularity is a major source of strength in gaining cooperation from Congress."

Presidents are correct in noting the reciprocal relationship involved; their legislative success depends in part on their public standing and their popularity depends in part on their legislative successes. Gains and losses in popularity play a role in the success of the presidents' proposals in Congress (Peterson, 1990; Marra, Ostrom, & Simon, 1990). In turn, foreign policy issues can be part of the successes, which can help make presidents more popular with the public (Bardes, 1995; Nincic & Hinckley, 1991).

The belief that public support and policy success are linked is a fourth reason why public opinion has an impact between elections. Abraham Lincoln once said that "with public sentiment, nothing can fail; without it nothing can succeed," and that view is still shared by presidents. As one State Department official recently put it, foreign policy makers "are people who have learned. . . . I think probably that the Sixites [the Vietnam war] were critical—that if you don't start with public opinion, you're going to end up losing" (Powlick, 1995:446).

One way to see the connection that policy makers believe exists between public support and policy success is to examine the degree to which presidents seek *consensus* (Meernik & Martinez, 1992; Wielhouwer, 1992). That consensus involves both public and congressional support because executive figures see the two as linked and reciprocal, with Congress both reflecting and helping to shape public opinion. A State Department official observed that it is "a great mistake . . . to lose Congress and the country—or the country and the Congress. You could take it in either order you want" (Rourke, 1983:117).

How Anticipating Public Opinion Affects Policy   It is difficult to show conclusively how anticipating public opinion affects foreign policy because presidents and other political leaders do not like to admit that they watch polls closely. Yet there is every evidence that policy makers take heed of public opinion as part of their complex political calculations. One State Department official disparaged the ability of yes-no type poll questions to reflect the complexities of policy choices, then added, "But by and large, polls do have an impact. They have a very noticeable impact" (Powlick, 1995:438). We can see this by looking at general public preferences, mass movements, and congressional reaction to public opinion using national security policy and a few other issues to provide examples of the informal power of public opinion.

General public preferences play a distinct role in determining national security policy (Hinckley, 1992; Blechman, 1990). The regular two-, four-, and six-year cycles of elections for the House of Representatives, the presidency, and the Senate tend to keep all political leaders focused on the domestic implications of foreign policy.

Research indicates that dramatic foreign policy initiatives tend to be rare during presidential election years, especially if an incumbent president is seeking reelection (Duncan, 1993; Kilgour, 1991). In fact, democracies are far more likely to get involved in wars shortly *after* elections than shortly before them because electoral pressures may force leaders to postpone inevitable entries into war until after elections (Gaubatz, 1991).

Public opinion is, of course, but one of many inputs that finally determine decisions in Washington, but it is possible to argue that public opinion has played a major restraint on actual or possible U.S. military interventions. General John Shalikashvili, chairman of the Joint Chiefs of Staff, recently told one unit of troops that, "like it or not, most of you will find yourselves in a place you never heard of, doing things you never wanted to do [such as fighting and dying]."[35] Perhaps, but that is less likely if the public has a say in the matter. The public had steadfastly opposed a number of possible U.S. interventions and is particularly adverse to having American soldiers killed in missions that the public finds dubious in the first place. After 18 army rangers were killed in Somalia, shocked public opinion forced President Clinton to announce a withdrawal date for U.S. forces from that country. Worry that a similar public reaction would take place if American troops were to suffer casualties in Haiti helped delay U.S. action against that country. "The threshold of casualties is so low," one official worried." You can lose 18 people if one helicopter goes down."[36] The same concern dampened the Clinton administration's early enthusiasm for sending troops to Bosnia. The problem, complained French general Philippe Morillon, is that Americans want "zero-dead wars."[37]

Some officials and other analysts complain about the public's supposed zero tolerance. "What struck me about Somalia was the appearance of shock and horror by many politicians that any Americans could die in service, as if now we're at a point in history where we regard death in the line of duty as abhorrent," worried one military historian.[38] That is not exactly the point, though. Rather, the point may well be that American tolerance for its sons and daughters returning home in body bags is at or near zero when the war is the result of a presidential initiative, rather than a national decision including strong public support and an authorization by Congress, or when the operation seems to have little chance of success.

If one assumes, however, that the operation is a multilateral one with a reasonable chance of success, the public's willingness to accept fatalities could increase sharply. Before the Dayton agreement for a Bosnia peace plan, an April 1995 poll asked respondents

> to imagine a scenario in which the United States participated in a large-scale U.N. intervention in Bosnia. In the scenario, 3,500 American troops are killed, but the operation succeeds in stopping ethnic cleansing and pacifying the region. Even with this number of fatalities, 60 per cent said they would feel that the U.N. had done "the right thing" by intervening. (Kull, 1996: 112)

So it may not be the case that Americans want "zero-dead wars." Instead, they insist that decisions to send U.S. troops into harm's way must be carefully planned to ensure reasonable chances for success. That planning process could be the result of national decisions which include input from Congress and the public, rather than just the president, or the careful deliberations of multilateral institutions like the UN or NATO.

In another area of national security, changes in levels of defense spending are based on shifts in U.S. public opinion, as well as on significant changes in the international environment (Hartley & Russett, 1991). Even more broadly, policies on arms control and disarmament, the use of military force, and other issues are adopted in large part because they gratify friends and disarm adversaries at home, not because they necessarily seem sensible in some abstract principle of the national interest abroad (Russett, 1990).

Congressional reaction to public opinion is also important to consider briefly before leaving the subject of how public opinion affects policy between elections. Congress gauges and anticipates public opinion, just as the executive branch does. Many members of Congress, just like other leaders, understand the usefulness of foreign aid and support it in theory. Those same legislators are also aware, though, of the public's antipathy to foreign aid and are hesitant about voting for it. This dilemma with respect to responding positively to the president's request for aid to Russia was explained by Representative David R. Obey (D-WI) after President Boris Yeltsin of Russia visited Congress. On the one hand, Obey noted, "the mood in the House is very receptive to Yeltsin." On the other hand, Obey continued, the mood is "still not very receptive to spending money abroad. . . . Conversations with Yeltsin don't impress people very much when you are back home in the district. . . . You still have to do a lot of hard work to bring people around to the idea of giving Russia aid."[39]

In general, the potential impact of public opinion on future elections is one of the key variables that concerns most members of Congress. When members favor a policy that the public opposes, the legislators ask themselves whether the voters will remember it during the next election and whether the unpopular stand will cost them their reelection. From this perspective, representatives and senators not only take into account the percentages of public opinion for or against a policy but also the intensity of the opinion. Many in Congress voted for the North American Free Trade Agreement (NAFTA), for example, even though they knew that public opinion opposed the measure. What made this negative opinion less worrisome to many legislators was the realization that the public was not intensely opposed to NAFTA. This was evident, among other places, in a poll taken just days before the vote. It found that of the respondents who were opposed to NAFTA, a reassuring 75 percent said that how their members of Congress voted on the NAFTA issue would not alone determine whether or not they would vote to reelect their representative or senator (Michaelson, 1995).

The nature of general public preferences as we have discussed them so far has been largely unstructured and generally passive, with politicians deriving cues from public opinion polls, letters, personal contacts with constituents, and through other ways in which opinion is conveyed. Sometimes, however, opinion becomes more organized and assertive in the form of mass movements.

Mass movements do not have the regular impact of general public preferences, but such movements can play a powerful role when they occur. A **mass movement** forms when a large segment of the public gets so aroused that those who advocate a change in government policy are able to organize it, begin media campaigns, and promote widespread demonstrations and other political activity to pressure governmental officials. In this way, regional and global conflict issues become matters of local interest, ensuring not only public activism but also public influence on policy makers (Cortright, 1993). We will examine mass movements by using three illustrations: the nuclear freeze, the anti–Vietnam War, and the pro–sanctions-on-South Africa movements.

The nuclear freeze campaign provides one good example of a mass movement (Hogan & Smith, 1991; Meyer, 1990). The notion of a bilateral, verifiable freeze on nuclear weapons acquisition and development arose in the late 1970s, then accelerated in reaction to President Reagan's reluctance to negotiate with the Soviets. In the 1980s, the "think globally, act locally" slogan motivated citizens in dozens of communities to press their city and state governments to take such actions as creating "nuclear-free zones" and endorsing a comprehensive ban on nuclear weapons tests (Hobbs, 1994). In 1982 referendums took place on the issue in 10 states, the District of Columbia, and 49 cities and counties, encompassing approximately 30 percent of all eligible voters. The results were strongly pro-freeze. Sixty percent of the voters endorsed a freeze in the legally nonbinding, but politically persuasive, referendums. They passed everywhere except in Arizona (Rourke, Hiskes, & Zirakzadeh, 1992). Additionally, hundreds of city councils also voted in favor of a nuclear freeze. Public support for the general concept of a freeze rose as high as 86 percent at one point. Reagan (1990:552) may have believed, as he sneered in his memoirs, that "well-meaning or not, the nuclear freeze movement had an agenda that could have been written in Moscow." But the movement had its impact. The effort worked especially to line up members of Congress behind the freeze campaign. The legislators, in turn, pressed the administration to negotiate more seriously in order to avoid legislative action (Overby, 1991). The House of Representatives in 1984 passed a concurrent resolution urging Reagan to negotiate a nuclear freeze. Such actions, coupled with the easing of the cold war, persuaded the administration to begin to negotiate more seriously with the Soviets. Reagan soon met with Soviet leader Mikhail Gorbachev, and in 1987 they signed the Intermediate-range Nuclear Forces (INF) Treaty. American and Soviet negotiators also began work on the first Strategic Arms Reduction Talks (START I), although the treaty did not reach fruition until 1991.

The Vietnam antiwar movement was an even more successful mass movement. Opposition to President Johnson's commitment of ground forces to Vietnam in 1965 began on college campuses and gradually spread outward to incorporate other elements of society. Soon chanting demonstrators were an almost constant presence in Lafayette Park, across from and within hearing distance of the White House. Johnson's daughter, Luci, remembers the chant: "I could hear it from my bedroom. I'd wake up in the morning with it—'Hey, hey, LBJ, how many kids did you kill today?' " The president could hear it too. He would go "over to the window" and come "back shaking his head," adviser Bill Moyers has recalled. " 'You know, they've attacked the country,' Johnson would say in anger and disbelief" (Miller, 1980:489).

Secretary of Defense Robert McNamara was also seared by the protests. Former first lady Jacqueline Kennedy exploded during one social conversation in which she and McNamara were discussing poetry. Turning suddenly on McNamara, she beat on his chest with her fists and cried out, "Do something to stop the slaughter!" Strangers also assailed the secretary of defense. A protester rushed up to McNamara, spat on him and shouted "Murderer!" while he was at a Seattle airport with his family. Another antiwar activist screamed "Baby burner! You have blood on your hands!" at McNamara as he ate in a restaurant with his wife. Most dramatically, a young Quaker, Norman R. Morrison, sat down on the grounds of the Pentagon within 40 feet of McNamara's office window, entrusted his infant daughter to the care of bystanders, doused himself with gasoline, and burned himself to death to protest the war. McNamara admits that he "reacted to the horror" by becoming tense and more reclusive; his wife, Marg, and his teenage son, Craig, developed ulcers.[40]

Even though a majority of Americans continued to support U.S. policy, the impact of the growing mass movement, according to White House journalist Max Frankel, was that "by late '66 early '67, the [president and his staff] felt beleaguered within this country. They felt themselves on the defensive on it all, and from the president on down" (Miller, 1980:488). By 1968 the combination of American combat losses in Vietnam and the chants of local antiwar groups were powerful enough to stop President Lyndon Johnson from running for reelection; presidential candidates thereafter debated how to get out of the war, not how to win it.

The new president, Richard Nixon, pledged withdrawal, but peace with honor was his standard. He pressed on and even intensified the war in an attempt to bomb the North Vietnamese into a malleable mood. As the war effort escalated, so did the opposition within the United States. The dissent experienced by the Johnson administration paled in comparison to the mass demonstrations and violence that rocked the Nixon White House. "The very fabric of the government was falling apart," national security adviser Henry Kissinger (1979:514) has recalled. "The Executive Branch was shell-shocked. After all, their children and their friends' children took part in the demonstrations" (1979:514). The mass movement encouraged and was reciprocally abetted by mounting opposition in Congress. Nixon and Kissinger knew they had to reach an agreement and get Americans out. They did.

A more recent and instructive example of a mass movement focused on the imposition of economic sanctions on South Africa. The Reagan policy of "constructive engagement" (quiet diplomatic persuasion) was not considered tough enough by many Americans who objected to South Africa's racist policy called apartheid. The efforts of blacks and other outraged Americans, led often by domestic civil rights groups (like the NAACP, the Urban League, and the Southern Christian Leadership Conference) and foreign policy groups (like TransAfrica), made opposition to investment in South Africa a popular issue (Solop, 1990). Popular pressure mounted on government and business to place sanctions on South Africa, including selling (divesting) all stocks, property, and other assets held in that country. Student protests became commonplace, prompting divestiture of university investments in South Africa. By the mid-1980s over 100 state and local governments had also divested, as had a number of corporations. As occurred with the nuclear freeze and the anti–Vietnam War mass movements, the upsurge of public sentiment activated Congress. Members who came from districts with liberal racial attitudes were especially likely to support sanctions. One study found, for example, that "the percentage of blacks in a congressional district strongly affected sanctions voting in Congress." Therefore, "Congressional votes for sanctions along domestic racial lines were 'rational' vis-à-vis [legislators'] constituents, who in the aggregate, thought along the same dimensions" (Hill, 1993:210). The result was that Congress enacted a series of economic sanctions against South Africa in 1986, then overrode the veto of President Reagan.

These three examples show that mass movements are like sandstorms in the desert. Though rare, they can significantly change the political landscape. On a more daily basis, nothing can hide the fact that what Americans think about foreign policy ultimately matters. These public preferences are watched carefully by executive and congressional actors with an eye to keeping within the realm of acceptable policy options. When the public goes to vote, foreign policy issues help guide them, whether they are choosing presidents or voting for members of Congress. The mix of officials elected affects the future direction of U.S. foreign policy, and the electoral cycle has its own foreign policy rhythms as well. Finally, between elections public opinion is constantly monitored by elected officials, and most try to stay comfortably within its confines of acceptable policy action.

Thus democracy is a force in foreign policy making just as it is in domestic policy making. It may not be tidy, and it may take a while to enact proposals acceptable to the majority, but it is evident that early studies that discounted any public role in foreign policy making were inaccurate. The testimony of policy makers and the considerable evidence amassed by scholars make two things clear. One is that public opinion counts in the foreign policy process. It regularly modifies, sometimes restrains, and occasionally prompts what the government does. It is also clear, however, that public opinion plays an inconsistent role. It is sometimes an active player; it is sometimes a passive audience. These realities bring us to our final major section and perhaps most important issue: What ought to be the role of public sentiment? Is its role about right? Should it be greater? Should it be diminished?

WHAT IS: THE QUALITY OF PUBLIC OPINION

To return to a point made earlier, there is a long-standing and intense debate over the degree to which democracy and foreign policy are compatible. There is almost no one who disputes the idea that the will of the people should play a strong role in domestic policy. At the same time, however, there are many who have doubts about how much popular input there should be into foreign policy. Speaking to a peacetime Parliament on November 11, 1947, British prime minister Winston Churchill contended that while "no one pretends that democracy is perfect or all wise," it is a better system of government than "all those other forms that have been tried from time to time." Yet it was the same Churchill who, earlier and amid the pressures of the German menace, could tell the House of Commons on September 30, 1941, that "nothing is more dangerous in wartime than to live in the temperamental atmosphere of a Gallup Poll, always feeling one's pulse and taking one's temperature." When leaders "keep their ears to the ground," the prime minister cautioned graphically, the nation "will find it very hard to look up to leaders who are detected in that somewhat ungainly posture."

Scholars who have written on the quality of public opinion and its proper role in foreign policy making are, like Churchill, divided. This diversity can be categorized, in broad terms, into two schools of thought, or images, about the public's foreign policy interest, knowledge, and insight. One image is a very dim view of the quality of public opinion and thus might be labeled the "public opinion as a great wasteland" thesis. The alternative image is a much more positive view of public opinion. This image can be termed the "public opinion as a fertile field" point of view. We will explore each of these images in turn, then ponder what they suggest about the role that opinion should play in foreign policy formation. To reiterate a point, the opinion we are discussing here is that held by the general public, as distinct from the elite.

Image I: Public Opinion as a Great Wasteland

During most of the post–World War II years, scholarship took a dim view of public opinion. The bulk of research findings have centered on two ideas. One is that the

FIGURE 13.1

Public Knowledge of Specific Information in 8 Countries

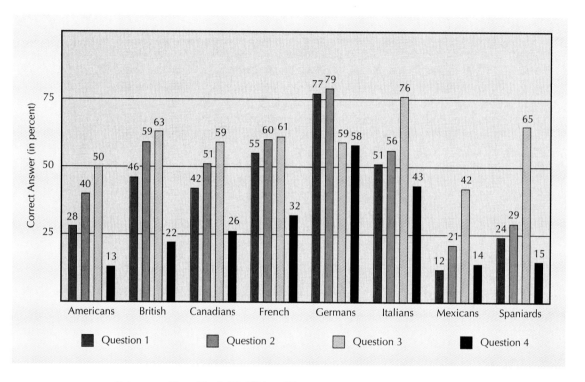

Data source: Time, March 28, 1994, p. 22.

Americans have poor specific information on world affairs and in a survey were less likely to answer the following four questions correctly in almost every case than were people in seven other countries: 1. Do you know the name of the ethnic group that has conquered much of Bosnia and has surrounded the city of Sarajevo? 2. Do you know the name of the group with which the Israelis recently reached a peace accord? 3. Who is the president of Russia? 4. Who is Boutros Boutros-Ghali?

public is apathetic—uninterested in and uninformed about foreign policy. The second is that, therefore, public opinion is unstable—irrational and volatile—and, as such, is an inadequate base on which to formulate foreign policy.

One recent and excellent review of public opinion and foreign policy traces the roots of skeptical scholarship on public opinion to what is called the *Almond-Lippmann consensus* (Holsti, 1992:439). This name is derived from the work of scholar Gabriel Almond and the views of pundit Walter Lippmann. Throughout the 1920s and 1930s, the Pulitzer Prize–winning columnist and author Walter Lippmann wrote several books, with titles such as *The Phantom Public* (1925), in which he scathingly denounced the quality of public opinion. Lippmann argued, for example, that "the unhappy truth is that the prevailing public opinion has been destructively wrong at critical junctions." What was more, he worried, "Mass opinion has acquired mounting power in this country. It has shown itself to be a dangerous master of decision when the stakes are life and death." Lippmann was no less contemptuous of politicians who responded to public opinion. He labeled those who "are sensitive to the vehemence and passion of mass sentiment" as "perpetual office seekers, always on trial for their political lives, . . . deprived of their independence" (Lippmann, 1935:20, 26).

Lippmann's journalistic view was given academic support by Almond, who published one of the earliest systematic studies of the relationship between public opinion and foreign policy in a 1950 book entitled *The American People and Foreign Policy*. Among other things, Almond's work showed that approximately 30 percent of the public knew virtually nothing about foreign policy issues. Another 45 percent had some limited knowledge, but only 25 percent could be called reasonably well-informed. Almond also concluded that the public was uninterested in foreign policy and that its opinions were unstable. "Often the public is apathetic when it should be concerned, and panicky when it should be calm," he later wrote (Holsti, 1992:443).

Ignorance is one characterization that has been used regularly to cast doubt on the quality of public opinion. The study of the public's factual knowledge has provided ample ammunition for those skeptical of public opinion. For one, Americans have a woeful grasp of geography. Surveys conducted in 1989 and 1995 by the National Geographic Society to test geography knowledge by asking people to locate places on a blank map yielded similar and dismal results. Among them, both surveys found an astounding 14 percent of American adults who could not point to the United States on the blank map. The 1989 survey showed that most people could not pinpoint (West) Germany, Japan, Sweden, or Vietnam. Twenty percent of those participating in the 1995 study could not name a single country in Europe.[41]

Knowledge about political events and actors is also often scanty. In the 1960s, only 25 percent of Americans knew China had a communist government; 25 percent were not aware that their country was fighting in Vietnam; 42 percent did not know that the United States was a member of the North Atlantic Treaty Organization (NATO); 38 percent thought that the Soviet Union was a NATO member.

Things have not improved. In 1993, just six weeks before Congress was to vote on the North American Free Trade Agreement (NAFTA), 62 percent of those polled said "no" when asked, "Do you know what NAFTA is?"[42] At about the same time, with U.S. troops fighting and dying in Somalia, 43 percent of the public did not know that Somalia was in Africa.[43] In 1994 only a third of the public knew that the leading candidate for the Mexican presidency had been assassinated, and just one in five Americans knew NATO air strikes had been launched against Bosnian Serb forces.[44] As Figure 13.1 shows, the foreign affairs knowledge of Americans does not compare very favorably with that of the citizens of other countries. Out of eight countries sampled in 1994, Americans finished somewhere between sixth and last in their ability to answer four current events questions.

This dearth of knowledge has policy ramifications, as the lack of popularity of foreign aid among Americans illustrates. Seventy-five percent of Americans believe that the United States spends "too much" on foreign aid; only 4 percent say "too little." That is not surprising in a way, because 41 percent of Americans think that aid is the single largest federal budget expenditure. Indeed, the average American thinks that foreign aid consumes 15 percent of the federal budget. If that were true, it would mean an annual aid budget in the $225 billion range, rather than the $15 billion or so that actually goes to aid, which is only 1 percent of the budget. When Americans were asked what would be about the right percentage of the budget to devote to foreign aid, the average answer was 5 percent. When asked to imagine that they had discovered that aid really accounts for only 1 percent of the budget, which is the actual percentage, most changed their negative view of the level of aid giving. In this case, 46 percent thought the amount was "about right" and 34 percent thought it was "too little."[45] What seems obvious, then, is that foreign aid would receive more public support and, by inference, congressional appropriations if the public knew how little of American wealth actually goes overseas in the form of aid. But the public does not, and that, complains J. Brian Atwood, the beset director of the U.S. Agency for International Development (USAID), means that "it has been possible for demagogues, isolationists, and populists—some all in the same person—to exploit public misperceptions to attack the aid program."[46]

Lack of interest is another reason cited by critics of a greater public role in foreign policy making, and it probably accounts for the ignorance of basic foreign affairs facts that have been detailed above. Surveys regularly show that foreign policy issues are normally low on the priority list of what concerns most Americans. Domestic issues, those that Americans see as directly affecting their lives, almost always rank higher. A series of surveys between 1981 and 1991, which asked Americans to name the most important issue facing the country, found that only an average of 9 percent of the respondents identified some international concern as the most crucial.[47] Even during times of military tension, public attention wanes. A survey taken on November 6, 1990, when the U.S. troop buildup for the Persian Gulf War was already under way, found that only about 6 percent of all respondents said that Iraq was the issue that "mattered the most." The environment, education, crime/drugs, and abortion were issues of greater concern to Americans.[48]

Another indicator of this lack of interest is reflected in Americans' attention to news in general. One media estimate of its own impact concluded glumly "that much of the American public has simply tuned out the news. . . . These people see journalists as messengers from a world that doesn't much interest them."[49] Most Americans do not read newspapers regularly, instead getting their news primarily from television and radio. Even then, their attention is focused primarily on local news events, sensational exposés (like the O. J. Simpson murder case), or tabloid and talk-show broadcasts rather than on routine coverage of national or international events. Only one in four Americans closely follow national and international news, and they are demographically atypical. They are markedly older, better educated, and higher paid than most other Americans; in short, they are a clear minority of the total population.

Unstable and irrational are yet other characterizations of the public by those who share the Almond-Lippmann consensus and deem public opinion to be a great wasteland. This is an attitude that has long persisted. Alexander Hamilton, for example, opposed direct popular control of the government on the grounds that "the people are turbulent and changing; they seldom judge or determine right" (McKenna, 1994:360). Some modern surveys can be used to support the skeptics' suspicions. Presidents, for example, ride a roller coaster of public opinion. President Carter's public approval rating varied by 45 percent in his four years in the White House; President Reagan's rating swung up and down 35 percent. Amid the glow of victory over Iraq in early 1991, George Bush's public approval rating approached 89 percent, the highest in known presidential history. Less than 2 years later, the voters dismissed him from office with just a little more than a third of the popular vote. Studies show that the public can also change its mind rapidly on some issues. Before the United States invaded Panama in December 1989, only 32 percent of the public supported such a move; 83 percent said that they agreed with the action once it had occurred (Jentleson, 1992:55).

There is, then, a wide variety of opinion, substantiated by considerable scholarship, that views the American public with great skepticism. Statesman and Pulitzer Prize–winning scholar George Kennan (1951:59) has derisively described democracy as "similar to one of those prehistoric monsters with a body as long as this room and a brain the size of a pin" that "lies there in his primeval mud and pays little attention to his environment." The inference is that the public would be slow to respond to threats or opportunities in the international environment, but when eventually motivated, it would react as mindlessly as Kennan imagined dinosaurs might. To those like Kennan and Walter Lippmann, greater public involvement in foreign policy making could be disastrous. The public simply does not know enough to be trusted with important foreign policy decisions. There are others, however, who disagree and who see public opinion as a fertile field rather than as a great wasteland. It is to this more optimistic assessment of the public that we can now turn our attention.

Image II: Public Opinion as a Fertile Field

Increasingly in recent years, the negative opinion of the public has been challenged by those who see public opinion as a fertile field that can and does provide a valuable input into the foreign policy process (Ripley, 1994; Peffley & Hurwitz, 1992). According to a number of recent studies, the mass public has not been given the credit it deserves (Kull, 1996; Nincic, 1992a; Popkin, 1991; Stimson, 1991). The political scientists who have written these works contend that the public does, in fact, possess enough knowledge to hold coherent views on foreign policy issues. The thrust of this literature, as one reviewer puts it, is that "as a general rule, popular preferences are sensibly related to the sound conduct of foreign policy" (Nincic, 1992b:772). Or, as another analyst put it after an extended study of public opinion and foreign policy, "There is plenty that suggests that the public as a whole will express structured and sensitive opinions on foreign policy matters" (Hinckley, 1992:131).

The shift in the view of many political scientists about public opinion is based in part on two factors. First, the end of the cold war changed the prioritization of foreign policy problems, and this allowed for greater public involvement in foreign policy. From 1949–1989, the biggest foreign policy threat was global annihilation as a result of a strategic nuclear war. This threat made the major focus of U.S. foreign policy "too dangerous," and its details "too technological," for the public to be trusted with a significant voice. After that strategic nuclear threat disappeared, the important issues in foreign policy became things like trade, aid, immigration, humanitarian concerns, and localized regional conflicts. Some of these topics affected many Americans in direct ways and mobilized them to speak out. Thus, foreign policy became less an elitist task and more a "grass-roots" activity (Clough, 1994).

Second, this greater appreciation for the importance of public opinion in foreign policy making also stems from a reevaluation of research methods (Gaubatz, 1993). Many of the studies that characterize public opinion as uninterested, ignorant, and volatile draw their inferences from readily available public opinion measures, such as questions about what is the "most important problem" facing the country, knowledge of factual information, and presidential support (popularity) scores. Scholars with a positive view of the public argue that it is necessary to go beyond such surface impressions of public opinion to evaluate it accurately. These scholars look at factors such as the stability of general public attitudes toward broad foreign policy orientations rather than specific policy details. This line of inquiry also tries to measure public attitudes against different policy options to see if the public is consistent and to measure changes in public opinion over time against changes in the political world to see if the shifts in public sentiment are reasonable reflections of dynamic global trends (Peffley & Hurwitz, 1993).

Stable is how studies increasingly characterize public opinion. One pair of scholars, for example, has focused on the public's responses to specific foreign policy alternatives (Page & Shapiro, 1992). By doing so, they have obtained a very different picture of public opinion. They show that mass public opinion about the specifics of foreign policy was quite stable over the 1935–1985 period. On broad orientations, such as internationalism and isolationism, changes in public opinion were relatively infrequent. Moreover, when shifts occurred, the degree of change was limited and gradual. On more specific issues, changes were reasonable. For example, the same two scholars in an earlier study looked at attitudes toward defense spending and discovered that the percentage of Americans in favor of more defense spending declined beginning in the late 1960s as Americans reacted against the Vietnam War and as President Richard Nixon and Soviet leader Leonid Brezhnev pursued a policy of détente. Support for more defense spending gradually increased (but remained a minority opinion) after a low in 1973, but then rose to a majority in the 1979–1980 period marked by the Iranian hostage crisis, the Soviet invasion of Afghanistan, and other foreboding events. Then, as events became less worrisome and as Soviet-American relations improved, American public support for more defense spending tailed off sharply. It is possible, of course, to argue interminably about the rights or wrongs of more, the same, or less defense spending. The point that these two scholars make, however, is that their research goes "a long way toward refuting any assertion that collective opinion moves in capricious or inexplicable ways." Instead, they found that "virtually all changes in Americans' foreign policy preferences over the last half century are understandable in terms of changing circumstances or changing information" (Shapiro & Page, 1988:243).

Other studies confirm such conclusions (Jordan & Page, 1992). One review of public attitudes over a 12-year period (1978–1990) on 11 different policy issues, ranging from containing communism, through protecting American business abroad, to preventing the spread of nuclear weapons, found relative opinion stability (Chittick, Billingsley, & Travis, 1993). The average spread over the years between the highest and the lowest percentages of the public that characterized each of the 11 policies as a "very important" foreign policy goal was only 12.2 percent. Of the 11 policies, five varied less than 10 percent and none varied more than 20 percent. Given the amazing changes in the international system during this period, as the cold war melted and then vanished, it would be odd if opinions had not varied somewhat! Finally, the stability of public opinion is evidenced further by the fact that during the same period and on the same 11 issues, the opinions of elites varied by an average of 14.8 percent, a 2.6 percent wider spread than that of the general public.

Reasonable is another adjective that some scholars apply to public opinion. According to one analyst, as the cold war eased and as the nuclear arsenals grew, most Americans gave up their desire for nuclear superiority and became "neither hawks nor doves, but . . . [wise] owls," who were "ready to settle for a balance of power in a realist's world" (Russett, 1991:537).

405

What Ought to
Be: Thinking
about Public
Opinion and
Policy

Recent research also finds the public generally responsible about the use of military force. After studying reactions to the possible use of force throughout the post–Vietnam War years, one scholar concluded that Americans are a "pretty prudent public" (Jentleson, 1992:49). Various analyses recognize that Americans are apt to rally to support a president in an acute crisis. More generally, though, recent research finds that the likelihood of a majority of Americans supporting the use of force depended on specific circumstances such as the source, target, and nature of a threat, the availability of peaceful and multilateral military options, and the anticipated costs and chances of success of a military intervention (Richman, 1995). Americans, the data shows, are most likely to support force when an antagonist had "gone beyond simply posing a standing threat and [had] initiated aggressive actions against American interests or citizens." This reaction is distinct from situations when the "principal objective" is to "remake the government of another country." In these cases, the American public is "disinclined to support the use of limited military force" (Jentleson, 1992:64). Such findings make the public's unwillingness to get directly involved in the civil war in Bosnia more easily understandable. The ability of the public to favor or oppose force based on a specific circumstance also is reflected in the fact that 65 percent of Americans in one survey were willing to use U.S. troops "to help move UN peacekeepers to safer positions in Bosnia."[50] A 1995 poll showed that 60 percent of the public would accept 3,500 U.S. casualties if they were part of a UN peacekeeping operation that ended the bloodshed and ethnic cleansing in the region. This general argument, that the public views such cases based on their specific circumstances, is further supported by the fact that Americans softened their opposition to intervention in Haiti, but a majority remained opposed to a U.S. military presence even after the intervention was carried out successfully.[51]

Based on such research, it is not surprising to take a stand that "question[s] the traditional view of the public as boorish, overreactive, and generally the bane of those who would pursue an effective foreign policy." It is possible to concede that most Americans do not make "sophisticated calculations" or have complex "analytical distinctions in their thought processes," yet still be confident that, however they arrive at it, and however they might attempt to articulate it, Americans do appear to have a much more pragmatic sense of strategy than they are given credit for (Jentleson, 1992:71). Insofar as this assessment is accurate, it means that the public may well be taking an approach to the world that is actually prudent when it comes to the use of military force.

The public response to noncrisis foreign policy issues has also been examined. The box entitled "The Stability of American Public Opinion" provides one example of public choices on a series of budgetary alternatives. Here again, the commentary supports the notion that public opinion is indeed coherent and stable.

WHAT OUGHT TO BE: THINKING ABOUT PUBLIC OPINION AND POLICY

As we conclude this chapter on public opinion and foreign policy, there are two things to think about. One is how the role of opinion may change in the future. The other is what you think the role of public opinion ought to be.

The Stability of American Public Opinion

One way to understand the stability of public opinion over time is to examine public support for federal budget options. The National Opinion Research Center (NORC) conducts a survey most years asking questions about 15 different portions of the federal budget, ranging from spending on foreign policy issues like military outlay and foreign aid to domestic issues, such as improving the educational system. The NORC surveys asked respondents to indicate whether they think the government is spending too little, about the right amount, or too much on each of the 15 or so budget items. Three of these are shown in Figure 13.2.

The NORC surveys show a striking degree of consistency in public opinion on foreign aid. From 1973 to 1994 the "spending too much" category was the strong majority position each year, with at least 66 percent of the respondents giving that answer. Moreover, in line with studies that link public preferences with foreign policy, it should not be surprising that foreign aid is unpopular on Capitol Hill or that U.S. foreign aid expenditures relative to gross national product rank the lowest among the advanced industrialized nations.

Responses regarding military spending are somewhat more volatile, but they do not change dramatically from year to year. Support seems to vary directly with general impressions of the nature of the international environment. For instance, 1980 (the year immediately following the Soviet invasion of Afghanistan and during the Iran hostage crisis) was the only year when a majority of the respondents felt that the United States was spending too little on defense. In all but 2 years, the "about right" category was the dominant response.

In a third budget category, it is interesting to note that concern over the environment is not some faddish development of the late 1980s and early 1990s. In every year since 1973, the spending "too little" category was the most frequently chosen response in the NORC survey. President Bush tried to paint then–vice presidential candidate Al Gore as an "econut," an environmental extremist, during the 1992 campaign. But, in fact, Gore was more in tune with public sentiments than was Bush.

Potential changes in the public role is the first point. One would be hard-pressed to deny that the cold war period was radically different from any the United States had previously experienced. First atomic weapons, then intercontinental ballistic missiles threatened to end civilization as we know it. The strength of the militarily powerful, ideologically inimical Soviet Union added to the sense of dread. A measure of gut-wrenching fear gave the United States the will to lead an international effort to protect itself and its friends. Postwar prosperity gave Americans the way to pay the costs of such leadership. The United States became a global superpower.

In that atmosphere and amid the anticommunist consensus, the public's voice was muted. The threat to national survival caused most Americans to place high levels of trust in their government, particularly the president, and in the foreign policy "experts" drawn from the intellectual establishment centered along a Yale-Harvard-New York-Washington corridor. But the political world has changed dramatically. According to one estimate:

> As long as the Cold War endured and nuclear Armageddon seemed only a missile away, the public was willing to tolerate such an undemocratic foreign policy making system. But . . . the world is no longer so menacing. . . . With

406

407

What Ought to
Be: Thinking
about Public
Opinion and
Policy

FIGURE 13.2   Public Opinion on Foreign Aid, Defense Spending,
and Environmental Spending

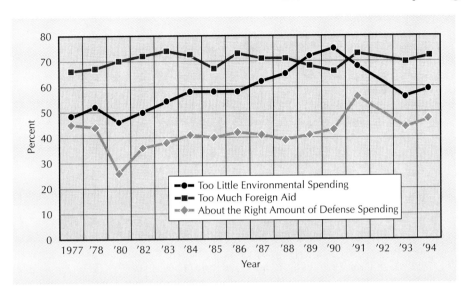

Note: The question asked, in part, was: "Are we spending too much, too little, or about the right amount on foreign aid, defense, and the environment?" The questions were not asked in 1979, 1981, and 1992.

Data source: NORC polls courtesy of the Roper Center, the University of Connecticut.

Surveys of public opinion on many issues are relatively stable over extended periods of time.

the Soviet Union residing in the dustbin of history and the United States reigning as the world's largest debtor . . . the public is no longer willing to trust the experts to make the right decisions when it comes to the lives of their sons and daughters, especially when the experts themselves are so deeply divided. The result is that the wall separating foreign affairs from domestic influences has come crumbling down. . . . And the old foreign policy making system, no longer insulated by fear and prosperity, is more susceptible than ever to societal pressures. (Clough, 1994:4)

These changes have produced two consequences. First, to resurrect a phrase from the 1920s, the end of the bipolar era of confrontation has brought about a sense of a "return to normalcy" for most Americans. Returning to normalcy includes a decline in the extraordinary willingness to give deference to executive authority. One indicator of such reduced deference is the public's increasing clamor for changes in the government's classification system. Displaying less trust in their political leaders than before, many Americans now want old secrets declassified and procedures changed to make it harder to classify new ones. It is difficult to criticize or change policy if "top secret" stamps keep citizens from learning what their government is doing. "When we invoke national security as the basis for classification, we are asking for public trust that what is being done is in the best interest of the nation and the people," a group of public officials recently noted. Unfortunately, the group's report continued, "that trust has been violated too many times."[52] Americans were appalled, for example, when they learned that their government had conducted 204 secret nuclear tests, about 20 percent of all such tests. The public might have accepted this in the cold war atmosphere. In the post–cold war era, Secretary of Energy Hazel R. O'Leary, whose agency conducts the tests, confessed that news of the tests "gave me an ache in my gut and my heart."[53] Increasingly, a presidential policy declaration no longer ends public debate on either a foreign policy issue or the appropriateness of the administration's response.

Second, the political empowerment of groups that have been long disenfranchised, legally or extralegally, is another factor that may well lead to greater public interest and participation in the foreign policy process. The chapter on interest groups noted, for instance, the rise in the political activity on foreign policy questions of African Americans and Latinos/as.

Women provide another apt illustration. Surveys dating from the 1940s and extending to the present continue to show that "fewer women than men are attentive to foreign affairs, at least measured by knowledge and awareness" (Brandes, 1993:3). But this gender gap reasonably may not be as wide as it seems. To the extent that it exists, the gap may result from persistent attitudes about appropriate male and female roles. Research indicates that men are more reluctant than women to admit that they are not interested in and do not know about foreign affairs. This is substantiated by the higher percentage of men who express opinions (so-called pseudo-opinions) on imaginary political matters sometimes inserted in surveys as control devices. Conversely, the lower overall sense of political efficacy (confidence that their political views count) in women may also mean that they underreport their interest in foreign policy. One clue that this may be true is the fact that women are more likely to express concern about national security issues. Men may say that they are more interested, but they are less likely to say that they "care" about the issue. This concern factor also shows up in factual knowledge. The data also shows that on factual questions about nuclear weapons and policy in the 1960s, virtually no gap existed between men and women.

These facts and trends relating to the gender gap seem to mean several things. One is that male-female differences may not be as wide as many surveys seem to show. As the same scholar advises, "one should be cautious in discussing gender differences. . . . Who cares . . . depends on how you ask the question" (Brandes, 1993:18). Second, as women move increasingly into the mainstream of all aspects of American political life, their political efficacy will rise, resulting in an increased willingness to make the effort to acquire information and to express an opinion.

Indications that the public and various segments of it are becoming more aware of and active on foreign policy are offset by other signs that interest and participation remain tentative or ambivalent. An upsurge of public support for a greater congressional role following the Vietnam War and Watergate was short-lived. By the late 1970s, polls found both an increasing number of people who blamed Congress for contributing to foreign policy failures and declining public support for a strong congressional role. Even more recent polls show that the public is still uncertain and divided when asked if Congress should be more influential in U.S. policy. One poll found that 49 percent of the respondents favored a greater legislative role; an equal 49 percent disagreed. Actually, just 26 percent had a strong opinion either way, while 74 percent "somewhat" thought yes or no or had no view (Myers, 1989). Similarly, a pair of polls found an increase from 22 percent to 28 percent between 1990 and

409

What Ought to
Be: Thinking
about Public
Opinion and
Policy

1994 in those who think that Congress has too much say in foreign policy. A small majority think that the balance is about right, and just over 20 percent believe Congress should play a stronger role (Rielly, 1995, 1991).

During the 1990–1991 Persian Gulf crisis, opinion reflected this division. One poll found that 68 percent of Americans thought that the president should use force only with congressional authorization.[54] Yet there was no general outcry against the president's failure to ask Congress for support until the last moment. The president's approval rating increased each time he moved decisively; and, in the glow of victory, 86 percent of Americans said that they had more confidence in the presidency than before the war.[55]

During the debate over intervention in Bosnia, the public once again favored congressional authorization as a prerequisite of the president's committing U.S. forces. Yet even though 60 percent of those surveyed took this position, there was little negative reaction when Clinton acted unilaterally.[56]

Thus it is unclear if there is any change in the offing for public opinion. The passing of the cold war and the concomitant easing of the sense of threat should increase the willingness of the public to differ with its political leaders. Yet the confidence of the public in its role and in the role of its elected representatives in Congress remains unsteady.

Desirable change is the second point to ponder. Given all you have just read, what do you think the role of the citizenry should be? One thing to avoid, when thinking about the debate over the quality and proper role of public opinion and policy, is the temptation to deride or exalt public opinion simply because you disagree or agree with it. Separating your values from your evaluation is tricky, and it may be that even scholars have been influenced by their own standards as well as by the evidence. Scholars, political leaders, and members of the elite are, as mentioned, much more likely than the public to be internationalists. As a result, commentators have sometimes assumed that the more nationalistic, even isolationist, leanings of average Americans mean that their judgment is deficient. Gabriel Almond, for one, fell into that trap, commenting in his 1950 book that "the undertow of withdrawal [from global affairs] is very powerful. Deeply ingrained [isolationist] habits do not die easy deaths." The American people, he feared, had not "fully digested" the "tragic lessons of the last decade" wrought by isolationism. Therefore, Almond concluded, "perhaps the gravest general problem confronting policymakers is that of the instability of mass moods," which threatened to lapse back into isolationism and destroy the newfound internationalist "policy stability" (Holsti, 1992:442).

Another common idea to avoid when deciding what ought to be the role of public opinion is to imagine that some sort of enduring, transcendent wisdom exists within the narrow geography of the nation's capital—inside the beltway. We have already pointed out too many questionable decisions by political leaders to belabor this point further.

Apart from avoiding these and a few other obvious pitfalls, there is no easy standard by which to decide about the appropriate public role in the foreign policy process. You need to think about that and decide for yourself based on your understanding of how democracy should work, your estimate of what the requirements of a successful foreign policy are, and your judgment of the quality of the citizenry as a whole.

To end where we began, the essential issue is one of democracy. Who should decide on the course of foreign policy? When making your judgments bear in mind that ignoring the global drama and not caring who writes the script for the American part does not mean that the play will stop or that the action will not affect you. Prince Klemens von Metternich, the great Austrian foreign minister during the Napoleonic era, once wrote that policy "is like a play in many acts, which unfolds inevitably once the curtain is raised. To declare then that the performance will not take place is an absurdity. The play will go on, either by means of the actors . . . or by means of the spectators who mount the stage" (Kissinger, 1957:41). The key question, then, is about your role: Will you be an actor or spectator?

SUMMARY

1. The examination of public opinion in foreign policy making is marked by two basic questions: *What is* the role of public opinion and *what ought* it to be?

2. Before examining public opinion's role, its fragmented nature must be recognized. Important divisions in public opinion exist: divisions between elites and masses, between demographic groups (based on traits like age, race, and gender), between liberals and conservatives, between belief structures (like the differences between isolationists, accommodationists, hard-liners, and comprehensive internationalists), and between unilateralists and multilaterists. Thus public opinion is really the amalgamation of the opinions of many different groups or publics.

3. What is the role of public opinion? At times it is passive. The public often serves as an audience, watching others such as the president in the presidential model, bureaucrats in the administrative model, and congressional, bureaucratic, and interest group representatives in the subgovernment model. This reactive role is well captured by the rally effect, the notion that public opinion temporarily jumps sharply in support of the president in times of crisis or great stress. At other times, the opinions of various publics play an active role in creating foreign policy. These cases are reflected in the political model.

4. How does public opinion affect foreign policy? First, public opinion affects who gets elected by highlighting popular candidates or candidates with popular ideas. As the people who make up the government change, what the government does in foreign policy usually changes as well.

5. The second way public opinion affects policy is through anticipated reaction between elections. Both the president and members of Congress try to anticipate general public opinion, or how their relevant specific publics feel about issues, and then act accordingly. Politicians do this for a variety of reasons: to help their own reelection chances, because they believe that popularity with the public enhances their political power or their chances for policy making success, or just because they believe in democracy. Occasionally mass movements arise regarding a foreign policy issue, a factor that makes assessing public attitudes very easy for political leaders.

6. What should the role of public opinion be in foreign policy making? Many studies show that the public often knows little about the details of foreign policy, and consequently some observers argue that public opinion should have little role in the policy process. However, when one gets past an emphasis on details and focuses on the bigger picture, new studies show that public attitudes about the general dimensions of foreign policy are far more consistent, rational, and prudent than most political scientists previously thought. From this point of view, public input into the foreign policy making process should be welcomed, as it veers policy away from extremes and keeps policy confined to centrist, moderate responses to foreign events.

7. The question for public opinion in the future is not whether it will continue to change as the international system changes, but how it should change. It is up to you to answer that question.

APPENDIX 1
WRITING THE GREAT AMERICAN TERM PAPER

Writing a term paper is one of the most common requirements for an upper-division course such as the one for which this book was probably assigned. Such term papers usually count for a significant part of your final grade. Yet many, perhaps most, students have never received formal instruction about how to write a good research report. The following pages are meant to help you write an A paper by giving you some guidelines about how to go about your research and writing.

Why do instructors assign papers? Answering this question is a good place to start thinking about term papers because if you know why papers are such a common assignment, then perhaps you can approach the task with added enthusiasm and dedication. Two goals usually motivate this assignment. One goal relates to the specific subject of the course; the other goal is based on your professional development. The first course-specific goal is to increase your expertise in some particular substantive area. The amount that you learn from this or almost any other course will be expanded significantly by doing research and by writing a paper. The effort will allow you to delve into the intricacies of a specific topic far beyond what is possible in the no doubt broad lectures that your instructor must deliver in class. Your research will go beyond the necessarily general commentary found in this text.

The second and probably more important goal behind a paper-writing assignment extends beyond the specific content of the course. The object is to sharpen your analytic and writing skills in preparation for the professional career that you may wish to pursue after graduation. Do not underestimate the importance of such thinking and communications skills. Most professional positions that college graduates seek will eventually require that you find information, analyze it, and convey your conclusions and recommendations to others, including your boss. You will be judged by your product. A survey of ranking business executives a few years ago asked them what accounted for the rise of their most successful young subordinates compared to the failure or slow progress of other junior executives. Communications skills was one of the factors most mentioned by the top executives. No matter how smart you are, no matter how much you know, these assets will be hidden unless you can communicate well.

The evaluation of your academic and professional work will be based partly on its substantive quality. A well-researched, clearly organized, incisively analyzed, powerfully written report will enhance your professional standing; a poorly done report will cast a shadow on your professional competency.

It is also important to realize that your report will be judged in part by such standards as neatness, grammar, and spelling, and other such technical criteria. It is not uncommon for university instructors to get papers that represent a good research and analytical effort but that are sloppy, contain numerous grammatical errors, are full of misspellings, or are burdened by other such technical deficiencies. Such short-comings make *you* look bad. It is very difficult for an instructor (or, later on, your boss) to be dazzled by your intellectual acumen while being simultaneously appalled by your English usage. Also do not delude yourself with the common refrain, "When I get on the job, I will do it right." It takes practice to do things well. That is true for rollerblading, shooting baskets, and playing the guitar. It is also true for doing a research paper. Now, in college, is the time to practice and learn. Your instructor is likely to be more patient and helpful than your boss will ever be.

Getting Started

Most successful efforts require some planning. Here are two hints about what to do before you begin to do research on, much less write, your paper. Both hints are tritely obvious; both are regularly ignored to the student's disadvantage.

1. *Follow instructions.* Your instructor will (or at least should) let you know what is expected. Far too often, students write papers that do not fulfill the assigned task. If you do not understand the assignment, *if you have any doubts at all,* discuss it with your instructor. It is not uncommon in class or on the job for a person to get in-structions, to not understand them, but to be reluctant to ask for clarification for fear of seeming "dumb." This is a significant error. In the first place, your boss will probably not think less of you for asking for clarification. In the second place, asking for supplementary instructions is far, far better than doing a report that does not meet the needs of your boss and is not what he or she wanted. That *really* makes you look dumb.

2. *Do not wait until the last minute.* Last-minute efforts usually read like last-min-ute efforts! Plan backward from the date the paper is due to allow plenty of time to get it done. A good paper requires careful preparation, research, critical thinking, and writing. These steps take time. Also, allow time for the unexpected. Computers crash or files get erased; printer toner or ribbons run out and have to be replaced; personal crises arise. You need to be able to cope with these and still get the paper done on time. "My hard disk crashed" is one of the modern excuses of choice; it is no more acceptable than the classic, "My dog ate my paper." Being late with reports in class or on the job is a very, very bad idea.

Choosing a Topic

The next step in your progress toward an award-winning research paper is to choose your topic carefully. If you are responsible for choosing your own topic, put some thought into this decision. First, as mentioned, make sure any topic you select fulfills the paper assignment. Second, if possible pick a topic that interests you. The more interested you are in a topic, the easier it will be for you to devote time and energy to studying it and to writing about it. Third, ensure that you select a topic that fits the length of the paper that you intend to write, the research resources that are available to you, and your analytical tools.

Length: If you attempt to write a 10-page paper entitled "The President and Congress Struggle for Power: Two Centuries of Constitutional Conflict," then your paper is destined to be "a mile wide and an inch deep," as they say. It is better to do something more narrowly focused and to do it well than to give a superficial treatment of a large subject.

Research Resources: Trying to write a paper on "Secret Military Operations in the Persian Gulf War" would also be a mistake because the government has not released the relevant information. You should take the holdings of your library into account. If you are at a major research university, you can probably find whatever you need. Even at large libraries, however, you may have trouble finding good sources to support a research paper on U.S.–Sri Lankan relations or U.S. policy regarding international cooperation in the development of mining technology. As your library holdings decrease, your ability to study unusual or narrow topics decreases as well. So be careful not to choose a topic that destines you to fail.

Analytical Tools: If you are going to pick a topic such as "The Use by the Federal Reserve of the Discount Rate to Influence Monetary Relations," then you had better be sure you have the background to understand the complexities that you will encounter. Similarly, ensure that you have the proper statistical skills if you are going to analyze votes in Congress to see whether length of service, party affiliation, constituency interest, or the margin of victory is most closely associated with a senator's support of presidential proposals.

For all of these issues, *rule number 1* here and throughout this writing guide is *check with the instructor* if there is any doubt in your mind. Indeed, it is a very good idea to write a paragraph on what you intend to analyze, show it to the professor, and get his or her reaction.

Doing the Research

Now the project begins in earnest. Good research is the foundation of your paper. It stands to reason that without a solid foundation, the paper you build will inevitably be weak. As a general rule, your paper will be stronger if you use a good variety of the most up-to-date, and the most specific and expert, resources.

The Library: The place to do research is the library. Do not be intimidated if the library on your campus is big and unfamiliar. Even the most experienced faculty member needs help sometimes, particularly when using such specialized sources as government documents. The good news is that assistance is readily available. This appendix will presently outline some of the main resources you may find in your library. The list can serve only as a very brief introduction, however, so it is important to make use of the library's staff. When you get lost, as we all do, ask the nearest librarian for help. Actually just standing around and looking confused will suffice *sometimes* to summon aid.

Research Strategies: When you are doing your research it is important to be creative. Here are a few tips:

1. *Start out by reading a general study or two on your subject.* This will give you a broad grasp of your topic and will help you identify what is important and on what you need to focus your research. Simply jumping in and beginning to do research in specialized studies can often waste a considerable amount of your time. Textbooks can also be helpful. For many topics, one starting point might be a U.S. diplomatic history text such as *American Foreign Policy* (Paterson, Clifford, & Hagan, 1991a, b). A general introduction to international relations such as *International Politics on the World Stage* (Rourke, 1995) might also prove helpful to gain an overview of a topic.

2. *Treat research like a detective story.* Search under a variety of subject headings when looking for sources in the physical or computerized card catalog, in an index, or any other finding aid. If, for example, you are doing a paper on Vietnam, do not limit yourself to looking under "V" for Vietnam. Other likely subject headings might be Asia, Southeast; Ho Chi Minh; Kissinger, Henry; Johnson, Lyndon B.; Nixon, Richard M.; U.S.–Foreign Relations; or U.S.–History.

3. *Look at the most recent books and journal articles first.* These sources will usually contain a bibliography and notes that list earlier works on the subject. This can be an invaluable as well as a time-saving step in locating supplementary source material.

4. *Photocopy important material.* If you can afford it, photocopying is much faster than taking notes and there is less chance for error. If you take written notes, use index cards. Larger cards are better than smaller ones. Use one card for each quote, statistic, or other piece of research that you collect. Cards work well because they can be arranged easily. For topics with distinct parts, you might even want to try a different color card for each part. Some people use portable computers to take notes. If you do, be sure to make a backup copy on a floppy disk.

5. *Make a careful and complete notation of the source of your material.* Later on we will cover why and how to cite material, but there is nothing more frustrating than having to go back to the library to look up a citation that you should have noted clearly and completely in the first place.

Research Resources

Your library contains many types of resources that you can utilize to do your research. The following list is a mere beginning. Use it, but also go to your library, wander about a bit looking at its various sections and the resources that each contains, and ask librarians about what is available. You may be surprised at how many resources you discover.

Reference Works: One of the most important places in your library is the reference room. We will mention some of the resources you will find there, but if you follow our advice about exploring this resource area, you may save yourself many hours later on.

The materials in the reference room are valuable resources for beginning to structure the basic outline of your topic. Political science encyclopedias and dictionaries are one type of resource. There are many. For an American foreign policy course you might wish to look at sources such as the *Dictionary of American Diplomatic History* (Findling, 1989) or, at the most general level of political science, you might wish to consult *The Encyclopedic Dictionary of American Government* (Dushkin, 1991). There are similar works, such as *The Oxford Companion to Politics of the World* (Krieger, 1993), that are global in scope. Then there are resources such as *Editorial Research Reports,* the *Political Handbook of the World,* or the *Index to International Public Opinion* that deal with particular topics, give summaries of various governments, or take other specialized approaches. Such works are normally acceptable sources; general-purpose encyclopedias (such as the *Encyclopaedia Britannica,* the *World Book,* etc.) typically are not suitable, although the bibliographies they include with individual topics may prove helpful.

In a U.S. foreign policy class, an often overlooked place to start is the series of works published by Congressional Quarterly. Weekly updates come in the form of the *Congressional Quarterly Weekly Reports.* Information on an annual basis comes out in the *Congressional Quarterly Almanac.* Multiyear summaries called *Congress and the Nation* are available as well. These contain the basics of most U.S. foreign policy actions. Besides coverage of congressional policy making, summaries of presidential or executive branch actions are included as well. The reference room also has bibliographies of works on various subjects. These are classified under "Z." Check with the reference librarians. They may save you time.

Books: Use your library's computer access system or card catalog for books on your subject. A good place to start is with the *Library of Congress Subject Headings* for ways to cross-reference your search for books. In the Library of Congress system, most U.S. history is under the letter E. For economics, look at H; for world history, consult books under D. Under H, the subsets of HC, HG, and HJ are particularly good for economics. The letter J encompasses most works on political science. As subsets, the letters JK focus on U.S. politics; JL, JN, and JQ cover other parts of the world; and JX covers international politics. Military affairs are under U. It is valuable to know these letters because sometimes it is worthwhile to simply go to the stacks where those letters are shelved and browse a bit to uncover resources that you may have missed in your computer or card catalog search. The shelves in the reference room are partly arranged using the Library of Congress system. Older books are also sometimes catalogued under the Dewey decimal system with the 300s and 900s of especial relevance to political science and history.

Scholarly Journal Articles: Some topics, like U.S. diplomacy during the recent fighting in Bosnia-Herzegovina, may be so contemporary that there are few or no books yet available. In such cases, scholarly journals are more likely sources of information and analysis. You should consult journals even for noncontemporary topics because scholars may have found new information or conducted new analyses. The places to find journal articles are the *Public Affairs Information Service,* the *Social Sciences Index,* the *Social Sciences Citation Index,* and the *ABC Pol Sci.* You should be able to find most, if not all of these, in your library's reference room. Just a few of the leading journals in foreign policy and international affairs are *Foreign Affairs, Foreign Policy, International Affairs, International Organization, International Security, International Studies Quarterly, Journal of Conflict Resolution, Journal of International Affairs, Orbis,* and *World Politics.* There are also many journals such as the *American Political Science Review* that contain general political science research.

Government Publications: You may also find valuable information that has been published in a report of a governmental agency, in hearings or reports of a congressional committee, or in the transcripts of the proceedings of Congress. The United Nations and a number of other international organizations also publish proceedings and reports. There are several indexes available. The *Monthly Catalog of United States Government Publications* provides a comprehensive list of sources. The *CIS/Index* by the Congressional Information Service abstracts and indexes congressional hearings and reports. Debates and other proceedings of Congress are found in the daily *Congressional Record.* At some schools, accessing government documents can be a challenge. See your reference librarians for help with government publications.

Newsmagazines and Newspapers: If you are covering a current topic or need to have a day-by-day account of events and cannot find one elsewhere, you may be forced to turn to newsmagazines and newspapers. Be sure, however, to check with your instructor to ensure that these are considered acceptable sources for your assignment. Mostly they are useful for facts or for contemporary quotes and are usually not good sources of analysis. Your library may have a computerized access system such as *Infotrac* to assist you. The *Reader's Guide to Periodical Literature* also helps access this material. Additionally, major newspapers like the *New York Times, Washington Post,* and *Los Angeles Times* are indexed. Some are now available on CD-ROM, allowing you to use the computer to search by subject and then print out the relevant stories. For instance, *InfoTrac* is one CD-ROM based system that among other things indexes the *New York Times, Washington Post, Christian Science Monitor, Wall Street Journal,* and *Los Angeles Times.* The *Lexis/Nexis* computer database will not only provide you with indexed citations of journalistic articles, but also with the text of the article in most instances. See the reference librarians for help with such resources. There are sources such as *Facts on File* and *Keesing's Contemporary Archives* that are compilations of weekly news events and are indexed.

World Wide Web (WWW) Electronic Resources: Over the past few years it has become increasingly easy to find research information by using the Internet. Until recently the Gopher system of data archives was the dominant form of Internet information access, but now most governmental and nongovernmental organizations, universities, and even many businesses have developed access to their research resources over the graphic environment on the World Wide Web. The following are a number of Web sites that will get you started in searching for information you may need in writing your research paper. Although some of the Uniform Resource Locators (URL) listed below are for specific information sources, most provide you with "hotlinked" lists that will get you to where you might want to look for information.

Government Bureaucracies
http://www.xnet.com/~blatura/suits.shtml

Government Homepages
http://www.semo.edu/government.html

The World ™ Guide to Government
http://www.theworld.com/law/governme/subject.htm

Networked Government Resources
http://www.ai.mit.edu/projects/iiip/government.html

U.S. Government Information
http://govtdoc.law.csuohio/usgov.html

U.S. Government Links
http://www.intergate.net/html/us.government.html

Roper Center for Public Opinion Research, University of Connecticut
http://www.lib.uconn.edu/RoperCenter/index.htm

International Simulations, University of Michigan
http://www.lib.umich.edu/libhome/Documents.center/intsim.html

Yahoo Political Science
http://www.yahoo.com/government/politics

It is important to note that URLs change frequently. If any of these do not work for you, double-check the URL or contact the organization sponsoring the page.

Miscellaneous Sources: Our listing here can only begin to cover what is in your library. There may be a map room. There may also be an audio-visual section. Some libraries contain archives or a rare book collection. Talk to a librarian or your professor for added information. Also realize that no library has everything. Consequently, you may find references to sources that are not found in your library. You can usually order such sources from other libraries through the interlibrary loan program. Check with your reference librarians to learn how to use this service. Be advised, however, that interlibrary loans take some time. So order any needed sources as early as possible.

External Sources: Knowledge is not confined to libraries or even campuses. A surprising number of students know someone who knows something about the specifics of some U.S. foreign policy issue. Even if you do not know someone personally, you might find it interesting and possible to conduct an interview with a decision maker or some other relevant person. Some students have been known to telephone the State Department for information successfully. Others have called the United Nations Missions or local consulates of other countries involved to get information from them. For advice on unconventional sources, see your instructor.

Organizing the Paper

The keys to effective papers are good organization and presentation of ideas and error-free technical skills. There are a number of sources that you can access to help you both organize and write your paper. Some are: *Writer's Guide: Political Science* (Biddle & Holland, 1987); *The Chicago Manual of Style* (1993); "The Write Stuff" (Cronin, 1986); *Writing with Power* (Elbow, 1981); *The Elements of Style* (Strunk & White, 1979); and *A Manual for Writers of Term Papers, Theses, and Dissertations* (Turabian, 1987). Our comments on writing a paper that follow may prove helpful to you, but they are not substitutes for the fuller discussions you will find in these writing guides.

There are three organizational issues to consider. They are the outline, the parts of the paper, and the approach.

Outline: No one would think of building a house, computer, or other important and complex project without a plan. Students regularly write papers without a plan. As a result, poor organization is a common weakness of undergraduate term papers. The best way to construct your plan and to organize information for maximum effect is to put together an *outline*. An outline serves to lay out your paper's structure, to ensure that it is complete and logical, and to prevent you from getting off the track. Determine what you wish to accomplish in the paper; then prepare an outline specifying every step from Introduction to Conclusion. Linear writing is crucial in professional papers and reports. A good outline also serves to help you later: It ensures that you stay on track, write an accurate summary for your conclusions, and cover all of the relevant information and arguments.

Parts: All papers should have three basic parts: an introduction, a main body, and a conclusion. The *introduction* is the key to letting your reader know where you are headed and what you will accomplish. Remember always that while the organization of your paper may be clear to you, it is not clear to your reader. Therefore, the introduction is something like a road map that acquaints the reader with the journey ahead. This will make it easier for the reader to understand what follows and will improve the reader's evaluation of your work. Tell the reader in concise terms (1) what the subject of the paper is, (2) what it is that you hope to find out, and (3) how you will go about it.

If you are writing an advanced, theoretical paper, your introduction might well also include a review of the existing scholarship on the subject, a section in which you identify how you collected your data and other information, and a discussion of the methodology you will use. Wolfinger (1993) is a guide for such advanced papers.

The *main body* is the largest part of the paper. It should have a logical organization. Especially if the paper is long, it is often a good idea to divide the main body into sections designated by headings and subheadings. Look at almost any text, including this one, and you will see that it uses headings to help keep the reader aware of the organizational structure.

Also with regard to your main body, do not assume knowledge on the part of the reader. Include all important information, explain its significance, and detail your logic. Write your paper as though its reader will be a reasonably intelligent and informed person but not an expert on your topic. Your instructor wants to know what you know and will not "read into" the paper information that is not there.

The *conclusion* should sum up what you have found and stress the evidence that supports your analysis. There is something very human about wanting to have things summed up, so do not leave your reader hanging without a conclusion.

Approach: There are several ways to approach your paper. A common organizational approach is a chronological one. The advantage of this approach is that it uses the passage of time as its organizing mechanism. The disadvantage of a chronological approach is that it can easily become a "laundry list" of events, both important and unimportant. Students often list everything they find, leaving it to the reader to determine which factors are most important. Chronologies are also no substitute for analysis. There is nothing wrong with a chronological approach if it is done well; just be sure to put more emphasis throughout on *why* things happened than on *what* happened.

A more analytic approach would be organized around a set of factors, or variables, that are important to the subject of the paper. This text, for example, organizes chapters 2 through 5 around levels of analysis and chapters 6 through 12 around the actors, including the president, Congress, and other foreign policy actors. Theoretical approaches can also be used to organize a paper. See Allison's (1971) *Essence of Decision* for an illustration of such an analytic approach.

Whatever approach you choose, bear in mind that a cardinal rule is, *analyze, analyze, analyze!* Summarizing your findings in the conclusion does not mean that this is the only place to put "you" in the paper. Your analysis should appear throughout the paper. A big error that many novice writers make is to use the main body of the paper to create a heap of facts and to wait until the conclusion to say what they mean. This approach is boring and will not impress your readers with your analytical ability. The best papers by far are those that draw data, events, and other material together and interpret them throughout.

Writing the Paper

Besides organization, the other hallmark of a good paper is clarity in writing. Remember that if a paper fails to communicate well, then its research—no matter how well done—will have little impact. There is an old piece of advice that says, "write like you speak." This is terrible advice, at least for formal papers. Good written communication is somewhat different from good verbal communication. When you speak to someone, especially face to face, you can convey meaning through voice inflection, gestures, and other methods in addition to your words. These methods are not available in written communications. Therefore, choice of words, punctuation, and other considerations are particularly vital when you write. Good writing can be divided into three parts: effort, style considerations, and technical matters.

Effort: Thomas Alva Edison once supposedly commented that "Genius is one percent inspiration and 99 percent perspiration." That is true whether one is inventing the lightbulb or creating an essay, a report, or a book. Writing and polishing drafts of a paper take time and effort. They cannot be done the night before the paper is due. If you sit down at your word processor the night before your report is due and write it into the wee hours of the morning, you will almost certainly leave your reader as bleary-eyed when he or she reads the paper as you were when you wrote it. Two things to do are to write drafts and to get others to read your paper.

1. *Write a draft, preferably more than one.* No professional writer would dream of sending a manuscript out for review or to press without writing multiple drafts. Drafts of this text, for example, were read at several stages by coauthors, reviewers, assistant editors, copy editors, and executive editors. Indeed, the more one writes, the more one feels the need to do drafts. Only undergraduates have the hubris to keyboard a paper into the computer, print a copy out, hand it in, and wait confidently for that rave review and A grade from the instructor. A better idea is to write a first draft. Note here that the adjective "rough" does not precede "draft." Your draft should be complete and carefully done. Once your smooth draft is done, put it aside for a few days so that you can gain perspective. Then reread it. You may be surprised at how many ways you find to improve what you have written when you look at it with "fresh eyes." The same is true for your third and subsequent drafts.

2. *Get help.* There are many people who can help you write a first-rate paper. One person is your instructor. Discuss your topic and your ideas with your professor. He or she may be able to help you refine your topic, avoid pitfalls, identify resources, or plan the paper's organization. Submit drafts to your professor far enough ahead of the deadline to give the instructor time to suggest revisions. It may prove helpful also to ask a classmate, a family member, or someone else to read your paper. Most people are not good judges of their own writing. We tend to read what we meant to say, not what we actually wrote. A fresh reader will be able to point out technical errors and lapses in your argument and organization. Writing centers are another source of help at many colleges and universities. You may have already paid for such assistance with your tuition dollars; you might as well use it.

Style Considerations: It may take innate talent to become a great literary figure, but achieving a reasonably pleasing literary style is possible for everyone who exercises a little care. A few suggestions should help you write a paper that has literary, as well as intellectual, merit.

1. *Watch your sentence structure.* Students and scholars too often seem to assume that long, complex sentences are symbolic of profundity. They are not; they are mostly just cumbersome. Simple, subject-verb-object sentences are best. They are powerful. Still, if you do not vary them occasionally, numerous short sentences do not "read" well. So, after several simple sentences, add a longer one. But do not go too far the other way. Consider "Rourke's Rule of 2s": "Sentences more than two lines long or with more than two commas are probably too long to be understood easily, especially if there have been two in a row."

2. *Rely on active tense, action verbs.* Avoid the passive tense (No: "Politicians are disliked by many people." Yes: "Many people dislike politicians."). Similarly, action verbs (made, jumped, went) are better than verbs of being (is, are, were). In general, active/action verbs generate more interest.

3. *Use standard English.* Colloquial English typically does not make a good impression unless you are writing fiction. Obscenities and other forms of gutter English are almost never acceptable.

4. *Avoid starting too many sentences with adverbial or adjectival clauses or phrases.* These are the short phrases (such as "In the morning, we went . . .") that are often followed by a comma. Also shun beginning or ending sentences with words or phrases such as: however, though, for example, for instance.

5. *Watch your paragraph length.* Paragraphs over one page in length are usually too long. They may contain redundant statements or more than one major idea. Rework such paragraphs to delete unnecessary text or to separate ideas into additional paragraphs. At the other extreme, one-sentence paragraphs are not acceptable. Remember that each paragraph should have a topic sentence.

6. *Rely on transitions between paragraphs.* Conventions like "On the other hand," "Still," "Also," "Nevertheless," "Thus," "However," or "As a result" help the reader get from one thought to another. They smooth the reading process.

7. *Avoid clichés.* "They fought like cats and dogs over which policy to adopt." Ugh!

8. *Get to the point.* Do not beat around the bush; save a tree; avoid word pollution.

Technical Matters: Your paper must be free of common writing mistakes. Cautions about some of these are:

1. *Avoid sentence fragments.* Every sentence must have a subject and a verb.

2. *Check your spelling.* Misspelled words make you appear uneducated, careless, or both. Keep in mind that misspelled words and typographical errors cannot be distinguished from each other by a reader. Both are unacceptable. Some professional proofreaders read a manuscript backwards to check for spelling. Try it. Do not rely on just your own sense of how words are spelled. Use a dictionary, a "spell check" program if you have a computer, and a second reader to proofread your drafts. Beware of spell checkers, though! Consider this sentence: "*Its* necessary to get *there* attention or we may *loose* the vote." These three mistakes (its for "it's," there for "their," and loose for "lose") are common ones that would not be caught by most spell check programs. Thus it is crucial to have a human scan your words.

3. *Make sure subjects and verbs agree.* Subject-verb disagreement is most likely to occur when the two are separated in the sentences by several other words.

4. *Be careful of verb tense.* Many poor writers use only present tense. Use past tense, future, and other tenses as appropriate. Also be careful to keep verb tense consistent within paragraphs.

5. *Make pronouns mean what they say.* Misuse of pronouns is very common. A pronoun refers to the last noun of the same person and gender. Consider the sentences, "John F. Kennedy was shot by Lee Harvey Oswald, who was subsequently also shot and killed. Many Americans wept at his death." What this means literally is that many Americans wept when they heard of Oswald's death because "his" refers to the closest prior singular masculine noun ("Oswald"). Also, do not normally use pronouns more than twice in a row to refer to the same noun. Use the noun or a variation thereof again for clarity. While we are on the subject of pronouns, it is seldom correct to use a gender-specific pronoun (he, she, him, her) to refer to an inanimate object. The United States, for example, is an "it," not a "she."

6. *Do not split infinitives.* Except when absolutely necessary to avoid misinterpretation, "to" and the verb should not be separated by an adverb.

7. *Avoid the use of contractions.* Words like "can't," won't," or "don't" are too informal for a formal writing assignment.

8. *Be careful of abbreviations.* Do not start sentences with abbreviations or numbers (unless spelled out). For countries, avoid using the abbreviation as a noun (No: The U.S. did . . .); but the abbreviation is acceptable as an adjective (Yes: Current U.S. foreign policy . . .). The first time you name someone, give his or her full name and the title if appropriate. Also do not use an acronym unless it is very common without first spelling out the full name, as in, the North Atlantic Treaty Organization (NATO).

9. *Do not end sentences with prepositions.* This rule is being relaxed, but repetitive use of prepositions at the end of sentences is indicative of poor sentence structure.

10. *Know when and how to use specific punctuation.* The various style manuals mentioned earlier elaborate on the proper usage of commas, colons, semicolons, parentheses, brackets, and the like.

Citations and References

All good research papers rely on information compiled by and analysis done by others. If you write a research paper without consulting other works, then you have written an essay, not a report. If you do rely in part on the work of other people and you do not cite them, you have failed in your responsibilities. A research paper *must* cite the work of others.

There are two reasons that citations are mandatory. The first is to allow the reader to explore the subject further by consulting the works that you have utilized. Without regular and complete citations, such further exploration by your reader is difficult or impossible. Second, intellectual honesty requires citations. Failure to use them is plagiarism, which is unacceptable in any form. Plagiarism is the theft of the thoughts, facts, or knowledge of others by not giving them proper credit.

When to Cite: Follow these guidelines to protect yourself:

1. *Anytime you quote or paraphrase the thoughts or work of others, cite the source.* It is incorrect to believe that only quotations require citations. You should also insert a note whenever you are relying on someone else's thoughts or research, even if you are only paraphrasing (putting it in your own words).

2. *Simple, commonly known facts need not be footnoted.* A rule of thumb is that if you did not know the information before you started the paper, then you should use a citation to show where you found the information. Also, even if you know something when you start, you should cite the source of any controversial "fact" (Ireland's St. Brenden and the Vikings came to the New World before Columbus).

3. *When in doubt, cite the source.* Plagiarism is unethical. Instructors and other readers take it very seriously. Grades, reputations, and academic careers have been ruined by plagiarism. Err on the side of safety. One citation too many is far better than one citation too few.

How to Cite: The use of a correct format for citations used in endnotes or footnotes and in a bibliography often seem a bit complex and cumbersome, but doing so has two good points. Those advantages are completeness and consistency. Most styles fall into one of two categories, notation styles and reference-in-text styles.

Notation style involves the use of numbers to indicate each citation. Each number's corresponding note may be at the bottom of the page as a footnote or at the end of the paper as an endnote. In either case, you should provide comprehensive information on each source the first time it appears as a footnote or an endnote, with shortened versions appearing in later footnotes or endnotes. At the end of the paper, a bibliography repeats the full documentation of these sources, listing them alphabetically by author. Bibliographies have their own formatting styles. A number of works demonstrate both citation and bibliography format styles, including *A Manual for Writers of Term Papers, Theses, and Dissertations* (Turabian, 1980) and *The Chicago Manual of Style* (1993).

A *reference-in-text* style has been used throughout this book. Such styles use the author's name and the year of publication of the work, which are placed in parentheses and inserted at the appropriate place in the text. A page number is also included for direct quotes and in some other cases. Then at the end of the paper or book there is a "References" or "Works Cited" section that contains the full documentation for all the sources cited throughout the body of the work. These sources are listed alphabetically by author. Reference-in-text styles are increasingly the norm in social science, and most are some variant of the style developed by the American Psychological Association (APA). For details of how to use such styles, see the APA's *Publication Manual of the American Psychological Association* (1983); *Writer's Guide: Political Science* (Biddle & Holland, 1987); or use this book as an illustration. Whatever citation style you choose, use it correctly and be consistent.

Presenting the Paper

Your job is not quite finished. After writing the paper, you must prepare its physical presentation. Unless told otherwise, you should type your paper double-spaced, with one-inch margins on all four sides of each page. Your paper should feature a title page, the body of the paper, and then the bibliography, "Works Cited," or "References" page(s). If your instructor prefers some variation of this model, that will usually be specified in advance. Once again, it is important to stress that a paper is a whole product. A paper that contains impeccable research, cogent analysis, and brilliant writing will still evoke a negative reaction from the reader if it is wrinkled, printed sloppily, or barely readable because the ink on the ribbon is exhausted. Some general guidelines include:

1. *Printed material is preferable.* Most instructors will not accept handwritten reports. Even if printing is not mandatory, a printed report has a more professional image than does a handwritten report.

2. *Make sure the print is easily legible.* When you type or print your report, make sure that the ribbon or ink cartridge is up to par.

3. *Do not play the margin, spacing, and font game.* Professors are not naive and have read veritable mountains of papers. Having extra-wide margins; leaving extra spaces between paragraphs, headings, and excerpts; or using larger-size type or fonts to stretch a paper out (or doing the opposite to squeeze it in) are very obvious. You will not fool the instructor or anyone else. So, why bother?

4. *Number your pages.* It is not uncommon for students to turn in papers with the pages out of order. Numbering the pages cuts down on this mistake. Also, unbound papers sometimes fall apart and must be reassembled. Numbered pages will facilitate this.

5. *Securely fasten the paper together.* Paper clips are a bad idea. Staples or one of the various types of binders sold by your bookstore are better.

6. *Read your paper one last time.* Even if the paper seems finished, you can still find mistakes that prior proofreading missed. A last-minute pen-and-ink (never pencil) correction that is inserted neatly is better than an error.

7. *Go home and relax.* Get a pizza, watch some television, catch a movie! You deserve it after working hard and writing a great paper. Congratulations!

APPENDIX 2
DEMOCRACY, FOREIGN POLICY, AND YOU: MAKING A DIFFERENCE

Democracy was literally the first word of the first chapter of this text. That initial chapter made several points about democracy and foreign policy. First, the foreign policy process affects the substance of foreign policy. That is, *who* decides has a significant impact on *what* gets decided. Second, there is often a gap between the foreign policy preferences of leaders and those of the public. Policies favored by the president, the secretary of state, and other top officials may not be the same as the policies favored by the majority of the public. Furthermore, even if the president and a majority of the public are in agreement, you personally may advocate an alternative approach. And you may be right! Third, foreign policy affects you regularly and intimately. As the saying goes, "you can run, but you can't hide." Trade decisions may supply you with less expensive goods or cost you your job. To a degree, college loans and scholarship money compete with defense spending in the federal budget. The government can decide to send you or someone in your family to the Persian Gulf, to Somalia, to Bosnia or to some other scene of conflict and dying. Fourth, you can affect foreign policy.

This last point is the most important for our discussion here. If, like most of the students who will use this book, you are an American citizen, that means that (1) you live in a democracy, and (2) you live in the world's most powerful country. These two points mean that (1) you often have an opportunity to influence your country's foreign policy and that (2) the influence you exercise will not only have a one-country impact, but may also have global consequences. For good or ill, as an example, public pressure on President Clinton from both sides is one of the reasons why his administration was so slow to get involved militarily in the Bosnian conflict. This slowness—some would call it caution—affected the American soldiers who ultimately did serve in Bosnia as part of the NATO intervention, the Bosnian Muslims who continued to be killed under the Serbian offensive, and many others in Europe and elsewhere who were trying to find a solution to this bloody conflict. Student political activism can be an important political force and is common internationally, as can be followed in the study, *Student Political Activism: An International Reference Handbook* (Altbach, 1989).

For all these reasons, then, getting involved in the foreign policy process is both possible and worthwhile. Indeed, it is incumbent on you as a citizen of a democracy to stay informed and to play a role. Doing so is not easy, though. Involvement requires effort. Playing a role also entails a bit of foreknowledge about how to become involved. It is to that end that the following suggestions are directed.

Stay Informed

The first thing that a responsible citizen in a democracy needs to do is to be informed. To do that on a daily basis, you must be aware of current events; the most complete information usually comes from newspapers. Because of their excellent coverage and because nearly everyone who makes policy reads them, the *New York Times* and the *Washington Post* are the two most influential newspapers in the country for coverage of national and international news. Both papers, especially the *Times,* are available across the country. The *Christian Science Monitor* is another good source of international news that is available nationally. The *Wall Street Journal* is good for economic news. Great Britain's *Financial Times* is a first-rate paper for general and economic international news (particularly about Europe), and your library may well subscribe to it. If you cannot get these papers, simply read all the national and international news in your local or regional paper.

There are also many sources of broadcast news and features available through radio and television stations. Especially as a news source, however, you should be cautious about relying too heavily on broadcast sources. One reason is that they are relatively brief. Everything said on the television network's evening 30-minute programs would not fill up even the front page of the *New York Times.* Another drawback of broadcast news for those who are relatively unfamiliar with global events and personalities is that names and places go by quickly and may be hard to remember. Names like that of Iran's president Hashemi Rafsanjani or even General John Shalikashvili, chairman of the U.S. Joint Chiefs of Staff, will, for instance, be much easier to remember when you see them written than when you hear them on the radio or on television. Still, broadcast news has its value for both immediacy and being able to hear or see individuals and events. All three commercial radio networks (ABC, CBS, and NBC) carry national and international news. The program *CBS World News Roundup* (broadcast Monday–Friday at 8:00 A.M. Eastern Time) is a good example. Even more detailed radio coverage is available on the National Public Radio. Not only are the major headlines presented, but more in-depth reports are provided in its early morning and late afternoon "drive-time" programs.

The most extensive daily coverage of national and international news on television comes from CNN. In many areas there is both a regular and a "headline" CNN channel. The ABC, CBS, and NBC television networks have national news programs during the late afternoon hours or early evening hours, and each has a "late night" program after 11:00 P.M. Eastern Time (ABC—*Nightline,* CBS—*CBS News Up to the Minute,* NBC—*NBC News Nightside*). In many parts of the country, those who speak Spanish and Italian can get national and international news from the Telemundo and Univision networks.

Other news sources are available on a weekly basis. In print you can find *Newsweek, Time,* and *U.S. News & World Report.* All three of these magazines provide international and national news. In your library, you may be able to read the *Congressional Quarterly Weekly Report,* the *National Journal,* and the *Washington Monthly.* On television, you can watch weekly news programs that may deal with foreign policy topics. Among these, Sunday programs often feature interviews, while Friday night programs feature panel discussions by journalists and other commentators. Another source of information, available on a biweekly basis, is the *New York Review of Books.* Although its name may not suggest it, this publication often includes review essays that provide in-depth summaries and analyses of major international issues.

A variety of journals dealing with foreign and defense topics are available for personal subscription or can be found in your library. These are detailed in the appendix on how to write term papers. Explore your library and see your periodicals librarian for help in identifying those relevant to your interests. You can also subscribe to these journals, and some, such as *Foreign Affairs* and *Foreign Policy,* are available on newsstands and in many town libraries.

Use Your Vote

Being informed is the foundation of action. The next level is to get active, and an obvious way to get involved in influencing foreign policy is through the electoral process. Every four years Americans get the chance to vote in presidential elections. All the major presidential candidates usually give some indications of the type of foreign policy that will come from their administration, if they are elected. *With occasional exceptions, we usually get what we vote for.* If the candidate of your choice wins the presidency, there is a good chance you will be pleased with the general direction of foreign policy coming from that president's administration.

Congressional elections occur every two years, with all the seats in the House of Representatives and approximately one-third of the seats in the Senate at stake. As our discussion of Congress shows, members annually vote on a variety of foreign policy issues. You should determine the general foreign policy positions of your legislators and candidates so that you can better choose whether to vote for their re-election or not. Members of Congress are rated on their foreign and defense policy votes by a number of organizations. These ratings are available in Michael Barone and Grant Ujifusa (1993), *The Almanac of American Politics 1994* (Washington, DC: National Journal). The *National Journal* also annually issues its ratings of the foreign and defense policy votes of legislators. You can also contact the office of legislators (detailed below) or candidates to ask them specific questions or to request their positions on foreign policy on a variety of issues.

Lobby Government Officials

Lobbying government officials involves trying to persuade them to act in accordance with your policy views. Elected officials are the most susceptible to public persuasion. But keep in mind from chapter 10 on bureaucracy that career officials also feel public opinion pressure.

Executive Branch Officials: The place to start is the White House. You can call both the president and vice president at the White House switchboard number: (202) 456-1414. The vice president's direct number is (202) 456-2326. While it is highly unlikely you will be able to speak directly to either of them, the White House keeps a count of phone calls for or against the hot issues at any time. You can also reach them via electronic mail. The president's Internet address is:

PRESIDENT@WHITEHOUSE.GOV.

The vice president's is:

VICE.PRESIDENT@WHITEHOUSE.GOV.

It may also be possible to reach them by commercial electronic networks, such as Prodigy. Letters to the president should be sent to:

The White House
1600 Pennsylvania Avenue, NW
Washington, DC 20500

Those to the vice president should be sent to:

The Office of the Vice President
Old Executive Office Building
Washington, DC 20501

For more information regarding contacting the president, vice president, and members of the White House staff, call the White House switchboard (202) 456-1414 and ask for the Office of Presidential Correspondence.

The president appoints a variety of top policy making officials who deal with foreign policy, and you can contact them as well. Some of the most relevant offices are listed below:

Department of State
Office of the Secretary of State
2201 C St., NW
Washington, DC 20520
(202) 647-4000

Secretary of Defense, Information
The Pentagon
Washington, DC 20301
(703) 545-6700

Office of National Security Affairs
National Security Adviser
Executive Office
The White House
1600 Pennsylvania Avenue, NW
Washington, DC 20500
(202) 395-3000

Office of the United States Trade
  Representative
Winder Building
600 17th St., NW
Washington, DC 20506
(202) 395-3000

Office of the Director of Central
  Intelligence
Central Intelligence Agency
McLean, VA 20505
(703) 482-1100

Depending on which issues you have chosen, you might contact other executive branch officials, such as Treasury officials for financial issues, Commerce officials for business issues, Agriculture officials for food and fiber exports, etc. For their phone numbers and addresses, see *The Federal Yellow Book* (1995) or contact your librarian. It is also worth noting that all the phone numbers listed in the appendix may change at any time, so if you run into any problems with the numbers listed here, you should consult the most recent edition of *The Federal Yellow Book*.

Whatever your method of communication and whomever you contact, there are some general rules of thumb to follow in order to be most successful. Keep your message short and simple. Use your own words. Focus on one issue only. Be specific about what you want the official to do and why. Communicate as an individual, not as a member of a group. Be polite; avoid making electoral threats. Physical threats are, of course, a federal felony. Try to reach the official *before* a decision has been made. When using the mail, you should send a letter rather than a postcard. Be sure to type or handwrite the letter; preprinted postcards or letters by interest groups are less effective. Sign your name and include your return address. For other hints, see the *Campaign for Global Security* (Zimmerman, 1991:15).

Members of Congress: The same general rules apply for lobbying your members of Congress. To find out who your elected legislators are, check the government pages of your local phone book, contact your local elections or voter registration administrator (usually an office of your local county government), or call your local office of the League of Women Voters. Once you know your legislators' names, you can get their local phone numbers in your phone book or their Washington phone numbers by calling the Capitol Hill switchboard at (202) 224-3121. You can call their offices to get their mailing addresses, or look them up in either Michael Barone and Grant Ujifusa's *The Almanac of American Politics 1994* (1993, Washington, DC: National Journal), or *Congressional Quarterly's Politics in America 1994* (1993, Washington, DC: CQ Press).

The same general guidelines exist for contacting legislators, as noted above for executive branch officials, with one addition. When discussing an upcoming piece of legislation, refer to the bill's number or legislative sponsors if possible. Many different versions of bills get considered in Congress, and you should be as specific as possible about which one concerns you. If you do not know the bill number, however, do not be put off. Contact your representatives and senators!

Among other reasons to lobby members of Congress is that it is easier to get direct access to them compared to executive branch officials. You can reach legislators at their offices in Washington, D.C., or at their district or state offices when they return during legislative recesses. If you call in advance to make an appointment, your chances of seeing them in person increase. If you cannot see your legislators personally, present your message to one their staff members. While that may not seem the same to you, representatives and senators rely heavily on their staffs for information and analysis.

In addition to contacting your local legislators, you can also contact the members of congressional committees relevant to your concerns. Some of the relevant committees are listed below, with their mailing addresses and phone numbers.

House International Relations
  Committee
2170 Rayburn House Office Building
Washington, DC 20515
(202) 224-4651

Senate Foreign Relations Committee
446 Dirksen Senate Office Building
Washington, DC 20515
(202) 224-4651

House National Security Committee
2120 Rayburn House Office Building
Washington, DC 20515
(202) 225-4151

Senate Armed Services Committee
228 Russel Senate Office Building
Washington, DC 20515
(202) 224-3871

House Intelligence Committee
House 405, The Capitol
Washington, DC 20515
(202) 225-4121

Senate Intelligence Committee
211 Hart Senate Office Building
Washington, DC 20515
(202) 224-1700

House Appropriations Subcommittees on:
Commerce, Justice, State, and the
  Judiciary
Defense
Foreign Operaitons, Export
  Financing, and Related Programs
Military Construction
House 218, The Capitol
Washington, DC 20515
(202) 225-2771

Senate Appropraitions Subcommittees on:
Commerce, Justice, State, and the
  Judiciary
Defense
Foreign Operations
Military Construction
Senate 128, The Capitol
Washington, DC 20515
(202) 224-3471

Take Individual Direct Action

The First Amendment to the Constitution bars the government from making any law "abridging the freedom of speech . . . or the right of the people peacefully to assemble, and to petition the Government for a redress of grievances." This means that you can not only write, phone, or fax your disagreements to the government, you can get out on the street and march, wave signs, chant, and generally attract attention to your views. Huge marches in Washington, D.C., which included many students, helped end U.S. involvement in the war in Vietnam. Protests put pressure on the Reagan administration to negotiate arms agreements with the Soviets. Even lone, individual efforts can make a statement because, in part, the press loves controversy and may well run a story or photograph about protest activity. So hit the street!

Or you can hit *etherspace*. Most of the governmental and non-governmental organizations listed in this appendix have now developed access to their offices and their resources through the World Wide Web (WWW) and other Internet tools such as the Gopher. Please refer back to the WWW URL addresses that we listed in the first appendix on term paper writing. All of those listed in that appendix will provide you with starting places for searching the Web for points of direct electronic access to governmental officials and lobbying groups.

Join Groups

If you want to learn more about foreign policy matters and possibly influence policy makers, a variety of groups exist that you may choose to join. As noted in our discussion of interest groups, these groups often lobby government officials on behalf of their members. Consequently, by belonging to one or more such groups, your foreign policy interests may be communicated to officials by group representatives. Various types of groups can be identified.

Multi-Issue Groups: Some foreign policy groups address a wide range of international issues. Many cities have **World Affairs Councils**; these can be found in your local phone book. They often have monthly meetings with featured speakers. These speakers might be officials from the State Department's public liaison section, foreign officials (like ambassadors, consuls, or others), or private citizens with expertise on specific international issues.

As noted in the interest groups discussion, the **Council on Foreign Relations** has long held a highly visible spot in U.S. foreign policy making. Its Washington address is 2400 N St., NW, Washington, DC 20037. Its phone number is (202) 862-7780.

Another multi-issue group is the **Citizens Network for Foreign Affairs**, a group that tries to help educate the U.S. public on the broad range of international issues facing the United States. Its mailing address is 1111 19th St., NW, Washington, DC 20036. Its phone number is (202) 296-3920.

A multi-issue group that focuses on a particular international institution is the **United Nations Association**. This group supports the role of the United Nations in U.S. foreign policy. Since the United Nations deals with a wide array of issues, so does the UNA. It can be reached at 1010 Vermont Avenue, NW, Washington, DC 20005 or by telephone at (202) 347-5004.

Single-Issue Groups: There is a vast range of groups that focus on specific issues. A few such concerns and some of the groups associated with them are:

Human Rights Groups: These groups address civil and political rights. Some such groups are:

Amnesty International (212-807-8400) works for the protection of political prisoners.

Freedom House (212-514-8040) monitors civil and political liberties globally.

Human Rights Internet (613-564-3492) acts as a clearinghouse for human rights information.

Human Rights Watch (202-972-8400) coordinates human rights organizations such as Africa Watch, Asia Watch, Americas Watch, Middle East Watch, Helsinki Watch, and the Fund for Free Expression.

Some human rights groups even focus on a specific country. A number of groups arose to oppose apartheid in South Africa and have continued to work on other issues of interest to a specific African country or region. These groups are also concerned with the current attempts to reform the system and achieve majority rule. For information and involvement, contact:

The Africa Fund (212-962-1210)

Fund for a Free South Africa (617-267-8333)

TransAfrica (202-797-2301)

Washington Office on Africa (202-546-7961)

Humanitarian Groups: A number of groups work to improve the quality of life in other societies. Some of those efforts are directed at ending hunger. Such groups include:

Bread for the World (800-82-BREAD)

The End Hunger Network (310-454-3716)

The Hunger Project (212-532-4255)

Interfaith Hunger Appeal (212-870-2035)

Oxfam America (617-482-1211) (617-728-2594)

World Hunger Year (212-629-8850)

Other humanitarian groups work to provide relief from natural disasters and other catastrophes. Some of these include:

American Red Cross (202-737-8300)

AmeriCares (800-486-4357/203-966-5195)

Catholic Relief Services (410-625-2220)

Direct Relief International (805-964-4767)

Doctors Without Borders (212-679-6800)

International Red Cross and Red Crescent Movement (202-728-6600)

International Rescue Committee (212-551-3000)

Migration and Refugee Service (202-541-3220)

U.S. Committee for Refugees (202-347-3507)

World Relief (800-535-5433)

Some groups target the needs of children in particular. Examples include:

CARE (212-686-3110)

Children International (800-888-3089)

Christian Children's Fund (804-756-2700)

Feed the Children (800-627-4556/405-942-0228)

Save the Children (203-221-4000/800-828-0175)

UNICEF (212-326-7000)

World Vision (818-357-7979/800-423-4200)

Other groups target global overpopulation. Some such groups include:

International Planned Parenthood Federation (212-995-8800)

Negative Population Growth (201-837-3555)

Population-Environment Balance (202-879-3000)

Population Institute (202-544-3300)

Zero Population Growth (202-332-2200)

Finally, some groups work on a wide variety of issues, all of which seek to improve the human condition. Examples of such groups include:

American Friends Service Committee (212-598-0958)

American Jewish World Service (212-683-1161)

Catholic Charities (703-549-1390)

Church World Service (219-264-3102)

Compassion International (800-336-7676)

Coordination in Development (212-870-3000)

Interaction/American Council for Voluntary International Action (212-667-8227)

Interfaith Impact for Justice and Peace (202-543-2800)

Lutheran World Relief (212-532-6350)

Overseas Development Council (202-234-8701)

Returned Volunteer Services (800-424-8580, Ext. 2284)

Environmental Groups: Given the state of the global environment, groups have arisen to address environmental needs. Some of those include:

Conservation International (202-429-5660)

Cousteau Society (804-523-9335)

Cultural Survival Inc. (617-621-3818)

EarthSave (800-362-3648)

Friends of the Earth (202-783-7400)

Greenpeace (202-462-1177)

Institute for Transportation & Development Policy (202-260-8144)

Mothers and Others for a Livable Planet (212-242-0010)

Rainforest Action Network (415-398-4404)

Rainforest Alliance (212-677-1900)

Union of Concerned Scientists (617-547-5552)

World Resources Institute (202-638-6300)

World Wildlife Fund (202-293-4800)

Worldwatch Institute (202-452-1999)

Peace Groups: A wide array of groups calling for a more peaceful world exist. Some focus on the need to stop the spread, testing, or emphasis on nuclear weaponry. Examples include:

Arms Control Association (202-463-8270

Concerned Educators Allied for a Safe Environment (CEASE) (617-864-0999)

Council for a Livable World (202-543-4100)

Institute for Defense and Disarmament Studies (617-354-4337)

Nuclear Age Peace Foundation (805-965-3443)

Other groups focus on the need for people-to-people diplomacy between historical rivals such as the United States and the former Soviet Union. Examples include:

American Field Service (AFS) Intercultural Inc. (212-949-4242)

Center for Citizen Initiatives (415-346-1875)

Peace Links (202-544-0805)

Finally, other groups deal with a wide range of peace-related issues, from opposing warfare and high defense spending to eradicating social injustices. Some of these groups include:

Beyond War (415-328-7756)

Bikes Not Bombs (212-260-8144)

Carnegie Endowment for International Peace (202-862-7900)

Center for Defense Information (202-862-0700)

Council on Economic Priorities (212-420-1133/800-729-4237)

Fellowship of Reconciliation (408-423-1626)

Fund for Peace (212-661-5900)

Women's International League for Peace and Freedom (215-563-7110)

World Federalist Association (202-546-3950)

World Policy Institute (212-229-5808)

Worldwatch Institute (202-452-1999)

Make a Personal Commitment

Finally, you can affect foreign policy by getting involved on a direct, personal level. This step involves making a personal commitment of your time, either on a short-term or long-term basis.

Short-Term Commitments: What if you cannot find a group expressing your foreign policy views? You can create one. Remember our illustration of a significant grassroots movement—the nuclear freeze movement. It started locally in Massachusetts and spread nationally. With luck and hard work, yours could too.

If you are willing to live in other countries for brief periods of time (thereby learning more about those societies and helping people there better understand yours), several of the groups listed above in the people-to-people diplomacy section are relevant. Examples include the Citizens Exchange Council (212-643-1985), and the School for International Trainings' College Semester Abroad Program (800-336-1616), the Youth Exchange Service (800-848-2121/714-955-2030), and the Volunteers for International Work Camps (802-259-2759). This last group operates international work camps, which are somewhat similar to the Peace Corps but without the long-term commitment.

Long-Term Commitments: You can also decide to take an extended role or make an extended commitment measured in years, rather than in weeks or months.

Governmental Positions: A popular place to start is the **Peace Corps** (800-424-8580). This program sends volunteers into other countries, normally for periods of two years. You live and work in that society; thus you might be teaching basic health care and nutrition to villagers in rural Paraguay, helping budding entrepreneurs start small businesses in Kenya, or promoting more environmentally sound agricultural practices in a variety of developing countries around the globe.

Other long-term commitments may involve making foreign affairs your career. One popular career option is to become a **Foreign Service Officer** in the State Department (703-875-7490). As an FSO, you could work in a variety of topical areas, such as administration, consular services, economic analysis, political affairs, information and cultural affairs, or commercial and business services. However, you should be realistic about a career as an FSO. According to State Department personnel, only about 15 percent of the annual applicants pass the required written exam and move onto the oral interview, the medical exam, and the background security check. At the end of this grueling process, only about 1 percent of the original applicants receive job offers. If you are hired, most of your career will involve the implementation of foreign policy decisions made by others. Only the most senior FSOs advance to ambassadorial rank, and relatively few advance to the top decision making positions in the State Department, which is the realm of presidential appointees. Still, many find being an FSO to be a highly rewarding career, filled with meaningful professional activity, interesting interchanges, and exciting cultural experiences.

Other executive branch departments also engage in foreign policy activities. Not all FSOs work at State; some are seconded (temporarily assigned) to departments like **Agriculture** or **Commerce** to work in the area of exports and imports. The **Treasury Department** needs people to help with international financial and economic policy. The **Defense Department** hires an array of civilian analysts to help with national security policy. Les Aspin, the Clinton administration's first secretary of defense, started his public service career as one of these civilian analysts in the Kennedy administration.

Executive branch agencies and offices also engage in foreign policy activities. The **National Security Council** needs staff personnel, as does the **Office of the United States Trade Representative**. The **Central Intelligence Agency** hires both analysts and field agents.

Congressional staff positions also offer a way to have a career in foreign policy. The most obvious place for hires is as a staffer for one of the foreign affairs committees or subcommittees in each chamber. See the listing of such committees in the above section regarding the lobbying of congressional committees. Some foreign policy analysts work as staffers for individual legislators who serve on these committees or who have a keen personal interest in national security or foreign affairs.

For any of these governmental positions, the normal educational prerequisite is a master's degree in international studies, politics, or foreign affairs, political science, economics, or a relevant public policy area.* There are many good master's programs around the country, although the ones in the greater Washington, D.C., area offer an obvious geographic advantage when seeking government employment. In a number of cases, having a master's degree may not be enough. Many who staff these governmental positions have doctoral degrees. See your class instructor or academic adviser for help in choosing graduate programs to consider.

One other option exists as well. You could run for elective office. As a member of Congress you could have a direct impact on foreign policy, particularly to the extent that you served on one of the foreign policy-relevant committees in your chamber. Or you could run for president. Don't laugh; who would have guessed, back when they were college undergraduates, that Bill Clinton, George Bush, Ronald Reagan, Jimmy Carter, Gerald Ford, or Richard Nixon would later become president?

Nongovernmental Positions: For those who want to influence U.S. foreign policy from the outside, a wide range of potential nongovernmental employers exists. Many of the **interest groups** identified earlier hire personnel to play a variety of roles: professional management of the group, membership and/or fund-raising activities, or professional lobbying of government officials.

Similar employee roles are often needed by research centers (or "think tanks") associated with foreign policy topics. A sampling of such think tanks would include:

ACCESS (617-720-5627)

American Defense Foundation (703-519-7000)

American Enterprise Institute for Public Policy Research (202-862-5800)

American Security Council (202-296-9500)

Atlantic Council of the United States (202-347-9353)

The Brookings Institution (202-797-6000)

Carnegie Endowment for International Peace (202-862-7900)

Center for Defense Information (202-862-0700)

Center for Security Policy (202-466-0515)

Center for Strategic and International Studies (202-887-0200)

Council on Foreign Relations (212-734-0400)

Ethics and Public Policy Center (202-682-1200)

Friends Committee on National Legislation (202-547-6000)

Hudson Institute (317-545-1000)

Institute for Policy Studies (202-234-9382)

National Peace Institute Foundation (202-223-1770)

Overseas Development Council (202-234-8701)

Rand Corporation (202-296-5000)

United States Global Strategy Council (202-466-6029)

*For a few positions, like Foreign Service Officers or CIA analysts or field agents, some may be hired with only an undergraduate degree. This usually happens only when that person offers something else of value, such as relevant military or work experience, experience in living abroad, or an unusual ability to learn foreign languages. Even then, that person will probably be advised to start working on a master's degree in order to have opportunities for future advancement.

Again, the typical minimum prerequisite for such positions is a master's degree in a relevant subject. Many staff personnel have doctoral degrees. A few of these research centers may accept significant and relevant military, governmental, or other work experience in lieu of graduate degrees. The names, addresses, and phone numbers of other think tanks are available in Zimmerman (1991) or the Congressional Quarterly's *Washington Information Directory* (published annually).

In summary, there are many things you can do to become involved in foreign policy. You can use your vote to choose officials whose foreign policy views mirror your own, lobby both elected and appointed officials on behalf of your policy views, join like-minded interest groups or even form your own, or make a personal commitment to the issues about which you feel deeply. You may even make foreign policy issues the focus of your career, whether as a governmental official or a professional associated with an interest group or think tank. Keep this thought in mind: *you can influence your country's foreign policy and world events only if you try.*

ENDNOTES

CHAPTER 1

1. *Time,* July 19, 1993, p. 17.
2. *National Journal,* February 11, 1995, p. 385.
3. *Boston Globe,* February 19, 1994, p. 6.
4. *New York Times,* March 3, 1995, p. A3.
5. *Congressional Quarterly Weekly Report,* March 26, 1994, p. 751.
6. *Hartford Courant,* May 9, 1995, p. A1.
7. *New York Times,* February 13, 1995, p. A19.
8. *New York Times,* November 14, 1994, p. A12.
9. The polls results and the Atwood quote are both from the *New York Times,* April 30, 1995, p. E4.
10. *New York Times,* November 24, 1994, p. A12.
11. Congressional Quarterly on-line service, transmitted: April 13, 1995.
12. *Newsweek,* September 26, 1994, p. 36.
13. *Washington Post,* September 3, 1993, p. A23.
14. *New York Times,* May 23, 1995, p. A9.
15. The Helms and Atwood quotes are from the *New York Times,* February 15, 1995, p. A5.
16. *New York Times,* May 23, 1995, p. A9.
17. *Hartford Courant,* December 1, 1990, p. A8.
18. *New York Times,* May 26, 1978, p. A10.
19. *New York Times,* December 16, 1981, p. A35. The columnist was Tom Wicker.
20. *Hartford Courant,* October 19, 1993, p. A1.
21. Brent Scowcroft, "The Limits of Congressional Power," *Hartford Courant,* August 22, 1993, p. C13.
22. *Congressional Quarterly Weekly Report,* on-line service, September 17, 1994.
23. All quotes are from the *Congressional Quarterly Weekly Report,* on-line service, September 17, 1994.
24. *Congressional Quarterly Weekly Report,* on-line service, September 17, 1994.
25. *New York Times,* August 4, 1994, p. A16.
26. *Congressional Quarterly Weekly Report,* on-line service, September 17, 1994.
27. *Congressional Quarterly Weekly Report,* on-line service, September 17, 1994.
28. Tobin Harshaw, "Unvindicating Oliver North," *New York Times Book Review,* November 13, 1994, p. 9.
29. *New York Times,* September 13, 1991, p. A10.
30. *Hartford Courant,* November 14, 1994, p. A1.
31. *Washington Post National Weekly Edition,* July 3–9, 1995, p. 14.
32. *New York Times,* January 13, 1995, p. A8.
33. *Time,* April 17, 1995, pp. 45–46 in an extended extract from Robert S. McNamara, *In Retrospect* (New York: Random House, 1995).
34. *Time,* April 17, 1995, pp. 45–46 in an extended extract from *In Retrospect.*

BOX, "Diplomats and Soldiers: Women and Foreign Policy," pp. 12–13

1. *New York Times,* November 25, 1995, p. A1.
2. The quote from the anonymous diplomat and the newspaper are from the *New York Times,* November 25, 1994, p. A1. The quote on Haiti is from *Time,* October 31, 1994, p. 31.
3. *Time,* October 31, 1994, p. 31.
4. *Time,* October 31, 1994, p. 20.
5. All quotes from *Time,* June 12, 1995, pp. 46–47.
6. *Newsweek,* September 10, 1990, p. 23.
7. Both the Gingrich and Schroeder quotes are from *Newsweek,* January 30, 1995, p. 17.
8. *Hartford Courant,* June 19, 1990, p. A7.
9. Both the White and Draude quotes are from the *Hartford Courant,* December 8, 1992, p. A6.
10. *American Enterprise,* March/April 1991, p. 87.
11. *Hartford Courant,* August 7, 1991, p. A3.

CHAPTER 2

1. *Los Angeles Times,* October 2, 1990, p. A6.
2. *Hartford Courant,* October 15, 1993, p. A1.
3. *New York Times,* October 13, 1993, p. A1.

CHAPTER 3

1. *New York Times,* January 29, 1992, p. A16.
2. *Time,* February 10, 1992, p. 23. The quip was not a Tsongas original. Reportedly (*Time,* December 2, 1991, p. 70) Soviet foreign ministry representative Gennadi Gerasimov used the line during a 1990 visit to the United States.
3. U.S. Department of State (1984). *Realism, Strength, Negotiation: Foreign Policy Statements of the Reagan Administration* (Washington, DC), p. 186.
4. *Hartford Courant,* November 4, 1991, p. A4.

Endnotes

5. *Time,* April 13, 1992, p. 28.
6. For more on this view, see Robert A. Manning, "Beyond Human Rights," *Orbis,* 38/3 (Spring, 1994), pp. 193–206.
7. *New York Times,* May 27. 1994, p. A8.
8. *New York Times,* May 24, 1994, p. A1.
9. *New York Times,* May 27, 1994, p. A8.
10. *New York Times,* December 12, 1994, p. A55.
11. *New York Times,* February 8, 1993, p. A8.
12. The aide was John P. Sears, quoted in Hendrick Smith, "Reagan," *New York Times Magazine,* April 30, 1995, p. E4.
13. Anatoly Dobrynin, *In Confidence* (New York: Random House, 1995), quoted in *Time,* September 18, 1995, p. 32. See also Nicholas Henderson, "Their Man in Washington," *New York Times Book Review,* September 17, 1995, p. 11.
14. *Time,* June 13, 1988, p. 13.
15. *Hartford Courant,* April 2, 1993, p. A1.
16. *New York Times,* June 7, 1995, p. A1.
17. *Hartford Courant,* December 11, 1991, p. A5.
18. *Time,* December 2, 1991, p. 71.
19. *New York Times,* May 29, 1995, p. A3. The official was Under Secretary of Commerce for International Trade Jeffrey E. Garten.
20. *Hartford Courant,* February 2, 1995, p. A8.
21. *Time,* November 27, 1995, p. 40.
22. *Time,* December 4, 1995, p. 33.
23. *New York Times,* September 22, 1995, p. A1.
24. *New York Times,* October 18, 1995, p. A1.
25. *Boston Globe,* February 19, 1994, p. A12
26. *New York Times,* May 18, 1995, p. D1.
27. *New York Times,* June 7, 1995, p. A1.
28. *New York Times,* May 14, 1995, p. D1.
29. The Juppé and Rexrodt quotes are both from the *New York Times,* May 3, 1995, p. A7.
30. May 25, 1995, p. A1.
31. *New York Times,* May 19, 1995, p. D1.
32. *New York Times,* May 29, 1995, p. A1.
33. Off-the-record interview with Mark Boyer.
34. *New York Times,* February 12, 1995, p. E5.
35. *Hartford Courant,* May 25, 1995, p. A5.
36. *New York Times,* December 11, 1994, p. A1.
37. *New York Times,* January 4, 1995, p. D4.
38. *New York Times,* May 2, 1994, p. A6.
39. *Dallas Morning News,* November 19, 1994, p. 24A.
40. *Christian Science Monitor,* January 29, 1992, p. 18.
41. *Los Angeles Times,* December 31, 1989, p. M5.
42. *Congressional Quarterly Weekly Report,* September 17, 1994, p. 2605.
43. *Christian Science Monitor,* March 31, 1995, pp. 1, 7.
44. *Christian Science Monitor,* March 31, 1995, p. 7. The analyst was John Bolton of the National Policy Forum.
45. *New York Times,* November 19, 1994, pp. A1.
46. *New York Times,* December 19, 1993, p. E4. The analyst was C. Fred Bergsten, director of the Institute for International Economics.
47. *New York Times,* December 2, 1994, pp. A1, A22.
48. *New York Times,* June 14, 1995, p. D1.
49. *New York Times,* April 25, 1995, p. A1. The analyst was C. Fred Bergsten.
50. *New York Times,* June 15, 1995, p. D1.
51. *Hartford Courant,* February 9, 1992, p. A14. The quote is from a declassified top-secret cable from acting Secretary of State Robert Lovett to the U.S. ambassador in Riyadh recounting a personal message that Truman gave to the Saudi crown prince to relate to his father, the king.
52. *New York Times,* January 25, 1980, p. A1.
53. *Maine Sunday Telegram,* June 27, 1993, p. A1.
54. *Time,* August 20, 1990, p. 21.
55. *New York Times,* August 25, 1992, p. A11.
56. *Hartford Courant,* September 14, 1993, p. A12. The comment is by Richard Haass, an adviser on the Middle East to President Bush.
57. *Congressional Quarterly Weekly Report,* March 26, 1994, p. 754.
58. *New York Times,* June 2, 1995, p. A1.
59. *Christian Science Monitor,* March 15, 1995, pp. 1, 18.
60. *New York Times,* May 16, 1995, p. A8.
61. *Hartford Courant,* December 20, 1991, p. A1.
62. George Will, "Why Bush Is Vulnerable on Foreign Policy," *Hartford Courant,* January 13, 1992, p. A11.
63. Charles Krauthammer, "The Man Who Loved Dictators," *Time,* October 14, 1991, p. 93.
64. *New York Times,* October 12, 1992, p. A21.
65. Clinton and the Cabinet members' quotes are from the *New York Times,* June 18, 1995, p. A12.
66. *New York Times,* June 18, 1995, p. A12.
67. All quotes are from the *New York Times,* June 18, 1995, p. A12.
68. *New York Times,* October 16, 1991, p. A10.

BOX, "U.S.–Japan Relations: Political Alliance and Economic Conflict?" pp. 68–69

1. *New York Times,* June 30, 1995, p. D5.
2. *New York Times,* June 30, 1995, p. D5.
3. *Christian Science Monitor,* June 30, 1995, p. 9.
4. Louis Ortmayer, "The FSX Agreement," Pew Case Study 350 (Institute for the Study of Diplomacy, Georgetown University), p. 2.
5. Louis Ortmayer, "The FSX Agreement," Pew Case Study 350 (Institute for the Study of Diplomacy, Georgetown University), p. 5.

CHAPTER 4

1. This chapter relies on several diplomatic histories, including Bailey (1974); Graebner (1964, 1985); Hartmann & Wendzel (1985); Jones (1988); LaFeber (1989); Paterson, Clifford, & Hagan (1995); Paterson and Merrill (1995); and Schlesinger (1986).
2. Henry Kissinger, "How to Achieve the New World Order," *Time,* March 14, 1994, p. 73. The article is an excerpt from Henry A. Kissinger, *Diplomacy,* New York: Simon & Schuster, 1994.
3. U.S. President, *Public Papers of the President of the United States: John F. Kennedy,* 1963, p. 503.
4. *New York Times,* January 6, 1992, p. A17; the television program *60 Minutes,* September 6, 1992.
5. *New York Times,* October 12, 1992, p. A16.
6. *Hartford Courant,* April 2, 1992, p. A1.
7. *New York Times,* September 16, 1994, p. A10.
8. *New York Times,* September 16, 1994, p. A10.
9. Department of State, Human Rights Report 1994, February 1995, Internet (DOSFAN).
10. *New York Times,* August 29, 1994, p. 94.
11. *Time,* May 30, 1994, p. 40.
12. *Hartford Courant,* June 19, 1995, p. A4.
13. The first quote is from the *New York Times,* December 12, 1992, p. A1. The second quote is from the *Washington Post National Weekly Edition,* January 18–24, 1993, p 4.
14. *Newsweek,,* June 26, 1995, p. 31.
15. St. Matthew 5:14.
16. *Hartford Courant,* April 10, 1993, p. A2. The expert was Steven Cohen.
17. Anthony J. Kane, codirector of the Center for Chinese and American Studies, jointly of Johns Hopkins University and Nanjing University, quoted in *New York Times,* November 11, 1991, p. A6.
18. Jerome A. Cohen, Chinese law specialist, New York University, *New York Times,* November 6, 1991, p. A6.
19. Both opinions on Somalia were reported in the *New York Times,* December 13, 1992, p. A16.
20. *Newsweek,* July 18, 1994, p. 47.
21. *New York Times,* May 18, 1994, p. A19, quoting H. R. Holdeman, *The Holdeman Diaries* (New York: G. P. Putnam's Sons, 1994).
22. *Newsweek,* August 9, 1993, p. 25.
23. *World Opinion Update,* January 1994, p. 2.
24. *Hartford Courant,* February 29, 1992, p. A4. The report by the U.S. Commission on Civil Rights is entitled "Civil Rights Issues Facing Asian-Americans in the 1990s."
25. *Time,* February 10, 1992, p. 20.
26. *New York Times,* December 3, 1991, p. A16.
27. *Hartford Courant,* March 4, 1992, p. A2.
28. *Newsweek,* November 27, 1993, p. 13.
29. *New York Times,* September 16, 1994, p. A10.
30. *Hartford Courant,* January 15, 1993, p. A8.
31. *Hartford Courant,* June 29, 1993, p. A1.
32. *Time,* July 5, 1993, p. 33.
33. Acheson cites Townsend Hoopes, "The Persistence of Illusion: The Soviet Economic Drive and American National Interest," *Yale Review,* Spring 1960, p. 325.
34. *Time,* February 13, 1989, p. 33. Baker was serving as Ronald Reagan's White House chief of staff at the time he made the remark.
35. *Hartford Courant,* March 6, 1992, p. A6.
36. *Washington Post,* August 30, 1991, p. A32.
37. Summary of *CQ Researcher,* July 15, 1994 (Internet).
38. *New York Times,* November 14, 1991, p. A6.
39. *Hartford Courant,* January 3, 1992, p. A1.
40. *Time,* November 16, 1992, p. 80. The observer was Michael Dewar of the International Institute for Strategic Studies in London.
41. *Time,* November 16, 1992, p. 78.
42. *New York Times,* February 7, 1992, p. A1. The analyst was Professor Michael Mandelbaum.
43. *Time,* November 16, 1992, p. 78.
44. *Dallas Morning News,* June 3, 1995, pp. 1A, 8A.
45. *Hartford Courant,* December 7, 1995, p. A1.
46. Charles M. Lichenstein, "The United Nations No Longer Serves U.S. Interests," *Hartford Courant,* May 3, 1995, p. A11. Lichenstein is a former alternative U.S. representative to the UN in the Reagan administration and is currently with the Heritage Foundation.
47. *Hartford Courant,* December 16, 1992, p. A8.
48. *New York Times,* September 28, 1993, p. A1.
49. *Time,* December 11, 1995, p. 60.
50. Dick Kirschetn, "Newt's Abstract Internationalism," *National Journal,* March 18, 1995, p. 716.
51. The Dole article was taken off the Internet. The page reference is to the Internet version, not the printed article in *Foreign Policy.*
52. *New York Times,* April 28, 1995, p. A12.
53. *New York Times,* June 27, 1995, p. A11.
54. *Christian Science Monitor,* March 14, 1995, p. 18.
55. The specific quote is taken from the *Christian Science Monitor,* March 14, 1995, p. 18.
56. *New York Times,* June 27, 1995, p. A11.
57. *CQ Researcher,* July 15, 1994, p. 2 (Internet). The first analyst was Andrew Kohut; the second was Daniel Yankelovich.
58. *New York Times,* October 31, 1993, p. A8.
59. *New York Times,* June 25, 1995, p. A1.
60. *Hartford Courant,* June 25, 1995, p. A3.

BOX, "Bill Clinton: Liberal Candidate, Pragmatic President," pp. 98–99

1. *New York Times,* August 14, 1992, p. A15.
2. *New York Times,* August 14, 1992, p. A15.
3. *New York Times,* February 11, 1993, p. A1.
4. *New York Times,* November 20, 1992, p. A1.
5. *New York Times,* March 3, 1993, p. A16.
6. Anthony Lewis, "The Clinton Doctrine?" *New York Times,* January 22, 1993, p. A24.
7. *Time,* November 16, 1992, p. 80.
8. *Hartford Courant,* April 1, 1993, p. A19.
9. *New York Times,* March 3, 1993, p. A16.
10. *New York Times,* March 3, 1993, p. A16.
11. *Dallas Morning News,* October 14, 1994, p. 1A; October 16, 1994, p. 1A.

CHAPTER 5

1. Quoted in *Newsweek,* April 17, 1995, p. 46 in an excerpt from McNamara's *In Retrospect* (New York: Random House, 1995).
2. *Time,* February 13, 1989, p. 31.
3. *Time,* June 7, 1993, p. 23.
4. *Time,* June 7, 1993, p. 23.
5. *National Journal,* February 11, 1995, p. 385.
6. Colin L. Powell, *My American Journey,* New York: Random House, 1995, excerpted in *Time,* September 18, 1995, p. 64.
7. Colin L. Powell, *My American Journey,* New York: Random House, 1995, excerpted in *Time,* September 18, 1995, p. 69.
8. *New York Times,* May 21, 1995, p. A8.
9. *New York Times,* October 31, 1993, p. A8.
10. *Time,* January 14, 1991, p. 14.
11. *Hartford Courant,* January 12, 1989, p. A9.
12. *Hartford Courant,* November 17, 1990, p. A1.
13. *Hartford Courant,* November 17, 1990, p. A5.
14. *Hartford Courant,* December 28, 1990, p. A10.
15. *Time,* December 31, 1990.
16. *Time,* January 25, 1993, p. 28.
17. *Hartford Courant,* October 9, 1995, p. A5.
18. *New York Times,* June 17, 1991, p. A10.
19. *Hartford Courant,* November 1, 1990, p. A1.
20. *Time,* August 20, 1990, p. 20.
21. *New York Times,* September 15, 1995, p. A26.

CHAPTER 6

1. *New York Times,* May 11, 1995, p. A5.
2. *New York Times,* April 6, 1995, p. A12.
3. *New York Times,* May 12, 1995, p. A1.
4. Editorial Research Reports, *Making Foreign Policy* (Washington, DC: CQ Press, 1988), p. 26.
5. *Christian Science Monitor,* August 20, 1993, p. 1.
6. *New York Times,* September 15, 1993, p. B12.
7. *New York Times,* September 15, 1993, p. B12.
8. *New York Times,* November 3, 1993, p. A9.
9. *New York Times,* October 5, 1993, p. B10.
10. *Hartford Courant,* November 9, 1993, p. A6.
11. *New York Times,* November 4, 1993, p. A19.
12. *Time,* July 16, 1990, p. 19.
13. *Hartford Courant,* October 18, 1993, p. A2.
14. *New York Times,* July 5, 1995, p. A1.
15. All quotes in this paragraph are from the *Hartford Courant,* June 17, 1993, p. A4. The dissenting analyst was William Arkin.
16. *Hartford Courant,* July 3, 1994, p. A17.
17. The text of Bush's address was reprinted in the *New York Times,* December 26, 1991, p. A16.
18. *New York Times,* October 7, 1995, p. A1.
19. Jeffrey E. Garten, "Even Before the Inauguration," op-ed piece in the *New York Times,* November 15, 1992, p. F13.
20. *New York Times,* December 23, 1992, p. A13.
21. The first quote is from *Newsweek,* July 10, 1995, p. 48; the Dole quote is from *Time,* July 10, 1995, p. 45.
22. *New York Times,* June 30, 1995, p. D5.
23. *New York Times,* September 15, 1993, p. B12. The analyst was Geoffrey Garin.

CHAPTER 7

1. Quote is by Christopher Lehmann-Haupt from a review of the latest edition of Neustadt's book, now entitled *Presidential Power and the Modern Presidents: The Politics of Leadership from Roosevelt to Reagan* (New York: Free Press, 1990), found in *New York Times,* November 1, 1990, p. C6.
2. In addition to the works cited in the pages, recent studies include Fisher (1995a); Rourke (1993); Draper (1992); Lehman (1992); Hall (1991); Keynes (1991); Nathan (1991); Turner (1991); Barney (1990); and Henkin (1990).
3. "Authority of the President to Repel the Attack in Korea," *Department of State Bulletin* 23 (July 31, 1950), p. 173.
4. McNamara's comment is in an excerpt of his *In Retrospect* (New York: Random House, 1995) published in *Newsweek,* April 17, 1995, p. 50.
5. U.S. Congress, 1983, p. 37.
6. *Wall Street Journal,* November 3, 1990, p. A10.
7. *Time,* November 19, 1990, p. 50.

8. Address at the dedication ceremony of the Social Sciences Complex at Princeton University, May 10, 1991, recorded in the *Weekly Compilation of Presidential Documents,* vol. 27, no. 19 (May 13, 1991), p. 590.
9. *New York Times,* October 23, 1994, p. A1.
10. *New York Times,* April 22, 1991, p. A1.
11. *Goldwater v. Carter,* 444 U.S. 996 (1979).
12. *Hartford Courant,* May 10, 1991, p. A14.
13. *Hartford Courant,* January 10, 1993, p. A4.
14. *New York Times,* May 20, 1995, p. A1.
15. *New York Times,* July 12, 1995, p. A8.
16. A transcript of Clinton's statement is in the *New York Times,* July 12, 1995, p. A9.
17. *United States v. Curtiss-Wright Export Corporation,* 299 U.S. 304 (1936).
18. *Manchester Guardian Weekly,* March 19, 1995, p. 6.
19. *Newsweek,* May 15, 1995, p. 19.
20. *New York Times,* May 23, 1995, p. A10.
21. *New York Times,* May 22, 1995.
22. *New York Times,* June 17, 1995, p. A5.
23. *New York Times,* May 24, 1995, p. A8.
24. *Hartford Courant,* January 25, 1993, p. A3.
25. *Hartford Courant,* August 12, 1993, p. A1.
26. The quotes on the Balkans and Somalia are from the *New York Times,* September 23, 1993, p. A1.
27. *Hartford Courant,* May 1, 1995.
28. *Hartford Courant,* February 23, 1992, p. A1.
29. *Newsweek,* February 13, 1995, p. 29.
30. *New York Times,* December 9, 1994, p. A19.
31. *New York Times,* December 25, 1992, p. A22.
32. *Hartford Courant,* November 15, 1990, p. A8.
33. *Hartford Courant,* December 14, 1990, p. A16.
34. Poll of January 10–11, 1991, reported in *Newsweek,* January 21, 1991, p. 19.
35. *Time,* January 7, 1991, p. 33.
36. *Time,* January 21, 1991, p. 32.
37. *Time,* March 6, 1993, p. 20.
38. Address at the dedication ceremony of the Social Sciences Complex at Princeton University, May 10, 1991, recorded in the *Weekly Compilation of Presidential Documents,* vol. 27, no. 19 (May 13, 1991), p. 590.
39. Walter Issacson, *Kissinger: A Biography* (New York: Simon & Schuster, 1993), quoted in Theodore Draper, "Little Heinz and Big Henry," *New York Review of Books,* September 6, 1992, p. 21.
40. Except as noted, the quotes relating to the *Mayaguez* incident are all drawn frm Vandenbroucke (1991:237–242).
41. George P. Shultz, *From Turmoil and Triumph: My Years as Secretary of State* (New York: Charles Scribner's Sons, 1993); excerpted in *Time,* February 9, 1993, p. 45.
42. *Time,* August 27, 1990, p. 16.
43. *Hartford Courant,* November 16, 1990, p. A13.

BOX, "William Jefferson Clinton and the War Power," pp. 176–177

1. The quote is from a letter from Jefferson to Michel Guillaume Jean de Crèvecoeur, August 9, 1788. It can be found in most compilations of Jefferson's writings.
2. *Time,* May 24, 1993, p. 22.
3. *Maine Sunday Telegram,* June 27, 1993, p. A1.
4. *Washington Post,* June 16, 1993, p. A14.
5. *Hartford Courant,* October 19, 1993, p. A1.
6. *New York Times,* October 19, 1993, p. A1.
7. *Time,* July 25, 1994, p. 22. The poll showed 50 percent agreeing, 39 percent disagreeing, and 11 percent unsure.
8. *New York Times,* September 15, 1994, p. A8.
9. *New York Times,* December 15, 1995, p. A20.
10. *New York Times,* December 13, 1995, p. A1.
11. *New York Times,* November 28, 1995, p. A14.
12. *New York Times,* November 29, 1995, p. A18.
13. *Hartford Courant,* December 7, 1995, p. A15. The poll was of residents of Connecticut and was conducted by the Institute for Social Inquiry at the University of Connecticut.
14. *Time,* December 18, 1995, p. 54.
15. *New York Times,* December 14, 1995, p. A1.
16. *New York Times,* October 22, 1995, p. A15.
17. *Hartford Courant,* October 18, 1995, p. A1.

CHAPTER 8

1. The language is part of an amendment to the State Department Authorization Act of 1973, P.L. 93–126, October 19, 1973, Sec. 13.
2. Kissinger was testifying before the Senate Select Committee on POW–MIA Affairs and was referring specifically to the issue of pressuring Hanoi in the 1972–1975 period to better account for unaccounted-for Americans.
3. *New York Times,* September 23, 1992, p. A8.
4. *Congressional Quarterly Weekly Report,* January 12, 1991, p. 66.
5. *Congressional Record,* January 11, 1991, p. S250.
6. *Congressional Record,* January 11, 1991, p. S278.
7. *Congressional Record,* January 10, 1991, pp. H150–51.
8. *Congressional Record,* January 10, 1991, p. H160.
9. *Congressional Record,* January 11, 1991, p. S251.
10. *Time,* January 14, 1991, p. 12.
11. *National Journal,* February 9, 1991, p. 350.
12. *New York Times,* July 29, 1995, p. A3.

Endnotes

13. *New York Times*, May 11, 1995, p. A6.
14. Emphasis in the original.
15. *New York Times*, December 14, 1995, p. A1.
16. Both the McCain and Dole quotes are from the *New York Times*, December 1, 1995, p. A1.
17. *Hartford Courant*, December 14, 1995, p. A1.
18. The Biden and Hamilton quotes are from the *Washington Post National Weekly Edition*, May 23–29, 1994, p. 12.
19. *Time*, October 30, 1005, p. 79.
20. *New York Times*, September 23, 1994, p. B18.
21. *New York Times*, September 21, 1994, p. A1.
22. *New York Times*, October 23, 1993, p. A2.
23. *New York Times*, September 22, 1994, p. A6.
24. *Dallas Morning News*, June 8, 1995, p. 11A; *Newsweek*, June 12, 1995, pp. 18–23.
25. *New York Times*, June 8, 1995, p. A11.
26. *New York Times*, June 8, 1995, p. A11.
27. *Hartford Courant*, June 8, 1995, p. A6.
28. Both quotes are from the *New York Times*, November 11, 1994, p. A9.
29. *New York Times*, February 1, 1995, p. A3.
30. Talbott's statements about Israel and Russia are both from the *New York Times*, February 4, 1994, p. A6.
31. *New York Times*, February 9, 1994, p. A13.
32. *Congressional Quarterly Weekly Report*, May 13, 1995, p. 1342.
33. *Time*, January 9, 1995, p. 36.
34. *Dallas Morning News*, November 11, 1994, p. A6.
35. *New York Times*, November 10, 1994, p. A17.
36. *New York Times*, July 28, 1995, p. A1, and July 27, 1995, p. A1.
37. Both the Cohen and Conrad quotes are from the *New York Times*, July 28, 1995, p. A1.
38. *New York Times*, August 2, 1995, p. A6.
39. *New York Times*, February 15, 1995, p. A19.
40. The Helms and Atwood statements are from the *New York Times*, February 15, 1995, p. A5.
41. *New York Times*, May 26, 1995, p. A6. The spokesperson was Tony Blankley.
42. *Immigration and Naturalization Service v. Chadha*, 454 U.S. 812 (1983). Other relevant cases were *Process Gas Consumers Group v. Consumer Energy Council (1983)*, and *United States v. Federal Trade Commission (1983)*.
43. Gingrich and Torricelli are quoted in the *Dallas Morning News*, April 4, 1995, p. A9.
44. Originally found in *The Annals of Congress*, 490–94 (1792) as quoted in U.S. Legislative Reference Service (1964), *The Constitution of the United States of America: Analysis and Interpretation* (Washington, DC: U.S. Government Printing Office), p. 105.

BOX, "The GOP Worldview: Newt, Bob, Jesse and Ben," pp. 236–237

1. *New York Times*, December 7, 1994, p. A10.
2. *New York Times*, December 7, 1994, p. A10.
3. The quotes are from the *New York Times*, December 7, 1994, p. A10; *Time*, December 5, 1994, pp. 35–37; and *Newsweek*, December 5, 1994, pp. 24–26.
4. *New York Times*, December 7, 1994, p. A10.
5. Both quotes are from the *New York Times*, November 23, 1994, p. A19.
6. Quoted in an op-ed piece "What Kind of Hawk?" by Owen Harries in the *New York Times*, June 15, 1995, p. A31.
7. All quotes are from the *New York Times*, March 1, 1995, p. A2, except the quote of deputy foreign minister Yossi Beilin, which is from the *New York Times*, March 4, 1995, p. A4.
8. *New York Times*, December 9, 1994, p. A5.
9. *New York Times*, November 23, 1994, p. A19.
10. *Dallas Morning News*, November 23, 1994, p. A1.
11. *Time*, December 5, 1994, p. 37.
12. *New York Times*, March 1, 1995, p. A2.
13. All quotes are from the *New York Times*, July 18, 1995, p. A1.

CHAPTER 9

1. Both quotes in this paragraph are from Paterson, Clifford, and Hagan. The diplomatic historian was Thomas A. Bailey writing in *The Man in the Street* (New York: Macmillan, 1948).
2. *New York Times*, October 8, 1995, p. E7.
3. *International Herald Tribune*, April 18, 1994, p. A1.
4. *Time*, October 22, 1990, p. 27.
5. *Fort Myers News-Press*, January 14, 1993, p. A9.
6. *New York Times*, February 8, 1993, p. A9.
7. *Time*, January 25, 1993, p. 29.
8. *New York Times*, March 22, 1993, p. A2.
9. *Time*, May 2, 1994, p. 56.
10. *Time*, October 31, 1994, p. 36.
11. *Congressional Quarterly Weekly Report*, June 10, 1989, p. 1642.
12. *New York Times*, September 26, 1993, p. D3.
13. *New York Times*, October 19, 1993, p. A1.
14. *New York Times*, July 28, 1995, p. A1.
15. *Washington Post National Weekly Edition*, May 23–29, 1994, p. 12.
16. *Washington Post National Weekly Edition*, May 23–29, 1994, p. 12.
17. *Hartford Courant*, October 3, 1993, p. A8. Conyers ultimately voted against NAFTA.
18. *Hartford Courant*, June 8, 1992, p. C9.
19. *Hartford Courant*, June 8, 1992, p. C9.
20. *Time*, February 7, 1994, p. 24.

21. The first scholar is Stephen J. Wayne of Georgetown University; the second is Stephen Hess of the Brookings Institution. Both quotes are from the *New York Times,* January 29, 1994, p. E3.
22. *Time,* May 3, 1993, p. 46.
23. Both quotes are from the *New York Times,* November 18, 1993, p. A20.
24. *New York Times,* February 24, 1992, p. 31.
25. *Time,* January 25, 1993, p. 28.
26. *Washington Post Weekly Edition,* April 11–17, 1994, p. 11.
27. Both quotes are from *Time,* February 7, 1994, p. 28.
28. *Time,* January 25, 1993, p. 28.
29. All quotes in this paragraph are from the *Washington Post Weekly Edition,* April 11–17, 1994, p. 11.
30. *Time,* February 7, 1994, p. 28.
31. *New York Times,* June 14, 1995, p. A13.
32. *Time,* September 27, 1993, p. 57.
33. *Time,* February 7, 1994, p. 28.
34. *New York Times,* October 31, 1993, Section 4, p. 1.
35. *Time,* June 7, 1993, p. 23.
36. *Time,* June 7, 1993, p. 23. The official was Thomas "Mack" McLarty.
37. *Newsweek,* June 13, 1994, p. 31. A total of 29 percent answered "seriously," 43 percent answered "somewhat."
38. *Washington Post National Weekly Edition,* February 20–26, 1995, p. 37.
39. *National Journal,* January 29, 1994, p. 262.
40. *Time,* January 31, 1994, p. 86.
41. *USA Today,* April 1, 1992, p. A11.
42. *New York Times,* April 23, 1995, p. E3. The scholar was historian Michael Beschloss.
43. *USA Today,* April 1, 1992, p. A11.
44. *New York Times,* January 24, 1993, p. E3.
45. *Time,* January 17, 1994, p. 24. The adviser was former defense secretary and CIA director James Schlesinger.
46. *New York Times,* September 26, 1993, p. D3.
47. *New York Times,* March 6, 1992, p. A1.
48. *New York Times,* January 8, 1993, p. A12.

CHAPTER 10

1. *New York Times,* April 13, 1994, p. A15.
2. *Time,* June 28, 1993, p. 22. The Hunt donations were reported in *Time,* January 31, 1994, p. 20.
3. *New York Times,* April 13, 1994, p. A15.
4. Off-the-record interview with Mark A. Boyer, November 1993.
5. Quoted in *Time,* September 18, 1995, p. 59.
6. *New York Times,* November 15, 1995, p. D1.
7. *Christian Science Monitor,* March 28, 1995, pp. 1, 4.
8. *Hartford Courant,* December 3, 1995, p. A11.
9. *Newsweek,* June 12, 1995, p. 35.
10. *Newsweek,* June 12, 1995, p. 34.
11. Editorial Research Reports, *Making Foreign Policy* (Congressional Quarterly, Inc.: Washington, DC, 1988), p. 25.
12. *Newsweek,* October 25, 1993, p. 23.
13. John DeParle, "The Man Inside Bill Clinton's Foreign Policy," *New York Times Magazine,* August 20, 1995, p. 34.
14. *Newsweek,* October 3, 1994, p. 36.
15. John DeParle, "The Man Inside Bill Clinton's Foreign Policy," *New York Times Magazine,* August 20, 1995, p. 46.
16. John DeParle, "The Man Inside Bill Clinton's Foreign Policy," *New York Times Magazine,* August 20, 1995, p. 37.
17. *New York Times,* October 16, 1994, p. A30.
18. Nixon is quoted in Oudes (1989); Johnson is quoted in *People,* February 2, 1987, p. 11.
19. *Time,* August 1, 1994, p. 22.
20. *The Arizona Republic,* March 8, 1992, p. A2.
21. *New York Times,* February 17, 1992, p. A8.
22. *New York Times,* February 17, 1992, p. A1.
23. *Time,* January 30, 1995, p. 41.
24. *USA Today,* June 14, 1994, p. A10.
25. *Time,* August 1, 1994, p. 22.
26. Woolsey's comments were reprinted in *Vital Speeches of the Day,* March 1, 1994, pp. 6–9.
27. *New York Times,* September 20, 1992, p. A1.
28. *New York Times,* March 5, 1995, p. A10.
29. Colin L. Powell, *My American Journey* (New York: Random House, 1995), excerpted in *Time,* September 18, 1995, p. 69, and quoted in the *New York Times,* September 17, 1995, p. A26.
30. *New York Times,* April 12, 1994, p. A10.
31. *Hartford Courant,* December 1, 1995, p. A4.
32. Colin L. Powell, *My American Journey,* New York: Random House, 1995, excerpted in *Time,* September 18, 1995, p. 64.
33. *Time,* April 20, 1992, p. 61.
34. *New York Times,* December 4, 1994, p. A28.
35. *New York Times,* October 16, 1994, p. A30.
36. *New York Times,* October 16, 1994, p. A30.
37. *New York Times,* December 4, 1994, p. A28.
38. Louis G. Sarris, "McNamara's War, and Mine," op-ed piece in the *New York Times,* September 5, 1995, p. A17.
39. *Hartford Courant,* May 21, 1992, p. A8.
40. *New York Times Book Review,* January 19, 1992, p. 3. The quote is from Richard M. Nixon, *Seize the Moment: America's Challenge in a One-Superpower World* (New York: Simon & Schuster, 1992), as quoted in a review by Richard Perle entitled "The

World According to Nixon." The CIA's estimate was given to Nixon during his trip in 1990 to the USSR.

41. *New Yorker,* December 30, 1991, pp. 23–24.

42. Both quotes are from Joseph Finder, "The Spy in the Gray Flannel Suit," a review of David Corn, *Blond Ghost: Ted Shackley and the CIA's Crusades,* in the *New York Times Book Review,* October 23, 1994, p. 22.

43. The Specter quote is from the *New York Times,* November 1, 1995, p. A1; The Deutch quote is from *Time,* November 13, 1995, p. 82.

44. *New York Times,* April 7, 1992, p. A26.

45. *New York Times,* May 5, 1993, p. A18.

46. *New York Times,* May 5, 1993, p. A18.

47. John DeParle, "The Man Inside Bill Clinton's Foreign Policy," *New York Times,* August 20, 1995, p. 45.

48. *Hartford Courant,* December 8, 1994, p. A17.

49. Lawrence J. Korb, "The Readiness Gap. What Gap?" The *New York Times Magazine,* February 26, 1995, pp. 40–41.

50. *New York Times,* September 2, 1994, p. A9.

51. U.S. General Accounting, Report HR–93–7, December 1992, taken from the Internet.

52. *New York Times,* January 16, 1993, p. A8.

53. *New York Times,* June 2, 1992, p. A1.

54. *New York Times,* July 5, 1992.

55. *New York Times,* April 32, 1992, p. A7.

56. All quotes on the Lemay memo are from the *New York Times,* July 13, 1992, p. A12.

BOX, "The Guatemalan Connection," pp. 280–281

1. *New York Times,* April 2, 1995, p. A1.

2. *New York Times,* March 30, 1995, p. A1.

3. *New York Times,* April 2, 1995, p. A1.

4. *New York Times,* March 30, 1995, p. A1.

5. *New Orleans Times-Picayune,* March 24, 1995, p. A2.

6. *New York Times,* April 2, 1995, p. A1.

7. *New York Times,* April 25, 1995, p. A6.

8. *New York Times,* September 30, 1995, p. A5.

9. *New York Times,* July 26, 1995, p. A1.

CHAPTER 11

1. *New York Times,* March 31, 1992, p. A3.

2. *Vital Speeches of the Day,* 58/13 (March 1992), p. 370.

3. *Time,* December 12, 1994, p. 47.

4. *New York Times,* October 27, 1993, p. A1.

5. *New York Times,* September 1, 1994, p. A1.

6. *New York Times,* May 25, 1995, p. A1.

7. *New York Times,* February 3, 1994, p. A5.

8. *New York Times,* September 10, 1994, p. A5.

9. All quotes are from the *New York Times,* May 19, 1995, p. A12.

10. *Dallas Morning News,* August 25, 1994, p. A8. The observer was Peter Hakim, director of the Inter-American Dialogue in Washington, DC.

11. *Congressional Quarterly Weekly Report,* September 17, 1994, Internet transmission, February 15, 1995.

12. *New York Times,* July 7, 1994, p. A10.

13. *Newsweek,* May 22, 1995, p. 47.

14. Both the Robinson and Payne quotes are from the *New York Times,* March 17, 1995, p. A10.

15. *New York Times,* May 10, 1995, p. A3.

16. Rochester (NY) *Democrat and Chronicle,* February 3, 1991, p. A1.

17. *Time,* February 4, 1991, p. 43.

18. *Time,* February 4, 1991, p. 43.

19. *Hartford Courant,* April 12, 1995, p. A14. The two scholars are Harvey Klehr of Emory University and John Earl Haynes of the Library of Congress. They have published the 1995 book *The Secret World of American Communism.*

20. *New York Times,* August 28, 1994, p. E5. The analyst was the Reverend J. Bruan Hehir, a Roman Catholic priest, professor at Harvard Divinity School, and a member of the Harvard Center for International Affairs.

21. *The American Enterprise* 2, No. 4 (July–August 1991): 86. The survey was taken in 1989.

22. Choate is quoted in *Time,* October 1, 1990, p. 106.

23. *Time,* October 1, 1990, p. 106. The columnist was Michael Kinsley.

24. *Time,* November 1, 1993, p. 36.

25. *Congressional Quarterly Weekly Report,* January 30, 1993, p. 231.

26. *Congressional Quarterly Weekly Report,* March 13, 1993, p. 622.

27. *New York Times,* November 10, 1992, p. A3.

28. *New York Times,* January 5, 1993, p. A11.

29. *New York Times,* January 5, 1993, p. A11.

30. *New York Times,* February 9, 1994, p. A13.

31. *Hartford Courant,* November 28, 1991, p. A1.

32. This and the quote in the previous paragraph are from the *New York Times,* May 8, 1995, p. A1.

33. Both preceding quotes are from the *New York Times,* July 23, 1995, p. A10. The second quote is by Jay Mallin, former news director of Radio Martí.

34. *Christian Science Monitor,* March 10, 1995, p. 5.

35. *New York Times,* August 27, 1995, p. A10.

36. *Fortune,* February 8, 1993, pp. 84, 86.

37. *Dallas Morning News,* February 26, 1995, p. 1A.

BOX, "The Jewish Lobby: David or Goliath?" pp. 330–332

1. *New York Times,* March 12, 1994, p. A5.
2. *New York Times,* September 30, 1995, p. A1.
3. All quotes from the *New York Times,* May 18, 1995, p. A1.
4. *Hartford Courant,* October 25, 1995, p. A1.
5. *Hartford Courant,* November 25, 1991, p. A1.

CHAPTER 12

1. Thomas Jefferson to Edward Carrington, January 16, 1787, available in most compilations of Jefferson's writings and letters.
2. John Quincy Adams diary entry, September 7, 1820.
3. Dana's article "What Is News?" appeared in the *New York Sun* in 1882.
4. Don Oberdorfer, "Government and the Media: Dependence and Distrust," *Washington Post National Weekly Edition,* April 26–May 2, 1993, p. 24.
5. *New York Times,* March 1, 1967, n.p.
6. *New York Times,* July 29, 1994, p. A12.
7. *Christian Science Monitor,* April 21, 1995, p. 4.
8. U.S. President, *Public Papers of the President of the United States: John F. Kennedy,* 1962 (Washington, DC: GPO, 1963), p. 376.
9. Thomas's remarks were broadcast on May 6, 1993, by C-Span, which was televising a testimonial dinner for Thomas.
10. The Hosler and Thomas quotes are from the *New York Times,* January 24, 1993, p. A20.
11. Richard Harwood, "The Press's Revenge . . . ," *Washington Post,* June 16, 1993, p. A21. The second, third, and fourth columnists are Stanley Cloud, James Perry, and Eleanor Clift, all quoted by Harwood.
12. *New York Times,* February 4, 1993, p. A10.
13. *New York Times,* May 31, 1993, p. 10. The reporter was R. W. Apple.
14. *New York Times,* September 23, 1994, p. A23.
15. Speake's comments were made on ABC television on January 31, 1987.
16. *Newsweek,* September 4, 1995, p. 17.
17. *New York Times,* May 4, 1994, p. A1.
18. *Washington Post National Weekly Edition,* April 3–9, 1995, pp. 7–9. The reporter was Howard Kurtz.
19. *Newsweek,* September 11, 1995, p. 38.
20. *CQ Researcher,* July 15, 1994, taken from the Internet, as transmitted February 2, 1995.
21. All quotes from the Times Mirror Center for the People and the Press report are from the *Hartford Courant,* November 4, 1995, p. A9.
22. *Washington Post National Weekly Edition,* May 29–June 4, 1995, p. 7.
23. *Dallas Morning News,* March 19, 1995, p. 1J. The journalist was Charles Madigan.
24. *Dallas Morning News,* December 30, 1995, p. 4A.
25. *Washington Post National Weekly Edition,* May 29–June 4, 1995, pp. 6–7.

BOX, "The Press Goes to War," pp. 362–364

1. *Hartford Courant,* January 18, 1991, p. A20.
2. *Time,* February 18, 1991, p. 32.
3. *Hartford Courant,* January 31, 1991, p. A1.
4. *Time,* January 21, 1991, p. 41.
5. *Time,* February 18, 1991, p. 39. The reporter was Thomas Giusto.
6. *Time,* February 18, 1991, p. 39.
7. *Hartford Courant,* March 2, 1991, p. A7.
8. *Hartford Courant,* January 22, 1991, p. A6.
9. *Hartford Courant,* January 22, 1991, p. A6.
10. *Hartford Courant,* January 22, 1991, p. A6.
11. Marvin Kalb, "Let's Not Kill the CNN Messenger in Baghdad," *Hartford Courant,* February 5, 1991, p. B11.
12. The Halberstam and Donaldson quotes are both from *Time,* Feburary 25, 1991, p. 55.
13. *Hartford Courant,* January 31, 1991, p. A1.
14. *Hartford Courant,* January 31, 1991, p. A1.

CHAPTER 13

1. *National Journal,* March 11, 1995, p. 642.
2. *Newsweek,* June 12, 1995, p. 20; *Washington Post National Weekly Edition,* June 12–18, 1995, p. 37.
3. *New York Times,* April 30, 1995, p. E4.
4. *Time,* March 18, 1991, p. 22.
5. *National Journal,* January 14, 1995, p. 130.
6. Yankelovich poll reported on by Reuter on the Internet, July 22, 1995; *Newsweek,* June 12, 1995, p. 23; *Washington Post National Weekly Edition,* June 12–18, 1995, p. 37.
7. All polls cited in this paragraph are from *Public Perspective,* July/August, 1994, p. 96.
8. *World Opinion Update,* September 1990, p. 101.
9. "A Roper Center Review of Public Opinion on the Gulf Crisis" (Roper Center for Public Opinion Research: The University of Connecticut at Storrs), January 24, 1991.
10. *Hartford Courant,* December 7, 1995, p. A15. The poll surveyed residents of Connecticut.
11. *American Enterprise,* March/April 1991, p. 85.
12. *World Opinion Update,* January 1994, pp. 2–3.
13. Using Wittkopf (1994) terminology to report Wittkopf (1990) data.

Endnotes

14. Wittkopf's (1994) categories are used in place of those in Hinckley and Wittkopf (1994).
15. The multilateralist percentage combines the Hinckley and Wittkopf (1994) categories of active and ordinary multilateralists.
16. *Time,* May 17, 1993, p. 74.
17. "An American Ruling Class?" *The Washington Spectator,* April 1, 1993, p. 1.
18. *New York Times,* June 29, 1993, p. A5.
19. *Time,* May 24, 1993, p. 22.
20. *Congressional Quarterly Weekly Report,* September 17, 1994, on the Internet.
21. *National Journal,* January 14, 1995, p. 130.
22. *National Journal,* January 14, 1995, p. 130, and March 11, 1995, p. 642.
23. *Dallas Morning News,* June 29, 1993, p. 7A. The polls were taken by the Gallup organization.
24. *National Journal,* March 11, 1995, p. 642.
25. *New York Times,* April 30, 1995, p. 4.
26. *Dallas Morning News,* July 12, 1995, p. 11A.
27. *Time,* June 12, 1995, p. 55.
28. *Time,* October 7, 1991, p. 26. The observer was William Galston, who served as Walter Mondale's issue director in the previous 1984 campaign.
29. *New York Times,* August 17, 1992, p. A9.
30. *New York Times,* October 22, 1992, p. A19.
31. *New York Times,* January 28, 1992, p. A1.
32. *New York Times,* August 2, 1992, p. E3.
33. *National Journal,* January 14, 1995, p. 130.
34. Excerpt from Colin Powell with Joseph E. Persico, *My American Journey* (New York: Random House, 1995), in *Time,* September 18, 1995, p. 69.
35. *Newsweek,* September 26, 1994, p. 36.
36. *Congressional Quarterly Weekly Report,* September 17, 1994, on the Internet.
37. *Newsweek,* September 26, 1994, p. 36.
38. *New York Times,* March 5, 1995, p. A10. This historian was Michael S. Sherry of Northwestern University.
39. Thomas L. Friedman, "With One Eye on Elections, House Balks at Russian Aid," *New York Times,* July 10, 1992, p. A10.
40. Excerpts from Robert S. McNamara, *In Retrospect* (New York: Random House, 1995), printed in *Newsweek,* April 17, 1995, p. 47.
41. *U.S. News & World Report,* May 29, 1995, p. 20.
42. *Hartford Courant,* November 9, 1989, p. A19.
43. *Time,* October 4, 1993, p. 20.
44. *Dallas Morning News,* May 19, 1994, p. 5A.
45. *Washington Post National Weekly Edition,* March 20–26, 1995, p. 37; *New York Times,* February 27, 1995, p. A6.
46. *New York Times,* February 27, 1995, p. A6.
47. Polls taken in 1981, 1982, 1987, 1988, 1989, 1990, and 1991 by various polling organizations as reported in *Public Opinion Perspective,* January/February 1992, p. 101. Data interpretation by the authors includes as a foreign concern those respondents identifying "foreign trade," which was listed in the journal as an economic issue.
48. *The American Enterprise,* March/April, 1991, p. 92.
49. *Washington Post National Weekly Edition,* May 29–June 4, 1995, p. 6.
50. *Time,* June 12, 1995, p. 55.
51. *National Journal,* January 14, 1995, p. 130.
52. David Morrison, "Whose Eyes Only?" *National Journal,* February 26, 1994, p. 473. The group is the National Classification Management Society.
53. *New York Times,* December 8, 1993, p. A20.
54. *Time,* November 26, 1990, p. 31.
55. *Time,* March 18, 1991, p. 22.
56. *Hartford Courant,* December 7, 1995, p. A15.

GLOSSARY

American exceptionalism The notion that the United States is not just different from, but is better than, other countries. **91**

Balance of payments The record of all transactions of goods and services in an economy. Maintenance of a balanced balance of payments was crucial to the stability of the Bretton Woods international economic system. A balance of payments deficit means more money is flowing out of an economy than is flowing into that economy. The reverse is true for a balance of payments surplus. **77**

Bipartisanship The idea that presidents should be able to count on foreign policy support from both Republicans and Democrats in Congress. **246, 391**

Bipolar An international system that is dominated by two powerful countries. **43**

Boland Amendments A series of amendments, beginning in 1982, which barred the expenditure of funds to topple the Ortega government in Nicaragua. **229**

Bretton Woods international economic system The international economic system designed in 1944 at Bretton Woods, New Hampshire, to remedy the sources of the Great Depression and to provide greater opportunities for the capitalist nations to prosper in the post-war world. Under Bretton Woods, the International Monetary Fund (IMF) and International Bank for Reconstruction and Development (renamed the World Bank) were created to provide financial support for post-war recovery and economic development. **50**

Capitalism An economic system based on the free market, the laws of supply and demand, and a respect for both private property and the profit motive. **97**

Carter Doctrine The policy enunciated by President Jimmy Carter that explicitly put the Soviets on notice that the Persian Gulf was a strategic American interest and that the United States would protect it militarily if required. The president's new outlook regarding defense needs mirrored American public opinion. This doctrine

was a direct response to the 1979 Soviet invasion of Afghanistan. **61**

Clark Amendment A 1975 amendment terminating financial support for CIA operations in Angola. **228**

Containment doctrine This policy, first enunciated by President Harry Truman in 1947, held that communism, especially backed by Soviet power, presented a deadly threat to the United States and the rest of the free world; that any communist advance was unacceptable; and, therefore, that the West, led by the United States, had to counter every communist thrust no matter where it occurred in the world in order to prevent the further spread of this threat. **52**

Cultural imperialism The imposition of one's cultural values and way of life on others. **102**

Democracy The concept from political philosophy that describes a system of government based on active participation of the citizenry in decision making. The American political system is often characterized as a democracy, but the degree of citizen participation varies considerably depending upon the issues involved, the level of government, and other factors. More accurately, the American political system can be described as a representative democracy, where the citizens popularly elect officials to make decisions for them. **16, 95**

Dependencia The theory that asserts that the wealthier capitalist nations cultivate policies that foster the dependence of developing nations on the industrialized, capitalist nations. See also **Neoimperialism. 50**

Détente The establishment of warmer relations during the cold war period between the United States and the Soviet Union. This policy was developed by the Nixon foreign policy team. **60**

Domino theory Held as true by many Americans during the cold war, this theory suggested that, like a row of on-end dominoes successively toppling by striking one another, one communist takeover would lead to another, then another, until the last free world domino, the United

xxxviii

Glossary

States, was imperiled. It was also part of the rationale for American intervention in Vietnam in the 1960s. **52**

Elite The few people in a society who exercise power directly and in inordinate proportion to their numbers. **374**

Executive agreements Agreements made with other governments not requiring Senate approval. **180**

Executive Agreements Act A 1972 act requiring presidents to inform Congress of agreements made with other countries within 60 days of the agreement's implementation. **214**

Extraterritoriality The international legal provision that allows citizens of one country that are accused of crimes in other countries to be tried before courts in the home country rather than the foreign country where the crime was committed. This provision was part of the Treaty of Wanghia with China signed in 1844. **47**

Foreign policy process The series of activities that takes place within and around the governmental system that produces foreign policy. The study of the foreign policy process is distinct from the general study of foreign policy itself by focusing on *how* foreign policy is made rather than on *what* foreign policy is. **5**

Foreign Service Officers (FSOs) The 3,500 or so U.S. governmental officials who constitute the diplomatic corps and also the upper echelons of the State Department. Traditionally, this group has been dominated by white, upper-class, Ivy League-educated males. They are also frequently referred to as *career diplomats* to distinguish them from the individuals holding diplomatic positions who are appointed for political reasons by the president. **278**

Gatekeeping Control of the flow of stories to the media, thereby determining what stories the press will report or largely ignore. **366**

Gender gap The difference between males and females along dimensions such as their attitudes toward foreign policy issues. **376**

General Agreement on Tariffs and Trade (GATT) The international agreement that created the organization of the same name as the principal institution working to ensure market access and liberalize trade policies among the capitalist countries after World War II. **50**

Good Neighbor Policy In 1933 Franklin Roosevelt used the traditional phrase "good neighbor" to denote his policy toward Latin America. The United States government was trying to soften the image of self-interested domination of its sphere of influence. The Good Neighbor Policy marked an end to prolonged, direct U.S. interventions, but the United States actively continued to foster pro-American regimes throughout Latin America. **45**

Group of Seven The seven largest economically free market countries: Canada, France, Germany, Great Britain, Italy, Japan, and the United States. **78**

Groupthink The pressure to achieve consensus within a small, face-to-face decisional group. **134**

Hughes-Ryan Amendment A 1974 amendment requiring the president to inform Congress of covert operations by the CIA. **228**

Human rights The belief that all individuals possess certain rights, such as civil rights and liberties, which should not be infringed upon by governments. **96**

Idealism The belief that peace and harmony are the natural states of humankind, and thus violence and conflict represent human failures and are not to be tolerated. **105**

Imperial overstretch Historian Paul Kennedy's theory that as a country becomes powerful economically, its international interests increase as well as the cost of defending those interests. The resultant military investment leads to a defeat of the original intent. **70**

Imperialist internationalism A more aggressive form of the belief that the United States has a stake in international affairs. This relates in particular to the growth of American commercial interests throughout the world. International economic involvement was perceived as the next logical step in American economic growth once American domestic markets became saturated. As a result, American business leaders looked outward for new and larger markets for their products. See also **Internationalism. 47**

Incremental policy Policy which evolves slowly as a series of minor steps or minor changes from previous policy. **159**

Intelligence Oversight Act A 1980 act requiring the president to report any covert intelligence operations to the House and Senate Intelligence Committees. **232**

Interest groups Nongovernmental associations of people with some shared commonality when that commonality has a political stake. **322**

International system The global social-economic-political-geographic environment. **33**

Internationalism The belief that the United States has a stake in the general shape of the international political system. It also implies the country's willingness to get actively involved on a regular basis in the political affairs of others. **41, 117**

Investigation The congressional power to require testimony before legislators and the transmission of information to Congress. **230**

Iron triangles Informal alliances among specific offices in the bureaucracy, congressional subcommittees and legislators, and private business and interest groups that have mutually supportive interests centered on a particular issue or problem. **157, 315**

Isolationism The belief that the United States should avoid becoming involved in the political affairs of other countries. **41, 114**

Issue areas Substantive categories of policies across which policy making processes vary and that must be considered when evaluating national interests. **160**

Legalism An orientation that emphasizes organizations, rules, agreements, procedures, and other such formal structures to judge and govern conduct. **100**

Legislative veto The process by which Congress reserves the right to terminate presidential actions by passage of concurrent resolutions that are not subject to presidential vetoes. **221**

Liberalism The belief in or commitment to individual liberty and the protection of private property; to limited government, the rule of law, natural rights, the perfectibility of human institutions, and to the possibility of human progress. **94**

Mandate A specific public endorsement of one or more foreign policy initiatives. **389**

Manifest Destiny The notion that Americans had the God-given right and duty to spread their benevolent rule over the North American continent and its native peoples. **102**

Marshall Plan The economic aid program for post–World War II Europe. Also known as the European Recovery Program. **44**

Mass The general public. **373**

Mass media The organizations that convey political news to the public, such as radio, television, and printed sources. **350**

Mass movement A large segment of the public gets so aroused that advocates of a change in government policy create supportive organizations, begin media campaigns, and promote widespread demonstrations and other political activity to pressure government officials. **396**

Messianism An urge, a sense of duty, to remake the world in one's own image, often including the right to save others, even from themselves. **102**

Micromanagement Occurs when a policy maker or policy making body becomes overly involved in how those who carry out policy implement it. The executive branch often accuses Congress of trying to micromanage foreign policy by putting restrictive details in legislation or by otherwise dictating to executive officials how to implement broad policy goals. **232**

Model An intellectual construct that represents what something is like or how it works. **147**

Monroe Doctrine Enunciated by President James Monroe in December 1823, this doctrine declared the New World off limits to further colonization by Old World powers and proclaimed American determination to stay out of Europe's affairs. President Monroe's démarche (a strong policy statement in diplomacy) was based on an idealistic mix of an isolationist sense of moral superiority to Europe and a realistic desire to keep European powers at bay and to establish and fortify the claim of the United States to influence in the Western Hemisphere. **44**

Moralism The need to justify political agendas and actions in moral terms and to judge outcomes against a set of moral values. **92**

Most favored nation (MFN) This term means granting another country a tariff rate that is no higher than the lowest rate accorded to any other country. This status benefits the recipient country by giving it competitive access to U.S. markets. **58**

Multilateralist An individual who believes that the United States establishes its foreign policy goals and carries them out by emphasizing international cooperation through multilateral institutions such as the United Nations. Multilateralists are' wary of a narrow focus on U.S. interests and of acting unilaterally to secure those interests. See **Unilateralist. 123**

Multinational corporations (MNCs) Companies that have production facilities and other operations in foreign countries. **324**

Multipolar An international system that is dominated by four or more powerful countries. The nation-state system most often identified as multipolar was the system centered in Europe throughout most of the nineteenth century. **38**

Glossary

Neoimperialist A description used by critics of U.S. foreign policy asserting that it uses foreign policy to create a continuing economic and political system that promotes dependency of the poorer nations on the richer nations of the world. Under this system, critics alleged, the rich get richer and the poor stay poor and remain dependent on the wealthier countries. See also **Dependencia. 50**

New world order Espoused by President George Bush after the end of the cold war, this idea focused on the creation of an international system based on international law and relying on international organizations such as the United Nations to settle international conflicts. **87**

Nixon Doctrine The policy enunciated by President Nixon that sought to minimize the role of the United States as world policeman, while still preserving American influence in critical regions of the world by using strategic allies as surrogate powers in the region. **54**

Nontariff barriers (NTBs) Barriers to free access to American markets that are not tariffs. Tariffs are taxes on imported goods that make those goods more expensive to domestic consumers. Nontariff barriers include voluntary export restraints, quotas, and health and packaging restrictions. Most NTBs have been outside the scope of GATT until very recently and have thus been used by many nations to avoid strict adherence to the free trade policies espoused under GATT. **77**

Open Door policy The U.S. administration policy (1899) that demanded that the other imperial powers already in China share that country's resources and markets with the United States. **48**

Operational reality What decision makers think is real, rather than what is real. **137**

Oversight The congressional authority to monitor the operations of the executive branch. **231**

Pluralism The notion that a political society is an amalgam of many different groups, each of which has its own interests. **322**

Political agenda The set of issues being widely and intensely discussed. **164, 364**

Political culture A society's historical experiences, traditional ways of looking at the world, and long-standing norms (values) that provide it a way to interpret political reality. **90**

Pragmatism The practice of dealing with problems on a case-by-case basis rather than with an eye on long-term planning or ideological values. **111**

Presidential wars The power of the president to decide unilaterally when and if, not just how, U.S. military forces will be used. **173**

Public opinion The opinions held by the wide range of Americans. **373**

Racism The conviction that one race is superior or inferior to others on the basis of real or imagined characteristics, e.g., skin color. **108**

Rally effect The sharp jump in presidential popularity at times of crisis. **192**

Reagan Doctrine This policy, enunciated by President Ronald Reagan, pledged that the United States would supply anticommunist forces everywhere in the world. At its root it was an interventionist doctrine. The president saw the U.S. role in the world as one of nourishing and defending freedom and democracy. **61**

Realism A belief that the major goal of states must be to take care of their interests by managing their power prudently. **105**

Role The notion that the way people act is partly determined by the job they hold. **133**

Roosevelt Corollary Enunciated by Theodore Roosevelt, this policy asserted the U.S. right to intervene in other Western Hemisphere nations to stop actions unacceptable to the United States. The American-claimed right to define such wrongdoing was a reflection of the political culture trait of American exceptionalism, or the tendency to view the United States as a unique and morally superior nation. The corollary justified to Americans repeated interventions, and at times occupying forces, in many Latin American countries. **45**

Smoot-Hawley Tariff Enacted in 1931 when Congress imposed very high duties on imported goods. This was a major barrier to foreign access to American markets. **49**

Social Darwinism The justification of racism and the oppression of other peoples based on the notions of the "law of the jungle" or "survival of the fittest." **108**

Sovereignty The concept that nation-states legally answer to no higher authority than themselves. As a result, the international system is organized horizontally. **34**

Spheres of influence Geographic areas over which particular nation-states exercise special influence. Spheres of influence usually develop as a result of international competition over international power, territory, and economic opportunities. **44**

Standard Operating Procedures (SOPs) These are the rules established within large bureaucracies that provide them with coherence, direction, and clear guidelines for action, especially in the face of uncertainty and ambiguous decision making situations. SOPs allow bureaucrats to fit the problem of the moment into a neat formula for action that is based on organizational tradition. In this way, the individual knows that he or she is operating within the parameters of what is considered "safe" for the organization. **153, 302**

Subgovernments Informal alliances in which bureaucratic substructures, interest groups, and members of Congress cooperate, conflict, or compromise to make policy decisions. **156**

Technocracy A government by technical experts. **154**

Technocrats Bureaucrats who are technical experts on one or another issue. **17**

Think tanks Privately funded public policy research centers. **336**

Transnational interest groups Interest groups which operate across national borders. **338**

Two-Level Game The concept that in order to arrive at satisfactory international agreements, a country's diplomats actually have to deal with (at one level) the other country's negotiators and (at the second level), legislators, interest groups, and other domestic forces at home. **3**

Truman Doctrine The policy of the Harry S. Truman administration of giving military and economic aid to those countries (Greece and Turkey specifically) seeking to resist Soviet pressure. The Doctrine also enunciated the policy of containment of Soviet influence throughout the world. **44**

Unilateralist An individual who believes that the United States should focus on its national (self-) interests and act alone when necessary to secure those interests. Unilateralists are wary of relying on multilateral diplomacy to set foreign policy goals or to carry them out. See **Multilateralist.** **123**

War Powers Resolution (WPR) A 1973 attempt by Congress to limit the president's unilateral ability to deploy U.S. forces into dangerous areas or order them into combat. **209**

ABBREVIATIONS

ACDA	Arms Control and Disarmament Agency
AFL-CIO	American Federation of Labor and Congress of Industrial Organizations
AID	Agency for International Development
AIPAC	American Israel Public Affairs Committee
ANC	African National Congress
ANZUS	Australia-New Zealand-United States Tripartite Treaty
APEC	Asian Pacific Economic Cooperation
BMD	Ballistic Missile Defense
CANF	Cuban American National Foundation
CFE	Conventional Forces in Europe (treaty)
CFR	Council on Foreign Relations
CIA	Central Intelligence Agency
CO2)	Carbon Dioxide
CoCom	Coordinating Committee
DCI	Director of Central Intelligence
DEFCON	Defense Condition
EU	European Union
FSO	Foreign Service Officer
FTAA	Free Trade Agreement of the Americas
G-7	Group of Seven
GAO	General Accounting Office
GATT	General Agreement(s) on Tariffs and Trade
GDP	Gross Domestic Product
GNP	Gross National Product
ICJ	International Court of Justice
IGO	Intergovernmental Organization
IMF	International Monetary Fund
INF	Intermediate-range Nuclear Forces
JCS	Joint Chiefs of Staff
LDC	Less Developed Country
MFN	Most Favored Nation
MIA	Missing in Action
MNC	Multinational Corporation
NAACP	National Association for the Advancement of Colored People
NAFTA	North American Free Trade Agreement
NAM	Nonaligned Movement
NATO	North Atlantic Treaty Organization
NGO	Nongovernmental Organization
NIC	Newly industrializing country
NORC	National Opinion Research Center
NPT	Nuclear Nonproliferation Treaty
NSC	National Security Council
NSC-68	National Security Council Paper Number 68
NTB	Nontariff Barrier
OAS	Organization of American States
OMB	Office of Management and Budget
OPEC	Organization of Petroleum Exporting Countries
PLO	Palestine Liberation Organization
POW	Prisoner of War
SAC	Strategic Air Command
SALT I	Strategic Arms Limitation Talks
SDI	Strategic Defense Initiative
SEATO	Southeast Asia Treaty Organization
SIGINT	Signal intelligence
SIOP-7	Strategic Integrated Operational Plan–7
SOP	Standard Operating Procedure
START	Strategic Arms Reduction Talks
STR	Special Trade Representative
UN	United Nations
UNCTAD	United Nations Conference on Trade and Development
UNDP	United Nations Development Program
USIA	United States Information Agency
USSR	Union of Soviet Socialist Republics
USTR	United States Trade Representative
WASP	White Anglo-Saxon Protestant
WHAM	"Winning Hearts and Minds"
WPR	War Powers Resolution
WTO	World Trade Organization

REFERENCES

Abelson, Donald E. (1995). "From policy research to political advocacy; The changing role of think tanks in American politics." *Canadian Review of American Studies 25*, 93–126.

Aberbach, Joel D., Mezger, Daniel B., & Rockman, Bert. (1991). "Bureaucrats and politicians: A report on the administrative elites project." *Australian Journal of Public Administration, 50*, 203–17.

Abramson, Paul R., Aldrich, John H., & Rohde, David W. (1990). *Change and continuity in the 1988 elections.* Washington, DC: CQ Press.

Achen, Christopher H. (1978). "Measuring representation." *American Journal of Political Science, 22*, 475–510.

Acheson, Dean G. (1969). *Present at the creation.* New York: W. W. Norton.

Adams, Gordon. (1988). "The iron triangle: Inside the defense policy process." In Charles W. Kegley Jr. & Eugene R. Wittkopf (Eds.), *The domestic sources of American foreign policy* (pp. 70–78). New York: St. Martin's.

Adler, David G. (1988). "The Constitution and presidential warmaking." *Political Science Quarterly, 103*, 1–36.

Aldrich, John H. (1991). "Power and order in Congress." In Morris P. Fiorina & David W. Rohde (Eds.), *Home style and Washington work: Studies of congressional politics* (pp. 219–52). Ann Arbor: University of Michigan Press.

Alger, Chadwick F. (1990, April). "U.S. public opinion on the UN: A mandate for more creative U.S. participation in the UN system?" Paper presented at the International Studies Association convention, Washington, DC.

Allen, Barbara, O'Loughlin, Paula, Jasperson, Amy, & Sullivan, John L. (1994). "The media and the Gulf War: Framing, priming, and the spiral of silence." *Polity, 27*, 255–84.

Allison, Graham T. (1971). *Essence of decision: Explaining the Cuban missile crisis.* Boston: Little, Brown.

Almond, Gabriel A. (1960). *The American people and foreign policy* (rev. ed.). New York: Praeger.

Altbach, Philip G. (Ed.). (1989). *Student political activism: An international reference handbook.* Westport, CT: Greenwood.

Ambrose, Stephen. (1991). *Nixon: The triumph of a politician, 1962–1972.* New York: Simon & Schuster.

Ambrose, Stephen. (1992). "The presidency and foreign policy." *Foreign Affairs, 70*, 120–37.

American Psychological Association. (1983). *Publication Manual of the American Psychological Association* (3rd ed.). Washington, DC.

Andrew, Christopher. (1995). *For the president's eyes only: Secret intelligence and the American presidency from Washington to Bush.* New York: HarperCollins.

Ansolabehere, Stephen, Behr, Roy, & Iyengar, Shanto. (1993). *The media game.* New York: Macmillan.

Arnold, R. Douglas. (1990). *The logic of congressional action.* New Haven, CT: Yale University Press.

Aukofer, Frank A. (1991). "The press collaborators." *Nieman Reports, 45*, 24–26.

Bailey, Thomas A. (1974). *A diplomatic history of the American people* (9th ed.). Englewood Cliffs, NJ: Prentice–Hall.

Ball, George W., & Ball, Douglas B. (1992). *The passionate attachment: America's involvement with Israel.* New York: W. W. Norton.

Banks, Jeffrey S., & Weingast, Barry. (1992). "The political control of bureaucracies under asymmetric information." *American Journal of Political Science, 36*, 509–24.

Barber, James D. (1985). *The presidential character: Predicting performance in the White House* (3rd ed.). Englewood Cliffs, NJ: Prentice Hall.

Bard, Mitchell. (1987). "Ethnic group influence on Middle East policy—how and when: The cases of the Jackson-Vanik Amendment and the sale of AWACS to Saudi Arabia." In Mohammed E. Ahari (Ed.), *Ethnic groups and U.S. foreign policy* (pp. 45–64). Westport, CT: Greenwood.

Bard, Mitchell. (1988). "The influence of ethnic interest groups on American Middle East policy." In Charles W. Kegley Jr. & Eugene R. Wittkopf (Eds.), *The domestic sources of American foreign policy: Insights and evidence* (pp. 57–69). New York: St. Martin's.

Bardes, Barbara A. (1995, August). "From the cold war to the Clinton years: The American public views a changing world." Paper presented at the American Political Science Association convention, Chicago.

Barilleaux, Ryan J. (1988). "Presidential conduct of foreign policy." *Congress & the Presidency, 15*, 1–25.

References

Barnet, Richard J. (1990). *The rockets' red glare: When America goes to war—the president and the people.* New York: Simon & Schuster.

Barone, Michael, & Ujifusa, Grant. (1993). *The Almanac of American Politics, 1994.* Washington, DC: National Journal.

Barrett, David M. (1993). *Uncertain warriors: Lyndon Johnson and his Vietnam advisers.* Lawrence: University of Kansas Press.

Bartels, Larry M. (1991). "Constituency opinion and congressional policy making: The Reagan defense buildup." *American Political Science Review, 85,* 457–74.

Bartels, Larry M. (1994). "The American public's defense spending preferences in the post–cold war era." *Public Opinion Quarterly, 58,* 479–508.

Bathurst, Robert B. (1993). *Intelligence and the mirror: On creating an enemy.* Thousand Oaks, CA: Sage.

Beck, Nathaniel. (1991). "The illusion of cycles in international relations." *International Studies Quarterly, 35,* 455–76.

Beckman, Peter R. (1984). *World politics in the twentieth century.* Englewood Cliffs, NJ: Prentice Hall.

Bendor, Jonathan. (1995). "A model of muddling through." *American Political Review, 89,* 819–40.

Bendor, Jonathan, & Hammond, Thomas H. (1992). "Rethinking Allison's models." *American Political Science Review, 88,* 301–22.

Bennett, Marc. (1993, March). "October surprise, November demise? An expected-utility approach to the rally effect." Paper presented at the International Studies Association convention, Acapulco.

Berman, Larry. (1990). "Presidential power and national security." In Howard E. Shuman & Walter R. Thomas (Eds.), *The Constitution and national security* (pp. 117–34). Washington, DC: National Defense University Press.

Berry, Nicholas O. (1990). *Foreign policy and the press: An analysis of the New York Times' coverage of U.S. foreign policy.* Westport, CT: Greenwood.

Beschloss, Michael R. (1992). *The crisis years.* New York: HarperCollins.

Betts, Richard K. (1978). "Analysis, war, and decision: Why intelligence failures are inevitable." *World Politics, 31,* 61–89.

Biddle, Arthur W., & Holland, Kenneth M. (1987). *Writer's guide: Political science.* Lexington, MA: D. C. Heath.

Blechman, Barry M. (1990). *The politics of national security: Congress and U.S. defense policy.* New York: Oxford University Press/Twentieth Century Fund.

Blechman, Barry M., & Kaplan, Stephen S. (1979). *Force without war: U.S. armed forces as a political instrument.* Washington, DC: Brookings Institution.

Bohlen, Charles. (1973). *Witness to history: 1929–1969.* New York: W. W. Norton.

Bond, Jon R., & Fleisher, Richard. (1990). *The president in the legislative arena.* Chicago: University of Chicago Press.

Bostdorff, Denise M. (1991). "The presidency and promoted crisis: Reagan, Grenada, and issue management." *Presidential Studies Quarterly, 21,* 737–50.

Bostdorff, Denise M. (1993). *The presidency and the rhetoric of foreign crisis.* Columbia: University of South Carolina Press.

Bostdorff, Denise M., & Goldzwig, Steven R. (1994). "Idealism and pragmatism in American foreign policy rhetoric: The case of John F. Kennedy and Vietnam." *Presidential Studies Quarterly, 24,* 515–30.

Boyd, Richard W. (1993, September). "Elections and crises: The influence of foreign affairs in the 1956 election." Paper presented at the American Political Science Association convention, Washington, DC.

Boyer, Mark A. (1993). *From enemies to benefactors: The G-7 negotiates Soviet aid.* Case study written for Pew Faculty Fellowship in International Affairs, Harvard University.

Boyer, Mark A. (1995). "Two-level games in the American foreign policy process." Unpublished manuscript. University of Connecticut.

Brace, Paul, & Hinckley, Barbara. (1992). *Follow the leader: Opinion polls and the modern presidents.* New York: Basic Books.

Bracken, Paul, & Johnson, Stuart E. (1993). "Beyond NATO: Complementary militaries." *Orbis, 37*(2), 205–21.

Brandes, Lisa C. O. (1993, March). "Who cares? Interest, concern, and gender in international security policy." Paper presented at the International Studies Association convention, Acapulco.

Brandes, Lisa C. O. (1994). "The liberal feminist state and war." Paper presented at the American Political Science Association convention, New York.

Briggs, Philip J. (1991). *Making American foreign policy: President-Congress relations from the Second World War to Vietnam.* Lanham, MD: University Press of America.

Brilmayer, Lea. (1994). *American hegemony: Political morality in a one-superpower world.* New Haven: Yale University Press.

Brinkley, Alan. (1994). "The view from the former top." A review of Robert C. McFarlane with Zofia Smardz, *Special Trust* (New York: Cadell & Davies, 1994). *New York Times Book Review,* November 13, 1994: 9.

Brody, Richard A. (1991). *Assessing the president: The media, elite opinion, and public support.* Stanford, CA: Stanford University Press.

Brody, Richard A. (1994). "Crisis, war, and public opinion: The media and public support for the president." In W. Lance Bennett and David L. Paletz (Eds.), *Taken by storm: The media, public opinion, and U.S. foreign policy in the Gulf War* (pp. 210–27). Chicago: University of Chicago Press.

Brown, Walton L. (1994). "Presidential leadership and U.S. nonproliferation policy." *Presidential Studies Quarterly, 3,* 563–76.

Bruening, Marijke. (1995, February). "Culture, history, and role: How the past shapes foreign policy now." Paper presented at the International Studies Association convention, Chicago.

Bruner, Michael, Ketcham, Allen, Preda, Michael, & Norwine, Jim. (1993). "Postmodern nationalism among university students in Texas." *Canadian Review of Studies in Nationalism, 20,* 35–43.

Burbach, David T. (1995, August). "Foreign policy preferences, presidential approval, and the use of force." Paper presented at the American Political Science Association convention, Chicago.

Burgin, Eileen K. (1991). "Representatives' decisions on participation in foreign policy issues." *Legislative Studies Quarterly, 16,* 521–46.

Burgin, Eileen K. (1992). "Congress, the War Powers Resolution, & the invasion of Panama." *Polity, 25,* 217–42.

Burke, John P., & Greenstein, Fred I. (1989). "Presidential personality and national security leadership: A comparative analysis of Vietnam decision-making." *International Political Science Review, 10,* 73–92.

Caldwell, Dan. (1989, March). "The SALT II ratification debate." Paper presented at the International Studies Association convention, London.

Caldwell, Dan. (1990, April). "The SALT II ratification debate." Paper presented at the International Studies Association convention, Washington, DC.

Callaghan, Karen J., & Virtanen, Simo. (1993). "Revised models of the 'rally phenomenon': The case of the Carter presidency." *Journal of Politics, 55,* 756–64.

Campbell, David. (1993a). *Politics without principle: Sovereignty, ethics, and the narratives of the Gulf War.* Boulder, CO: Lynne Rienner.

Campbell, James E. (1993b). *The presidential pulse of congressional elections.* Lexington: University Press of Kentucky.

Carrol, Nancy Ann. (1992, April). "The fall of the shah: Not a question of if, but when." Paper presented at the International Studies Association convention, Atlanta.

Carruth, Gorton. (1991). *What happened when: A chronology of life and events in America.* New York: Signet.

Carter, Ralph G. (1986). "Congressional foreign policy behavior: Persistent patterns of the postwar period." *Presidential Studies Quarterly, 16,* 329–59.

Carter, Ralph G. (1991, October). "Congressional defense spending behavior: Changing patterns of postwar politics." Paper presented at the Annual Research Seminar of the Association for Public Policy Analysis and Management, Bethesda [revised version forthcoming in Paul E. Peterson (Ed.), *Congress and the making of foreign policy.* Norman: University of Oklahoma Press].

Carter, Ralph G. (1992, April). "Capitol Hill versus the White House: Changing patterns in defense spending decisions." Paper presented at the International Studies Association convention, Atlanta.

Carter, Ralph G. (1994). "Budgeting for defense." In Paul E. Peterson (Ed.), *The president, the Congress, and the making of foreign policy* (pp. 161–78). Norman: University of Oklahoma Press.

Chan, Steve, & Mintz, Alex. (Eds.). (1992). *Defense, welfare and growth: Perspectives and evidence.* London: Routledge

Chicago manual of style, The. (14th ed.). (1993). Chicago: University of Chicago Press.

Chittick, William O., Billingsley, Keith R., & Travis, Rick. (1993, March). "Persistence and change in foreign policy attitudes." Paper presented at the International Studies Association convention, Acapulco.

Chittick, William O., Billingsley, Keith R., & Travis, Rick. (1995). "A three-dimensional model of American foreign policy beliefs." *International Studies Quarterly, 39,* 313–32.

Choate, Pat. (1990). *Agents of influence.* New York: Knopf.

Christopher, Warren. (1995). "America's leadership, America's opportunity." *Foreign Policy, 98,* 6–28.

Cimbala, Stephen J. (1992). "Behavior modification and the Cuban missile crisis: From brinksmanship to disaster avoidance." *Arms Control, 13*(2), 252–84.

Cingranelli, David Louis. (1993). *Ethics, American foreign policy, and the third world.* New York: St. Martin's.

Citrin, Jack, Haas, Ernest B., Mute, Christopher, & Reingold, Beth. (1994). "Is American nationalism changing? Implications for foreign policy." *International Studies Quarterly, 38,* 1–32.

Clark, Michael T. (1990). *Thinking about world change.* Washington, DC: Center Report, Center for the Study of Foreign Affairs, Foreign Service Institute, U.S. Department of State Publication 9795.

Clifford, J. Garry. (1989, December 12). "Remember the Monroe Doctrine?" *Hartford Courant,* p. D15.

References

Clifford, J. Garry. (1991). "A second chance for Zionists." *Reviews in American History, 19,* 426–31.

Clifford, J. Garry. (1993). "Juggling balls of dynamite." *Diplomatic History, 17,* 633–36.

Clough, Michael. (1994). "Grass-roots policymaking: Say good-bye to the 'wise men.'" *Foreign Affairs, 73,* 2–7.

Cogan, Charles G. (1990). "Not to offend: Observations on Iran, the hostages, and the hostage rescue mission—ten years later." *Comparative Strategy, 9,* 414–32.

Cohen, Jeffrey E. (1995). "Presidential rhetoric and the public agenda." *American Journal of Political Science, 39,* 87–107.

Cohen, Raymond. (1991). *Negotiating across cultures: Communication obstacles in international diplomacy.* Washington, DC: United States Institute for Peace.

Cohen, Warren I. (1994). *The Cambridge history of American foreign relations. Vol. IV, America in the age of Soviet power, 1945–1991.* New York: Cambridge University Press.

Cole, Timothy M. (1994). "Congressional investigation of American foreign policy: Iran-Contra in perspective." *Congress and the Presidency, 21,* 31–47.

Collier, Ellen O. (1991, February 26). "War Powers Resolution: Presidential compliance." *CRS Issue Brief* (#IB81050). Washington, DC: Congressional Research Service (of the Library of Congress).

Collier, Ellen O. (1994). "The War Powers Resolution: Twenty years of experience." *CRS Report for Congress,* January 11, 1994. Washington, DC: Congressional Research Service (of the Library of Congress).

Congressional Quarterly Almanacs. (1946–1994). Washington, DC: Congressional Quarterly.

Congressional Quarterly Weekly Report. (1995). Washington, DC: Congressional Quarterly.

Conover, Pamela Johnston, & Virginia Sapiro. (1993). "Gender, feminist consciousness, and war." *American Journal of Political Science, 37,* 1079–99.

Conti, Delia B. (1995). "Reagan's trade rhetoric: Lessons for the 1990s." *Presidential Studies Quarterly, 25,* 91–108.

Cooper, Richard N. (1987). "Trade policy as foreign policy." In Robert M. Stein (Ed.), *U.S. trade policies in a changing world economy* (pp. 291–336). Cambridge: MIT Press.

Cortright, David. (1993). *Peace works: The citizen's role in ending the cold war.* Boulder, CO: Westview.

Corwin, Edward S. (1957). *The president: Office and powers, 1787–1957.* New York: New York University Press.

Crabb, Cecil V., Jr., & Holt, Pat M. (1989). *Invitation to struggle: Congress, the president, and foreign policy* (3rd ed.). Washington, DC: CQ Press.

Crabb, Cecil V., Jr., & Mucahy, Kevin V. (1991). *American national security: A presidential perspective.* Pacific Grove, CA: Brooks/Cole.

Craig, Allen Smith, & Smith, Kathy B. (1994). *The White House speaks: Presidential leadership as persuasion.* Westport, CT: Praeger.

Cronin, Thomas E. (1970, October). "Superman: Our textbook presidency." *The Washington Monthly,* 47–54.

Cronin, Thomas E. (1986). "The write stuff." *News for Teachers of Political Science, 49,* 1–4.

Culver, John (1990). "The War Powers Resolution." In Howard E. Shuman and Walter R. Thomas (Eds.), *The Constitution and national security* (pp. 233–42). Washington, DC: National Defense University Press.

Cunliffe, Marcus. (1987). *The presidency.* New York: American Heritage.

Cunningham, Jennifer, & Moore, Michael K. (1995, August). "Mass and elite foreign policy attitudes: Is anyone leading the parade?" Paper presented at the American Political Science Association convention, Chicago.

Dalby, Simon. (1990). "American security discourse: The persistence of geopolitics." *Political Geography Quarterly, 9,* 177–88.

Dallek, Robert. (1983). *The American style of foreign policy: Cultural politics and foreign affairs.* New York: Oxford University Press.

David, Charles-Philippe, Carrol, Nancy Ann, & Selden, Zachary A. (1993). *Foreign policy failure in the White House: Reappraising the fall of the shah and the Iran-Contra affair.* Lanham, MD: University Press of America.

Davis, Edward B. (1995). "Changing national security policy in the Clinton administration." Paper presented at the American Political Science Association convention, Chicago.

Davis, Richard. (1992a). "The foreign policy making role of Congress in the 1990s: Remote sensing technology and the future of congressional power." *Congress & the Presidency, 19,* 175–92.

Davis, Richard. (1992b). *The press and American politics: The new mediator.* New York: Longman.

Davis, Richard. (1993). "Technology, news, and national security: The media's increasing capability to cover war." *Journal of Political Science, 21,* 69–89.

Dawson, Joseph G., III. (Ed.). (1994). *Commanders in chief: Presidential leadership in modern wars.* Lawrence: University of Kansas Press.

DeConde, Alexander. (1992). *Ethnicity, race, and American foreign policy: A history.* Boston: Northeastern University Press.

DeCosse, David E. (Ed.). (1992). *But was it just? Reflections on the morality of the Persian Gulf War.* New York: Doubleday.

Deering, Christopher J. (1991). "Congress, the president, and war powers: The perennial debate." In James A. Thurber (Ed.), *Divided democracy* (pp. 171–97). Washington, DC: CQ Press.

Demchak, Chris C. (1991). *Military organizations, complex machines: Modernization in the U.S. armed services.* Ithaca, NY: Cornell University Press.

Destler, I. M., Gelb, Leslie H., & Lake, Anthony. (1984). *Our own worst enemy: The unmaking of American foreign policy.* New York: Simon & Schuster.

Di Leo, David L. (1991). *George Ball, Vietnam, and the rethinking of containment.* Chapel Hill: University of North Carolina Press.

DiClerico, Robert E. (1979). *The American president.* Englewood Cliffs, NJ: Prentice Hall.

Diehl, Paul F. (1991). "Ghosts of arms control past." *Political Science Quarterly, 105,* 597–615.

Dixon, William J. (1993). "Democracy and the management of international conflict." *Journal of Conflict Resolution, 37,* 42–68.

Dixon, William J., & Gaarder, Stephen M. (1992). "Presidential succession and the cold war: An analysis of Soviet-American relations, 1948–1988." *Journal of Politics, 54,* 156–75.

Dixon, William J., & Moon, Bruce E. (1993). "Political similarity and American foreign trade patterns." *Political Research Quarterly, 46,* 5–26.

Dobriansky, Paula J., & McCaffrey, Diana A. (1995). "Do the media make foreign policy?" In Annual Editions series, *American foreign policy, 95/96* (pp. 102–5). Guilford, CT: Dushkin Publishing/Brown & Benchmark Publishers.

Dole, Robert. (1995). "Shaping America's global future." *Foreign Policy, 98,* 29–43.

Donahue, Thomas R. (1991). "The case against a NAFTA." *The Columbia Journal of World Business, 26,* 91–95.

Doran, Charles F. (1993). "America's changing role in a transforming world." *SAIS Review, 13,* 69–85.

Draper, Theodore. (1991). *A very thin line: The Iran-Contra affair.* New York: Touchstone/Simon & Schuster.

Draper, Theodore. (1995, May 7). "Capturing the Constitution." A review of Louis Fisher, *Presidential War Power* (Lawrence: University of Kansas Press). *New York Times Book Review,* 3–6.

Drew, Elizabeth. (1994). *On the edge: The Clinton presidency.* New York: Simon & Schuster.

Duffy, Michael, & Goodgame, Dan. (1992). *Marching in place: The status quo presidency of George Bush.* New York: Simon & Schuster.

Dumbrell, John. (1990). *The making of U.S. foreign policy.* Manchester, UK: Manchester University Press.

Duncan, Dean F. (1993, September). "The election cycle in foreign policy activity." Paper presented at the American Political Science Association convention, Washington, DC.

Dye, Thomas R. (1993). "The friends of Bill and Hillary." *PS: Political Science & Politics, 26,* 693–95.

Dye, Thomas R. (1995). *Who's running America? The Clinton years* (6th ed.). Englewood Cliffs, NJ: Prentice Hall.

Edwards, George C. III. (1980). *Presidential influence in Congress.* San Francisco: W. H. Freeman.

Edwards, George C., III, & Gallup, Alec M. (1990). *Presidential approval: A sourcebook.* Baltimore, MD: The Johns Hopkins University Press.

Edwards, George C., III, Mitchell, William, & Welch, Reed. (1995). "Explaining presidential approval: The significance of issue salience." *American Journal of Political Science, 39,* 108–34.

Edwards, George C., III, & Swenson, Tami. (1994). "Who rallies?: The anatomy of a rally event." Paper presented at the Midwest Political Science Association convention, Chicago.

Edwards, George C., III, & Wayne, Stephen J. (1985). *Presidential leadership in Congress.* New York: St. Martin's.

Elbow, Peter. (1981). *Writing with power.* New York: Oxford University Press.

Elkin, Steven L. (1991). "Contempt of Congress: The Iran-Contra affair and the American Constitution." *Congress & the Presidency, 18,* 1–16.

Elshtain, Jean Bethke. (1995). "Exporting feminism." *Journal of International Affairs, 48,* 541–55.

Ely, John Hart. (1993). *War and responsibility: Constitutional lessons of Vietnam and its aftermath.* New Haven: Yale University Press.

Emery, Christine V., & Deering, Christopher J. (1995, February). "Congress and foreign policy: Substantive and procedural legislation in the post-war era." Paper presented at the International Studies Association convention, Chicago.

Englehardt, Tom. (1995). *The end of victory culture: Cold war America and the disillusioning of a generation.* New York: Basic Books.

Enloe, Cynthia. (1993). *The morning after: Sexual politics at the end of the cold war.* Berkeley: University of California Press.

Evans, Peter B., Jacobson, Harold K., & Putnam, Robert D. (Eds.). (1993). *Double-edged diplomacy: International bargaining and domestic politics.* Berkeley: University of California Press.

Eveland, William P., Jr., McLeod, Douglas M., & Signorielli, Nancy. (1995). "Actual and perceived U.S. public opinion: The spiral of silence during the Persian Gulf War." *International Journal of Public Opinion Research, 7,* 91–109.

References

Farkas, Steve. (1995). "Mixed messages: A survey of the foreign policy views of American leaders." A working paper. New York: Public Agenda.

Fascell, Dante B. (1991). "Learning from the past without repeating it: Advice for the new president." In Greg Schmergel (Ed.), *U.S. foreign policy in the 1990s* (pp. 14–33). New York: St. Martin's.

Fearon, James D. (1994). "Domestic political audience and the escalation of international disputes." *American Political Science Review, 88,* 577–93.

Federal yellow book: Who's who in federal departments and agencies, The. (1993, Summer). Washington, DC: Monitor.

Fenno, Richard F., Jr. (1973). *Congressmen in committees.* Boston: Little, Brown.

Findling, John E. (1989). *Dictionary of American diplomatic history* (2nd ed.). Westport, CT: Greenwood.

Fischer, Frank (1991). "American think tanks: Policy elites and the politization of expertise." *Governance: An International Journal of Policy and Administration, 4,* 332–53.

Fisher, Louis. (1981). *The politics of shared power: Congress and the executive.* Washington, DC: CQ Press.

Fisher, Louis. (1990). "The legitimacy of the congressional national security role." In Howard E. Shuman & Walter R. Thomas (Eds.), *The Constitution and national security* (pp. 243–58). Washington, DC: National Defense University Press.

Fisher, Louis. (1993). *The politics of shared power: Congress and the executive* (3rd ed.). Washington, DC: CQ Press.

Fisher, Louis. (1995a). "Congressional checks on military initiatives." *Political Science Quarterly, 109,* 739–62.

Fisher, Louis. (1995b). "The Korean War: On what legal basis did Truman act?" *American Journal of International Law, 89,* 21–39.

Fisher, Louis. (1995c). *Presidential war power.* Lawrence: University of Kansas Press.

Flanigan, William H., & Zingale, Nancy H. (1991). *Political behavior of the American electorate* (7th ed.). Washington, DC: CQ Press.

Forsythe, David P. (1990). "Human rights in U.S. foreign policy: Retrospect and prospect." *Political Science Quarterly, 105,* 435–54.

Fox, Thomas C. (1991). *Iraq: Military victory, moral defeat.* Kansas City, MO: Sheed & Ward.

Franck, Thomas M. (1991). "Courts and foreign policy." *Foreign Policy, 83,* 66–86.

Franck, Thomas M. (1992). *Political questions/judicial answers: Does the rule of law apply to foreign affairs?* Princeton, NJ: Princeton University Press.

Franck, Thomas M., & Patel, Faiza. (1991). "UN police action in lieu of war: The old order changeth." *American Journal of International Law, 85,* 63–73.

Franck, Thomas M., & Weisband, Edward. (1979). *Foreign policy by Congress.* New York: Oxford University Press.

Frankel, Charles. (1968). *High on Foggy Bottom: An outsider's inside view of the government.* New York: Harper & Row.

Friedberg, Aaron L. (1992). "Is the United States capable of acting strategically? Congress and the president." In Charles W. Kegley and Eugene R. Wittkopf (Eds.), *The future of American foreign policy* (pp. 95–111). New York: St. Martin's.

Friedberg, Aaron L. (1994). "The future of American power." *Political Quarterly, 109,* 1–22.

Fukuyama, Francis. (1989). "The end of history." *The National Interest, 16,* 3–18.

Fulbright, J. William. (1964). *Old myths and new realities.* New York: Random House.

Fulbright, J. William. (1972). *The crippled giant: American foreign policy and its domestic consequences.* New York: Random House.

Gamson, William A. (1992). *Talking politics.* New York: Cambridge University Press.

Gant, Michael M., & Lyons, William. (1993). "Democratic theory, nonvoting, and public policy: The 1972–1988 presidential elections." *American Politics Quarterly, 21,* 185–204.

GAO. U.S. General Accounting Office. National Security and International Affairs Division. (1992, September). *Security assistance: Observations on post–cold war program changes.* Report: GAO/NSIAD-92-248. Washington, DC.

Gaubatz, Kurt. (1991). "Election cycles and war." *Journal of Conflict Resolution, 35,* 212–44.

Gaubatz, Kurt Taylor. (1993, September). "Intervention and intransitivity: Public opinion, social choice, and the use of military force abroad." Paper presented at the American Political Science Association convention, Washington, DC.

Gaubatz, Kurt Taylor. (1995). "Intervention and intransitivity: Public opinion, social choice, and the use of military force abroad." *World Politics, 47,* 534–54.

Geller, Daniel S. (1992). "Capability, concentration, power transition, and war." *International Interactions, 17,* 269–84.

Genovese, Michael A. (1990). *The Nixon presidency.* Westport, CT: Greenwood.

Gergen, David R. (1991). "Diplomacy in a television age: The dangers of a teledemocracy." In Simon Serfaty (Ed.), *The media and foreign policy* (pp. 47–64). New York: St. Martin's.

Geyelin, Philip L. (1991). "The Strategic Defense Initiative: The president's story." In Simon Serfaty (Ed.), *The media and foreign policy* (pp. 19–32). New York: St. Martin's/Foreign Policy Institute.

Geyer, Alan, & Green, Barbara G. (1992). *Lines in the sand: Justice and the Gulf War*. Louisville, KY: Westminster/John Knox Press.

Gibson, Martha Liebler. (1992). *Weapons of influence: The legislative veto, American foreign policy, and the irony of reform*. Boulder, CO: Westview.

Gibson, Martha Liebler. (1994). "Managing conflict: The role of the legislative veto in American foreign policy." *Polity, 26*, 442–72.

Gibson, Martha Liebler. (1995). "Issues, coalitions, and divided government." Unpublished manuscript. Storrs: University of Connecticut.

Gilbert, Robert E. (1989). "President versus Congress: The struggle for public attention." *Congress & the Presidency, 16*, 83–97.

Gilmour, Robert, & Minkoff, Eric. (1994). "Producing a reliable weapons system: The advanced medium-range air-to-air missile (AMRAAM)." In Robert S. Gilmour and Alexis A. Halley (Eds.), *Who makes public policy? The struggle for control between Congress and the executive* (pp. 195–218). Chatham, NJ: Chatham House.

Glad, Betty (1989). "Personality, political and group process variables in foreign policy decision making: Jimmy Carter's handling of the Iranian hostage crisis." *International Political Science Review, 10*, 35–61.

Gleijeses, Piero. (1995). "The CIA and the Bay of Pigs." *Journal of Latin American Studies, 27*, 18–42.

Glennon, Michael J. (1991a). "The Constitution and Chapter VII of the United Nations Charter." *American Journal of International Law, 85*, 74–88.

Glennon, Michael J. (1991b). "The Gulf War and the Constitution." *Foreign Affairs 70*, 84–101.

Goldberg, David Howard. (1990). *Foreign policy and ethnic interest groups: American and Canadian Jews lobby for Israel*. Westport, CT: Greenwood.

Goldman, Emily O., & Diaz, Alfonso S. (1993). "Adapting defense decision-making to the new security environment: Eliminating the policy analysis mismatch." *Defense Analysis, 9*, 137–58.

Goldstein, Joshua S. (1991). "The possibility of cycles in international relations." *International Studies Quarterly, 35*, 477–80.

Goldstein, Martin E. (1984). *America's foreign policy: Drift or decision*. Wilmington, DE: Scholarly Resources.

Gottlieb, Gideon. (1993). *Nation against state*. New York: Council on Foreign Relations Press.

Gowing, Nik. (1994). "Instant TV and foreign policy." *The World Today, 50*, 187–91.

Graber, Doris A. (1993). *Mass media and American politics* (4th ed.). Washington, DC: CQ Press.

Graebner, Norman. (Ed.) (1964). *Ideas and diplomacy*. New York: Oxford University Press.

Greenstein, Fred. (1995). "Political style and political leadership: The case of Bill Clinton." In Stanley A. Renshon (Ed.), *The Clinton presidency: Campaigning, governing, and the psychology of leadership* (pp. 137–48). Boulder, CO: Westview.

Gregg, Robert W. (1993). *About face? The United States and the United Nations*. Boulder, CO: Lynne Rienner.

Gunther, Albert C. (1992). "Biased press or biased public? Attitudes toward media coverage of social groups." *Public Opinion Quarterly, 56*, 147–67.

Gurr, Ted Robert, & Harff, Barbara. (1994). *Ethnic conflict in world politics*. Boulder, CO: Westview.

Guth, James L. & Fraser, Cleveland R. (1993, September). "Religion and foreign policy attitudes: The case of Christian Zionism." Paper presented at the American Political Science Association convention, Washington, DC.

Haass, Richard N. (1994). *Intervention: The use of American military force in the post–cold war world*. Washington: Carnegie Endowment for International Peace.

Hadar, Leon. (1994). "Covering the new world disorder: The press rushes in where Clinton fears to tread." *Columbia Journalism Review, 33*, 26–30.

Hafner, Donald. (1994). "Presidential leadership and the foreign policy bureaucracy." In David A. Deese (Ed.), *The New Politics of American Foreign Policy* (pp. 36–58). New York: St. Martin's.

Hagan, Joe D. 1994. "Domestic political systems and war proneness." *Mershon International Studies Review*, a supplement to the *International Studies Quarterly, 38* (supplement 2), 183–209.

Hamby, Alonzo L. (1992). *Liberalism and its challengers*. New York: Oxford University Press.

Haney, Patrick J. (1992, April). "Organizing for foreign policy: Presidents, advisers, and crisis decision-making." Paper presented at the International Studies Association convention, Atlanta.

Hansen, Wendy L. (1990). "The International Trade Commission and the politics of protectionism." *American Political Science Review, 84*, 21–46.

Hansen, Wendy L., & Park, Kee Ok. (1995). "Nation-state and pluralistic decision making in trade policy: The case of the International Trade Administration." *International Studies Quarterly, 39*, 181–211.

Hantz, Charles. (1995). "Ideology, pragmatism, and Ronald's world view: Full of sound and fury, signifying . . . ?" *Presidential Studies Quarterly*, forthcoming.

Hargrove, Erwin C. (1988). *Jimmy Carter as president*. Baton Rouge: Louisiana State University Press.

References

Hartley, Thomas, & Russett, Bruce. (1991, March). "Public opinion and the common defense: Who governs military spending in the United States?" Paper presented at the International Studies Association convention, Vancouver.

Hastedt, Glenn P. (1987, April). "Controlling intelligence: Values and perspectives of administration." Paper presented at the International Studies Association Convention, Washington, DC.

Hastedt, Glenn P. (1991). *American foreign policy: Past, present, future* (2nd ed.). Englewood Cliffs, NJ: Prentice Hall.

Henkin, Louis (1990). *Constitutionalism, democracy, and foreign affairs.* New York: Columbia University Press.

Henrikson, Alan K. (1991). "Mental maps." In Michael J. Hogan & Thomas G. Paterson (Eds.), *Explaining the history of American foreign relations* (pp. 177–92). Cambridge: Cambridge University Press.

Herek, Gregory M., Janis, Irving L., & Huth, Paul. (1987). "Decision-making during international crises: Is the quality of process related to the outcome?" *Journal of Conflict Resolution, 31,* 203–36.

Herman, Edward S. (1993). "The media's role in U.S. foreign policy." *Journal of International Affairs, 47,* 23–46.

Herrera, Cheryl Lynn, Herrera, Richard, & Smith, Eric R. A. N. (1992). "Public opinion and congressional representation." *Public Opinion Quarterly, 56,* 185–205.

Hershberg, James G. (1990). "Before 'the missiles of October.' " *Diplomatic History, 14,* 182–97.

Hill, Kevin A. (1993). "The domestic sources of foreign policymaking: Congressional voting and mass attitudes toward South Africa." *International Studies Quarterly, 37,* 195–214.

Hilsman, Roger. (1990). *The politics of policy making in defense and foreign affairs* (2nd ed.). Englewood Cliffs, NJ: Prentice Hall.

Hinckley, Barbara. (1994). *Less than meets the eye: Foreign policy making and the myth of the assertive Congress.* Chicago: University of Chicago Press.

Hinckley, Ronald H. (1992). *People, polls, and policymakers: American public opinion and national security.* New York: Lexington.

Hinckley, Ronald H. & Eugene R. Wittkopf. (1994). "The domestication of American foreign policy: Public opinion in the post–cold war era." Paper presented at the International Studies Association convention, Washington, DC.

Historical Tables, Budget of the U.S. Government, FY1994. Washington, DC: Office of Management & Budget.

Hobbs, Heidi H. (1994). *City Hall goes abroad: The foreign policy of local politics.* Beverly Hills: Sage.

Hocking, Brian. (1990). "Bringing the 'outside' in: The role and nature of foreign interest lobbying." *Corruption and Reform, 5,* 219–33.

Hoffmann, Stanley. (1995). "The crisis of liberal internationalism." *Foreign Policy, 98,* 159–77.

Hofstede, Geert. (1991). *Cultures and organizations.* London: McGraw-Hill.

Hogan, J. Michael, & Smith, Ted J., III. (1991). "Public opinion and the nuclear freeze." *Public Opinion Quarterly, 55,* 534–69.

Hoge, James F., Jr. (1994). "Media pervasiveness." *Foreign Affairs, 73,* 136–44.

Holland, Lauren (1991, August–September). "The influence of the president in weapons acquisition decisions: Process and policy considerations." Paper presented at the American Political Science Association convention, Washington, DC.

Holsti, Kalevi J. (1991). *Peace and war: Armed conflicts and international order.* Cambridge: Cambridge University Press.

Holsti, Ole R. (1991). "International systems, system change, and foreign policy: Commentary on 'changing international systems.' " *Diplomatic History, 15,* 83–90.

Holsti, Ole R. (1992). "Public opinion and foreign policy: Challenges to the Almond-Lippmann consensus." *International Studies Quarterly, 36,* 439–66.

Holsti, Ole R. (1995). "Theories of international relations and foreign policy: Realism and its challengers." In Charles W. Kegley Jr. (Ed.), *Controversies in international relations theory: Realism and the neoliberal challenge* (pp. 35–66). New York: St. Martin's.

Holsti, Ole R., & Rosenau, James N. (1988). "The domestic and foreign policy beliefs of American leaders." *Journal of Conflict Resolution, 32,* 248–94.

Holsti, Ole R., & Rosenau, James N. (1990). "The emerging U.S. consensus on foreign policy." *Orbis, 34,* 579–93.

Holt, Pat M. (1995). *Secret intelligence and public policy: A dilemma of democracy.* Washington: CQ Press.

Hoogland, Eric. (1992). "Iran." In Peter J. Schraeder (Ed.), *Intervention into the 1990s: U.S. foreign policy in the third world* (pp. 303–20). Boulder, CO: Lynne Rienner.

Hook, Steven W. (1995). *National interest and foreign aid.* Boulder, CO: Lynne Rienner.

Howes, Ruth, & Stevenson, Michael. (Eds.). (1993). *Women and the use of military force.* Boulder, CO: Lynne Rienner.

Hudson, Valerie M. (1995, February). "Culture and foreign policy: Developing a research agenda."

Paper presented at the International Studies Association convention, Chicago.

Hummel, Ralph P., & Isaak, Robert Allen. (1986). *The real American politics: Changing perspectives on American government.* Englewood Cliffs, NJ: Prentice Hall.

Hunt, Michael H. (1987). *Ideology and U.S. foreign policy.* New Haven, CT: Yale University Press.

Hybel, Alex Roberto. (1993). *Power over rationality: The Bush administration and the Gulf crisis.* Albany: State University of New York Press.

Ikenberry, G. John, & Kupchan, Charles A. (1990). "Socialization and hegemonic power." *International Organization, 44,* 283–315.

Immerman, Richard H. (1992). *John Foster Dulles and the cold war.* Princeton, NJ: Princeton University Press.

Iriye, Akira. (1993). *The Cambridge history of American foreign relations, Vol. III, The globalizing of America, 1913–1945.* New York: Cambridge University Press.

Iyengar, Shanto, & Simon, Adam. (1994). "News coverage of the Gulf crisis and public opinion." In W. Lance Bennett & David L. Paletz (Eds.), *Taken by storm: The media, public opinion, and U.S. foreign policy in the Gulf War* (pp. 167–85). Chicago: University of Chicago Press.

Jackman, Robert W., & Miller, Ross A. (1995). "Voter turnout in the industrial democracies during the 1980s." *Comparative Political Studies, 27,* 467–92.

Jackson, Thomas M. (1993, September). "The unwritten constitution of presidential war: A conception of public law perceiving limits." Paper presented at the American Political Science Association convention, Washington, DC.

Jacobs, Lawrence R., & Shapiro, Robert Y. (1995). "Public opinion in President Clinton's first year: Leadership and responsiveness." In Stanley A. Renshon (Ed.), *The Clinton presidency: Campaigning, governing, and the psychology of leadership* (pp. 195–215). Boulder, CO: Westview.

Jacoby, William G. (1995). "The structure of ideological thinking in the American electorate." *American Journal of Political Science, 39,* 314–35.

Jacoby, William G., & Valentine, John P. (1995, August). "Ideological issue conflict within the American electorate: The importance of issue saliences." Paper presented at the American Political Science Association convention, Chicago.

James, Patrick, & Hristoulas, Athanasios. (1994). "Domestic politics and foreign policy: Evaluating a model of crisis activity for the United States." *Journal of Politics, 56,* 327–48.

James, Patrick, & Oneal, John R. (1991). "The influence of domestic and international politics on the president's use of force." *Journal of Conflict Resolution, 35,* 307–32.

Janis, Irving L. (1982). *Groupthink: Psychological studies of policy decisions and fiascos.* Boston: Houghton Mifflin.

Jeffreys-Jones, Rhodri. (1995). *Changing differences: Women and the shaping of American foreign policy, 1917–1994.* New Brunswick, NJ: Rutgers University Press.

Jentleson, Bruce W. (1990). "American diplomacy: Around the world and along Pennsylvania Avenue." In Thomas E. Mann (Ed.), *A question of balance: The president, Congress and foreign policy* (pp. 146–200). Washington, DC: Brookings Institution.

Jentleson, Bruce W. (1992). "The pretty prudent public: Post-Vietnam American opinion on the use of military force." *International Studies Quarterly, 36,* 49–73.

Jentleson, Bruce W. (1994). *With friends like these: Reagan, Bush, and Saddam, 1982–1990.* New York: W. W. Norton.

Jervis, Robert. (1990). "Foreign policy and congressional/presidential relations." In Howard E. Shuman and Walter R. Thomas (Eds.), *The Constitution and national security: A bicentennial view* (pp. 37–54). Washington, DC: National Defense University Press.

Johnson, James Turner, & Weigel, George. (1991). *Just war and the Gulf War.* Washington: Ethics & Public Policy Center.

Johnson, Loch K. (1989). *America's secret power: The CIA in a democratic society.* New York: Oxford University Press.

Johnson, Loch K. (1991). *America as a world power: Foreign policy in a constitutional framework.* New York: McGraw Hill.

Johnson, Loch K., Gelles, Erna, & Kuzenski, John C. (1992). "The study of congressional investigations: Research strategies." *Congress & the Presidency, 19,* 137–56.

Johnson, Lyndon B. (1971). *The vantage point: Perspective of the presidency, 1963–1969.* New York: Holt, Rinehart & Winston.

Johnston, Alastair Ian. (1995). "Thinking about strategic culture." *International Security, 19,* 32–64.

Jones, Howard. (1988). *The Course of American Diplomacy* (2nd ed.). Chicago: Dorsey.

Jordan, Donald L. (1993). "Newspaper effects on policy preferences." *Public Opinion Quarterly, 57,* 191–204.

Jordan, Donald L., & Page, Benjamin I. (1992). "Shaping foreign policy opinions: The role of tv news." *Journal of Conflict Resolution, 36,* 227–41.

References

Kaiser, Robert G. (1991). *How Gorbachev happened.* New York: Simon & Schuster.

Kalb, Marvin. (1991). "Foreword." In Simon Serfaty (Ed.), *The media and foreign policy* (pp. xiii–xvii). New York: St. Martin's/Foreign Policy Institute.

Karsh, Efraim, & Rautsi, Inari. (1991). "Why Saddam Hussein invaded Kuwait." *Survival, 33,* 18–30.

Katzman, Robert A. (1990). "War powers: Toward a new accommodation." In Thomas E. Mann (Ed.), *A question of balance: The president, the Congress, and foreign policy* (pp. 35–69). Washington, DC: Brookings Institution.

Kaufman, Natalie Hevener (1991). *Human rights treaties and the Senate: A history of opposition.* Chapel Hill: The University of North Carolina Press.

Kearns, Doris. (1976). *Lyndon Johnson and the American dream.* New York: Harper & Row.

Kegley, Charles W., Jr. (1995). "The neoliberal challenge to realist theories of world politics: An introduction." In Charles W. Kegley Jr. (Ed.), *Controversies in international relations theory: Realism and the neoliberal challenge* (pp. 1–24). New York: St. Martin's.

Kennan, George F. (as "X"). (1947). "The sources of Soviet conduct." *Foreign Affairs, 25,* 566–82.

Kennan, George F. (1951). *American Diplomacy, 1900–1950.* New York: New American Library.

Kennan, George F. (1995, March/April). "On American principles." *Foreign Affairs 74,* 116–127.

Kennedy, Paul. (1993). *Preparing for the twenty-first century.* New York: Vintage.

Kennedy, Robert F. (1969). *Thirteen days: A memoir of the Cuban missile crisis.* New York: W. W. Norton.

Kerbel, Matthew Robert. (1991). *Beyond persuasion: Organization efficiency and presidential power.* Albany: State University of New York Press.

Kerbel, Matthew Robert. (1994). *Edited for television: CNN, ABC, and the 1992 presidential campaign.* Boulder, CO: Westview.

Kerry, Richard J. (1990). *The star-spangled mirror: America's image of itself and the world.* City Savage, MD: Rowman & Littlefield.

Kessler, Ronald. (1992). *Inside the CIA: Revealing the secrets of the world's most powerful spy agency.* New York: Pocket Books.

Kilgour, D. Marc. (1991). "Domestic political structure and war behavior: A game-theoretic approach." *Journal of Conflict Resolution, 35,* 266–84.

Kissinger, Henry A. (1957). *The World Restored: Castlereagh, Metternich, and the Restoration of Peace, 1812–1822.* Boston: Little, Brown.

Kissinger, Henry A. (1979). *The White House years.* Boston: Little, Brown.

Klingberg, Frank L. (1990). "Cyclical trends in foreign policy revisited in 1990." *International Studies Notes, 15,* 54–58.

Kneffel, Peggy Davids, & Schwartz, Carol A. (Eds.). (1994). *Encyclopedia of Associations.* Detroit: Gale Research.

Koh, Harold Hongju. (1990). *The national security constitution: Sharing power after the Iran-Contra affair.* New Haven, CT: Yale University Press.

Krasner, Stephen D. (1988) "Are bureaucracies important? A re-examination of accounts of the Cuban missile crisis." In Charles W. Kegley Jr. & and Eugene R. Wittkopf (Eds.), *The domestic sources of American foreign policy* (pp. 215–26). New York: St. Martin's.

Kreiger, Joel. (Ed.). (1993). *The Oxford companion to politics of the world.* New York: Oxford University Press.

Krosnick, Jon, & Tehlami, Shibley. (1995). "Public attitudes toward Israel: A study of attentive and issue publics." *International Studies Quarterly, 39,* 535–54.

Kull, Steven. (1995, March/April). "Misreading the public mood." *The Bulletin of the Atomic Scientists,* 55–59.

Kull, Steven. (1996). "What the public knows that Washington doesn't." *Foreign Policy, 101,* 102–15.

Kurth, James R. (1989). "A widening gyre: The logic of American weapons procurement." In John G. Ikenberry (Ed.), *American foreign policy: Theoretical essays* (pp. 14–37). Glenview, IL: Scott, Foresman.

Kux, Dennis. (1995, March). "In the eye of the storm." *Foreign Service Journal,* 22–25.

Kuzma, Lynn. (1993, March). "After the cold war: Change in U.S. foreign policy beliefs." Paper presented at the International Studies Association convention, Acapulco.

Ladd, Everett Carll. (1993). "The 1992 U.S. national election." *International Journal of Public Opinion Research, 5,* 1–21.

LaFeber, Walter. (1981). "The last war, the next war, and the new revisionists." *Democracy, 1,* 98–115.

LaFeber, Walter. (1989). *The American age: United States foreign policy at home and abroad from 1750 to the present.* New York: Norton.

LaFeber, Walter. (1993). *The Cambridge history of American foreign relations, Vol. II, The American search for opportunity, 1865–1913.* New York: Cambridge University Press.

Lagon, Mark P. (1992, September). "The breakdown of consensus revisited: Elite beliefs and post–cold war U.S. foreign policy." Paper presented at the American Political Science Association convention, Chicago.

Lake, David A. (1992). "Powerful pacifists: Democratic states and war." *American Political Science Review, 86,* 24–37.

Lance, Bennett W., & Paletz, David L. (Eds.). (1994). *Taken by storm: The media, public opinion, and U.S. foreign policy in the Gulf War*. Chicago: University of Chicago Press.

Larson, James F. (1990). "Television and U.S. foreign policy: The case of the Iran hostage crisis." In Doris A. Graber (Ed.), *Media power in politics* (2nd ed.) (pp. 301–12). Washington, DC: CQ Press.

Lebovic, James H. (1994.) "Before the storm: Momentum and the onset of the Gulf War." *International Studies Quarterly, 38*, 447–74.

Leffler, Melvyn. (1994). *The specter of communism: The United States and the origins of the cold war, 1917–1953*. New York: Hill & Wang.

Leogrande, William M., & Brenner, Philip. (1993). "The House divided: Ideological polarization over aid to the Nicaraguan 'Contras.' " *Legislative Studies Quarterly, 18*, 105–36.

Lian, Bradley, & Oneal, John R. (1993). "Presidents, the use of military force, and public opinion." *Journal of Conflict Resolution, 37*, 277–300.

Lind, Michael. (1995). *The next American nation: The new nationalism and the fourth American revolution*. New York: Free Press.

Lindsay, James M. (1990). "Congressional oversight of the Department of Defense: Reconsidering the conventional wisdom." *Armed Forces & Society, 17*, 7–34.

Lindsay, James M. (1991, August). "Congress, foreign policy, and the new institutionalism." Paper presented at the American Political Science Association convention, Washington, DC.

Lindsay, James M. (1993). "Congress and foreign policy: Why the hill matters." *Political Science Quarterly, 107*, 607–28.

Lindsay, James M. (1994). "Congress, foreign policy, and the new institutionalism." *International Studies Quarterly, 38*, 281–304.

Lindsay, James M., & Ripley, Randall B. (1992). "Foreign and defense policy in Congress: A research agenda for the 1990s." *Legislative Studies Quarterly 17*, 417–49.

Lindsay, James M., Sayrs, Lois W., & Steger, Wayne P. (1992). "The determinants of presidential foreign policy choice." *American Politics Quarterly, 20*, 3–25.

Lineberry, Robert L., Edwards, George C., III, & Wattenberg, Martin P. (1994). *Government in America* (6th ed.). New York: HarperCollins.

Link, Arthur S. (1965). *Wilson: Campaigns for progressivism and peace*. Princeton, NJ: Princeton University Press.

Link, Arthur S. (Ed.). (1988). *The papers of Woodrow Wilson. Vol. 58*. Princeton, NJ: Princeton University Press.

Lippmann, Walter. (1925). *The phantom public*. New York: Harcourt Brace.

Lippmann, Walter. (1935). *Essays in the public philosophy*. Boston: Little, Brown.

Livingston, Steve G. (1994). "The limits of high politics: When national security and international economic goals conflict in American foreign policymaking." *Polity, 26*, 417–41.

Lohmann, Susanne, & O'Halloran, Sharyn. (1994). "Divided government and U.S. trade policy: Theory and evidence." *International Organization, 48*, 595–632.

Lomperis, Timothy J. (1993). *The war everyone lost—and won. America's intervention in Viet Nam's twin struggles* (rev. ed.). Washington, DC: CQ Press.

Lowenthal, Abraham F. (Ed.). (1991). *Exporting democracy: The United States and Latin American themes and issues*. Baltimore, MD: Johns Hopkins University Press.

Lowi, Theodore J. (1989). "Making democracy safe for the world: On fighting the next war." In G. John Ikenberry (Ed.), *American foreign policy: Theoretical essays*. Glenview, IL: Scott, Foresman.

Lumsdaine, David Halloran. (1993). *Moral vision in international politics: The foreign aid regime, 1949–1989*. Princeton, NJ: Princeton University Press.

Lundestad, Geir. (1990). *The American "empire."* Oxford: Oxford University Press/Norwegian University Press.

Luttwak, Edward N. (1994, January). "2020." *Across the Board*, 12–15.

Lutz, James M. (1991). "Determinants of protectionist attitudes in the United States House of Representatives." *The International Trade Journal, 5*, 301–24.

Lynn, Naomi B., & McClure, Arthur F. (1973). *The Fulbright premise*. Lewisburg, PA: Bucknell University Press.

Mackenzie, G. Galvin. (1995). "Resolving policy differences: Foreign aid and human rights." In Robert S. Gilmour & Alexis A. Halley (Eds.), *Who makes public policy? The struggle for control between Congress and the executive* (pp. 261–88). Chatham, NJ: Chatham House.

Madison, James. (1987). *Debates in the federal convention of 1787. Vols. I and II*. Buffalo, NY: Prometheus. Also frequently cited elsewhere as *Madison's notes*.

Mahan, Alfred T. (1890). *The influence of seapower on history*. New York: Hill & Wang (copyright 1957).

Maître, H. Joachim. (1991). "Journalistic incompetence." *Nieman Reports, 45*, 10–15.

Mandelbaum, Michael. (1993, April 5). "By a thread: Yeltsin survives—but only just." *National Review, 208*, 19–25.

References

Mann, Thomas E. (1990). "Making foreign policy: President and Congress." In Thomas E. Mann (Ed.), *A question of balance: The president, the Congress, and foreign policy* (pp. 1–34). Washington, DC: Brookings Institution.

Maoz, Zeev. (1991). "Framing the national interest: The manipulation of foreign policy decisions in group settings." *World Politics, 73*, 77–110.

Maoz, Zeev, & Russett, Bruce. (1993). "Normative and structural causes of democratic peace, 1946–86." *American Political Science Review, 87*, 624–38.

Marcus, Jonathan. (1990). "Discordant voices: The U.S. Jewish community and Israel during the 1980s." *International Affairs, 66*, 545–58.

Marder, Murray. (1991). "Operation Washington shield." *Nieman Reports, 45*, 3–9.

Marra, Robin F., Ostrom, Charles W., Jr., & Simon, Dennis M. (1990). "Foreign policy and presidential popularity: Creating windows of opportunity in the perpetual election." *Journal of Conflict Resolution, 34*, 588–623.

Martin, Joseph. (1978). *My first fifty years in politics.* New York: McGraw-Hill.

Mayer, Frederick M. (1992). "Managing domestic differences in international negotiations: The strategic use of internal side-payments." Mayer, Frederick W. (1992). "Managing domestic differences in international negotiations: The strategic use of internal side-payments." *International Organization, 46*, 793–818.

Mayer, Kenneth R. (1991). *The political economy of defense contracting.* New Haven, CT: Yale University Press.

McCain, John. (1993). "Preserving international stability in the post–cold war era." *Strategic Review, 21*, 7–19.

McCalla, Robert M. (1992). *Uncertain perceptions: U.S. cold war crisis decision making.* Ann Arbor: University of Michigan Press.

McCartney, James. (1994). "Rallying around the flag." *American Journalism Review, 16*, 40–47.

McClintock, Michael. (1992). *Elements of statecraft: U.S. guerrilla warfare, counter-insurgency, and counter-terrorism, 1940–1990.* New York: Pantheon.

McCool, Daniel. (1989). "Subgovernments and the impact of policy fragmentation and accommodation." *Policy Studies Review, 8*, 264–87.

McCormick, James M., & Wittkopf, Eugene R. (1992). "At the water's edge: The effects of party, ideology, and issues on congressional foreign policy voting, 1947–1988." *American Politics Quarterly, 20*, 26–53.

McElroy, Robert W. (1992). *Morality and American foreign policy.* Princeton, NJ: Princeton University Press.

McGlen, Nancy E., & Sarkees, Meredith Reid. (Eds.). (1993). *Women in foreign policy.* New York: Routledge.

McKenna, George (1994). *The drama of democracy: American government and politics* (2nd ed.). Guilford, CT: Dushkin.

McKenney, James W. (1995). "The Clinton foreign policy: Problems and prospects." Paper presented at the International Studies Association convention, Chicago.

Mead, Walter Russell (1995, Winter). "Lucid stars: The American foreign policy tradition." *World Policy Journal, 11*, 1–17.

Mearsheimer, John J. (1990). "Back to the future: Instability in Europe after the cold war." *International Security, 15*, 5–56.

Meernik, James. (1993). "Presidential support in Congress: Conflict and consensus on foreign and defense policy." *The Journal of Politics, 55*, 569–87.

Meernik, James. (1994). "Presidential decision making and the political use of military force. *International Studies Quarterly, 38*, 121–38.

Meernik, James, & Martinez, Valerie. (1992, September). "American foreign policy attitudes and the Persian Gulf War: Public support for a new world order?" Paper presented at the American Political Science Association convention, Chicago.

Melanson, Richard A. (1991). *Reconstructing consensus: American foreign policy since the Vietnam War.* New York: St. Martin's.

Merrill, Dennis. (1994). "The United States and the rise of the third world." In Gordon Martel (Ed.), *American foreign relations reconsidered, 1890–1993* (pp. 166–86). London: Routledge.

Meyer, David S. (1990). *A winter of discontent: The nuclear freeze and American politics.* Westport, CT: Praeger.

Michalak, Stanley, Jr. (1992). *Competing conceptions of American foreign policy.* New York: HarperCollins.

Michelson, Melissa R. (1995, August). "Explorations in public opinion–presidential power linkages: Congressional action on unpopular foreign agreements." Paper presented at the American Political Science Association convention, Chicago.

Miller, Merle. (1980). *Lyndon: An oral biography.* New York: G. P. Putnam's Sons.

Mintz, Alex. (1993). "The decision to attack Iraq: A noncompensatory theory of decision-making." *Journal of Conflict Resolution, 37*, 595–618.

Mitchell, Neil J. (1995). "The global policy: Foreign firms' political activity in the United States." *Polity, 27*, 447–63.

Mo, Jongryn. (1994). "The logic of two-level games with endogenous domestic coalitions." *Journal of Conflict Resolution, 38*, 402–22.

Moens, Alexander. (1990). *Foreign policy under Carter: Testing multiple advocacy decision making.* Boulder, CO: Westview.

Moens, Alexander. (1991). "President Carter's advisers and the fall of the shah." *Political Science Quarterly 106,* 211–37.

Mondak, Jeffery J. (1995). "Newspapers and political awareness." *American Journal of Political Science, 39,* 513–27.

Moreno, Dario. (1990). *U.S. policy in Central America: The endless debate.* Miami, FL: Florida International University Press.

Morgan, H. Wayne. (1965). *America's road to empire.* Lexington, MA: D. C. Heath.

Morgan, T. Clifton, & Bickers, Kenneth N. (1992). "Domestic discontent and the external use of force." *Journal of Conflict Resolution, 36,* 25–52.

Morrow, James D. (1991). "Conceptual problems in theorizing about international conflict." *American Political Science Review, 85,* 923–29.

Mouw, Calvin J., & MacKuen, Michael B. (1992). "The strategic agenda in legislative politics." *American Political Science Review, 86,* 87–105.

Mueller, John. (1994). *Policy and opinion in the Gulf War.* Chicago: University of Chicago Press.

Mulcahey, Kevin. (1995). "Rethinking groupthink: Walt Rostow and the national security advisory process in the Johnson administration." *Presidential Studies Quarterly, 25,* 237–50

Muravchik, Joshua. (1992). *Exporting democracy: Fulfilling America's destiny* (rev. ed.). Washington, DC: AEI.

Murray, Shoon. (1993). *American elites' reaction to the end of the cold war: A 1988–1992 panel study.* Unpublished dissertation, Yale University.

Murrell, Peter. (1992). "Privatization complicates the fresh start." *Orbis, 35,* 323–32.

Myers, Robert J. (1989). "The Carnegie poll on values in American foreign policy." *Ethics and International Affairs, 3,* 297–302.

Myerson, Marilyn, & Northcutt, Susan Stoudinger. (1994). "The question of gender: An examination of selected textbooks in international relations." *International Studies Notes, 19,* 19–25.

Nacos, Brigitte Lebens. (1990). *The press, presidents, and crises.* New York: Columbia University Press.

Nacos, Brigitte Lebens. (1994). "Presidential leadership during the Persian Gulf conflict." *Presidential Studies Quarterly, 24,* 543–61.

Nathan, James. (1993). "Salvaging the War Powers Resolution." *Presidential Studies Quarterly, 23,* 235–68.

National Opinion Research Center (NORC). (1991). *General social survey.* Storrs: University of Connecticut, Roper Center Archives.

Neal, Steven. (1978). *The Eisenhowers: Reluctant dynasty.* Garden City, NY: Doubleday.

Nelson, Michael, & Tillman, Thomas. (1984). "The presidency, the bureaucracy, and foreign policy: Lessons from Cambodia." In Michael Nelson (Ed.), *The presidency and the political system* (pp. 494–518). Washington, DC: CQ Press.

Neuchterlein, Donald E. (1993). *America recommitted: United States' national interests in a restructured world.* Lexington: University of Kentucky Press.

Neuman, W. Russell, Just, Marion R., & Crigler, Ann N. (1992). *Common knowledge: News and the construction of political meaning.* Chicago: University of Chicago Press.

Neumann, Robert G. (1993). "This next disorderly half century: Some proposed remedies." *Washington Quarterly, 16,* 33–49.

Neustadt, Richard E. (1960). *Presidential power: The politics of leadership.* New York: Wiley.

Neustadt, Richard E., & May, Ernest R. (1986). *Thinking in time: The uses of history for decision makers.* New York: Free Press.

Nice, David C. (1992). "Peak presidential approval from Franklin Roosevelt to Ronald Reagan." *Presidential Studies Quarterly, 22,* 119–26.

Nincic, Miroslav. (1990). "U.S. Soviet policy and the electoral connection." *World Politics, 42,* 370–96.

Nincic, Miroslav. (1992a). *Democracy and foreign policy: The fallacy of political realism.* New York: Columbia University Press.

Nincic, Miroslav. (1992b). "A sensible public: New perspective on popular opinion and foreign policy." *Journal of Conflict Resolution, 26,* 772–89.

Nincic, Miroslav, & Hinckley, Barbara. (1991). "Foreign policy and the evaluation of presidential candidates." *Journal of Conflict Resolution, 35,* 333–55.

Nivola, Pietro S. (1990). "Trade policy: Refereeing the playing field." In Thomas E. Mann (Ed.), *A question of balance: The president, Congress, and foreign policy.* Washington, DC: Brookings Institution.

Nixon, Richard M. (1978). *RN: The memoirs of Richard Nixon.* New York: Grosset & Dunlap.

Nixon, Richard M. (1980). *The real war.* New York: Warner.

Nokes, R. Gregory. (1991). "Libya: A government story." In Simon Serfaty (Ed.), *The media and foreign policy* (pp. 33–46). New York: St. Martin's/Foreign Policy Institute.

Nolan, Stanley, D., & Quinn, Dennis P. (1994). "Free trade, fair trade, strategic trade, and protectionism in the U.S. Congress, 1987–1988." *International Organization, 48,* 491–525.

Normandy, Elizabeth L. (1994). "African-Americans and U.S. policy on Africa: Research trends." *International Studies Notes, 19,* 10–18.

References

Norrander, Barbara, & Wilcox, Clyde. (1993). "Rallying around the flag and partisan change: The case of the Persian Gulf War." *Political Research Quarterly, 46,* 759–70.

Northcutt, Susan Stoudinger. (1992). "An analysis of Bush's war speech." *International Social Science Review, 67,* 123–29.

Nye, Joseph S., Jr. (1990). "The changing nature of world power." *Political Science Quarterly, 105,* 177–92.

O'Loughlin, Michael G. (1990). "What is bureaucratic accountability and how can we measure it?" *Administration and Society, 22,* 275–302.

Oneal, John R., & Bryan, Anna Lillian. (1993, September). "The rally 'round the flag effect in U.S. foreign policy crises, 1950–1985." Paper presented at the American Political Science convention, Washington, DC.

Organski, A. F. K. (1990). *The $36 billion bargain: Strategy and politics in U.S. assistance to Israel.* New York: Columbia University Press.

Orman, John. (1991, August). "George Bush and the macho presidential style." Paper presented at the American Political Science convention, Washington, DC.

Ornstein, Norman J., & Schmitt, Mark. (1990). "Dateline campaign '92: Post–cold war politics." *Foreign Policy, 79,* 169–86.

Oudes, Bruce. (Ed.). (1989). *From the president: Richard Nixon's secret files.* New York: Harper & Row.

Overby, L. Marvin. (1991). "Assessing constituency influence: Congressional voting on the nuclear freeze, 1982–1983." *Legislative Studies Quarterly, 16,* 297–308.

Ovsiovitch, Jay S. (1992, April). "A distorted image?: Factors influencing the media's coverage of human rights." Paper presented at the International Studies Association convention, Atlanta.

Pacy, James S., & Henderson, Daniel B. (1992). "Career versus political: A statistical overview of presidential appointments of the United States chiefs of mission since 1915." *Diplomacy and Statecraft, 3,* 382–403.

Page, Benjamin I., & Shapiro, Robert Y. (1992). *The rational public: Fifty years of trends in Americans' policy preferences.* Chicago: University of Chicago Press.

Park, Bert E. (1994). *Ailing, aging, addicted: Studies of compromised leadership.* Lexington, KY: University Press of Kentucky.

Parry, Geraint. (1993). "The interweaving of foreign and domestic policy-making." *Government & Opposition, 28,* 143–51.

Parsons, Karen Toombs. (1994). "Exploring the "two president" phenomenon: New evidence from the Truman administration." *Presidential Studies Quarterly, 24,* 495–514.

Pastor, Robert A. (1980). *Congress and the politics of U.S. foreign economic policy, 1929–1976.* Berkeley: University of California Press.

Pastor, Robert A. (1992). "George Bush and Latin America: The pragmatic style and the regionalist option." In Kenneth A. Oye, Robert J. Lieber, & Donald Rothchild (Eds.), *Eagle in a new world.* New York: HarperCollins.

Paterson, Thomas G. (1979). "Presidential foreign policy, public opinion, and Congress." *Diplomatic History, 3,* 1–18.

Paterson, Thomas G. (Ed.). (1989). *Major problems in American foreign policy. Vol II: Since 1914.* Lexington, MA: D. C. Heath.

Paterson, Thomas G., Clifford, J. Garry, & Hagan, Kenneth J. (1991a). *American foreign policy. Vol. I: To 1914* (3rd ed.). Lexington, MA: D. C. Heath.

Paterson, Thomas G., Clifford, J. Garry, & Hagan, Kenneth J. (1991b). *American foreign policy. Vol. II: Since 1900* (3rd ed.). Lexington, MA: D. C. Heath.

Paterson, Thomas G., Clifford, J. Garry, & Hagan, Kenneth J. (1995a). *American foreign relations: A history. Vol. I: To 1914.* (4th ed.). Lexington, MA: D. C. Heath.

Paterson, Thomas G., Clifford, J. Garry, & Hagan, Kenneth J. (1995b). *American foreign relations: A history. Vol. II: Since 1895* (4th ed.). Lexington, MA: D. C. Heath.

Paterson, Thomas G., & Merrill, Dennis. (Eds.). (1995). *Major problems in American foreign relations. Vol. I: To 1920. Vol. II: Since 1914* (4th ed.). Lexington, MA: D. C. Heath.

Payne, Richard J. (1995). *The clash with distant cultures: Values, interests, and force in American foreign policy.* Albany: State University of New York Press.

Pearce, David D. (1995). *Wary partners: Diplomats and the media.* Washington, DC: CQ Books.

Peffley, Mark, & Hurwitz, Jon. (1992). "International events and foreign policy beliefs: Public response to changing Soviet–U.S. relations." *American Journal of Political Science, 36,* 421–61.

Peffley, Mark, & Hurwitz, Jon. (1993). "Models of attitude constraint in foreign affairs." *Political Behavior, 15,* 61–90.

Pelz, Stephen. (1991). "Changing international systems, the world balance of power, and the United States." *Diplomatic History, 15,* 47–82.

Peterson, Mark A. (1990). *Legislating together: The White House and Capitol Hill from Eisenhower to Reagan.* Cambridge: Harvard University Press.

Peterson, Paul E. (Ed.). (1994a). *The president, the Congress, and the making of foreign policy*. Norman: University of Oklahoma Press.

Peterson, Paul. (1994b). "The president's dominance in foreign policy making." *Political Science Quarterly, 109,* 215–34.

Peterson, V. Spike, & Ronyan, Anne Sisson. (1993). *Global gender issues.* Boulder, CO: Westview.

Petracca, Mark P. (Ed.). (1992). *The politics of interests: Interest groups transformed.* Boulder, CO: Westview Press.

Petras, James, & Morley, Morris. (1994). *Empire or republic? American global power and domestic decay.* New York: Routledge.

Pfiffner, James P. (1991). "Divided government and the problem of governance." In James A. Thurber (Ed.), *Divided democracy: Cooperation and conflict between the president and Congress* (pp. 39–60). Washington, DC: CQ Press.

Pika, Joseph A., & Thomas, Norman C. (1992). "The presidency since mid-century." *Congress & the Presidency, 19,* 43–52.

Pilger, John. (1993). "The U.S. fraud in Africa: Operation Restore Hope is part of new age of imperialism." *New Statesman and Society, 6* (No. 234), 10–11.

Pitsvada, Bernard T. (1991). *The Senate, treaties, and national security, 1945–1974.* Landham, MD: University Press of America.

Poe, Steven C. (1990). "Human rights and U.S. foreign aid: A review of quantitative studies and suggestions for future research." *Human Rights Quarterly, 12,* 499–512.

Popkin, Samuel L. (1991). *The reasoning voter: Communication and persuasion in presidential campaigns.* Chicago: University of Chicago Press.

Porter, Roger B. (1988). "The president, Congress, and trade policy." *Congress & the Presidency, 15,* 169–83.

Powell, Charles, Purkitt, Helen E., & Dyson, James W. (1987). "Opening the black box: Cognitive processing and optimal choice in foreign policy decision making." In Charles F. Hermann, Charles W. Kegley Jr., & James N. Rosenau (Eds.), *New directions in the study of foreign policy* (pp. 203–20). Boston: Allen & Unwin.

Powlick, Philip J. (1991). "The attitudinal bases for responsiveness to public opinion among American foreign policy officials." *Journal of Conflict Resolution, 35,* 611–41.

Powlick, Philip J. (1995a, August). "Public opinion in the foreign policy process: An attitudinal and institutional comparison of the Reagan and Clinton administrations." Paper presented at the American Political Science Association convention, Chicago.

Powlick, Philip J. (1995b). "The sources of public opinion for American foreign policy officials." *International Studies Quarterly, 39,* 427–52.

Prados, John. (1991) *Keepers of the keys: A history of the National Security Council from Truman to Bush.* New York: Morrow.

Press, Charles, & VerBerg, Kenneth. (1988). *American politicians and journalists.* Glenview, IL: Scott, Foresman.

Prindle, David F. (1991). "Head of state and head of government in comparative perspective." *Presidential Studies Quarterly, 21,* 55–72.

Purkitt, Helen E. (1990). "Political decision making in the context of small groups: The Cuban missile crisis revisited—one more time." Typescript provided to the author of a forthcoming article in Eric Singer and Valerie Hudson (Eds.), *Political psychology and foreign policy.* Boulder, CO: Westview.

Putnam, Robert. (1988). "Diplomacy and domestic politics: The logic of two-level games." *International Organization, 42,* 427–60.

Radway, Laurence Ingram. (1993, November). "Social status, public opinion, and Nixon's Vietnam decision." Paper presented at the Northeastern International Studies Association convention, Newark.

Raymond, Gregory A. (1994). "Democracies, disputes, and third-party intermediaries." *Journal of Conflict Resolution, 38,* 24–42.

Reagan, Ronald W. (1990). *An American life.* New York: Simon & Schuster.

Reardon, Betty. (1990). "Feminist concepts of peace and security." In Paul Smoker, Ruth Davies, & Barbara Munske (Eds.), *A reader in peace studies* (pp. 136–43). Oxford: Pergamon.

Regens, James L., Gaddie, Ronald Keith, & Lockerbie, Brad. (1995). "The electoral consequences of voting to declare war." *Journal of Conflict Resolution, 39,* 168–92.

Rehbein, Kathleen A. (1995). "Foreign-owned firms' campaign contributions in the United States." *Policy Studies Journal, 23,* 41–61.

Reingold, Beth. (1994). Review of Paul Brace and Barbara Hinckley, *Follow the leader: Opinion polls and the modern president.* New York: Basic Books, 1992. In *American Political Science Review, 88,* 754–56.

Reisman, W. Michael, & Baker, James E. (1992). *Regulating covert action.* New Haven, CT: Yale University Press.

Reiter, Howard L. (1990). "Unmobilized constituencies: Public opinion of the Nicaraguan war." *New Political Science, 18/19,* 125–46.

Renka, Russell D., & Jones, Bradford S. (1991). "The 'two presidencies' thesis and the Reagan administration." *Congress & the Presidency, 18,* 17–33.

Renshon, Stanley A. (Ed.). (1993). *The political psychology of the Gulf War: Leaders, publics, and the process of conflict.* Pittsburgh: University of Pittsburgh Press.

Renshon, Stanley, A. (1995). "Character, judgment, and political leadership: Promise, problems, and prospects of the Clinton presidency." In Stanley A. Renshon (Ed.), *The Clinton presidency: Campaigning, governing, and the psychology of leadership* (pp. 57–90). Boulder, CO: Westview.

Rhodes, Edward. (1994). "Do bureaucratic politics matter? Some disconfirming findings from the case of the U.S. Navy." *World Politics, 47,* 1–41.

Ricci, David M. (1993). *The transformation of American politics: The new Washington and the rise of think tanks.* New Haven: Yale University Press.

Richman, Alvin. (1995 April/May). "When should we be prepared to fight?" *The Public Perspective, 6(3),* 44–47.

Rielly, John E. (1987). "America's state of mind." *Foreign Policy, 66,* 39–56.

Rielly, John E. (1991). "Public opinion: The pulse of the '90s." *Foreign Policy 82,* 79–96.

Rielly, John E. (1995). "The public mood at mid-decade." *Foreign Policy, 98,* 76–95.

Ripley, Brian D. (1994, March). "Setting agendas: Citizen participation in U.S. foreign policy." Paper presented at the International Studies Association convention, Washington.

Ripley, Randall B., & Lindsay, James M. (1993). *Congress resurgent: Foreign and defense policy on Capitol Hill.* Ann Arbor: University of Michigan Press.

Risse-Kappan, Thomas. (1991). "Public opinion, domestic structure, and foreign policy in liberal democracies." *World Politics, 43,* 479–512.

Rose, Richard. (1988). *The postmodern president: The White House meets the world.* Chatham, NJ: Chatham House.

Rosenthal, Joel H. (1991). *Righteous realists: Political realism, responsible power, and American culture in the nuclear age* (pp. 682–83). Baton Rouge: Louisiana State University Press.

Rosner, Jeremy D. (1995). "Clinton, Congress, and assistance to Russia and the NIS." *SAIS Review, 15,* 15–35.

Rossiter, Clinton (1960). *The American presidency* (2nd ed.). New York: Harcourt Brace Jovanovich.

Rourke, Frances E. (1993). "Whose bureaucracy is this, anyway? Congress, the president and public administration." *PS: Political Science & Politics, 26,* 687–92.

Rourke, John T. (1983). *Congress and the presidency in U.S. foreign policymaking: A study of interaction and influence, 1945–1982.* Boulder, CO: Westview.

Rourke, John T. (1990). *Making foreign policy: United States, Soviet Union, China.* Pacific Grove, CA: Brooks/Cole.

Rourke, John T. (1995). *International politics on the world stage* (5th ed.). Guilford, CT: Dushkin.

Rourke, John T., & Carter, Ralph G. (1989, March). "Dueling presidencies: Assessing the relative roles of Congress and the presidency in American foreign policy making." Paper presented at the International Studies Association and British International Studies Association joint convention, London.

Rourke, John T., Hiskes, Richard P., & Zirakzadeh, Cyrus Ernesto. (1992). *Direct democracy and international politics.* Boulder, CO: Lynne Rienner.

Roy, Denny. (1990). "The U.S. print media and the conventional military balance in Europe." *Armed Forces & Society, 16,* 509–28.

Rusk, Dean, as told to Richard Rusk. (1990). *As I saw it.* New York: W. W. Norton.

Russell, Greg. (1990). *Hans J. Morgenthau and the ethics of American statecraft.* Baton Rouge: Louisiana State University Press.

Russett, Bruce M. (1990). *Controlling the sword.* Cambridge: Harvard University Press.

Russett, Bruce M. (1991). "Doves, hawks, and U.S. public opinion." *Political Science Quarterly, 105,* 515–38.

Russett, Bruce M., Hartley, Thomas, & Murray, Shoon. (1994). "The end of the cold war, attitude change, and the politics of defense spending." *PS: Political Science & Politics, 27,* 17–21.

Russett, Bruce M., & Starr, Harvey. (1992). *World politics: The menu for choice* (4th ed.). San Francisco: W. H. Freeman.

Said, Edward W. (1993). *Culture and imperialism.* New York: Knopf.

Salinger, Pierre, & Laurent, Eric. (1991). *Secret dossier.* New York: Penguin.

Saunders, Robert M. (1994). "History, health and herons: The historiography of Woodrow Wilson's personality and decision-making." *Presidential Studies Quarterly, 24,* 57–77.

Schampel, James H. (1993). "Change in material capabilities and the onset of war: A dyadic approach." *International Studies Quarterly, 37,* 395–408.

Schlesinger, Arthur M., Jr. (1967). *A thousand days: John F. Kennedy in the White House,* Greenwich, CT: Fawcett.

Schlesinger, Arthur M., Jr. (1973). *The imperial presidency.* Boston: Houghton Mifflin.

Schmitt, John. (1995). "NAFTA, the press and public opinion: The effect of increased media coverage on the formation of public opinion." *International Journal of Public Opinion Research, 7,* 203–21.

Schneider, William. (1992). "The old politics and the new world order." In Kenneth A. Oye, Robert J. Lieber, & Donald Rothchild (Eds.), *Eagle in a new world*. New York: HarperCollins.

Schoenbaum, David. (1993). *The United States and the state of Israel*. New York: Oxford University Press.

Schraeder, Peter J. (1992). "U.S. intervention in perspective." In Peter J. Schraeder (Ed.), *Intervention into the 1990s: U.S. foreign policy in the third world* (pp. 385–405). Boulder, CO: Lynne Rienner.

Schraeder, Peter J. (1994). *United States foreign policy toward Africa*. New York: Cambridge University Press.

Schubert, James N. (1993, March). "Realpolitik as a male primate strategy." Paper presented at the International Studies Association convention, Acapulco.

Schudson, Michael. (1995). *The power of news*. Cambridge: Harvard University Press.

Schulzinger, Robert D. (1989). *Henry Kissinger: Doctor of diplomacy*. New York: Columbia University Press.

Scolnick, Joseph M., Jr. (1995). "Prologue to policy: Clinton's foreign policy activities during the transition period." Paper presented at the American Political Science Association convention, Chicago.

Scott, James M. (1994). "Branch rivals: The Reagan doctrine, Nicaragua, and American foreign policy making." Paper presented at the International Studies Association convention, Washington, DC.

Scott, James M. (1995). "Shifting constellations: Actors and influence in American foreign policy making." Paper presented at the International Studies Association convention, Chicago.

Secrest, Donald, Brunk, Gregory G., & Tamashiro, Howard. (1991). "Moral justifications for resort to war with Nicaragua: The attitudes of three American elite groups." *Western Political Quarterly, 44,* 541–59.

Semetko, Holli A., Brzinski, Joanne Bay, Weaver, David, & Willnat, Lars. (1992). "TV news and U.S. public opinion about foreign countries: The impact of exposure and attention." *International Journal of Public Opinion Research, 4,* 18–36.

Serfaty, Simon. (1990). *The media and foreign policy*. New York: St. Martin's.

Shain, Yossi. (1995). "Ethnic diasporas and U.S. foreign policy." *Political Science Quarterly, 109,* 811–42.

Shapiro, Catherine R., Brady, David W., Brody, Richard A., & Ferejohn, John A. (1990). "Linking constituency opinion and Senate voting scores: A hybrid explanation." *Legislative Studies Quarterly, 15,* 597–620.

Shapiro, Robert Y., & Page, Benjamin I. (1988). "Foreign policy and the rational public." *Journal of Conflict Resolution, 32,* 211–47.

Sherrill, Robert. (1979). *Why they call it politics*. New York: Harcourt Brace Jovanovich.

Shoemaker, Christopher C. (1991). *The NSC staff: Counseling the council*. Boulder, CO: Westview.

Shull, Steven A. (Ed.). 1991. *The two presidencies: A quarter century of assessment*. Chicago: Nelson-Hall.

Silverstein, Gordon. (1994). "Judicial enhancement of executive power." In Paul E. Peterson (Ed.), *The president, the Congress, and the making of foreign policy* (pp. 23–45). Norman: University of Oklahoma Press.

Sinclair, Barbara. (1992). "The emergence of strong leadership in the 1980s House of Representatives." *Journal of Politics, 54,* 657–84.

Skidmore, David. (1993). "Foreign policy interest groups and presidential power: Jimmy Carter and the battle over ratification of the Panama Canal treaties." *Presidential Studies Quarterly, 23,* 477–98.

Skidmore, David, & Hudson, Valerie M. (Eds.). (1992). *The limits of state authority: Societal groups and foreign policy formation*. Boulder, CO: Westview.

Skowronek, Stephen. (1993). *The politics presidents make: Leadership from John Adams to George Bush*. Cambridge, MA: Harvard University Press.

Smith, James A. (1991). *The idea brokers: Think tanks and the rise of the new policy elite*. New York: Free Press.

Smith, Steve. (1984). "Groupthink and the hostage rescue mission." *British Journal of Political Science, 15,* 117–26.

Smith, Tony. (1994). *America's mission: The United States and the worldwide struggle for democracy in the twentieth century*. Princeton: Princeton University Press.

Smoke, Richard. (1987). *National security and the nuclear dilemma* (2nd ed.). New York: Random House.

Snyder, Louis L. (1977). *Varieties of nationalism*. New York: D. Van Nostrand.

Sobel, Richard. (Ed.). (1993). *Public opinion in U.S. foreign policy: The controversy over Contra aid*. Lanham, MD: Rowman & Littlefield.

Soderlund, Walter C., Wagenberg, Ronald H., & Pemberton, Ian C. (1994). "Cheerleader or critic? Television news coverage in Canada and the United States of the U.S. invasion of Panama." *Canadian Journal of Political Science, 27,* 581–605.

Solop, Frederic I. (1990). "Public protest and public policy: The anti-apartheid movement and political innovation." *Policy Studies Review, 9,* 307–26.

Sorensen, Theodore. (1963). *Decision-making in the White House: The olive branch or the arrows*. New York: Columbia University Press.

Sorensen, Theodore. (1965). *Kennedy*. New York: Harper & Row.

References

Sorensen, Theodore C. (1995). "Foreign policy in a presidential democracy." *Political Science Quarterly,* 109, 515–28.

Spanier, John, & Hook, Steven W. (1995). *American foreign policy since World War II* (13th ed.). Washington: CQ Press.

Spanier, John, & Uslander, Eric M. (1994). *American foreign policy making and the democratic dilemmas.* (6th ed.). New York: Macmillan.

Sparrow, B.H. (1993, September). "The news media, the executive branch, and the Gulf War: An institutional perspective." Paper presented at the American Political Science Association convention, Washington, DC.

Spear, Joanna, & Williams, Phil. (1988). "Belief systems and foreign policy: The cases of Carter and Reagan." In Richard Little & Steve Smith (Eds.), *Belief systems and international relations* (pp. 190–208). New York: Basil Blackwell.

Spiegel, Steven L. (1987). "Ethnic politics and the formulation of U.S. policy toward the Arab-Israeli dispute." In Mohammed E. Ahari (Ed.), *Ethnic groups and U.S. foreign policy* (pp. 23–44). Westport, CT: Greenwood.

Stanley, Harold W., & Niemi, Richard G. (1988). *Vital Statistics on American politics.* Washington, DC: CQ Press.

Stanley, Harold W., & Niemi, Richard G. (1992). *Vital Statistics on American politics* (3rd. ed.). Washington, DC: CQ Press.

Starr, Harvey (1992). "Democracy and war: Choice, learning and security communities." *Journal of Peace Research,* 29, 207–13.

Steinbruner, John D. (1974). *The cybernetic theory of decision: New dimensions of political analysis.* Princeton, NJ: Princeton University Press.

Stern, Eric, & Bengt, Sundelius. (1994). "The essence of groupthink." *Mershon International Studies Review,* 38, 101–07.

Stimson, James A. (1991). *Public opinion in America: Moods, cycles, and swings.* Boulder, CO: Westview.

Stockton, Paul. (1991). "The new game on the hill: The politics of arms control and strategic force modernization." *International Security,* 16, 146–70.

Stockton, Paul. (1995). "Beyond micromanagement: Congressional budgeting for a post–cold war military." *Political Science Quarterly,* 110, 233–60.

Stoessinger, John G. (1985). *Crusaders and pragmatists: Movers of modern American foreign policy* (2nd ed.). New York: W. W. Norton.

Strong, Robert A. (1991). "Jimmy Carter and the Panama Canal treaties." *Presidential Studies Quarterly,* 21, 269–91

Strunk, William, & E. B. White. (1979). *The elements of style* (3rd ed). New York: Macmillan.

Stuckey, Mary E. (1990). *Playing the game: The presidential rhetoric of Ronald Reagan.* New York: Praeger.

Stuckey, Mary E. (1992). *The president as interpreter-in-chief.* Chatham, NJ: Chatham House.

Summary, Larry J., & Summary, Rebecca M. (1994, April). "Foreign agents and foreign influence in the United States." Paper presented at the Midwest Political Science Association convention, Chicago.

Swansbrough, Robert H. (1991, August). "Wimp or warrior: The interaction of President Bush's personality and style in the Panama and Gulf crises." Paper presented at the American Political Science convention, Washington, DC.

Sylvan, Donald A., Ostrom, Thomas A., & Gannon, Katherine. (1993, September). "Case-based, model-based, and explanation-based styles of reasoning in foreign policy." Paper presented at American Political Science Association convention, Washington, DC. This paper was scheduled to appear in *International Studies Quarterly,* 38 (March 1994).

Sylvan, Donald A., & Thorson, Stuart J. (1990). "Ontologies, problem representation, and the Cuban missile crisis." *Journal of Conflict Resolution,* 36, 709–32.

Sylvester, Christine. (1994). *Feminist theory and international relations in a postmodern era.* New York: Cambridge University Press.

Taira, Koji. (1991, January). "Japan, an imminent hegemon?" *Annals of the American Academy of Political and Social Sciences,* 513, 151–63.

Taylor, Andrew J., & Rourke, John T. (1995). "Historical analogies in the congressional foreign policy process." *Journal of Politics,* 57, 460–68.

Taylor, William J., Jr., & Petraeus, David H. (1987). "The legacy of Vietnam for the U.S. military." In George K. Osborn, Asa A. Clark IV, Daniel J. Kaufman, and Douglas E. Lute (Eds.), *Democracy, strategy, and Vietnam: Implications for American policymaking.* Lexington, MA: Lexington.

Thompson, Jake H. (1994). *Bob Dole: The Republican's man for all seasons.* New York: Donald I. Fine.

Thompson, Loren. (Ed.). (1991). *Defense beat: The dilemmas of defense coverage.* New York: Lexington.

Thurber, James A. (1991). "Introduction: The roots of divided democracy." In James A. Thurber (Ed.), *Divided democracy: Cooperation and conflict between the president and Congress* (pp. 1–8). Washington, DC: CQ Press.

Tickner, J. Ann. (1992). *Gender in international relations: Feminist perspectives on achieving global security.* New York: Columbia University Press.

Togeby, Lisa. (1994). "The gender gap in foreign policy attitudes." *Journal of Peace Research,* 31, 375–92.

Tolley, Howard, Jr. (1991). "Interest group litigation to enforce human rights." *Political Science Quarterly, 109,* 617–36.

Tonelson, Alan. (1991, July). "What is the national interest?" *The Atlantic Monthly,* 35–52.

Trubowitz, Peter. (1992). "Sectionalism and American foreign policy: The political geography of consensus and conflict." *International Studies Quarterly, 36,* 173–90.

Truman, Harry S. (1955). *Year of decision.* Garden City, NY: Doubleday.

Turabian, Kate L. (1987). *A manual for writers of term papers, theses, and dissertations* (5th ed.). Chicago: University of Chicago Press.

Turner, Robert F. (1991). *Repealing the War Powers Resolution.* McLean, VA: Brassey's.

Twombly, Jim. (1995, January 3). Political science research and teaching list. Electronic mail communication.

U.S. (CIA) Central Intelligence Agency. (1994). *The world factbook, 1994–95.* Washington, DC: Brassey's.

Valentine, Douglas. (1990). *The Phoenix program.* New York: Avon.

Vandenbroucke, Lucien S. (1991). *Perilous options: Special operations in U.S. foreign policy.* Unpublished dissertation, the University of Connecticut. A manuscript based on Vandenbroucke's revised dissertation was published in 1993 under the same title, *Perilous options: Special operations as an instrument of U.S. foreign policy* by Oxford University Press.

Verdier, Daniel. (1994). *Democracy and international trade: Britain, France, and the United States, 1860–1990.* Princeton, NJ: Princeton University Press.

Vlahos, Michael. (1991). "Culture and foreign policy." *Foreign Policy, 82,* 59–78.

Vogel, Ezra F. (1992). "Japanese American relations after the cold war." *Daedalus, 121,* 35–59.

Von Vorys, Karl. (1990). *American national interest: Virtue and power in foreign policy.* New York: Praeger.

Waller, Wynne Pomeroy, & Ide, Marianne E. (1995). "The polls—poll trends: China and human rights." *Public Opinion Quarterly, 59,* 133–43.

Walters, Vernon. (1978). *Silent mission.* Garden City, NY: Doubleday.

Waltz, Kenneth N. (1995). "Realist thought and neorealist theory." In Charles W. Kegley Jr. (Ed.), *Controversies in international relations theory: Realism and the neoliberal challenge* (pp. 67–82). New York: St. Martin's.

Weaver, David. (1991). "Issue salience and public opinion: Are there consequences of agenda-setting?" *International Journal of Public Opinion Research, 3,* 53–68.

Weissman, Stephen R. (1995). *Congress's failure of leadership in foreign policy.* New York: Basic Books.

Wiarda, Howard J. (1990). *Foreign policy without illusion.* Glenview, IL: Scott, Foresman/Little, Brown.

Wielhouwer, Peter W. (1992, April). "The reconstruction of consensus? George Bush and the selling of Operation Desert Shield." Paper presented at the International Studies Association convention, Atlanta.

Wilcox, Clyde, & Allsop, Dee. (1991). "Economics and foreign policy as sources of Reagan support." *Western Political Quarterly, 44,* 941–58.

Wilcox, Clyde, Ferrara, Joseph, & Allsop, Dee. (1993). "Group differences in early support for military action in the Gulf: The effects of gender, generation, and ethnicity." *American Politics Quarterly, 21,* 343–59.

Wildavsky, Aaron. (1966). "The two presidencies." *Trans-action, 4,* 7–14.

Winter, David G. (1995). "Presidential psychology and governing styles: A comparative psychological analysis of the 1992 presidential candidates." In Stanley A. Renshon (Ed.), *The Clinton presidency: Campaigning, governing, and the psychology of leadership* (pp. 113–36). Boulder, CO: Westview.

Wirls, Daniel. (1991). "Congress and the politics of military reform." *Armed Forces & Society, 17,* 487–512.

Wittkopf, Eugene R. (1990). *Faces of internationalism: Public opinion and American foreign policy.* Durham, NC: Duke University Press.

Wittkopf, Eugene R. (1993, March). "Faces of internationalism in a transitional environment." Paper presented at the International Studies Association convention, Acapulco.

Wittkopf, Eugene R. (1994). "Faces of internationalism in a transitional environment." *Journal of Conflict Resolution, 38,* 376–401.

Wolfe, Robert. (1991). "Atlanticism without the wall: Transatlantic cooperation and the transformation of Europe." *International Journal, 46,* 137–63.

Wolfers, Arnold. (1962). "The pole of power and the pole of indifference." In Arnold Wolfers (Ed.), *Discord and collaboration* (pp. 3–35). Baltimore, MD: The Johns Hopkins University Press.

Wolfinger, Raymond E. (1993). "Tips for writing papers." *PS: Political Science & Politics, 26,* 87–88.

Wood, B. Dan, & Waterman, Richard W. (1991). "The dynamics of political control of the bureaucracy." *American Political Science Review, 85,* 801–28.

Woodward, Bob. (1991). *The commanders.* New York: Simon & Schuster.

Woodward, Bob. (1994). *The agenda: Inside the Clinton White House*. New York: Simon and Schuster.

Wooten, Jim. (1995, January 28). "The conciliator." *The New York Times Magazine,* 48 et seq.

Wright, Jim. (1993). *Worth it all: My war for peace*. Washington, DC: Brassey's (U.S.).

Wyden, Peter. (1979). *Bay of Pigs: The untold story*. New York: Simon & Schuster.

Yeric, Jerry L., & Todd, John R. (1996). *Public Opinion: The visible politics* (3rd ed.). Itasca, IL: Peacock Press.

Zaller, John. (1994a). "Elite leadership of mass opinion." In W. Lance Bennett and David L. Paletz (Eds.), *Taken by storm: The media, public opinion, and U.S. foreign policy in the Gulf War* (pp. 186–209). Chicago: University of Chicago Press.

Zaller, John. (1994b). "Strategic politicians, public opinion, and the Gulf crisis." In W. Lance Bennett and David L. Paletz (Eds.), *Taken by storm: The media, public opinion, and U.S. foreign policy in the Gulf War* (pp. 250–74). Chicago: University of Chicago Press.

Zhongdang, Pan, & Kosicki, Gerald M. (1994). "Voters' reasoning processes and media influences during the Persian Gulf War." *Political Behavior, 16,* 117–51.

Zimmerman, Richard. (1991). *What can I do to make a difference? A positive action sourcebook*. New York: Plume.

Index

Page numbers in **boldface** refer to glossary terms.

CREDITS